Second Edition

Reading Sociology
Canadian Perspectives

Edited by

Lorne Tepperman

Angela Kalyta

Published in partnership with

**THE CANADIAN SOCIOLOGICAL ASSOCIATION
LA SOCIÉTÉ CANADIENNE DE SOCIOLOGIE**

OXFORD
UNIVERSITY PRESS

OXFORD
UNIVERSITY PRESS

Oxford University Press is a department of the University of Oxford.
It furthers the University's objective of excellence in research, scholarship, and education by publishing world-wide. Oxford is a registered trade mark of Oxford University Press in the UK and in certain other countries.

Published in Canada by
Oxford University Press
8 Sampson Mews, Suite 204,
Don Mills, Ontario M3C 0H5 Canada

www.oupcanada.com

Database right Oxford University Press (maker)
First Edition published in 2007
Second Edition published in 2012

Library and Archives Canada Cataloguing in Publication
Reading sociology : Canadian perspectives / edited by Lorne Tepperman, Angela Kalyta. — 2nd ed.

"Published in partnership with the Canadian Sociological
Association / La société canadienne de sociologie".
ISBN 978-0-19-544129-1

1. Sociology—Canada—Textbooks. 2. Canada—Social
conditions—1991– —Textbooks. 3. Sociology—Textbooks.
I. Tepperman, Lorne, 1943– II. Kalyta, Angela III. Canadian Sociological Association

HM586.R43 2011   301   C2011-905213-X

Cover image: Morgan David de Lossy / Veer

This book is printed on permanent (acid-free) paper ∞.

Printed and bound in Canada.
1 2 3 4 — 15 14 13 12

Contents

Note: Most papers could have been placed in more than one section. To help students and instructors, we have listed the names of those other sections under each title. For ideas on how to use these tools, see the introduction on page xi.

Introduction

This is the second edition of a book that started out in 2004 with the goal of teaching introductory sociology students something about the field of sociology in Canada. We believed that a short book of readings could be useful in two-term introductory sociology courses—whether at universities or community colleges—to complement the main textbook.

We also believed that many instructors of introductory sociology at Canadian colleges and universities would ask their students to read such a book if the selection and editing were effective. Such a book would introduce new Canadian sociology to undergraduate students in small, manageable pieces, and it would let professional sociologists know about some of the newer work emerging at Canadian colleges and universities. Ideally, this book would be revised every few years, to reflect new developments in Canadian sociology. All royalties would go to the Canadian Sociological Association (CSA).

The popular response to the first edition has supported our optimistic belief: the book was a success and was used in many classrooms. So now we are back with new articles and a new edition.

Like the first edition, the second edition of *Reading Sociology: Canadian Perspectives* is organized around the major topic of sociology. It includes pieces selected from the best papers submitted and chosen for presentation at the 2010 CSA Conference in Montreal. As with the first edition, we followed a simple course: presenters were asked to send a brief, readable précis of their paper (roughly 2,000 words long). We, the book editors, checked them for quality and readability, and requested speedy revisions where needed. We then assembled the revised papers into a manuscript and provided it to the publisher a mere three months after the conference: something of a record in academic publishing.

Still, the book in your hands is the result of extensive collaboration between the book editors and the authors of the more than 60 pieces it contains, and between the CSA and Oxford University Press. The book departs in only a few ways from what we originally imagined. Specifically, in some sections, we have included shortened versions of papers recently published in the *Canadian Review of Sociology* (CRS)—the journal of the CSA—to round out the selection.

Unlike the first edition, this second one includes a cross-referencing system to help instructors and students. As instructors are well aware, social processes, and sociological inquiry into them, are not easy to categorize into the simple, focused topics of the introductory text book. In fact, the strength of much sociological research is precisely in its revealing of connections between multiple processes. As such, most of the articles included could have been placed into a number of different sections. Conversely, a grouping of four or five articles could never perfectly reflect the depth and variability of research going on in any one topic. But by considering overlap of topics within chapters, readers can get a broader idea of how Canadian sociologists are thinking about culture, globalization, or any of the other topics.

Instructors and students can use the section titles listed under each article title in the table of contents to consider how any one article is connected to other conceptual topics in the book. Instructors: you can use this system to generate discussion questions, and to help you decide what articles to teach and when. So, if, for example, you don't like some of the papers that we have chosen to place in the States and Government section, you can easily locate other articles to substitute. Perhaps one of the other chapters is closer to your research interests, and thus more interesting to teach. This system simplifies the searching process, saving the time required to read all of the papers. Students: you can use the system when studying. The cross-references can draw your attention to the processes going on in a paper besides the main topic of focus—aspects that you might not have noticed during your first reading. Instead of just trying to memorize what an article is saying, you can ask yourself, What does this chapter tell me about inequality? work? the life course? or whatever other topics the chapter is cross-referenced with. This thinking process can help you remember more about the chapter.

In the long run, being able to read course materials in this way (conceptually) is useful, regardless of what major you end up choosing. Test graders are always impressed when students demonstrate creative and critical thinking by using their course work in unique ways to formulate answers. And as you go on in academia, such creative, lateral thinking is ever more important. It helps you discover the anomalies, contradictions, or outright voids in existing research that inspire essay ideas in later classes, and research ideas later in your academic career. Some of the connections we have drawn are obvious, and others more conceptual. Practise seeing the connections we have noted, and also remember that there are many more possible conceptual connections among the pieces than we have highlighted. Now that you know what we mean by 'seeing the connections' among different pieces, try finding conceptual connections among sections and chapters that we haven't suggested. We hope that this new element in the second edition proves useful to students and instructors alike.

In preparing this book, we have received wonderful co-operation from the authors of the pieces included: thank you, authors, for your patient help. More importantly, thank you for your insight and creativity—as revealed in the pages of this book. The reader will note that many of the included pieces are by new scholars—doctoral candidates and junior faculty members throughout Canada. The energy and imagination of our youngest sociologists gives us a great deal to look forward to in years to come.

To judge from the papers in this book, Canadian sociology is in a state of creative ferment right now. Here we see evidence of many theoretical and methodological approaches, and a smorgasbord of topics, ranging from the obvious to the surprising. Readers of this book will be struck by the energy, curiosity, and ambition of our authors. So sit back, dip into the book, enjoy, and reflect.

In preparing the book, we received great help from Adrianna Robertson, a recent graduate of the University of Toronto, who assisted with correspondence and administration of the project. Adrianna ensured that everything we received was reviewed and revised, and that nothing got lost. She also invested a great deal of time in putting together the glossary and drafting questions. Thank you, Adrianna.

At Oxford University Press, Allison McDonald developed a plan for the book and made sure that we stayed on track; and after her departure, we were guided by Tamara Capar, who was also helpful and encouraging. Thank you, Allison and Tamara. You made the birth of this book easier, and were fun to work with. In the last stages, we were helped and advised by Tara Tovell, who copy-edited the large, unruly manuscript, bringing it into conformity with scholarly expectations. Thank you, Tara, for making this book finally have the appearance (as well as content) of an Oxford University Press book. We enjoyed working with you.

Thanks go, finally, to the various presidents of the CSA—especially Harley Dickinson and John Goyder—who provided the institutional encouragement a project like this needs.

As expected, the editorial collaboration was an education in itself, with each editor learning something from the other. Mostly it was fun, and we hope you enjoy the book!

Lorne Tepperman
University of Toronto

Angela Kalyta
McGill University

Contributors

Adams, Tracey L., University of Western Ontario

Adorjan, Michael C., University of Hong Kong

Aitken, Rob, University of Alberta

Albanese, Patrizia, Ryerson University

Ali, Harris, York University

Andersen, Robert, University of Toronto

Armstrong, Pat, York University

Arnold, Robert, University of Windsor

Baker, Maureen, University of Auckland

Barron, Christie, University of Calgary

Beagan, Brenda L., Dalhousie University

Beaujot, Roderic, University of Western Ontario

Beauregard, Diane, University of Ottawa

Beauregard, Nancy, University of Montreal

Benoit, Cecilia, University of Victoria

Berenson, Carol, University of Calgary

Bischoping, Kathy, York University

Boyd, Monica, University of Toronto

Brayton, Jennifer, University of Ottawa

Chen, Shaun, OISE, University of Toronto

Chira, Sinzania, Dalhousie University

Clément, Dominique, University of Alberta

Colaguori, Claudio, York University

Corrigall-Brown, Catherine, University of British Columbia

Crichlow, Wesley, University of Ontario Institute of Technology

Curtis, Bruce, Carleton University

Curtis, Josh, University of Toronto

Denis, Jeffrey S., Harvard University

DeVault, Marjorie, Syracuse University

Deveau, J.L., Agriculture and Agri-Food Canada

Doucet, Andrea, Carleton University

Drakulic, Slobodan, Ryerson University

Eglin, Peter, Wilfrid Laurier University

Fanelli, Carlo, Carleton University

Funk, Laura M., University of Manitoba

Garlick, Steve, University of Victoria

Haan, Michael, University of Alberta

Hallgrimsdottir, Helga Kristin, University of Victoria

Hardy Kristin A., York University

Helmes-Hayes, Rick, University of Waterloo

Ilcan, Suzan, University of Windsor

Karakayali, Nedim, Bilkent University

Kennelly, Jacqueline, Carleton University

Knezevic, Ivanka, University of Toronto Scarborough

Knudson, Sarah, University of Toronto

Kobayashi, Karen M., University of Victoria

Lacombe, Dany, Simon Fraser University

Lalu, Nirannanilathu, University of Alberta

Lange, Matthew, McGill University

Laxer, Emily, University of Toronto

Leyden, Myra, University of Guelph

Lombardo, Anthony, University of Toronto

MacDonald, Laura, Dalhousie University

McGuire, Patricia D., University of Saskatchewan

McLaren, Arlene Tigar, Simon Fraser University

Myers, Daniel J., University of Notre Dame

Nakhaie, Reza, University of Windsor

Netting, Nancy S., University of British Columbia (Okanagan)

Neves, Katja, Concordia University

Ollivier, Michèle, University of Ottawa

Olstead, Riley, St. Francis Xavier University

O'Shaughnessy, Sara, University of Alberta

Parnaby, Patrick F., University of Guelph

Parusel, Sylvia, Simon Fraser University

Paulson, Justin, Carleton University

Peekhaus, Wilhelm, University of Illinois

Phillips Rachel, University of Victoria

Quirke, Linda, Wilfrid Laurier University

Ravanera, Zenaida, University of Western Ontario

Ridzi, Frank, Syracuse University

Riggins, Stephen Harold, Memorial University of Newfoundland

Robbins, Wendy, University of Ottawa

Roth, Reuben N., Laurentian University

Satzewich, Vic, McMaster University

Sauvé, Geneviève, University of Ottawa

Scott Rebecca, Queen's University

Shaffir, William, McMaster University
Shaver, Frances, Concordia University
Simmons, Alan, York University
Steiner, Sherrie, Booth College
Stepnisky, Jeff, Grant MacEwan University
Stoddart, Mark C.J., Dalhousie University
Taylor, Lisa, Bishop's University
Tézli, Annette, University of Calgary
Torres, Carlos, York University
Trovato, Frank, University of Alberta

Vardy, Mark, Queen's University
Venkatesh, Murali, Syracuse University
Voyageur, Cora J., University of Calgary
Walby, Kevin, Carlton University
Wallace, Jean, University of Calgary
Warren, Jean-Philippe, Concordia University
Wilkes, Rima, University of British Columbia
Young, Marisa, University of Toronto
Young, Nathan, University of Ottawa

Part I

What Is Sociology?

Like all scientists, sociologists have their own set of theoretical and methodological tools for studying the world. When we are working through assumptions about *how the world is*, we are dealing with theory. All of us use theories every day. We need accurate assumptions about how the world works to navigate it—to move toward the things we want and avoid the things that we don't. They are tools, like flashlights: amid the mess of reality, they highlight where we should look for causal explanations. For example, you may have chosen to come to university on the assumption that a post-secondary education would help you get a better job.

All sciences have basic theoretical foundations that guide them to examine some causal relationships over others. For example, psychologists explain human action by referring to how the human brain works. They may talk about biological processes like the nervous system, or chemical and hormonal reactions, by way of explanation. Sociologists' theoretical commitment to social context leads them to look at very different things, among them, cultural understandings and practices, positions within a social structure and the relationships that bind them, and distribution of opportunities and constraints.

But the relationship between the external reality around us and the ideas that we have about it is not a simple one. Our ideas—our theories—can be more or less accurate. Just because you assume that school will get you a good job does not make it so. As humans, much of our success is due to being able to constantly go back and forth between theories and reality, bringing our ideas about how the world works closer to how it actually does work so we can act more effectively on it. When we are doubting *how we know what we know*, we are dealing with *methodology*. The way that science resolves these doubts is through empirical observation. For this, we develop methods for extracting information from the world around us. Throughout this book, you will read articles that use various sources of data to make an argument about the social world, including statistical surveys, interviews, historical documents, and cultural texts (newspapers, songs, etc).

But the challenge isn't over once we have information. After that, we must interpret what it means—what it tells us about the world we are trying to understand. In this first section of the book, Bruce Curtis reminds us that data, even seemingly straightforward statistics, do not explain themselves. The sociological interpretation of statistics is always a narrative construction, and sometimes an ideological act. Alone, data are nothing more than fragments of reality that have been snipped apart for us to more easily see and think about. They are merely pieces of the puzzle. When we are trying to put the pieces together into a bigger picture, we must use theoretical assumptions. Curtis argues that we need to uphold constant vigilance, or in his words, be reflexive: we need to remain willing to interrogate our assumptions of what our data represent and how to make sense of it. We too are social beings, and our context provides us with interpretive habits that we must be aware of. Jean-Philippe Warren helps to make this point by exploring how French- and English-Canadian sociologists produce very different kinds of work, based on different methodological and theoretical practices. Patricia McGuire ponders how mainstream sociological assumptions and practices are rooted in a European way of knowing and making sense of the world. She explores how sociology might be enriched by Aboriginal ways of knowing. There was a widespread feeling among conference attendees that McGuire was at the 'cutting edge' of indigenous studies and was saying much of what needed to be said, however simply.

But there is an even bigger problem of interpretation. We said above that knowing the world makes it easier to act on it effectively, to manipulate the external world in a way that produces a needed result. This is a problem for sociologists: what information should we look for? How should we use the information we find? This is a *normative* dilemma. Doctors are privileged by having a unified idea of the goal of their work: preserving human health—prolonging life, postponing death, curing illness, etc. Few humans would deny this is a worthwhile goal. However, people are often divided about the goals of sociological research, so there can be large political implications when sociologists uncover evidence that favours a particular side. Unlike the molecules, masses, and tissues that other scientists study, our subject matter can hear what we say about it, and use that information to change itself. And so, sociologists are forced to consider the broader social implications of their findings. In doing so, they must decide whether they want to uncover information that works toward one result or another, as well as which discussions they want to stay out of. For sociologists, there is no way out of this normative dilemma.

Throughout the book, we see debates about which methods and theories best clarify specific phenomena. However, in this section, we devote most of our attention to the normative debate about purpose: namely, what is the ultimate goal of sociology (and sociologists)? Eglin describes three different perspectives on the role of the sociologist. Helmes-Hayes, almost by way of illustration, explores the contribution of one prominent Canadian sociologist, John Porter, reminding us of the important role sociologists can play as public intellectuals. Warren explains how and why French- and English-Canadian sociologies have diverged in the later decades of the twentieth century. McGuire displays her commitment to a broader social cause, advocating for an Aboriginal sociology that could create information that helps rather than hinders Aboriginal communities. Curtis reminds us that statistics never speak for themselves—in fact, we have to speak for them; and Warren explains why different communities of sociologists tend to tell different kinds of stories.

CHAPTER 1

Intellectual Citizenship and Incarnation: A Reply to Stanley Fish

Peter Eglin

My subject is the problem of 'intellectual citizenship'—how to live the academic life in the contemporary Northern university—from the point of view of moral/political economy. I begin by critiquing **Stanley Fish**'s position on the responsibility of intellectuals before arguing my own Chomskian position via a brief case study, and explicating the concept of incarnation, the intended main contribution of the paper.

Critique of Fish

Fish argues that 'Neither the university as a collective nor its faculty as individuals should advocate personal, political, moral, or any other kind of views except academic views' (Fish, 2008: 19), the 'university can protect the integrity of its enterprise only if it disengages entirely from the landscape of political debate, if it says, in effect, we do academic, not political business, here' (85) and 'the only obligation to which [academics] must be faithful is the obligation to present the material in the syllabus and introduce students to state-of-the-art methods of analysis' (97). Fish does, however, allow that 'after hours, on their own time, when they write letters to the editor or speak at campus rallies, [professors] can be as vocal as they like about anything and everything' (29). He echoes **Max Weber** (1974 [1917]: 48): 'university teaching achieves really valuable effects only through specialized training by specially qualified persons. Hence "intellectual integrity" is

the only specific virtue which universities should seek to inculcate'.

I agree with Fish that where non-academic practical evaluations enter the classroom the teacher's job is to *academicize* them, and that just because we use the same term to refer to them does not mean that all politics are the same ('Once you realise that while politics is everywhere, it isn't the same politics, the cash value of saying that everything is political disappears' [Fish, 2008: 174]) and that 'there are many things to be true or false about, and not all of them fall within the university's sphere' (34). I disagree, however, that 'the truths the university is pledged to establish and protect are truths about matters under academic study' (34).

The question as to whether the *university* should confine itself to pursuing and conveying specialized knowledge and analytic skills is surely moot insofar as universities have from their beginning had practical missions. Fish himself says that the university 'can and should take collective (and individual) action on those issues relevant to the educational mission—the integrity of scholarship, the evil of plagiarism, and the value of a liberal education' (19). Though he denies it (55–59), 'the value of a liberal education' is surely not confined to academic values, but has broader moral and, indeed, political significance in the society at large. Even Weber's (1958: 147) famous dictum that 'the primary task of a useful teacher is to teach his students to recognize "inconvenient" facts—I mean facts that are inconvenient for their party opinions' imports a political motive into teaching, though not a partisan one.

The standard liberal response is to say that politicizing the university is disastrous for its academic mission. But, as Fish says, not all politics are the same sorts of things. Indeed, let us simply refer to the conventional liberal distinction between fundamental human rights ('politics 1') and partisan contention in a parliamentary democracy ('politics 2'). Notice that in liberal democracies these are separated by putting the first in some constitutional form, as in Canada's Charter of Rights and Freedoms, where it is protected *as law*, typically by a Supreme Court, from the disputatious character of the second, which is located in a parliament, elections, and civil society generally. Moreover, the separation acknowledges that partisan politics—what Weber and Fish are hung up on—depends upon the entrenchment of human rights in law. Yes, my position amounts to the politicization of the university, but only in the sense of politics 1, and who can object to that?

Chomsky

On the other hand, **Noam Chomsky** argues that 'The intellectual responsibility of the writer, or any decent person, is to tell the truth . . . it is a moral imperative to find out and tell the truth *as best one can*, about things *that matter*, to *the right audience*' (Chomsky, 1997: 55). Indeed, he goes even further, asserting that 'The responsibility of the writer as a *moral agent* is to try and bring the truth about *matters of human significance to an audience that can do something about them*. That is part of what it means to be a moral agent rather than a monster' (56). He continues, 'The moral culpability of those who ignore the crimes that matter by moral standards is greater to the extent that the society is free and open, so that they can speak more freely, and act more effectively to bring those crimes to an end. And it is greater for those who have a measure of privilege within the more free and open societies, those who have the resources, the training, the facilities and opportunities to speak and act effectively: the intellectuals, in short' (65).

For his part, Fallis notes that 'Although some professors and students see themselves as "activists" and welcome the role of critic, most professors and students are uneasy' (Fallis, 2008: 21) with such talk of moral responsibility for 'crimes that matter'. It smacks altogether too much of that other vocation, politics, that is surely beyond our academic remit; it is demanding enough to be responsible teachers and researchers. Life would certainly be easier for me if I could see it this way. But I can't.

Not only is pronouncing on non-academic matters of fundamental human rights a legitimate exercise of academic freedom, it is the *responsibility* of professors and universities to do so. It may be done on or off campus, though rarely in the classroom itself. The obligation to do so arises from the academic vocation to tell the truth in the context of both the *values* ('the pursuit of truth is . . . *the* central purpose of the university' [Fish, 2008: 119]), and the material *incarnation* of exploitation, that underlie and sustain the academic enterprise (Eglin, 2010).

(A) Academic Values: Truth-Seeking Is a Moral Activity

In my view, pursuing truth in free inquiry into our subjects ('things that matter'), with and for colleagues and students, is itself moral action, and thereby part of the same family of activities that includes telling the truth about the 'crimes that matter'.

If it is important to figure out how, say, Robert Frost's 'Fire and Ice' achieves its remarkable locutionary meaning, illocutionary force and perlocutionary effects, and to communicate and teach those findings and the methods for arriving at them, it is so because they have human significance. But 'human significance' is a moral idea. If then these inquiries are important by virtue of the morality of human significance, then how much more so are the actual bodies, lives, and real circumstances of oppressed and suffering people? If we have a responsibility to find out and tell the truth about matters of human significance in our subjects of inquiry, to the right audience of our colleagues and students, then we have a responsibility to find out and tell the truth about the crimes that matter to an audience that can do something about them. An irreducible part of intellectual citizenship is responsibility for politics 1.

Case Study:
Colombia and My University

On June 14, 2010, Canada ratified a free trade agreement with Colombia. Yet, of 101 trade unionists murdered world-wide in 2009, '48 were killed in Colombia . . . . Twenty-two of the Colombian trade unionists who were killed were senior trade union leaders and five were women, as the onslaught of previous years continued' (ITUC, 2010). According to Human Rights Watch, army-backed Colombian paramilitaries murdered an estimated 15,000 trade unionists, peasants and local leaders from 1994 to 2003. In 2002, the teaching trade union FECODE lost 70 members to assassins (see Roger, 2003; Gordon, 2008a, 2008b).

Cashing in on the climate of terror are transnational corporations, including mining companies from Canada, and Coca-Cola. An enterprising student in one of my courses, Jordan Leith, investigated what was 'behind the Coca-Cola® brand'. He discovered that his own student union (WLUSU) had an exclusive marketing agreement with Coke (Leith, 2003: 8), and that the School of Business and Economics at WLU uses a Harvard business case called *Cola Wars Continue: Coke vs. Pepsi in the 1990s* (Yoffie and Foley, 1994). The case notes that profit margins are higher in some international markets than in the United States.

Leith discovered that 'in July [2001], the United Steelworkers of America and the International Labour Rights Fund filed suit in US court against Coca-Cola and some bottlers in Colombia on behalf of their workers, alleging that the companies 'hired, contracted with or otherwise directed paramilitary security forces'. The companies denied the charges, [yet] one high-ranking labour official says simply, 'Everyone knows that Coca-Cola works with the paramilitaries' (Roston, 2001: 34). 'Operating in an environment where union involvement is life risking gives employers huge

power. It severely diminishes resistance against inhumane labour practices. Does this create the "cost advantages" that the Harvard case touched upon? Coke's agreement with WLUSU constrains change-provoking discussions about these issues at Laurier' (Leith, 2003: 17). Notice that the student union acts very much like a company—secretive and indifferent to the ghastly human fate of the leaders of the unions that valiantly struggle for basic decency, dignity, and human rights for the workers whose work makes the profits for companies such as Coke that corporate operations like Laurier's student union can profit from for the reputed benefit of students. Meanwhile the university's faculty vegetate as future business 'leaders' are trained in the tradition, and Colombian faculty union and student leaders are terrorized.

The Colombian Coke case ties university teaching and learning here to terrorism and murder there. Not just knowing about but indirectly benefiting from such violations makes one's responsibility as an intellectual citizen to respond that much more compelling.

(B) Incarnation: Truth-Seeking Is Steeped in Others' Blood and Sweat

My problem, then, is not simply a matter of being unwilling to stand by as fellow human beings—not least educational workers—are terrorized, or of the competing, twin, moral demands of intellectual responsibility for technical inquiry and the defence of human rights. Rather, it comes from the *incarnate* connections between the stable, peaceful, and affluent conditions of my 'free' sociological inquiry and the exploited, terrorized, and impoverished circumstances of others' lives.

Incarnation arises from the labour theory of value and of commodity fetishism (Marx and Engels, 1976 [1867]: 163ff.; Shawn, 1991: 19–21; Cohen, 1997: 12–14, 199–252; Barndt, 2002: 31–32). The value of a commodity is an expression of the human labour that has gone into its production. That the labour is incarnate in the commodity affords a social relationship between producer and consumer of the commodity. As I read this paper written on paper, I am linked to the paper's producers, and by extension to all others embedded in the global social relations that comprise the political economy in which the paper gets made, distributed, and sold (Marx and Engels, 1987 [1848]: 23–25).

What concerns me is their moral dimension. In order that some may write their thoughts on paper, others may have to be killed, tortured, impoverished, and exploited, while still others will have to be enriched and empowered. The political economy and social relations of global corporate capitalism afford a grotesquely skewed distribution of human rights.

'The costs of adjusting to greater openness are borne exclusively by the poor, regardless of how long the adjustment takes' (Kim, 2001, citing World Bank, 1999 [Lundberg and Squire, 2003]; see Wright, 2008: 209; York, 2009). My intellectual life as a sociologist is incarnate in the moral-political economy of global corporate capitalism. My university's material infrastructure that grounds my free inquiry into the social embodiment of social facts is bought with the exploited and impoverished lives of countless other bodies (and the enrichment of a few). Taking this seriously requires radically changing the moral organization of inquiry in the university.

References

Barndt, Deborah. 2002. *Tangled Routes: Women, Work and Globalization on the Tomato Trail*. Lanham, MD: Rowman and Littlefield.

Chomsky, Noam. 1997. 'Writers and Intellectual Responsibility'. In *Perspectives on Power: Reflections on Human Nature and the Social Order*. Montreal: Black Rose, pp. 55–69.

Chomsky, Noam. 2010. *Hopes and Prospects*. Chicago: Haymarket Books.

Cohen, Leah Hager. 1997. *Glass, Paper, Beans: Revelations on the Nature and Value of Ordinary Things*. New York: Doubleday Currency.

Eglin, Peter. 2010. *Intellectual Citizenship and the Problem of Incarnation*. Unpublished manuscript.

Fallis, George. 2008. 'Professors as Public Intellectuals', *Academic Matters*, Oct.–Nov., 19–22.

Fish, Stanley. 2008. *Save the World on Your Own Time*. New York: Oxford University Press.

Gordon, Todd. 2008a. 'Building Its Ties to Colombia: Canada's Imperial Adventure in the Andes', *The Bullet*, 110 (27 May): www.socialistproject.ca/bullet/bullet110.html.

Gordon, Todd. 2008b. 'Disaster in the Making: Canada Concludes its Free Trade Agreement with Colombia', *The Bullet*, 112 (11 June): www.socialistproject.ca/bullet/bullet112.htm

Herman, Edward S. and David Peterson. 2010. *The Politics of Genocide*. New York: Monthly Review Press.

International Trade Union Confederation (ITUC). 2010. *Annual Survey*: www.ituc-csi.org/ituc-annual-survey.html (accessed on June 11, 2010).

Kim, Janice. 2001. 'Reasons to Protest', *Imprint* [University of Waterloo], November 30, p. 8.

Leith, Jordan. 2003. 'Searching for 'The Real Thing'®': Behind the Coca-Cola® Brand'. Term paper for Sociology 410

Theory and Practice: The Political Economy of Inquiry. Waterloo, ON: Wilfrid Laurier University.

Marx, Karl and Friedrich Engels. 1976 (1867). 'The Fetishism of the Commodity and Its Secret'. In *Capital: A Critique of Political Economy*, vol. 1. Harmondsworth, Middlesex: Penguin, pp. 163–177.

Marx, Karl and Friedrich Engels. 1987 (1848). *The Communist Manifesto*, ed. Jack Wayne. Toronto: Canadian Scholars' Press.

Roger, Angela. 2003. 'Commentary: My Trip to Hell', *CAUT Bulletin*, September, A11.

Roston, Adam. 2001. 'It's the Real Thing: Murder', *Nation*, 273, no. 7, September 3.

Shawn, Wallace. 1991. *The Fever*. New York: Noonday Press.

Weber, Max. 1958 (1922). 'Science as a Vocation'. In H.H. Gerth and C. Wright Mills (Eds.), *From Max Weber: Essays in Sociology*. New York: Oxford University Press, 1958, pp. 129–156.

Weber, Max. 1974 (1917). 'The Meaning of "Ethical Neutrality" in Sociology and Economics'. In Edward Shils (Ed.), *Max Weber on Universities: the Power of the State and the Dignity of the Academic Calling in Imperial Germany*. Chicago: University of Chicago Press, pp. 47–54.

World Bank. 1999. 'The Simultaneous Evolution of Growth and Inequality'; published version by Lundberg, Mattias and Lyn Squire. 2003. *The Economic Journal* 113 (April): 326–344.

Wright, Ronald. 2008. *What Is America? A Short History of the New World Order*. Toronto: Knopf Canada.

Yoffie, David B. and Sharon Foley. 1994 (since updated). *Cola Wars Continue: Coke vs. Pepsi in the 1990s*. Cambridge: Harvard Business School.

York, Geoffrey. 2009. 'Financial Crisis Pushes Millions More into Hunger', *Globe and Mail*, June 12, A16.

CHAPTER 2

Anticipating Burawoy: John Porter's Public Sociology

Rick Helmes-Hayes

In the analysis below, I outline Burawoy's position. As well, I compare his argument about the superiority of a social democratic public sociology with a similar claim put forward in the 1970s by Canadian sociologist John Porter (1921–1979), author of *The Vertical Mosaic* (1965), widely regarded as the most influential book in the history of Canadian sociology. The comparison serves two purposes: first, it illustrates the point that the debate is a recurrent one in the discipline. Second, it allows me to draw the attention of current Canadian undergraduates to at least part of John Porter's remarkable legacy. Students may be surprised to discover that even though Porter dealt with the issue of the place of values in sociology a full 30 years ago, his ideas about a morally committed sociology, citizenship, equality, and social justice remain relevant to this day.

I: Burawoy on 'Legitimate' Public Sociology

In his presidential address, Burawoy argued that current sociology has four 'faces'—professional, critical, policy, and public. Professional sociology, best represented by mainstream, highly quantitative, 'scientific' sociology, is the dominant and most prestigious form of sociological practice. Its audience is the scholarly community. Policy sociology is applied professional sociology commissioned by a client and directed at the solution of some problem the client has identified. Clients are most often governments and corporations because they have the resources to pay. Critical sociology is likewise directed at a scholarly audience but is 'reflexive', concerned to address fundamental value questions—often from a 'radical', left-wing perspective. Examples would be Marxism and non-liberal forms of **feminism**. Public sociology is applied critical sociology. There are two types. The first is traditional public sociology, which is best exemplified by newspaper opinion pieces or scholarly books written by scholars for a mass, educated public. The other type is organic public sociology. Rather than speaking 'at' publics, organic sociologists enter into dialogic relations (conversations) with disadvantaged or oppressed groups with the goal of helping them to solve their problems. Examples would be sociologists who work with street people, immigrant groups, and marginal workers (2005a).

According to Burawoy's vision of the discipline, outlined in 'For Public Sociology' and more than a score of essays since, these four types of sociology can and should be combined under the umbrella of public sociology to create a type of discipline—a 'value science' (2005d: 158–9)—that would contribute to solving the world's problems. It was this claim—that sociology could and should be a 'value science'—that sparked the international furore.

From the outset, his vision of public sociology has been methodologically ecumenical and deeply concerned to include the best of professional sociology. Unlike many Marxists, feminists, humanists, and postmodernists who distrust science or, at the least, scorn professional sociology for being methodologically and statistically sophisticated but substantively bankrupt, Burawoy has placed professional, scientific sociology at the core of public sociology. He is highly critical of it for sometimes devolving into a 'pathological' enterprise characterized by 'methodological fetishism and an obsession with trivial topics' (2005a: 15) but, nonetheless, argues that it is central to the public sociology project: 'I believe that an effective public sociology, far from being incompatible with science, depends on the best of science' (2005e: 515).

That said, there is one part of professional sociology that Burawoy argues must be jettisoned: the doctrine of value neutrality. In his view, sociologists must be accountable to society *as a whole*, not just to the scientific community and the internal norms of science. Sociology, he says, must be 'post-positivist'; it must 'recognize its own implication in the world it studies' (2005e: 515–6). 'The social sciences are at the intersection of the humanities and the natural sciences because they necessarily partake in both instrumental and reflexive knowledge. Here are research programs that are deeply embedded in value premises that need to be critically fleshed out and become the object of public debate' (2005e: 514–5; see also 2005d). But he goes well beyond the rejection of value freedom. In addition, he argues that public sociology must be based on a set of social democratic values that he holds to be *objectively good*. Only social democratic political views, he argues, serve 'humanity's interest' (2004: 125). He offers a long list of specific injustices that public sociology should oppose— e.g. 'the erosion of civil liberties, . . . the degradation of the environment, . . . and deepening inequalities' (2004: 125)—but argues that its ultimate goal is to provide people around the globe with an expanded set of guaranteed universal human rights (2006: 1, 9; see also 2005d: 157–8, 2008a, 2008b: 358). The existing narrowly conceived property rights of the **neo-liberal** market and the existing narrowly conceived political rights of the **neo-liberal** state are, he claims, are inadequate. In their extant form,

he says, they simply 'commodify . . . everyday life and . . . privatiz[e] all things public' (2005d: 155, 2007, 2008a: 437), thereby creating and exacerbating rather than solving problems related to global human emancipation (2006: 4-6).

II: John Porter and the New Liberalism

John Porter, Canada's most celebrated sociologist, guaranteed himself a place in the pantheon of Canadian sociology in 1965 when he published **The Vertical Mosaic**, a monumental, pioneering analysis of the structure of class and power in Canada. (For a detailed discussion of Porter's life and work, see my recent biography of Porter: R. Helmes-Hayes, *Measuring the Mosaic: An Intellectual Biography of John Porter.* Toronto: University of Toronto Press, 2010.)

The Vertical Mosaic decimated the prevailing myth that Canada was a democratic, largely classless nation where people from all ethnic backgrounds enjoyed the benefits of equal opportunity. The volume created an instant sensation and established Porter as the country's premier sociologist. In subsequent years, he went on to collaborate on a series of major quantitative studies in the areas of occupational prestige, educational opportunity, and social mobility (Pineo and Porter, 1967; Porter, Porter and Blishen, 1982; Boyd et al., 1985). Always a political progressive, near the end of his career Porter wrote a series of essays—some published, some not—in which he elaborated on the elements of a highly sophisticated, quantitative **macrosociology** based on the New Liberal social democratic scholarly and political principles he had internalized at the LSE (see Porter, 1973, 1974, 1975a,b, 1977, 1979a,b,c,d,e). In many respects, this perspective—reflexive and morally committed, based on solid science, politically engaged and 'practical'—anticipated arguments Burawoy made years later in promoting his more modern version of public sociology.

III: Porter's New Liberal 'Public Sociology'

i) Reflexive and Morally Committed

The philosophical/methodological approach Porter developed in his late-career essays melded the four faces of Burawoy's public sociology by combining the sophisticated methodological techniques of professional sociology with the critical, practical, and value-laden aspects of the three other faces of sociology. Porter started from the premise that while it was important to be objective in the process of gathering and reporting data (1979c), the doctrine of value neutrality had to be rejected. 'The argument that values have no place in social scientific inquiry is in my view incorrect for *the central question of that inquiry relates to the conditions and capacities that a society needs to move itself in the direction of the social good*' (Porter, 1975b: 2; emphasis added). The social scientist's freedom to pursue research—a societally granted privilege—carried with it the responsibility to use that freedom in the service of society. Sociologists were duty-bound to assess and criticize any social order that served particular rather than general interests. 'To me, the major task of social science is to abstract from the confused flow of events perspectives which clarify and which permit some judgement about society in the light of moral principles' (1975b: 2; see also 1973: 467, 1979c: 2). Not only that, but like Burawoy years later, he claimed it was possible to use philosophical/sociological reasoning to identify *objective standards of moral worth* that could and should then be scientifically operationalized and used as a standard against which to measure progress. Burawoy talked about it in terms of 'humanity's interest'; Porter talked about it using Hobhouse's phrases: societal 'organic harmony' and 'the unity of mankind.' This is where Porter's view of sociology as a 'science' comes in.

ii) Based on Solid Science

I do not have space here to review all the elements of the methodological orientation Porter proposed in his unfinished, unpublished essays on macrosociology, but a few key terms and illustrations will make the point.

1. His methodological approach would be *grand in scale and synthetic*. Here he had in mind the *omnium gatherum* political economy and moral philosophy of the nineteenth century.
2. Properly practised, sociology would be *comparative* in orientation and *international in scope*. His basic unit of analysis would be the nation-state, and would take into account unique features of the development of individual nations, but he argued that particular nation-states should be studied as examples of a wider *type of society* developing along a common *type or path of development* (1975b: 1). Modern neo-liberal societies would constitute one such type.
3. It would be as *quantitatively sophisticated* as possible. 'The macrosystem can be viewed as one in evolution, and the appropriate macrodata to trace out this evolution are to be found in time-series and ultimately expressed in complex mathematical models' (1970: 153). In one of his later-life unpublished essays, he specified some of the details. What he was looking for, he said, was a set of empirical indicators of '*social development*' equivalent to those employed by economists to describe *economic* development. His model specified 12 'common elements' of modern industrialized societies which he wanted to operationalize as 'variables.' Four of these variables—a just reward system, an open and democratic political process, the widest possible distribution of citizenship rights, and the stewarding of the environment—constituted his preferred outcomes. Together, they constituted 'progress' operationalized (1975a: 6–7, 20–1).

iii) Politically Engaged and Practical

For Porter, this was not an exercise in professional model-building; he wanted to use these empirical measures of progress for a political purpose. In his view, social development and moral progress were two sides of the same coin. Just as societies had achieved greater and lesser degrees of economic progress, so too had they achieved varying degrees of moral progress. 'Not all cultures have equal claims on our moral support,' he wrote. '[I]n the course of social evolution some principles of social life have emerged which are more morally supportable than others' (1979d: 130). In this respect, he had no qualms about pointing an accusatory finger at neo-liberal cultures. He valued some elements of classical liberalism and harboured meritocratic liberal sensibilities throughout his career, but in these later-life essays he concluded that modern neo-liberal society— what he called 'neo-conservative' society—was deeply and irremediably flawed.

Indeed, in 1979, the year he died, he issued the following judgment—sounding exactly like Burawoy does today: '[W]estern capitalism ha[s] reached a critical point of slow growth giving the state an increasingly ambiguous task of intervention to maintain or re-establish climates favourable for capitalist enterprise. In this context has arisen the new conservatism . . . . The new conservatism is both economic and political; it warns us of an inescapable trade-off between equality and economic efficiency and equality and political liberty, since the redistributive objectives which

equality requires can be reached only through increased state encroachment and control' (1979c: 4). This is exactly what Burawoy has referred to as the 'colonizing' agendas of markets and states (2006 1, 2005d: 157-8).

Conclusion: Porter's Relevance to the Public Sociology Debate

The paragraphs above indicate that the substance and political/scholarly intent of Porter's work is in many respects very similar to Burawoy's. Indeed, despite the fact that he died over 30 years ago, Porter's writings have substantial contemporary relevance. There is no doubt that some parts of his work are dated, but his later-life essays in particular offer some specific and (for some of us at least) appealing ideas about directions that a legitimate public sociology might take. The key for Porter, as for Burawoy, is that the doctrine of value freedom is not an appropriate basis for the discipline. It is not enough, he wrote, for sociology 'to understand . . . how a society in its totality works and how it got to be where it is.' It should also 'be able to judge whether or not it is moving in the direction of maximizing human welfare' (1979c: 2).

References

Blau, K. and K. Iyall Smith (eds.). 2006. *Public Sociologies Reader*. Lanham, MD: Rowman and Littlefield.

Boyd, M., J. Goyder, F. Jones, H. McRoberts and J. Porter. 1985. *Ascription and Achievement*. Ottawa: Carleton University Press.

Burawoy, M. 2004. 'Manifesto for public sociologies,' *Social Problems* 51 (1): 124–9.

_____. 2005a. 'For public sociology,' *American Sociological Review* 70 (February): 4–28.

_____. 2005b. 'The critical turn to public sociology,' *Critical Sociology* 31 (3): 313–26.

_____. 2005c. 'Rejoinder: Toward a critical public sociology,' *Critical Sociology* 31 (3): 379–90.

_____. 2005d. 'Third-wave sociology and the end of pure science,' *The American Sociologist* 35 (3-4): 152–65.

_____. 2005e. 'Provincializing the social sciences,' in *The Politics of Method in the Human Sciences*, pp. 508–25, G. Steinmetz, ed. Durham, NC: Duke University Press.

_____. 2006. 'Introduction: A public sociology for human rights,' in *Public Sociologies Reader*, pp. 1–18, J. Blau and K. Iyall Smith, eds. Lanham, MD: Rowman and Littlefield.

_____. 2007 'Public sociology versus the market,' *Socio-Economic Review* 5: 356–67.

_____. 2008a. 'What is to be done? Theses on the degradation of social existence in a globalizing world,' *Current Sociology* 56 (3): 357–9.

_____. 2008b. 'Rejoinder: For a subaltern global sociology?' *Current Sociology* 56 (3): 435–44.

Collini, S. 1979. *Liberalism and Sociology*. Cambridge: Cambridge University Press.

Helmes-Hayes, R. 1990. '"Hobhouse Twice Removed": John Porter and the LSE Years,' *Canadian Review of Sociology and Anthropology* 27 (3): 357–88.

_____. 2009. 'Engaged practical intellectualism: John Porter and "new liberal" public sociology,' *Canadian Journal of Sociology* 34 (3): 831–68.

_____. 2010. *Measuring the Mosaic*. Toronto: University of Toronto Press.

Helmes-Hayes, R. and N. McLaughlin (eds.). 2009. *Canadian Journal of Sociology*, Special Issue on Public Sociology 34 (3).

Hobhouse, L. 1924. *Social Development*. New York: Henry Holt.

———. 1927. *Development and Purpose*. London: Macmillan.

———. 1964. *Liberalism*. London: Oxford. [orig. 1911]

Macpherson, C. B. 1973. *Democratic Theory*. Oxford: Clarendon.

Marshall, T. H. 1950. *Citizenship and Social Class and Other Essays*. Cambridge: Cambridge University Press.

Pineo, P. and J. Porter. 1967. 'Occupational prestige in Canada,' *Canadian Review of Sociology and Anthropology* 4 (1): 24–40.

Porter, J. 1965. *The Vertical Mosaic*. Toronto: University of Toronto Press.

———. 1970. 'Research biography of a macrosociological study: *The Vertical Mosaic*,' in *Macrosociology*, pp. 149–81, J. Coleman, A. Etzioni, and J. Porter, eds. Boston: Allyn and Bacon.

———. 1973. 'The limits of sociology,' *Contemporary Sociology* 2 (5): 463–7.

———. 1974. 'Macrosociology: Some problems with the nation state as the unit of analysis,' Carleton University, Sociology 602 (unpublished draft) (W. Clement Papers).

———. 1975a. 'Towards a macrosociology: Further notes,' Carleton University, Sociology 602 (unpublished draft) (W. Clement Papers).

———. 1975b. 'Notes as a commentator on the macrosociological issues,' presented at the Annual Meetings of the CSAA; Library and Archives Canada, John Porter Papers, vol. 6 #14.

———. 1977. 'Address by John Porter,' in *Options for Canada*, pp. 56–67. Ottawa: St. Patrick's College and Carleton University.

———. 1979a. 'Education and the just society,' in J. Porter, *The Measure of Canadian Society*, pp. 263–80. Toronto: Gage.

———. 1979b. 'Education and equality: The failure of a mission,' in J. Porter, *The Measure of Canadian Society*, pp. 242–62. Toronto: Gage.

———. 1979c. 'Prologue,' in J. Porter, *The Measure of Canadian Society*, pp. 1–5. Toronto: Gage.

———. 1979d. 'Ethnic pluralism in Canadian perspective,' in J. Porter, *The Measure of Canadian Society*, pp. 105–37. Toronto: Gage.

———. 1979e. Introduction to 'Research biography of a macrosociological study: *The Vertical Mosaic*,' in J. Porter, *The Measure of Canadian Society*, pp. 7–9. Toronto: Gage.

Porter, J., M. Porter and B. Blishen. 1982. *Stations and Callings*. Toronto: Methuen.

CHAPTER 3

Indigenous Spaces in Sociology

Patricia D. McGuire

Theory generation is a human activity. It takes place within a social context for different subjective purposes. Theories are based on and reflective of social realities. Contemplation and questioning of why the social world is as it is inform all theoretical development. Western social theory has been privileged as the pinnacle of theory with its clearly delineated descriptions, explanations, and evaluations as they are widely dispersed within the modern world (Reynolds 1971, Neilsen 1990, Shadjahan 2005). That social scientists make their observations within a socially mediated framework of their own cultural meanings and symbols is evident: their realities assist in the development of theory (Semali & Kincheloe 1999, Mason 2004, Kanaiaupuni 2005). Feminist, post-colonial, and multicultural theorists have argued that theories and methods developed as a social process to rationalize and extend a distinct cosmology on all societies and with all peoples (Said 1979, Denzin & Lincoln 1998, Smith 1999, Shadjahan 2005). Critiques of social theory arise from this idea of intellectual colonialism. That there must be and are different realities is unmistakable.

In Canadian sociology, there exists a great deal of descriptive information about indigenous people(s) social issues. Statistical analysis is given on social indicators prevalent in and across indigenous societies. High rates of violent death, suicides, car accidents, infant mortality, and other indicators of social imbalance proliferate. In many ways, the focus is on deficits and problems in indigenous societies, with little discussion of strengths and positive aspects of the same societies (Doxtater 2004, Kanaiaupuni 2005). Canadian sociology is very Canadian in that respect: it generally offers only a marginal recognition to the contributions of **Aboriginal Canadians**. This marginalization is not unique—for example, Australian sociology is critiqued in the same manner (McIlwraith 2006). How indigenous people either think of or conceptualize their relationship within Canada is less known. How indigenous peoples view or consider social change processes is unfamiliar terrain. This situation raises questions about the place of Aboriginal perspectives within Canadian society and whether a space exists or can be created to include such developing perspectives. This requires asking some difficult questions of the discipline.

Can sociological theory be developed that does not take Western philosophy as its vantage point? Does rational discourse, as determined in Western systems, have to be the starting point? Can there be other conceptions of rationality that exist in other cultures, times, and places? Does indigenous sociology mean only the translation of Western terms into indigenous languages and vice versa? Does a dialogue on world views facilitate sociological theory and the social study of change processes in other cultures? What would social change theories look like if based in indigenous knowledge(s)? These are important questions requiring discussion on foundational issues within the discipline. Base ideas about land, progress related to modernity, and the current deficit lens placed on Aboriginal peoples must be examined. The continuing impact and interrelationships between colonialism, knowledge production, and social change must also be scrutinized. The starting point for this discussion may be to look at how knowledge itself is created and influenced.

Theories, in the most basic sense, help us make sense of and understand the world around us. Scientific theory answers such questions as why things happen but not why things exist (Smith D. 1974/1990). The latter question is left for philosophical inquiry. There is a separation of knowledge(s). Scientific knowledge provides a method for organizing and categorizing things (typologies), predictions of future events, explanations for past events, and a sense of understanding what may cause events (Reynolds 1971, Neilsen 1990, Smith D. 1974/1990, Smith L. 1999). These methods are the basis for scientific knowledge of the world. Knowledge systems construct the world that they describe and study. This is a dynamic process based on perceptions of reality.

The power of Western science is its ability to depict its findings as universal knowledge. This includes the ability to determine what legitimate knowledge is and is not and to advance what is considered legitimate. This 'power lies in the use of knowledge to advance one understanding of the world as opposed to another' (Kanaiaupuni, 2005: 32). This view, while dominant, is only one of many knowledges. The modernist way of constructing reality and producing knowledge is one of a multitude of local ways of knowing—it is a local knowledge system that denies this, so as to produce universal knowledge which then becomes true regardless of context (Smith D. 1974/1990, Collins 1990, Semali & Kincheloe 1999, Smith L. 1999, Shadjahan 2005). Yet, alternative knowledge(s) exist in spite of this situation.

Knowledge, in order to be meaningful, needs to be rooted in the very realities that it is attempting to explain (Kanaiaupuni 2005). Indigenous knowledge as discussed in English is a modernist dichotomous discussion at risk of pan-indianism, yet the Canadian indigenous sociology conversation has to start on some common ground for dialogue to occur.

To begin this dialogue within sociology, we must discuss indigenous knowledge as an object, while remembering that all knowledge is rooted in one's realities and is contextual. Indigenous knowledge differs in substantive ways from what is called Western knowledge. It is a diverse and elusive term. 'Indigenous knowledge . . . might be a thing or a body of knowledge, but to Indigenous peoples, it is much more' (Wilson, 2004: 363). It is both a relationship with life and a way of life. It is combined thought of the land, the people, and metaphysics, that is, dreams, vision, spirit, and the emotive (Cajete 1994, Monture-Angus 1995, Castellano 2000, Barnes 2003, Atleo 2004, Bastion 2004, Rose 2005). Dei, Hall and Rosenberg (2000) state that indigenous knowledge 'refers to the traditional norms and values, as well as the mental constructs that guide, organize, and regulate' people's ways of making sense of their worlds' and further, that indigenous knowledge is a 'body of knowledge that is diverse and complex given the histories, cultures, and lived realities of peoples' (6). For some scholars like Battiste (2002), indigenous knowledge provides a counter discourse that completes and fills in the gaps of Western knowledge(s).

> Indigenous scholars discovered that Indigenous knowledge is far more than the binary opposition of western knowledge. As a concept, Indigenous knowledge benchmarks the limitations of Eurocentric theory—its methodology, evidence, and conclusions—reconceptualizes the resilience and self-reliance of Indigenous peoples, and underscores the importance of their own philosophies, heritages, and educational processes. Indigenous knowledge fills the ethical and knowledge gaps in Eurocentric education, research and scholarship (5).

Indigenous knowledge(s) are evident in Canada. The main difference between these systems is one of recognition, authority, and place within the academy. How does this apply to Canadian sociology and the creation of an indigenous sociology?

The idea that one culture determines what counts as truth and reality is unrealistic, as all cultures accumulate knowledge. It is intellectual arrogance to think otherwise. Sociology as a discipline is self-reflexive, so discourse about indigenous sociology is available within the discipline, (McIlwraith 2006). The creation of an indigenous sociology can be seen in a variety of ways: as a counter-force to the dominant discourse, as folk knowledge, as a conservative reaction to the modern, as a response for cultural preservation, as a nationalist exercise, and as a need for tradition and spirituality in a world where it no longer exists. Yet, no matter how one views indigenous knowledge(s), it will not and cannot be ignored.

One of the main advocates for the development of indigenous sociology in the 1980s and 1990s was Akiwowo (1999). He argued that globalization processes would result in the indigenization of sociology. This is similar to Patel's (2006) premise that global processes make opportunities for the 'play of plural perspectives, so that all traditions of doing sociology are placed on equal levels and given equal significance' (383). Debate and dialogue continue about the evolutionary change of sociology into either one discipline that covers all people, in all places, and in all times or sociologies that are diverse and localized to specific societies in the world, sociologies that grow from the parent culture. These ideas, universalism or particularism, are the crux of this debate.

Sociology can be enriched by insights brought forward from oral-based cultures, in general and in specific populations (Kusch 1970/ 2010, Akiwowo 1999). Sociological propositions, Akiwowo (1999) argued, assist in the development of indigenous African sociology. A critique is that an indigenous sociology can only be based in terms of Western philosophy and that more than translating Western concepts into indigenous languages must be done. This should be based on rigour and precision in indigenous concepts used. In spite of this, Akiwowo argued that African languages 'provide systematically linguistic and metaphysical representations of knowledge for the development' of explanatory sociological principles (116). The problems that arise are the issues of communicability and the limits of universalism. **Relativism** is a key part of this debate as well.

Sociology as a discipline examines its foundational knowledge as a matter of course. It is a critical element of sociology to constantly question itself. Perhaps it is time for sociology to test its boundaries and look at the contested terrain of the creation of indigenous sociology. It will require reflexivity and a radical reassessment of its base.

Self-sociologies need to break open the binaries on which they were constructed, interrogate the divisions embodied in the construction of knowledge of society, move away from the universalism of classical theorists of early modernity and assess the many different ways to understand the consequences of this modernity both in terms of social processes and their knowledge systems. (Patel, 2006: 393)

Arguing that sociology has universal application in the world is problematic due to the ideas of progress and modernization within the discipline. Moving beyond a deficit-based discussion of Aboriginal peoples in Canada will require intellectual curiosity and openness to alternative knowledge(s). For Aboriginal peoples, it will require the same, as well as trust. It is unfortunate that the appropriation of cultural systems of practice and ideas has been a feature of the scientific relationship with indigenous peoples. Even when discussing how the current system can accommodate alternative ways of knowing, some place the discussion in appropriation of language. 'There is much more to be gained from further mining of the fertile ground that exists within Indigenous knowledge systems' (Barnhardt & Kawagley, 2005: 15).

This can create mistrust. There is much that can be thought of and created by working together to envision different ways of seeing. The binary between Western and indigenous knowledge is a false one. To create knowledge in a responsible manner requires that both views work together. It is imperative

[t]hat we address these issues in a two way transaction. Native people need to understand Western society but not at the expense of what they already know and the way that they have come to know it. . . . (Western) people too need to recognize the coexistence of multiple worldviews and knowledge systems, and find ways to understand and relate to the world in its multiple dimensions and varied perspectives. (Barnhardt & Kawagley, 2005: 9)

This is the challenge in exploring alternatives to the dominant discourse in sociology. It will require considerable openness and reflexivity from both indigenous and sociological perspectives on the world to begin this dialogue in Canada.

Indigenous views about knowledge influence how we are seen and how we see as well. Indigenous peoples can redefine and negotiate their space of knowing. In this process, knowledge production can be an empowering exercise. There is a space within sociology to look at alternative ways of being. The premise of social theory as a social construction facilitates efforts in this regard. Resulting indigenous-based theories will help in describing, understanding, and evaluating indigenous social life, as it will be embedded in specific indigenous social realities. Indigenous theory creation is fraught with controversy in both Canadian sociology and within indigenous societies themselves. Even as I wrote this essay in English, questions arose about its purpose and intent. However, controversy should not discourage such exploration, as writing creates a place in which indigenous social theory can imagine a different way of being, one that is rooted in our past but meets our collective future with confidence.

References

Akiwowo, Akinsola. (1999) 'Indigenous Sociologies—Extending the Scope of the Argument'. *International Sociology*. Volume 14 (2): 115–138.

Atleo, E. Richard. (2004) *Tsawalk—A Nuu-chad-nulth Worldview*. British Columbia: UBC Press.

Barnes, Judy Iseke. (2003) 'Living and Writing Indigenous Spiritual Resistance'. *Journal of Intercultural Studies*. Volume 24 (3): 211–238.

Barnhardt, Ray & Kawagley, Angayuqaq. (2005) 'Indigenous Knowledge Systems and Alaska Native Ways of Knowing'. *Anthropology and Education Quarterly*. Volume 36 (1): 8–23.

Bastien, Betty. (2004) *Blackfoot Ways of Knowing—The Worldview of the Siksitaitsitapi*. Alberta: University of Calgary Press.

Battiste, Marie. (2002) *Indigenous Knowledge and Pedagogy in First Nations Education—A Literature Review with*

Recommendations. National Working Group on Education: Indian and Northern Affairs Canada. Accessed May 31, 2010 http://www.usask.ca/education/people/battistem/ikp_e.pdf.

Battiste, Marie & Henderson, James (Sa'ke'j) Youngblood, eds. (2000) *Protecting Indigenous Knowledge and Heritage—A Global Challenge.* Saskatchewan: Purich Publishing Ltd.

Cajete, Greg. (1994) *Look to the Mountain: An Ecology of Indigenous Education.* Skyland: Kivaki Press.

Castellano, Marlene Brant. (2000) 'Updating Aboriginal Traditions of Knowledge', in Dei, George, Hall, B., Rosenberg, D., eds., *Indigenous Knowledge in Global Contexts: Multiple Readings of Our World.* Toronto: University of Toronto Press.

Collins, Patricia Hill. (1990). *Black Feminist Thought: Knowledge, Consciousness and the Politics of Empowerment.* London: HarperCollins.

Sefa Dei, G.J., Hall, B.L., Rosenberg, D.G., eds. (2000) *Indigenous Knowledges in Global Contexts: Multiple Readings of our World.* Toronto: University of Toronto Press.

Sefa Dei, G.J. (2000) 'Rethinking the Role of Indigenous Knowledges in the Academy'. *Inclusive Education.* Volume 4 (2): 111–132.

Denzin Norman K., Lincoln Yvonne S., eds. (1998). *The Landscape of Qualitative Research—Theories and Issues.* Thousand Oaks, CA: Sage Publications, Inc.

Doxtater, Michael G. (2004) 'Indigenous Knowledge in the Decolonial Era'. *American Indian Quarterly.* Volume 28 (3 & 4): 618–633.

Kana'iaupuni, Shawn Malia. (2005) 'Ka'akalai Ku Kanaka: A Call for Strengths-Based Approaches from a Native Hawaiian Perspective'. *Educational Researcher.* Volume 34 (5): 32–38.

Kusch, Rodolfo. (1970). *Indigenous and Popular Thinking.* Translated 2010, Maria Lugones and Joshua M. Price. Durham, NC: Duke University Press.

Mason, Jennifer. (2004) *Qualitative Researching.* 2nd ed. London: Sage Publications.

McLeod, Neil. (2007). *Cree Narrative Memory—From Treaties to Contemporary Times.* Saskatoon: Purich Publishing Ltd.

McIlwraith, Kathleen Butler. (2006) '(Re)presenting Indigeneity—The Possibilities of Australian Sociology'. *Journal of Sociology.* Volume 42 (4): 369–381.

Monture-Angus, Patricia. (1995). *Thunder in My Soul—A Mohawk Woman Speaks.* Halifax: Fernwood Publishing.

Nielsen, Joyce McCarl. (1990). 'Introduction', in *Feminist Research Methods: Exemplary Readings in the Social Sciences*, ed. J.M. Nielsen, 1–37. Boulder CO: Westview Press.

Patel, Sujata. (2006) 'Beyond Binaries'. *Current Sociology.* Volume 54 (3): 381–395.

Reynolds, Paul Davidson. (1971) *A Primer in Theory Construction.* Needham Heights, MA: Allyn and Bacon.

Rose, Deborah. (2005) 'An Indigenous Philosophical Ecology: Situating the Human'. *The Australian Journal of Anthropology*, Volume 16 (3): 294–305.

Said, Edward. (1979). *Orientalism.* New York: Random House.

Semali, Ladislaus & Kincheloe, Joe L. (1999) *What is Indigenous Knowledge? Voices from the Academy.* New York: Falmer Press.

Shahjahan, Riyad Ahmed. (2005) 'Mapping the Field of Anti-Colonial Discourse to Understand Issues of Indigenous Knowledges: Decolonizing Praxis'. *McGill Journal of Education.* Volume 40 (2): 213–240.

Simpson, Leanne R. 'Anticolonial Strategies for the Recovery and Maintenance of Indigenous Knowledge'. *American Indian Quarterly.* Volume 28 (3 & 4): 373–384.

Smith, Dorothy. (1974/1990). *The Conceptual Practices of Power: A Feminist Sociology of Knowledge.* Boston: Northeastern University Press.

Smith, Linda Tuhiwai. (1999). *Decolonizing Methodologies—Research and Aboriginal Peoples.* New York: St. Martin's Press.

Wilson, Angela, Waziyatawin. (2004) 'Indigenous Knowledge Recovery Is Indigenous Empowerment'. *American Indian Quarterly.* Volume 28 (3 & 4): 359–372.

CHAPTER 4

Reading Reflexively

Bruce Curtis

This discussion begins with **narratives** because of one of the most interesting developments in sociology and the other social sciences over the last two decades: the recognition of the inescapably narrative quality of our accounts of the social (for instance White, 1987; Somers, 1994). I propose that this awareness extends to that seemingly least narrative of objects: numerical *census* returns. A great many developments both in and outside the academy have undermined the credibility of sociology's earlier attempts at master narratives, as in **systems theory** or **Marxism**. The growing awareness of the existence of a multiplicity of narratives has increased interest in the ways in which narratives are constructed, work, become **hegemonic**, and are discredited.

From the sociology side, the use of new data sources and the multiplication of historical voices encouraged critical interrogation of the dominant accounts of social development. For instance, in the historical sociology of education, the reigning account of the origins of public education, until the late 1960s, was one in which progressive bourgeois, or middle-class, intellectuals fought against the dark forces of oligarchy and privilege to bring the light of learning into the humble homes of the people. Any opposition to public education or to the school was a defence of ignorance or, as **Talcott Parsons** put it, simply sour grapes on the part of those unable to adapt to the needs of modern society (Parsons, 1964).

Some critics at the time did point out that the claims about popular literacy levels depended on dubious assumptions about the meaning of entries on census forms (Mays and Manzl, 1974). There was, and continues to be, concern among many sociologists, economic historians, and historical demographers about the internal coherence of the Canadian manuscript censuses that many researchers embraced enthusiastically. As the so-called quantitative history took off, a few people, such as Marvin McInnis from Queen's, were suggesting that some of the censuses were suspect, and were calling for a systematic investigation of census execution. But such cautions tended not to be heard and the census returns themselves were assimilated into scholarly practice, with generations of history graduate students and junior faculty now joining their sociological counterparts and finding themselves constrained to use the census or to deal with others who did.

Remarkably, while there have been literally hundreds of studies in Canadian social history and historical sociology that have drawn on manuscript and aggregate census data, until *Politics of Population*, no one attempted to give a systematic account of 'how the census was done', nor to investigate the effects of practices of census knowledge production on the substance of the returns.

We can identify reasons for such neglect, but without a working understanding of the organization of knowledge production, one cannot locate the traces of it. And one typically has to read through, over, and around the official documentary system to construct defensible inferences about what actually was done, especially since government departments often destroy their guilty secrets. There is a kind of craft knowledge involved here that entails learning about how official documentary systems are constructed and mobilized for purposes other than the ones that might interest us, and then patching surviving pieces together to construct a credible narrative. And this is often monk's work: too slow for a dissertation, too big for anyone without secure employment, and unlikely to captivate most researchers.

There are other good reasons for the failure to scrutinize census-making. Aggregate returns carry the sanction of the state. Sovereign authority commonly works to construct and enforce truths, and census returns are made into truths practically, in that people's life chances are often determined by policies that draw on census information. As Bourdieu pointed out (1999, 2001), sociologists are dependent on the state in order to be critical of the state and, so, without **epistemological** vigilance, concepts and practices of state tend to colonize our thinking. As well, of course, aggregate returns are largely expressed in numbers, seemingly the furthest possible from narrative, and the closest possible to objective truth. My recent work shows that the numbers are indeed narratives, and it has been revealing to me to see how shocking it is to some researchers when first they notice that census numbers were in fact reports of reports of reports with oral history accounts at the bottom, given the denigration of popular memory by those who want to privilege the numerical form as 'hard data'.

One might respond to variations in a population data set by investigating the circumstances and the mechanics of the process of enumeration and revision; one might deal with provenance. Of course, this would demand a collective research project for world population data. Keilman instead turns inwards toward the data set and proposes that data quality can be evaluated by 'measuring the extent to which historical estimates have been revised in later years' at the national level. He proposes that 'a large spread' in estimates contained at different moments within the data source 'indicates large problems with data quality, and, by hypothesis, low accuracy' (2001: 152). So Keilman seeks to validate the data by using criteria internal to the data set—his main criterion is internal consistency. The best national census data sets are those without wildly fluctuating revisions, or those whose population reports remain relatively constant: these are the ones we should most trust. And I think that the invocation of the notion

of 'accuracy', although Keilman does not elaborate on it, is an implicit theory of reference. That is, smooth data sets that repeat a story consistently without wild fluctuations best capture the nature of the reality to which they refer; they are the most accurate. Because Keilman invokes no empirical evidence to sustain his position, I believe his is an aesthetic choice.

Phrased in this way, the claim cannot sustain critical scrutiny. A strong refutation comes from Peter Uvin's (2002) essay, 'On Counting, Categorizing, and Violence in Burundi and Rwanda'. In Rwanda, there were mass killings of Tutsi in 1962 and 1963, with about 10,000 people being murdered, and with somewhere between 140,000–250,000 fleeing to neighbouring countries. In late 1972, between 100,000 and 150,000 Hutu were killed by the Tutsi army in Burundi, with as many more fleeing that country. Uvin shows that 'both Rwandan and Burundian **population statistics** manage to hide these instances of mass violence,' which should have been clearly evident in countries where annual increments were about 60,000. Instead, 'all sets of Rwandan population data indicate that population increases continued exactly on trend.' In the Burundian case, the census scheduled for 1972 was dropped. No census was conducted for 7 years and then the returns showed a gradual decline. 'In order to make [the census total] compatible with older data, a ten-year-long decline in population growth was invented (and then reproduced by the United Nations)—and the selective genocide had disappeared with a statistical sleight of hand' (2002: 153–4). Smoothness in data sets, a constant theme with limited variations, then, is by no means a criterion for a reliable portrayal of violently uneven events.

An additional level of complexity lies in the fact that those who actually do the work of census enumeration cannot possibly ever see everyone, even if we wanted to privilege the vision of an enumerator as the measure of reality. In practice, enumeration takes place—in the periods before mail-in self-enumeration—by some kinds of people going around asking some other kinds of people about a third category of people. In fact, the census is not simply a discovery project. Who is to count as a person, where they are to be found, and who is to provide information about them are modelled, more or less coherently, conceptually before the enumeration begins and census managers then translate the model, more or less efficiently, into field measures. Yet census returns also result from negotiated understandings between enumerators and informants mediated by the text of enumeration schedule and other documents, and by the physical, environmental, and cultural aspects of the encounter. Informants may not co-operate. Informants may not command the information sought. Enumerators may not be able to write outdoors in winter and may copy more or less vaguely remembered information onto schedules later. The categories mobilized by the census may clash with the categories used by informants. The conceptual model drives observational practice, which is not to say that observed objects or relations fit with it.

I have been referring repeatedly and positively to **reflexive sociology**. In keeping with many others who are interested in the 'practice turn' in sociology, (among others, Bryant, 1995; Flyvbjerg, 2001) I am an advocate for a version of it about which I want to say a few words in conclusion. In Bourdieu's terms, the inherently controversial nature of our discipline compels us to exercise a particular form of epistemological vigilance. For him, that meant we need to operate our categories and interrogate them at the same time, and we need also to be able to relate the strategies of knowledge production that we adopt as individuals and as members of specialties to our own positions and investments in the sociological field (Bourdieu, 2001). Practically, from my point of view, such vigilance must also involve alertness to the areas in which we are invited to suspend disbelief so that our narratives will work, attention to the aesthetic qualities of practices and relations, and cognizance of the dependence of knowledge claims on contextual elements. The refusal to suspend disbelief is relatively easy; often we need only to be alert to foundational assumptions and narrative devices.

The issue of aesthetics invites us to be alert to our reactions and to those of others to research questions and research materials. I do not have a therapeutic agenda in this matter, even if I do think that the capacity to adopt a stance of moral and political agnosticism is one dimension of **reflexivity**. Rather, we don't want any guilty secrets; we need to know about what strikes us as the startling, the monstrous, the gripping, because such things define the contours of our conceptual postulates, and point to powerful zones of normativity. At the same time, for many of us, what doesn't fit, what is out of place, what won't work in the ways we're accustomed to things working can be instructive if we're prepared to notice. Category slippage, Bourdieu reminds us, is our bread and butter. And I am also thinking of things as simple as strange idioms: One enumerator describing his work in Canada in 1861 claimed that 'many of the heads of families, when comeatable, did not know how to answer my questions about acres of land, quantities of crops, etc.' Where does 'comeatable' fit? In a world where polling, questionnaires, forms, and surveys have not made it commonplace for just anyone to walk up to just anyone else and start asking questions? A world that has not yet been remade in the image of sociology (see Osborne and Rose, 1999)?

I'm not interested in saying we should jettison the numerical and statistical in favour of the literary. Sociology, in my view, needs to identify regularities and to analyze effects of structure. It depends on systematic social observation. Yet a reflexive sociology has to be cognizant of the ways in which the numerical and statistical decontextualize local particulars and enlist them in attempts to recontextualize. These practices are selective, disciplinary, and potentially violent. We need to be aware of the ways in which the local and particular are worked up into the general and abstract; and we need to be aware of the degrees of fit present when the abstract and general returns to confront the local and particular. We need to know things because when we don't know is when next it may blow up a gale.

References

Bourdieu, P. 2001. *Science de la science et réflexivité*. Cours du Collège de France. 2000–2001. Paris: Éditions Raisons d'Agir.

Bryant, C.G.A. 1995. *Practical Sociology. Post-empiricism and the Reconstruction of Theory and Application*. Oxford: Basil Blackwell.

Curtis, B. 2001. *The Politics of Population: Statistics, State Formation, and the Census of Canada, 1840–1875*. Toronto: University of Toronto Press.

Flyvbjerg, B. 2001. *Making Social Science Matter: Why Social Inquiry Fails and How It Can Succeed Again*. Cambridge: Cambridge University Press.

Keilman, N. 2001. 'Data Quality and the Accuracy of United Nations Population Projections, 1950–95', *Population Studies* 55: 149–64.

Mays, H.J., and H.F. Manzl. 1974. 'Literacy and Social Structure in Nineteenth Century Ontario: An Exercise in Historical Methodology', *Histoire sociale/ Social History*: 33–45.

Parsons, T. 1964. 'The School Class as a Social System: Some of its Functions in American Society', in *Social Structure and Personality*, pp. 129–54. New York: Free Press.

Uvin, P. 2002. 'On Counting, Categorizing, and Violence in Burundi and Rwanda', in *Census and Identity*, pp. 148–75, D.I. Kertzer and D. Arel, eds. Cambridge: Cambridge University Press.

CHAPTER 5

Francophone and Anglophone Sociologists in Canada: Diverging, Converging, or Parallel Trends?

Jean-Philippe Warren

As a specialist in the history of Quebec society in the twentieth century, I've occasionally been puzzled by the indifference French- and English-Canadian scholars seem to show toward one another (G. Rocher 1992). How, I have often asked myself, can sociology be so deeply divided in this country when scientific knowledge supposedly knows no cultural or political boundaries?

Many assume that English Canadians' indifference toward Quebec stems from the latter's demographic, political, and economic decline, relative to other provinces. There is of course a kernel of truth to this explanation, but there are other factors at play that I wish to consider. In particular, I will discuss how the normal growth of science contributes to the development of two antagonistic, paradoxical forces. One can link the development of these two antagonistic forces to a more specific

question about the relationship of French-Quebec and English-Canadian sociologists.

On the one hand, the evolution of science rests on the creation of national institutions devoted to scientific enterprise. Universities and research centres are usually directly linked to national ambitions and aspirations. On the other hand, science is driven by a universal principle that ideally transcends national boundaries and the politics of states. This double influence imposes a self-contradictory impetus to the expansion of science. As scientific research progresses, it becomes more national and more international *at the same time*.

Exploring this hypothesis, I wish to schematically present a few trends that have affected the development of sociology in French Quebec and the rest of Canada from the 1970s to the present day. Through this very brief history, we shall realize that neither the forces behind nationalization nor internationalization have—in this particular case—worked to foster a dialogue between the two linguistically divided scholarly communities.

Nationalization Trends

Fuelled by a boom in education and the economy, Canadian universities in the '60s had the resources to support a community of scholars devoted to a better understanding of their society. French-Quebec and English-Canadian sociologists enthusiastically aspired to gain greater autonomy vis-à-vis (principally) French, British, and U.S. institutions. However, during this period, sociologists in both English and French Canada encountered three acute areas of frustration.

First, people decried a congested job market. Such a critique was far more pronounced in English Canada than in French Quebec, where competition from U.S. or European scholars was never overwhelming. Around two-thirds of full-time English-Canadian sociologists had received their highest degree in a U.S. university in 1970. In 1970, 63 per cent of faculty had received their highest diploma from a U.S. institution, 18 per cent from a Canadian institution, and 8 per cent from a British institution.

Second, some scholars protested against the handing-out of syllabi for undergraduate courses and the publication of scientific research predominantly focused on U.S. society. They spoke in alarming terms of 'the extinction of the Canadian university' slowly and progressively swallowed up by the U.S. education system. In Quebec, Fernand Dumont (Warren 1998) argued in favour of a 'connaissance d'ici', a knowledge of the local produced by local scholars that would replace a picture of Quebec hitherto portrayed by foreign social scientists (Everett. C. Hughes, Horace Miner, Raoul Blanchard).

Third, many scholars believed that the epistemological perspective adopted by those practising within the walls of the academy was also at stake. They pleaded in favour of a genuinely Canadian approach that would be rooted in Canadian identity. The 'quest for a Canadian sociology' (Hiller 1979) became the object of intense discussions.

Were Quebec and Canadian sociologies more historical, macrosociological, and interdisciplinary compared to the allegedly more presentist, **quantitative**, and **microsociological** sociology practised in the United States (Hiller 1980)? Should they be?

The ultimate objective, in French Quebec and in English Canada, was to establish a science of society that would be fully nationalized. Professors would be home-trained. Research would be focused on locally rooted realities. Theories and methodologies would be elaborated in a Quebec or Canadian perspective.

Although the third never materialized, the first two aspects of the nationalist program enjoyed some success. In the last 40 years, the proportion of Canadian faculty with a foreign diploma has decreased steadily over time. At the beginning of the twenty-first century, after a quarter of a century of Canadianization (Cormier 2004), Canadian-trained sociologists were at last predominant in their departments in Quebec and in the rest of the country (Gingras and Warren 2006). Also, the study of Canadian society made formidable inroads in academia. Courses on Quebec and Canadian societies were offered. Well-funded research projects devoted to a global analysis of the two nations' features were completed. Books and articles on Canadian and Quebec studies filled up libraries.

A Growing Separation

The first obvious result of the Quebec-ization movement and the Canadianization movements was to isolate the two linguistically distinct scientific communities (F. Rocher 2007). French-Canadian sociology professors regrouped themselves into their own disciplinary society, the Association canadienne des sociologues et anthropologues de langue française, created in 1969. They launched their own journals, *Recherches sociographiques* in 1960 and *Sociologie et Sociétés* in 1969. They organized their own research centres and conferences under the umbrella of the Association canadienne-française pour l'avancement de la science.

Whereas French Quebecers adopted a strict unilingual principle, English-Canadian sociologists kept the official bilingual policy of their journals, conferences, and associations when, in fact, these journals, conferences, and associations had *de facto* become English-only venues. For example, the CSA has been, for a very long time, an English-dominated institution. Only twice in its entire history did the CSA award an outstanding achievement award to a French-Quebec sociologist.

Consider two other indicators of this academic divorce. The first indicator is the institution of higher learning in which Canadian university professors of sociology obtain their PhDs. Those who have studied in English Canada teach in English Canada, and reciprocally, those who have obtained their degree in a French-Canadian institution are hired by French-Quebec universities. The second indicator is interprovincial collaboration. Looking at the most recent period, one can observe how isolated from French universities English-Canadian sociology is. For an English-Canadian sociologist living anywhere outside Quebec, the likelihood of co-authoring an article with a researcher in the United States or the United Kingdom is incomparably greater than it is with a researcher from French Quebec.

In brief, in the last 40 years, English- and French-Canadian sociologists have moved away from one another because of the growing nationalization of the sociological field. But, if my central hypothesis holds any truth, we should *at the same time* be able to observe trends toward the internationalization of the discipline. Indeed, data shows that the two solitudes are not working in isolation; it's just that they don't work with one another (Gingras, Godin and Foisy 1999). In other words, sociologists do not turn away from international collaborations—only away from collaborations across the French Canada/English Canada boundary. Having a choice, French-Quebec and English-Canadian sociologists prefer to co-author their publications with U.S., British, French, Israeli, Italian, or German colleagues.

Internationalization Trends

While the nationalization of the sociological field was providing scholars with the means to research, publish, and travel, its internationalization was channelling sociologists' research away from their society. Of course, other external factors were at stake—to name a few: globalization, U.S. imperialism, and the neo-liberal agenda. But here I wish to insist only on the internal dynamics of science; dynamics that have recently come to challenge the Quebec-ization and Canadianization movements.

Nowhere is the impact of internationalization clearer than in the language used by French-Quebec sociologists. For a growing number of them, English has now become the language of exchange and publication. Today, fewer than 50 per cent of the social science articles listed in Quebec, Belgian, and French databases are published in French (Gingras 2008). From 1990 to 1999, according to citation counts from the Web of Science, about half of all the books cited by French-Quebec sociologists were English; the proportion is now close to 80 per cent.

But the effect of internationalization on sociologists goes further than language. To 'be' international, one must appeal to international audiences. The decision to publish in English is not enough to attract the attention of foreign colleagues. And—let us face reality—the readership of prestigious peer-reviewed journals, the attendees of international conferences organized in glamorous metropolises around the globe, the researchers in Ivy League schools are generally not interested in Quebec- or Canada-specific issues.

This may explain why scientific journals founded in Quebec since the 1990s do not bear a title explicitly mentioning 'Quebec', or why a number of respected journals changed their titles to erase the words 'Québec' or 'Canada français' from their titles. This may also explain why Canadians both inside and outside Quebec have started to talk more about U.S. society, where the top-ranked journals are edited, and less about their own society. 'United States' is now one of the top-30 terms used in the titles of Canadian sociologists' articles. Moreover, this may help us understand why, in English Canada, over half of tenured and tenure-track professors of sociology who obtained their degree after 2004 obtained it from a U.S. university, a percentage not far away from the one recently decried by Groarke and Fenske (2009) in philosophy departments.

Let us dig deeper. It seems that the internationalization of the field affects Canadian sociology's major intellectual influences. Looking at the authors most cited by Canadian sociologists, one notices the rising domination of non-Canadian scholars. In the 1980s, among the 10 most cited authors were, according to citation counts from the Web of Science, John Porter, John Hagan, Wallace Clement, and Seymour Martin Lipset—scholars who devoted some part of their career to understanding Canada. In the 1990s and 2000s, Dorothy Smith and John Hagan were the only 'Canadian' sociologists on this top-10 list, and even they didn't fully qualify. By the early 2000s, Hagan was back in the United States and Dorothy Smith was formulating a feminist sociology of knowledge that didn't focus on Canada.

Looking at these facts, some might say that Canadian sociology is being increasingly swallowed into international sociology, losing its identity in the process. That may be. But my main point is elsewhere. What I wish to draw attention to is the fact that French-Quebec sociologists and English-Canadian sociologists have—ironically—never been so isolated from one another as they are now that their works are increasingly influenced by the same authors and the same sources. Academic cross-fertilization between English-Canadian and French-Quebec sociologists is as low as ever, and yet their common integration into the international scientific field has perhaps never been greater. The two solitudes are dancing with the same partner, so to speak.

Clashing Point

Many scholars fail to apprehend the intertwined nationalization and internationalization of a discipline. The former involves the development of national institutions (universities, research centres, prizes, journals, etc.). The latter denotes integration into a field that is not specific to any nation and in which concepts, methodologies, and theoretical approaches are shared, or at least acknowledged, by all members of the scientific community.

From 1970 to 2000, the Quebec-ization and Canadianization movements made enormous gains in Quebec and in the rest of the country. French Quebec and English Canada now benefit from well-funded academic institutions, strong undergraduate and graduate programs, peer-reviewed journals, disciplinary associations, and so forth.

At the same time, Canadian sociologies were always under pressure to internationalize. The invitations to write in English, to publish in international journals, to present papers in European and U.S. colloquia, and to seek foreign collaborations resonate louder and louder in the academy. From the standpoint of science alone, this trend seems inescapable. For example, the once-distinct field of Canadian physics doesn't exist anymore. It has been abolished by the evolution of science. In 2010, notwithstanding their numerous debates, physicists from all over the globe belong to one and only one world community.

It appears that we have now reached a clashing point. Scholars are increasingly asked to choose between, on the one hand, supporting the Quebec-ization or Canadianization movement and, on the other hand, working toward the continuous strengthening of internationalization. Science per se does not give them a choice. But perhaps a science of society does.

References

Cormier, Jeffrey. 2004. *The Canadianization Movement. Emergence, Survival, and Success*. Toronto: University of Toronto Press.

Gingras, Yves. 2008. « Les langues de la sciences: le français et la diffusion de la connaissance. » in Jacques Mauret et al. (eds.), *L'avenir du français*. Paris: Éditions des archives contemporaines: 95–97.

Gingras, Yves, Benoît Godin and Martine Foisy. 1999. 'The Internationalization of Univerity Research in Canada'. In Sheryl Bond and Jean-Pierre Lemasson (eds.), *A New World of Knowledge. Canadian Universities and Globalization*. Ottawa: IDRC: 77–98.

Gingras, Yves and Jean-Philippe Warren. 2006. 'A British Connection? A Quantitative Analysis of the Changing Relations Between American, British and Canadian Sociologists'. *Canadian Journal of Sociology*, 31 (4): 509–522.

Groarke, Louis and Wayne Fenske. 2009. 'PhD. To What End?' *University Affairs* 50, November 9: Accessed online at http://www.universityaffairs.ca/phd-to-what-end.aspx.

Hiller, Harry H. 1979. 'The Canadian Sociology Movement: Analysis and Assessment'. *Canadian Journal of Sociology* 4: 125–150.

Hiller, Harry H. 1980. 'Paradigmatic Shifts, Indigenization, and the Development of Sociology in Canada'. *Journal of the History of Behavioral Sciences* 16: 263–274.

Rocher, François. 2007. 'The End of the 'Two Solitudes'? The Presence (or Absence) of the Work of French-Speaking Scholars in Canadian Politics'. *Canadian Journal of Political Science* 40 (4), December: 833–857.

Rocher, Guy. 1992. 'The Two Solitudes Among Canadian Sociologists'. In William K. Carroll and al. (eds.), *Fragile Truths. Twenty-Five Years of Sociology and Anthropology in Canada*. Ottawa: Carleton University Press.

Warren, Jean-Philippe. 1998. *Un Supplément d'âme. Les intentions primordiales de Fernand Dumont (1947–1970)*. Sainte-Foy: Les Presses de l'Université Laval.

Questions for Critical Thought

CHAPTER 1

1. What is the trouble with trying to differentiate between political and academic views, or to determine which truths matter for academia? Based on the various arguments in this paper, what are some potential dangers in working too hard to keep some truths out of academia, and conversely, not working hard enough to maintain academic integrity?
2. Discuss the three different perspectives on the role of the sociologist that Eglin describes. What are the strengths and weaknesses of each?
3. What is the difference between politics 1 and politics 2? Do you think this distinction is an effective way around the politics/academia dilemma? Explain.
4. Discuss with your classmates the signs of intellectual citizenship on campus. Which role of the sociologist/intellectual citizen do you think is practised at your college/university? In your department? In your classroom?
5. Compare Eglin's concept of incarnation with Mills' concept of the sociological imagination. Discuss any similarities and differences.

CHAPTER 2

1. What are Burawoy's four faces of sociology? What does he mean by value science, and which values does he argue that we should reach toward?
2. Describe the four variables with which Porter operationalizes progress. Do you think that these are sufficiently specific operationalizations? Are there other important variables that you can think of that weren't included?
3. Compare Burawoy's and Porter's visions of public sociology. How are they similar and different?
4. Recall the epistemological vigilance that Curtis called for in his piece. Using this vigilance, consider the chapter on methods and theory in your introductory sociology textbook. Look for the assumptions it makes about the role/purpose of the sociologist. Do you think the chapter endorses the principles of Porter's public sociology? Does it endorse any other roles explored in Eglin's or Helmes–Hayes' papers in this section? If not, what message do you think it sends about the role and purpose of sociology?
5. How does Helmes-Hayes' article build on Eglin's analysis of the varying sociological roles?

CHAPTER 3

1. By studying Aboriginals as problems rather than legitimate contributors to Canadian society, McGuire argues that most Canadian sociologists studying Aboriginals enact the cultural biases of their society and take part in the very marginalization that they aim to study. What unique methodological and ethical challenges does this interconnectedness between sociologists and the phenomena they study pose for the sociologist trying to

pursue 'objective' knowledge? Be sure to discuss the effects of both society on socio-logical knowledge, and sociological knowledge on its research subjects and society.

2.   What does McGuire mean when she says that Western and indigenous knowledge are not binary, mutually exclusive categories? Based on what McGuire has said and what you have seen of sociology so far, what parts of sociological thinking are compatible with the indigenous knowledge she describes? What parts are not?

3.   In this article, much is made of the tension between particular/relative and general/uni-versal types of knowledge. Discuss the strengths and weaknesses of each, and how Mc-Guire suggests that they should relate to each other.

4.   What is the purpose of creating a social theory rooted in indigenous views? Which role of the sociologist (as presented in Eglin's and Helmes-Hayes' articles) do you think McGuire fills most closely?

5.   This article brings up the problem of insider (in this case local, indigenous) and outsider (general, Eurocentric) perspectives. What are the opportunities and dangers in producing knowledge about other groups and about our own groups? Would insiders and outsiders be able to see different things? Explain.

6.   Consider McGuire's use of the term 'reflexivity'. Does she mean the same thing as Curtis does? Why or why not?

CHAPTER 4

1.   What are some problems that Curtis points out with assuming that the numerical data speak for themselves, or are more certain than other kinds of data? Why are numerical data not as simple to interpret as they seem? Provide examples from the article, especially concerning how census data is actually collected.

2.   What are some of the limitations with judging the quality and validity of data on it's internal consistency? If internal validity is misleading, how else can we judge the quality of data?

3.   What does it mean to have epistemological vigilance?

4.   Reread Curtis's article. Can you find places where he has not been vigilant enough in his analysis? Are there places that surprise you, or make you suspicious of his argument? Does he defend them effectively? Do these omissions weaken his argument?

5.   Curtis brings up some important weaknesses of census data, but he doesn't propose that they are entirely useless. Despite the weaknesses, how are census data valuable for soci-ologists and society?

CHAPTER 5

1.   Explain what Warren means by scientific research in Canada expanding both nationally and internationally. How has this created conflict for the francophone and anglophone sociologists of Canada?

2.   Compare the 'quest for [English- and French-] Canadian sociology' to McGuire's call for indigenous sociology. How are the concerns at the core of both movements similar and different?

3. According to Warren, what was the first growing separation between the French and English Canadians? How did this come about? Be sure to provide evidence from the paper.
4. Does Warren argue that French and English sociologists are different in how they do sociology? Explain how English and French Canadians still contribute to ongoing sociology even though they have ceased working together at a national level.
5. This article also touched on the dilemma of particular versus universal knowledge, but in a different way from McGuire's paper. What are the strengths and weaknesses of studying issues on a more international level rather than on a national level?

Part II

Culture

Just as with theories and methods, the idea that the sociological study of culture can be fully addressed within one section of this volume may be misleading, as every chapter deals with culture in one way or another. Humans are cultural creatures, and so there is hardly anything that we do that does not involve culture. What exactly does it mean to be a cultural creature? Put simply, it means that our behaviour is not set for us by biological instincts alone. But what about all of our biological functions? Yes, it is true, there are no societies in which people do not breathe, eat, and bleed, no matter how different their cultures are. But this doesn't mean that we all think about breath, food, and blood in the same way. And our differences are not limited to ideas. We have very different practices surrounding our seeming biological similarities. Consider the central meditative role of breath in eastern religion, or seclusion rituals performed during menstruation in some ancient and current religions. Compare these with modern Christianity's considerable silence on both breathing and menstruating. Furthermore, what we eat and the technologies we develop to prepare and eat it are so different across cultures that they can repel us from one another.

So what is culture? In the biggest sense, it is everything about our existence that is not biologically determined. But this definition is hardly helpful for sociological investigation. Some useful tools for narrowing our scope (fine-tuning our theoretical flashlights) might be to think about ideas/symbols and actions/practices. Much of cultural studies in sociology focuses on symbolic genres, such as national poems, self-help books, and pornography. It can analyze the symbolic content: the assumptions made within, and messages communicated through, such genres. For example, in this section of the book, Sarah Knudson explores the changing assumptions about equality in heterosexual romantic relationships as reflected in advice given in self-help books.

Cultural studies also investigates the production and spread of ideas. Slobodan Drakulic considers the folk-song origins of the various Balkan nationalities. He challenges the popular thesis that national identities are created by political elites to unify their subjects against external groups. He points out that political elites draw from the cultural context around them rather than just spinning an identity out of thin air.

Cultural studies often interrogates everyday practices that we entirely take for granted. The goal of such work is to articulate the assumptions or purposes underlying these practices, or to consider their unintended, unnoticed effects. Stephen Riggins contemplates our practices of collecting and presenting objects in our homes. He outlines a methodology for investigating social status through these practices—exploring aspects such as how we use them (or don't), how we display them, and how we aggregate them into groups.

But ideas and practices are not entirely separate from one another. Steve Garlick explores how a symbolic message is changed when it is received through a different practice. Specifically, he investigates the practice of accessing the pornographic genre through searching the Internet rather than by watching videos or looking through magazines. Garlick argues that men's ideas about themselves, women, and sex are shaped differently when they access the pornography genre through the Internet. The very process of online navigation cultivates assumptions that leave their impressions on the sexual experiences that it mediates.

CHAPTER 6

Maintaining Control?
Masculinity and Internet Pornography

Steve Garlick

While it is widely acknowledged that gender is a key category in **pornography**, the relation of porn to contemporary masculinities remains relatively obscure. With few exceptions (Brod, 1990; Barron & Kimmel, 2000; Kimmel, 2005; Cook, 2006), the connection between the **social construction** of **masculinity** and the consumption of pornographic images has been more often presumed than examined. There is a substantial literature that debates the merits of men's use of pornography in terms of its contribution to gender inequality, but surprisingly little work attempts to understand how pornographic representations are involved with the production of hegemonic masculinities. This lacuna becomes more apparent when juxtaposed with the profusion and proliferation of Internet porn in recent years.

This paper aims to contribute to a more sustained analysis of 'techno-porn'. Rather than entering into existing anti- or pro-porn debates, however, I wish to move in a different direction and to pose a different set of questions about the relationship between masculinity, technology, and pornography. As starting points, I offer two critical comments in relation to Robert Jensen's (2007) **radical feminist** critique of pornography. First, while Jensen recognizes that the Internet has revolutionized the delivery of pornography, he does not consider whether this technology might be more than simply a means of delivering an existing product. By contrast, in what follows, I explore the question of whether the Internet may in fact produce a qualitative change in the way in which viewers are affected by pornography. Second, for Jensen, technology is important insofar as it increases men's ability to control the experience of porn and, in turn, to control women's bodies. I will argue that while he is correct in his identification of the centrality of control to the pornographic imagination, it is not merely the control of women's bodies that is at stake in contemporary pornography. Rather, porn participates in a larger drama involving the technological confrontation between men and nature—one in which the meaning of masculinity is perpetually at stake.

Modern Pornography

It is important to note that, while sexual acts have been represented throughout history and across cultures, pornography as we now recognize it has not always existed. Lynn Hunt (1993) has shown that the beginnings of something resembling contemporary 'pornography' first emerged in European societies alongside print culture in the sixteenth century. These texts and images were considered to be a form of social and religious criticism associated with an Enlightenment sensibility that rejected conventional moralities and religious orthodoxies. Historical evidence suggests that the early part of the nineteenth century was the crucial period for defining modern pornography. At this time, porn lost its politically subversive qualities and became merely a means of displaying women's bodies for the purposes of men's sexual arousal (Hunt, 1993: 42). The specific character of modern pornography began to crystallize around the pleasures that men could take in the explicit display of women's bodies. At the same time, porn became more widely available—a move that led to attempts to restrict its circulation in the name of preserving public morality from the threat of 'obscenity'.

A key factor here was the invention of photography. Although it scarcely features in conventional histories of the medium, photography has always manifested a strong desire for sex. Plentiful evidence of the explosion of explicit photographic images of women from the 1840s onwards is available to those who look for it (Ovenden & Mendes, 1973). Here, technology is not merely a neutral medium for the transmission of sex; rather, it changes both how we see and what we see. Early photography appeared to offer truthful, empirical knowledge about human bodies, and this was crucial to its role in pornography (Pultz, 1995). Photography promised objective truth without the contaminants of subjectivity and, in this context, the pornographic image potentially held the power to define sexual difference—to tell the *truth* of sex by allowing it to show itself. It thereby also promised men the power to take control of sex.

The modern pornographic imagination has always been wedded to technology, whether the medium is photography, film, video, or the Internet. The question is whether porn remains the same across these different media, or whether the affective force of sex changes along with the emergence of new technologies.

Masculinity, Techno-porn, and Nature

Internet pornography, I want to suggest, may be profitably theorized as an example of what Martin Heidegger (1977) refers to as 'modern technology' in his classic essay 'The Question Concerning Technology'. For Heidegger, technology should not be conceived in instrumental terms as a mere technical means of achieving a given end. Rather than simply a category of mechanical devices,

technology is a particular 'way of revealing' (1977: 12). It refers to a historical mode of bringing forth the energies of nature into culture. According to Heidegger, modern technology is primarily concerned with 'enframing' nature, or with the regulating and securing of natural forces. It is a call to order, a ceaseless program of challenging-forth, categorizing, and disciplining nature. Heidegger believes that because enframing presents itself as a transparent relation to nature, it diminishes our ability to recognize that modern technology is a contingent historical mode of revealing. Moreover, it blocks our ability to recognize singularity, complexity, and difference within the natural world.

I suggest that as pornography has moved online, its character as a form of modern technology has become more apparent. Consider almost any pornographic website—when navigating the site, you are presented with an array of categories. Bodies, acts, body parts are called to order—'Asian', 'anal', 'ass'—technologically revealed within a preexisting framework that collapses differences even as it seemingly multiplies them. Complexities of desire, emotion, and bodily response are swept up into these categories of 'standing reserve'—available at the click of a mouse. Internet technology promises to fulfill viewers' desire to see the truth of sex as it is challenged-forth to presence and brought under control.

Jensen claims that the most important thing to recognize 'is how central the concept of control—of women by men—is to pornography' (2007: 114). Yet, he also asserts that the pornographic imagination creates a fantasy world in which all women always want sex, and, if at first they don't realize this, they can easily be persuaded because it is *in their nature* (2007: 57). Men's control, therefore, appears to be less the exertion of an external power of dominance than it is the ability to call forth that which is allegedly inherent to women's nature. From this perspective, the gender politics of porn may be said to turn upon the *enframing* of nature—its calling to order. Moreover, I contend that this connection between gender and the politics of nature is crucial to understanding the role of technology and Internet pornography in the production of hegemonic masculinities. This is not simply a matter of men's domination over women; rather, mainstream pornography stages a confrontation between Man and nature—one in which the ongoing desire to establish control over nature by bringing it to order is central to the status of masculinity.

A paradox appears, however: Internet pornography promotes standardization, and yet the ongoing proliferation of sex online continually threatens to fragment the visual field. The pornographic experience is more fragmentary on the Net, due both to the fact that viewers 'surf' from site to site or image to image, and to a change in the way that the pornographic content on offer is produced and distributed. Of particular interest here is the rise of not-for-profit, amateur pornography on the Internet. For example, on freely available, mixed-content websites such as xtube.com or youporn.com, commercial 'teasers' and user-generated images and videos exist side by side. Because amateur netporn is often produced in fragments—obscure images or video clips that begin at an arbitrary moment in the scene and don't necessarily bring it to the conventional conclusion of the 'money shot'—the effect is to disrupt the conventional narratives of commercial 'hard core' porn.

It is perhaps from this perspective that we may begin to grasp the distinctive features of Internet porn. Indeed, I argue that it is in the elusive and fragmentary quality of its technovision that Internet pornography effects a shift from previous modes of pornographic representation. Although the Internet can be a means of delivering conventional video content, the technological interface is such that it breaks down the expectation that a narrative structure exists to guide the viewer's pleasure.

Of central importance here is the contention that the Internet has promoted what Brian McNair (2002) refers to as the 'democratization of desire'. Digital technologies have lowered barriers to production and allowed almost anyone with access to a video camera and an Internet connection to become a participant in the world of pornography. This, in turn, has widened the sphere of pornographic representation and opened it up to more unconventional bodies and desires (Lehman, 2006). It is not simply the advent of

amateur content that is significant, however; it is the technovision of the Internet that allows pornography to be presented *as fragments* of people's everyday experience—affective images unencumbered by the guidelines of narrative. This is significant because it might at first seem as though the path that leads to a freeing up of vision would of necessity turn away from technologically enframed modes of seeing. Yet, this is not what Heidegger suggests. On the contrary, he claims that 'the coming to presence of technology harbors in itself what we least suspect, the possible arising of the saving power' (1977:32). Could amateur porn break the narratives of mainstream porn and 'save' porn viewers from the constraints of hegemonic masculinity? How can amateur porn break the effects of online enframing *even from within that very same enframing*?

Sex and Boredom

Harry Brod observes that pornographic representations of sex reduce and narrow desires to the extent that they become *boring* (1990: 194). Internet pornography, if its proponents are to be believed, is supposed to overcome such problems by offering greater interactivity and a much wider diversity of sexual representations. Yet, there are good reasons to think that pornography may have actually become more boring through its shift online.

To claim that pornography is boring may seem somewhat perverse. After all, if there is one feature of pornographic representations that might be said to hold the genre together, then it is surely the capacity to excite and arouse desire. What could be less boring than a vast sexual smorgasbord ready and awaiting the tap of a keyboard? Yet, the ever-escalating catalogue of extreme sexual acts perhaps reveals that Internet pornography does become increasingly boring over time. A quality of sameness overtakes the images as acts and body parts are endlessly repeated, catalogued, and circulated as resources around the globe. This sameness drives pornographers to search for ever-new representations of what is 'hot' or 'nasty' this week, but the cycle is ultimately self-defeating and a state of boredom is engendered. As Arthur

Kroker observes: 'It is the age of the bored eye: the eye which flits from situation to situation, from scene to scene, from image to image, from ad to ad, with a restlessness and high-pitched consumptive appetite that can never really ever be fully satisfied' (2004: 167). Internet porn is a spearhead of this culture of boredom.

As noted above, Heidegger does not advocate the rejection of technology, but sees possible resistance to 'enframing' as arising from reflection upon technology itself. Similarly, he claims that we should not try to push boredom away (through busying ourselves by clicking on the next image), but rather we need to experience what it tells us about the condition of our lives. We need to attune ourselves to 'the *fundamental emptiness that bores us*' (Heidegger, 1995: 164). For Heidegger, if we are able to experience the boredom that pervades our technological culture for what it is—a sign of danger—then we can take a step toward freeing ourselves from it.

What if Internet porn were a pre-eminent place wherein we may experience the boredom of our contemporary sexual culture, and thereby reflect upon what it tells us? Surely, it would tell us something about our current gender order—about how masculinity is produced through the enframing of nature and how this blocks other potential ways of being. Moreover, what if the emergence of amateur porn on the Net is a sign of a turning away from enframing? What if these fragments of sexual life began to challenge the masculine position of control? Certainly, this is no sure thing. Notably, 'amateur' pornography is increasingly commodified as capital moves online; what was one day a site of user-generated content may the next day be a commercial for-profit venture. Moreover, there is no guarantee that amateur sex does anything more than reproduce the gendered models of the conventional pornographic imagination. Clearly, it is important to retain a critical lens on all forms of pornography. Yet, insofar as marginal forms of online porn are able to break away from the profit-driven imperative to reinforce the existing gender order and, instead, to give us glimpses of sex that rupture the usual narratives of gender and sexuality, they thereby alert us to the sway of technological enframing and potentially disrupt the production of hegemonic masculinity within the pornographic imagination.

References

Barron, Martin & Michael Kimmel. 2000. Sexual Violence in Three Pornographic Media: Towards a Sociological Explanation. *Journal of Sex Research* 37 (2):161–9.

Brod, Harry. 1990. Eros Thanatized: Pornography and Male Sexuality. In *Men Confront Pornography*, ed. Michael Kimmel, 190–206. New York: Crown.

Cook, Ian. 2006. Western Heterosexual Masculinity, Anxiety, and Web Porn. *The Journal of Men's Studies* 14 (1):47–63.

Heidegger, Martin. 1977. The Question Concerning Technology. In *The Question Concerning Technology and Other Essays*. Trans. William Lovitt, 3–35. New York: Harper & Row. Originally published as Die Frage nach der Technik, in *Vorträge und Aufsätze* (1954).

------. 1995. *The Fundamental Concepts of Metaphysics: World, Finitude, Solitude*. Trans. William McNeill & Nicholas Walker. Bloomington: Indiana University Press. Originally published as *Die Grundbegriffe der Metaphysik. Welt—Endlichkeit—Einsamkeit* (1983).

Hunt, Lynn. 1993. Introduction: Obscenity and the Origins of Modernity, 1500–1800. In *The Invention of Pornography: Obscenity and the Origins of Modernity, 1500–1800*, ed. Lynn Hunt, 9–45. New York: Zone Books.

Jensen, Robert. 2007. *Getting Off: Pornography and the End of Masculinity*. Cambridge: South End Press.

Kimmel, Michael. 2005. Pornography and Male Sexuality. *The Gender of Desire: Essays on Male Sexuality*. Albany: SUNY Press.

Kroker, Arthur. 2004. *The Will to Technology and the Culture of Nihilism: Heidegger, Nietzsche, and Marx*. Toronto: University of Toronto Press.

Lehman, Peter. 2006. Introduction: 'A Dirty Little Secret'—Why Teach and Study Pornography? In *Pornography: Film and Culture*, ed. Peter Lehman, 1–20. New Brunswick: Rutgers University Press.

McNair, Brian. 2002. *Striptease Culture: Sex, Media and the Democratization of Desire*. London: Routledge.

Ovenden, Graham & Peter Mendes. 1973. *Victorian Erotic Photography*. London: Academy Editions.

Pultz, John. 1995. *The Body and the Lens*. New York: Harry N. Abrams.

What a Girl Wants, What a Girl Needs: Examining Cultural Change and Ideas about Gender Equality in Relationship Self-Help Books, 1960–2009

Sarah Knudson

Introduction: The Case for Studying Relationship Self-Help

Changes in advice book messages over the past 50 years reflect and speak to the many cultural and structural changes that have affected how heterosexual men and women think about and live out their intimate lives. Sociologists can therefore turn to relationship self-help to illuminate changing gender relations, social structures, and ideologies. As key social structures in North America where individuals once sought guidance about their relationships—for instance, the church and extended families—lose cultural potency (Bellah et al., 1985), and insecurities about social and economic structures—namely our families, our intimate relationships, our jobs and career trajectories—become increasingly insecure or unclear (McGee, 2005), people are turning to alternative sources of advice, of which self-help books are a readily available example. Their accessibility and low cost, along with the privacy they offer readers, suggest that they will remain a popular source for relationship advice in the coming years (Schudson, 1989; Simonds, 1992; Starker, 1989).

Self-Help Amid the 'Chaos' of Contemporary Love

Though the popularity of self-help literature and relationship advice is widely acknowledged in sociological research (see Carpenter, 2008; Neville, 2007; Whelan, 2004), sociologists disagree about the nature of relationship advice books' content and their impact on intimate relationships. Most researchers (e.g. Boynton, 2003; Clarke and Rúdólfsdóttir, 2005; Coontz, 2005; Ericksen, 1999; Hazleden, 2003, 2004; Hochschild, 1994; Jamieson, 1998; Ménard and Kleinplatz, 2008; Siegel, 2000) suggest that advice literature champions conservative or even regressive approaches to developing and sustaining relationships. Anthony Giddens (1992), however, opposes these views and argues that advice books help men and women expect and achieve more egalitarian relationships. We are thus confronted with varying ideas about continuity, change, and promotion of gender equality in book content over time. This existing body of research invites more in-depth, longitudinal study that identifies changes in the genre's messages and situates them against a backdrop of macro-level social change in order to address why the shifts have occurred.

The past half-century is of particular sociological interest because intimate relationships have altered profoundly during this 'late modern era' (see Bauman, 2000; Beck and Beck-Gernshiem, 2004; Stocks, 2007: 3; Wilson and Stocks, 2004: 72). Couples now marry later, cohabitation has grown in popularity, and relationships are becoming more egalitarian in terms of power and resources (Ambert, 2006). Increasingly, couples come from mixed ethnic and socio-economic backgrounds, divorce has lost much of its cultural stigma, and there has been a marked increase in the number of single-parent households and blended families (Coontz, 2005; Gross, 2005). These changes have made love and loving in the late modern era 'chaotic', as couples try to build successful relationships in a culture where multiple scripts for loving (the traditional, the modern, and the postmodern) coexist (Beck and Beck-Gernsheim, 1995). It also creates a climate ripe for individuals to seek out relationship guidance.

Data and Method

A sample of bestselling relationship advice books from 1960–2009 was created using a stratified random sampling technique. Ten books were selected from each decade, drawn from a master list consisting of all relevant titles found in *Publishers Weekly* and *New York Times* bestseller book lists. Exceptionally, only three books published in the 1960s met the criteria for inclusion, making the total sample size forty-three books. Qualitative content analysis techniques were used to examine the data, with a focus on themes and an interest in authors' explicit and implicit messages.

Findings

Cluster 1 (1960s and 1970s): Openness and Joy: New Frontiers in Intimate Life

The sample's earliest books demonstrate a striking optimism concerning changes in intimate life, broader social changes, and their impact on heterosexual relationships. Authors (1) emphasize that partners should be seen as equals, (2) endorse exploration of new relationship forms, (3) promote couples' investment in ensuring women's sexual satisfaction, and (4) stress the need for open and honest communication. Authors also speak excitedly about the women's movement and encourage women's increasing financial independence through labour force involvement. Authors speak confidently about the possibility of breaking away from traditional models of dating and marriage and experimenting with tailor-made intimate arrangements. George and Nena O'Neill's *Open Marriage* typifies the period's ideas: 'Equality in open marriage is a state of mind, supported by respect and consideration for each other's wishes and needs. Roles can thus be flexible and interchangeable' (1972: 52). Some voices in the sample, however, advocate a contradictory mixture of tradition and change in patterns of intimate living; Helen Gurley Brown (1962), for instance, promotes single women's sexual experimentation, but suggests maintenance of traditional roles within the framework of marriage.

Cluster 2 (1980s to mid-1990s): Be Your Own Prince!: Cautionary Tales of Being Burned

By the early 1980s, a marked shift in the advice books' emphases is evident. Optimism about and interest in exploration in relationships give way to calls for women's caution and introspection. Books also demonstrate an increasingly myopic view of relationships, focusing on couples or the woman only, while backgrounding social context. Five foci are characteristic of this cluster: (1) emphasis on the relationship of the self with self, (2) promotion of women's self-love above all relationship concerns, (3) a vocabulary of dysfunction and pathology for framing relationship challenges, (4) caution to women vis-à-vis emotional investment in relationships, and (5) greater sexual conservatism. These foci appear alongside an overarching emphasis on the need for women to be seen and treated as equals, but authors show less confidence in the reality of equal partnerships.

Authors stress that a willingness to get to know and love oneself better is a prerequisite to a willingness to fall in love (DeAngelis, 1992; Hendrix, 1992; Russianoff, 1982), and that men are 'just desserts'—a cherry meant to crown a woman's already satisfying life (Friedman, 1983). In *The Cinderella Complex*, Colette Dowling informs readers that a prince is not coming to rescue them; women will instead have to be their own princes, filled with self-love instead of waiting to be rescued and validated (1981: 215–216). The imperative to love oneself above all and the quest to find a selfless lover coexist uncomfortably in this cluster's messages. In this cluster, neo-liberal ideology also creeps into the books (see Rimke, 2000). Women are asked to be self-conscious, to self-regulate and to take responsibility for their successes and failures in relationships; authors tell them to refocus their energies inward, prioritizing the self in a genre ostensibly about relationships.

Cluster 3 (mid-1990s to late 2000s): Cheetah Boys and Creatures Unlike Any Other: The Return of Romance . . . among Equal Partners

Another shift in advice book content gains momentum in the mid-1990s. Books from this cluster (1) promote so-called egalitarian relationships but emphasize the need for distinctly feminine and masculine personae within them (a model of gender equality *without* gender uniformity), (2) voice displeasure at the outcomes of the feminist movement and the perceived erosion of family values, (3) promote romance, a return to chivalry and male leadership, and (4) emphasize the importance of God, religion, and spirituality in intimate relations. Neo-liberal discourses also intensify in this cluster's titles, and a post-feminist view of gender relations becomes dominant, whereby neo-conservative arguments about gender and sexuality and a focus on individualism are used to claim that equality has been achieved and feminism is no longer needed (McRobbie, 2009: 8–12).

Books from this period continue to bracket broader structural issues affecting intimate relations, and considerable tension is evident between authors' insistence on men and women's formal equality and their belief that men and women must have different roles and personae in relationships. As Ellen Fein and Sherrie Schneider stress in *The Rules*,

> We understand why modern, career-oriented women have sometimes scoffed at our suggestions. They've been MBA-trained to 'make things happen' and to take charge of their careers. However, a relationship with a man is different from a job. In a relationship, the man must take charge. He must propose. We are not making this up—biologically, he's the aggressor (1995: 9).

The solution, according to the authors, lies in men assuming their 'Cheetah Boy' persona—leading, providing, protecting—and women being 'Creatures Unlike Any Other'—coy, hard-to-get, nurturing (Fein and Schneider, 1995; McGraw, 2005).

The major foci of this cluster appear contradictory, but cohere when viewed through the theoretical lenses of neo-liberalism and post-feminism. Yet to the average reader, unversed in these theoretical ideas, this cluster's messages would appear to work at cross-purposes.

Discussion

The Personal Is Political: A 'Rising Spiral' of Cultural Change and Advice Book Content

A careful study of ideological trends in advice books and the broader social context reveals that *the personal is political*: even when books apparently ignore social context, writing about relationships in individualistic terms, they are still shaped by broader social forces. Although three distinct ideological clusters are evident in the advice over time, each cluster nonetheless demonstrates internal tensions between ideas favouring progress/equality and tradition/inequality in gender relations, and tensions persist across clusters. I suggest that these tensions reflect ongoing debates surrounding the major social changes of each period and of the past half-century more broadly. At the same time, each cluster bears the imprint of shifting ideological currents.

The first cluster's books coincide, arguably, with the period of most profound change for North American gender relations. Interest in alternative lifestyles grew while fertility levels dropped sharply, abortion was legalized, and the birth control pill became available (Levy, 2005; Rubin, 2004; Treas, 2004). New Social Movements, notably feminism, enjoyed great momentum, changes to Canadian and U.S. frameworks for divorce made marital dissolution easier, and U.S. Congress' Equal Pay Act banned sex-based workplace discrimination (Allen, 2004; Paetsch et al., 2004). Some people and institutions were hesitant to fully embrace all changes at the outset, however, resulting in mixed promotion of continuity and change.

Cluster 2's books coincide with a period of reactionary neo-liberalism in North America, during which fewer gender-sensitive policies were made, the women's movement lost momentum and women's work was increasingly seen as a necessity, not a choice indicating liberal attitudes (Coleman et al., 2004). HIV/AIDS appeared, contributing to cultural disapproval of casual sex,

and in-vitro fertilization now reduced women's reliance on men in family formation (Richards, 2004; Treas, 2004).

By the mid-1990s (cluster 3), the political climate was still dominated by a shift to the right and conservative policies. Conservative views on the family were promoted in some academic (e.g. Popenoe, 1996; 2007) and much mainstream writing. The resilience of religious culture—particularly in the U.S.—fuelled the New Christian Right, the Marriage Movement, and Covenant Marriages' promotion of traditional family values (Sanchez et al., 2001; Smith, 2000). Meanwhile, post-feminist ideology enjoyed mainstream promotion through pop culture products like *Sex and the City* and *Bridget Jones's Diary* (Budig, 2004; McRobbie, 2009). Despite the cultural shift to the right, however, many individuals and couples were committed to moving beyond traditional forms of intimate life.

What is visible across these advice book clusters is, in short, a *rising spiral* of ideas about relationships; some traditional ideas about intimacy persist or resurface while new, progressive ones appear, always in slightly new packaging, to reflect changes in macro-level social structure and ideology.

References

Allen, Katherine. 2004. 'Feminist Visions for Transforming Families: Desire and Equality Then and Now'. Pp. 192–203 in Coleman, Marilyn and Lawrence H. Ganong (Eds.), *Handbook of Contemporary Families: Considering the Past, Contemplating the Future*. Thousand Oaks: Sage.

Ambert, Anne-Marie. 2006. *Changing Families: Relationships in Context*. Toronto: Pearson, Allyn and Bacon.

Bauman, Zygmunt. 2000. *Liquid Modernity*. Cambridge: Polity.

Beck, Ulrich and Elisabeth Beck-Gernsheim. 2004. 'Families in a Runaway World'. Pp. 499–512 in Coleman, Marilyn and Lawrence H. Ganong (Eds.), *Handbook of Contemporary Families: Considering the Past, Contemplating the Future*. Thousand Oaks: Sage.

———. 1995. *The Normal Chaos of Love*. Cambridge, MA: Polity Press.

Bellah, Robert N., Richard Madsen, William M. Sullivan, Ann Swidler, and Steven M. Tipton. 1985. *Habits of the Heart: Individualism and Commitment in American Life*. New York: Harper and Row.

Boynton, Petra. 2003. 'Abiding by the Rules: Instructing Women in Relationships'. *Feminism & Psychology* 13(2): 237–245.

Budig, Michelle. 2004. 'Feminism and the Family'. Pp. 420–432 in Scott, Jacqueline, Judith Treas, and Martin Richards (Eds.), *The Blackwell Companion to the Sociology of Families*. Maldon, MA: Blackwell.

Carpenter, Caitlin. 2008. 'Self-Help Books Get the "Tough Love" Treatment'. *The Christian Science Monitor*. 7 February 2008, http://www.csmonitor.com/2008/0207/p17s02-lign.html.

Clarke, Victoria and Annadís G. Rúdólfsdóttir. 2005. 'Love Conquers All? An Exploration of Guidance Books for Parents, Family and Friends of Lesbians and Gay Men'. *The Psychology of Women Section Review* 7(2): 37–48.

Coleman, Marilyn and Lawrence H. Ganong (Eds.). 2004. *Handbook of Contemporary Families: Considering the Past, Contemplating the Future*. Thousand Oaks: Sage.

Coontz, Stephanie. 2005. *Marriage, a History: How Love Conquered Marriage*. Toronto: Penguin.

Ericksen, Julia. 1999. *Kiss and Tell: Surveying Sex in the Twentieth Century.* Cambridge: Harvard UP.

Giddens, Anthony. 1992. *The Transformation of Intimacy.* Stanford: Stanford University Press

Gross, Neil. 2005. 'The Detraditionalization of Intimacy Reconsidered'. *Sociological Theory* 23(3): 286–311.

Hazleden, Rebecca. 2004. 'The Pathology of Love in Contemporary Relationship Manuals'. *The Sociological Review* 52(2): 201–217.

———. 2003. 'Love yourself: The Relationship of the Self with Itself in Contemporary Relationship Manuals'. *Journal of Sociology* 39(4): 413–428.

Hochschild, Arlie. 1994. 'The Commercial Spirit of Intimate Life and the Abduction of Feminism: Signs From Women's Advice Books'. *Theory, Culture and Society* 11(2): 1–24.

Jamieson, Lynn. 1998. *Intimacy: Personal Relationships in Modern Societies.* Cambridge: Polity Press.

Levy, Ariel. 2005. *Female Chauvinist Pigs: Women and the Rise of Raunch Culture.* Toronto: Free Press.

McGee, Micki. 2005. *Self-Help Inc.: Makeover Culture in American Life.* London: Oxford University Press.

McRobbie, Angela. 2009. *The Aftermath of Feminism: Gender, Culture and Social Change.* Washington, DC: Sage.

Ménard, A. Dana and Peggy J. Kleinplatz. 2008. 'Twenty-one Moves Guaranteed to Make His Thighs Go Up in Flames: Depictions of "Great Sex" in Popular Magazines'. *Sexuality & Culture* 12: 1–20.

Neville, Patricia. 2007. 'Helping Self-Help Books: Moving Towards a Sociological Analysis'. Paper presentation at Beyond the Book: Contemporary Cultures of Reading Conference, September 2, Birmingham, UK.

Paetsch, Joanne et al. 2004. 'Trends in the Formation and Dissolution of Couples'. Pp. 306–319 in Scott, Jacqueline, Judith Treas and Martin Richards (Eds.). *The Blackwell Companion to the Sociology of Families.* Maldon, MA: Blackwell.

Popenoe, David. 2007. 'What Is Happening to the Family in Developed Nations?' Pp. 186–190 in Loveless, A. Scott and Thomas B. Holman (Eds.), *The Family in the New Millennium: World Voices Supporting the 'Natural' Clan, Volume 1: The Place of Family in Human Society.* Westport, CT: Praeger.

———. 1996. 'Modern Marriage: Revisiting the Cultural Script'. Pp. 247–270 in D. Popenoe, J. Elshtain and D. Blankenhorn (Eds.), *Promises to Keep.* Lanham, MD: Rowman and Littlefield.

Richards, Martin. 2004. 'Assisted Reproduction, Genetic Technologies, and Family Life'. Pp. 481–491 in Scott, Jacqueline, Judith Treas and Martin Richards (Eds.). *The Blackwell Companion to the Sociology of Families.* Maldon, MA: Blackwell.

Rimke, Heidi Marie. 2000. 'Governing Citizens through Self-Help Literature'. *Cultural Studies* 14(1): 61–78.

Rubin, Roger. 2004. 'Alternative Lifestyles Today: Off the Family Studies Screen'. Pp. 23–32 in Coleman, Marilyn and Lawrence H. Ganong (Eds.), *Handbook of Contemporary Families: Considering the Past, Contemplating the Future.* Thousand Oaks: Sage.

Sanchez, L. et al. 2001. 'The Implementation of Covenant Marriage in Louisiana'. *Virginia Journal of Policy and the Law* 23: 192–223.

Schudson, Michael. 1989. 'How Culture Works: Perspectives from Media Studies on the Efficacy of Symbols'. *Theory and Society* 18: 153–180.

Siegel, Carol. 2000. *New Millennial Sexstyles.* Bloomington, IN: Indiana University Press.

Simonds, Wendy. 1992. *Women and Self-Help Culture: Reading between The Lines.* New Brunswick, NJ: Rutgers University Press.

Smith, Christian. 2000. *Christian America? What Evangelicals Really Want.* Berkeley: University of California Press.

Starker, Stephen. 1989. *Oracle at the Supermarket: The American Preoccupation with Self-Help Books.* New Brunswick, NJ: Transaction.

Stocks, Janet, Capitolina Díaz and Björn Halleröd (Eds.). 2007. *Modern Couples Sharing Money, Sharing Life.* New York: Palgrave MacMillan.

Treas, Judith. 2004. 'Sex and Family: Changes and Challenges'. Pp. 398–407 in Scott, Jacqueline, Judith Treas and Martin Richards (Eds.). *The Blackwell Companion to the Sociology of Families.* Maldon, MA: Blackwell.

Whelan, Christine. 2004. *Self-Help Books and the Quest for Self-Control in the United States, 1950–2000.* Doctoral thesis. Oxford University.

Wilson, Frank and Janet Stocks. 2007. 'The Meaning of Breadwinning in Dual-Earner Couples'. Pp. 72–97 in Stocks, Janet, Capitolina Díaz and Björn Halleröd (Eds.). *Modern Couples Sharing Money, Sharing Life.* New York: Palgrave MacMillan.

Appendix A: Advice Books

1961: Life With Women and How to Survive It - Joseph H. Beck

1962: Sex and the Single Girl - Helen Gurley Brown

1964: Games People Play - Eric Berne

1971: The Sensuous Woman - 'J' (published anonymously by a female author)

1971: Any Woman Can! - David Reuben

1972: Open Marriage - George O'Neill and Nena O'Neill

1972: The Joy of Sex - Alex Comfort

1973: More Joy of Sex - Alex Comfort

1973: The Total Woman - Marabel Morgan

1974: Creative Divorce - Mel Kranzler

1976: Your Erroneous Zones - Wayne W. Dyer

1978: The National Love, Sex & Marriage Test: Are You As Good a Mate as You Think You Are? - Rubin Carson

1978: How to Get Whatever You Want Out of Life - Joyce Brothers

1981: The Cinderella Complex: Women's Hidden Fear of Independence - Colette Dowling

1981: What Every Woman Should Know about Men - Joyce Brothers

1982: Why Do I Think I Am Nothing without a Man? - Penelope Russianoff

1982: How to Make Love to a Woman - Michael Morgenstern

1982: How to Make Love to Each Other - Alexandra Penney

1983: Men Are Just Desserts - Sonya Friedman

1985: Smart Women, Foolish Choices: Finding the Right Men and Avoiding the Wrong Ones - Connell Cowan and Melvyn Kinder

1985: Women Who Love Too Much - Robin Norwood

1986: Men Who Hate Women and the Women Who Love Them - Susan Forward and Joan Torres

1987: How to Marry the Man of Your Choice - Margaret Kent

1990: Secrets about Men Every Woman Should Know - Barbara DeAngelis

1991: Light Her Fire - Ellen Kreidman

1992: Keeping the Love You Find - Harville Hendrix

1992: Men Are from Mars, Women Are from Venus - John Gray

1992: Are You the One for Me? - Barbara DeAngelis

1994: Ten Stupid Things Women Do to Mess Up Their Lives - Laura Schlessinger

1995: Mars and Venus in the Bedroom - John Gray

1995: The Rules: Time-Tested Secrets for Capturing the Heart of Mr. Right - Ellen Fein and Sherrie Schneider

1997: Mars and Venus on a Date - John Gray

1998: In the Meantime - Iyanla Vanzant

2000: The Hard Questions: 100 Essential Questions to Ask before You Say 'I Do' - Susan Piver

2000: Relationship Rescue - Philip McGraw

2001: The Worst-Case Scenario Survival Handbook: Dating and Sex - Joshua Piven, David Borgen and Jennifer Worick

2001: 10 Stupid Things Couples Do to Mess Up Their Relationship - Laura Schlessinger

2004: The Proper Care and Feeding of Husbands - Laura Schlessinger

2004: He's Just Not That Into You - Greg Behrendt and Liz Tuccillo

2005: It's Called A Breakup Because It's Broken - Greg Behrendt and Amiira Ruotola-Behrendt

2005: Love Smart - Philip McGraw

2006: Lies at the Altar - Robin L. Smith

2009: Act Like a Lady, Think Like a Man - Steve Harvey

CHAPTER 8

The Bonds of Things

Stephen Harold Riggins

The Beat poet Allen Ginsberg tells this story about moving out of a university residence. He and a friend returned to his room to pick up his last possessions:

> We were talking about the phantomlike, ghostly nature of moving from place to place and saying farewell to old apartments and rooms. And so we walked up the seven flights, and I picked up whatever gear I hadda get, and then turned and bowed and saluted the door as I left, and then saluted the hallway and said, 'Goodbye, beautiful steps. Goodbye, second step. Goodbye, third step.' And so on, as we went down the seven flights. And so we [Jack Kerouac and I] got into a rapport over the sense of mortal transience, because he said, 'Ah, I do that, too, when I say goodbye to a place' (Gifford and Lee 1999: 42).

When people are moving, they often make an effort to remember their old home at the end of their stay by paying close attention to its appearance, describing it in writing, or photographing it. Ginsberg is not sentimental, however. Saying goodbye to a home without making any real or mental snapshots could be understood as the genuine acceptance of transitoriness. But he mockingly plays with the idea that objects are powerful *agents* which shape us. Otherwise, why talk to them?

Contemporary sociologists who specialize in the study of material culture assume that people constantly engage in silent *dialogues with objects*. Objects bind people, generations, castes, and classes. They symbolize the kind of people we are or the kind we aspire to be. They help individuals and societies remember the past. This chapter provides a methodology for studying such human–object interaction. Although I focus on domestic artifacts, the terminology should be applicable to most human environments (Emmison and Smith 2000). Human–object interaction is relevant to several academic specialties, variously called the sociology of consumption (Bocock 1993), material culture studies (Woodward 2007), thing theory (Brown 2009), and the socialness of things (Riggins 1994). The theme of self-identity in this research comes from **symbolic interactionism**.

The research I describe requires photographs, interviews, and a sociologist's knowledge of the history of objects and decoration. Photographs are the basic data that substantiate interpretations. The interview begins by asking about the personal meaning of a prominent object and then proceeds systematically throughout the room. These interviews are quite invasive because people talking about their possessions are talking about themselves (Miller 2008). Ethical problems can be minimized by concentrating on a few highly symbolic possessions—*epiphany objects* (Woodward 2001) or *evocative objects* (Turkle 2007)—which interviewees think represent their taste or social bonds. The alternative, which I prefer, is long interviews documenting as many objects as possible. Interviewees are then *co-researchers*. They have the right to read draft versions of the study and control the content before it appears in print.

A basic idea of this research is that the same object can have different meanings depending on how it is used or conceptualized by people. In that sense, my terminology is flexible. (For studies using my terminology, see Riggins [1994] or Mitchell and Reid-Walsh [2002].) Domestic artifacts serve as entry points for telling stories about the self and social relationships. Interviewees' comments thus fall into two categories: mapping and referencing. *Mapping* is the information interviewees provide about the way objects plot their social network and represent their cosmology and ideology. *Referencing* is reserved for their comments about the history, aesthetics, and customary uses of objects. In general, interviewees are the authority with respect to mapping while the investigator knows more about referencing.

The concept of *agency* is used to distinguish between the active and passive use of objects. Some objects are meant to be handled, others to be contemplated. *Intrinsically active* refers to objects that were intended to be physically manipulated—for example, a corkscrew. *Intrinsically passive* refers to objects which are supposed to be contemplated (a poster or painting). The symbolic treatment of objects, however, may not correspond with these intentions. *Mode* provides a more subtle differentiation. *Active mode* refers to objects that are touched, caressed, or moved regardless of intended use. *Passive mode* refers to objects that are contemplated irrespective of original intentions. An old coffee grinder is an intrinsically active object. But if it is displayed as an heirloom, its mode is probably passive. Conversely, an intrinsically passive object like a small sculpture can be treated in the active mode as a paperweight.

Normal use and *alien use* also point to the shifting of categories in the use of artifacts, but they are more narrow concepts than agency and mode. Alien use refers to any non-standard use that may vary from objects recycled because of poverty to objects refashioned in response to creative concerns. An ashtray that serves as a receptacle for loose change is an example of alien use. A 'found object', perhaps battered and weathered, displayed as art is an extreme example of alien use.

Objects can be interpreted as indices of status. Since all domestic artifacts express a style of life and cultural values, *status objects* yield information relevant to the ranking of people. All domestic objects could thus be conceptualized as serving political functions. Since actual cost may not be ascertainable, *apparent cost* may be the more appropriate term. *Esteem objects* symbolize the personal self-esteem an individual has achieved in the intimate spheres of life, such as parenthood or marriage, or they indicate public recognition and communal gratitude. Displays of greeting cards, trophies, and children's art are common examples.

Domestic artifacts can also represent ties with groups outside the family. *Collective objects* include national symbols, memorabilia from social movements, and signs of membership in voluntary associations. Family heirlooms fall in this category if they are considered by interviewees to represent ethnicity, religion, or tradition, and not just personal or family identity.

Households contain *stigma objects*, things associated with 'spoiled' identities. Probably the most common examples in homes are objects associated with aging. Other illustrations include medical supplies, items used in 'disreputable pleasures', and signs of poverty. Living rooms contain relatively few stigma objects; more can be found in the private areas of a house, notably bathrooms and bedrooms. Tidying up a room often means removing stigma objects.

Artifacts can deliberately misrepresent. *Disidentifying objects* are things that make false claims—for instance, those that inflate status. Fake antiques and books no one reads may be the most common. Informants may distance themselves from a variety of social categories, one of which could be status. Sometimes the overall flavour of a home contributes to such misrepresentation.

Social facilitators are any thing that people use to turn each other into temporary partners and opponents or to facilitate public demonstrations of skill and knowledge (e.g. card games and puzzles). Social facilitators structure face-to-face interaction in the immediate present. The display of *occupational objects* is not uncommon in living room decoration. These tools may be somehow atypical, antique, handmade, or constructed in unusual dimensions. They may orient conversations toward a topic that members of the household know best. Households also contain both locally made and foreign-made goods. The proportion of *exotic objects* to *indigenous objects* provides information about an informant's reference groups and attitudes toward local society, as well as their status.

Time indicators refer to any sign of time in the decoration—for instance, stylistic features of objects that place them in an historical era. *Temporal homogeneity* refers to a room in which most artifacts appear to have been made at the same time. *Temporal heterogeneity* refers to the mixing of objects of obviously different historical eras. Time indicators tell sociologists about the self's position in time (attitudes toward history, tradition, change, and continuity); and the active presence of several generations in the house. Davidson (2009) uses the concept *haunting* for any sign within a home of previous owners or absent family members. Time indicators also include artifacts pointing to the future, such as romantic posters of rock stars in the bedrooms of pre-adolescents girls.

The size of objects has an impact on their meaning. Objects of *non-standard sizes* or *proportions* carry a different meaning than those of customary sizes. *Miniaturization* and *monumentality* represent the extremes of the category. *Way of production* distinguishes between handmade and machine-made objects. Although most domestic artifacts are now commercially manufactured, the home remains a refuge for handmade artifacts because they embody individuality, esteem, and personal bonds. They tend to be a fertile source of narratives.

The next set of categories introduces *display syntax*—that is, the way objects are displayed in relation to each other. The meaning of an artifact is influenced by the qualities of the surrounding or *co-located artifacts*. The same artifact may elicit radically different readings depending upon the setting in which it is displayed.

Artifacts within homes cannot be displayed in such a way that each attracts equal attention; some things must be more prominent than others. *Highlighting* specifies techniques of display that attract attention to objects: hanging objects at eye level, framing pictures, putting plants on stools, setting something at the centre of a mantelpiece, and putting one antique in a contemporary setting. *Understating* specifies any technique of display that deflects attention away from artifacts: placing something above or below eye level or in an obscure corner. Consciously displaying an expensive artifact in an apparently casual manner may reinforce claims to prestige. Such understating may paradoxically result in the self's status being highlighted.

Clustering and *dispersing* point to the manipulation of space that separates objects. Artifacts are clustered when they are grouped together. Scattering objects in a large volume of space, one artifact on a bare table for example, is referred to as dispersing. Clustering may highlight a group of objects. Dispersing may highlight individual objects.

When most objects in a room convey the same level of status because all are apparently expensive or inexpensive, the room is characterized by *status consistency*. However, many homes seem to be a mixture of costly things and those that are precious for sentimental reasons. Such homes display *status inconsistency*. The concepts tell us something about egalitarianism and elitism.

Degree of conformity refers to the extent to which a household conforms to the current common-sense rules of interior decoration. Even though there is evidence today of a wide diversity of styles of interior decoration, shared notions of appropriateness remain, such as those relating to functional specialization, orderliness, colour, comfort, and decorative complexity. Some styles of design and decoration that might have undermined these notions most dramatically—for example, the playfulness of postmodernism or the pseudo-primitive style of environmentalists—have not succeeded in attracting a wide public.

The general impression conveyed by a room is its *flavour*. It refers to taste, a sense which for most people is less developed than sight. The flavour of a room is the product of a range of identifiable but elusive qualities whose reality is undeniable. Examples include: cozy, conservative, impersonal, chaotic, formal, etc. All of these terms are subcategories of flavour.

Sociological inquiries into social status usually focus on objective measures such as income, but they provide a rough grid. The same type of inquiry, using the approach recommended in this paper, has the advantage of being more refined. It is not because research into domestic artifacts is based on anecdotes that it cannot provide valid statistics and objective grounds for generalizations. The approach sounds impressionistic, but numbers can be extracted through a large sample of interviews. The ideas summarized here thus provide a sort of microscopic version of macroscopic statistics.

References

Bocock, Robert (1993) *Consumption.* London: Routledge.

Brown, Bill (2009) 'Thing Theory'. In Fiona Candlin and Raiford Guins (Eds.) *The Object Reader.* London: Routledge, 139–152.

Davidson, Tonya (2009) 'The Role of Domestic Architecture in the Structuring of Memory'. *Space and Culture*, 12(3), 332–342.

Emmison, Michael and Philip Smith (2000) *Researching the Visual: Images, Objects, Contexts and Interactions in Social and Cultural Inquiry.* Thousand Oaks, CA: Sage.

Gifford, Barry and Lawrence Lee (1999) *Jack's Book: An Oral Biography of Jack Kerouac.* Edinburgh: Rebel Inc.

Miller, Daniel (2008) *The Comfort of Things.* Cambridge: Polity Press.

Mitchell, Claudia and Jacqueline Reid-Walsh (2002) *Researching Children's Popular Culture: The Cultural Spaces of Childhood.* London: Routledge.

Riggins, Stephen Harold (1994) 'Fieldwork in the Living Room: An Auto-ethnographic Essay'. In Stephen Harold Riggins (Ed.) *The Socialness of Things: Essays on the Socio-semiotics of Objects.* Berlin: Mouton de Gruyter, 101–148.

Turkle, Sherry (Ed.) *Evocative Objects: Things We Think With.* Cambridge, MA: MIT Press.

Woodward, Ian (2001) 'Domestic Objects and the Taste Epiphany: A Resource for Consumption Methodology'. *Journal of Material Culture*, 6(2), 115–136.

Woodward, Ian (2007) *Understanding Material Culture.* Los Angeles: Sage.

CHAPTER 9

Nationalism from Below

Slobodan Drakulic

A long-standing orthodoxy maintains that **nationalism** was invented by European cultural elites and passed down to the masses by propagandists. John Acton (1972 [1862]: 141) ascribed its engendering to 'men of speculative or imaginative genius'. To Carlton Hayes (1933: 62), 'the elaboration of a doctrine of nationalism by . . . "intellectuals"—philologists, historians, anthropologists, economists, philosophers, and litterateurs' was the '[f]irst and fundamental' of three factors involved '[i]n the propagation of nationalism'. The second are 'citizens who discover in it satisfaction and refreshment for their souls and sometimes an advantage to their pockets'. The third is the 'the popular mind', shaped by 'mass-education'.

Hans Kohn (1971: 16) found 'the first full manifestation of modern nationalism . . . in the writings of John Milton', and this 'liberal English nationalism', eventually influenced 'the French *philosophes*' (18) and revolutionaries. Elie Kedourie saw nationalism as an **ideology** (1993: xiii), or 'a doctrine invented in Europe' (1) by intellectuals, such as Herder, Kant, or Fichte (43–48), and passed on to the likes of Mazzini and the *Carbonari* (91–92).

Miroslav Hroch systematized Hayes' trickle-down scheme (1985: 22), maintaining that national revivals begin with Phase A, or 'the period of scholarly interest', in 'the language, the culture, the history of the oppressed nationality', by 'intellectuals'. Phase B is 'the period of patriotic agitation', and Phase C 'the rise of a mass national movement' (Ibid: 23).

Ernest Gellner's fable of Ruritanian nationalism arising within Magalomania follows the same sequence (1983: 58–62). The Ruritanians were peasants harbouring 'griefs . . . recorded in their lament-songs' (58), but 'a careful analysis of the folk songs' discloses little 'evidence of any serious discontent' concerning 'their linguistic and cultural situation' (59). Peasants migrating to the cities encountered 'Ruritanian lads destined for the church', but, 'influenced by the new liberal ideas', went to the university, and became 'journalists, teachers and professors'. They themselves 'received encouragement from a few foreign . . . ethnographers, musicologists and historians' exploring Ruritania (59–60). And likewise Anthony Smith (1998: 56): 'Most nationalisms are led by intellectuals and/or professionals'; the former 'furnish the basic definitions and characterisations of the nation'; the latter 'are the main disseminators of the idea and ideals of the nation'.

However, the history of revolutions shows that their supposed intellectual leaders were often misplaced when their supposed followers rose up (e.g. Lenin in 1917). Furthermore, intellectuals, professionals, and the masses are not parties in the Weberian sense, but social aggregates with limited behavioural uniformity. The image of cultural elites leading the masses is doubly erroneous: it conflates social movements with social division of labour and postulates what must be ascertained by research.

Such research has been conducted by the studies in Serbo-Croatian oral traditions, for instance—largely unnoticed by the students of nationalism—which reveal that the Croatian elite protonationalists held the folk traditions in high esteem. A Latinist Juraj Šižgoriċ (ca 1420–1509) 'praised the folk songs of his homeland' (Kombol 1945: 45), and lamented the devastation of his 'sweet fatherland' by the Ottoman 'barbarians' (Šižgoriċ 1966: 37–39 Croatian, 101–4 Latin). Patrician Petar Hektoroviċ (1487–1572), recorded two folk songs sung by some fishermen in 1555 (Kombol 1945: 125; Hektoroviċ 1953 [1568]: 12; 1979: 24; 1997: 67), and was as Turko-phobic as Šižgoriċ. A Croatian *ban* (viceroy), Count Petar Zrinski (1621–1671)—a famous Turk-fighter executed by the Habsburgs for sedition—possessed a manuscript with an old heroic song (Bogišiċ 1878: 120–22; Miletich 1990: 125–31). Instead of the trickle-down, Svetozar Koljeviċ speaks of 'the rich and fascinating interplay of literary and oral culture in the central Balkans', or their 'complex give-and-take relationship' (1980: 2).

Researchers have also unearthed a nexus between the folk traditions and ethnic identity. Maximilian Mügge notes (1916: 1) that folk songs 'ensured the continuance of the Serbian language' and 'kept alive the spirit of nationality' under the Ottomans. Vojislav Đuri (1954: v–vi) argues that oral tradition has influenced written literature and inspired 'Yugoslav socialist patriotism'—charging that claims about the folk poetry being handed down from the feudal elites to plebeians betray disbelief 'in the creative capacities of the working masses' (xx). Peter Levi (Pennington and Levi 1984: viii) argues that folk songs 'were a principal expression of national identity, and to some degree of national resistance' to the Ottomans. Milne Holton and Vasa Mihailovich (in Karadžiċ, 1997: 134) suggest that folk poetry represented 'a guide to conduct for a colonized people'.

My research into premodern Croatian nationalism likewise indicates that its propagation occurred within complex interactions between the elite and folk traditions, not within one of them (Drakulic 2008). That prompted me to delve into folk traditions, represented by the heroic or 'male' folk songs of the Serbo-Croatian speakers. I have heretofore examined 434 songs in seven of the nine volumes in the collection by Vuk Stefanoviċ (1787–1864), leaving the two volumes of 'female' and 'love songs' aside.

The songs speak of places and personages from across Europe and the Middle East, debunking the presumed geopolitical idiocy of medieval peasantry. The idiocy claims are further undermined by the songs' frequent mention of the written exchanges between their characters—often *hajduks* and *uskoks*, social bandits or mere brigands (Hobsbawm 2000).

Karadžič was an autodidact peasant from Herzegovina who joined the failed Serbian Revolution of 1804–1813, fled to Austria, and became an ethnographer, linguist and pan-Serb nationalist. Being Serbo-centric, his collection marginalizes Croatian and Slavic Muslim traditions, and thus makes my picture of premodern folk nationalisms incomplete.

Karadžič has produced a rough chronological classification of the songs, allowing us to reconstruct historical trends in the emergence of nationalism from below. The songs of 'the oldest times', as he called them, cover the period of roughly the fourteenth and fifteenth centuries; those of 'the middle times', the sixteenth and seventeenth centuries; and those of 'the newer times', the eighteenth and nineteenth centuries.

The first period coincides with the Ottoman invasion of the Balkans and Venetian acquisition of Dalmatia. The second covers the Ottoman conquest of the region; the peak of their power; their rout at Vienna (1683); and their retreat south of the Save and Danube. The last period witnesses a growing Christian resistance to the Ottomans, and emergence of modern Balkan nationalisms and polities.

The presence of ethnocentrism in folk songs is confirmed by derogatory terms concerning an ethnic, racial, or religious other, and/or praise of one's ethnic self. The presence of patriotism, by the praise of one's own homeland—past, present or proposed. Šižgorič's lament over the Turkish barbarians devastating his fatherland reflects both ethnocentrism and patriotism. The songs of the oldest times contain frequent **ethnocentric** and infrequent patriotic expressions. Both multiply in the songs of the middle times, with the former still more prominent. The two entwine and approximate modern nationalism in the songs of the newer times.

Most songs of the oldest times deal with the Battle of Kosovo (1389) and its aftermath (Subotič 1932: 141). They reveal ethnocentrism, patriotism (laments over the lost Serbian empire), and racism. Karadžič's collection contains 147 songs of the oldest times, found in his volumes two and six. Ethnocentric and/or patriotic expressions appear in 100 of them, or 68 per cent.

Ethnocentrism aims mostly at the Muslims, and more at the Arabs than the Turks or Muslim Slavs. The Arabs are regularly 'black', removed from the Christian Slavs by religion and race—this last apparently making them aesthetically and erotically repugnant. A Serbian prince freed from a dungeon by an Arab princess thus kills her after a night together, loathing her black face and white teeth (Karadžič II 1932: 349; Low 1968: 106). The Turks are reviled but feared; their Sultan is mostly 'illustrious' or 'honourable;' and they are less alien than the Arabs.

The songs' images of the non-Muslims vary. The Latins (mainly Italians) and Greeks are crafty and untrustworthy; Magyars, or Hungarians, are more trusty. An 'accursed Jewish emperor' is grudgingly recognized as fast in his faith for refusing to reveal where the true cross is even under torture, but his empress succumbs—after the Byzantines begin to roast her child (Karadžič II 1932: 76–79). Patriotism primarily emerges in the laments over the ephemeral Serbian empire of Stefan Dušan (circa 1308–1355)—evanesced within a generation but kept alive by the folk tradition for centuries.

The 180 songs of the middle times are found in volumes three, six and seven, and ethnocentric and less frequent patriotic expressions appear in 154 of the songs, or 86 per cent of them. Inasmuch as the folk tradition reflects the **collective consciousness** of the people, this indicates that their ethnocentrism was historically ascending. The theatre of events had meanwhile expanded from Macedonia, Kosovo and Serbia, to Croatia and Montenegro, where cross-border raids and ambuscades are fought between the Christians and Muslims. The 'Turks' (often Slav Muslims) and especially 'black Arabs' remain the main antagonists—despised, reviled, and feared. The

Slavic-Latin and Slavic-Greek animosity remains, but muted by the necessity of unity against the Ottomans. Magyars appear less, but fare better than the Latins or Greeks.

Differential distancing between the self and diverse others emerges in middle times songs' frequent accounts of female abductions or elopements. Abducted or eloping brides were converted to their groom's faith and thus made suitable, but their abduction or elopement dishonoured their kin. Abductions and elopements within Christendom were less stigmatized. The Christian–Muslim fighting continued for unerotic reasons as well—revenge, honour, possessions—or *la guerre pour la guerre*. A Christian hero thus complains about the long peace that makes his arm crave war, and his sabre thirst Turkish blood (Karadžič VI 1940: 321).

The Turks remain the principal antagonists one should shun or resist. Those maligning their 'brethren to the Turk, the filthy power' sin against God (Karadžič VI 1940: 1–5; Brkič 1961: 47). One should not pay tribute to the Turks, especially in virgins, as that is sinful and shameful. The tribe of Piperi in Montenegro thus withstood an Ottoman invasion for withholding eight maids requested by some Tahir-Pasha (Karadžič IV 1932: 27–31; Brkič 1961: 86). One should not accept abuse from the Turks. A poor highlander Novak became a *hajduk* after slaughtering seven Turks trying to rob him after he fed them (Karadžič VII 1935: 293–97). Another peasant, Bajo, became an *uskok* after beheading an *aga* for calling him a 'whore's son' and striking him for being late to work (Brkič 1961: 87; Karadžič VII 1935: 297–98).

Sporadic ethno-religious clashes of the middle times meanwhile grew into open conflict.

Karadžič's volumes eight and nine contain 107 newer songs, with 96, or 90 per cent of them, ethnocentric and/or patriotic. The main characters are freedom fighters and their leaders from Montenegro, Herzegovina, and Serbia, seeking independence from the Ottomans. The songs' geopolitical horizons widen to despicable English monarchs and bankers financing the decaying Ottoman empire; benevolent but distant emperor Peter and empress Catherine of Russia; and faithless Napoleon who invades Kotor (coveted by Montenegro) but not Turkey.

In the newer songs, elite and folk traditions entwine, as the literati turned to composing them—most famously in the surrogate folk songs and tales penned by Fra Andrija Kačič-Miošič (1690–1760). He maintained that 'it is in human nature to praise, elevate and aggrandize one's own people', and did so in plebeian ways (1942 [1756; 1759]): 5), confirming that the elites and masses were not separated but interrelated.

Karadžič's description of popular gatherings on Christian holy days illustrates this point well (1969 [1827]: 171). In fair weather, 'thousands of people . . . gather around some monasteries', where 'barmen pour wine and brandy; butchers roast and sell lamb, sheep, goat and pig meats; the blind . . . sing heroic songs, old and new; lads eye the maids', and godfathers, friends, acquaintances and sometimes notables 'make diverse agreements'. And while 'people mostly go to the monasteries nearest to them . . . they also go to the more distant ones . . . from all over Serbia, and from Bosnia and Herzegovina.' This account reveals the elites and masses not as worlds apart, but as parts of a complex yet common cultural universe.

References

Acton, John Emerich Edward Dalberg. 1972. *Essays on Freedom and Power*. Gloucester, MA: Peter Smith.

Bogišič, Valtazar. 1878. *Narodne pjesme is starijih, najviše primorskih zapisa*. Belgrade: Glasnik srpskog učenog društva, drugo odeljenje, knjiga deseta.

Brkič, Jovan. 1961. *Moral Concepts in Traditional Serbian Epic Poetry*. The Hague: Mouton.

Drakulic, Slobodan. 2008. 'Premodern Croatian Nationalism?', *Nationalism and Ethnic Politics*, vol. 14, no. 4 (2008), pp. 523–48.

Đurič, Vojislav, ed. 1954. *Antologija narodnih junačkih pesama*. Belgrade: Srpska književna zadruga.

Hayes, Carlton J. H. 1933. *Essays on Nationalism*. New York: Russell & Russell.

Hektorovič, Petar. 1953 [1568]. *Ribanye i ribarscho prigovaranye i razliche stvari ine sloxene po Petretu Hectorovichiv*

Hvaraninv. Zagreb: Jugoslavenska akademija znanosti i umjetnosti.

————. 1979 [1568]. *Fishing and Fishermen's Conversation*, translated by Edward D. Goy. Bristol: BC Review, no. 15.

————. 1997 [1568]. *Ribanje i ribarsko prigovaranje—Fishing and Fishermen's Conversations*, translated by Edward D. Goy. Stari Grad: Faros.

Hobsbawm, Eric. 2000. *Bandits*. Second edition. London: Weidenfeld & Nicolson.

Hroch, Miroslav. 1985. *Social Preconditions of National Revival in Europe: A Comparative Analysis of the Social Composition of Patriotic Groups among the Smaller European Nations*. Cambridge: Cambridge University Press.

Kačič-Miošič, Andrija. 1942 [1756; 1759]. *Razgovor ugodni*, edited by Tomo Matič. Zagreb: Hrvatska akademija znanosti i umjetnosti.

Karadžič, Vuk Stefanovič . 1932 (II). *Srpske narodne pjesme: knjiga druga u kojoj su pjesme junačke najstarije*. Belgrade: Državna štamparija.

————. 1929 (III). *Srpske narodne pjesme: knjiga treča u kojoj su pjesme junačke srednjijeh vremena*. Belgrade: Državna štamparija.

————. 1932 (IV). *Srpske narodne pjesme: knjiga četvrta u kojoj su pjesme junačke novijih vremena o vojevanju za slobodu*. Belgrade: Državna štamparija.

————. 1940 (VI). *Srpske narodne pjesme: knjiga šesta u kojoj su pjesme juna ke najstarije i srednjijeh vremena*. Belgrade: Državna štamparija.

————. 1935 (VII). *Srpske narodne pjesme: knjiga sedma u kojoj su pjesme juna ke srednjijeh vremena*. Belgrade: Državna štamparija.

————. 1936 (VIII). *Srpske narodne pjesme: knjiga osma u kojoj su pjesme junačke novijih vremena o vojevanju za slobodu i o vojevanju Crnogoraca*. Belgrade: Državna štamparija.

————. 1936 (IX). *Srpske narodne pjesme: knjiga deveta u kojoj su pjesme junačke novijih vremena o vojevanju Crnogoraca i Hercegovaca*. Belgrade: Državna štamparija.

————. 1969 [1827]. 'Geografičesko-Statističesko opisanije Srbije', in V. S. Karadžič , *Sabrana dela Vuka Karadžič a VIII: Danica 1826 • 1827 • 1828 • 1829 • 1834* (Belgrade: Prosveta), 126–76.

————. 1997. *Songs of the Serbian People: From the collections of Vuk Karadžič*, translated and edited by Milne Holton and Vasa D. Mihailovich. Pittsburgh PA: University of Pittsburgh Press.

Kedourie, Elie. 1998. *Nationalism*, fourth edition. Oxford: Blackwell Publishers.

Koljevič, Svetozar. 1980. *The Epic in the Making*. Oxford: Oxford University Press.

Kombol, Mihovil. 1945. *Poviest hrvatske književnosti do narodnog preporoda*. Zagreb: Matica Hrvatska.

Low, D. H. 1968 [1922]. *The Ballads of Marko Kraljevič*. Westport CT: Greenwood Press.

Miletich, John S. 1990. *The Bugarštica: A Bilingual Anthology of the Earliest Extant South Slavic Folk Narrative Song*. Edited and translated by J. S. Miletich. Urbana and Chicago: University of Illinois Press.

Mügge, Maximilian August. 2010 [1916]. *Serbian Folk Songs, Fairy Tales and Proverbs*. LaVergne, TN: Bibliolife.

Pennington, Anne and Peter Levi, eds. 1984. *Marko the Prince: Serbo-Croat Heroic Songs*. London: Duckworth.

Smith, Anthony D. 1998. *Nationalism and Modernism: A Critical Survey of Recent Theories of Nations and Nationalism*. London: Routledge.

Šižgorič, Juraj Šibenčanin. 1966. *Elegije i pjesme*. Selected, translated and edited by Nikola Šop. Zagreb: Jugoslavenska akademija znanosti i umjetnosti.

Subotič, Dragutin. 1932. *Yugoslav Popular Ballads: Their Origin and Development*. Cambridge: Cambridge University Press.

Questions for Critical Thought

CHAPTER 6

1. How does Garlick modify Jensen's argument that porn is about controlling women's bodies?
2. How is the man/nature divide played out in porn? How does this relate to the socialization of gender and gender relations?
3. According to Heidegger, what is the danger in how modern technology 'enframes nature'?
4. In this paper, Garlick considers a phenomenon common in social life: that experiences are in some ways 'called to order', while in others they are pulled apart into fragments. How is order produced in online porn? And how is order disrupted?
5. If porn is boring, and we should contemplate what this boredom tells us about the condition of our lives, what is it about online porn that makes it so boring, according to Garlick? Can you think of other things that make it boring that his theory doesn't catch?
6. What does Garlick have to say about amateur porn? How does he think it might change the relationship between porn and gender? What reservations does he have about making this assumption?
7. Garlick considers the effect of online porn only on male viewers. Given Garlick's observations, how do you think online porn could change how women think about themselves sexually?

CHAPTER 7

1. Why does Knudson argue that loving is chaotic in the late-modern period?
2. According to Knudson, how have self-help books become a reliable source for broader cultural assumptions about gender relations?
3. How are each of the three periods Knudson discusses distinct or similar from the others? How are they related to the broader social changes that surround them?
4. Have all of the ideas about romantic relationships changed in a linear fashion—that is, in a straight line of continual progress toward some new ideal? Or is there evidence of circularity, or even regression? Explain with evidence from Knudson's paper.
5. Another notorious cultural form that contains messages about romantic relationships is the romantic comedy movie genre. Do you think the way these movies portray romantic relationships contradicts or conforms to any of the ideals that Knudson finds in self-help books (in any of the three periods)? Explain.

CHAPTER 8

1. Explain what Riggins means by normal use and alien use. Give two examples of objects in your life that you could categorize this way.
2. What is the methodology Riggins has devised for analyzing objects and how they are culturally significant? How does the relationship with research subjects differ from most research?

3. What does Riggins mean by *status inconsistency*? How does this reflect on an individual?
4. Consider Riggins' concept of representing selfhood through objects in a historical context. Do you think we have always been able to engage in this type of representation as much as we do now? How does our broader contemporary cultural context provide the opportunities/incentives to express ourselves through objects?
5. The idea that the objects with which we surround ourselves convey information about our status in the greater social ranking is a provocative one. But what about the criticism that the same objects can be ranked differently by different people: do you think Riggins' methodology can sustain such a critique? Why or why not?

CHAPTER 9

1. What problems does Drakulic point out in the theory that cultural elites lead the masses in creating nationalist ideas?
2. How did the content of folk songs from the three consecutive time periods that Drakulic discusses reflect the political, cultural, and social changes of those times?
3. How did the folk songs express and create symbolic divisions between 'us' and 'them'?
4. Consider, as Curtis does, the conditions of the production and recording of the data on this subject. What are some limitations of assuming that folk songs reflect the collective consciousness of the Balkan identities explored? What else might they mean? What are the folk songs' strengths compared to other cultural products of the time?
5. Can you think of any contemporary cultural forms that serve the same role in Canada now as folk songs did in the Balkan nations during the time periods Drakulic analyzed? Where and how do people build cultural identities today? Are there any cultural forms that are the basis of a Canadian identity?

Part III

Socialization

If one of the central assumptions of sociology is that human behaviour is not purely biologically determined, then how else do we pick up our habits, ideas, and hopes and dreams? The sociologist's answer is that we learn them from interacting with other humans and the cultural objects and systems that they create. While we are born with a lot of malleability, our possible positions on subjects such as God, the opposite sex, or the savoury merits of squid get narrowed down as we become a member of our community. We are born with the ability to learn many different skills, but we will develop only a few of those, depending on the community we grow up in. Most basically, we are socialized to understand and take part in the culture around us—taught which god to worship, what is right and wrong, how to be a girl or boy, and of course, how to communicate with others. It could be said that the process of socialization is roughly akin to downloading software (culture—knowledge, values, skills, etc.) onto hardware (our brains and bodies). But this metaphor is loose and only suggestive. Socialization is not a packaged, planned process, even though parents, teachers, and others try hard to shape what is absorbed. We are socialized in many different ways and by many different agents, some more purposeful than others.

Much of our general cultural learning happens through our family. However, the family is only one agent of socialization, and it can provide us with content that is very different from the world around us. Nedim Karakayali's piece in this section explores how second-generation immigrants are often socialized to become two different kinds of people, able to manage in two very different cultures—that of their parents' home country and that of their current country. The result is flexibility, perhaps, but also a split social personality.

In any event, we never go through the socialization process and come out fully formed at a particular age, ready for what ever else life may throw at us. As life wears on, we invariably have to develop new skills and knowledge for navigating new challenges. Anthony Lombardo's piece describes how online communities socialize gay men, giving them skills that mainstream, heterosexual culture does not. He points out that these communities teach their members how to successfully navigate a men-who-have-sex-with-men world. This includes such skills as how to manage their identity and tell what they are looking for in ways that others will understand, so they can find the partners that they are looking for. No particular individual in these communities is responsible for teaching these skills, and no one does it purposefully. Men learn about the culture of this online world through trial and error, as they move through it.

On the other hand, secondary socialization can take the form of formal purposeful training, as in schools of all kinds. Brenda Beagan examines how modern medical schools produce doctors not only by providing the medical knowledge needed to cure patients, but by also teaching them how to act like doctors, exuding competence and earning the trust and respect of their patients.

Finally, even formal socialization has informal, non-purposeful aspects, and we often learn un-intended behaviours during formal training. As you have probably noticed already, only part of the learning you enjoy in post-secondary school happens through the official curriculum. Nancy Beaure-gard, Andrée Demers, and Louis Gliksman explain the various factors involved in socializing post-secondary students into a particular drinking culture. This is usually not the socialization intended by higher education institutions. Rather, many different circumstances combine to make binge drinking an important part of being a student at some post-secondary schools.

Online Interactions among Men Who Have Sex with Men: Situated Performances and Sexual Education

Anthony P. Lombardo

The Internet is a popular place for men who have sex with men (MSM) to find sexual partners, fostering a growing research area. Quantitative research has focused mainly on risk behaviours among MSM who do and do not seek sex online (see, e.g. Liau Millett, & Marks, 2006). **Qualitative** research has focused on how men use the Internet in their sexual lives for learning about gay culture and social networking, and their experiences seeking sex online (see, e.g. Brown, Maycock, & Burns, 2005; Davis, Hart, Bolding, Sherr, & Elford, 2006; Engler, Frigault, Léobon, & Lévy, 2005; Sanders, 2008).

This qualitative work has also noted the development of diverse 'subcultures' of MSM online (e.g. Brown et al., 2005), and the role of the online environment in men's socialization into gay culture (e.g. Sanders, 2008). This chapter presents findings from a study that followed in the tradition of the qualitative work in this area, with a focus on the role of the Internet in the sexual lives of MSM (Lombardo, 2009). The analysis presented here focuses not so much on how men used their online interactions to learn about gay culture, but rather highlights how men learned to participate and interact in the online sex-seeking process. The findings also speak to the role of men's online interactions in sexual education.

It draws upon **Erving Goffman**'s (1959) notions of the '**presentation of self**' in analyzing men's online interactions.

Method

The study was an ethnographic exploration of the experiences of 23 MSM in the Greater Toronto Area (Ontario, Canada) who use the Internet for same-sex sexual purposes. Thirteen of the participants identified as gay, five as bisexual, and two as straight; others did not identify in these particular categories. The youngest participant was 20 years of age and the oldest was 61, with an average age of 38 years. Fifteen of the men were HIV-negative, six were HIV-positive, and two were of unknown HIV status. The majority of participants were born in Canada and identified as Caucasian. Men were recruited and interviewed both online and offline. Participants are cited herein by interview number, age, sexual orientation, and HIV status: positive (HIV+), negative (HIV–), and unknown (HIV?). The study received ethics approval from the University of Toronto.

Findings

Men's accounts showed how they learned to give 'legitimated performances' of self in their online interactions—presentations of selves (Goffman, 1959) that were appropriate to the particular online setting and purpose. For instance, one participant recalled his experience in defining his mannerisms as portrayed through his online profile:

> I'm looking for masculine, butch. And everyone is. And no one puts feminine [in their profile]. . . . *And that's sort of the way it is online.* And when I first went online, people would be like, 'are you masc[uline]?' and I was like, not really . . . and then *I realized that, in that context, yes, I am'.* (003: 26, gay, HIV−)

Another noted,

> You can put in a little bio-line, so I'll put my age, my height, my weight, my stats . . . *which is how big your dick is.* And then anything else you want to put in stat wise, like . . . there's this one-percentage of body fat . . . body mass index. (009: 35, gay, HIV−)

These examples demonstrate certain 'rules' that govern how a man should present his 'front' in the online sexual search, even if it is at odds with how he actually perceives himself. These rules also highlight the dominance of certain physical characteristics, similar to the offline sex-seeking world.

It was also the case that different sites permitted different performances of self:

> I have a few different ads. I have one on *collarme.com* which is sort of just a general BDSM [bondage / sado-masochism] type of ad . . . I have two on *men4sexnow.com*, which is [to] attract responses from guys, I have one on *bondage.com* which is more of a heterosexual ad, and I have one on *plentyoffish.com* which is a heterosexual ad. (013: 30, bisexual, HIV−)

Examples such as this one demonstrate the possibility afforded by the online environment to present numerous and diverse 'selves', each one appropriate to the particular setting.

Men also had to learn to construct the 'selves' of their potential partners. Clues about the fit of a potential partner were given through active and passive means. For instance, one man remarked, 'if the first question they ask is how hung are you [size of penis], I usually pass. . . . That would be an indication that they're not interested in me, they're just interested in my dick' (005: 49, gay, HIV+). Sometimes this process was more intricate, as in this case of an older Caucasian man with an interest in younger Asian men:

> Basically in the Asian [chat]room where I spend most of my time, *I'm older than most of them want,* so I don't tend to *make a nuisance of myself,* chasing after these young guys. . . . The exception I make to that is if I'm in the 'Mature' [chat]room, and somebody that's of my liking comes into that room . . . *the feeling is that they're almost fair game, if they're in a room that's frequented by mostly older guys, they must be interested in somebody older,* so occasionally I will private them. (002: 56, gay, HIV−)

Goffman's (1959) concepts of the 'given' and the 'given off' are instructive here, where men must be careful about not only what they 'give' and 'give off' through their own actions, but also what is 'given' and 'given off' by their potential partners, and how those signals shape the social interaction and its possibilities. This example likewise highlights 'rules' around relations by age and race.

Finally, in addition to learning to interact in this process, online interactions came to be a conduit for sexual education for some men, especially for those new to same-sex relations. Men learned about sexual health and risk through websites, but—importantly—also through their online interactions with other MSM:

> I discuss [with potential partners] that I am in an experimental phase, and they discuss with me too. . . the guys understand more, and give me general information about hooking up, etc. [I have learned] *safe sex with men, more about exploring, and that there is a risk to everything, and to be safe.* (017: 21, straight, HIV?)

These conversations represent an important source of sexual education, especially where such information might be difficult to obtain elsewhere (e.g. Kubicek, Beyer, Weiss, Iverson, & Kipke, 2010).

Discussion

In contrast to earlier research on Internet communication and relationship-building (e.g. McKenna & Bargh, 2000; Turkle, 1995), these findings show that men were somewhat restricted in how they could present their self in the online sexual search. Men learned to give 'e-presentations' of self that were structured by discourses reflecting sexual desire in gay communities more generally, including physical attractiveness, age, race, and so on (Adam, Sears, & Schellenberg, 2000; Green, 2008a; Jones, 2005; Seal et al., 2000), as well as the nature of the specific website. Further, men's online interactions were influenced by active and passive constructions of potential partners. Men's online presentations of selves and interactions were thus 'situated' within certain online norms, which the men came to learn as a function of their experiences online. These findings illuminate norms of an online sex-seeking subculture—which mirror those of traditional offline gay communities—and a process of socialization into them.

A key question is how men build and maintain 'erotic capital' (Green, 2008b) in online settings and the implications for sexual behaviour. For instance, it has been noted that men who feel 'disadvantaged' in the sexual search due to certain characteristics (e.g. perceived unattractiveness) may 'trade off' safer sex for the sake of keeping a sexual partner (Adam, Husbands, Murray, & Maxwell, 2005; Ames, Atchinson, & Rose, 1995; Green, 2008a). With the continued emphasis on the physical in the presentation of self online, online sex-seeking may exacerbate, rather than diminish, this particular issue, warranting further inquiry.

Men's online interactions with other MSM also emerged as a place of sexual education for men in this study, as similarly noted elsewhere (e.g. Sanders, 2008). However, less is known about what men actually learn about sexual risk through these interactions—in other words, sexual socialization—and whether that knowledge promotes or inhibits safer sex. Future work should explore the role of these interactions in how men develop 'folk knowledges' (Kubicek et al., 2008) of sexual risk and safety, and how the interactions themselves may represent an opportunity for health promotion, especially through Web 2.0 social media applications (Rietmeijer & McFarlane, 2009).

Overall, these findings illuminate some of the 'rules of engagement' that men learned to seek sex online, and the role of men's online interactions as a tool for sexual education. Cyberspace holds the potential for many diverse 'subcultures' in the sexual realm (Brown et al., 2005); thus future research must consider how men interact in other cyberspaces, and how HIV prevention might work within those spaces in innovative and resonant ways.

References

Adam, B. D., Husbands, W., Murray, J., & Maxwell, J. (2005). AIDS optimism, condom fatigue, or self-esteem? Explaining unsafe sex among gay and bisexual men. *Journal of Sex Research, 42*(3), 238–248.

Adam, B. D., Sears, A., & Schellenberg, E. G. (2000). Accounting for unsafe sex: Interviews with men who have sex with men. *Journal of Sex Research, 37*(1), 24–36.

Ames, L. J., Atchinson, A. B., & Rose, D. T. (1995). Love, lust, and fear: Safer sex decision making among gay men. *Journal of Homosexuality, 30*(1), 53–73.

Brown, G., Maycock, B., & Burns, S. (2005). Your picture is your bait: Use and meaning of cyberspace among gay men. *Journal of Sex Research, 42*(1), 63–73.

Davis, M., Hart, G., Bolding, G., Sherr, L., & Elford, J. (2006). E-dating, identity and HIV prevention: Theorising

sexualities, risk and network society. *Sociology of Health & Illness, 28*(4), 457–458.

Engler, K., Frigault, L.-R., Léobon, A., & Lévy, J. J. (2005). The sexual superhighway revisited: A qualitative analysis of gay men's perceived repercussions of connecting in cyberspace. *Journal of Gay & Lesbian Social Services, 18*(2), 3–37.

Goffman, E. (1959). *The presentation of self in everyday life*. Garden City, NY: Doubleday.

Green, A. I. (2008a). Health and sexual status in an urban gay enclave: An application of the stress process model. *Journal of Health and Social Behavior, 49*(4), 436–451.

Green, A. I. (2008b). The social organization of desire: The sexual fields approach. *Sociological Theory, 26*(1), 25–50.

Jones, R. H. (2005). 'You show me yours, I'll show you mine': The negotiation of shifts from textual to visual modes in computer-mediated interaction among gay men. *Visual Communication, 4*(1), 69–92.

Kubicek, K., Beyer, W. J., Weiss, G., Iverson, E., & Kipke, M. D. (2010). In the dark: Young men's stories of sexual initiation in the absence of relevant sexual health information. *Health Education & Behavior, 37*(2), 243–263. doi: 10.1177/1090198109339993

Kubicek, K., Carpineto, J., McDavitt, B., Weiss, G., Iverson, E. F., Au, C. W., et al. (2008). Integrating professional and folk models of HIV risk: YMSM's perceptions of high-risk sex. *AIDS Education and Prevention, 20*(3), 220–238. doi: 10.1521/aeap.2008.20.3.220

Liau, A., Millett, G., & Marks, G. (2006). Meta-analytic examination of online sex-seeking and sexual risk behavior among men who have sex with men. *Sexually Transmitted Diseases, 33*(9), 576–584.

Lombardo, A. P. (2009). *Sex and cyberspace: The Internet in the sexual lives of men who have sex with men* (Doctoral dissertation, University of Toronto, Toronto, ON). Retrieved from http://hdl.handle.net/1807/19056

McKenna, K. Y. A., & Bargh, J. A. (2000). Plan 9 from cyberspace: The implications of the Internet for personality and social psychology. *Personality and Social Psychology Review, 4*(1), 57–75.

Rietmeijer, C. A., & McFarlane, M. (2009). Web 2.0 and beyond: Risks for sexually transmitted infections and opportunities for prevention. *Current Opinion in Infectious Diseases, 22,* 67–71.

Sanders, T. C. (2008). M4M chat rooms: Individual socialization and sexual autonomy. *Culture, Health & Sexuality, 10*(3), 263–276.

Seal, D. W., Kelly, J. A., Bloom, F. R., Stevenson, L. Y., Coley, B. I., & Broyles, L. A. (2000). HIV prevention with young men who have sex with men: What young men themselves say is needed. *AIDS Care, 12*(1), 5–6.

Turkle, S. (1995). *Life on the screen: Identity in the age of the Internet.* New York: Simon & Schuster.

CHAPTER 11

The Ecology of College Drinking: Revisiting the Role of the Campus Environment on Students' Drinking Patterns

Nancy Beauregard, Andrée Demers, and Louis Gliksman

Perhaps one of the most critical transitions in life is the passage from adolescence to adulthood. For many youth, a core component of this transition is the shift from secondary schools to higher education institutions (Gore et al. 1997). Vocationally, higher education institutions transmit multiple capital pivotal to students' societal participation (Bourdieu 1979). In light of the pervasive public health concern that constitutes college drinking, it is now recognized that higher education institutions contribute to youth health capital (National Center on Addiction and Substance Abuse at Colombia University 2007). Yet, the nature of the specific pathways through which higher education institutions shape student drinking culture is debated. Anchored in **social practice theory**, this paper seeks to address this issue with an empirical investigation of Canadian undergraduates.

The Social Dynamics of Post-secondary Drinking

Since **Émile Durkheim**'s 'Suicide' (1897), a basic tenet in sociology contends that human activity defines and is defined by the social environment. So far, the literature on post-secondary drinking has carried forward this idea by examining the contribution of higher education institutions through the specific pathways of social norms and alcohol control mechanisms.

According to social norms theory, students' appraisals of descriptive and injunctive drinking norms characterizing their campus environment modulate their drinking patterns. These norms respectively represent students' perceptions of the typicality (e.g. quantity) and moral acceptability (e.g. social expectations) of drinking behaviours commonly displayed by student peers (Perkins 2002). Empirically, consistent support has been demonstrated for an association between students' own subjective perceptions of overly typical and permissive norms and riskier drinking patterns (Larimer et al. 2004; Weitzman, Nelson and Wechsler 2003). However, far less is known about the collective aspects of social norms. Collective aspects of social norms are present when social norms perceptions are shared by a given group of students exposed to the same normative environment. Preliminary multilevel studies were supportive of the relevance to concomitantly and distinctively investigate both subjective and collective aspects of social norms (Trockel, Williams and Reis 2003).

Relative to alcohol control mechanisms, subjectively perceived ease in alcohol availability on campus and supportiveness toward permissive alcohol control policies have been identified as individual-level risk factors for alcohol drinking patterns (Wechsler et al. 2000; Wechsler et al. 2001; Weitzman, Nelson and Wechsler 2003; Lavigne et al. 2008). At the collective level, reports of decreased institutional rates in problematic students' drinking due to stricter enforcement (Knight et al. 2003) and availability policies (Wechsler et al. 2004) were noted, though not consistently (Shaffer et al. 2005). Such discrepancy in findings may result from unacknowledged concomitant sources of variability in post-secondary drinking tributary to individual and contextual-level factors (Kawachi and Berkman 2003).

In sum, two areas may be targeted to comprehensively address the social dynamics of post-secondary drinking: (1) the integration of plural institutional pathways (e.g. normative, regulatory) under a unified scheme; (2) the specification of their analytical levels (e.g. subjective, collective).

Contextualizing Post-secondary Drinking: Bridging Pathways and Analytical Levels

A promising approach can be found in social theory and its conceptualization of health lifestyles (Cockerham 2005). Health lifestyles are not random behaviours reflecting deliberate individual choices. Rather, they represent socially conditioned patterns at the junction of individuals' life chances and choices. Life choices, viewed as 'a process of agency by which individuals critically evaluate and choose their course of action' (Cockerham, 2005: 60), are constantly enabled or constrained by life chances—namely the opportunities structures conferred to individuals following their location in the social structure. Health lifestyles thus anchor the shared social practices routinely adopted by groups of individuals characterized by structural proximity in their life chances and choices.

While informative of the dynamic relationship between agency and structure, we contend that the concept of health lifestyles and its contribution to the understanding of the specific nature of the pathways through which agency and structure intersect can be further clarified in light of Giddens' work (1984). For Giddens, human activity is comprised of three specific modalities: normative, political, and semantic. We believe that post-secondary drinking can heuristically be conceived as a health lifestyle governed by such modalities. These modalities reflect as many pathways from which higher education institutions influence post-secondary drinking.

In substance, the normative pathway stresses the centrality to display a skilled performance in the negotiation of drinking-related sanctions (e.g. peer pressure). The political pathway directs attention to the impact of administrative power relationships on post-secondary students' alcohol consumption through alcohol policies control led by campus authorities. Lastly, the semantic pathway underlies the performative components of the act of drinking whose definition rests on commonly held assumptions by members of a given student community about the meaning of this lifestyle. In line with Giddens, interdependent links between these pathways are postulated even though their operationalization implicates separate measures. Analytically, such pathways are deemed to operate at the subjective and collective level with distinct emergent properties (Archer 1995; Kawachi and Berkman 2003). The subjective level incorporates students' individual representations of the social environment, while the collective level incorporates the sharedness in such representations proper to members of a given student community.

Lastly, we consider that the notion of place here tackles interwoven social influences organized around institutional and academic membership. Disparities between higher education institutions and academic disciplines in prestige, selectivity, and overall organizational capacity influence students' assets and returns (Bourdieu 1979; van de Werfhorst and Kraaykamp 2001). Arguably, students' differential position in the institutional and academic structure distinctively defines their life chances through the facilitation or limitation in access and mobilization of resources affecting their health-related choices. In light of the above, the following research questions were examined:

> Research question 1: What is the nature of the pathways characterizing the association between alcohol-related practices on campus and students' drinking patterns?

> Research question 2: Do alcohol-related practices on campus shape students' drinking patterns from a subjective or a collective level of analysis?

Method

Sample

The data were drawn from the *Canadian Campus Survey* (CCS), a project examining the social determinants of addiction and mental health among full-time undergraduates enrolled in Canadian universities (for extensive details on sample design: Adlaf, Demers and Gliksman 2005). For this study, the data followed a hierarchical

structure in which students were nested in their academic environments. Academic environments combined university campus and field of study affiliation (i.e., Arts/Humanities, Medicine). To maximize assessment of academic environment-level indicators, only academic environments with 5 students or more were included. After excluding residual cases with missing data, lifetime and past year abstainers, the final sample was comprised of 4,641 students from 249 academic environments.

Dependent Variables

Heavy episodic drinking (HED) was derived from a one item-question ('On the days when you drank, how many drinks did you usually have?'). Caseness was set up at five or more drinks per occasion.

Independent Variables

Student-level variables

Subjective alcohol-related practices were adapted from Perkins and Wechsler's (1996) index of campus alcohol norms. Items measured in a **Likert scale** (1=strongly disagree to 5=strongly agree) respondents' perceptions about prevailing alcohol-related practices on their campus ('To what extent do you agree with the following statements about alcohol use at your campus?'). Two items measured semantic pathways ('students here admire non-drinkers' (reverse coded); 'drinking is an important part of the university experience'), two items normative pathways ('you can't make it socially in this university without drinking'; 'it's important to show how much you can drink and still hold your liquor'), and two other items political pathways ('university rules about drinking are almost never enforced', 'alcohol is easily available on campus').

Covariates

Gender, years in program, living arrangement, recreational-oriented activities profile, and intellectual-oriented activities profile were used as covariates, as these were associated with differential drinking dynamics (Demers et al. 2002; Gliksman et al. 1997).

Academic environment-level variables

Collective alcohol-related practices were aggregated scores at the academic environment units of the individual scores obtained from subjective alcohol-related practice measures.

Analytical Procedure

Multilevel statistical techniques were used to assess the joint contribution of subjective and collective alcohol-related practices on HED. Estimation of multilevel logistic regressions model parameters relied on iterative generalized least squares using a predictive quasi-likelihood method with second order Taylor expansion (PQL-2) (Snidjers and Bosker 1999). Confirmatory analyses were conducted on the 1998 data to corroborate the stability in the observed dynamics across CCS samples. Multilevel analyses were performed with MlWin 2.0 (Rasbash et al. 2004) and descriptive analyses with SPSS 15.0 (SPSS 2006). Both subjective and collective alcohol-related practices indicators were dichotomized above the median to emphasize riskier perceived practices.

Results

Summarily, of the 4,641 respondents: 36.2 per cent were male, 30.4 per cent in their first year, 17.9 per cent lived on campus, and 30.6 per cent reported past-year HED. The variance component model indicated that 11.8 per cent of the total variation in the risk for HED was attributable to academic environments. For subjective alcohol-related practices, non-drinkers being undervalued and being part of the university experience increased the risk for HED after adjustment for covariates. For collective alcohol-related practices, to hold liquor in public and social acceptance based on alcohol consumption were risk factors for HED, while weak rules of enforcement were a protective factor after adjustment for covariates. Results were unchanged after all factors were accounted for. Comparative analyses across CCS cycles led to stable results in risk associations between subjective and collective alcohol-related practices and HED (data not shown).

Table 11.1 Results of Multilevel Logistic Regression Models Explaining Heavy Episodic Drinking in Canadian Undergraduate Students (Odds Ratios and 95% Confidence Intervals: CCS, 2004)

	MODEL 1	MODEL 2	MODEL 3	MODEL 4
	OR (95%CI)	OR (95%CI)	OR (95%CI)	OR (95%CI)
Intercept	0.421*** (0.376–0.470)	0.241*** (0.203–0.285)	0.294*** (0.232–0.373)	0.250*** (0.194–0.322)
STUDENT-LEVEL				
Subjective alcohol-related social practices				
Non-drinkers undervalue[a]		1.157* (1.005–1.333)		1.174* (1.019–1.351)
Drinking as part of university experience[a]		1.564*** (1.345–1.818)		1.559*** (1.338–1.816)
Hold liquor in public[b]		1.150 (0.991–1.335)		1.129 (0.972–1.310)
Social acceptance based on alcohol consumption[b]		0.904 (0.768–1.064)		0.877 (0.744–1.034)
Weak rules of enforcement[c]		0.944 (0.779–1.143)		0.957 (0.790–1.160)
Alcohol availability on campus[c]		0.820 (0.664–1.014)		0.837 (0.676–1.036)

Table 11.1 (continued)

	MODEL 1	MODEL 2	MODEL 3	MODEL 4
	OR (95%CI)	OR (95%CI)	OR (95%CI)	OR (95%CI)
ACADEMIC ENVIRONMENT LEVEL				
Collective alcohol-related social practices				
Non-drinkers undervalue			.828 (.656–1.045)	.804 (.633–1.021)
Drinking as part of university experience			1.045 (.812–1.346)	.968 (.747–1.253)
Hold liquor in public			1.344* (1.054–1.714)	1.309* (1.020–1.679)
Social acceptance based on alcohol consumption			1.372* (1.078–1.746)	1.398** (1.092–1.790)
Weak rules of enforcement			.709** (.567–.886)	.711** (.565–.894)

	MODEL 1	MODEL 2	MODEL 3	MODEL 4
	OR (95%CI)	OR (95%CI)	OR (95%CI)	OR (95%CI)
Alcohol availability on campus			0.937 (0.746–1.176)	0.935 (0.741–1.181)
RANDOM PART				
Wald test	41.324 (1)***	41.647 (1)***	33.985 (1)***	35.078 (1)***
Academic environment variance	0.442***	0.489***	0.375***	0.395***
Intraclass correlation	0.118	0.129	0.102	0.107
GOODNESS-OF-FIT				
X^2 (df)		325.273 (11)***	308.254 (11)***	347.629 (17)***

Note: N=4,641 students from N=249 academic environments. All models were adjusted for the following individual-level covariates: gender, years in program, living arrangement, recreational-oriented activities profile, and intellectual-oriented activities profile.

[a] Semantic pathways

[b] Normative pathways

[c] Political pathways

*p<.05 **p<.01 ***p<.001

Discussion

By positing post-secondary drinking as a health lifestyle, this study sought to revisit the role of higher education institutions as social contexts for drinking. Findings corroborate the relevance of studying academic environments as a proxy for the disciplinary subcultures and campus settings to capture social variations in students' life choices, chances, and lifestyles. Academic environments were associated through normative, political, and semantic pathways to HED among students. Noteworthy is the stability of these associations over a multisample examination.

A closer look at the configuration of alcohol-related practices corroborated the plurality of their pathways and analytical levels in association with HED. According to our results, a significant amount of academic environments' variability in HED was connected to collective alcohol-related practices, independent of their subjective measures and other individual correlates. To illustrate, results for the normative pathways indicated that the collective but not the subjective measures (i.e., social acceptance based on drinking, hold liquor in public) emerged as risk factors for HED, therefore supporting emergent properties of the collective level of analysis (Kawachi and Berkman 2003).

Alternatively, the semantic pathways investigated were associated with HED, and were so through their subjective measures only. Individual perceptions that drinking is a highly valued practice and a common way to experience post-secondary life were shown to put students at risk. These results are in line with studies suggesting that alcohol consumption is meaningfully constructed by students as a functional, integrative, and inherent social practice of post-secondary life (Guise and Gill 2007; Workman 2001). The fact that no collective effects for the semantic pathways were found may pertain to the presence of modifying relationships between students and academic environments factors not examined in this study.

The political pathway revealed that students were at greater risk for HED in campus environments where drinking regulations were collectively perceived as being strongly enforced, contradicting preliminary evidence (Weitzman, Chen and Subramanian, 2005). One possible explanation for this resides in the potential tension between institutional responses to excessive students' drinking and students' adaptation to such measures. Given that most student drinking takes place off campus where campus rules do not apply and that disciplinary actions are marginal practices (Wechsler et al. 2002), clarifications on this particular point are warranted. Ease of alcohol availability did not associate with HED in its subjective or collective measure, contrary to other studies (Wechsler et al. 2000; Wechsler et al. 2001; Weitzman, Chen and Subramanian 2005). Again, this finding may raise the importance of considering academic environments from multiple concomitant rather than isolated pathways.

Despite these novel contributions, some limitations apply. First, the CCS data rests on self-reports, a well-known limitation in alcohol studies notably implying social desirability. Second, the cross-sectional nature of the data did not allow for causal inferences to be drawn. More research combining multilevel and longitudinal designs is highly warranted.

Conclusion

Higher education institutions are powerful learning environments for youth health capital. As suggested by this study, important steps in knowledge advancements may be achieved through a comprehensive appreciation of students–higher education institutions exchanges at the heart of the social dynamics of post-secondary drinking.

References

Adlaf, Edward, Andrée Demers, and Louis Gliksman. 2005. 'Canadian Campus Survey 2004'. edited by Edward Adlaf, Andrée Demers, and Louis Gliksman. Toronto, On: Center for Addiction and Mental Health.

Archer, Margaret S. 1995. *Realist Social Theory: The Morphogenetic Approach*. New York: Cambridge University Press.

Bourdieu, Pierre. 1979. *La Distinction. Critique Sociale Du Jugement*. Paris: Éditions de Minuit.

Cockerham, William C. 2005. 'Health Lifestyle Theory and the Convergence of Agency and Structure'. *Journal of Health and Social Behavior* 46:51–67.

Demers, Andrée, Sylvia Kairouz, Edward M. Adlaf, Louis Gliksman, Brenda Newton-Taylor, and Alain Marchand. 2002. 'Multilevel Analysis of Situational Drinking among Canadian Undergraduates'. *Social Science and Medicine* 55:415–24.

Giddens, Anthony. 1984. *The Constitution of Society, Outline of the Theory of Structuration*. Cambridge: Polity Press.

Gliksman, Louis, Brenda Newton-Taylor, Edward Adlaf, and Norman Giesbrecht. 1997. 'Alcohol and Other Drug Use by Ontario University Students: The Roles of Gender, Age, Year of Study, Academic Grades, Place of Residence and Programme of Study'. *Drugs: Education, Prevention and Policy* 4:117–129.

Gore, Susan, Robert Aseltine, Mary Ellen Colten, and Bin Lin. 1997. 'Life after High School: Development, Stress and Well-Being'. Pp. 197–214 in *Stress and Adversity over the Life Course: Trajectories and Turning Points*, edited by Ian H. Gotlib and Blair Weaton. Cambridge: Cambridge University Press.

Guise, Jennifer M. F., and Jan S. Gill. 2007. 'Binge Drinking? It's Good, It's Harmless Fun': A Discourse Analysis of Accounts of Female Undergraduate Drinking in Scotland'. *Health Education Research* 22:895–906.

Hirschfeld, Lindsay M., Karin L. Edwardson, and Mark P. Mcgovern. 2005. 'A Systematic Analysis of College Substance Use Policies'. *Journal of American College Health* 54:169–176.

Kawachi, Ichiro, and Lisa F. Berkman. 2003. *Neighborhoods and Health*. New York: Oxford University Press.

Knight, John R., Sion K. Harris, Lon Sherritt, Kathleen Kelley, Shari Van Hook, and Henry W. Wechsler. 2003. 'Heavy Drinking and Alcohol Policy Enforcement in a Statewide Public College System'. *Journal of Studies on Alcohol* 64:696–703.

Larimer, Mary E., Aaron P. Turner, Kimberly A. Mallett, and Irene Markman Geisner. 2004. 'Predicting Drinking Behavior and Alcohol-Related Problems among Fraternity and Sorority Members: Examining the Role of Descriptive and Injunctive Norms'. *Psychology of Addictive Behaviors* 18:203–212.

Lavigne, Andrea M., Caren Francione Witt, Mark D. Wood, Robert Laforge, and William DeJong. 2008. 'Predictors of College Student Support for Alcohol Control Policies and Stricter Enforcement Strategies'. *American Journal of Drug and Alcohol Abuse* 34:749–759.

National Center on Addiction and Substance Abuse at Colombia University. 2007. 'Wasting the Best and the Brightest: Substance Abuse at America's Colleges and Universities'. edited by National Center on Addiction and Substance Abuse at Colombia University. New York.

Perkins, H. Wesley. 2002. 'Social Norms and the Prevention of Alcohol Misuse in Collegiate Contexts'. *Journal of Studies on Alcohol*:164–72.

Perkins, H. Wesley , and Henry Wechsler. 1996. 'Variation in Perceived College Drinking Norms and Its Impact on Alcohol Abuse: A Nationwide Study'. *Journal of Drug Issues* 26:961–974.

Rasbash, John, Fiona Steele, William Browne, and Bob Prosser. 2004. *Mlwin Version 2.0*, London, UK: Multilevel Models Project, Institute of Education, University of London.

Shaffer, Howard J. , Antony N. Donato, Richard A. Labrie, Rachel C. Kidman, and Debi A. Laplante. 2005. 'The Epidemiology of College Alcohol and Gambling Policies'. *Harm Reduction Journal* 2:1.

Snidjers, Tom A. B., and Roel J. Bosker (Eds.). 1999. *Multilevel Analysis : An Introduction to Basic and Advanced Multilevel Modeling*. London: SAGE.

SPSS Inc. 2006. *Spss Base 15.0 for Windows User's Guide*, Chicago, IL: SPSS Inc.

Trockel, Mickey , Sunyna S. Williams, and Janet Reis. 2003. 'Considerations for More Effective Social Norms Based Alcohol Education on Campus: An Analysis of Different Theoretical Conceptualizations in Predicting Drinking among Fraternity Men'. *Journal of Studies on Alcohol* 64:50–9.

van de Werfhorst, Herman G., and Gerbert Kraaykamp. 2001. 'Four Field-Related Educational Resources and Their Impact on Labor, Consumption, and Sociopolitical Orientation'. *Sociology of Education* 74:296–317.

Wechsler, Henry W., Meichun Kuo, Hang Lee, and George W. Dowdall. 2000. 'Environmental Correlates of Underage Alcohol Use and Related Problems of College Students'. *American Journal of Preventive Medicine* 19:24–29.

Wechsler, Henry W., Jae E. Lee, Jeana Gledhill-Hoyt, and Toben F. Nelson. 2001. 'Alcohol Use and Problems at Colleges Banning Alcohol: Results of a National Survey'. *Journal of Studies on Alcohol* 62:133–41.

Wechsler, Henry W., Jae E. Lee, Toben F. Nelson, and Meichun Kuo. 2002. 'Underage College Students' Drinking Behavior, Access to Alcohol, and the Influence of Deterrence Policies - Findings from the Harvard School of Public Health College Alcohol Study'. *Journal of American College Health* 50:223–236.

Wechsler, Henry W., Mark Seibring, I-Chao Liu, and Marylin Ahl. 2004. 'Colleges Respond to Student Binge Drinking: Reducing Student Demand or Limiting Access'. *Journal of American College Health* 52:159–168.

Weitzman, Elissa R. , Ying-Yeh Chen, and S. V. Subramanian. 2005. 'Youth Smoking Risk and Community Patterns of Alcohol Availability and Control: A National Multilevel Study'. *Journal of Epidemiology and Community Health* 59:1065–71.

Weitzman, Elissa R., Toben F. Nelson, and Henry W. Wechsler. 2003. 'Taking up Binge Drinking in College: The Influences of Person, Social Group, and Environment'. *Journal of Adolescent Health* 32:26–35.

Workman, Thomas A. 2001. 'Finding the Meanings of College Drinking: An Analysis of Fraternity Drinking Stories'. *Health Communication* 13:427–447.

Duality and Diversity in the Lives of Immigrant Children: Rethinking the 'Problem of the Second Generation' in Light of Immigrant Autobiographies

Nedim Karakayali

Introduction

In an article published at the dawn of the twentieth century, the renowned social statistician Richmond Mayo-Smith (1894) identified three major groups among what he called 'the whites' in America. First, there were 'the native-born of native parentage', the 'true Americans' who constituted 'a homogeneous body, and to this body the others of more recent arrival tend to be assimilated'. Then, there were 'the whites of foreign birth, the immigrants . . . the real element to be assimilated'. Finally, there were the 'the native-born of foreign parents . . . the second generation of immigrants, so to speak'. Second-generation immigrants, Mayo-Smith wrote, 'stand half-way . . . between the native and the foreign element. . . . They represent the process of assimilation in the act' (437–8).

Although few researchers today, if any, would proceed with such a simplistic scheme, MayoSmith's remarks are far from being obsolete. In fact, most social research on children of immigrants in the twentieth century has unfolded in the broader context of the integration of immigrant groups. More specifically, the idea that children of immigrants are caught between the 'worlds' or 'cultures' of their parents and the host society remains relevant.

This paper is an examination of the **two-worlds thesis** in light of autobiographies written by children of immigrants in twentieth-century North America. The major issues addressed will focus on

duality. First, although the experience of duality is expressed in almost all the autobiographies, once we begin to zoom into the 'worlds' of immigrant children, we also observe an immense diversity. Children of immigrants 'live' in many—not just two—worlds. In this respect, my findings concur with recent ethnographic studies in multiethnic contexts in Western Europe (Ålund, 1995; Back, 1995; Qureshi and Moores, 1999; Soysal, 2001). By focusing on the experience of duality, the two-worlds thesis depicts an existence shaped by uncertainty and ambivalence. It is this condition that constitutes 'the problem of the second generation' (Hansen, 1952). Autobiographies, however, also reveal the presence of dreams and a desire for a different kind of life. The second argument of this paper is that the realization of these dreams is an equally important aspect of the 'problem'. I will also therefore suggest that the so-called 'problem of the second generation' should be located in the tension between diversity and duality, rather than in being caught between two worlds.

Data Sources and Limitations of the Study

Autobiographies as a Data Source

Children of immigrants can neither be defined as a class, an ethnic group, or an age group. The classic proponents of the two-worlds thesis justify this categorization on the grounds that children of immigrants share a common subjective experience (Stonequist, 1937; Hansen, 1952).

That 'immigrant autobiographies' can provide a key for understanding the 'experience' of immigrants was first stressed in the pioneering work of Boelhower (1982). We should nevertheless note that not all immigrant autobiographies deal with the experience of migration, nor do they always focus on children. In fact, it might be quite misleading to treat them as a unified genre. We have no reason to assume that there is a unified 'experience' associated with being a second-generation migrant.

Methodological Limitations

Since the main objective in the limited space of this study is to show in what ways the accounts given in the autobiographies diverge from the two-worlds thesis, there is little emphasis on the ways in which the autobiographies differ from each other. I try to reveal the multiplicity of relationships and potentials that often remain invisible from the point of view of the two-worlds thesis. It is nevertheless important to note that immigrant children—depending on race, ethnicity, and gender—articulate these relationships and potentials in different ways.

Data Sources and the Historical Period

In this study I have consulted some 30 autobiographical sources from North America (Canada and the United States), though only about half of them are cited/quoted here. Most of these sources are published autobiographies written almost exclusively by children of immigrants. The publication dates of the autobiographies analyzed range from 1925 to 1998.

A Brief History of the Two-Worlds Thesis

The two-worlds thesis states that immigrants will bring with them 'the principles of the governments they leave. . . . These principles, with their language,

they will transmit to their children. In proportion to their numbers, they will share legislation with us. They will infuse into it their spirit, warp or bias its direction, and render it a heterogeneous, incoherent, distracted mass' (Jefferson, 1964: 152).

In How Many Worlds Do Children of Immigrants Live?

In autobiographies written by children of immigrants, individuation begins with the immediate family. For the immigrant child, the relation between his or her mother and father is at least as important as how the two together relate to the society at large. In certain cases, the mother and father, as two different personalities, complement each other (Maynard, 1972; Antin, 1997: 155). In others, they develop deep conflicts. Sometimes the lot of the immigrant child consists of a despotic father and a helpless mother who 'did not count for much . . . except to take the beatings when things went wrong in the home' (Ruddy, 1975: 11). In other cases, one of the parents might be completely missing and the focus shifts to the relations between the single parent and his or her partners (Santiago, 1998). Parents also differ from each other in terms of their attitudes towards the host society. Horn (1997: 47) notes that, while his father considered the decision to immigrate to Canada from the Netherlands as the 'greatest blunder of his life', his mother was comfortable in her position as an immigrant since, having been raised in Java, she was 'less rooted in the Netherlands'. Similar observations can be made about brothers, sisters, and grandparents.

Not only do autobiographies shatter the image of the 'immigrant family' as an undifferentiated entity, but they also reveal that there is no uniform, 'typical' relationship between the immigrant child and his or her family. Furthermore, the composition of the 'immigrant family' changes over time and, especially for poor families, harsh living conditions often entail death and remarriage, and hence the need to form new relations—a typical theme in many autobiographies (Kohut, 1925; Adamic, 1969; Covello, 1970).

Finally, while the children might be highly conscious of the barriers between their ethnic community and host society, these two domains cannot be understood in terms of a simple opposition. Indeed, the desire to take part in the society at large is often induced by encounters in the ethnic community itself.

Becoming 'Someone Else': Diversity, Desire, and the Secret Life of Immigrant Children

Almost invariably, autobiographic sources indicate that an immigrant child, especially in his or her adolescent years, is likely to develop a myriad of relationships and participate in many different 'lives'. It is worth noting here that researchers identify a positive potential—'projects' and 'dreams'—emerging out of this complexity. In this sense the autobiographies of immigrant children can be seen as the stories of a new person—if not a new people—in the making. Autobiographies are not mere inventories of a myriad of encounters and disjointed worlds; in them, these separate parts are woven into a narrative and become elements of a singular life. As Deleuze and Guattari (1986: 17) insist, 'marginality' does not have to be a completely crippling condition: 'If the writer is in the margins or completely outside of his or her fragile community, this situation allows the writer all the more possibility to express another possible community and to forge the means for another consciousness and another sensibility.'

Why Do Children of Immigrants Feel That They Live in Two Worlds?

Why, then, do children of immigrants themselves often feel that they are caught between two worlds? On the basis of the autobiographies analyzed, we propose one straightforward answer. If the theme of two worlds is omnipresent in them, this is mainly because it is omnipresent in the everyday life of immigrant children. Almost from the day they are born, the distinction between a 'homeland' and a 'new land' permeates their lives, even seeping through the tales they hear, for example when grandparents would tell stories of their homelands to grandchildren.

Some of the proponents of the two-worlds thesis come very close to observing the division that cuts through the everyday life of immigrant children and how such divisions become a source of tension. 'The sons and the daughters of immigrants,' writes Hansen (1952: 494), 'were subjected to the criticism and taunts of the native [sic] Americans and to the criticism and taunts of their elders as well. . . . The source of all their woes . . . lay in the strange dualism into which they had been born.'

Concluding Remarks

The real problem with the two-worlds thesis is not its argument that immigrant children feel caught between two worlds, but its failure to note that this experience follows from the condition of living in a world where most people believe that there are only two worlds. By depicting this belief—this constructed reality—as the only reality of immigrant children, the two-worlds thesis unwittingly contributes to its reproduction. Moreover, to state, as Hansen does, that all the 'woes' of immigrant children can be located in the 'duality into which they were born' is to miss the point that there is also a desire to escape this duality—a desire for a new identity. The actualization of this desire is no less a 'problem' than the experience of being caught up between two worlds.

References

Adamic, L. 1969. *Laughing in the Jungle*. New York: Arno Press.

Ålund, A. 1995. 'Alterity in Modernity', *Acta Sociologica* 38, 4: 311–22.

Antin, M. 1997. *The Promised Land*. New York: Penguin Books.

Back, L. 1995. 'X Amount of Sat Siri Akal!: Apache Indian, Reggae Music and Intermezzo Culture', in *Negotiating Identities*, A. Ålund and R. Granqvist, eds. Amsterdam: Rodopi.

Boelhower, W. 1982. *Immigrant Autobiography in the United States*. Verona, Italy: Essedue edizioni.

Covello, L. 1970. *The Teacher in the Urban Community, or The Heart Is the Teacher*. Totowa, NJ: Littlefield, Adams and Co.

Deleuze, G., and E. Guattari. 1986. *Kafka: Toward a Minor Literature*. Minneapolis: University of Minnesota Press.

Hansen, M.L. 1952. 'The Problem of the Third Generation Immigrant', *Commentary* 14, 4: 492–500.

Horn, M. 1997. *Becoming Canadian*. Toronto: University of Toronto Press.

Jefferson, T. 1964. *Notes on the State of Virginia*. New York: Harper & Row.

Kohut, R. 1925. *My Portion: An Autobiography*. New York: T. Seltzer.

Maynard, F.B. 1972. *Raisins and Almonds*. Toronto: Doubleday Canada.

Mayo-Smith, R. 1894. 'Assimilation of Nationalities in the United States', *Political Science Quarterly* 9, 3: 426–44.

Qureshi, K., and S. Moores. 1999. 'Identity Remix: Tradition and Translation in the Lives of Young Pakistani Scots', *European Journal of Cultural Studies* 2, 3: 311–30.

Ruddy, A.C. 1975. *The Heart of the Stranger*. New York: Arno Press.

Santiago, E. 1998. *Almost a Woman*. Reading, MA: Perseus Books.

Soysal, L. 2001. 'Diversity of Experience, Experience of Diversity: Turkish Migrant Youth Culture in Berlin', *Cultural Dynamics* 13, 1: 5–28.

Stonequist, E., ed. 1937. *The Marginal Man*. New York: Charles Scribner's Sons.

CHAPTER 13

'Even If I Don't Know What I'm Doing, I Can Make It Look Like I Know What I'm Doing': Becoming a Doctor in the 1990s

Brenda L. Beagan

Introduction

When students enter medical school, they are nothing more than normal lay people with some science background. When they leave four years later they have become physicians; they have acquired specialized knowledge and taken on a new identity of medical professional. What happens in those four years? What processes of **socialization** go into the making of a doctor?

Most of what we know about how students come to identify as future physicians derives from research conducted when students were almost exclusively male, white, middle or upper class, young, and single—for example, the classics *Boys in White* (Becker, Geer, Strauss, and Hughes, 1961) and *Student Physician* (Merton, Reader, and Kendall, 1957). When women and students of colour were present in this research it was in token numbers. Even when women and non-traditional students were present, as in Sinclair's (1997) recent **ethnography**, their impact on processes of professional identity formation and the potentially distinct impact of professional socialization on these students have been largely unanalyzed. What does becoming a doctor look like now, when many students are female, are of diverse backgrounds, are working-class, gay, and/or parents?

This study draws on survey and interview data from students and faculty at one Canadian medical school to examine the processes of professional identity formation and how diverse undergraduate medical students in the late 1990s experience these processes. As the results will show, the processes are remarkably unchanged from those documented 40 years ago.

Research Methods and Participants

This research employed three complementary research strategies: a survey of a third-year class (123 students) at one medical school, interviews with 25 students from that class, and interviews with 23 faculty members from the same school. Third-year students were chosen because in a traditional medical curriculum the third year is a key point for students; it is an important transition as they move out of the classroom to spend the majority of their time working with patients—patients who may or may not call them 'doctor', treat them as doctors, and reflect them back to themselves as doctors (cf., Coombs, 1978; Haas and Shaffir, 1987).

Survey respondents also identified faculty members who they believed were 'especially interested in medical education'. Twenty-three faculty interviews were conducted. All interviews took 60–90 minutes following a semi-structured interview guide, and were tape-recorded and transcribed.

Processes of Identity Formation

First Experiences Become Commonplace

When identifying how they came to think of themselves as medical students, participants described a process whereby what feels artificial and unnatural initially comes to feel natural, simply through repetition. For many students, a series of 'first times' were transformative moments.

Constructing a Professional Appearance

Students are quite explicitly socialized to adopt a professional appearance: 'When people started to relax the dress code a letter was sent to everybody's mailbox, commenting that we were not to show up in jeans, and a tie is appropriate for men.' Most students, however, do not require such reminders; they have internalized the requisite standards. Dressing neatly and appropriately is important in order to convey respect to patients, other medical staff, and the profession. It probably also helps the patients consider the students seriously (survey comment). When asked whether or not they ever worry about their appearance or dress at the hospital, 41 per cent of the survey respondents said they do not, while 59 per cent said they do.

Changes in Language, Thinking, and Communication Skills

Acquiring a huge vocabulary of both new words and old words with new meanings—what one student called 'medical-ese'—is one of the central tasks facing medical students, and one of the major bases for examining them (Sinclair, 1997). Students were well aware of the importance of adopting the formal language of medicine.

The language of medicine is the basis for constructing a new social reality. Even as it allows for communication, language constructs 'zones of meaning that are linguistically circumscribed' (Berger and Luckmann, 1966: 39). Medical language encapsulates and constructs a world wherein reducing a person to body parts, organs, and systems becomes normal, 'the only reasonable way to think' (C... 1993: 98–9). Students describe... pare away 'extraneous' infor... life to focus on what is c...

Not surprisingly, students may simultaneously lose the communication abilities they had upon entering medical school.

Learning the Hierarchy

Key to becoming a medical student is learning to negotiate the complex hierarchy within medicine, with students positioned at the bottom. A few faculty saw this hierarchy as a fine and important tradition facilitating students' learning. Students, and most faculty members, were far less accepting of this traditional hierarchy—particularly of students' place in it. Both faculty and students pointed out the compliance the hierarchical structure inculcates in students, discouraging them from questioning those above them. For students, being a 'good medical student' means not challenging clinicians. Although virtually every student described seeing things on the wards they disagreed with, as long as there was no direct harm to a patient they stayed silent and simply filed away the incident in their collection of 'things not to do when I am a doctor'. These students had developed a sense of alliance with other members of the profession rather than with lay people and patients—a key to professional socialization.

Relationship to Patients

As students are learning their r¹   the hierarchy w¹   taneously
                                          patients.
                                        el power-
                                        nts, even
                                        r. In the
                                        iews on
                                        ʳsicians

                                        ection
                                        al dis-
                                        1957,
                                        ell' as
                                        over-
                                        ment
                                        ʳous.
                                        athy

and objectivity, learning to overcome or master their emotions (Haas and Shaft, 1987; Conrad, 1988): 'I only become of use if I can create some distance so that I can function.' In contrast, several faculty members rejected the 'emotional distancing' approach to medicine in favour of one based in egalitarian connection.

Playing a Role Gradually Becomes Real

Along with emotional distancing, Fox (1957) identified 'training for uncertainty' as key to medical socialization, including the uncertainty arising from not knowing everything, and not knowing enough. Alongside gathering the knowledge and experience that gradually reduces feelings of uncertainty, students also grow to simply tolerate high levels of uncertainty. At the same time, they face routine expectations of certainty—from patients who expect them 'to know it all' and faculty who often expect them to know far more than they do and who evaluate the students' competence (Haas and Shaffir, 1987). Students quickly learn that it is risky to display lack of certainty; **impression management** becomes a central feature of clinical learning (Conrad, 1988). Haas and Shaffir (1987: 110) conclude that the process of professionalization involves, above all, the successful adoption of a cloak of competence such that audiences are convinced of the legitimacy of claims to competence.

Responses from Others

The more others treat students as if they really were doctors, the more the students feel like doctors (cf., Coombs, 1978). In particular, the response from other hospital personnel and patients can help confirm the student's emerging medical professional identity.

For many students, patients were the single most important source of confirmation for their emerging identity as physicians. Simply being called 'doctor' by others, especially by patients, is one response that has a tremendous impact (Konner, 1987; Shapiro, 1987). Survey results show that 68 per cent (n = 48) of students had been called 'doctor' at least occasionally by people other than family or friends. All but two fully recalled the first time they were called 'doctor' and how they felt about it. Not being referred to as a doctor—especially when your peers are—can be equally significant. In previous accounts, being white and being male have greatly improved a medical student's chances of being identified as a doctor (Gamble, 1990; Dickstein, 1993; Lenhart, 1993; Kirk, 1994). In this study, although social class background, minority status, and first language made no difference, significantly more men than women were regularly called doctor and significantly more women had never been called doctor.

Secondary Socialization: Subsuming the Former Self?

The fact that **roles** carry with them established expectations heightens the potential for clashes with the identity characteristics of new incumbents. Education processes, which are inevitably processes of secondary socialization, must always contend with individuals' already formed and persistent selves, selves established through primary socialization. In this research, most students indicated that medicine had largely taken over the rest of their lives, diminishing their performance of other responsibilities. While 55 per cent of survey respondents thought they were doing a good job of being a medical student, many thought they were doing a poor to very poor job of being a spouse (26 per cent) or family member (37 per cent); 46 per cent gave themselves failing grades as friends. Fewer than a quarter of respondents thought they were doing a good job of being an informed citizen (18 per cent) or a member of their religion, if they had one (17 per cent). What emerged from most interviews and from the survey was a picture of medical school dominating all other aspects of daily life. Overwhelmingly, students talked about sacrifice.

Thus, some students do not or cannot integrate their medical student identities with their former sense of self; rather they let go of parts of themselves, bury them, abandon them, or put

them aside, at least for a while. Another option for students who experience incongruities between their medical student identities and other aspects of themselves is to segregate their lives. Because human beings have the ability to reflect on our own actions, it becomes possible to experience a segment of the self as distinct, to 'detach a part of the self and its concomitant reality as relevant only to the role-specific situation in question' (Berger and Luckmann, 1966: 131). In this research, 31 per cent of survey respondents felt they are one person at school and another with friends and family.

Difference as a Basis for Resistance

Elsewhere I have argued that intentional and unintentional homogenizing influences in medical education neutralize the impact of social differences students bring into medicine (Beagan, 2000). Students come to believe that the social class, 'race', ethnicity, gender, and sexual orientation of a physician are not—and should not be—relevant during physician–patient interactions. Nonetheless, at the same time those social differences can provide a basis for critique of and resistance to aspects of medical professional socialization. A study of medical residents found that those most able to resist socialization pressures minimized contact and interaction with others in medicine, maintained outside relationships that supported an alternative orientation to the program, and entered their programs with a 'relatively strong and well-defined orientation' (Shapiro and Jones, 1979: 243). Complete resocialization requires 'an intense concentration of all significant interaction within the [new social] group' (Berger and Luckmann, 1966: 145); it is also facilitated by minimal contradictions between the previous social world and the new world.

Conclusion

What is perhaps most remarkable about these findings is how little has changed since the publication of *Boys in White* (Becker et al., 1961) and

Student Physician (Merton et al., 1957), despite the passage of 40 years and the influx of a very different student population. The basic processes of socializing new members into the profession of medicine remain remarkably similar, as students encounter new social norms, a new language, new thought processes, and a new world view that will eventually enable them to become full-fledged members of 'the team', taking the expected role in the medical hierarchy.

Finally, this research shows that the same sources of differentiation that mark some students as not quite fitting in also serve as sources of resistance against medical socialization. Older students, gay students who refuse to be closeted, and students who come from poverty or from working-class backgrounds, may be more likely than others to 'do medical student' differently. Whether that translates into 'doing doctor' differently is a matter for further empirical research. Future research needs to examine how these 'different' students, these resisting students, experience residency and professional practice, and whether and how they remain in medical practice.

References

Beagan, B.L. 2000. 'Neutralizing Differences: Producing Neutral Doctors for (almost) Neutral Patients', *Social Science of Medicine* 51, 8: 1253–65.

Becker, H.S., B. Geer, A.L. Strauss, and E.C. Hughes. 1961. *Boys in White: Student Culture in Medical School*. Chicago: University of Chicago Press.

Berger, P.L., and T. Luckmann. 1966. *The Social Construction of Reality: A Treatise in the Sociology of Knowledge*. New York: Doubleday.

Conrad, P. 1988. 'Learning to Doctor: Reflections on Recent Accounts of the Medical School Years', *Journal of Health and Social Behavior* 29: 323–32.

Cooley, C.H. 1964. *Human Nature and the Social Order*. New York: Schocken.

Coombs, R.R. 1978. *Mastering Medicine*. New York: Free Press.

Dickstein, L.A. 1993. 'Gender Bias in Medical Education: Twenty Vignettes and Recommended Responses', *Journal of the American Medical Women's Association* 48, 5: 152–62.

Fox, R.C. 1957. 'Training for Uncertainty', in *The Student-Physician: Introductory Studies in the Sociology of Medical Education*, pp. 207–44, R.K. Merton, G.G. Reader, and P.L. Kendall, eds. Cambridge: Harvard University Press.

Gamble, V.N. 1990. 'On Becoming a Physician: A Dream not Deferred', in *The Black Women's Health Book: Speaking for Ourselves*, pp. 52–64, E.C. White, ed. Seattle: Seal Press.

Goffman, E. 1959. *The Presentation of Self in Everyday Life*. New York: Doubleday.

Good, B.J. and M.J. DelVecchio Good. 1993. '"Learning medicine": The Constructing of Medical Knowledge at Harvard Medical School', in *Knowledge, Power, and Practice: The Anthropology of Medicine and Everyday Life*, pp. 81–107, S. Lindbaum and M. Lock, eds. Berkeley: University of California Press.

Haas, J., and W. Shaffir. 1987. *Becoming Doctors: The Adoption of a Cloak of Competence*. Greenwich, CN: JAI Press.

Kirk, J. 1994. 'A Feminist Analysis of Women in Medical Schools', in *Health, Illness, and Health Care in Canada*, 2nd ed., pp. 158–82, B.S. Bolaria and H.D. Dickenson, eds. Toronto: Harcourt Brace.

Konner, M. 1987. *Becoming a Doctor: A Journey of Initiation in Medical School*. New York: Viking.

Lenhart, S. 1993. 'Gender Discrimination: A Health and Career Development Problem for Women Physicians', *Journal of the American Medical Women's Association* 48, 5: 155–9.

Mead, G.H. 1934. *Mind, Self, and Society: From the Standpoint of a Social Behaviorist*. Chicago: University of Chicago Press.

Merton, R.K., G.G. Reader, and P.L. Kendall. 1957. *The Student Physician: Introductory Studies in the Sociology of Medical Education*. Cambridge: Harvard University Press.

Shapiro, M. 1987. *Getting Doctored: Critical Reflections on Becoming a Physician*. Toronto: Between the Lines.

Shapiro, E.C., and A.B. Jones. 1979. 'Women Physicians and the Exercise of Power and Authority in Health Care', in *Becoming a Physician: Development of Values and Attitudes in Medicine*, pp. 237–45, E. Shapiro and L. Lowenstein, eds. Cambridge: Bellinger.

Sinclair, S. 1997. *Making Doctors: An Institutional Apprenticeship*. New York: Berg.

Questions for Critical Thought

CHAPTER 10

1. Explain how the Internet provides unique opportunities for impression management for the men whom Lombardo interviews. Compare this with the offline world. What are some advantages of online dating over cruising only in the offline world?

2. How do online communities structure how men can present themselves? Be sure to talk about the generalized other and the situated self, using examples from Lombardo's paper.

3. How do men interpret other men's presentations of selves to find their ideal partner? What kinds of things do they look for? What kind of decorum is expected?

4. How are these online communities especially helpful for new and exploring men who have sex with men?

5. What are Lombardo's findings about sexual health? What kinds of folk knowledges do participants learn online about safe sex? Could sexual health campaigns for men who have sex with men be more successful by targeting online communities?

6. The men whom Lombardo interviews are very clear about why they manipulate their identity online: to find partners. But we all manipulate our identity on- (and off)line. Consider the ways that you manage your identity online (on Facebook, Twitter, or other social network media). What are you trying to communicate about yourself? Why? Who is your audience? Where have you learned how to present yourself?

CHAPTER 11

1. Explain what Beauregard , Demers, and Gliksman mean by 'health lifestyles'.

2. Which specific institutional properties do each of the three pathways—semantic, normative, and political—direct our attention to?

3. Compare the results of the three pathways. Did they all generate significant results? What did each of these pathways point to as a significant predictor of heavy episodic drinking?

4. Compare the results of the individual- and institutional-level variables. Did they perform similarly? Was one level a better predictor than the other? Explain why or why not.

5. Consider your institutional context. Do you think your campus culture encourages heavy episodic drinking? Explain why or why not.

CHAPTER 12

1. According to Karakayali, what are the benefits and hindrances of using autobiographies as a data source?

2. Is the second-generation child caught in only two worlds? Is the immigrant family a cohesive unit, unified against the host country in a homogeneous way? Explain using examples from the text.

3. According to Karakayali, why is it that children of immigrants feel caught between two worlds?

4. Why is it problematic for second-generation immigrants to believe that they are trapped between only two worlds?

5. Immigrant children are not the only children to be caught 'between worlds'. Explain how other marginalized cultures that children can be part of—in their family, with friends, or in their personal lives—would give them experiences similar to those of second-generation immigrants.

CHAPTER 13

1. Beagan wanted to expand the information available on how people with marginalized identities (women, visible minorities, etc.) experience medical professionalization. What did she discover about their experiences compared to those of white, male medical students? Provide examples from the article.

2. How do Beagan's findings replicate previous findings? How are they different from past studies?

3. According to Beagan, what are some of the most important parts of performing the medical student's identity?

4. Why do medical students have to know how to pretend that they know what they are doing? How does this relate to training for uncertainty?

5. How do other people help medical students feel more confident in their doctor identity, and less like they are pretending?

6. Does medical school re-socialize students into entirely new people? What are some of the ways that students navigate the conflict between their new doctor identity and their previously existing identities?

Part IV

Deviance

We have all engaged in acts of deviance. At times, we have done things we should not have—things that have made us ashamed, anxious, or that gave us a secret thrill. Though our actions may not have seemed deviant to us at the time, the stigma surrounding them made them deviant from a social perspective. What is most likely to interest a sociologist, then, is not the deviant behaviour itself, but how deviance and conformity are related to each other: how conformists treat deviance. Deviance, as we shall see, is another aspect of social order. *Society creates deviance* by expecting, insisting on, and enforcing social order.

Deviance is not a special topic of study but a measure of how strictly a society is organized and how reliably it enforces its norms and laws. Every area of social life provides a chance to deviate. Deviance ranges from murder at one extreme to pushing to the head of a line of people waiting for a bus at the other. Deviance also includes keeping a dog off-leash in restricted areas, taking one's clothes off in the lobby of a doctor's office, bargaining at a department store, and eating poached worms in Regina.

Behaviours termed 'deviant' all threaten what members of one group or another feel are their cherished values or their security. To sociologists, then, *deviance* is a general term referring to any behaviour that leads to a negative reaction by some part of the community. When no one feels threatened by an uncommon behaviour—for example, by the wearing of a polka-dot bow tie—people are likely to see it as simply an expression of individuality.

All the papers in this section focus on public reactions to crime, not on causes of the crime itself. Reactions to uncommon behaviour depend largely on how the behaviour is viewed. Still, perception by itself is not enough; for an act to be deviant, perception must be turned into action. How much weight that action carries will depend on how much power people have to *enforce* their own views of acceptable behaviour. In this section, we see a variety of approaches to deviance and efforts by the public—especially policy-makers—to control it. The article by Christie Barron and Dany Lacombe asks whether highly publicized incidents of crime or delinquency by girls and women represent a major social change or merely a moral panic about the rise of 'nasty girls'. Similarly, Michael Adorjan examines the moral panic fed by newspapers and other mass media in their discussions of youth crime in Alberta.

The two remaining papers in this section address official reactions to behaviours deemed deviant—especially when such behaviours have generated a moral panic. Frances Shaver discusses the debate about how to handle sex work as a public issue in Canada—whether to address it through harm reduction or through criminalization and law enforcement and, if the latter, whether to punish the sex providers, their pimps, or the people who buy their services. Patrick Parnaby and Myra Leyden's paper applies Robert Merton's well-known typology of adaptations to anomie to understanding police deviance as a seemingly inevitable outcome of clashing rules and public demands for crime control.

Emotions Contests and Reflexivity in the News: Examining Discourse on Youth Crime in Canada

Michael C. Adorjan

In this paper, I examine how two Canadian newspapers, the *Alberta Report* and the *Calgary Herald*, address appropriate reactions to youth **crime**. I focus particular attention to the argument that the media play a significant role in generating moral panics regarding youth crime, especially by promoting public fear that youth crime is increasingly serious and spiralling out of control (Goode and Ben-Yehuda 1994; Cohen 2002 [1972]). I also address arguments that the media react to moral panics in increasingly complex ways (McRobbie and Thornton 1995; Garland 2008; Altheide 2009). I contribute to this literature by focusing primarily on whether or not rhetoric related to youth crime takes on emotional or rational forms, as well as on the news 'awareness contexts' (Glaser and Strauss 1964) that involve reactions to emotions as a central aspect of the social problem.

News Reflexivity and Emotions Discourses

Numerous studies have examined crime coverage in the news. The vast majority of this research suggests that disproportionate, needlessly exaggerated representations of crime in newspapers are indicative of distortion and ideology (Fishman 1978; Hall, Critcher, Jefferson, Clarke and Roberts 1978; Gorelick 1989; Barlow, Barlow and Chiricos 1995; Sacco 1995; Welch, Fenwick and Roberts 1997). Related studies found little evidence of 'rational' contextualizing information in news reports, including the absence of any discussion of crime causation (Tuchman 1978, 192; Marsh 1991, 76; Altheide 1997, 662–663).

However, moral panic theorists who have observed the public's longstanding focus on youth crime as a target for the channelling of broader anxieties are cognizant of the complexity of these processes (Zatz 1987; Welch, Price and Yankey 2002). Rather than positing a top-down model in which media puppet-masters disseminate moral panics from above and a gullible public is easily swayed by the media's machinations, these scholars point to 'social differentiation', 'audience segmentation', and an array of 'disparate perspectives' facilitated by a wider range of media sources (McRobbie and Thornton 1995, 564, 568). Today's moral panics are 'more knowing and self-reflexive', with the media more frequently commenting on their own practices, 'often making a story of the story' (Garland 2008, 12, 18).

Recent studies of Canadian moral panics over youth crime have largely neglected to address these advances. Some have argued that the Canadian media are involved in a 'politics of child-hating' that involves a 'deliberately constructed . . . conspiracy against the marginalized', whereby media rhetoric 'decontextualizes' youth crime stories in an effort to 'direct and control public perception' (Schissel 2001, 85; Schissel 2006, 106). In contrast, constructionist scholars have recently pointed to more ambiguous formulations that often play out as 'victim contests' (Holstein and Miller 1997), drawing upon 'broader cultural [and emotional] discourses'—of young offenders as either 'cold-blooded, calculating predators, incapable of remorse' or as 'innocent victims of the social conditions that had robbed them of youthful innocence' (Spencer 2005, 48, 55).

Whereas emotional reactions to youth crime remain a central analytic concern for these studies, I draw more explicit attention to how emotions discourses are formulated, reacted to, and resisted within Canadian newspapers. Emotions contests involve claims-making *about* emotions. Media reflexivity undergirds these processes, as journalists who are often acutely aware of their competitors' representational strategies seek to undermine emotional discourses through rational rejoinders, or vice versa. I explore *how* media reactions to emotions discourses highlight the processes through which ideology is accomplished (Fine and Sandstrom 1993), and how newspapers reflexively react to emotions as objects themselves within media discourse. Such an analysis responds to Loseke's (2003) suggestion that constructionists pay more attention to how emotions discourses (e.g. condemnation or sympathy) are associated with rendering deviant 'people types'.

While the *Calgary Herald* underscored rational assessments of youth crime, the *Alberta Report* favoured emotional responses; in fact, for the latter such responses were themselves viewed as rational. In highlighting representative examples from each paper, I challenge scholarship suggesting that media often decontextualize social problems or that sensationalistic coverage necessarily permeates them.

Emotional vs. Rational Assessments of Youth Crime

Emotions Discourses as Rational

For the *Alberta Report*, brutal violence committed by young offenders justifies outrage. One article (Byfield 23 May 1994), ostensibly aware of its usage of emotions discourses to criticize youth crime policy and assess the severity of youth crime, began with this description:

> One Thursday evening early this month Rodney Bell, 44, was driving in the town of Oyama, B.C., between Kelowna and Vernon, when a car full of teenagers ran a stop sign and he narrowly avoided a collision. He followed the youngsters to a service station, where he thoroughly berated them.
>
> The next day one of the teenagers warned Mr. Bell's son that his dad had 'messed with the wrong guys', and at about 11:30 the following night, Saturday, the family was awakened by a gang outside their home. Mr. Bell came out to reason with them. His wife heard 'this really loud thwack', then found her husband lying on the lawn bleeding while the teens fled.
>
> He had been hit over the head with an axe and his skull smashed in. The kids didn't kill him—quite. But he can communicate only by squeezing his wife's hand, and his left side is likely permanently paralysed. . . . Two 16-year-olds have been charged, one for kicking him as he lay prone.

The writer then addresses the reader directly:

> What you may be sensing after hearing these facts is described by our federal minister of Justice as 'an emotional reaction', by which he means that your opinion must be discounted. We must look at youth crime 'realistically', he says, not 'emotionally'.
>
> A curious assertion indeed. It implies that anyone exposed to the physical realities of a situation makes a doubtful adviser. Direct experience invalidates opinion. . . . The

opinions of the sociologists on juvenile crime are valid. The opinions of people whose neighbour was butchered by an uncontrolled kid are merely 'an emotional reaction'.

The article suggests awareness that others, such as sociologists and politicians, do not favour 'emotional reactions' to violent youth crime. In contrast, emotional reactions are here constituted as legitimate through the article's normative position. The article also evidences awareness of other news media which would also potentially attack the position that emotional reactions are legitimate: 'Finally, the day before Mr. Bell's skull was bashed in, the *Edmonton Journal* began a three-part series on the youth crime problem', the article states. The *Edmonton Journal* is criticized for relying upon the advice of social workers, youth lawyers, psychologists, and sociologists, among others, to conclude, 'If you look carefully at the statistics, there is no problem.' However, these positions are quickly discounted: '(Notice that their intimacy with youth crime does not disqualify their opinions. Presumably that's because they don't get "emotional" about it.)'. The article ends by again criticizing the *Edmonton Journal*'s assurance that 'everything in the garden is lovely—if only you read the statistics right. Well it isn't. Just ask Rodney Bell.'

The act of perpetuating a moral panic is, in this article, taken as an object, with reference to dissenting expert sources as well as other media outlets. The *Alberta Report* reproduces sensational and emotive discourse, attracting attention to a social problem its editors and writers putatively view to be a serious affliction upon society, but does so with an acute awareness of how others perceive such arguments—both academics and journalists alike. Rather than merely *reproducing* a theme of 'exaggeration' (Kappeler and Potter 2005, 18), the article above *actively reacts to* the theme itself and *constitutes* emotional responses to youth crime as authentic, legitimate, and most significantly, rational.

Contesting Emotional Responses to Youth Crime

Such representations are frequently offset within the *Calgary Herald* through appeals to contextualizing

factors that strain youth toward deviance, and perhaps more significantly, a rejection of emotional reactions to youth crime. This paper's criticism facilitates a reflexive awareness of representational practices within the media, especially in relation to competitors.

One article (Cooney 14 May 1991) begins by addressing *its own* headlines: 'Last weekend's headlines made the morning coffee a little bitter. "Kid next door" could be violent. Bored youths bide time with beer, baseball bats. Attack at LRT station shatters teen's peace of mind.' The headlines 'spoke forcefully', it is stated:

> Raw, poignant, revealing, they spoke for themselves. The other stories more quietly revealed something about what our kids are up against. Behind the front page Saturday, a headline read April bad month for city's jobless. Unless you are looking for a career in fast food, the view from high school doesn't look too promising these days. Now pick a youth crime story. Any one will do. It doesn't take a sociologist to make a connection.

After a section reviewing a sample of movie titles and ratings from its own entertainment section, it is stated:

> Back in the real world, this small item appeared deep on A11 Saturday under the headline Protest mother guilty of assault. 'Three Hills (CP) - An Elnora mother who complained that a school mistreated her children has been convicted of assaulting the youngsters with a belt'. Mom's murder preliminary set. 'A preliminary hearing will be held Oct. 7 for a mother charged with first-degree murder in the shooting deaths of her two daughters'. Enough of the real world.

This article contains two salient interpretive aspects. Emotions of sympathy toward young offenders as victims are generated by pointing to external social forces that exacerbate the conditions youth face and, it is implied, 'push' them into deviancy. In this case, some mothers are *themselves* cast as the victimizers at fault. Moreover, instead of being 'punks' or 'predators', youth are innocent 'mistreated children' when cast as victims. This article suggests not only a cognizance of social forces that temper the individual pathologization of young offenders, but a reflexive awareness of the putative role of media in generating these panics, going so far as to 'deconstruct' its own narratives and offering a reflexive rejoinder from an insider's standpoint.

Similarly, another *Calgary Herald* article (30 April 1994) also offers a reflexive 'debunking' of sensationalistic media presentations of youth crime: 'Young offenders provide a perfect diversion. The public is jittery following a few isolated incidences of violent crimes involving young offenders and, egged on by sensational news stories, and pandering politicians, is anxious for a simple, easy solution.' Such sensational stories can be found, it is implied, in *other* papers.

What is especially salient in these examples from the *Calgary Herald* is not only a position that challenges emotionally infused renditions of young offender identity that, some argue, obfuscate the contexts that mediate such criminal behaviour, but an awareness—ironically from *within* the media—of the media's tendency to incite moral panics through sensationalistic crime coverage. Emotional descriptions are downplayed here in favour of a sober analysis of youth crime that critiques emotionally infused rhetoric and panicked reaction.

Discussion

The *Calgary Herald* and the *Globe and Mail* contrast in their *reactions to* reactions regarding emotional and rational responses to youth crime. The emotions contests generated are related to broader victim contests that frame young offenders as victims or victimizers, and that elicit and direct emotions of sympathy or condemnation toward individual young offenders and/or their social and environmental circumstances. While emotions discourses *are* sometimes judged as more significant and authentic than cognitive-rational assessments of social problems (see Loseke 2003, 127), emotions discourses were only presented as legitimate responses to youth crime within the *Alberta Report*. Such responses, on the other hand, were illegitimate for those who viewed young offenders more as victims than victimizers. Both papers demonstrate how the reflexive nature of Canadian news media relates to such strategies.

In sum, rather than finding simplicity and uniform distortion, Canadian news articles are polymorphous and reflexive. This reflexivity, perhaps the norm within late modern mass media, has led to intriguing narratives demonstrating the ability of media to not only adopt the rhetoric of moral panics but also adapt to it in novel ways. The media generates emotions contests given the central aspect emotional reactions play within the moral panic narrative. What renders these cultural clashes vibrant is their unpredictability. News remains an 'artful accomplishment' (Tuchman 1978, 216) that takes both society and itself as an object.

References

'If It Ain't Broke', *Calgary Herald* 30 Apr 1994, A4.

Altheide, David. 1997. 'The News Media, the Problem Frame, and the Production of Fear'. *The Sociological Quarterly* 38(4): 647–668.

Altheide, David. 2009. 'Moral Panic: From Sociological Concept to Public Discourse'. *Crime Media Culture* 5(1): 79–99.

Barlow, Melissa, David Barlow and Theodore Chiricos. 1995. 'Economic Conditions and Ideologies of Crime in the Media: A Content Analysis of Crime News'. *Crime & Delinquency* 41(3): 3–19.

Byfield, Ted. 'A Father Is Axed, a Mother Knifed, as Ottawa Deplores "Emotionalism"', *Alberta Report* 23 May 1994, 44.

Cohen, Stanley. 2002 [1972]. *Folk Devils and Moral Panics* (3rd ed.). London: Routledge.

Cooney, Roman. 'Society Sends Teens Wrong Message', *Calgary Herald* 14 May 1991, A4.

Fine, Gary and Kent Sandstrom. 1993. 'Ideology in Action: A Pragmatic Approach to a Contested Concept'. *Sociological Theory* 11(1): 21–38.

Fishman, Mark. 1978. 'Crime Waves as Ideology'. *Social Problems* 25(5): 531–543.

Garland, David. 2008. 'On the Concept of Moral Panic'. *Crime Media Culture* 4(1): 9–30.

Glaser, Barney G. and Anselm L. Strauss. 1964. 'Awareness Contexts and Social Interaction'. *American Sociological Review* 29(5): 669–679.

Goode, Erich and Nachman Ben-Yehuda. 1994. *Moral Panics: The Social Construction of Deviance*. Oxford, UK: Blackwell.

Gorelick, Steven. 1989. 'Join Our War: The Construction of Ideology in a Newspaper Crimefighting Campaign'. *Crime & Delinquency* 35(3): 421–436.

Hall, Stuart, Charles Critcher, Tony Jefferson, John Clarke and Brian Roberts. 1978. *Policing the Crisis: Mugging, the State, and Law and Order*. London: Macmillan.

Holstein, James A. and Gale Miller. 1997. 'Rethinking Victimization: An Interactional Approach to Victimology'. Pp. 25–47 in *Social Problems in Everyday Life: Studies of Social Problems Work*, edited by G. Miller and J. A. Holstein. London: JAI Press Inc.

Kappeler, Victor and Gary Potter. 2005. *The Mythology of Crime and Criminal Justice* (4th ed.). Long Grove: Waveland.

Loseke, Donileen. 2003. 'Constructing Conditions, People, Morality, and Emotion: Expanding the Agenda of Constructionism'. Pp. 120–129 in *Challenges and Choices: Constructionist Perspectives on Social Problems*, edited by J. A. Holstein and G. Miller. New York: Aldine De Gruyter.

Marsh, Harry. 1991. 'A Comparative Analysis of Crime Coverage in Newspapers in the United States and Other Countries from 1960–1989: A Review of the Literature'. *Journal of Criminal Justice* 1967–79.

McRobbie, Angela and Sarah Thornton. 1995. 'Rethinking "Moral Panic" for Multi-Mediated Social Worlds'. *British Journal of Sociology* 46(4): 559–574.

Sacco, Vincent. 1995. 'Media Constructions of Crime'. *Annals of the American Academy of Political and Social Science* 539(1): 141–154.

Schissel, Bernard. 2001. 'Youth Crime, Moral Panics, and the News: The Conspiracy Against the Marginalized in Canada'. Pp. 84–103 in *Canadian Youth Justice*, edited by R. Smandych. Toronto: Harcourt Canada.

Schissel, Bernard. 2006. *STILL Blaming Children: Youth Conduct and the Politics of Child Hating*. Halifax: Fernwood Publishing.

Spencer, Jack. 2005. 'It's Not as Simple as It Seems: Ambiguous Culpability and Ambivalent Affect in News Representations of Violent Youth'. *Symbolic Interaction* 28(1): 47–65.

Tuchman, Gaye. 1978. *Making News: A Study in the Construction of Reality*. New York: The Free Press.

Welch, Michael, Melissa Fenwick and Meredith Roberts. 1997. 'Primary Definitions of Crime and Moral Panic: A Content Analysis of Experts' Quotes in Feature Newspaper Articles on Crime'. *Journal of Research in Crime and Delinquency* 34(4): 474–494.

Welch, Michael, Eric Price and Nana Yankey. 2002. 'Moral Panic over Youth Violence: Wilding and the Manufacture of Menace in the Media'. *Youth & Society* 34(1): 3–30.

Zatz, Marjorie. 1987. 'Chicano Youth Gangs and Crime: The Creation of a Moral Panic'. *Crime, Law and Social Change* 11(2): 129–158.

CHAPTER 15

Dirty Harry and the Station Queens: A Mertonian Analysis of Police Deviance

Patrick F. Parnaby and Myra Leyden

In this paper, we take advantage of the versatility inherent in **Robert Merton**'s 1938 article on social structure and **anomie** by applying his model to the realm of policing, where the cultural definitions of success and the opportunity structure are different. Specifically, we argue that police **deviance** can be understood as a function of an anomic social structure in which an exuberant cultural emphasis on police as noble, masculine 'crime fighters' (see Niederhoffer 1967; Manning 2001) occupies a disproportionate relationship to the availability and/or efficacy of institutionally accepted means. The outcomes, we argue, are forms of deviant behaviour among officers that coincide closely with Merton's four classifications—namely innovation, retreatism, rebellion, and ritualism.

Machismo, Heroism, and the Thin Blue Line

North America's preoccupation with the drama, machismo, and adventure of policing is well known and well documented (Doyle 2006; Rabehemp 2008). A cursory review of prime-time television often reveals officers chasing dangerous suspects into alleyways, hanging from helicopters, and racing through city streets in a desperate bid to fight crime. Policing, therefore, is constructed as a non-stop adrenaline rush in which the lines between good and evil are relatively clear and where, more often than not, the cops always seem to 'get their man' (see Surette 2007). It is perhaps not surprising that young recruits cite the job's excitement and the opportunity to 'fight' crime when asked why they initially wanted to become police officers (Ranganella and White 2004). Thus, despite the somewhat tepid reality of day-to-day police work, evidence appears to suggest that incipient officers partially internalize the cultural construction of police as crime fighters. In Mertonian terms, the North American social system is promoting a value system that equates successful policing with fighting crime; however, the extent to which the opportunity structure accommodates officers in their struggle varies as a function of several overarching forces.

The Structural Impediments to Crime Fighting

Here we argue that the opportunity structure varies as a function of three overlapping phenomena: (a) the organizational capacity of police departments to respond effectively to criminal activity as a function of their resource base; (b) the extent to which the legitimate means are supported by other criminal justice institutions; and (c) the willingness and/or capacity of communities to assist the state in the greater project of order maintenance. Each factor is outlined below.

The Economics of Fighting Crime

Police departments have very different organizational capacities and degrees of efficacy that are, in part, functions of the overlapping economic structures within which they operate. Although spending on law enforcement in Canada has increased steadily for decades (Statistics Canada 2008), police departments are not flush with money. In fact, the recurring need to do more with less has become an organizational mantra as departments look to scale back expenditures. Across the United States, economic instability has led to reduced patrol hours, fewer new recruits, and civilian staffs being told to work more efficiently (Luhby 2010). Fiscal restraint also means the best talent cannot be recruited, technological improvements are deferred, and crime prevention programs are shut down. It is no wonder civilian staff and front-line officers feel like they are working with one hand tied behind their backs when budgets are cut.

Institutional Support

According to Bennett and Schmitt (2002), soon after joining the police service, officers realize they are unable to bring about permanent reductions in criminal activity. For many officers, the system fails to prosecute, convict, and sentence offenders in ways commensurate with their perceived standards of justice. For example, in Johnson's (2004) study of police frustration with domestic violence calls, officers identified the underhanded tricks of defence lawyers and the unwillingness of courts to prosecute batterers as key sources of personal cynicism and frustration. Moreover, for decades officers have complained when courts, in lieu of prison crowding, have handed down lesser sentences (Goldschmidt 2008) or, as is currently the case in Canada, when court backlogs result in the dismissal of cases that might have otherwise ended with an offender being held accountable for his or her actions (see Green 2003). In short, when understood in relation to our culture's unbridled emphasis on fighting crime, the variable extent to which other criminal justice institutions are willing and/or able to maintain the integrity of due process contributes to the anomic disconnect in question.

Public Assistance

Although popular culture still clings to the idea that crimes are solved by officers working in isolation with only their finely tuned detective skills at the ready, the truth is more prosaic; the police need the public's help (Moskos 2009). In fact, agencies are acutely aware of how important community-based social networks are in the fight against crime (Maguire and Katz 2002; Ortiz et al. 2007); however, the extent to which these opportunity structures yield useful information is a function of broader social forces. Pre-existing racial tensions and decades of social disorganization, for example, sometimes turn communities into anti-police areas, effectively closing down the vital channels of communication that are instrumental in the fight against crime (see Anderson 1990; Davis 1992; Herbert 1996; Parenti 1999; Harris 2005). Officers become frustrated when witnesses fail to come forward, when community meetings yield little information, or when the spread of misinformation leads to unnecessary anxiety and tension among citizens. Police agencies often spend years trying to re-establish functional relations with the alienated communities in their midst.

Our intention thus far has been to highlight, in rather broad strokes, how the unbridled cultural emphasis on police as crime fighters is sometimes at odds with the legitimate opportunity structure. Thus, on the basis of Merton's theoretical model, we argue that various forms of police deviance are probabilistic outcomes of these structural conditions.

The Innovator

In his 2004 autobiography, Juan Lopez (1994) revisits the seven years he spent policing Chicago's streets. His experiences are saturated with anger, frustration and, at times, a sense of sheer hopelessness as he lays bare the extent to which fellow officers employed unethical and sometimes malicious tactics to fulfill objectives that were, in and of themselves, noble. In fact, Lopez claims to have threatened and beaten suspects in order to acquire intelligence; unfortunately, such behaviour is not uncommon among officers. For example, in 2003, members of the Toronto Police Service who were already facing charges of corruption faced additional accusations that they had brutally abused a suspected marijuana dealer during his interrogation, leaving him bleeding and unable to breathe on his cell floor (CBC News Online 2003).

The adoption of questionable means to achieve noble ends is more prevalent, and likely more systemic, under less extreme circumstances. Skolnick and Fyfe (1993), for example, argue that the use of deceptive practices is common in police work, especially when officers are seeking a confession. Similar findings emerged in Goldschmidt's (2008) research on police dishonesty insofar as officers admitted to planting narcotics, falsifying reports, and searching without just cause. Not surprisingly, Goldschmidt's participants sought to legitimize their activity by emphasizing the noble cause that was alleged to have been their objective; in a Mertonian sense, they are classic innovators.

Rebellion

In November 1990, Neil Stonechild, a 17-year-old Aboriginal man, froze to death in a remote industrial area north of Saskatoon, Saskatchewan. Neil was a victim of a 'starlight tour'. Police officers had dropped him off on the city's outskirts so he could sober up while walking home. The temperature that night was −28.1 degrees Celsius, according to the judicial inquiry (Wright 2004).

The violence exacted upon Stonechild reflected a complete and utter disregard for human rights in favour of a violent discriminatory social order where the institutionally legitimate means of exercising social control and the culturally celebrated goal of being a noble, masculine crime fighter were summarily dismissed. This form of street justice, wherein a desire for revenge supplants an officer's pursuit of a more noble cause, clearly fulfills the principle components of Merton's rebellion category.

Police brutality is not rebellion's only manifestation, however. The institutionally accepted means and culturally proscribed goals are cast aside similarly when officers engage in self-interested corruption. Buying and selling narcotics, theft, taking bribes, and negotiating kickbacks all reflect a willingness to let personal gain trump the ethical standards of public service (see Punch 2000).

The Ritualist

While accepting the institutionalized means that ritualists scale back the goals so as to render them more readily achievable, rarely do they 'go the extra mile' in their bid to meet normative expectations. Ritualists are not hard to find in any North American police organization. Here, we examine female police officers and officers approaching retirement.

Finding their place in the male-dominated field of law enforcement is difficult for women. Indeed, most are unavoidably confronted with the choice of being a *police*woman (officer first/female second) or a police*woman* (female first/officer second) (Martin 1980). Female officers who identify as police*woman* eschew the aggressive and violent behaviours attributed to male police work by scaling back the crime fighting ideal, preferring to adopt more feminine roles that involve caretaking, softness, and empathy (Carlan and McMullan 2009; Rabe-hemp 2008). Those who embrace the role of *police*woman are also ritualists in so far as they *strictly* observe the formal regulations and standardized procedures amenable to crime fighting to avoid being seen as either soft on crime by their co-workers or as pushovers by the public (see Rabe-hemp 2008).

Research has long shown that men identify closely with their work; therefore, retirement means a loss of job, identity, and colleagues. In many police organizations, soon-to-be retirees often choose assignments that are less risky or opt for supervisory duties that keep them off the beat while becoming sticklers for procedure (Brown et al. 1996; Paoline 2004). One becomes an 'old timer' whose occupational distance from the street becomes the subject of derisive humour. As Herbert (1996) notes in his analysis of the Los Angeles Police Department, 'station queens', a label sometimes applied to crime prevention officers, are those who no longer fight the good fight, opting instead for the safety of a desk and the predictability of bureaucratic routine. These ritualists soothe their discomfort by scaling back the cultural goals while preparing for their inevitable transition out of work.

Retreatists

Unable to live up to the culturally celebrated definition of success, the retreatist finds him- or herself in a reclusive world outside the bounds of conventional society. For police officers thwarted in their attempts to sustain the crime fighter persona, retreatism is often reflected in substance abuse or in stress-related illness.

Myriad studies have demonstrated that policing is a stressful occupation (see Violanti and Aron 1995). Behaviourally congruent with Merton's retreatist, officers suffering from stress-related illnesses often find themselves emotionally isolated from co-workers, friends, and family, eventually withdrawing into a world of drugs, alcohol, depression, or suicide (Chapin et al. 2008; Ouimette et al. 2010; Violanti 1995). That said, the retreatist is deviant on two levels: first, officers experience the stigmatization that accompanies mental and physical illness and, second, they find themselves living a life that no longer resembles the idealized image that helped lure them to the occupation in the first place. It is no wonder that over-stressed and/or ill officers refer to themselves as 'incompetent' and 'damaged' (see Tolin and Foa 1999: 530).

Conclusion

Admittedly, this model has departed slightly from Merton's original thesis insofar as he did not conceptualize systemic anomie in terms of how a narrow slice of the population adapts to the limited availability and/or efficacy of acceptable means. However, we believe our argument is consistent with Mertonian logic and that it has transcended traditional levels of analysis by conceptualizing the etiology of police deviance in terms of discordant structural conditions.

References

Anderson, Elijah. 1990. *Streetwise: Race, Class, and Change in an Urban Community*. Chicago: University of Chicago Press.

Bennett, Richard R. and Erica L. Schmitt. 2002. 'The Effect of Work Environment on Levels of Police Cynicism: A Comparative Study'. *Police Quarterly* 5(4): 493–522.

Brown, Jennifer, Cary Cooper, and Bruce Kirkcaldy. 1996. 'Occupational Stress among Senior Police Officers'. *British Journal of Psychology* 87(1): 31–42.

Carlan, Philip E. and Elizabeth C. McMullan. 2009. 'A Contemporary Snapshot of Policewomen Attitudes'. *Women & Criminal Justice* 19(1): 60–79.

CBC News Online. 2003. 'Police report says suspect beaten by drug squad,' 15 September. http://www.cbc.ca/canada/toronto/story/2003/09/15/to_siureport20030915.html. Accessed March 9, 2009.

Chapin, Mark, Stephen J. Brannen, Mark I. Singer and Michael Walker. 2008. 'Training Police Leadership to Recognize and Address Operational Stress'. *Police Quarterly* 11(3): 338–352.

Davis, Mike. 1992. *City of Quartz*. New York: Vintage.

Doyle, Aaron. 2006. 'How Not to Think About Crime in the Media'. *Canadian Journal of Crime and Criminal Justice* 48(6): 867–884.

Goldschmidt, Jona and Anonymous. 2008. 'The Necessity of Dishonesty: Police Deviance, "Making the Case", and the Public Good'. *Policing and Society* 18(2): 113–135.

Green, Mariana. 2003. '2003 Annual Report of the Office of the Provincial Auditor of Ontario: 3.01 Court Services'. Ministry of the Attorney General.

Harris, David. 2005. *Good Cops: The Case for Preventive Policing*. New York: The New Press.

Herbert, Steve. 1996. 'The Normative Ordering of Police Territoriality: Making and Marking Space with the Los Angeles Police Department'. *Annals of the Association of American Geographers* 86(3): 567–582.

Johnson, Richard R. 2004. 'Police Officer Frustrations about Handling Domestic Violence Calls'. *The Police Journal* 77: 207–219.

Lopez, Juan. 2004. *Brotherhood of Corruption*. Chicago: Chicago Review Press.

Luhby, Tami. 2010. 'Police Officers Feel State Budget Cut Squeeze' http://ca.finance.yahoo.com/personal-finance/article/cnnmoney/police-officers-feel-state-budget-cut-squeeze-20100526. Accessed May 28, 2010.

Maguire, Edward R. and Katz, Charles M. 2002. 'Community Policing, Loose Coupling, and Sensemaking in American Police Agencies'. *Justice Quarterly* 19(3): 503–536.

Manning, Peter K. 2001. 'Theorizing Policing: The Drama and Myth of Crime Control in the NYPD'. *Theoretical Criminology* 5(3): 315–344.

Martin, Susan E. 1980. *Breaking and Entering: Policewomen on Patrol*. Berkeley: University of California Press.

Merton, Robert K. 1957. *Social Theory and Social Structure*. 1957 enl. ed. New York: Free Press [1968].

_____. 1938. 'Social Structure and Anomie'. *American Sociological Review* 3: 672–682.

Moskos, Peter. 2009. *Cop in the Hood: My Year Policing Baltimore's Eastern District*. New Jersey: Princeton University Press.

Niederhoffer, A. 1967. *Behind the Shield*. Garden City. NY: Doubleday.

Ortiz, Christopher W., Nicole J. Hendricks. and Naomi F. Sugie. 2007. 'Policing Terrorism: The Response of Local Police Agencies to Homeland Security Concerns'. *Criminal Justice Studies* 20(2): 91–109.

Ouimette, P., J.P. Read, M. Wade and V. Tirone. 2010. 'Modeling Associations between Posttraumatic Stress Symptoms and Substance Use'. *Addictive Behaviors* 35: 64–67.

Paoline, Eugene A. 2004. 'Shedding Light on Police Culture: An Examination of Officers' Occupational Attitudes'. *Police Quarterly* 7(2): 205–236.

Parenti, Christian. 1999. *Lockdown America: Police and Prisons in the Age of Crisis*. New York: Verso.

Punch, Maurice. 2000. 'Police Corruption and Its Prevention'. *European Journal on Criminal Policy and Research* 8: 301–324.

Rabe-hemp, Cara E. 2008. 'POLICEwomen Or PoliceWOMEN?: Doing Gender and Police Work'. *Feminist Criminology* 4(2): 114–129.

Raganella, Anthony J. and Michael D. White. 2004. 'Race, Gender, and Motivation for Becoming a Police Officer: Implications for Building a Representative Police Department'. *Journal of Criminal Justice* 32: 501–513.

Skolnick, Jerome H. and James J. Fyfe. 1993. *Above the Law: Police and the Excessive Use of Force*. Toronto: The Free Press.

Statistics Canada. 2008. *Police Resources in Canada*. Catalogue: 85-225-X.

Surette, R. 2007. *Media, Crime, and Criminal Justice: Images, Realities, and Policies*. California: Thomson Wadsworth.

Tolin, David F. and Edna B. Foa. 1999. 'Treatment of a Police Officer with PTSD using Prolonged Exposure'. *Behavior Therapy* 30(3): 527–538.

Violanti, John M. and Fred Aron. 1995. 'Police Stressors: Variations in Perception Among Police Personnel'. *Journal of Criminal Justice* 23(3): 287–294.

Wright, D. H. 2004. *Commission of Inquiry into Matters Relating to the Death of Neil Stonechild*. Government of Saskatchewan.

CHAPTER 16

Legislative Approaches to Prostitution: A Critical Introduction

Frances M. Shaver

This chapter provides a brief introduction to the four most common legislative approaches to **prostitution**. It includes a critical evaluation of each for the promotion of security, health, and human rights of people working in the sex industry (PWSI) and the communities in which they live and work. Together, they provide a useful framework for the analysis of sex work and the sex industry.

The Regulation of Sex Work

The most common approach to prostitution is *criminalization*. From this perspective, sex work is usually regarded as an immoral activity that should be prohibited (as in most of the United States and South Africa), or tolerated (as it is in Canada and England). In the United States and South Africa, laws are designed to prohibit all forms of sex work, including the buying and selling of sexual services. In Canada, the exchange of sexual services for money does not violate any statutes of the Criminal Code of Canada (CCC 1985). However, activities associated with the buying and selling of sexual services violate several sections of the Code. Briefly stated, these include: keeping or being found in a common bawdy house (s. 210), providing directions to or transporting someone to a bawdy house (s. 211), procuring or living on the avails of prostitution (s. 212), communication in a public place for the purpose of prostitution (s. 213), and purchasing sexual services from someone under 18 years of age (s. 212(4)). Some forms of sex work are also affected by sections dealing with obscenity (s. 163), engaging in an immoral theatrical performance (s. 167), performing an indecent act in a public place (s. 173), and public nudity (s. 174).

The second option, referred to as *the Swedish model*, is in operation in Sweden, Norway, and Finland. Prostitution is regarded as a social ill and a form of men's violence against women. Criminal law is used to regulate clients, managers, and owners/operators, but not PWSI. Legislation criminalizes the purchase of sexual services, procurement, working indoors, working with others, advertising, and profiting from the sexual labour of others.

The remaining two options each make sex work legal but in very different ways. Under *legalization*—where sex work is generally regarded as a morally repugnant but inevitable activity—some forms of sex work are criminalized while others are licensed. Current practices include the licensing of workers, compulsory medical check-ups for PWSI, registration and size limitations on bawdy-houses, maintenance of procuring and pimping criminal laws, and limitations on street prostitution. Prostitution activities are legalized in Nevada, United States; Amsterdam, Netherlands; and some states in Germany and Australia.

When sex work is seen as a private matter between consenting adults, *decriminalization* is the preferred model. It regulates PWSI and sex work activities without using criminal law while recognizing labour rights and responsibilities. Prostitution activities are decriminalized in New Zealand and

New South Wales, Australia, where workers, managers, and business establishments are regulated using labour standards legislation; occupational, health, and safety codes; and zoning regulations.

In spite of the dissimilar moral perspectives and regulatory variations embedded in the first three models, there are remarkable similarities in their consequences for PWSI (Scoular 2010). In Sweden, for example, the practical effects of the new law—in place since 1999—led to a temporary reduction in street work, the displacement of women and men into more hidden forms of sex work, and the worsening of conditions for those who remained on the streets (p.18). Furthermore, despite the fact that purchasing sex was criminalized irrespective of location, the law has been selectively enforced, with the main focus being on the highly visible spaces of street-based prostitution (p. 19). Scoular's study also revealed similar patterns under legalization in Holland and criminalization in San Francisco.

Research from New Zealand (Abel et al. 2010) indicates that this pattern is unlikely to occur under *decriminalization*. Since the passage of the Prostitution Reform Bill in 2003, New Zealand's sex industry has been operating under health and safety regulations. Workers, managers, and business establishments are regulated using provincial labour standards legislation, occupational health and safety codes, and zoning regulations. Only the most disruptive and abusive activities associated with some sex work—coercion, kidnapping, physical assault, sexual assault, unlawful confinement—are regulated using criminal law.

This combination of factors has reinforced the ability of PWSI to ensure safe sex and secure their work environments through the provision of occupational, employment, and legal rights. Decriminalization thus reduces the risks and dangers associated with the other approaches. Risks to emotional health as a result of the stigmatization attached to sex work are not addressed, however (Abel et al. 2010: 234). Addressing them requires social programs designed to alter the negative perceptions and behaviours of the public, members of the judicial system, and policy-makers toward the sex industry and PWSI (Shaver et al. 2011).

The Debate

The debate regarding the most appropriate and effective policy option continues to flourish. In Canada, both the Fraser Committee in 1985 and the House of Commons Subcommittee on Solicitation Laws (SSLR) in 2005 addressed these issues with a view to possible reform. Neither was able to move forward to develop effective policy. The SSLR committee in particular was divided by the two conflicting models of law reform proposed during the hearings: 'sex work as victimization' and 'sex work as work' (Canadian HIV/AIDS Legal Network 2007).

Lowman (2009: 16) sums up both models succinctly. Those favouring the 'sex work as victimization' perspective (e.g. Farley 2004, Raymond 2003, 2004) argue that

> the distinction between forced and voluntary prostitution is largely spurious; prostitution is female sexual slavery; prostitution is violence against women; women do not 'consent' to prostitution; very few women would choose to prostitute if they really had choices; selling sex harms the prostitute, [and] because it treats women as sex objects, prostitution harms all women.

As a consequence they usually favour the *Swedish model,* prohibiting the purchase of sexual services, procuring, and living on the avails.

Those who see prostitution as work (i.e., as a legitimate revenue-generating activity) support *decriminalization* and the use of generic criminal laws to control violence and exploitation in the industry, and civil laws (e.g. causing a disturbance) to control the nuisances associated with street prostitution. They argue that forced prostitution should be distinguished from voluntary prostitution; cross-border trafficking should be distinguished from migration; a person's right to control her/his body includes the right to sell sexual services; and regardless of whether money changes hands, adults who consent to engage in sex should not be subject to criminal penalty. They also argue that violence, pimp exploitation, nuisance, and low self-esteem are caused or exacerbated by the criminalization and stigmatization of prostitution, not by the act of selling sexual services (Lowman 2009:16).[1]

The Terminology

The language used to talk about PWSI and what they do can reinforce discrimination and abuse. Words like 'prostitution' and 'prostitute', for example, carry intense social stigma (Jeffrey and MacDonald 2006). This is one reason why those who support prostitution as work prefer to use the terms 'sex work' and 'sex worker'. Obviously, just changing the words cannot eliminate the stigma that PWSI continue to face, even under decriminalization. But using these terms focuses attention on the fact that sex work is a legitimate revenue-generating activity and that sex workers deserve rights and protection in their jobs like other workers.

Shifting our gaze away from the moralist language of prohibitionists and toward human rights is likely to increase opportunities for respecting and protecting the health and rights of sex workers. Focusing on these rights makes it easier to avoid the debate and acknowledge the diversity within the industry. One way to begin is to examine the benefits of the four legal approaches from the perspectives of several stakeholders, including the experiences of PWSI.

Legislative Approaches and Their Benefits

Table 16.1 facilitates this shift in perspective by examining each of the four legislative approaches in relation to the benefits most often identified by various stakeholders (e.g. PWSI, residents, service providers). The symbols within each cell indicate the likelihood of achieving the identified benefit under each approach.

The concerns of PWSI are identified in the first three rows. They are related to removing stigma and fostering respect, securing safe

Table 16.1 Legislative Approaches and Their Benefits

	CRIMINALIZATION	SWEDISH MODEL	LEGALIZATION	DECRIMINALIZATION
Concerns of PWSI				
Remove stigma/foster respect	x	x	x	✓?
Safe/secure work locations	x	x	✓?	✓
Health and well-being				
- clean needles	✓?	x	✓	✓
- condom use	✓?	x	✓?	✓
- access to health and legal services	✓?	✓?	✓?	✓
Labour rights and protections	x	x	x	✓
Economic security	x	✓?	✓?	✓
Concerns of Residents				
Less street noise and nuisance	✓?	✓?	✓?	✓
Safe/secure neighbourhoods	✓?	✓?	✓?	✓
Social Programs				
Labour, health, and safety standards	x	x	x	✓
Eliminate/reduce stigma	x	x	x	✓?
Educate public, police, and policy-makers	x	✓?	x	✓

x = unlikely
✓? = questionable
✓ = likely

work environments, good health and well-being, obtaining labour rights and economic security—concerns appropriate for all Canadians. Some of these benefits are supported by legislation grounded in criminal law (the first three approaches) but the prognosis for their successful application is poor. Eliminating stigma and fostering respect are highly unlikely since the goal is to prohibit prostitution (or at least some kinds of prostitution) entirely. In addition, PWSI are treated differently from other workers, and their clients are criminalized and often 'shamed'. In the case of legalization, a two-tiered system is built directly into the model (e.g. some PWSI are legitimated and others are not). Secure work locations—next to impossible under the first two models—may be possible under legalization, but client choice is not always guaranteed and medical checks are required by law even though the majority of PWSI get check-ups as part of their own health care regime (van der Meulen & Durisin 2008). Clean needles and condoms—and in Vancouver, a safe-injection site—are available, but there is an ✓? in the cells, indicating that that police sometimes 'stake out' the facilities—particularly harm reduction programs that provide condoms and needle exchanges—and when workers exit, they are 'harassed', 'frisked for drugs', and 'pulled into' police cars for background checks and 'questioning' (Shaver et al. 2011: 58). Under legalization, mandatory testing may lead to a false sense of security and less condom use; hence, the ✓? and the **x**s in the comparable cells under the Swedish model indicate the complete lack of state support for harm reduction programs relating to condoms or clean needles. It is possible for PWSI to access health and legal services under the first three options, but studies show that the ongoing stigma and marginalization limit their access to both (Jeffrey & MacDonald 2006; STAR 2006). Labour rights are overlooked entirely since sex work is not seen as a legitimate revenue-generating activity,

and economic security, while possible, is difficult to achieve since long-term economic security is jeopardized through 'proceeds of crime' legislation that hinders workers' capacity to save or invest for the future (Lewis et al. 2005: 17).

Residents' concerns regarding street nuisance and the safety of their neighbourhoods are often addressed under the first three models. Unfortunately, the measures most often adopted by the police tend to ensure the security of the public, while ignoring the security concerns of PWSI (Shaver et al. 2011: 55).

The full implementation of key social programs is most likely to occur with decriminalization. In fact, they are essential since legal reform on its own is not enough to dispel the myths about sex work and PWSI or to improve relations between residents and workers. An overall examination of the table reveals that only two key areas remain problematic under decriminalization: the ongoing stigma and marginalization of PWSI and opportunities to develop social programs to eliminate/reduce it. Thus, the decriminalization of prostitution between consenting adults must be coupled with social reforms promoting the health, human, and labour rights of PWSI and the health of communities. To a large extent these depend on programs promoting the education of the public, police and policy-makers about the realities of the sex industry and PWSI.

Conclusion

Shifting away from stigmatizing terminology and examining the four legal models from the perspective of several stakeholders makes it possible to move into a more productive discussion about the positive and negative outcomes related to each. Moving to a decriminalization model—while beneficial to all stakeholders—still leaves critical issues unaddressed. To be effective, decriminalization must be combined with a full array of social programs.

Notes

1. Canadian research supporting this position includes Shaver (1985, 2005), Jeffrey & MacDonald (2006), Canadian HIV/AIDS Legal Network (2005), STAR (2006), and van der Meulen and Durisin (2008).

References

Abel, G., L. Fitzgerald, and C. Healy with A. Taylor (eds.) 2010. 'Part Two: Implementation and Impact of the 2003 Prostitution Reform Act: The First Five Years'. In *Taking The Crime Out Of Sex Work: New Zealand Sex Workers' Fight For Decriminalisation*. Briston: The Policy Press, pp. 105–264.

Criminal Code, R.S.C. 1985, c. C-46.

Farley, M. 2004. 'Bad for the Body, Bad for the Heart: Prostitution Harms Women Even If Legalized or Decriminalized'. *Violence Against Women* 10 (10): 1087–1125.

Canadian HIV/AIDS Legal Network. 2007. *Not up to the Challenge of Change: An Analysis of the Report of the Subcommittee on Solicitation Laws*. Available online at http://www.aidslaw.ca/EN/publications/index.htm.

Canadian HIV/AIDS Legal Network. 2005. *Sex, Work, Rights: Changing Canada's Criminal Laws to Protect Sex Workers' Health and Human Rights*. Available online at http://www.aidslaw.ca/EN/publications/index.htm.

Jeffrey, L.A. & G. MacDonald. 2006. *Work, Stigma, and Resistance: Sex Workers in the Maritimes Talk Back*. Vancouver: UBC Press.

Lewis, J., E. Maticka-Tyndale, F. M. Shaver and K. Gillies. 2005. *Health, Security and Sex Work Policy*. Invited presentation to the House of Commons Subcommittee on Solicitation Laws (SSLR), Ottawa Canada. Retrieved 22 August 2009 from http:// www.uwindsor.ca/star.

Lowman, J. 2009. Deadly Inertia: A History of Constitutional Challenges to Canada's *Criminal Code* Sections on Prostitution. Unpublished manuscript, School of Criminology, Simon Fraser University.

Raymond, J. 2004. 'Prostitution on Demand'. *Violence Against Women* 10 (11):1156–1186.

Raymond, J. 2003. *10 Reasons for Not Legalizing Prostitution*. Coalition Against Trafficking in Women International (CATW). Retrieved 20 June 2006 from http://www.rapereliefshelter.bc.ca/issues/prostitution_legalizing.html.

Scoular, Jane. 2010. 'What's Law Got to Do with It? How and Why Law Matters in the Regulation of Sex Work'. *Journal of Law and Society* 37 (1):12–39.

Shaver, F.M. 2005. *Sex Work Policy: An Integrated Approach*. Invited presentation to the House of Commons Subcommittee on Solicitation Laws (SSLR), Ottawa Canada. Available online at http://francesmshaver.ca.

Shaver, F.M. 1985. 'Prostitution: A Critical Analysis of Three Policy Approaches'. *Canadian Public Policy* 11 (3): 493–503.

Shaver, F.M., J. Lewis and E. Maticka-Tyndale. 2011. 'Rising to the Challenge: Addressing the Concerns of People working in the Sex Industry'. *Canadian Review of Sociology* 48 (1):47–65.

Sex Trade Advocacy & Research (STAR). 2006. *Safety, Security and the Well-Being of Sex Workers: A Report Submitted to the House of Commons Subcommittee on Solicitation Laws (SSLR)*. Windsor, ON. Available online at http://www.uwindsor.ca/star.

van der Meulen, E. and E. M. and Durisin. 2008. 'Why Decriminalize? How Canada's Municipal and Federal Regulations Increase Sex Workers' Vulnerability'. *Canadian Journal of Women and the Law* 20: 289–311.

Recommended Readings

Abel, G., L. Fitzgerald, C. Healy with A. Taylor (eds). 2010. *Taking the Crime out of Sex Work: New Zealand Sex Workers' Fight for Decriminalisation*. Briston: The Policy Press.

Jeffrey, L.A. and B. Sullivan. 2009. 'Canadian Sex Work Policy for the 21st Century: Enhancing Rights and Safety, Lessons from Australia'. *Canadian Political Science Review* 3 (1), 57–76.

Lewis, J., E. Maticka-Tyndale, F.M. Shaver & H. Schramm. 2005. 'Managing Risk and Safety on the Job: The Experiences of Canadian Sex Workers'. *Journal of Psychology and Human Sexuality, Special Issue* 17 (1/2): 147–167.

Shaver, F.M. 2005. 'Sex Work Research: Methodological and Ethical Challenges'. *Journal of Interpersonal Violence* 20 (3): 296–319. Available online at http://www.uwindsor.ca/star.

Weitzer, Ronald. 2010. 'The Mythology of Prostitution: Advocacy Research and Public Policy'. *Sex Research Social Policy* 7: 15–29.

CHAPTER 17

Moral Panic and the Nasty Girl

Christie Barron and Dany Lacombe

This paper examines why, despite evidence to the contrary, recent incidents of female violence have been interpreted as a sign that today's girls are increasingly nasty. We argue that the 'nasty girl' phenomenon is the product of a **moral panic**. While girl violence has always existed, today's discussion is dominated by the concept of risk. Reform initiatives resulting from the panic consist of disciplinary mechanisms acting on the body of the individual delinquent, and techniques that regulate individuals through the fostering of **risk society** and a culture of risk management and security consciousness. Finally, we situate the panic in the current backlash against feminism.

Female violence became a topic of much discussion in the mid-1990s in the wake of the gruesome sexual murders of teenagers by the infamous Ontario couple Paul Bernardo and Karla Homolka. But it was the murder of Reena Virk by a group of mostly female teens, in a suburb of Victoria in November 1997, that led Canadians to believe that something had gone terribly wrong with teenage girls. However, the belief that girl violence is rampant is a social construction. According to Statistics Canada, the annual youth charge rate for violent crime dropped 5 per cent in 1999, signalling a decline for the fourth year in a row (Statistics Canada, 2000). Moreover, Doob and Sprott (1998) have shown that the severity of youth violence did not change in the first half of the 1990s. Questioning the federal government's concern about the increase in girls' participation in

violent and gang-related activities, Reitsma-Street (1999) indicates that the number of girls charged for murder and attempted murder has been constant for the past 20 years and that such charges are infrequent. Although statistics indicate a phenomenal increase in the number of young women charged with minor or moderate assault over the past 10 years (from 710 charged under the Juvenile Delinquents Act in 1980 to 4,434 under the Young Offenders Act in 1995–6), several researchers indicate that the increase is more a reflection of the youth justice system's change in policy and charging practices than a 'real' change in behaviour (Doob and Sprott, 1998; Reitsma-Street, 1999). Yet the public continues to believe that youth violence, particularly girl violence, is increasing at an alarming rate and necessitates immediate attention (Chesney-Lind and Brown, 1999). This perception prompts the important question: Why, despite evidence to the contrary, are recent isolated incidents of female violence interpreted as a sign that today's girls have become increasingly 'nasty'?

We argue that the recent alarm over girl violence is the product of a moral panic that has had a significant impact on social, educational, and legal policy-making. All moral panics identify and denounce a personal agent responsible for the condition that is generating widespread public concern. As Schissel explains, 'folk devils are inherently deviant and are presumed to be self-seeking, out of control and in danger of undermining the stability of society . . .' (1997: 30). Hence, during the 'warning phase' of a panic there are, as shown in the documentary *Nasty Girls*, predictions of impending doom, sensitization to cues of danger, frequent overreactions, and rumours speculating about what is happening or what will happen (Cohen, 1980: 144–8). Subsequently, a large part of the public becomes sensitized to the threat, and, as in the case of the nasty girl, when confronted with an actual act of girl violence their perception of danger and risk solidifies.

It is not surprising; therefore, that the beating and murder of 14-year-old Reena Virk by a group of seven girls and one boy would become the event that provided evidence that girl violence had become a significant problem in Canada.

As is often the case in a moral panic, the media distorted and exaggerated the extent of isolated acts of girl violence following Virk's death. For example, newspaper and magazine headlines associated the case with a larger trend in girl violence: 'Bad Girls: A Brutal BC Murder Sounds an Alarm about Teenage Violence' (Chisholm, 1997), 'Spare the Rod and Run for Cover: When Students Hold the Cards, School Violence Grows, Especially among the Girls' (McLean, 1999), 'When She Was Bad: Violent Women and the Myth of Innocence' (Chesney-Lind, 1999), 'Virk's Death Triggers Painful Questions: Girls' Involvement "Exacerbates Rage"' (Mitchell, 1997), and 'In Reena's World, being a "Slut" Can Get You Killed' (Anon., 1997).

Also central to the creation of a climate of fear is statistical manipulation of crime data to establish the amplitude of girl violence. As journalist Nolan astutely recognizes in her analysis of the media reporting of the Virk case, '"experts" and authors were appearing on TV and radio talk shows trumpeting—with the solemn self-importance that always accompanies adult laments about the various wickedness of youth—the shocking fact that, according to the Canadian Centre for Justice Statistics, crime by young girls had increased 200 per cent since 1986' (1998: 32). However, most articles failed to recognize that the increase was in reference to minor assaults, such as pushing or slapping, which did not cause serious injury.

The panic over the nasty girl has had a significant impact on legal, educational, and social policy in Canada. The result has been an increase in both formal and informal mechanisms of control. While proposals for legal reform mostly consist of repressive measures targeted at delinquent youths, social and educational programs contain informal mechanisms of control targeting society more generally. Proposals for reform are not only disciplinary mechanisms of power acting on the body of the individual delinquent, but are also part of the more recent governmental techniques of power which regulate and manage free individuals through the fostering of a culture of risk management, public safety and security consciousness (Foucault, 1982; Cohen, 1985; O'Malley, 1996; Garland, 1997).

Following the Virk case and other high-profile youth crimes, state policies on violent youth have become punitive. The Youth Criminal Justice Act (YCJA) came into effect on 1 April 2003 and, although it offers positive measures to reduce the number of youths being incarcerated, its clear distinction between 'non-violent', 'violent', and 'seriously violent' offences reflects public desire to deal harshly with violent youth.

Of even more concern for girls specifically is the passage of the Secure Care Act (Bill 25) in British Columbia. Following the lead of Alberta's Protection of Children Involved In Prostitution Act (PCHIP), the Secure Care Act is intended 'to provide, when other less intrusive means are unavailable or inadequate, a means of assessing and assisting children who have an emotional or behavioural condition that presents a high risk of serious harm or injury to themselves and are unable to reduce the risk. . . . These conditions may [include] severe substance misuse or addiction or the sexual exploitation of a child' (Section 2 [1], cited in Busby, 2001). In essence, this legislation, meant to protect children, ultimately blames victims of sexual exploitation and permits the apprehension and incarceration of girls—who will be targeted more than boys due to their differential involvement in prostitution.

While harsh legal policy is aimed at incapacitating both violent boys and girls, informal mechanisms of control targeting young girls in particular have also resulted from the panic over girl violence. This groundwork has produced new definitions of violence and new methods of controlling both young females and society in general.

The expansion in definitions of violence is most obvious in relation to what goes on at school—a site where the threat of the violent girl is most apparent. Pepler, who was commissioned by the Ontario and Canadian Governments to prepare strategies for aggressive girls, helped foster a new rationality of bullying—teasing, gossiping, and quarrelling—as an intolerable act of aggression.

The new rationality and concern over bullying is not only targeting the aggressive girl. It also actively seeks the participation of school authorities in the informal control of girls. For example, Pepler and Sedighdeilami's caution that '[g]irls in families with violence, ineffective parenting, and high levels of conflict should be identified for supportive interventions' encourages school staff to observe and detect signs of risk in girls.

Why did the reaction to girl violence take the particular form and intensity it did during the late 1990s? The moral panic literature emphasizes that, during a panic, the anxieties the public experiences are real, but their reaction is often misplaced. Hence, the object of the panic—the violent girl—is not always the source of people's anxiety.

We start our attempt at contextualizing the moral panic over the violent girl by examining the larger structural forces characterizing our present. According to Young (1999), the transition from modernity (the 'Golden Age' of the post-war period) to the present late modernity (late 1960s and onwards) resulted in significant structural and psychological changes that produced social anxieties.

The shift primarily entailed a movement from an inclusive to an exclusive society: from a society that incorporated its members and enjoyed full (male) employment, rising affluence, stable families, and conformity, to an exclusive society arising from changes in the labour force. These changes included a shift from a more social-based, communitarian labour force to one of individualism stemming from the new knowledge-based, technology society. As late-modern society became increasingly characterized by a plurality of values, self-reflexivity, multiculturalism, and scientific and political relativism, the solid foundation of modernity began to melt. Material certainty and shared values shattered, leaving us with a heightened sense of risk and uncertainties. In such a precarious climate, crime acquires a powerful symbolic value. If we could only control crime better, we would bring safety into one aspect of our disrupted lives. It is not surprising that our quest for security often translates into a projection of our fears onto specific scapegoats who are made responsible for our feelings of insecurity.

Although the moral panic framework has much utility in understanding the recent concerns about girl violence, it also has the potential to dismiss them. The framework can be used simply to deconstruct the sources of fear for the purpose of demonstrating that the societal concern is unfounded. We think, however, it should be used to uncover how the configuration of ideas surrounding a phenomenon has come into being and has moulded our life, customs, and science (Doyle and Lacombe, 2000). In this way, we would be in a better position to resist the insidious effects of a moral panic.

References

Anon. 1997. 'In Reena's World, Being a "Slut" Can Get You Killed', *Toronto Star*, 6 December: E1, E4.

Busby, K. 2001. 'Protective Confinement of Children Involved in Prostitution: Compassionate Response or Neo-criminalization?' Notes for a presentation at the Women Behind Bars Conference. University of New Brunswick, Fredericton, New Brunswick, 9 February.

Chesney-Lind, M. 1999. 'When She Was Bad: Violent Women and the Myth of Innocence', *Women and Criminal Justice* 10, 4: 113–18.

Chesney-Lind, M., and M. Brown. 1999. 'Girls and Violence: An Overview', in *Youth Violence: Prevention, Intervention and Social Policy*, D. Flannery and C.R. Huff, eds. Washington, DC: American Psychiatric Press.

Chisholm, R. 1997. 'Bad Girls: A Brutal BC Murder Sounds an Alarm about Teenage Violence', *Maclean's*, 8 December: 12.

Cohen, S. 1980. *Folk Devils and Moral Panics: The Creation of the Mods and Rockers*. New York: St Martin's Press.

———. 1985. *Visions of Social Control*. New York: Oxford University Press.

Doob, A., and J.B. Sprott. 1998. 'Is the "Quality" of Youth Violence Becoming More Serious?', *Canadian Journal of Criminology and Criminal Justice* 40, 2: 185–94.

Doyle, K., and D. Lacombe. 2000. 'Scapegoat in Risk Society: The Case of Pedophile/Child Pornographer Robin Sharpe', *Studies in Law, Politics and Society* 20: 183–206.

Foucault, M. 1982. *The Subject and Power*, 2nd ed., H.L. Dreyfus and R. Rabinow, eds. Chicago: Chicago University Press.

Garland, D. 1997. '"Governmentality" and the Problem of Crime: Foucault, Criminology, Sociology', *Theoretical Criminology* 1, 2: 173–214.

Justice for Girls. 2001. 'Statement of Opposition to the Secure Care Act'. Available at http://www.moib.com/ jfg/ publications/p_sca.htm.

McLean, C. 1999. 'Spare the Rod and Run for Cover: When Students Hold the Cards, School Violence Grows, Especially among the Girls', *British Columbia Report* 10, 9: 52–4.

Mitchell, A. 1997. 'Virk's Death Triggers Painful Questions: Girls' Involvement "Exacerbates Rage"', *Globe and Mail*, 28 November: A1, A8.

Nolan, N. 1998. 'Girl Crazy: After the Brutal Murder of Reena Virk, the Media Whipped the Country into a Frenzy over a Supposed "Girl Crime Wave"', *This Magazine* 31, 5 (March/ April): 30–5.

O'Malley, R. 1996. 'Risk and Responsibility', in *Foucault and Political Reason*, pp. 189–208, A. Barry, T. Osborne, and N. Rose, eds. Chicago: University of Chicago Press.

Pepler, D. 1998. 'Girls' Aggression in Schools: Scenarios and Strategies'. Unpublished paper. Ministry of Training and Education, Government of Ontario.

Pepler, D.J., and F. Sedighdeilami. 1998. *Aggressive Girls in Canada*. Working papers. Hull, QC: Applied Research Branch, Strategic Policy, Human Resources Development Canada.

Reitsma-Street, M. 1999. 'Justice for Canadian Girls: A 1990s Update', *Canadian Journal of Criminology and Criminal Justice* 41, 3: 335–64.

Schissel, B. 1997. *Blaming Children: Youth Crime, Moral Panics and the Politics of Hate*. Halifax, NS: Fernwood Publishing.

Statistics Canada. 2000. 'Crime Statistics', *The Daily* 18 July. Available at http://www.statcan/Daily/ English/000718/ d00718a.htm.

Questions for Critical Thought

CHAPTER 14

1. Compare Adorjan's article with Barron and Lacombe's. What similarities and/or differences do you see in the arguments put forth?
2. According to Adorjan, how have news coverage of moral panics become more sophisticated?
3. What are 'emotions contests' in the news?
4. Discuss the differences and similarities in how each newspaper (the *Alberta Report* and the *Calgary Herald*) portrays youth crimes. Use examples from the text.
5. Recall the reflexivity discussed in Curtis's paper in Part I. What does Adorjan's article add to the concept of reflexivity? Can we still be as optimistic about the ability of reflexive sociology to improve academic research, or should our optimism be more measured? Explain.
6. This article highlights the problem of emotions intervening in attempts to interpret social life. Based on the debate between the perspectives presented in the paper, what are some problems with knee-jerk emotional reactions? On the other hand, what are some dangers of ignoring our feelings about the social world?

CHAPTER 15

1. According to Parnaby and Leyden, what is the value system that informs policing? What goals and ideals do police officers have about policing when they enter the force? What do Parnaby and Leyden argue is the source of these expectations?
2. What are the three structural impediments that Parnaby and Leyden point out, and how do they each impede officers from securing their standard of justice? Use examples from the article.
3. Discuss the four types of deviance that occur within the police force as presented by Parnaby and Leyden. Use examples to demonstrate how they each deal with (accept or reject) the ends and means of policing.
4. Three papers in this section have credited media with much responsibility for creating both the illusion of deviance and deviant acts. Why do you think the media are so important in discussing the creation of order and thus deviance? It could be said that focusing too much on media might also lead us to miss other important explanatory tools. What other institutions might also be important in creating order and deviance?
5. Policing is not the only realm where the achievement of cultural ideals is made impossible by practical structures. Think of other areas of life where this is true. Explain one of these, describing the ideals and how the relevant structures make them difficult to attain.

CHAPTER 16

1. Compare the policies and laws of the two models that make sex work illegal: criminaliza-tion and the Swedish model. What does each approach assume about sex work, work-ers, and consumers? Which actions and actors are subject to which kinds of law?
2. Compare the policies and laws of the two models that make sex work legal: legalization and decriminalization. What does each approach assume about sex work, workers, and consumers? Which actions and actors are subject to which kinds of law?
3. Compare the effects of each policy approach on the various stakeholders involved: sex workers, clients, residents, etc.
4. Compare the positions on sex work—sex work as victimization and sex work as work—within the sex work debate. Which position do you think underpins each of the four legislative approaches?
5. While Shaver is clearly in favour of one model—decriminalization—over the others, she does not argue that it solves all of the problems presented by sex work. What critical is-sues are left unaddressed by any of the legislative models? What does Shaver suggest to address these issues?

CHAPTER 17

1. According to Barron and Lacombe, what is a moral panic? How is a climate of fear created?
2. What evidence do Barron and Lacombe offer as proof that violence perpetrated by girls is not a 'real' problem in Canada? Do you think this is strong evidence, or that more in-formation could be helpful to their argument? Explain.
3. How have policy changes in the youth justice system made it seem like there is more girl violence than before?
4. Some people may argue that these are just harmless stories that Barron and Lacombe are taking too seriously. How has the perception of a girl violence problem affected vari-ous policies, which have in turn affected the lives of young girls?
5. According to Barron and Lacombe, if our social anxiety does not really come from a fear of girl violence, what are we really anxious about? What is the danger of diverting this anxiety toward scapegoats like violent girls? Be sure to talk about the concept of a risk society.

Part V

Families

Family life has undergone major transitions over the past century. Given the multiplicity of current models, sociologists and policy-makers continue to debate exactly what a 'family' is meant to be and how people should carry out this family ideal in practice. Indeed, the meanings of *family* and *marriage* continue to change, especially in response to changes in the economy. With industrialization and urbanization, we see increases in rates of cohabitation and divorce, later average ages of marriage, and lower rates of childbearing. All of these changes, in turn, revise our understanding of the institution we call 'family', as well as traditional family practices such as mate selection.

In the last 50 years, we have seen a shift from the traditional breadwinner–caregiver type of family to a two-earner family model characterized by greater equality between husbands and wives. However, data still reveal inequalities in the sharing of housework and caregiving between partners in this two-earner household. So, even though some changes have promoted equality and choice in marriage and family, barriers and traditional views (especially in the rural and immigrant populations) tend to slow legislation that would help non-traditional families.

The chapters in this section explore this evolution of the family's links with community, work, and equality. Patrizia Albanese reminds us that the report of the Royal Commission on the Status of Women in 1970 drew a clear connection between the quality of family life and the quality of relations between men and women in Canadian society. Briefly, conflict and inequality in one predicted conflict and inequality in the other. As Albanese notes, 'The Royal Commission adopted four principles in its report: (1) that women should be free to choose whether or not to take employment outside their homes; (2) that the care of children is a responsibility to be shared by the mother, the father and society; (3) that society has a responsibility for women because of pregnancy and child birth, and special treatment related to maternity will always be necessary; and (4) that in certain areas women will for an interim time require special treatment to overcome the adverse effects of discriminatory practices (p. xii).'

To repeat, this meant that society—not the individual family, much less individual women—had a prime responsibility for ensuring that children were parented well, and that fathers and mothers would have an equal responsibility in this process. By this reckoning, the burden and cost of parenting should not fall unequally on women's shoulders, preventing them from exercising the same right to education and paid employment as their mates enjoyed. This said, the articles by Albanese and

Andrea Doucet show that the argument over this issue continues today. We continue to debate whether, between husbands and wives, gendered differences amount to gendered inequalities; and if so, how and when we will solve these problems as a society—for example, through readily accessible, low-cost, high-quality daycare.

But we should not get caught up in talking about families as a homogeneous, abstract idea. In reality, family experiences are varied, and all families face many specific challenges other than deciding who will take care of the children. Nancy Netting shows us how globalization has made mate selection an even more difficult process than usual for young people in India, as they are caught between the traditions of arranged marriage and imported marriage ideals. And finally, Annette Tézli describes the difficulties homeless Canadian families face in trying to preserve 'normal' family relations in the fish-bowl-like atmosphere of an emergency family shelter in Calgary. Here, equality issues take a back seat to the basic survival of families.

The More Things Change . . . the More We Need Child Care: On the Fortieth Anniversary of the *Report on the Royal Commission on the Status of Women*

Patrizia Albanese

The *Report of the Royal Commission on the Status of Women* (1970) and I are roughly the same age. And while the fact that a woman from a working-class immigrant background has written this chapter and is enjoying a career in academia may appear to be evidence that the Royal Commission was a success, and its recommendations fulfilled, that interpretation would not be accurate. I do not have young children to care for, to worry about and educate, and to place in developmentally appropriate, high-quality care. I did not have to book a child care spot at $80 plus tax, per day, per child, in a facility near Concordia University, to present this paper at the Canadian Sociology Association annual meeting, in spring 2010.

Many of my colleagues, students, and other women across Canada have to worry, wait, pay, juggle, and run, in order to keep their jobs and feed their families. That is evidence that many of the recommendations have never been put into action, including the one calling for the creation of a national daycare program.

Since the report's call for the creation of a National Day Care Act, the number of women with young children in the labour force has skyrocketed (Marshall, 2006; Luffman, 2006; Roy, 2006). Partly by choice, and in part due to economic necessity created by the rise of precarious, low-waged employment, a growing number of women with young children find themselves in the labour force (Bezanson & Luxton, 2006; Silver et. al, 2005; Hughes & Lowe, 2000; Statistics Canada, 1998). The need for non-parental child care increased; and at specific junctures, diverse federal governments appeared willing, and even ready, to respond to this.

National Child Care Strategies Since the Royal Commission

In 1966, Canada introduced the Canada Assistance Plan (CAP), a federal–provincial cost-sharing agreement aimed at improving the lives of lower-income earners. Through CAP, federal funds were assigned to child care services, as part of social welfare provisions for 'needy' families. While limited, CAP stimulated the development of child care services. With the Royal Commission's report, child care came to be widely seen as a necessary step toward gender equality—for all women, not just the poor. Since then, there have been a number of (mostly failed) attempts by federal governments to develop more comprehensive national approaches to child care.

In 1984, Pierre Trudeau's Liberals set up the Task Force on Child Care. In 1986, Brian Mulroney's Progressive Conservatives established a Special Committee on Child Care. This was followed by Jean Chrétien's Liberal Red Book promises in 1993 (see Scherer, 2001). Each step highlighted the importance of child care beyond its role as part of social welfare. And each failed to deliver a national strategy.

Changing political and economic currents ushered in new federal–provincial cost-sharing arrangements that in the name of increased provincial autonomy, and against the wishes of a number of women's organizations, did away with CAP and established the Canada Health and Social Transfer. This gave the federal government less power to interfere in provincial matters, and made the provinces less accountable for how they spent public funds. Many provinces tightened eligibility requirements and introduced cuts to social welfare rates—moves that disproportionately harmed women and children (see Little, 1998; Albanese, 2010; Raphael, 2007). The hope for the creation of a national child care strategy was slipping as provincial programs were being eroded (Friendly, Beach and Turiano, 2002). Hope was lost when the election of a Conservative federal government in 2006 resulted in the creation of the Universal Child Care Benefit. Stephen Harper's government scrapped billion-dollar child care agreements with the provinces and began delivering to parents an individual, pre-tax cash payment of $100 per month per child under the age of six.

When UNICEF (Adamson, 2008) published the first international study to rank the quality, access, financing, and policies of early childhood education programs, Canada ranked at the very bottom of the 25 developed countries that were compared—tied with Ireland. While Canada as a whole falls short compared to other industrialized nations, individual provinces have been attempting to improve access and quality at the provincial level. Quebec, for example, began to provide funds, other than fee subsidies, to child care centres to reduce operating costs or to improve employee wages in 1979. Beginning in 1997, it brought in a publicly funded (reduced-fee, $5/day; later $7/day) early childhood education program, full-day kindergarten, and low-fee, after-school day care spaces for school-aged children—for all families regardless of income (Albanese, 2006; Tougas, 2002; 2002a). That said, high-quality, affordable child care remains out of reach for many Canadians.

A Look at the Ottawa Valley

My research sought to understand the ways in which neo-liberal reconfigurations of non-urban economies have affected the lives of employed, non-urban women with young children, and the strategies and networks they have adopted to cope with these changes. I found that despite rapid social and economic changes that have increasingly called upon mothers of young children to (re)enter the labour force, precious little has been done, especially outside Quebec, to facilitate the changes, particularly when it comes to child care.

I conducted 55 interviews—22 in Quebec and 33 in Ontario—with mothers of young children living and employed in separate policy jurisdictions, on the two sides of the Ottawa Valley. This was a non-probability purposive sample of employed mothers working near the Ontario–Quebec border. This paper focuses on the responses of mothers who resided in Ontario, who seemingly have more obstacles and challenges when managing their child care needs.

The Royal Commission adopted four principles in its report:

- that women should be free to choose whether or not to take employment outside their homes;
- that the care of children is a responsibility to be shared by the mother, the father and society;
- that society has a responsibility for women because of pregnancy and child birth, and special treatment related to maternity will always be necessary; and
- that in certain areas women will for an interim time require special treatment to overcome the adverse effects of discriminatory practices (p. xii).

I found that women are actually *not* free to choose whether or not to take employment outside their homes. The Ottawa Valley, like other parts of Canada, has been spiralling into economic crisis for years, with the decline of relatively well-paid, male-dominated jobs in the wood products industries. Increasingly, families rely on women's employment to make ends meet. Rather than have 'special' treatment, many mothers have to bend and stretch, skip lunch, lose wages, take on challenging shifts, reduce the number of hours they work, etc., to meet the challenges associated with child care.

The inaction around the development of a national child care strategy reminds us that these principles require attention 40 years after being put to paper. The report's recommendation 115 states: 'We recommend that fees for the care of children in day-care centres be fixed on a sliding scale based on the means of the parents' (p. 411). While there is a subsidy system in Ontario, and many of the licensed spots in Renfrew County are subsidized, many of the women I spoke to were ineligible to receive subsidies, had lost their subsidy, or could not find a subsidized spot in their communities. One mother admitted:

> Right now we're paying almost $1,000 a month in childcare; like that's a mortgage . . . we don't qualify for subsidies, but we're still paying student loans . . . it's very hard when you can't qualify . . . but at the same time, you need quality care for your child (2-008).

Many of the women I spoke to had their child(ren) in less-than-ideal unlicensed care arrangements. Even these arrangements cost mothers upwards of $30 and $40 dollars per day. Cost of care was a common answer when I asked mothers to identify the most challenging thing when balancing paid work and family life. One mother stated:

> Number one for me is financial. . . . Daily, I sit back and think is this really worth [it]? . . . We're not really making that much money . . . maybe I should just be staying at home with my kids. But how can we financially, as a family, do that? We can't. That's the point (2-021).

A mother of four who was originally from Quebec, then moved to Ontario, and finally returned to Quebec, in part because of child care, said:

> So I had a babysitter. . . . I forget what I paid her a day, but when it worked out, I made

$11 a day; and that didn't take into account driving there . . . and the price of gas last summer . . . so I just had to keep reminding myself that it was short term. But basically, last summer I worked for free . . . I might as well have quit . . . . but I needed to work, and I really loved my job (1-005).

She added that once she moved to Quebec from Ontario, and got access to $7-a-day child care:

> I was able to go from full-time work to part-time work . . . and have the same amount of disposable income. And I went from making a decent wage, to less, because you make less money here [in Quebec]; like I lost $5 an hour. I was able to work less hours for less pay, and still have the same amount of income (1-005).

Her move to Quebec allowed her to work fewer hours, spend more time with her children, and financially support her family. In Ontario, the cost of child care made this impossible, even when she worked longer hours at higher wages.

The *Report of the Royal Commission* and other declarations, including the *UN Convention on the Rights of the Child*, to which Canada is a signatory, decree that the care and well-being of children is a responsibility to be 'shared' by the mother, the father, and society, but Canadian social policy does not reflect this. Mothers scramble, often in distress, to manage paid work and family responsibilities.

To this day, children and child care are treated as private matters and individual lifestyle 'choices'. Children are not socially valued and mothers continue to disproportionately bear the weight of social reproduction. In order to stay employed and raise their families, the mothers I spoke to sacrificed a great deal, including sleep, having more children, and working the number of hours they wanted or needed to work. With too few social supports in place, far too many of these women sounded defeated. One mother said:

> I keep telling myself this is temporary, and I'm not the first one that has gone through this . . . but I'm living it now and I'm having difficulty (2-009).

The child care situation is miserable in this country, especially outside of Quebec. After 40 years, now more than ever, we need an affordable, flexible, high-quality national child care strategy. This would assist women in their choices and access to paid work, and in their ability to fulfill some of their career goals without putting at risk their own and their family's well-being.

References

Adamson, Peter. (2008). *The Child Care Transition: A League Table of Early Childhood Education and Care in Economically Advanced Countries.* Innocenti Report Card 8. Florence: Innocenti Research Centre, UNICEF.

Albanese, Patrizia. (forthcoming 2010). 'Balancing Paid Work and Family Responsibilities: Lessons on Family Policy from Quebec' in *Demystifying the Family/Work Contradiction: Challenges and Possibilities*, Catherine Krull and Justyna Sempruch (eds). Vancouver: UBC Press. p. TBA.

———. (2006). 'Small Town, Big Benefits: The Ripple Effect of $7/day Child Care'. *Canadian Review of Sociology and Anthropology* 43(2): 125–140.

Bezanson, Kate and Luxton, Meg (eds). (2006). *Social Reproduction: Feminist Political Economy Challenges Neoliberalism.* Montreal: McGill-Queen's University Press.

Friendly M., Jane Beach and Michelle Turiano. (2002). *Early Childhood Education and Care in Canada 2001.* Toronto: Childcare Resource and Research Unit, University of Toronto.

Hughes, Karen and Graham Lowe. (2000). 'Surveying the "Post-Industrial" Landscape: Information Technologies and Labour Market Polarization in Canada'. *Canadian Review of Sociology and Anthropology* 37(1): 29–53.

Little, Margaret Hillyard. (1998). *No Car, No Radio, No Liquor Permit: The Moral Regulation of Single Mothers in Ontario.* Toronto: Oxford University Press.

Luffman, Jacqueline. (2006). 'Core-Age Labour Force'. *Perspectives On Labour and Income* (Statistics Canada) 7(9): 5–11.

Marshall, Katherine. (2006). 'Converging Gender Roles'. *Perspectives On Labour and Income* (Statistics Canada) 7(7): 6–17.

Raphael, Dennis. (2007). *Poverty and Policy in Canada.* Toronto: Canadian Scholars' Press.

Roy, F. (2006). 'From She to She: Changing Patterns of Women in the Canadian Labour Force'. *Canadian Economic Observer.* (Statistics Canada). Catalogues No. 11-010, pp. 3.1–3.10

Royal Commission on the Status of Women. (1970). *Report of the Royal Commission on the Status of Women.* Ottawa: Information Canada.

Scherer, Rebecca Kelley. (2001). 'Federal Child Care Policy Development: From World War II to 2000' in *Changing Child Care*, Susan Prentice (ed). Halifax: Fernwood. pp. 187–198.

Silver, S., J. Shields and S. Wilson. (2005). 'Restructuring of Full-time Workers: A Case of Transitional Dislocation or Social Exclusion in Canada? Lessons from the 1990s'. *Social Policy & Administration* 39(7): 786–801.

Statistics Canada. (1998). '1996 Census: Labour Force Activity, Occupation and Industry, Place of Work, Mode of Transportation to Work, Unpaid Work'. The *Daily*, March 17.

Tougas, Jocelyne. (2002). 'Reforming Quebec's Early Childhood Care and Education: The First Five Years'. Toronto: Childcare Resource & Research Unit, Centre for Urban & Community Studies. Occasional Paper 17.

Tougas, Jocelyne. (2002a). 'Quebec's Family Policy and Strategy on Early Childhood Development and Childcare.' *Education Canada* 39(4): 20–22.

UNICEF. 1990. *Convention on the Rights of the Child.* New York: United Nations.

CHAPTER 19

Keeping the Family Intact: The Lived Experience of Sheltered Homeless Families

Annette Tézli

In this paper, I present preliminary results of research that explores the lived experience of homeless families sheltered at the Emergency Family Shelter (a pseudonym— henceforth EFS), located in Calgary. This paper aims at contributing to the existing literature on homeless families by exploring how the social organization of the EFS shapes the lived experience of homeless families.

For my research, I collected ethnographic data relying on both **participant observation** as well as in-depth interviews with shelter guests, staff, and board members to explore the social organization of the EFS in particular and the shelter system in Calgary in general. I am further interested in how the social organization of the shelter—that is its policies, rules, and practices—helps shape the lived experience of homeless families housed at the EFS.

The Families:
In Their Own Words

The families whose accounts this paper is based on came from a variety of backgrounds. They all had in common a history of residential instability and often cited high rents and the shortage of affordable housing in Calgary as the main reason for not being able to maintain housing. Most of them did not come to the shelter directly after losing their home but initially utilized other resources such as staying with family or friends, couch surfing or doubling up. Overcrowding, stress and conflict

with hosts or roommates were the most frequently cited reasons for leaving the shared living arrangement and turning to a shelter for accommodation, which was often the last resort after all other options had been exhausted. Most families I talked to came to the EFS specifically because they could stay together as a family.

Interpersonal Relationships and Family Dynamics within Shelter Life

Just as varied as the backgrounds of the families at the EFS, so are their interpersonal relationships and family dynamics. Some families experienced few problems while staying at the EFS while others struggled with interpersonal relationship problems and living in the shelter environment. Just as in any other setting, some relationships were stronger than others and some parents got along with their children better than others.

One of the fathers, Ryan, was attending literacy classes to improve his grade 2–level reading skills. When I asked him whether he was enjoying learning how to read and write, he answered: 'No. I just wanna do it 'cause I wanna be able to read to my daughter when she's older 'cause every parent wants to do that.'

On entering the EFS, Ryan also agreed to spend 28 days in a rehab facility to get sober and overcome his anger management problems. Despite all the interpersonal problems they encountered while staying at the EFS, Mona, Ryan's fiancé, stated: 'I think it's made my relationship with Ryan stronger. . . . yeah I guess it gets stressful at times and yeah we argue about it but at the same time it's making us stronger.' When I asked her how the situation is making them stronger she replied: ''Cause it's a hard time in our life and we're doing this together and we're trying to like do better for our family and we're doing it together, right?'

Similarly, Edith, whose partner's gambling addiction contributed to her family's homelessness, encouraged her partner to make some changes upon entering the EFS. She stated:

> I spoke to one of the workers and I addressed the issue. . . . And so we made a plan to talk to him and we talked to him and then uhm addressed the issue of what's gonna happen if he didn't make changes in his life and if things weren't gonna get better I said I was gonna up and leave and I was gonna start over without him and I was gonna build my life without him. And so he agreed to go and get himself checked into an addiction program.

One positive aspect of having a partner by their side that some couples mentioned was the support they were getting from their partner. Raheem, who had suffered a stroke and was partially paralyzed, physically depended on his wife's support to accomplish the most mundane tasks such as getting dressed or taking a shower. He explained:

> I cannot go to the washroom, I cannot open my bottom and I cannot put on my shoes or put on my pants, so I need everything her help, even for the showering. When I want to go to shower, I need her help. . . . She come with me, she puts some chairs over there in the men's washroom for me so I can sit on that and she wait out there and she stand outside and calling me after every two, three minutes 'Are you ok?' 'Everything is ok.'

Dana, who stayed at the EFS with her husband Brian and their two children, pointed out:

> I guarantee you, without my husband I would have killed myself by now . . . his big thing is he doesn't feel like a real man anymore 'cause he's not able to support his kids. . . . I know he feels like crap right now and I tell him all the time I'm like 'Look honey, you're still here. You're a lot better than most other guys who just walk away. They would. Most other guys would just walk away from here.'

Similarly, Natalie also pointed to the positive side of their shelter experience and the importance of having her husband going through the experience with her:

> It definitely made us tighter as a family. We appreciate each other more. I mean I appreciate him for sticking by, I mean, like he could have walked away any moment, you know? . . . I realized how strong my marriage really is. He could have walked away at any moment and chose to stand by and, you know, endure all with us.

Negative Aspects of Shelter Life

Being at the shelter as a two-parent family is not in all cases a benefit. A staff member pointed out: 'I think having a two-parent family can be more beneficial and sometimes having a single-parent family can be more beneficial depending on what the situation is.' (staff member, personal conversation, November 8, 2009). Living in a confined space, the entire family housed in a small cubicle with no privacy, can be a challenging and stressful experience for couples and can strain their relationship.

As one staff member put it: 'I think it gets challenging for a couple when they're in a little bit of a feud, they have no privacy or if they want to show affection they have no privacy . . . ' (staff member, personal conversation, November 8, 2009). In addition, having two parents does not always mean that the work of caring for the children is shared.

Several participants talked about the challenges they had to face while living at the shelter as a couple. One issue that arose repeatedly was conflict with one's partner. Altercations between partners is an almost daily occurrence, and disagreement often arises over the distribution of chores, child-rearing responsibilities and approaches, the need for personal space, and the exchange of physical intimacy. Many of these conflicts can be observed in most households, but in a shelter setting, the issues have to be fought over and resolved in public under the watchful eyes of staff who readily intervene to re-establish peace and order. The lack of privacy and personal space inevitably takes its toll on couples' relationships.

One couple, Mona and Ryan, mentioned the negative impact shelter life had on their relationship. When I asked Mona why they were fighting, she answered:

> Uhm just stupid reasons really. Just little stupid fights . . . we're both really stressed out and havin' a new baby and things like that and he didn't agree with some of the ways that I wanted to raise a baby and things like that.

To the same question, Ryan responded:

> Like if I wanna go in my room, you know, I can't and I gotta sit in this little room with her and if I wanna go out, I gotta go outside and when I'm up there she comes and asks for cigarettes and I can't get away from her (laughs). It's not good.

Other research participants talked about how their partner's behaviour at the shelter caused problems for the family as a whole. Janice mentioned how her boyfriend's attitude drew staff's attention on them as a couple:

> . . . my boyfriend, like he speaks his mind and they don't like that about him, so . . . you know. They always write to our family worker down here, like things that my boyfriend says to them or whatever, or if he's talking to me and they overhear it and they go like tell on us and then we get in trouble . . . I always tell him to quit but he doesn't listen to me.

Didier and his family ended up leaving the EFS because his wife got barred from the facility for bad behaviour. From informal conversation with several staff members, I gathered that staff found Didier's wife to be rude, unco-operative, and verbally abusive. Once his wife got barred from the EFS, the family decided to seek shelter at the Salvation Army even though the EFS told the remaining family members they could stay. However, after a couple of months, Didier and his children returned to the EFS without his wife. He explained that they had gotten into an argument and his wife had lost her temper, so he had decided to leave her and work things out on his own.

Some women at EFS struggled with the situation of abusive partners staying with them at the shelter. Janice stated that her boyfriend was verbally abusive and often made her feel worthless. She continued, 'Every time I try to talk to him about it, he just ignores me, swears at me and walks away. . . . He tells me that he loves me every day. But sometimes when he's mad at me, he tells me that he doesn't love me.' When I asked her why she was staying with him, she responded that it made her feel good when he told her that he loved her and that it ' . . . would make me feel like a bad mother taking his [her son's] dad away from him.'

Similarly, Destinie struggled with the relationship between her and her husband. She and her two daughters had followed him to Canada after a year of separation. However, on her arrival in Canada, Destinie found out that, while they were apart, her husband had been seeing another woman, with whom he had had a child. Destinie stated that she did not want to leave her husband because not being a landed immigrant left her unable to work and financially dependent on his income. In addition, she said she was so used to having him around that the thought of leaving him was painful. Finally, she did not want their daughters grow up without their father. So Destinie stayed, despite all the reasons not to.

Conclusion

Few family shelters in Alberta are currently accommodating families that are headed by mixed-gender couples. However, shelters housing all types of families are an important resource for homeless families who otherwise would have to separate and seek accommodation through different institutions separating couples as well as teenage and adult children from their parent(s). When families are in trouble, it can be beneficial for couples to be housed together and jointly work on overcoming their problems rather than being forced to seek shelter in separate facilities, which might break up already vulnerable families.

Yet, despite homeless shelters' attempts to the contrary, shelterization can have a negative impact on the families and their interpersonal relationships. This serves to underline the well-known sociological observation that, often, social planning has unintended consequences—however positive the intentions of planners.

Shelterization may serve to keep together families that otherwise might have separated; and it may cause tensions that break apart families that otherwise might have stayed together.

References

Anderson, E. A., & Koblinsky, S. A. (1995). Homeless Policy: The Need to Speak to Families. *Family Relations*, 44(1), 13–18.

Averitt, S. S. (2003). 'Homelessness Is Not a Choice!' The Plight of Homeless Women With Preschool Children Living in Temporary Shelters. *Journal of Family Nursing*, 9(1), 79–100.

Baker, S. G. (1994). Gender, Ethnicity, and Homelessness: Accounting for Demographic Diversity on the Streets. *The American Behavioral Scientist*, 37(4), 476–504.

Banyard, V. L. (1995). 'Taking Another Route': Daily Survival Narratives from Mothers Who Are Homeless. *American Journal of Community Psychology*, 23(6), 871–891.

Barge, F. C., & Norr, K. F. (1991). Homeless Shelter Policies for Women in an Urban Environment. *Journal of Nursing Scholarship*, 23(3), 145–150.

Bentham, J. (1995). Panopticon. In M. Bozovic (Ed.), *The Panopticon Writings*. London: Verso.

Bourdieu, P. (1998). *Acts of Resistance: Against the Tyranny of the Market*. New York: The New Press.

———. (2003). *Firing Back: Against the Tyranny of the Market 2*. London: Verso.

Boxill, N. A., & Beaty, A. L. (1990). Mother/Child Interaction among Homeless Women and Their Children in a Public Night Shelter in Atlanta, Georgia. In N. A. Boxill (Ed.), *Homeless Children: The Watchers and the Waiters* (pp. 49–64). New York: The Haworth Press.

Cairns, K. V., & Gardiner, H. P. (2003). *Solutions: Strategic Initiatives to Create an Organized Path Out of Homelessness in Calgary*. Calgary: Calgary Homeless Foundation.

Calgary Committee to End Homelessness. (2008a). *The 10-Year Plan to End Homelessness*. Calgary: Calgary Committee to End Homelessness.

———. (2008b). *Calgary's 10 Year Plan to End Homelessness*. Calgary: Calgary Committee to End Homelessness.

Choi, N. G., & Snyder, L. J. (1999a). Homeless Families with Children. *Journal of Poverty*, 3(2), 43–66.

———. (1999b). *Homeless Families with Children: A Subjective Experience of Homelessness*. New York: Springer Publishing Company.

———. (1999c). Voices of Homeless Parents. *Journal of Human Behavior in the Social Environment*, 2(3), 55–77.

Cosgrove, L., & Flynn, C. (2005). Marginalized Mothers: Parenting without a Home. *Analyses of Social Issues and Public Policy*, 5(1), 127–143.

Decter, A. (2007). *Lost in the Shuffle: The Impact of Homelessness on Children's Education in Toronto*. Toronto: Community Social Planning Council of Toronto.

Denzin, N. K. (1997). *Interpretive Ethnography: Ethnographic Practices for the 21st Century*. Thousand Oaks, CA: Sage.

DeOllos, I. Y. (1997). *On Becoming Homeless: The Shelterization Process for Homeless Families*. New York: University Press of America.

Eberle, M., Kraus, D., Pomeroy, S., & Hulchalski, D. (2001). *Homelessness—Causes & Effects. Volume 2. A Profile, Policy Review and Analysis of Homelessness in British Columbia*. Victoria: Ministry of Social Development and Economic Security.

Friedman, D. H. (2000). *Parenting in Public: Family Shelter and Public Assistance*. New York: Columbia University Press.

Gerstel, N., Bogard, C. J., McConnell, J. J., & Schwartz, M. (1996). The Therapeutic Incarceration of Homeless Families. *The Social Service Review*, 70(4), 543–572.

Gubrium, J. F., & Holstein, J. A. (1990). *What Is Family?* Mountain View, CA: Mayfield.

Haber, M. G., & Toro, P. A. (2004). Homelessness among Families, Children, and Adolescents: An Ecological-Developmental Perspective. *Clinical Child and Family Psychology Review*, 7(3), 123–164.

Holstein, J. A., & Gubrium, J. F. (1995). *The Active Interview*. Thousand Oaks, CA: Sage.

———. (2002). Active Interviewing. In D. Weinberg (Ed.), *Qualitative Research Methods* (pp. 112–126). Oxford, UK: Blackwell.

Jacobs, F. H. (1994). Defining a Social Problem: The Case of Family Homelessness. *American Behavioral Scientist*, 37(3), 396–403.

Kraus, D., & Dowling, P. (2003). *Family Homelessness: Causes and Solutions*. Ottawa: Canada Mortgage and Housing Corporation.

Laird, G. (2007). *Shelter—Homelessness in a Growth Economy: Canada's 21st Century Paradox*. Calgary: Sheldon Chumir Foundation for Ethics in Leadership.

Liff, S. R. (1996). *No Place Else to Go: Homeless Mothers and Their Children Living in Urban Settings*. New York: Garland.

Lyon-Callo, V. (2004). *Inequality, Poverty, and Neoliberal Governance: Activist Ethnography in the Homeless Sheltering Industry*. Peterborough, ON: Broadview Press.

Marvasti, A. B. (2003). *Being Homeless: Textual and Narrative Constructions*. Lanham, MA: Lexington Books.

McChesney, K. Y. (1995). A Review of the Empirical Literature on Contemporary Urban Homeless Families. *The Social Service Review*, 69(3), 429–460.

McMullin, J. (2010). *Understanding Social Inequality: Intersections of Class, Age, Gender, Ethnicity, and Race in Canada* (2nd ed.). Don Mills: Oxford.

Miller, J., & Glassner, B. (1997). The 'Inside' and the 'Outside'—Finding Realities in Interviews. In D. Silverman (Ed.), *Qualitative Research: Theory, Method and Practice* (pp. 99–112). Thousand Oaks, CA: Sage.

Novac, S., Brown, J., & Bourbonnais, C. (1996). *No Room of Her Own: A Literature Review on Women and Homelessness*. Ottawa: Canada Mortgage and Housing Corporation.

O'Connor, A. (2001). *Poverty Knowledge: Social Science, Social Policy, and the Poor in Twentieth-Century U.S. History*. Princeton, NJ: Princeton University Press.

Presser, H. B., & Cox, A. G. (1997). The Work Schedules of Low-Educated American Women and Welfare Reform. *Monthly Labor Review*, 120(4), 25–35.

Presser, L. (2004). Violent Offenders, Moral Selves: Constructing Identities and Accounts in the Research Interview. *Social Problems*, 51(1), 82–101.

Rossi, P. H. (1994). Troubling Families: Family Homelessness in America. *American Behavioral Scientist*, 37(3), 342–395.

Schütz, A., & Luckmann, T. (1973). *The Structures of the Life-World*. Evanston, IL: Northwestern University Press.

Shinn, M., & Weitzman, B. C. (1996). Homeless Families Are Different. In J. Baumohl (Ed.), *Homelessness in America* (pp. 109–122). Phoenix, AZ: Oryx.

Statistics Canada. (2008a). *Canada Year Book 2007* (No. 11-402-XPE). Ottawa: Statistics Canada.

———. (2008b). *Families in Low Income before and after Tax, by Age and Sex of Major Income Earner, Canada, Provinces and Select CMAs* (No. Table 2020803). Ottawa: Statistics Canada.

———. (2008c). *Persons in Low Income, Canada, Provinces and Select CMAs* (No. Table 2020802). Ottawa: Statistics Canada.

———. (2010). *Labour Force, Employed and Unemployed, Numbers and Rates, by Province* (No. Table 282-0002). Ottawa: Statistics Canada.

Susser, I. (1993). Creating Family Forms: The Exclusion of Men and Teenage Boys From Families in the New York City Shelter System, 1987–91. *Critique of Anthropology*, 13(3), 267–283.

The Emergency Family Shelter. (2004). *2004 Annual Report*. Calgary: The Emergency Family Shelter.

———. (2008a). *2007 Annual Report*. Calgary: The Emergency Family Shelter.

———. (2008b). *Employee Manual*. Calgary: The Emergency Family Shelter.

———. (2008c). *The Family Shelter Fact Sheet*. Calgary: The Emergency Family Shelter.

———. (2008d). *The Family Shelter Family Expectations*. Calgary: The Emergency Family Shelter.

———. (2008e). *News from the Emergency Family Shelter*. Calgary: The Emergency Family Shelter.

———. (2009). *2008 Annual Report*. Calgary: The Emergency Family Shelter.

Thomas, J. (1993). *Doing Critical Ethnography*. Newbury, CA: Sage.

Wacquant, L. J. D. (2008). *Urban Outcasts: A Comparative Sociology of Advanced Marginality*. Cambridge: Polity Press.

Waegemakers Schiff, J. (2004). Community Collaboration for Housing Homeless Families: Results From the Field. *Canadian Review of Social Policy, Fall 2004*(54), 103–107.

———. (2007). Homeless Families in Canada: Discovering Total Families. *Families in Society*, 88(1), 131–140.

Willis, P., & Trondman, M. (2000). Manifesto for Ethnography. *Ethnography*, 1(1), 5–16.

CHAPTER 20

Love and Arranged Marriage in India Today: Negotiating Adulthood

Nancy S. Netting

Until the present time, Indian society has maintained the tradition of **arranged marriages** (Dion and Dion, 1993; Derné, 1995), even among highly educated professional youth who are fluent in English, adept at electronic communication, and very familiar with global youth culture. Since this group is clearly exposed to conflicting values, their continued adherence to Indian marriage customs becomes problematic. The research discussed here asks what is happening to the arranged-marriage tradition in the current environment of rapid economic change.

This paper examines two opposing hypotheses offered by sociological theory. **Modernization theory** predicts the collapse of the arranged marriage system and its replacement with Western-style individual choice; ideologies of individualism and romantic love are intricately imbedded in the global market system (Inkeles and Smith, 1974; Illouz, 1997; Nolan and Lenski, 1999). Neo-traditionalism predicts that Indian youth will instead see individualism as destructive of Indian family and religion, and thus strengthen their support of customs like arranged marriage. Commentators on contemporary Indian society provide various examples of such reaction (Derné, 1995; John and Nair, 1998; Kishwar, 1999; Harriss-White, 2001). This study also addresses a gap identified by Patricia Uberoi, who wrote, 'Our sociological reflection on family and kinship . . . is [missing] the qualitative dimension of love, sex, marriage, and family life . . . the [whole] emotional tenor of [Indian] family relations' (Uberoi, 1993: 36).

This research is based on intensive **open-ended interviews** with 30 never-married upper-middle-class educated youth in their twenties from Vadodara (formerly known as Baroda), a prosperous city in the west Indian state of Gujarat. The sample consisted of 15 men and 15 women, chosen via the snowball procedure. They ranged from 22 to 29 years years of age; most had professional bachelor's or master's degrees. Twenty-five were Hindu, two were Christian, and one came from each of the Jain, Muslim, and Sikh faiths. Questions covered parental marriage type; respondents' romantic history; attitudes on mate selection and desirable qualities in a mate; and opinions about premarital sexual experiences, dowry, horoscopes, women's employment and residence after marriage, number of desired children, and individualism. The results showed that arranged marriages, as they exist in today's India, are a product of ongoing evolution. It is still socially expected that marriages will be arranged, but the process has changed considerably over the past generation.

Arrangements have evolved into a system of introductions, in which parents first pre-approve potential partners, and then formally introduce the young people. Parental criteria are based on education, income (especially of the man), religion, **caste**, and reputation of the other family. The potential bride or groom can veto someone at the start, or, if they think a match is possible, can hold several subsequent private sessions. When such meetings—more like interviews than dates—have continued for about six weeks, the pair are expected to announce their engagement. During the engagement period, the couple is allowed to go out together frequently but is expected to refrain from sexual activity. While there is more free choice at every stage than in the past, parents still expect to initiate the courting process and reserve the right to terminate any relationship of which they disapprove. There also exists in Indian cities a competing 'underground' system of romantic relationships, in which young people meet at college or work and sometimes develop serious feelings for each other. Two-thirds, or 20, of the respondents had been involved in at least one romantic relationship that they judged important. Over half (13/23) of these self-chosen couples were not traditionally acceptable in Indian culture: 10 because the partners came from different castes, and another 3 because their partners were from different religions. If parents disapproved, the usual reason was incompatibility of the partner's family. The second most frequent cause was that the boy was too young and without a stable job. Most (16/26) of the relationships had broken by the time of the interview, 13 for reasons internal to the couple. Three had been forced apart by disapproving parents, while another three were struggling with parental objections and admitted they were likely to separate. In this sample, no respondents believed they would marry if their parents continued to disapprove.

Most respondents (16) preferred a love match, provided they could eventually get parental approval, but only nine expected one. Although a self-chosen marriage provided more equality and intimacy, they recognized that a parental introduction guaranteed similarity of backgrounds and ongoing parental support, while still offering them a degree of choice.

In many ways, the predictions of modernization theorists have been realized. Parents still play a decisive role in most marriages, but they put more emphasis on achieved characteristics such as education and occupation, rather than on ascribed ones. Arranged marriage has evolved to allow more input from youth, and there also exists a parallel system of dating that is growing in prevalence. To a lesser extent, neo-traditionalism is present as well; horoscopes, premarital virginity, and the requirement of parental support remain important.

Mainly, the interviews showed young people living within the intersections of the familial and the individualistic systems, and at times attempting to create and navigate structures that are qualitatively different from any pre-existing model. One such innovation is the self-arranged marriage, in which a young person accepts the rules and values of an arrangement, but manages to control the procedure. More common is the 'love-cum-arranged' scenario, widely considered the best possibility. This includes the emotional high of falling in love, continues into an extended period of getting to know each other, and concludes with the winning of parental support. Whether either of these combinations, or some other possibility, will emerge as a stable norm, or whether they simply represent intermediate points on the way to Westernization, is, as yet, impossible to predict.

It is also apparent from the respondents' replies that decisions about marriage do not occur in isolation; they are made in the context of changes in the pace and pattern of growing up. Long years of education have brought India's middle-class youth more physical independence, modern skills, and intellectual sophistication than earlier generations ever experienced. Their desire for a greater share in the marriage decision is part of a growing demand for more equality in general. Young women want the rights to continue their careers, to have a small number of children, and to maintain responsibility for their own parents (instead of their husband's) after marriage. Men want more freedom of sexual expression for themselves and their partners, not only before but also during marriage. Youth of both sexes insist they will use their newfound voices not as selfish individualists but as responsible members of a family unit. They will listen to their parents, but they also want their parents to listen to them. In short, they want to be treated as full adults. If youth of both sexes, and eventually women of all ages, gain this equality, then Indian families will be qualitatively different from their predecessors.

In the respondents' replies, love emerged not only as romantic passion but also as the quiet trust that grows slowly between classmates or during a family-directed engagement. An ongoing theme was the need to prevent emotion from carrying the self into unknown, dangerous territory. Instead, the emphasis fell on mutual understanding and respect. Respondents spoke of their hopes to create an intimate space where emotion, sexuality, ideas, and needs, could be safely expressed. Such a conjugal relationship is problematic in India because it is not a major goal of the **patrilocal multigenerational family** (Singh and Uberoi, 1994). Today, however, both men and women want a partner who is caring, understanding, honest, and respectful. Compatibility of backgrounds, interests, values, and education were valued by the respondents because they made intimacy possible.

The prevailing tone expressed by Indian youth approaching marriage is not one of defiance or rebellion, but of conscious attention to their own needs and empathy for those of their parents. They do not want to abandon a cherished home, but to renovate it to accommodate modern requirements. Freer communication between generations, based on respect and trust, as well as assured space for intimacy between marriage partners, are key goals to be achieved. As this study demonstrates, Indian youth of today are embarking on this great task of cultural reconstruction with confidence and courage.

References

Derné, S. 1995. *Culture in Action: Family Life, Emotion, and Male Dominance in Banaras, India.* Albany, NY: SUNY Press.

Dion, K.K., and K.L. Dion. 1993. 'Individualistic and Collectivistic Perspective on Gender and the Cultural Context of Love and Intimacy', *Journal of Social Issues* 49, 3: 53–69.

Harriss-White, B. 2001. 'Gender-cleansing: The Paradox of Development and Deteriorating Female Life Chances in Tamil Nadu', in *Signposts: Gender Issues in Post-independence India*, pp. 125–54, R.S. Rajan, ed. New Brunswick, NJ; London: Rutgers University Press.

Illouz, E. 1997. *Consuming the Romantic Utopia: Love and the Cultural Contradictions of Capitalism.* Berkeley, CA: University of California Press.

Inkeles, A., and D.H. Smith 1974. *Becoming Modern: Individual Change in Six Developing Countries.* Cambridge, MA: Harvard University Press.

John, M.E., and J. Nair. 1998. *A Question of Silence? The Sexual Economies of Modern India.* London and New York: Zed.

Kishwar, M. 1999. *Off the Beaten Track: Rethinking Gender Justice for Indian Women.* Delhi: Oxford University Press.

Nolan, P., and G. Lenski. 1999. *Human Societies: An Introduction to Macrosociology*, 8th ed. New York: McGraw-Hill.

Singh, A.T., and P. Uberoi. 1994. 'Learning to "Adjust": Conjugal Relations in Indian Popular Fiction', *Indian Journal of Gender Studies* 1, 1: 93–120.

Gender Equality and Gender Differences: Parenting, Habitus, and Embodiment (The 2008 Porter Lecture)

Andrea Doucet

Social and Political Landscapes: Men and Mothering

In the past three decades, scholarly and policy interest in fathering has gone from being relatively ignored in the 1980s, to a 'hot topic in the 1990s' (Marsiglio 1993), to a burgeoning field in the early years of the twenty-first century. Within this scholarship, there is a small but growing group of researchers who have studied shared or primary caregiving fathers (see Crittenden 2001; Deutsch 1999; Dienhart 1998; Ehrensaft 1987; Kimball 1988; Risman 1987; Smith 1998). It is interesting to note that most or all of these studies take the position that when men are taking on much or most of the family caregiving, then they are mothering. The most frequently cited proponent of the men and mothering position is Sara Ruddick. One of the aims of her book, *Maternal Thinking,* was to challenge and disrupt the binary distinction between mothers and fathers and the taken-for-granted ideological and discursive lapse between mother/carer/homemaker and father/provider/breadwinner.

This large project of attempting to radically alter gender relations is something that has preoccupied feminists for many decades. Yet, it is intriguing to note that there are opposing feminist positions on the 'do men mother?' question as well as more broadly on issues of gender equality and differences in mothering and fathering. On the one hand, the argument that gender should not matter in parenting is grounded in the basic tenets of equality feminism and liberal feminism, which underpin most research on gendered divisions of labour and on primary caregiving fathers (see Doucet 1995). That is, most of these studies are informed by the view that gender differences are to be avoided, and that gender equality is the gold standard to which couples should strive.

On the other hand, both feminists and fathers' rights groups also unwittingly join together in taking a position that 'men do not mother'. For feminists, a position that recognizes gender differences in parenting is theoretically informed by 'difference feminism', or what feminist theorists have referred to as 'the difference category' (Scott 1988). Particular manifestations of this position can be found in historical and contemporary arguments for wages for housework and the valuing of women's unpaid work, as well as feminists working on issues of child custody and divorce who accept and reinforce caregiving differences, largely based on the unequal social and political positioning of women and men. Fathers' rights groups also fall into this category.

In exploring the specific question 'do men mother?' in my study of men as primary caregivers, my research required not only a wide theoretical approach to men and mothering; it also needed to settle on a definition of maternal responsibilities that could be translated into empirical research questions.

Researching Men and Mothering

For a definition of maternal responsibilities, I drew directly on Ruddick's (1995) threefold conception of maternal demands—'preservation, growth, and social acceptability' (pp. 17–25)—and explored them, not as demands, but as responsibilities: emotional, community, and 'moral'. I investigated if, how, and when men took on these responsibilities, as well as the conditions and social contexts that promoted fathering and responsibility.

Emotional Responsibility

A first maternal responsibility is rooted in a vast body of feminist work on the ethic of care in which care is defined partly as 'knowledge about others' needs', which the carer acquires through 'attentiveness to the needs of others' (Tronto 1989: 176–78; see also Gilligan 1982; Noddings 2003). It refers to everyday conceptions of care as nurturing, and is akin to Susan Walzer's (1998) discussion of 'parental consciousness' and 'thinking about the baby' (p. 15). The assertion that men can take on emotional responsibility is confirmed by a large body of research attesting to how fathers can be nurturing, affectionate, and responsive to their children (see Dienhart 1998; Dowd 2000; Lamb 2000).

My work confirms many cross-cultural longitudinal studies that have demonstrated that fathers use play as a way of connecting with their infants and young children (Coltrane 1996; Lamb 2000). Second, the overwhelming majority of fathers in my study referred to how they, in the words of Aaron, 'made a point of going out every day' with their children, doing a lot of physical activities, and being very involved with their children's sports (see Brandth and Kvande 1998; Plantin, Månsson, and Kearney 2003). A third form of paternal nurturing is found in how fathers actively promote their children's independence. Recurring, everyday examples in fathers' accounts include strongly encouraging their kids to be involved in housework, make their own lunches, tie their own laces (shoes or skates), and carry their own backpacks to school.

Community Responsibility

A second maternal responsibility is community responsibility, which connects the domestic realm to the community and involves social networking, coordinating, balancing, negotiating, and orchestrating those others who are involved in children's lives.

One avenue for exploring the issue of fathers and community responsibility is to look to their creation and maintenance of community networks, as these networks often establish relations that tie into all other aspects of community responsibility. More specifically, community playgroups are one of the main forums in which parents of young children make connections with other parents. Yet, many stay-at-home fathers face difficulties gaining full acceptance in these playgroups (see Smith 1998; Doucet 2000, 2006a). For example, Peter, a stay-at-home father of two young boys, highlighted how community networking has 'gotten easier' over the course of being home for six years. Nevertheless, he added that 'to me as a man, that was a pretty alien environment and it continues to be'.

Thus, how do fathers network around children, and how do they facilitate or promote children's social development? While fathers are beginning to form networks as they stand in sites where children cluster—schoolyards, playgrounds, and at the doors of music or karate lessons—there are several other ways that fathers form networks, two of which are mentioned here.

First, fathers connect with mothers in extra-domestic spaces. If many fathers find it difficult, at least initially, to attend mother-dominated community playgroups, other fathers readily offer their own observations on the possible tensions involved with meeting up in other women's homes.

A second venue for fathers' networking is around their children's sports. While typically not included in studies that look at parents and networking around children, this is a social site through which fathers comfortably connect with each other. While fathers are increasingly becoming involved in children's sports activities, many men nevertheless pointed to how the 'alien environment' of mother-dominated social settings, particularly with young children, still leaves them feeling either excluded or marginalized.

'Moral' Responsibility

The supposedly moral responsibilities of mothering, and of fathering, embrace the former two responsibilities, but they are also rooted in the wider meanings, ideologies, and discourses through which men and women come to take on care work. They relate to people's identities as moral beings and how they feel they ought to and should act in society. That is, any individual is always 'actively working out his or her own course of action' from within a social and cultural location and 'with reference to other people' (Finch and Mason 1993:61).

This 'reference to other people' occurs especially in relation to earning and caring for fathers. Each and every stay-at-home father interviewed in my study of fathers as primary caregivers referred in some way to the moral responsibilities he felt weighing on him to be a family breadwinner or to earn at least some part of the family wages.

In addition to fathers being judged on their earning capacity within families, they are also sometimes judged negatively as carers. Within communities, there is a covert level of surveillance as men are scrutinized as carers of children. While many examples within fathers' interviews occur across different parenting sites, the most frequently mentioned were women-centred postnatal venues (e.g. community centres and schoolyards), and girls' sleepovers. With regard to the latter, single fathers of teenage girls feel particularly scrutinized. Girls' sleepovers are the window through which many men express their awareness of the fact that they have to be very careful around preteen and teenage girls.

Despite many good intentions by parents to alter gender relations, men's and women's lives as carers and earners are cut with deeply felt moral and social scripts about what women and men should do within and outside of household life.

Discussion

From my study of fathers as primary caregivers, comprising interviews with over 100 fathers and

14 heterosexual couples, many reasons emerged for gendered divisions in parental responsibilities. Key among these were: hegemonic masculinities (see Doucet 2006a, 2005); **embodiment** (Doucet 2006b); maternal gatekeeping (Doucet 2008); gendered friendship patterns; **habitus**; and gender ideologies. In the years since my book *Do Men Mother?* was published, I have continued to elaborate on some of these explanations, both theoretically and empirically, from my recent research with mothers and fathers, including interviews with a further 96 fathers and 26 mothers. Two explanations for continuing gender differences in parenting are further touched on below. These are first, habitus, and second, intersections between embodiment, space, and time.

Fathering and Habitus: 'I Grew Up as a Guy'

The tendency for fathers to exhibit traditionally masculine qualities in their enactment of emotional and community responsibilities is not surprising given that most boys grow up in cultures that encourage sport, physical and emotional independence, and risk-taking (Connell 2001; Messner 2002). Devon, a technician and the sole-custody father of his seven-year-old son, said that he promoted risk-taking because he 'grew up as a guy. We did dangerous things. That's what little boys do.' In contrast to Devon, as well as to her own husband Peter, Linda takes a more cautious parenting approach, rooted partly in having 'grown up as a girl':

> I don't know if boys take more physical risks than girls. I suspect that they do. Having grown up as a girl, you know you see the boys on the highest bars at the park, or riding their bikes on one wheel. I think that has some bearing on it.

Traditional sociological explanations for such statements point to these as evidence of gendered socialization. Yet, it is more than this. As Patricia Yancey Martin (2003) has recently written, gendering processes are deeply ingrained so that they 'become almost automatic'.

My argument here is that the gendered habitus of 'growing up as a girl' or 'growing up as a guy' is informed by deeply ingrained assumptions about gendered embodiment and about women as primary carers and men as secondary caregivers. There are certainly variations in how this plays out across class, ethnicity, age, and generation, and there is increasing evidence that these ideologies and norms are changing over time. Nevertheless, beneath the surfaces of everyday practices, there is still a constant pull back to those primary assumptions. In my study of fathers as primary caregivers, as well as in my recent study on fathers and parental leave, there is a strong sense that women feel guilty about leaving their child to go back to work and men feel guilty about leaving their work to care for their child. Put differently, mothers feel pulled toward care and connection while fathers feel pulled toward paid work and autonomy.

Fathering, Embodiment, Space, and Time

Fathers' narratives reveal that there are embodied differences in parenting, as expressed through fathers' use of physical play with infants and toddlers and athletic activities with older children. There are also different social perceptions of fathers' and mothers' acceptable physicality with children. While the early years of fathering infants and preschool children provide fathers with ample opportunity to freely hug and hold their children, many fathers of preteen and teenage boys and girls note that they are more closely scrutinized. In relation to boys, Brendan, a sole-custodial father of four, drew links between hegemonic masculinity and homophobia (Connell 1995, 2001) when he said: 'I mean I hug and kiss them, but it's not the same. And frankly I'm not as comfortable hugging the big guys as the little guys. Like the older guys go "hey man!" . . . I mean we're not homophobic, but it's something you're raised with.'

Similarly, most of the single fathers of preteen and teenage girls pointed to how public displays of close physical affection could be misinterpreted. Henry, a sole-custodial father, reflected on how he was always 'nervous' and 'conscious' of what he did around his 13-year-old daughter because his actions could be misinterpreted.

In my research on fathers as primary caregivers, I have noted that when a father is attending to children—by cuddling, feeding, reading, bathing, or talking to them—gendered embodiment can be largely negligible. At other times, and in other spaces, however, the social gaze upon men's movements with children is tinged with suspicion and surveillance as men move in female-dominated community spaces. That is, there are intersections between embodiment, time, and social spaces. The social sites where embodiment of fathers matters include recent versions of the moms-and-tots groups (community playgroups), schoolyards, classrooms, and other female-dominated venues, as well as instances when single fathers host girls' sleepover parties. From my recent research on new fathers, including fathers who take some parental leave, men expressed how they feel especially scrutinized as carers of infants.

Conclusions

Drawing on key findings from my research on primary caregiving fathers (2000 to 2004) and my book *Do Men Mother?* and pointing to new results emerging from recent research projects (2004 to 2008), I offer five concluding points. First, while there has been much excellent work on the gender division of household tasks, the issue of *responsibility* is the one area where gender differences have stubbornly persisted in mothering and fathering. A focus on responsibilities reveals how gender differences in parenting are deeply embedded in habitus, supposedly moral identities, embodiment, and in diverse spatial and time-framed contexts.

Second, the assumption that gender differences are negative features in domestic life requires greater attention. The large majority of studies conducted by feminist scholars assume that gender differences are to be avoided and that couples espousing discourses or practices of equality are, as Deutsch (1999) argues, 'the stars' of such studies.

Third, a key argument that continues to emerge from my work is that listening to, and theorizing from, fathers' narratives through a maternal lens means that paternal forms of nurturing are ignored or obscured (see also Stueve and Pleck 2003). For example, with regard to the issue of emotional responsibility, a maternal lens misses the ways in which fathers promote children's independence, and their playfulness, physicality, and outdoors approach to the care of young children are viewed only as second-best, or invisible, ways of caring.

A fourth point is that, while I am arguing for the importance of attending to some differences between mothers and fathers' enactments of parental responsibilities, these also vary across class, ethnicity, and sexuality. The particularities of these issues for distinct groups of fathers over generational and biographical time call for greater research attention. In Canada, this call has begun to be taken up by the Father Involvement Research Alliance.

Finally, while, theoretically speaking, it is useful to deconstruct mothering and fathering as distinct practices and identities, I argue that they nevertheless recur at the level of community and inter-household practices as embodied identities, and within social relations and discourses. As captured in Rich's (1986) oft-repeated observation, there is a distinction between the experience and the institution of mothering.

One of the main conclusions emanating from my research on gender equality and gender differences in parenting is that, rather than using a maternal lens and comparing fathers to mothers, what is required are novel ways of listening to and theorizing about fathers' approaches to parental responsibilities and how they are radically reinventing what it means to be a man and a father in the twenty-first century.

References

Brandth, Berit and Elin Kvande. 1998. 'Masculinity and Child Care: The Reconstruction of Fathering'. *Sociological Review* 46:293–313.

Coltrane, Scott. 1996. *Family Man: Fatherhood, Housework and Gender Equality*. New York and Oxford: Oxford University Press.

Connell, Robert W. 1995. *Masculinities*. Cambridge, UK: Polity Press.

Connell, Robert W. 2001. *The Men and the Boys*. Berkeley, CA: University of California Press.

Crittenden, Ann. 2001. *The Price of Motherhood: Why the Most Important Job in the World Is Still the Least* Valued. New York: Holt.

Deutsch, Francine M. 1999. *Having It All: How Equally Shared Parenting Works*. Cambridge, MA: Harvard University Press.

Dienhart, Anna. 1998. *Reshaping Fatherhood: The Social Construction of Shared Parenting*. Thousand Oaks, CA: Sage.

Doucet, Andrea. 1995. 'Gender Equality and Gender Differences in Household Work and Parenting'. *Women's Studies International Forum* 18:271–84.

Doucet, Andrea. 2000. '"There's a Huge Difference Between Me as a Male Carer and Women": Gender, Domestic Responsibility, and the Community as an Institutional Arena'. *Community Work and Family* 3:163–84.

Doucet, Andrea. 2005. '"It's Almost Like I Have a Job, But I Don't Get Paid": Fathers at Home Reconfiguring Work, Care, and Masculinity'. *Fathering: A Journal of Theory, Research, and Practice about Men as Fathers* 2:277–303.

Doucet, Andrea. 2006a. *Do Men Mother? Fathering, Care and Domestic Responsibilities*. Toronto: University of Toronto Press.

Doucet, Andrea. 2006b. 'Estrogen-Filled Worlds: Fathers as Primary Caregivers and Embodiment'. *The Sociological Review* 23:695–715.

Doucet, Andrea. 2008. 'Fathers, Mothers and Maternal Gatekeeping'. Keynote Address. Father Involvement Research Alliance (FIRA) Conference. Toronto. Ontario, 26–28 October.

Dowd, Nancy E. 2000. *Redefining Fatherhood*. New York: New York University Press.

Ehrensaft, Diane. 1987. *Parenting Together: Men and Women Sharing the Care of Their Children*. London: Collier Macmillan Publishers.

Finch, Janet and Jennifer Mason. 1993. *Negotiating Family Responsibilities*. London: Routledge.

Gilligan, Carol. 1982. *In a Different Voice: Psychological Theory and Women's Development*. Cambridge, MA: Harvard University Press.

Kimball, Gayle. 1988. *50–50 Parenting: Sharing Family Rewards and Responsibilities*. Lexington, MA: Lexington Books.

Lamb, Michael E. 2000. 'The History of Research on Father Involvement: An Overview'. *Marriage and Family Review*. 29:23–42.

Marsiglio, William. 1993. 'Contemporary Scholarship on Fatherhood: Culture, Identity and Conflict'. *Journal of Family Issues* 14:484–509.

Martin, Patricia Yancey. 2003. '"Said and Done" Versus '"Saying and Doing": Gendering Practices, Practicing Gender at Work'. *Gender and Society* 17:342–66.

Messner, Michael. 2002. *Taking the Field. Women, Men, and Sports*. Minneapolis, MN: University of Minnesota Press.

Morrison, Toni. 1987. *Beloved: A Novel*. New York: Knopf.

Noddings, Nel. 2003. *Caring: A Feminine Approach to Ethics and Moral Education*. 2d ed. Berkeley, CA: University of California Press.

Plantin, Lars, Sven-Axel Månsson and Jeremy Kearney. 2003. 'Talking and Doing Fatherhood: On Fatherhood and Masculinity in Sweden and England'. *Fathering: A Journal of Theory, Research, and Practice about Men as Fathers* 1:3–26.

Rich, Adrienne. 1986. *Of Woman Born: Motherhood as Experience and Institution*. 2d ed. New York: Norton.

Risman, Barbara J. 1987. 'Can Men Mother? Life as a Single Father'. *Family Relations* 35:95–102.

Ruddick, Sara. 1995. *Maternal Thinking: Toward a Politics of Peace*. 2d ed. Boston. MA: Beacon.

Scott, Joan W. 1988. *Gender and the Politics of History*. New York: Colombia University Press.

Smith, Calvin D. 1998. '"Men Don't Do this Sort of Thing": A Case Study of the Socialization of House husbands'. *Men and Masculinities* 1:138–72.

Stueve, Jeffrey L. and Joseph H. Pleck. 2003. 'Fathers' Narratives of Arranging and Planning: Implications for Understanding Parental Responsibility'. *Fathering: A Journal of Research, Theory, and Practice* 1:51–70.

Tronto, Joan C. 1989. 'Women and Caring: What Can Feminists Learn about Morality From Caring?' Pp. 172–87 in *Gender/Body/Knowledge: Feminist Reconstructions of Being and Knowing*, edited by A.M. Jaggar and S. Bordo. New Brunswick, NJ: Rutgers University Press.

Walzer, Susan. 1998. *Thinking about the Baby: Gender and Transitions into Parenthood*. Philadelphia, PA: Temple University Press.

Questions for Critical Thought

CHAPTER 18

1. Why have some of the programs that Albanese writes about (e.g. the Canada Assistance Plan) been shut down? What kind of impact has this had on women and their families?
2. According to Albanese's research, why are women not able to choose whether or not to go to work? What sacrifices do they have to make in order to be able to work? Be sure to consider the contradictory pressures of larger-scale economic changes and the cost of child care.
3. According to Albanese, how is Quebec different from the rest of Canada in its handling of day care policy? Compare the effects of each approach on families, and be sure to include evidence from Albanese's findings.
4. According to Albanese, is Canadian policy holding up to its commitment made in declarations such as the *Report of the Royal Commission* or the *UN Convention on the Rights of the Child*? Why or why not? Be sure to discuss the specific commitments, policies, and effects.
5. The child care problem discussed by Albanese rests on the assumption that our economy usually requires both parents to work. Consider how our economy and working lives could be arranged differently, to allow adults to both contribute to the economy and raise future members of our communities. Feel free to think of very macro aspects such as corporations and government, as well as more micro aspects such as specific workplace policies or family arrangements.

CHAPTER 19

1. Tézli found that families exhaust all other options before going to shelters as a last resort. Explain those other options and why they don't work out.
2. What are some of the benefits of living together in the Emergency Family Shelter (as opposed to other shelters that would separate family members based on age and sex) that Tézli's respondents reported?
3. What are the challenges of living together in the Emergency Family Shelter that Tézli's respondents reported?
4. 'I think having a two-parent family can be more beneficial and sometimes having a single-parent family can be more beneficial depending on what the situation is' (staff member, personal conversation, November 8, 2009). Explain what this staff member means by 'depending on what the situation is'. Make connections to the benefits and challenges explored in questions 2 and 3.
5. Brainstorm some ideas of how you would change homeless shelters to make them a more beneficial environment for families.

CHAPTER 20

1. How is arranged marriage traditionally practised? How is it different from North American marriage practices?
2. How has globalization impacted the understandings, expectations, and practices of young people in courtships in India? How have relationships initiated outside of the arrangement process changed and stayed the same?
3. How has the arranged marriage process evolved to allow more input from youth? What kind of input are they allowed to offer?
4. What are the various paths that Indian youth have created as options? What are some advantages and disadvantages of pursuing the various models of marriage? Which model is preferred and why?
5. Compare the predictions of the modernization and neo-traditionalism theses. Do Netting's findings provide evidence for either, neither, or both? Explain.

CHAPTER 21

1. Explain the similarities and differences between equality feminism and difference feminism, particularly with respect to the question, Do men mother?
2. How does gender socialization produce mothers and fathers who prefer and choose to take on some parenting responsibilities over others?
3. Doucet's informants point out that even when men break socialized norms and try to take a more maternal role, there are substantial barriers to their being able to do so legitimately. What unique challenges do men face in taking on maternal responsibilities (emotional, community, moral)?
4. According to Doucet, how do embodiment (socialized masculinity), time, and social space interact to heighten the suspicion of, and danger for, fathers performing maternal care throughout their life course? As a result of this uneven suspicion, what kinds of parenting activities are practically impossible for male primary caregivers to perform at certain times and in certain spaces?
5. How does using a maternal lens to measure and evaluate parenting ignore and marginalize important aspects of parenting done by fathers? How does Doucet suggest researchers overcome these limitations in order to better understand the evolving role of fathers?

Part VI

Education

Educational institutions act as repositories for much of our collective knowledge. They help transfer the knowledge gained from generations past to the current generation, bringing young people 'up to speed', in a way, on the world they are born into. Sociologists study education because it plays a vital role in socializing individuals, transmitting social values, and providing young people with the skills that they need to function within the economy. Given these huge responsibilities, educational institutions (and the content of their lessons) have the power to create docile, path-following citizens, or citizens who are armed with the tools and inclination to change everything around them. This means that these institutions can quietly reproduce the social world around them, or radically disrupt it. Given what is at stake, exactly what schools teach and how they teach it is often contentious and subject to the power struggles of the society around them. It is hard to find anyone who has a position on what society should be like who does not turn their attention to education.

The sociologists featured in this section use various approaches to understand the present-day social role of education. However, the underlying theme of their papers is the interaction between social inequality and formal education. To what extent and under what circumstances does formal education, and the schools that make it possible, reduce and mitigate existing social inequalities in society? How could schools better enable equality? We see these themes addressed clearly in Shaun Chen's paper about the debate around Africentric schools: whether such schools will help improve the performance of black Canadian students or merely segregate them. The suggestion here is that groups that have suffered disadvantage and discrimination require special strategies to overcome their social and educational disadvantages.

Of all educational institutions, higher education is expected to play a special role in the functioning of a modern society. Academics are paid to investigate and think about the world around them, and so they are often expected to provide us with insights that we don't have time to discover for ourselves. We especially think this way about scientific/medical departments of the university. However, social science departments are also well known for outspokenly spreading their ideas among the broader population. For example, Matthew Lange's paper suggests that formal education factored significantly in promoting ethnonationalist conflict in Quebec over the last 50 years, though other factors moderated the eruption of this conflict into violence. That being said, educational institutions are not enlightened utopias leading us forth toward 'progress' by their pristine example, and they may fail to play their expected role as instruments of social change. Even as universities can be filled with critical insights into the social world around them, they are not immune to the very same social processes that their social science departments may disparage. Maureen Baker, for example, shows in her paper that, for a variety of reasons, women academics in research-intensive universities have failed to overcome traditional limits on their career mobility. Likewise, Sinziana Chira shows that international students—even if considered 'ideal Canadian citizen' material—fail to receive the support they need to realize their own, and society's, goals.

CHAPTER 22

The Rise of the 'Research University': Gendered Outcomes

Maureen Baker

Introduction

This paper investigates the impact of university restructuring on the academic gender gap, analyzing relations among globalizing workplaces, personal life, and professional success. The paper argues that the current focus on research, internationalization, and entrepreneurship perpetuates the gap, which has recently diminished. The term **gender gap** refers to that fact that more men occupy full-time tenured university jobs with higher ranks and salaries, and report greater satisfaction with mentoring, workloads, and advancement opportunities (Probert, 2005; White, 2004; Nakhaie, 2007; CAUT, 2008).

Gender differences are most notable at 'senior' academic ranks. In the 'liberal' states[1], men occupy between 76 and 82 per cent of senior positions[2], down from 90 to 95 per cent in the 1960s (Carrington & Pratt, 2003; NZ, 2008; Sussman & Yssaad, 2005; AAUP, 2006). The gap is attributed to there being fewer qualified women in the past but also to academic practices, gendered family roles, and their interactions (Bassett, 2005; Bracken et al., 2006; Comer & Stites-Doe, 2006; Drakich & Stewart, 2007; Baker, 2010).

This paper draws on a literature survey and interviews with academics in New Zealand, where university practices are similar to the other liberal states, relying on international recruitment, benchmarking, and rankings. Many academics in the country are foreign-born, receive qualifications and experience overseas, and disseminate their research internationally (Baker, 2009). Interview participants included 30 men and women with doctorates, working in permanent positions in two universities. One of the schools is more research-intensive and prestigious, while the second is newer and emphasizes teaching. The next section examines university restructuring before discussing the gendered findings.

The Rise of the 'Research University'

Universities shift their priorities to accommodate enrollments and costs, student/staff diversity, and changing state/public expectations. Historically, governments based university funding mainly on enrollments, but some are now 'capping' enrollments and providing grants for 'research productivity'. Also, governments are encouraging universities to support innovation in the globalizing economy and to become more attuned to employer needs (Mohrman et al., 2008). Generally, state transfers have not kept pace with increasing enrollments or operating costs (CAUT, 2009). To compensate, universities have expanded fundraising, raised fees, recruited international students, closed academic units, and hired less-expensive temporary teachers

(Larner & LeHeron, 2005; Fisher et al., 2009). Non-academic managers have gained more control over strategic goals and their implementation, leading to concerns about 'hyper-bureaucracy' and diminishing academic freedom (Tahir, 2010).

Some universities always valorized research, but more are hiring research chairs and temporary teachers, widening the teaching/research dichotomy. Research chairs can raise the university's profile by attracting external funds, international publicity, and postgraduate students (Side & Robbins, 2007). 'Teaching universities' still concentrate on undergraduate education and hire more women (Fletcher et al., 2007). However, most universities now expect new academics to arrive with a doctorate, teaching experience, and publications. The historic differences between universities have been especially altered by national research assessment, introduced over the last few decades in New Zealand, Australia, and the United Kingdom.

New Zealand's assessment exercise provides a prime example of the intensifying focus on research. The country's 1990s governments encouraged private tertiary providers and introduced a loan system, increasing enrollments but elevating state contributions (Baker, 2009). Partly to ration resources, the Performance-Based Research Fund (PBRF) introduced competitive funding for postgraduate completions, external research income, and staff research productivity in 2002. Academics are now required to document their publications, peer esteem,[3] and research contributions for regular assessment by senior academics.

University 'quality' has also been compared internationally (Fletcher et al., 2007). The Times Higher Education-QS World University Rankings system is based largely on peer reviews but also on citations and international staff/students. In contrast, the Shanghai Jiao Tong University ranking system favours research in science and engineering—disciplines in which fewer women work (Taylor & Braddock, 2007). These schemas produce different scores for the same university, promoting debate about what they actually measure.

Research assessment tends to influence what researchers study and how they disseminate results, encouraging academics to present themselves as researchers rather than as teachers (Beck & Young, 2005; Sikes, 2006). High-scoring academics argue for greater recognition and managers use institutional scores for marketing and individual scores to raise productivity, promoting the growth of competition and 'managerialism'.

Restructuring and Gender

Although academic managers focus on 'merit', promotion decisions often favour research over teaching and service, and display a hierarchy of publication venues. Peer-reviewed articles in high-impact journals and scholarly books are more important than textbooks or edited collections, but assessment exercises heighten these judgments (Harding, 2002; Sikes, 2006). Women tend to occupy lower ranks in institutions/disciplines focusing on teaching and service. They publish fewer peer-reviewed articles, win fewer scholarly prizes, display less academic confidence, and work shorter hours (Nakhaie, 2007; Monroe et al., 2008). They also receive lower scores in research assessment exercises (Middleton, 2009). In contrast, more men occupy senior positions, including that of research chair. As of February 2009, in Canada, 83.5 per cent of Tier 1 research chairs (for full professors) and 68.8 per cent of Tier 2 research chairs (for intermediate scholars) were awarded to men (CAUT, 2009).

The stronger emphasis on market forces rewards entrepreneurs who develop large-scale projects with multiple collaborators and external funding. However, women's projects are smaller and more applied, relying more on qualitative research and female participants (Knights & Richards, 2003). Men more often become principle investigators on funded projects with travel allocations, due to seniority and more grant application (Waisbren et al., 2008).

Curtis (2005) argued that feminized fields have been disproportionately retrenched. Redundancies are often 'voluntary', but more women accept part-time work and early retirement (Tizard & Owen, 2001). With the focus on internationalization, mothers become disadvantaged because more women are sole parents and retain child care responsibilities even in couple households (Fox, 2005; O'Laughlin & Bischoff, 2005). As universities experience tighter budgets and restrict hiring, redressing the gender imbalance becomes less likely, especially with later retirement (Acker & Armenti, 2004).

Participant Reactions to Restructuring

Growing Bureaucracy

Many of the study's participants from the teaching university noted that their institution was 'changing too fast'. One female senior lecturer commented:

> I have been here 13 years and I've had 11 Heads of School. I have prepared about 250 different lectures because my teaching keeps getting changed. I'm often stressed but I am never bored [laughter].

These participants also reported 'unreasonable' research expectations and newcomers gaining faster promotion.

Participants from both universities mentioned that their love of scholarship was being destroyed by 'hyper-bureaucracy'. A senior male at the research university said:

> I've become unhappy with the way this university seems to be managed these days . . . the creeping managerial style, or the way in which human resources seems to be dictating what we are able to do.

A senior woman justified her early retirement decision when she commented:

> It is not the wonderful job that it used to be. . . . There's so much monitoring and inventing justifications and descriptions of what one is doing [laughter] . . . Under that heading, I'm including filling in PBRF forms.

Women seemed more concerned than men about the restructuring's negative impact. University downsizing can create obstacles for everyone, but especially for academics who lack job security or have few publications. Women academics have less job security than men and are less likely to publish peer-reviewed articles (Nakhaie, 2007).

Family-Friendly Policies?

Mothers in particular told disheartening stories of juggling parental leave with teaching, organizing breastfeeding between classes, and resolving day-care problems, especially during conferences and periods of child illness. Most mothers reported little support from managers or colleagues, and some received little family assistance. One mother described the deterioration of family-friendly practices when she said:

> I'm teaching across six classes, initially three were at 4:00 p.m. or later. When I pointed out that it was too difficult because I couldn't physically put [her daughter] in child care and get to her before it closed, because the class ended at 6:00 p.m., the response was not terribly good. One senior colleague actually said: 'I'm so damned tired of you people with kids', as if there was a choice in this. In the past, it was more negotiable. So, although there is a 'family friendly policy', it's being nibbled away at the edges.

Participants agreed that parenthood makes a huge impact on women's careers. Consequently, many women felt that having children was too challenging and made such comments as: 'I only had one (child) because it was far too hard.'

Working Long Hours

Scholarship entails long hours but can be particularly isolating if academics believe their research is undervalued or feel excluded from networks. A senior man mentioned the consuming nature of academic work: 'Research questions never go away and the next book project is always on your mind, which is very different from a lot of professions.' Many academics report that they are now working harder without 'getting ahead' (Menzies & Newson, 2008).

Women seemed to object more than men to the long working hours, such as this senior woman: 'I started to get a bit stressed about the way in which I was working right through every weekend as well as often quite late at night.' A junior woman said:

> I had to take stress leave, and all I wanted to do was get out . . . And then I started to realize that it wasn't the job that was the problem, it was the management and the structures. . . . I was good at my job. I just didn't feel it because I didn't get any recognition. Still don't.

The heightened productivity requirements are particularly challenging for mothers with young children. In the interviews, half of the mothers but none of the fathers were parenting alone.

Internationalization

Many participants came from overseas, but men in particular acknowledged their partner's support in relocating, while women spoke of the challenges of relocating alone or as sole parents. This sole mother expressed a concern typical of the women in the study when she said:

> Men seem to have no problems setting roots as young academics because they have women to look after them. I needed a wife, if that makes sense. . . . I mean for me, it's a high-pressure kind of job and to be in a foreign country . . . .

Many of the men assumed that they would relocate again to further their career, and some reported using overseas job offers to improve their circumstances, such as this senior man:

> Recently, I've had two job offers from other places and I have used those here to get better money and for extra leave. . . . In my experience, it's the only time that the university will offer you anything.

Several men doubted that they could move because their wives refused to relinquish their jobs or disrupt family life. This was particularly challenging for 'head-hunted' academics, but more men reported overseas opportunities or implied that relocation would be desirable. Some women seemed unaware that job offers could become bargaining chips and most disapproved of this tactic.

Male participants showed greater confidence about promotion. In many cases, women downplayed their scholarship, but some also made disparaging comments about 'overconfident' male colleagues, like this woman:

> I think a lot of people pad up their work big time and they put a showcase out to the dean saying 'this is what I'm doing and it's so wonderful and fabulous and I'm top of the class', and they're not.

Yet success within the current entrepreneurial and international environment relies largely on confidence and peer esteem.

Conclusion

Since the 1960s, universities have made notable inroads in employment equity, but they continue to reward academics who publish widely and remain fully employed until retirement, which more men do (Baker, 2009). Currently, universities are restructuring to deal with socio-political changes, but the new priorities tend to augment the gender gap. Interview participants lamented the growth of hyper-bureaucracy and the heightened research expectations. Most believed that they worked hard and deserved greater recognition. However, fewer women wanted to compete in an individualistic or managerial work environment, saying they preferred a more 'balanced life' (Baker, 2010).

More men accepted the long-hours culture and values inherent in the promotion system. The 'corporatized' university that privileges research and international prestige tends to favour masculinized behaviour that is competitive and sometimes confrontational. This suggests that the gender gap will persist even as more women rise through the ranks.

Notes

1. Canada, Australia, New Zealand, United Kingdom, and the United States.
2. In North America, 'senior' is defined as a full professor; in Australia, New Zealand, and the UK it refers to associate professor and professor.

3. The concept of 'peer esteem' is used in New Zealand and some other countries to refer to citations, positive reviews, awards, prizes, honours, fellowships, or any indicator from colleagues that they think an academic's work is of high quality.

References

AAUP (Association of American University Professors). (2006). *AAUP Faculty Gender Equity Indicators 2006*. Washington: AAUP.

Acker, S. & C. Armenti (2004). Sleepless in Academia. *Gender and Education*, 16, 1, 3–24.

Baker, Maureen (2010). Motherhood, Employment and the 'Child Penalty', *Women's Studies International Forum*, 33, 215–224.

———. (2009). Gender, Academia and the Managerial University. *New Zealand Sociology*, 24, 1, 24–48.

Bassett, Rachel Hile (2005). *Parenting and Professoring*. Vanderbilt University Press.

Beck, J. & M.F.D. Young (2005). The Assault on the Professions and the Restructuring of Academic and Professional Identities. *British Journal of Sociology of Education*, 26, 2, 183–197.

Bracken, Susan J., Jeanie K. Allen & Diane R. Dean, eds. (2006). *The Balancing Act: Gendered Perspectives in Faculty Roles and Work Lives*. Sterling, Virginia: Stylus Publishing.

CAUT (Canadian Association of University Teachers) (2008). Narrowing the Gender Gap: Women Academics in Canadian Universities. *CAUT Equity Review* 2, March. http://www.caut.ca/uploads/EquityReview2-en.pdf.

CAUT (2009). *CAUT Almanac of Post-Secondary Education 2009–2010*. Ottawa: Canadian Association of University Teachers.

Carrington, K. & A. Pratt (2003). How Far Have We Come? Gender Disparities in the Australian Higher Education System. *Current Issues Brief 31*. Canberra: Information & Research Services, Dept. of the Parliamentary Library.

Comer, Debra R. & Susuan Stites-Doe (2006). Antecedents and Consequences of Faculty Women's Academic-Parental Role Balancing. *Journal of Family and Economic Issues*, 27, 495–512.

Curtis, John W. (2005). Inequalities Persist for Women and Non-Tenure-Track Faculty: The Annual Report on the Economic Status of the Profession 2004–2005. *Academe*, 91, 2, 20–98.

Drakich, Janice & Penni Stewart (2007). Forty Years Later, How are University Women Doing? *Academic Matters*, February, 6–9.

Fisher, Donald, K. Rubenson, G. Jones & T. Shanahan (2009). The Political Economy of Post-Secondary Education: A Comparison of British Columbia, Ontario and Québec. *Higher Education*, 57, 549–566.

Fletcher, Catherine, R. Boden, J. Kent & J. Tinson (2007). Performing Women: The Gendered Dimensions of the UK New Research Economy. *Gender, Work and Organization*, 14, 5 (2007) September, 433–453.

Fox, Mary (2005). Gender, Family Characteristics, and Publication Productivity among Scientists. *Social Studies of Science*, 35, 131–150.

Harding, S. (2002). The Troublesome Concept of Merit. In *Gender, Teaching and Research in Higher Education: Challenges for the Twenty-First Century*, edited by G. Howie and A. Tauchert, 248–261. Aldershot: Ashgate.

Knights, D. & W. Richards (2004). Sex Discrimination in UK Academia. *Gender, Work and Organization*, 10, 2, 213–238.

Larner, Wendy & Richard LeHeron (2005). Neo-Liberalizing Spaces and Subjectivities: Reinventing New Zealand Universities. *Organization*, 12, 6, 843–862.

Menzies, Heather & Janice Newson (2008). Time, Stress and Intellectual Engagement in Academic Work: Exploring Gender Difference. *Gender, Work and Organization*, 15, 5, September, 504–522.

Middleton, Sue (2009). Becoming PBRF-able. In *Assessing the Quality of Educational Research in Higher Education*, edited by Tina Besley, 193–208. Rotterdam: Sense Publishers.

Mohrman, Kathryn, W. Ma & D. Baker (2008). The Research University in Transition: The Emerging Global Modal. *Higher Education Policy*, 21, 5–27.

Monroe K., S. Ozyurt, T. Wrigley & A. Alexander (2008). Gender Equality in Academia: Bad News from the Trenches, and Some Possible Solutions. *Perspectives on Politics*, 6, 2, 215–233.

Nakhaie, M. Reza (2007). Universalism, Ascription and Academic Rank: Canadian Professors, 1987–2000. *Canadian Review of Sociology and Anthropology*, 44, 3, 361–386.

New Zealand, Human Rights Commission (2008). *New Zealand Census of Women's Participation*. Wellington, New Zealand. http://www.neon.org.nz.

O'Laughlin, E.M. & L.G. Bischoff (2005). Balancing Parenthood and Academia: Work/Family Stress as Influenced by Gender and Tenure Status. *Journal of Family Issues*, 26, 79–106.

Probert, Belinda (2005). 'I Just Couldn't Fit It In': Gender and Unequal Outcomes in Academic Careers. *Gender, Work and Organization*, 12, 1, 50–72.

Side, Katherine & Wendy Robbins (2007). Institutionalizing Inequalities in Canadian Universities: The Canada Research Chairs Program. *NWSA Journal*. Special Issue: *Women, Tenure, and Promotion*, 19, 3, 163–81.

Sikes, P. (2006). Working in a 'New' University: In the Shadow of the Research Assessment Exercise? *Studies in Higher Education*, 31, 5, 555–568.

Sussman, Deborah & Lahouaria Yssaad (2005). The Rising Profile of Women Academics. *Perspectives*, February, 6–19.

Tahir, Tariq (2010). The Irresistable Rise of Academic Bureaucracy. *The Guardian*, 30 March. http://www.guardian.co.uk.

Taylor, P. & R. Braddock (2007). International University Ranking Systems and the Idea of University Excellence. *Journal of Higher Education Policy and Management*, 29, 3, 24–260.

Tizard, Barbara & Charlie Owen (2001). Activities and Attitudes of Retired University Staff, *Oxford Review of Education*, 27, 2, 253–270.

Waisbren, Susan E. et al. (2008). Gender Differences in Research Grant Applications and Funding Outcomes for Medical School Faculty. *Journal of Women's Health*, 17, 2, 207–214.

White, K. (2004). The Leaking Pipeline: Women Postgraduate and Early Career Researchers in Australia. *Tertiary Education and Management* 10, 3, 227–241.

CHAPTER 23

Education, Ethnonationalism, and Non-violence in Quebec

Matthew Lange

Education is popularly viewed as a cure for a number of social ills, including ethnic violence. Yet, Lange and Dawson (2010) find that a country's level of education is actually positively related to its level of ethnic violence. In particular, through a cross-national time-series analysis of 121 countries, they find that three different measures of education are positively and significantly related to ethnic violence, but that the findings are driven by low- and medium-income countries, with education being unrelated to ethnic violence among wealthy countries.

In this paper, I analyze Quebec to begin to explore potential reasons why education does not promote ethnic violence in wealthy countries. The analysis includes two parts: first, it describes the role of the educated in the Quebec **separatist** movement and the reasons for their strong support. Next, it investigates factors that prevented the movement from turning violent.

Education and the Quebec Independence Movement

From its very beginning and continuing to this day, the Quebec nationalist movement has been dominated by the educated elite. For example, several quantitative analyses of Parti Québécois (PQ) support show that the educated are greatly overrepresented among PQ supporters (Cuneo and Curtis 1974; Hamilton and Pinard 1976; McRoberts and Posgate 1980). Pinard and Kowalchuk (forthcoming) provide the most thorough analysis to date and find that the educated have dominated party administration and are the strongest support base of the PQ. In particular, they find that educated members of the intelligentsia and provincial public service have played among the most influential roles in the movement.

In line with the active involvement of the educated in the separatist movement, the movement became a powerful force in Quebec only after the educational system expanded dramatically and produced an increasingly large number of educated individuals. Per capita expenditure on education in constant dollars increased from a measly $3.85 in 1945 to $23.28 in 1960. By 1970, it had risen to $89.83, a level of per capita spending over 23 times greater than just 25 years earlier (Latouche 1974). An expansion of enrollment coincided with growing expenditure. The first area to expand was elementary education, and its student body grew by as much as 25 per cent annually in the late 1940s (Behiels 1985: 152). A similar but slightly later expansion occurred in secondary education. In 1952, only 4 per cent of francophones of secondary-school age attended school (Behiels 1985: 168). Shortly thereafter, however, public secondary schools were constructed throughout the province, and private schools were subsidized (Behiels 1985: 170; Linteau, Durocher, Robert, and Ricard 1991: 245). Through these efforts, the number of secondary students skyrocketed throughout the 1950s and 1960s, and the province approached universal secondary attendance by the late 1960s.

Education and educational expansion are linked to the separatist movement in different ways. For one, independence was often more in the economic, political, and social interests of the educated. Public sector provincial employees, for example, appear to have supported independence disproportionately—in part because it was in their personal interests and because they believed it would be best for Quebec (Behiels 1985: 44; Breton 1964; Gagnon and Montcalm 1990: 68; Heintzman 1983: 39). Considering the latter, the public sector has been very active in promoting state economic management in an effort to modernize Quebec and improve the economic position of francophone Quebeckers. And they saw independence as a means of giving themselves full control to do just this. Similarly, independence would place more power and resources in the hands of the public sector and would promote even further public sector expansion, thereby increasing the economic opportunities of educated francophones (Breton 1964).

Other analyses find that the frustration of educated francophones over their limited economic opportunities promoted their active and disproportionate support. Indeed, the opportunities of the francophone population in business and the federal administration were quite limited in the 1950s and 1960s, and studies find that anglophones held top positions and earned considerably more than francophones. Based on data from the 1970 census, for example, anglophone males earned between 11 and 25 per cent more than francophone males, and the earning differentials went up with education level, meaning that the educated francophones experienced a greater gap in income than less-educated francophones (Shapiro and Stelcner 1987: 98–100). Coinciding with this reality, a survey of francophone Québécois from 1970 to 1971 found that perceptions of inequality increased significantly with education level: the educated were more likely to believe that linguistic inequalities are real and that francophones face disadvantages in the labour market. The data also show that francophones with more education were more likely to report having experienced discrimination in the workplace and were much more likely to say that something needed to be done to address language-based inequality (Laczko 1987). Several qualitative analyses make similar arguments about the frustration of the educated over economic opportunities and their support for the separatist movement (Clift 1982: 22; Gagnon and Montcalm 1990: 9; Guindon 1964: 155; McRoberts and Posgate 1980: 119–121).

The Impediments of Ethnonationalist Violence in Quebec

While grievances and interests pushed many educated individuals to organize and support the Quebec separatist movement, the political and economic environment severely constrained grievances and reduced incentives for ethnonational militancy. In particular, the political and economic environment increased the costs of radicalism, diminished the benefits of radicalism, and helped reduce frustration. As a result, the separatist movement remained moderate and opposed militant action that would lead to ethnonationalist violence.

Despite periods of economic slowdown, post-World-War-II Canada (including Quebec) has experienced steady economic growth, and it currently has one of the highest living standards in the world: its UNDP Human Development Index was ranked fourth in the world in 2009. Along with general prosperity, the particularly advantaged economic position of the educated also suppressed movement radicalism. Education has been strongly and negatively related to unemployment in Quebec, meaning that the educated are well *under*-represented among the unemployed (Government of Quebec 2010). Even in 1982, a particularly difficult period of economic slowdown that affected the educated and less-educated alike, the unemployment rate of individuals in Quebec aged 25 and older with eight or fewer years of education was 13.6 per cent, but this rate declined steadily and consistently to only 5.8 per cent among individuals with university diplomas (Fortin 1984: 434).

The relatively deprived position of the francophone community vis-à-vis the anglophone community improved after World War II, and this is another factor that helps to explain the limited violence of the separatist movement. For instance, while significant earnings differentials existed between francophone and anglophone Québécois as late as 1970, these differentials had already improved considerably by that time and virtually disappeared by 1980. In fact, while educated francophones were most affected by inequality in 1970, by 1991 the economic returns of education were actually greater among francophones (Lian and Matthews 1998). Vaillancourt, Lemay, and Vaillancourt (2007) also found that the percentage of firms owned by francophones increased from 47 per cent in 1961 to 67 per cent in 2003. Thus, not only has the economic situation of francophones in Quebec improved in absolute terms, but it has also improved greatly relative to anglophones, and both of these changes limited the radicalism of the nationalist movement by reducing powerful grievances that can motivate violence. Along these lines, Stevenson (2006) describes how

the improved economic position of nationalists caused the movement to become increasingly moderate: 'By the mid-1970s, Quebec nationalists were becoming older and more affluent than they had been during the Quiet Revolution, and they had more to lose than before from economic uncertainty, disorder, and violence' (306).

The wavering support from university students for the **Front de libération de Québec (FLQ)** helps demonstrate this point. Many university students supported the FLQ at the beginning of the October Crisis (as demonstrated by participation in demonstrations). Yet, once the Canadian government enacted the **War Measures Act** in 1970 in reaction to the FLQ's kidnappings, the government clamped down on students, and student support dried up almost instantly. Bédard (1998) points to two main reasons for their rapid disengagement. First, the eventual death of Quebec minister of labour Pierre Laporte at the hands of his FLQ captors repulsed students, showing that their grievances were not powerful enough for them to support violent militantism (188). Second, continued support of the FLQ posed potential dangers to the students because the government was now arresting people associated with the FLQ (187). And, because students had great potential for mobility and risked it by joining a militant movement, they chose to disassociate themselves from it. Thus, government forces keeping surveillance over students shortly after the War Measures Act was declared concluded that student radicalism had disappeared: 'Students are concerned now about their examinations and are not in the mood for extra curricular meetings' (Bédard 1998: 171).

Besides the general availability of resources and the improving economic situation of the Québécois, the case also suggests that effective democratic government—which is strongly related to national wealth—limited ethnonationalist violence in several ways. For one thing, the Canadian state—at all levels—used very little coercion in dealing with the separatist movement and therefore did not spark violence through its own violent methods. Indeed, state violence against particular ethnic communities commonly instigates or intensifies ethnic violence, but the Canadian state did not use physical violence against the separatist movement.

An example that highlights the limited use of violence most clearly is, somewhat ironically, the enactment of the War Measures Act by Prime Minister Pierre Trudeau's government in 1970 after the FLQ's kidnapping of British diplomat James Cross and Pierre Laporte. After the declaration, the Canadian military had a strong presence in Quebec, and 497 people were incarcerated (of whom 62 were eventually charged and 32 refused bail). The act was only declared after the premier of Quebec and mayor of Montreal demanded it, showing how wary the federal government was of using coercion. In addition, the fact that nearly all of those detained were quickly released, that the act was only used temporarily, and that the police and military did not beat or kill people all helped contain radicalism. In other countries with less democratic and less effective governments, states of emergency pose much greater risks of violence because of a greater willingness of the government to resort to violence and because of the ineffectiveness of government to maintain law and order.

Besides very limited state violence, neither the Canadian nor the Quebec government has formally discriminated against francophone Canadians in the post-World-War-II period, and this restraint is a second way through which the political institutions limited violence. Several recent works have found that formal discrimination designates individuals as subordinate and outside the political community and is therefore an important source of ethnonationalist grievances and, consequently,

violence. In Quebec, this lack of formal political discrimination therefore deterred violence. In fact, political reforms actually sought to increase the presence of francophones in both the public and private sector, a policy that limited even further the willingness of individuals to resort to radicalism in pursuit of independence.

Finally, yet likely of greatest importance, political institutions have limited ethnic violence in Quebec by providing a clear means for disgruntled actors to address their grievances. For example, the federal government has consistently attempted to accommodate Québécois nationalism by treating Quebec fairly in its distribution of equalization payments (a practice that some provinces would say in fact gives Quebec an unfair advantage), by making a concerted effort to increase the place of French within the federal government, and by allowing a separatist party (the Bloc Québécois) to participate in the national parliament. More importantly, the federal system of government allowed francophone Québécois to control provincial politics and thereby implement policy to address ethnonational grievances. Bill 101, with its efforts to improve and protect the use of French in the public and private sectors as well as in public education, is a notable example. In this way, most francophones desiring change have sought to pursue it peacefully through formal politics, not violence. As a consequence, the leaders of the separatist movement—although sympathizing with the FLQ's grievances—spoke out strongly and unequivocally against the organization's use of violence and sought change through peaceful means.

References

Bédard, Éric. 1998. *Chronique d'une insurrection appréhendée: la crise d'octobre et le milieu universitaire*. Saint-Laurent: Septentrion.

Behiels, Michael. 1985. *Prelude to Quebec's Quiet Revolution: Liberalism versus Neo-Nationalism, 1945–1960*. Montreal: McGill-Queen's University Press.

Breton, Albert. 1964. 'The Economics of Nationalism.' *Journal of Political Economy*, 72 (4): 376–386.

Clift, Dominique. 1982. *Quebec Nationalism in Crisis*. Montreal: McGill-Queen's University Press.

Cuneo, Carl, and James Curtis. 1974. 'Quebec Separatism:

An Analysis of Determinants within Social-Class Levels.' *Canadian Review of Sociology*, 11 (1): 1–29.

Fortin, Pierre. 'Le Chômage de jeunes au Québec: aggravation et concentration, 1966–1982.' *Industrial Relations*, 39 (3): 419–448.

Gagnon, Alain, and Mary Beth Montcalm. 1990. *Quebec Beyond the Quiet Revolution*. Toronto: Nelson Canada.

Government of Quebec. 2010. 'The Labour Market: Integration of Graduates into the Labour Market.' Retrieved 24 March, 2010. http://www.mels.gouv.qc.ca/STAT/indic01/indic01A/ia01603.PDF.

Guindon, Hubert. 1964. 'Social Unrest, Social Class, and Quebec's Bureaucratic Revolution.' *Queen's Quarterly*, 71:150–162.

Guntzel, Ralph. 2000. '"Rapprocher les Lieux du Pouvoire": The Quebec Labour Movement and Quebec Sovereigntism, 1960–2000.' *Labour/Le Travail*, 46: 369–395.

Hamilton, Richard, and Maurice Pinard. 1976. 'The Bases of Parti Québécois Support in Recent Quebec Elections.' *Canadian Journal of Political Science*, 9 (1): 3–26.

Heintzman, Ralph. 1983. 'The Political Culture of Quebec, 1840–1960.' *Canadian Journal of Political Science*, 16 (1): 3–59.

Laczko, Leslie. 1987. 'Perceived Communal Inequalities in Quebec: A Multidimensional Analysis.' *Canadian Journal of Sociology*, 12 (1/2): 83–110.

Lange, Matthew, and Andrew Dawson. Forthcoming. 'Education and Ethnic Violence: A Cross-National Time-Series Analysis.' *Nationalism and Ethnic Politics*.

Latouche, Daniel. 1974. 'La vrai nature de . . . la Revolution Tranquille.' *Canadian Journal of Political Science*, 7 (3): 525–536.

Linteau, Paul-André, René Durocher, Jean-Claude Robert, and François Ricard. 1991. *Quebec Since 1930*. Trans. Robert Chodos and Ellen Garmaise. Toronto: James Lorimer & Co.

Lian, Jason, and David Matthews. 1998. 'Does the Vertical Mosaic Still Exist? Ethnicity and Income in Canada, 1991.' *Canadian Review of Sociology and Anthropology*, 35 (4): 461–481.

McRoberts, Kenneth, and Dale Posgate. 1980. *Quebec: Social Change and Political Crisis*. Toronto: McClelland and Stewart Limited.

Pinard, Maurice and Lisa Kowalchuk. Forthcoming. 'New Middle Class or Intellectuals, as Class Bases of the Quebec Movement: An Empirical Assessment.' In Maurice Pinard, *The Quebec Independence Movement*. Montreal: McGill-Queen's University Press.

Shapiro, D.M., and M. Stelcner. 1987. 'Earnings Disparities among Linguistic Groups in Quebec, 1970–1980.' *Canadian Public Policy*, 13 (1): 97–104.

Stevenson, Garth. 2006. *Parallel Paths: The Development of Nationalism in Ireland and Quebec*. Montreal: McGill-Queen's University Press.

Trudel, Marcel, and Genevieve Jain. 1970. *Canadian History Textbooks: A Comparative Study*. Ottawa: Queen's Printer.

Vaillancourt, Francois, Dominique Lemay, and Luc Laillancourt. 2007. 'Laggards No More: The Changed Socioeconomic Status of Francophones in Quebec. No. 103.' C.D. Howe Institute.

CHAPTER 24

From International Universities to Diverse Local Communities? International Students in Halifax and Beyond

Sinziana Chira

Introduction

Highly skilled migrants are often construed as populations to be attracted by competing developed nations (Li, 2008; Castles, 2002; Urry, 1995). Their desirability is based on the assumption that **human capital** (Bourdieu, 1986) assures successful post-migratory integration, while keeping the costs of integration low for the host state.

This line of argument has practically translated into a series of shifts in the immigration policies of the democracies of the Global North since the late 1980s—shifts often characterized as neo-liberal (Sassen, 2007; Harvey, 2004; Boyd, 2000). Most notably, the move toward introducing the points system as the basis for immigrants' selection has, in effect, empowered governments in the Global North to shape migration flows, giving rise to 'designer immigrants' (Simmons, 1999). However, as Urry (1995) predicted in his analysis of modern global capitalism, national governments no longer hold the monopoly on attracting, selecting, or bearing the costs for integrating skilled migrants. Increasingly, non-governmental actors, from transnational corporations to localized businesses and universities, have taken up roles to assure that they hold a competitive advantage when it comes to benefiting from the inflow of bright foreign minds. This stance has opened spaces for negotiation between states and private actors regarding duties, roles, and accountability vis-à-vis migrants' integration success.

This paper investigates the dynamics of such spaces by considering the cases of two Atlantic Canadian universities that have become increasingly instrumental in attracting and retaining highly skilled international graduates to Halifax, Nova Scotia. The Halifax example undermines the myth of the 'cost-effective' highly skilled immigrant by illustrating that integration processes demand resource mobilization in ways that have to match the socioeconomic complexities of incoming populations.

Study Methodology

This analysis relies on data that emerged from 14 semi-structured interviews conducted in Halifax in 2009. Among the interviewed were federal and provincial government officials, staff and administration from two of the city's largest and most international universities, and representatives of non-governmental organizations (NGOs) operating in the city's business and immigration settlement sectors. The interviews were designed to parallel a study conducted in Moncton, New Brunswick, by Wade and Belkhodja (forthcoming) and to address the implications of international students' rising numbers for the region's demographic challenges. The Halifax study was commissioned by

the Association of Atlantic Universities (AAU) in collaboration with the Atlantic Metropolis Centre.

Demographics in Halifax and Nova Scotia

Atlantic Canada is a region traditionally associated with the out-migration of youth and low immigrant attraction and retention rates (Murphy & de Finney, 2008). While Nova Scotia makes up about 2.9 per cent of Canada's population, between 2001 and 2006 it received on average only 0.7 per cent of Canada's immigrants—a decline from 1.2 per cent for the 1991–1996 period (Denton et al., 2009, p. 11). The consequence is an aging population and a diminishing labour force.

In 2006, the average age in the province was 41, while the labour force under 25 made up only 17 per cent of the population (Denton et al., 2009). The province is also lacking in diversity: 94.6 per cent of Nova Scotians were born in Nova Scotia, while only 6 per cent are first-generation Canadians, compared to the national average of 23.8 per cent. Only 4.2 per cent of Nova Scotians self-identify as a visible minority (Statistics Canada Census, 2006). In this backdrop, the province stands out through its success in attracting international students. Currently, Nova Scotia ranks as the fifth most popular destination for international students Canada-wide, hosting just under 7,000 young foreigners (CIC, 2009). In fact, both Halifax and Nova Scotia as a whole host about twice as many international students as permanent residents, a situation that is not mirrored on the national scale. Table 24.1 and Figures 24.1 and 24.2 illustrate these trends.

Table 24.1 International Students (IS), Permanent Residents, (PR) and the Population of Halifax and Nova Scotia (2009)

TERRITORY	POPULATION (POP)	PERMANENT RESIDENTS (PR)	PR/POP %	INTERNATIONAL STUDENTS (IS)	IS/POPULATION %
Halifax	398,000	1,792	0.45	4,702	1.18
NS	938,200	2,424	0.26	6,614	0.71
Canada	33,739,900	252,124	0.75	196,227	0.58

Source: Population numbers: StatsCan Population Estimates and Projections, 2009; Immigrant and International student numbers: CIC, Facts and Figures, 2009.

Note: Figure 24.1 situates the numbers presented in Table 24.1 in temporal perspective, illustrating a comparison between the numbers of permanent residents and international students from 1999 to 2009

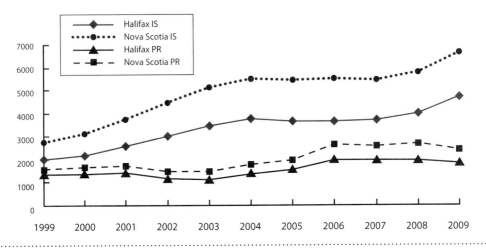

Figure 24.1 Numbers of International Students (IS) and Permanent Residents (PR) in the Province of Nova Scotia and the City of Halifax between 1999 and 2009

Source: CIC, Facts and Figures 2009.

Note: Figure 24.2 further illustrates those trends in comparison, this time on the national scale.

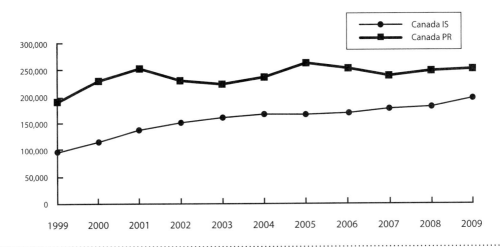

Figure 24.2 Numbers of International Students (Is) and Permanent Residents (PR) in Canada between 1999 and 2009

Source: CIC, Facts and Figures 2009.

Most students studying on the campuses included in this research come from China, while students from the United States, Korea, Japan, the Caribbean, and the Middle East together total about the same number of students. This trend is consistent with provincial rates (Akbari et al., 2007, p. 48).

Discussion and Conclusions

The region's success in attracting international students is, according to those interviewed for this study, the result of sustained investments from the province's top universities, which have created lucrative international recruitment strategies. Private sector organizations, such as EduNova and the AAU, have also been active in positioning Nova Scotia as a brand in the international education market.

In the interviews I conducted, it became clear that private sector involvement was seen as a response-solution to the lack of support from governmental branches, which have been reluctant to invest in adequately promoting Canada on the international education market. Thus, while governments in countries such as Australia and the UK have been building strong national brands for their higher education systems for the last 20 years, Canada's national brand came out only in 2008, in a manner described by university strategists and recruiters as 'timid at best'. Nonetheless, the presence of international students in growing numbers has sparked the interest of stakeholders outside universities. Therefore, Canada's government has shifted its citizenship policies to fast-track applications from international graduates of Canadian universities.

In 2008, Citizenship and Immigration Canada (CIC) launched the Canadian Experience Class stream, which offers permanent residence to international graduates with relevant work experience in Canada. Similarly, the Nova Scotia Office of Immigration (NSOI) has its Provincial Nominee International Graduate stream, which offers international graduates fast-track permanent residence with the condition that they secure permanent job contracts in the province. Also since 2008, international students have been able to work off-campus while studying and to apply for temporary work-permits after graduation without pre-existing job offers. Those interviewed at NGOs and on university campuses said that these changes reflect years of negotiations between universities, NGOs, employer groups, and government representatives. University staff noted that the off-campus work permit was a change they were particularly involved with as it offers students the opportunity to gain Canadian work experience and it helps pay tuition fees. In effect, universities took on direct involvement in the administration of off-campus work permits.

Currently, staff on university campuses across Canada devote university resources toward the evaluation of work permit applications from their international students. Only the university-approved applications reach CIC. Meanwhile, NGO representatives involved with the local business sectors underlined their lobbying activities regarding the post-graduation work permits, which, in theory, are supposed to give local businesses a competitive advantage in retaining bright foreign minds. This argument speaks to a growing literature on 'the ideal immigrant' in the Atlantic Canadian context, which points to the classed, gendered, and racialized nuances of such descriptions of desirability (Barber, 2008; Dobrowolsky, 2007; Tastsoglou et al., 2007).

In this context, international students theoretically fit the bill of 'ideal immigrant' better than other immigration streams. They are young, trained in Canada and mostly involved in high-tech, science, or entrepreneurial sectors, as, based on the data I obtained from the universities in the study, the majority of international students are working toward their science, engineering, and business administration degrees. Thus, they promise to become highly productive workers in the knowledge economy, while guaranteeing to be least burdensome on social services. Through their education in Canada, not only should they be able to bypass lengthy and costly processes of language skills and education recognition (Reitz, 2007), they are also supposedly familiar with Canadian life, and more anchored in Canadian communities than other categories of migrants.

Such characteristics, matched with recent results of the Canada First survey (Humphries

& Knight-Grofe, 2009), which notes that about one in two international students intend to stay in Canada after graduation (p. 16), should in theory position Nova Scotia at an advantage with regard to attracting highly skilled new migrants. However, as Akbari et al. (2007) illustrate, the province continues to lag behind in attracting new migrants, and especially those deemed 'highly skilled'. To a certain extent, this may reflect points of disconnect between discourse, policy, and practice among the various government agencies involved. As recruiters interviewed noted, incoming students are encouraged to understand their stay in Canada as temporary by border agencies, as any statements of long-term immigration plans translate into immediate rejection for student visa applicants.

Furthermore, in the Halifax case, international students' adaptation to Canadian life has not been going smoothly. Incoming students are visible and audible minorities, standing out in the homogeneous academic and social environments of Halifax. Anecdotes of racism in the classroom and on the streets of the city marked some of the interviews with university staff. Meanwhile, NGOs and university career services underlined that international graduates face challenges in finding adequate jobs despite their in-demand skills and Canadian degrees. The most cited impediment was the graduates' 'lack of ties to the community'.

Staff on university campuses noted that in many fields, jobs are not even advertised in Halifax, as positions are filled through socially established ties. This observation is in line with survey results released by the province's largest university, Dalhousie, where 67.5 per cent of graduates stated that they made use of their social networks (family, friends) in their job search, while 33.8 per cent actually obtained their job through their social network (Destinations Survey, 2009, p. 6). Moreover, NGO representatives who work with the city's business community note that employers are often reluctant to hire graduates because of 'foreign accents' as well as confusion regarding the legal status of foreign youths in Canada.

Such issues are not surprising given Halifax's lack of ethnic diversity as well as the novelty of the changes regarding the status of international graduates in Canada. Meanwhile, NGO workers noted they are in the process of lobbying the government for funding to start programs that aim to both educate employers and help match graduates with available jobs. Their efforts are undermined by the status of international students and graduates as temporary residents in Canada. The local and federal government branches respond by encouraging community actors to cover the costs of integrating international graduates into the local communities. Universities are cast as the designated solution, particularly as they are collecting differential fees from international students.

However, the extent of the universities' involvement in regulatory processes is a matter of debate on and beyond the campus. For example, policy changes concerning off-campus work permits have led interviewees to note that university resources are currently stretched and stressed by external needs. Moreover, faculty and administration seem to have increasingly divergent views of how university resources should be managed regarding the recruitment of international students, with faculty raising concerns about ethics and the roles of for-profit actors in bringing students to Canada. There are also contradictions between recruitment activities initiated by universities and regional immigration retention goals. Thus, university leaders underlined that they focus on attracting as many successful international students as possible.

However, in this context, successful international students are not necessarily successful future Canadian citizens. For example, on both campuses, staff in charge of recruiting noted that they plan to intensify activities in countries where governments are willing to pay for citizens' tuition abroad, despite the fact that this arrangement is generally conditional upon the return of the graduate to the home country upon graduation. Therefore, such students are not eligible for permanent residence in Canada. Similar tensions also characterize the post-graduation integration part of the process. Government representatives note that it should be universities and employer groups that invest in matching graduates with jobs, because they have the most to gain from the graduates' success.

Consequently, the government supports various projects aimed at convincing universities and other private sector actors to invest in graduates' integration. So far, one such initiative, the Halifax Regional Immigration Leadership Council, dissolved in 2008 and another, the Halifax Pilot, was started in 2010, currently partially funded by the government in collaboration with a business sector NGO and aiming to foster mentoring initiatives between universities and local employers. The government's stance toward limited involvement is framed by an understanding of 'the ideal Atlantic Canadian citizen' in terms that are in line with the academic analyses of neo-liberalism outlined earlier in this chapter.

Thus, one NSOI representative described the 'ideal immigrant' for the province as follows:

> We want people who are motivated and who, hmm . . . some people come here and, for example, say 'You say you want immigrants, find me a job!' No, we want you [the immigrant] to bring the expertise

that we need and you find a job and now we have the need for you to stay here if it works out.

In line with this view, the costs of integration for international graduates are recast as the responsibility of incoming immigrants, as well as various non-governmental actors, from universities to NGOs. The Halifax example highlights some larger trends in Canadian immigration policies, which are in turn integrated within global approaches to migrant populations and rising practices to alleviate integration costs by bringing in 'designer' immigrants. However, as this analysis shows, cost-to-benefit calculations become nuanced by various power dynamics as well as socially shaped characteristics such as race and class, which in turn reconstruct the success of 'the ideal immigrant'. In Halifax, spaces of negotiation between the needs and duties of governmental branches and private stakeholders continue to shape the success of international graduates in becoming Canadian citizens.

References

Akbari, A. H., Lynch H., McDonald, J. T. and W. Rankaduwa. 2007. *Socioeconomic and demographic profiles of immigrants in Nova Scotia*. Halifax: Metropolis Project.

Barber, P. G. 2008. The ideal immigrant? Gendered class subjects in Philippine-Canada migration. *Third World Quarterly*, 29(7): 1265–1285.

Bourdieu, P. 1986. The forms of capital. In J. Richardson (Ed.) *Handbook of theory and research for the sociology of education*. New York: Greenwood Press, 241–258.

Boyd, M. 2000. *Matching workers to work: The case of Asian immigrant engineers in Canada*. Working paper 14. San Diego: The Centre for Comparative Immigration Studies.

Castles, S. 2002. Migration and community formation under conditions of globalization. *International Migration Review*, 36(4): 1143–1168.

CIC Facts and Figures: *Immigration overview, Permanent and temporary residents*. 2009. Ottawa: Citizenship and Immigration Canada.

Destination Survey. 2009. Halifax: Dalhousie University Career Service Centre.

Denton, T.F., Feaver, C.H. and B.G. Spencer. 2009. An economic future with smaller numbers: The population and labour force outlook for the Atlantic region. Halifax: Atlantic Institute for Market Studies.

Dobrowolsky, A. 2007. (In)Security and citizenship: Security, im/migration and the shrinking citizenship regimes. *Theoretical Inquiries in Law*, 8: 629–661.

Harvey, D. 2005. *A brief history of neoliberalism*. Oxford: Oxford University Press.

Humphries, J. and J. Knight-Grofe. 2009. *Canada first: The 2009 survey of international students*. Winnipeg: Canadian Bureau for International Education.

Li, P. S. 2008. Immigration from China to Canada in the age of globalization: Issues of brain gain and brain loss. *Pacific Affairs*, 81(2): 217–239.

Murphy, T. and J. de Finney. 2008. Introduction. Our diverse cities: Atlantic region. *Our Diverse Cities*, 5: 3–8.

Reitz, J. G. 2007. Immigrant employment success in Canada. Parts I & II. *International Migration and Integration*, 8: 11–62.

Sassen, S. 2007. *A sociology of globalization*. New York: W.W. Norton and Co.

Statistics Canada Census: Nova Scotia profile. (2006). Ottawa: Statistics Canada.

Statistics Canada Population Estimates and Projections. (2009). Ottawa: Statistics Canada.

Simmons, A. B. 1999. Economic integration and designer immigrants: Canadian policy in the 1990s. In M. J. Castro (Ed.) *Free markets, open societies, closed borders? Trends* in international migration policy in the Americas. Miami: University of Miami Press, 53–71.

Tastsoglou, E., Crocker, D., Dobrowolsky, A., Keeble, E. and C. C. Moncayo. 2007. *Security and immigration, changes and challenges: Immigrant and ethnic communities in Atlantic Canada, presumed guilty?* Gatineau:

Department of Canadian Heritage, the Government of Canada.

Urry, J. 1995. *Consuming places.* London: Routledge.

Wade, M. and C. Belkhodja. (publication forthcoming). Managing a new diversity on a small campus: The case of l'Université de Moncton (Canada).

CHAPTER 25

Segregation versus Self-Determination: A Black and White Debate on Canada's First Africentric School

Shaun Chen

On January 29, 2008, the Toronto District School Board (TDSB) holds a special meeting to consider a controversial plan to combat a staggering 40 per cent dropout rate of black students in Toronto. After hearing from 22 delegations of parents, community leaders, educators, and researchers, the board of trustees approve Canada's first-ever **Africentric** alternative school by a vote of 11 to 9. I am one of the trustees in favour. While the meeting is meant to give closure to the contentious debate, I am left with many more questions than answers. The conscience of a nation is set on the Africentric school, which has provoked a plethora of public discourses on race, **racism**, and education. Filled with rhetoric and dichotomies, it is a running battle of conflicting words and statements, fuelling further confusion in an already complicated and discursive debate.

In this paper, I offer a critical analysis of the Africentric school debate within an equity framework that attempts to make sense of the diverse and divergent views presented by trustees, delegations, and the print media. Such a framework recognizes that schooling has 'largely failed in its promise to promote a more egalitarian society' and instead, 'in

content and process, contributes to the subordination of substantial segments of the population' (Wotherspoon, 2009, p. 33). The education of black students must therefore be understood in the context of social practices that maintain or reinforce racial hierarchy. Making sense of the Africentric school debate requires careful consideration of the racialized realities faced by black students.

Exploring Lived Experiences

Indeed, the final board decision was political, fuelled by a flurry of forceful arguments from both sides. What was often ignored in the ensuing hysteria was a critical discussion of race and racism in the current school system. **Critical race theory** suggests there is a collective 'voice' (Delgado, 1990, p. 98) spoken by people of colour from racialized experiences (Tate, 1997). Academics have used this theory in educational research 'not to determine whether racism exists but to determine the manner in which racial meanings and identities provide the basis for action, that being educational decision making for students of colour' (Evans, 2007, p. 166). The ideas stemming from critical race theory form a theoretical framework for this paper. The lived experiences of black students provide a lens through which the Africentric school debate is analyzed and understood.

Existing research confirms common threads in the educational experiences of black children across North America. A study involving three U.S. high schools, for example, identified struggles faced by black students, such as negative stereotypes, colour-blindness, and prevailing school images and curriculum that served the interests of those in power (Evans, 2007). Similarly, a Toronto-area study of black students uncovered day-to-day experiences of differential treatment and low expectations, as well as a lack of black teachers and the absence of diverse cultural knowledge in schools (Dei, 1996). Black Canadian students have been disengaged to the point of leaving school in part because of the absence of Africentricity, 'a world-view embraced in opposition to the subjugation of non-White peoples by Eurocentrism' (Dei, 1996, p. 181).

The narratives of black students paint a dire reality of biases and exclusion in their educational experiences. While the dominant discourse affirms those in power by presenting an illusion of integration, the experiences of white people and people of colour continue to differ in all facets of life, including education (Bell, 2003). Different from such earlier forms of racism as slavery and institutionalized segregation, present-day racism in Canada and other liberal democratic societies is less overt yet 'deeply embedded in the collective belief system and practices that operate within social, cultural, political and economic systems' (Tator & Henry, 2000, p. 124). Those who fall outside of 'the mythical norms that define "Canadianness"—that is, to be White, male, heterosexual, Christian and English-speaking' (Tator & Henry, 2000, p. 123)—experience a tension between their lived experiences as people of colour and the dominant discourses of 'democratic racism' (Henry, Tator, Mattis, & Rees, 2000, p. 19).

Analyzing the Debate

To begin, I transcribed the speeches by trustees and delegations and assembled a collection of newspaper articles, editorials, and letters to the editor concerning the Africentric school published in the *Toronto Star*, the *Globe and Mail*, and the *National Post*—the three most-circulated English-language newspapers in Canada (Penney, 2009)—as well as the local black community newspaper *Share* (circulated in the GTA). Then, I applied a content analysis to the arguments found in the artifacts, using an inductive approach to identify broader themes arising out of similar or related arguments (Berg, 2007).

As a result, I identified three main themes in favour of the Africentric school: (a) presence of racism in the mainstream school system; (b) self-determination; and (c) equity. I also identified three main themes against the Africentric school: (a) absence of racism in the mainstream school system; (b) segregation; and (c) formal **equality**. The ordering of these themes is deliberate as they are in direct contrast and contradiction to one another, thus forming three contesting pairs: (a) presence of racism versus absence of racism; (b) self-determination versus segregation; and (c) equity versus formal equality.

Presence of Racism versus Absence of Racism

Africentric school supporters point to the presence of racism in the mainstream school system. Black students are consistently viewed and treated differently, resulting in their higher rates of suspensions and expulsions. Trustee Sheila Cary-Meagher says discipline is disproportionately applied to young black men, who also face low expectations from educators. Looking back on his schooling, black teacher Nigel Barriffe recalls, 'They told our parents we should be streamlined into (a lower level) and that maybe you guys should be a tradesperson.' Other Africentric school proponents cite the overall disengagement and alienation experienced by black students. Trustee Bruce Davis says part of the problem is a lack of diverse educators: 'I go into a school and I sit up on the stage with the teachers and the staff, they are White, and I look at the gym floor and I see the United Nations. That (discrepancy) has got to change.'

On the other hand, the arguments in the absence of racism theme suggest that racial discrimination in the mainstream school system is insignificant or simply does not exist. One-third of all the arguments used by Africentric school opponents fall under this theme. Some of the most compelling points focus on social, cultural, individual, and familial factors outside the educational system—but through a colour-blind lens that fails to acknowledge the realities of racialized experiences. Second World War veteran Henry Raston says race is irrelevant because student success is only possible when 'parents are fully involved'. Others put the blame on the greater societal issues of poverty and illiteracy, as well as individual factors such as personal discipline and decision making. Implied in this discourse of denial is the assumption that 'because Canada is a society that upholds the ideals of a liberal democracy, it could not possibly be racist' (Henry et al., 2000, p. 26).

Self-Determination versus Segregation

Speaking at a delegation, black community leader Angela Wilson proclaims, 'It's not about segregation, it's about self-determination.' Like Wilson, many supporters describe the Africentric school as a place for enablement. June Veecock reminds readers in her 7 February 2008 letter to *Share* that 'no parent will be forced to send their child or children to this school.' For those who choose to attend, the Africentric school promises a safe space where students can experience that sense of belonging often missing in regular schools (Dei, 1997, p. 266). Proponents also point to the various forms of separation that currently exist in schools and communities. 'Mystified' by public cries of segregation, Michael Milech writes in his 1 February 2008 letter to the *National Post*: 'No one claims that Catholic schools or Greek schools are the second coming of apartheid; why would black schools be any more deleterious?'

Under the opposing theme, the Africentric school is indeed likened to institutionalized segregation. States the *National Post* editorial on 31 January, 2008: 'Segregating black students in a

separate-but-equal building . . . will merely serve to turn the school into one long, endless field trip back to 1954.' The segregated schools of the Jim Crow era, however, were designed to subordinate black children by force. Nonetheless, opponents contend that an Africentric school inadvertently removes diversity. Trustee Gerri Gershon asserts, 'Our public school system in Canada is the one institution where kids of every colour, culture and religion can come together . . . to gain an appreciation of one another.' Multiculturalism can undoubtedly promote understanding, but 'declarations of the need for tolerance and harmony tend to conceal the messy business of structural and systemic inequality' (Henry et al., 2000, p. 30).

Equity versus Formal Equality

Accounting for 45 per cent of all arguments made in support of the Africentric school, equity is by far the most popular theme in the whole debate. One of the theme's central arguments is that student needs are met in different ways. Recognizing Eurocentricity as the status quo in the mainstream school system, Africentric school proponents argue for more inclusive and culturally relevant curriculum and pedagogy. Donna Harrow, co-author of the Africentric school proposal put forth by the community, reminds trustees of the board's long-standing process for establishing alternative programs. Referring to the 40 existing specialized schools at the TDSB, trustee Bruce Davis says, 'Parents who are fighting to keep their children in school have alternatives if they believe their current school is not meeting their children's needs.'

Meanwhile, opponents use arguments in the formal equality theme to suggest that an Africentric school does not support student success for all. They contend that approval of the school will place the board on a slippery slope toward segregation across the system. 'Mark my words, if we allow this type of model to be implemented we will have many groups before us,' warns trustee Chris Tonks. Delegation Henry Raston says the equality provisions under the **Canadian Charter of Rights and Freedoms** mean that the board 'will not be able to refuse' separate schools for other groups. Equality, however, does not imply treating everyone the same. Equity is 'a pathway to achieving equality' (p. 11), where people may be treated differently in order to reduce social hierarchy (Burke & Eichler, 2006). Specific consideration must therefore be given to the ways in which underachievement is compounded by the racialized realities faced by black students.

Conclusion

As with **liberalism**, the Africentric school debate is 'full of paradoxes and contradictions and assumes different meanings, depending on one's social location and angle of vision' (Henry et al., 2000, p. 30). Emerging on one side of the debate are the Africentric school opponents, reiterating the dominant discourses of race and racism. Their arguments can range from the subtleness of an underlying racist tone to the explicitness of outright racist statements, but it is their defence of such liberal ideals as multiculturalism, harmony, and tolerance that is perhaps most intriguing. Herein lie some of the most convincing, well-intentioned and seemingly progressive arguments made against the Africentric school.

Through the interpretive lens of equity and critical race theory, such arguments used against the school are juxtaposed against the hidden narratives of black students' lived experiences of racism. It becomes clear, then, that the perspectives put forth by opponents rest on misinformation and false assumptions of what the school will be and for whom. The arguments fail to address the underlying impetus of improving black student outcomes. They also fail to understand the direness of current racialized realities and the means through which equality is achieved. Instead, they serve to help demonstrate how racism is deeply embedded within ostensibly liberal claims to racial equality.

References

Bell, L. A. 2003. Telling tales: What stories can teach us about racism. *Race Ethnicity and Education*, 6(1), 3–28.

Berg, B. L. 2007. *Qualitative research methods for the social sciences* (6th ed.). Boston: Pearson Education.

Burke, M. A., & Eichler, M. 2006. *The BIAS FREE framework*. Geneva: Global Forum for Health Research.

Dei, G. J. S. 1996. The role of Afrocentricity in the inclusive curriculum in Canadian schools. *Canadian Journal of Education/Revue canadienne de l'éducation*, 21(2), 170–186.

Dei, G. J. S. 1997. The social construction of a 'drop-out': Dispelling the myth. In G. J. S. Dei, J. Mazzuca, E. McIsaac, & J. Zine (Eds.), *Reconstructing 'drop-out': A critical ethnography of the dynamics of black students' disengagement from school* (pp. 263–273). Toronto: University of Toronto Press.

Delgado, R. 1990. When a story is just a story: Does voice really matter? *Virginia Law Review*, 76(1), 95–111.

Evans, A. E. 2007. School leaders and their sensemaking about race and demographic change. *Educational Administration Quarterly*, 43(2), 159–188.

Henry, F., Tator, C., Mattis, W., & Rees, T. 2000. *The colour of democracy: Racism in Canadian society* (2nd ed.). Toronto: Harcourt Brace and Company.

Penney, S. 2009. *Circulation data report 2008*. Toronto: Canadian Newspaper Association.

Tate, W. F. 1997. Critical race theory and education: History, theory, and implications. *Review of Research in Education*, 22, 195–247.

Tator, C., & Henry, F. 2000. The role and practice of racialized discourse in culture and cultural production. *Journal of Canadian Studies*, 35(3), 120–137.

Wotherspoon, T. 2009. *The sociology of education in Canada* (3rd ed.). Toronto: Oxford University Press.

Questions for Critical Thought

CHAPTER 22

1. Like Warren in his paper in Part I, Baker observes an internationalizing trend in universities. How does her explanation of the rise of the research university help us to understand recent changes in the university's structure and practices? Be sure to consider changes in government and the economy.

2. Discuss the research/teaching dichotomy in university institutions. How do universities focusing on research differ from universities focusing on teaching? Who do they hire and what do they work toward achieving?

3. According to Baker, do the changes in the university affect everyone the same way? Who is most affected, how, and why?

4. How do Baker's respondents report that the changes have affected their work satisfaction?

5. Recall Albanese's paper in Part V. Compare Baker's findings regarding the challenges women face in juggling both work and family in the educational context to Albanese's findings. Is academia a more, less, or similarly family-friendly place to work compared with other workplaces in the economy?

6. Recall the debates in Part I regarding the purpose/roles of sociologists, and of academics more generally. Which roles do the changes reported by Baker facilitate and impede? What assumption about the purpose of academia do these changes reveal?

CHAPTER 23

1. Explain how the relationship between education and ethnic violence differs in wealthy and lower-income countries.

2. Why were educated francophones more likely to support the separatist movement? How were their labour market experiences different from less-educated francophones? What did they stand to gain by independence?

3. How does effective democracy (lack of state violence/coercion/discrimination) affect ethnic conflict? Describe some specific formal procedures that Lange highlights as very consequential.

4. As time wore on, how did francophones' position in the opportunity structures (market, government, etc.) change? How did this affect their radicalism?

5. What is the War Measures Act? How did this act deter students' support of the FLQ? Why didn't it spark more radical opposition? How was it initiated and carried out?

6. Lange set out to explain why ethnic conflict in wealthy countries doesn't erupt into violence. However, he partially attributes the lack of radicalism to individual wealth, which, by itself, is a circular argument (wealthy countries don't suffer violence because people

are wealthy). What is it about the condition of wealth that reduces political radicalism? More importantly, what other processes de-escalated ethnic conflict in Canada? According to this case, what is it about wealthy countries that keeps ethnic conflict peaceful?

CHAPTER 24

1. What are 'designer/ideal immigrants'? According to Chira, why have Canadian immigration policies shifted toward preferring immigrants with human capital? What assumption does this rest on?
2. What specific barriers do immigrants face in being integrated into the Canadian labour market, despite having high human capital?
3. According to Canadian government representatives, why should the government not bear the cost of integrating highly educated immigrants into the labour market and local communities?
4. Despite not taking responsibility for integrating highly educated immigrants, the government has not entirely ignored the challenge. What policy approaches has it taken to help retain and integrate highly educated immigrants? Have these been helpful alone? What are some problems with these approaches?
5. If the government does not bear the cost of integrating highly educated immigrants into local communities and job markets, then who does? Identify the various actors that have been involved and describe some of the solutions they have initiated.

CHAPTER 25

1. What is critical race theory? How does Chen use it to develop and defend his position on the first Africentric school?
2. Why was the Africentric school established? What problems and failures was it meant to overcome?
3. Discuss the first set of divergent views: presence or absence of racism. What does each view assume? What evidence does each rely on? What are the strengths and weaknesses of both positions given the evidence?
4. Discuss the second set of divergent views: self-determination versus segregation. What does each view assume? What evidence does each rely on? What are the strengths and weaknesses of both positions given the evidence?
5. Discuss the third set of divergent views: equity versus formal equality. What does each view assume? What evidence does each rely on? What are the strengths and weaknesses of both positions given the evidence?

Part VII

Work

This section explores one major way in which we experience the economy—through work. You can think of the economy as the system our society has organized so that we can get what we need. Different economies create different ways for people to get what they need and different ways of doing the various kinds of work that need to be done. Historically, some of the most popular types of economies have included hunting and gathering, cultivating land and animals, exchanging goods, eliciting gifts and favours, maintaining/managing slaves, and pillaging neighbours for booty. The way that we usually think of work here in North America is in terms of exchanging labour for money, since most of the resources that we need (like food, shelter, clothes, health care, occupational education, etc.) are mostly available in markets that are mediated through money and prices. Rather than working to gather our own resources directly (by, for example, hunting for our own dinner), we are embedded within a complex set of social relationships that organizes labour and resources. In order to have access to these exchange relationships, we need money, and to get money, we perform jobs.

While almost all of us have to work in some way, the experience of work differs widely depending on what we do. Jobs are embedded within diverse social relationships, which bring with them unique sets of privileges, powers, risks, and expectations. The constellations particular to each job can have drastically different effects on the people doing the work.

Professions have traditionally been the quintessential examples of jobs that have many desirable advantages. However, changes in the economy have made these jobs increasingly difficult to distinguish from other jobs, leading some to argue that 'profession' is no longer a very useful category of work. In her paper, Tracey Adams argues that an examination of powers and privileges granted by the state to various occupational groups shows that there is still a small portion of jobs that have many more privileges than others. For example, such occupational categories have the power of self-regulation as well as various special legal exemptions and statuses, which makes them more attractive than other, deceptively similar kinds of work.

At the other end of the work spectrum, Reuben Roth considers a form of labour that has a disproportionate exposure to physical risk: working as a caregiver in a group home. Roth relates that receiving violence graciously and constructively is accepted as an inevitable aspect of working in group homes. Incentives (in the form of raises and promotions) are even given to workers who receive violence particularly well:

. . . 'sucking it up' and promptly returning to work following a violent incident is more than likely the reason these supervisors and managers were actually *selected* and *promoted* to their current positions. . . . Workers who want the added salary and perks of a supervisor know that this is the model of behaviour that gets them what they need.

Even as paid jobs dominate our ideas of work in contemporary society, there is still much work that is done outside of the parameters of traditional wage work. The remaining two papers in this section explore these invisible kinds of work. They especially highlight the inequalities that result when we pretend that invisible work isn't real work, and let it fall disproportionately to less powerful groups of people. In their paper, Jean Wallace and Marisa Young tackle the most well-known forms of invisible work: housework and child care. The authors compare the hours of paid and unpaid work performed by male and female lawyers and study the effects of these work hours on time spent in leisure activities. Their findings show that the effects are different for men and women, partially because of the differences in the kinds of work that men and women are responsible for in the household.

For their part, Marjorie DeVault, Murali Venkatesh, and Frank Ridzi examine the unique kinds of work involved in accessing pooled resources without money. The citizens of many countries have decided (by voting for politicians who promise to make policies) to pool resources through taxation in order to provide a collective safety net for individuals who aren't able to access needed resources. In some sense, this pooling frees resources so that they can move where they are needed without being limited by price and people's ability to pay. But these resources aren't entirely 'free'. This form of distribution requires different forms of work both by individuals on behalf of the government (which has to find ways of judging eligibility) and by applicants (who have to do extensive document collecting in order to prove their eligibility). The government rarely acknowledges the unpaid eligibility work done by applicants as real work. The work is made difficult and inefficient by the applicants' lack of knowledge of the complicated bureaucratic process and by their suffering from the various challenges that make them need the resources in the first place. DeVault, Venkatesh, and Ridzi document the process and consequences of revising the responsibility for invisible eligibility work so that it is shared by applicants and paid case workers. They find that once eligibility work is acknowledged and treated as real work that requires knowledge and skills, and professionals with these skills become involved, the result is a more efficient application process and improved access to resources for eligible individuals.

'Suck it Up Buttercup': A Culture of Acceptable Workplace Violence in Group Homes

Reuben N. Roth

When we think of work-related violence, most of us tend to envision the work of police officers, prison guards, youth group-home workers, and social workers. We rarely think of caregivers who work with the elderly or developmentally disabled, who in fact are often victims of violence while performing their jobs. For the purposes of this study, **workplace violence** is defined as:

> . . . any act in which an employee is abused, threatened, intimidated or assaulted during the course of, or as a result of employment [and includes] threatening behaviour—such as shaking fists, destroying property or throwing objects; verbal or written threats—any expression of intent to inflict harm; harassment—any behaviour that demeans, embarrasses, humiliates, annoys, alarms, and includes sexual harassment; verbal abuse—swearing, insults or condescending language; physical attacks—hitting, shoving, kicking, spitting, biting (Canadian Centre for Occupational Health and Safety, 2005).

While workplace violence has been a long-standing issue in Canada, its status as a health and safety concern is relatively recent. A review of the literature suggests that workplace violence gained recognition as an issue only as recently as the late 1980s and 1990s. Moreover, whereas this category of violence once encompassed mainly physical harm, it now includes a broad range of psychological injuries, such as harassment and verbal abuse (Montgomery and Kelloway, 2002).

National statistics show that violence in Canadian workplaces may be on the rise. The Association of Workers' Compensation Boards of Canada (AWCBC) reported a rise from 4,164 lost-time injuries caused by on-the-job assaults and violent acts by persons in 1996 to 5,227 lost-time injuries in 2004.

Simonowitz (1996) notes that workplace violence is a major problem in the United States and points out that most measures taken to address problems of societal violence have typically been after the fact, punitive, and poorly aimed at reducing workplace violence in particular. The same author notes that 'Type II' violence, defined by California's Occupational Health and Safety Association as 'an act of violence directed at staff by a client, customer or patient' (Cal/OSHA, 1995), occurs in health care settings on a *daily* basis and that the risks are higher for nursing aides, less experienced female workers, and workers in frequent and close contact with patients or residents.

Montgomery and Kelloway (2002) report that the most frequent forms of workplace violence include hitting, kicking, and biting. They cite International Labour Organization (ILO) statistics showing that Canadian workers tend to report work-related assaults more than U.S. workers do. This suggests either that Canadians are subject to more incidents of workplace assault than Americans, or that Canadians are more likely to report incidents of violence. The latter explanation may be suggestive of higher union density among Canadian public sector workers, resulting in greater protection for these workers.

Violence in the Ontario Community Care Group Home Sector

The population studied here includes 130 workers—support workers and maintenance workers employed by a publicly funded community care organization that operates five regional group homes for developmentally disabled persons. Survey data were collected via a self-administered, anonymous, confidential, voluntary mail-back survey questionnaire. The data were collected between January and May 2006, with a response rate of 59 per cent. Of the 76 workers who responded to the survey questionnaire, 90 per cent reported having been personally subjected to an act of workplace violence (as defined above) within the past year. For this reason, only 90 per cent of respondents are included in the analyses that follow.

Table 26.1 shows both the category of violence experienced as well as the frequency of on-the-job violence. Respondents reported a high frequency of violence. Main categories of violence they were subjected to included physical gestures and having objects thrown at them; verbal or written threats; physical and/or verbal sexual harassment; swearing and insults; being hit, shoved or pushed; being kicked; and being spat upon.

Questions in our study were formulated to gauge the intensity or impact of the violence experienced personally. They addressed whether a respondent who had experienced violence within the past year had required medical attention, debriefing/counselling, or had lost time from work. Cross-tabulations were used to examine whether there was a relationship between the *intensity* of violence experienced and the respondent's *sex, age, job category,* and *shifts* worked. An outstanding pattern of significant relationships was apparent for the 4:00 p.m. to midnight shift. There were statistically significant relationships with all three intensity variables and the combination intensity variable. In all cases, the nature of the relationship was such that respondents who *did not* work the 4:00 p.m. to midnight shift also experienced a lower-than-expected intensity of violence. In contrast, respondents who worked

Table 26.1 Category of Violence Experienced by Frequency

Category of Violence	FREQUENCY			
	Never	**Once**	**2–10 times**	**>10 times**
Physical gestures, throwing things	10% (7)	2% (1)	18% (12)	70% (48)
Verbal or written threats	19% (13)	2% (1)	23% (16)	56% (38)
Humiliated, demeaned, alarmed	18% (12)	9% (6)	32% (22)	41% (28)
Physical sexual harassment	49% (33)	3% (2)	19% (13)	30% (20)
Verbal sexual harassment	53% (36)	3% (2)	18% (12)	26% (18)
Swearing, insults, etc.	13% (9)	3% (2)	15% (10)	69% (47)
Hit	10% (7)	3% (2)	21% (14)	66% (45)
Shoved or pushed	10% (7)	3% (2)	27% (18)	60% (41)
Kicked	21% (14)	4% (3)	22% (15)	53% (36)
Bitten	35% (24)	18% (12)	12% (8)	35% (24)
Spat upon	24% (16)	2% (1)	16% (11)	59% (40)

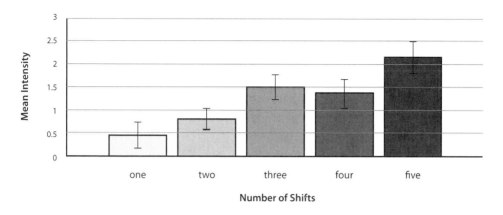

Figure 26.1 Intensity of Violence by Number of Shifts Worked

the 4:00 p.m. to midnight shift at least some of the time reported a higher-than-expected intensity of violence (i.e., violence requiring medical attention, debriefing/counselling, lost time, or a combination). As well, the number of shifts a respondent worked explains 15 per cent of the variance in combination intensity variable scores. Figure 26.1 provides an illustration of the mean intensity level of violence for different numbers of shifts worked.

The results show that *the more shifts a respondent works*, the more likely he or she will experience violence that requires medical attention or debriefing/counselling, or that results in lost time from work. When examining all the analyses undertaken involving shift variables and intensity variables, a significant relationship points to a problem with the 4:00 p.m. to midnight shift and, to a lesser degree, the 3:00 to 11:00 p.m. shift.

The Focus Groups: Workers' Voices

In a second study, we analyzed transcripts of two focus groups: managers and front-line workers. It is these data that are of particular interest here. Both the managers and the workers who participated in the focus groups were vocal, and respondents in both groups had, to a person, personally experienced workplace violence at least once. In fact, every participant in this focus group agreed

that they had experienced violent incidents on a daily basis, that this was the norm in extended institutional health care settings, and that many experiences were similar to the one described here:

> . . . you know, I myself am working with autistic adults . . . and . . . they tend to lash out, striking out, physically hitting. And, you know, it's . . . absolutely . . . not acceptable [but] you do begin to accept the fact that this kind of thing is going to happen. For example, . . . before 8:00 this morning, I went into work . . . and one of our clients comes through and just . . . punches another staff . . . in the hallway . . . and . . . I mean, I wasn't the recipient, but it's like, oh, here we go again, you know, [laughs] it's another day.

This description conveys the intensity of violence workers face, how ordinary daily incidents of violence have become among this group of workers, and how workers are acculturated to accept these violent incidents as a daily part of their work tasks.

The Focus Groups: Managers' Voices

Perhaps most surprising was the collective experience of the management focus group, which made no secret of the fact that they too had regularly experienced violence during the course of their daily duties. One manager opened the focus group with the admission, 'I've had my nose fractured—twice . . . and I've had my teeth broken.' From that point onward, it was the consensus among manager-participants that they were aware from the very beginning of their careers that being on the receiving end of resident violence was indeed an *expected* part of the job:

> Manager 1: . . . I've been in the field over 20 years. And I think *we all understood,* going [into] the field . . . that, you're dealing with people, people aren't predictable, you're dealing with people who may not 'get it' all the time and so sometimes you don't know what's going to come at you, and that part of the *thrill* was, you're walking into—you don't know what you're walking into every day.

> Manager 2: Adrenalin junkies. [laughter]

> Manager 1: . . . like Adrenalin junkies, right? We know we're going to be dealing with people who are trying to assault us regularly. So it's not a surprise to us that we get . . . not anymore, I mean we're all management now, [laughs] but that we get . . . that when we were front-line we were getting . . . assaulted.

Most startling from an outsider's perspective is the traditional male notion that 'taking it like a man' (Paap, 2006) is viewed as the only rational coping strategy among this group:

> Manager 1: . . . I'm such an old-school mind, that—[voices overlap . . . laughter] right, exactly . . . suck it up, buttercup.

Moreover, 'sucking it up' and promptly returning to work following a violent incident is more than likely the reason that these supervisors and managers were actually selected for and promoted to their current positions. From a materialist standpoint, this makes perfect sense. Workers who want the added salary and perks of a supervisor know that this is the model of behaviour that gets them what they need.

What Is to be Done about Workplace Violence?

The issues examined in this paper through the lens of workers and managers include forms of workplace violence and shifts worked. Our findings also include the observation that the path from front-line worker to manager depends largely on one's response to daily workplace violence. Those who 'suck it up' and take their medicine without a whimper are precisely those who are promoted upward through the ranks.

The issue of shift work should be more closely studied in the future to determine the cause of an apparent increase in the intensity of violence experienced during daytime shifts. Based on anecdotal evidence, we suspect there may be both a *higher frequency* of violence as well as an *increased intensity* of violence during these shifts in particular, simply because this is a moment of increased activity, as residents tend to gather for collective mealtimes during these shifts. In short, additional staff during daytime shifts are needed if we are to stave off an epidemic of violence in our extended health care sector.

In Gates's (1999a; 1999b) studies of violence experienced by workers in six nursing homes, one workplace was the exception. Here, caregivers reported that they felt supported, respected, and cared for by the administration and by the head nurses. In this home, caregivers frequently communicated with supervisors and did not hesitate to report violence. They were also included in all initiatives that dealt with violence. The director of this particular nursing home pointed out that the establishment maintained an **open-door policy** between staff and management and a team approach to dealing with workplace problems. The solution to the problem of workplace violence is clear: faced with a growing population of seniors and other chronic care patients who will eventually end up living in group home environments, this is the time to open the public purse and fund the staffing of group homes much more generously, for safety's sake.

References

CCOHS (Canadian Centre for Occupational Health and Safety). 2005. Violence in the Workplace: OSH Answers. Canadian Centre for Occupational Health and Safety (CCOHS). Retrieved from the Web at: http://www.ccohs.ca/oshanswers/psychosocial/violence.html

Gates, D., Fitzwater, E., Succop, P. & Sommers, M.S. 1999a. 'Reducing Violence against Caregivers in Nursing Homes.' Unpublished working paper for the National Institute for Occupational Safety and Health. Retrieved from the Web at: http://www2a.cdc.gov/nioshtic-2/BuildQyr.asp?s1=Reducing+Violence+Against+Caregivers+in+Nursing+Homes&f1=%2A&Startyear=&Adv=0&terms=1&EndYear=&Limit=10000&sort=&D1=10&PageNo=1&RecNo=1&View=f&

Gates, D., Fitzwater, E., Meyer, U. 1999b. 'Violence Against Caregivers in Nursing Homes: Expected, Tolerated, and Accepted'. *Journal of Gerontological Nursing*, Apr. 1999, 25(4), pp. 12–22.

Koomans, Cayley. 2007. 'Workplace Violence in Group Homes for the Mentally Disabled: Making Informed Recommendations to Deal with and Reduce Violence in the Workplace'. Unpublished paper. Sudbury, Ontario: Laurentian University.

Montgomery, J. & Kelloway, K. 2002. *Management of Occupational Health and Safety*, 2nd ed. Nelson Thompson Learning: Scarborough, Ontario.

Paap, Kris. 2006. *Working Construction: Why White Working-Class Men Put Themselves—and the Labor Movement—in Harm's Way*. Ithaca: ILR Press.

Peek-Asa, C. & Howard, J. 1999. 'Workplace-Violence Investigations by the California Division of Occupational Safety and Health, 1993–1996'. *Journal of Occupational and Environmental Medicine*, Aug. 1999, 41(8), pp. 647–653.

Rioux, Diane. 2004. 'Working Alone: A Review of OHS Policies and Initiatives'. Unpublished paper. Sudbury, Ontario: Laurentian University.

———. 2006. 'Workplace Violence in Group Homes for the Mentally Disabled: Identifying the Potential Risk of Violence for Group Home Workers'. Unpublished paper. Sudbury, Ontario: Laurentian University.

Simonowitz, J.A. 1996. 'Health Care Workers and Workplace Violence'. *Occupational Medicine*, Apr.–Jun. 1996, 11(2), pp. 277–291.

CHAPTER 27

'Let's Be Friends':
Working within an Accountability Circuit

Marjorie DeVault, Murali Venkatesh, and Frank Ridzi

In any public assistance program, determining eligibility for benefits is a surprisingly complex matter of examining an individual to check whether she or he fits the circumstances envisioned in the legislation that created the program. The public sector agencies mandated to perform that work have been characterized as complex 'rule-bound, paper-driven' bureaucracies (Lens and Pollack 1999). In recent years, these organizations have undergone significant changes, as policy-makers and administrators have promoted principles of a 'new public management' (Osborne and Gaebler 1992;

Bumgarner and Newswander 2009) emphasizing efficiency, delegation of responsibilities to local government, cost containment, and accountability. Although restructuring has been introduced from 'above', we have investigated how it has also developed through the actions of local administrators.

Our research focuses on county-level determination of eligibility for benefits in the chronic care strand of the U.S. Medicaid program, which provides financial support for health care (including nursing home care) for people with very low incomes. We examine the efforts of Medicaid staff in one New York county to respond to pressures for more efficient case processing. We argue that strategies adopted by local administrators have had the effect of inventing a new kind of public–private partnership. Nursing homes have become partners with Medicaid in the work of front-line case processing, and the partnership has sped up payments to those facilities who participate. The interpenetration of public and private interests we see in this case, and the business principles of efficiency and customer service that accompanied the changes, are characteristic of contemporary managerial restructuring in the public sector.

The Textual Constitution of Eligibility

Chronic care applications for Medicaid are heavily text-mediated. Front-line Medicaid eligibility staff are required to perform an exhaustive verification of the applicant's income and financial resources going back three years. One worker explained that she is trained to take literally *every* entry on the application to be a claim that must be verified (see also Zimmerman 1970), noting, 'Once we get satisfactory documentation then it flips and becomes a fact.'

The eligibility determination process (Figure 27.1) begins when the applicant submits her application and schedules an interview, during which the income maintenance (IM) worker assigned to the case may ask a few or many questions depending on how complete and compelling the application is. At the end of the interview, the worker writes up a *pending letter*, which lists all missing documents, and the applicant is allowed up to four weeks to produce the missing documents (a process that may be extended and repeated if the application is not successfully completed). When she deems the application to be complete, the IM worker reviews the evidence and makes a decision.

For applicants, this process can be quite daunting; one of our respondents referred to an 'information traffic jam', and a New York State report observed that applicants not infrequently 'end up lost in the Medicaid maze' (NYAHSA 2003). In complex cases, the application with all its supporting documents may amount to a file 15 to 20 centimetres thick. Preparing such a file can take many weeks and requires a great deal of skilled 'application work'. When this work is performed by applicants themselves, it is rarely acknowledged as work, perhaps because it is uncompensated and perhaps also because applicants are typically 'one-shotters' (Heimer 2006) who undertake the work only once. Thus, applicants and front-line staff are positioned quite differently.

Medicaid and Long-Term Care in the United States

In the United States, people who have resources must seek long-term care in a private marketplace and pay for it themselves. Many Americans who enter nursing homes on a private-pay basis quickly exhaust their resources and then look to public assistance programs like Medicaid. It is only when they have exhausted their private resources that they become eligible for any public assistance.

Medicaid legislation looks ahead toward this trajectory of impoverishment. The law includes provisions for sheltering assets such as a family home, and some individuals who foresee 'spending down' their assets make gifts to children or others before they deplete their resources. The program legislation has been crafted so as to allow, but also to limit sharply, such attempts to shelter assets, and these provisions explain why the application process includes such an extensive audit of the applicant's circumstances.

The events we analyze here involved significant changes in the work routines of program staff, made within the constraints of the legislation that created the program—changes that we think of, following Smith (2005), as a 'boss text'. The changes were introduced by a new administrator, who in 1997 was charged with improving the difficult relations between the county Medicaid agency and local facilities. A large and growing backlog of pending cases had become a matter of considerable urgency for these facilities; they were admitting residents who appeared to be eligible for Medicaid support but whose eligibility

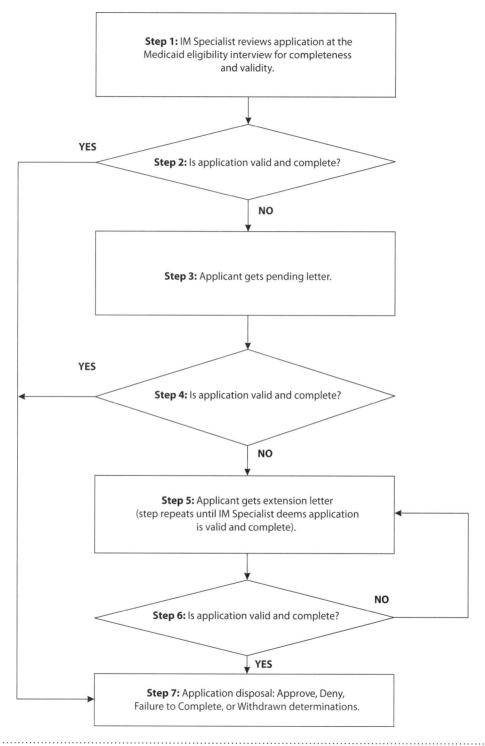

Figure 27.1 The Eligibility Determination Process

remained undetermined for many months. Once a resident was deemed eligible, the facility could apply for reimbursement for only three months of care already provided. Thus, delays in processing could have very significant budgetary effects.

Our analysis is based on fieldwork conducted by Venkatesh since 2005.[1] We draw on the institutional ethnography approach, which allows us to show how front-line work activities both are shaped by 'ruling relations' (Smith 2005) and also activate those relations in ways that are consequential elsewhere.

Reorganizing the Work of Eligibility Determination

In 1997, the county's new Medicaid director established a specialized entity, the Medicaid Chronic Care Unit (hereafter the Unit), to handle long-term care applications. The Unit's managers then adopted several strategies to speed up eligibility determination. These included a new co-operative approach that designated facilities as partners; the establishment of a training program for workers at the nursing homes; and support texts that guided the preparation of a properly filed application. Later, the Unit introduced Internet video interviewing to enhance the efficiency of the eligibility interview.

Intake in Medicaid and other U.S. means-tested programs has often been a matter of harsh, personalized scrutiny. The new mandate was that a hyper-skeptical, even forensic, approach should be replaced by a more sympathetic and co-operative spirit. The director adopted the slogan 'Let's be friends' to convey to her own staff and those in the nursing homes what she intended. Rather than leaving applicants on their own to file applications—which were inevitably incomplete, at best—she wished to provide concrete, useful guidance as to how such application work should proceed. Most applicants are not only 'one-shotters' but also require assistance with the application process due to the health or cognitive problems that have brought them to long-term care. Thus, the reforms were designed to recruit (and allow) nursing home

casework staff to provide assistance with application work. While such a procedure would introduce new tasks for facility caseworkers, taking up those tasks would benefit the facility, since complete and valid applications were meant to lead to quicker eligibility determinations. The slogan 'Let's be friends' was a headline for the business themes that imbued the new idea of partnership. The Unit administrator talked of the reforms as improving 'customer service', with 'customer' referencing both the applicant and the facility (and merging their interests).

In addition, Unit managers began to encourage the facilities to appoint a specialized caseworker trained in the intricacies of chronic care to assist residents applying for Medicaid and recommended that this caseworker report not to the facility's social services office but to the business office. Three of the four facilities we studied followed this recommendation.

At training sessions, these facility caseworkers worked through an application packet, learning how the Unit's staff would read the application so that they understood how to file it properly, with the appropriate supporting documents. Included in the packet were 'support texts' that could be used as worksheets guiding the preparation of various parts of the application. These locally designed worksheets not only indicated what information was needed but also provided instructions about how it could be obtained most easily.

Later, the Unit began to offer a video interviewing option in facilities with trained caseworkers. Applicants who chose video interviewing did not need to leave the facility for the eligibility interview, and the caseworker who was helping to assemble the application could easily participate. Thus, the three parties involved—the Unit's eligibility staff, applicant, and caseworker—could have a real-time conversation centred on the application in order to resolve questions and determine what documentation was still needed for a complete and valid application.

These reforms reorganized the relations of application work. What had previously been a two-way interaction, involving the applicant and Medicaid staff, became a triangular interaction, which includes the applicant and front-line staff from both organizations. The 'Let's be friends' idea suggested that applicants would be seen as presumably worthy individuals in need of assistance, rather than as potential scam artists. But 'Let's be friends' also signalled a new kind of co-operation between the Medicaid Unit and the facilities, and this organizational 'friendship' is the more enduring one.

The Unit and most local facilities see the reforms as successful. It remains to be seen, however, whether they can be sustained. A new Deficit Reduction Act has introduced a layer of 'boss text' regulations for Medicaid eligibility, and facilities have begun to grumble at taking on so much of the work of pre-screening and application assembly, a burden they feel should more appropriately be borne by the Unit. Thus, what we see in this reform effort is a delicately balanced set of accountabilities and their fragility in a changing political and economic context.

Unit managers came to understand the facilities as 'customers' to whom the Unit was accountable, using the term 'customer service' to refer to a value they wished to pursue. At the same time, the Unit was pushing facilities to reorganize their Medicaid casework function and tie it to their financial bottom line. The facilities were certainly aware of this tie (and because they were, they had brought pressure to bear on county Medicaid in the first place). However, the Unit offered to help them concretely with their cash flow concerns, and this was a first. In its legislative outline, Medicaid is aimed at helping the poor defray their healthcare costs, not assisting facilities with their financial bottom-line. Thus, the Unit was breaking new ground in this regard.

Realignments of Public and Private Sector Work

To the extent that the rearrangement of work we examine here has been successful, we suggest that it realigns the state's provision for long-term care so as to address more adequately than in the past the concerns of private sector facilities. Thus, it represents a change that seems a straightforward matter of efficiency and better service but in fact produces a new form of public–private partnership. Cost-cutting is a fact of life in contemporary organizations, and this fact has prompted long-term care facilities to take unprecedented steps in order to better manage their costs and risks.

The applicant has a rather ghostly presence in eligibility determination, as the target of benefits but not the direct recipient of them. Overall, these reforms seem to have had positive effects for applicants and their families; certainly, the reform allows for a quicker resolution of the financial uncertainties of nursing home care. However, applicants are unorganized and do not have the collective power of facilities to bring pressure on the Unit to make or retain such changes. They benefit primarily when their interests coincide with those of the organizations involved.

Conclusion

Medicaid is one of the major entitlement programs that has contributed to an increasingly unsustainable budget deficit in the United States, and the program undergoes continual scrutiny and revision with an eye to cost containment. In this overall context, the reforms we studied stand out, because they seem designed to facilitate, rather than impede, Medicaid eligibility.

Our analysis suggests that the local reformers we studied are working within two **accountability circuits**. On the one hand, they are accountable to the 'boss text' of program legislation: they must work within the parameters of enabling regulations. On the other hand, they have responded to a different set of local accountabilities, working with those in other organizations (the hospitals and long-term care facilities in the county) also charged with the provision of care for the elderly. By responding not only to their legal mandate but also to the concerns of the facilities that depend on Medicaid reimbursement, these reformers have forged and strengthened a local, horizontal accountability circuit that links organizational entities in the county in unprecedented new ways.

Notes

1. The data include in-depth interviews with county Medicaid and facility directors and staff; six short interviews with applicants and family members; observations of training sessions for facility staff; review of program documents; and material from an earlier study, conducted in 2000–2001 when the agency piloted a video interviewing procedure for program intake.

References

Bumgarner, J. and Newswander, C.B. (2009). The irony of NPM: The inevitable extension of the role of the American state.' *American Review of Public Administration* 39 (2): 189–207

Heimer, C.A. (2006) Conceiving children: How documents support case versus biographical analysis. In A. Riles (Ed.), *Documents: Artifacts of modern knowledge*, 95–126. Ann Arbor, MI: University of Michigan Press.

Lens, V., and Pollack, D. (1999). Welfare reform: Back to the future! *Administration in Social Work*, 23 (2): 61–77.

New York Association of Homes and Services for the Aging (NYAHSA). (2003) *Preserving long term care for the long term future*. Albany, New York.

Osborne D., & Gaebler, T. (1992). *Reinventing government: How the entrepreneurial spirit is transforming the public sector*. New York: Penguin Books

Smith, D.E. (2005). *Institutional ethnography: A sociology for people*. Lanham, MD: AltaMira.

Zimmerman, D.H. (1970). Record keeping and the intake process in a public welfare agency. In S. Wheeler (Ed.), *On record: files and dossiers in American life*, 319–354. Albany, NY: Russell Sage.

CHAPTER 28

Profession: A Useful Concept for Sociological Analysis?

Tracey L. Adams

In common parlance, the term *profession* typically refers to paid employment or any occupation; its sociological usage to refer to a special kind of occupation with **status** and privileges appears increasingly divorced from social reality. Some scholars have argued that professions are in a state of decline, becoming subordinate and indistinguishable from other forms of expert labour (Leicht and Fennell 2001; Ritzer and Walczak 1988; Rothman 1984).

In the sociological literature, this dim view may also be the legacy of one of the last great American works on professions, Andrew Abbott's (1988) *System of Professions*. Abbott sought to shift the course of research on professions toward the work that professionals did, and their ability to lay claim to a scope of practice, or jurisdiction, as well as interprofessional conflict for control of jurisdictions. While Abbott's shift of focus was valuable, his emphasis on jurisdiction appears to apply equally to any occupation with a claim to expertise in a specific field of endeavour. In his work, there are no apparent differences between expert occupations with professional status, and those without it (Adams 2004; Sciulli 2005). Status—one of the key characteristics traditionally argued to distinguish professions from other expert occupations (Vollmer and Mills 1965)—is largely forgotten.

This paper presents the preliminary findings of a historical research project examining professional regulation in Canada. As I reviewed the legislation regulating occupational groups, it became clear that professions could be distinguished from others by the self-governance and authority they were granted, and typically by the training required for entry to practice.

Defining Professions

Defining professions is not a simple task and, over the past half-century, many definitions have been provided. Research published in the 1950s and 1960s tended to follow a 'trait approach', providing a list of characteristics that distinguished professions from other occupations. For instance, Vollmer and Mills (1965:481), following Foote (1953), stressed work that required 'a specialized technique supported by a body of theory', the pursuit of careers supported by professional associations, and 'status supported by community recognition' (pp. 371–80).

Definitions advanced beginning in the 1970s emphasized power. Thus, for Freidson (1970), Johnson (1972), and others, what distinguished professions from other occupations was practitioners' ability to control their occupation, their work, and the labour of those who worked with them.

Although the power approach has been very influential, it has not contributed a widely accepted, alternative definition of 'professions'. Typically, power approaches did not completely reject trait definitions and still tended to view professions as elite, organized occupations with specialized expertise and extensive training.

In response to the theoretical ambiguity, many researchers have adopted Freidson's (1983) recommendation and treated profession as a folk concept (Gidney and Millar 1994; Heap, Millar, and Smyth 2005; Neal and Morgan 2000). As Freidson argued, there may not be a definition of *profession*

that works across time and place. Rather, he suggested, researchers should explore how people in specific social-historical contexts 'determine who is a professional and who is not, and how they "make" or "accomplish" professions by their activities' (p. 27). The label *profession* is socially valued, and its application is socially contested. As groups struggle to have this label applied to them, they may stretch and alter its meaning. Freidson's approach reminds us that the term *profession* is socially constructed, and hence is variable, and the subject of social struggle and debate. Furthermore, it reminds us of the importance of status to professions.

Professions are **status groups** in the Weberian sense. According to Weber (1978), occupational status groups emerge when people sharing a status situation—'a position of positive or negative privilege in social esteem' associated with their lifestyle and occupation—form an association, claim status, and typically pursue 'certain special monopolies on the grounds of their status' (p. 60). Two different types of status have traditionally been crucial for professions (Adams and Welsh 2007:255). First is the nebulous dimension of 'social status'; successful professions are, on average, held in high esteem by members of the public. Second is legal status: In Canada and other Western countries, most groups studied as professions by researchers and regarded with high esteem by the public are regulated by the state. It is generally through legal avenues that professionals seek to secure the 'special monopolies' noted by Weber. Many professions, then, have a privileged legal status that grants them rights of self-regulation and shapes professionals' responsibilities to their clientele (Haug 1980; Rubin 1980).

Combining the insights of Freidson (1983), Weber (1978), and others, we can see that while exactly what a profession is may vary across time and place, the definition of profession need not be free floating. In essence, professions are organized occupational groups with a (somewhat) accepted claim to legal and/or social status. Exactly which groups are granted this status, and what this status entails, will vary. To understand who is a 'professional' and who is not in any given context, then, requires **empirical research**. Once this research is done, we may be in a position to develop a more accurate, empirically based sociological concept of profession.

The Study

This study focused on legislation regulating professions and occupations passed in five Canadian provinces from the time of Confederation (1867) until 1961. The five provinces were selected for their diversity and geographical dispersion across the country: Nova Scotia, Quebec, Ontario, Saskatchewan, and British Columbia (BC). I selected the end date of 1961 because it was a census year that predated the extensive federal and provincial reviews of professional regulation that began in the mid-1960s and resulted in legislative change soon after. I reviewed published collections of the acts passed annually by the legislatures in each province to identify legislation regulating occupations and professions.

Once identified, the regulatory legislation was examined to determine the nature of the regulation. Was there a regulatory body established or recognized by the act? Was the body granted the right to pass by-laws and regulate itself, and/or practice in a field more broadly? Was entry to practice restricted? Did the act establish penalties for those who practised counter to the act? I considered these and many other dimensions common to such regulatory legislation to explore differences among regulated occupational and professional groups.

This present paper addresses two principal research questions:

1. What professions were regulated historically, and when were they regulated?
2. What factors appear to distinguish professional regulation from the regulation of other occupations?

Regulated Professions and Occupations

A review of the legislation regulating occupational groups in all five provinces revealed clear differences between professional and other occupational regulation. Although there are many lines across which regulated groups historically differed in specific provinces and time periods, only two characteristics were universal across 'professions': (1) the establishment of a regulatory body, at least partially composed of practitioners, to govern the profession; and (2) the limitation of the right to practise or to utilize a restricted title to those with a demonstrated level of competence. In contrast, legislation regulating other groups included establishing a system of licensing, without creating a separate regulatory body and/or competency requirements. . . .

Generally, all who wanted to practise could do so, as long as they took the trouble to obtain a license; there were rarely any specified entry requirements. This regulation enabled state actors to oversee work in these fields, but little active regulation beyond the issuing of licenses is evident.

Under professional regulation, the state delegated authority to a regulatory board of practitioners who were given the right to govern practice (subject to certain limitations). Professional bodies established under legislation were empowered to pass by-laws to regulate their activities and the practitioners they governed. Their areas of governance typically included entry to practice, education and examinations, registration, practitioner conduct and discipline, occasionally professional fees, and other aspects of service provision. These professional bodies, then, had delimited legislative powers: their by-laws had the force of law, and affected practitioners and consumers alike. The privilege of self-regulation was granted to a relatively small number of groups who restricted access to such authority and to practice to a selected group of individuals who had distinguished themselves through their training, education, and/or examinations, as well as, generally, through their moral character. Historically in Canada, professions were special status groups demarcated by their training and education in a specific field, and their moral rectitude.

Utilizing these criteria, one can distinguish 36 professional groups regulated in the provinces of Nova Scotia, Quebec, Ontario, Saskatchewan, and BC before 1961. This finding is striking given that attempts to define professions in the past have been based predominantly on a handful of professions, and especially medicine and law.

Overall, legislation regulating professions before 1961 delineated practice rights and privileges and specified criteria and processes for entry to practice. The summary analysis shows that such legislation also served two other purposes. First, it granted status to professional groups: the legislation recognized them as a special category of workers and citizens, delegated limited governance rights to professional organizations, and granted practice privileges. Additional privileges were also common, such as limitations on malpractice suits and jury duty exemptions. Clearly professions had a special status in society; their special legal status was often, but not always, accompanied by considerable social and cultural status. Occupational groups—whether regulated or not—did not have status of this kind.

Discussion

My approach was to take Freidson's (1983) advice and consider which occupations were regarded as 'professions' in a specific social-historical context. Professions are, ultimately, status groups, and if one examines which occupations have status in certain locations and at certain points in time, one should be able to identify professions. Although both legal and social status are important to the making of professions, I chose, for simplicity's sake, to focus on legal status and consider which groups have been legally regulated as 'professions' in the past. This is not a perfect approach: not every regulated profession has a significant amount of social status. For instance, few Canadians would even know what a 'shorthand reporter' or 'agrologist' was, let alone hold them in high esteem. At the same time, many well-respected occupations, such as scientists, university professors, and managers,

are not regulated. Nevertheless, the approach undertaken here did allow me to identify groups of occupations that were granted a similar level of legal status and regulated in similar ways.

Professional powers are regulated, quite often by the state, and professionals' privileges and obligations to others are clearly delineated. A focus on the dynamics of these power relations, and how they are structured, enables us to acknowledge variations in levels of power across profession and across time period. A decline in power need not signal the end of professions, because it is the fact that these power relations exist and are structured—rather than the absolute level (or quantity) of power granted—that historically has distinguished professions.

More empirical research is needed to explore professional status—both legal and social status and the interconnections between them—and professional relationships in different times and places, before a more useful sociological conceptualization can be further specified. Nevertheless, I argue that considering professions as organized status groups, and exploring the ways in which their status is acquired, and the ways in which their relationships with the state, the public, and other workers are structured, is an approach that promises to move research forward. It not only facilitates our ability to operationalize and identify professions, it also opens up many avenues for research. It focuses attention on a broader range of professional groups, and hence, may enhance our understanding of professional activity in new and unknown ways. It also enables us to explore the ways in which professions and professional work change over time. Perhaps most importantly, such an approach returns our focus to issues of status, status-group formation, and status power in society—issues at the core of the establishment and maintenance of professions that have been brushed aside in recent research (Sciulli 2005).

References

Abbott, A. 1988. *The System of Professions*. Chicago, IL: University of Chicago Press.

Adams, T. and S. Welsh. 2007. 'Professions.' Pp. 252–69 in *The Organization and Experience of Work*. Toronto: Thomson Nelson.

Adams, T.L. 2004. 'Interprofessional Conflict and Professionalization: Dentistry and Dental Hygiene in Ontario.' *Social Science and Medicine* 58:2243–52.

Foote, N. 1953. 'The Professionalization of Labor in Detroit.' *American Sociological Review* 58:371–80.

Freidson, E. 1970. *Profession of Medicine*. New York, NY: Harper and Row.

———. 1983. 'The Theory of Professions: State of the Art.' Pp. 19–27 in *The Sociology of Professions*, edited by R. Dingwall and P. Lewis. New York: Macmillan.

Gidney, R.D. and W.P.J. Millar. 1994. *Professional Gentlemen*. Toronto: University of Toronto Press.

Haug, M. 1980. 'The Sociological Approach to Self-Regulation.' Pp. 61–80 in *Regulating the Professions*, edited by R.D. Blair and S. Rubin. Lexington, MA: Lexington Books, DC Heath and Company.

Heap, R., W. Millar and E. Smyth, eds. 2005. *Learning to Practise: Professional Education in Historical and Contemporary Perspective*. Ottawa: University of Ottawa Press.

Johnson, T. 1972. *Professions and Power*. New York: Macmillan.

Leicht, K.T. and M.L. Fennell. 2001. *Professional Work*. Malden, MA: Blackwell.

Neal, M. and J. Morgan. 2000. 'The Professionalization of Everyone? A Comparative Study of the Development of the Professions in the United Kingdom and Germany.' *European Sociological Review* 16:9–26.

Ritzer, G. and D. Walczak. 1988. 'Rationalization of Physicians.' *Social Forces* 67:1–22.

Roth, J.A. 1974. 'Professionalism: The Sociologists' Decoy.' *Work and Occupations* 1:6–23.

Rothman, R.&. 1984. 'Deprofessionalization: The Case of Law in America.' *Work and Occupations* 11:183–206.

Rubin, S. 1980. 'The Legal Web of Professional Regulation.' Pp. 29–60 in *Social Class and the Division of Labour*, edited by R.D. Blair and S. Rubin. Lexington, MA: Lexington Books, DC Heath and Company.

Sciulli, D. 2005. 'Continental Sociology of Professions Today: Conceptual Contributions.' *Current Sociology* 53:915–42.

Vollmer, H. and D.L. Mills. 1965. 'Some Comments on the Professionalization of Everyone?' *American Journal of Sociology* 70:480–81.

Weber, M. 1978. 'Classes, Status Groups and Parties.' Pp. 4341 in *Weber: Selections in Translation*, edited by W.G. Runciman Translated by E. Matthews. Cambridge, UK: Cambridge University Press.

CHAPTER 29

Work Hard, Play Hard?: A Comparison of Male and Female Lawyers' Time in Paid and Unpaid Work and Participation in Leisure Activities

Jean E. Wallace and Marisa C. Young

How we allocate our time to different activities can be viewed in terms of choices and trade-offs, since time is a finite resource (Hilbrecht, Zuzanek, and Mannell 2008). The time availability perspective suggests that the more time is spent in one role, the less time is available for another. For example, more time allocated to meeting work, home, and family obligations results in less time available for leisure. This is consistent with the idea of **role strain** that is often used in examining the difficulty in simultaneously fulfilling the competing demands associated with work and family roles.

As more women are employed than ever before, even when they become mothers, more attention has been paid to the impact of having a busy life on free time or leisure for both men and women. Terms such as 'the double shift' and the 'time squeeze' suggest that the combination of work and family roles are squeezing out time for leisure and negatively affecting North Americans' quality of life (Hochschild 1989, 1997; Schor 1991). Recent research highlights these trends among Canadian men and women (Duxbury and Higgins 2001). As professionals increasingly place priority on both their work and family roles and responsibilities, this may compromise the time and energy they have left over for leisure activities. Based on the trends reported in the literature, our first hypothesis is that *Greater time spent in paid and unpaid work will be negatively related to participation in leisure activities*.

The amount of time spent in paid and **unpaid work** and **leisure** may differ for men and women. Societal expectations of women's commitment to the domestic sphere can influence their participation in leisure activities (see Blair-Loy 2003; Hays 1996). As well, gender inequalities in leisure may be a product of different societal constraints placed on women's and men's paid and unpaid work as certain behaviours associated with being a 'man' or 'woman' are acted and re-enacted according to prescribed gender norms (see Connell 2002; Ferree 1991; Hochschild 1989 for more discussion on gender construction in domestic and paid labour).

Hays (1996) articulates the common understandings of motherhood as intensely child-focused and completely selfless. Personal leisure may not necessarily align with these expectations of intensive mothering because the leisure activities are self-rewarding, personally fulfilling, and individually oriented. The disjuncture between definitions of motherhood and leisure activities suggest mothers are less likely to participate in leisure compared with fathers, and Hill and Stafford's (1980) research supports these claims. The authors found that an employed mother's ability to work and care for her children was financed by reductions both in her personal care

time, including sleeping, and in passive leisure, such as watching television.

As a result of their heavier caregiving responsibilities, women experience not only less total leisure time than men but also lower quality leisure time (Mattingly and Bianchi 2003). Women have less time to relax from the demands of paid and unpaid work, and the time they do spend in leisure often involves other activities that are related to their primary responsibilities of housework and child care. These trends are particularly acute among professional women but may vary by age (Duxbury and Higgins 2001; Gauthier 2002). A recent Canadian study highlights that professional and managerial women spend approximately 12 hours more on child care per week compared with professional and managerial men *and* compared with women in more blue- or pink-collar types of occupations (Duxbury and Higgins 2001). Duxbury and Higgins suggest that these trends may reflect professional women's personal expectations to be 'super moms' and outperform others when it comes to child care.

Whereas men appear to be better at protecting their free time from their family responsibilities, women are more likely to have their leisure interrupted, intertwined, and fragmented because of their family's needs. Although women have increased their participation in the labour force, both Canadian and U.S. data suggest that men spend more time in paid work with higher wages and in more prestigious jobs, in addition to more time in leisure activities (Beaujot and Lui 2005; Frederick 1995; Mattingly and Bianchi 2003; Spain and Bianchi 1996; Zukewich 2003). Thus, our second hypothesis is that *Women will spend more time in household and child care activities than men, whereas men will spend more time in paid work and participate in more leisure than women*.

Even though men have increased the amount of time they spend in child care and housework, Canadian and U.S. data suggest that women continue to spend roughly seven hours more in these unpaid activities per week (Bianchi et al. 2000; Marshall 2006; Sayer 2005). Moreover, the household activities that men perform can generally be done when it is convenient for them (e.g.

yard work, household repairs) in contrast to the tasks that women remain largely responsible for (e.g. tending to children's needs, cooking dinner), which often require daily attention, usually at specific times. Thus, the time men spend on household activities generally offers more flexibility and opportunity for leisure activities. As well, research shows that women have less free time than men and that employment, marriage, and children restrict women's free time more than men's (Sayer 2005). Since women face a more significant time shortage compared with men, because their work time limits their household and family time, women may find it more difficult to set aside their family tasks for a leisure activity (Hochschild 1989). As a result, we expect that women's work and family responsibilities may have a stronger negative impact on women's leisure participation compared with men's. Our third hypothesis, then, is that *Greater time spent in paid and unpaid work will result in a stronger negative relationship with leisure for women compared with men*.

Control Variables

We control for a number of different conditions in our multivariate analyses. First, we control for three family status variables: marital status, number of children, and the presence of preschool-aged children. Second, we control for two physical characteristics: health and age. We expect that healthier adults are more likely to participate in leisure activities, particularly active leisure (Bird and Fremont 1991). As people age, their obligatory time commitments associated with work and family generally lessen as the most intense periods of work-family demands are behind them (Gauthier 2002; Mattingly and Sayer 2006). Third, we control for three work-related variables: work setting, income, and work salience. Work setting is taken into account as the ebbs and flow of legal practice vary significantly across different places where lawyers may work.

While law firms generally require longer work hours than corporate or government offices, they usually offer more flexibility in terms of when those hours are worked (Kordana 1995; MacEachen,

Polzer, and Clarke 2008). Higher income may provide greater resources to outsource household labour and child care and thereby reduce unpaid work demands (Mattingly and Sayer 2006). In addition, it may allow for participation in leisure activities that are more expensive in terms of membership, special equipment, or other accessories. Work salience captures the extent to which work is central to an individual's definition of self and may be related to working long hours as well as to placing a lower priority on leisure activities.

The data are from the 2000 'Juggling It All' survey, which collected information on practising lawyers' work and family experiences and attitudes. The survey was distributed to all practising lawyers in the Province of Alberta. Of the 5,921 lawyers contacted, 1,829 completed the survey, yielding a 31 per cent response rate. A comparison of the sample data to the provincial figures from the Law Society of Alberta using chi-square tests indicates that similar proportions of lawyers are represented in the survey data by gender, work setting, and city. For the purposes of this paper, the sample is restricted to lawyers working full time, which includes respondents working 35 or more hours per week ($N=1,451$).

The 14 leisure items included in the questionnaire were constructed from 120 lawyers' responses to an open-ended interview question from an earlier study that asked how they usually spend their leisure time (refer to Wallace 2002 for a detailed description of this study). Each participant identified, on average, three or four leisure activities, and in total they identified 56 different activities. The items constructed for the questionnaire were based on the most popular activities reported by the 120 interview participants.

Work hours were measured in several ways in this study. We included self-report measures of respondents' average *total hours worked,* including time spent working at the office and at home. Average weekly hours *worked in the evenings* and *on weekends* were also reported by respondents. Together, these three indicators of work hours provide a comprehensive representation of the hours worked by respondents in a given week. To measure weekly time spent in household and child care activities, respondents were asked to answer the following questions separately for weekdays and weekends: 'About how much time do you spend on home chores, such as cooking, cleaning, repairs, shopping, yard work, banking?' and 'About how much time do you spend with your children, taking care of them, playing with them, feeding them, etc.?' The weekday figures were multiplied by five and the weekend figures by two. These total figures were then summed to produce two weekly averages: one for *weekly hours spent on household activities* and one for *weekly hours spent on child care activities*. Those who did not have any children were assigned a value of zero for the time spent on child care activities.

Work setting was coded 1 for those working in law firms and values of 0 were assigned to those working in other settings (e.g. government, private corporations, or solo practice). To measure *annual income*, respondents were asked to report their total annual earnings from the practice of law in the year before the survey before taxes and other deductions were made. Finally, *work salience* was measured by a scale created from three items: 'I am very absorbed in my work'; 'My work is a very important part of who I am'; and 'I am deeply committed to my work.' Responses ranged from 'strongly disagree' (coded 1) to 'strongly agree' (coded 5). Responses were summed and divided by three to compute a mean score; higher scores correspond to greater work salience (α=.733)

Results

The results for the control variables reveal several important patterns. The family status control variables show that women who are married participate in less passive and social leisure than unmarried women, whereas married men participate less in social leisure but participate to the same degree in active or passive leisure as unmarried men. Women with preschool-aged children are less engaged in active or passive leisure than women without young children, whereas whether men have preschool-aged children is unrelated to their leisure activities. The results for the physical characteristics show that, for both women and

men, health is positively related to participation in active and social leisure and age is negatively related to active leisure. The work-related control variables show that working in a law firm may be positively related to active and social leisure activities, whereas income is unrelated to leisure. Work salience appears positively related to leisure, particularly social leisure, which may suggest that this form of leisure could be work related.

We hypothesized that the more time spent in paid and unpaid work would be negatively related to participation in leisure activities, particularly for women. An interesting pattern in our findings reveals that even though men spend more time in paid work, only working on weekends seems relevant in limiting their leisure activities. The longer hours they work over the entire workweek or in the evenings are not significant in explaining the degree to which they participate in leisure. In contrast, for women, work time is negatively related to their leisure activities, particularly in terms of their total work hours and social leisure and working in the evenings and their passive leisure.

Another unexpected set of findings is that the time men spend in housework or child care is either unrelated or positively related to their leisure participation, while the time women spend in housework is unrelated to their leisure participation. As predicted, the time women spend in child care is negatively related to their active and passive leisure. These results suggest that men's greater overall opportunities for leisure compared with women's stem from unanticipated relationships between men's involvement in housework and child care and their leisure activities.

In addition to the gendered relationships of paid and unpaid work time and leisure, we also found that marital status and the presence of preschool-aged children are differentially related to leisure for women and men. For women, being married or having preschool-aged children is negatively related to their leisure activities, but for men these family status variables are less relevant or unrelated to their leisure. This pattern of findings is consistent with the notion that family obligations, whether captured through time spent in housework or child care or the control variables of being married or having young children, are more important in restricting women's participation in leisure than men's. We explore several possible explanations for these findings in greater detail below.

One explanation for the pattern of findings that unpaid obligations are either unrelated or positively related to men's leisure but negatively related to women's may be because men 'earn' more leisure time when they help out around the house. Fathers may feel more entitled to rewards for their contributions for both their paid and unpaid work in the form of more time for themselves and their leisure pursuits, whereas mothers may have a greater sense of responsibility for taking care of the household and children that is not seen to deserve special recognition in the form of more free time (Deutsch 1999). At the same time, men's contributions to unpaid work are generally more highly valued than women's (Thompson 1991). That is, when husbands contribute to housework or child care, it is often viewed as a more significant and valued contribution than women's day-to-day performance of the same activities. As a result, husbands and wives may believe that men's contributions deserve more praise, appreciation, and rewards (Sanchez 1994; Thompson 1991). A time out from the demands of paid and unpaid work may be one of the ways in which men are rewarded for their family contributions (Nomaguchi, Milkie, and Bianchi 2005). Future research might explore the extent to which women and men feel they earn or deserve free time for themselves.

In addition, explanations of the gendered interrelationships among family and work roles may help us to better understand the gendered links between family and leisure roles. Simon (1995) convincingly demonstrated that work and family roles are more interconnected and compatible for men as they fulfill their familial role of breadwinner through their work role, whereas for women the roles are more independent and incompatible as they feel that performing their work role prevents them from adequately fulfilling the nurturing roles of mother and spouse. Along similar lines, we might argue that men's family and leisure roles may be more overlapping and compatible compared with women's.

Last, the negative relationship between being married and participating in leisure was particularly striking, especially for women. Perhaps the combination of the negative relationships of marital status and preschool-aged children for women indicates that it is more difficult for married women and those with young children to leave their home responsibilities to engage in family-free leisure activities (Lee and Bhargava 2004). It is unclear though why married men report less leisure time compared with single men. However, household production and time allocation theories provide a generalized explanation for why both married men and women engage in less leisure compared with single individuals. Bryant's (1990) theory of household production and Becker's (1965) time allocation theory argue that married households spend less time on leisure because of the additional time necessary for household production in maintaining marital (and other) functions and relations. Previous studies report such findings (Lee and Bhargava 2004; Robinson and Godbey 1997), suggesting that married and single individuals have different resources, tastes, and time toward leisure activities, which accounts for the gap between these two groups.

In closing, there are several limitations of this study that should be noted. First, the data in this study are cross-sectional and, as a result, we must be cautious in making causal claims. It is possible that, for some people, leisure is a priority that limits the time they spend in paid and unpaid work rather than the reverse (Nomaguchi and Bianchi 2004). Second, this paper focused on a single, high-status, professional occupation—namely, lawyers. Some of the findings presented in this paper may be limited to this particular occupation under study or to professionals more broadly. Third, from the results of our study we do not know the extent to which respondents spend all or some of their different leisure activities by themselves or with other people, such as their children, spouse, colleagues, or people unrelated to their work or family. Parents may choose to engage in activities that involve their children and that their children will enjoy (Mattingly and Bianchi 2003).

Conclusion

The results of this study suggest that the relationships between the work, family, and leisure domains differ for women and men. While it was not surprising to find that men spend more time in paid work and leisure and women spend more time in housework and child care, we did discover several unexpected results. The extent to which men's participation in housework and child care enhances their participation in different forms of leisure points to several avenues for future research. One is to explore the meaning of work, family, and leisure roles in greater depth in order to examine whether men's and women's participation in paid and unpaid work contributes to a sense of earning or deserving leisure time and feeling guilty or guilt free in their leisure pursuits. Another is to examine the degree to which parents in particular involve their children or spouse in their leisure activities as a way of combating the time squeeze while still enjoying leisure and fulfilling family roles. By better understanding the gendered meanings of leisure and its interconnectedness to other work and family roles, perhaps we will be able to comprehend more fully the benefits of leisure for men's and women's health and well-being.

References

Beaujot, R. and J. Lui. 2005. 'Models of Time Use in Paid and Unpaid Work'. *Journal of Family Issues* 26:924–47.

Becker, G.S. 1965. 'A Theory of Time Allocation'. *Economic Journal* 75:293–317.

Becker, P.E. and P. Moen. 1999. 'Scaling-Back: Dual Career Couples' Work-Family Strategies'. *Journal of Marriage and the Family* 61:995–1007.

Bianchi, S.M. 2000. 'Maternal Employment and Time with Children Dramatic Change and Surprising Continuity?' *Demography* 37:401–14.

Bianchi, S.M., M.A. Milkie, L.C. Sayer and J.P. Robinson. 2000. 'Is Anyone Doing the Housework? Trends in the Gender Division of Household Labor'. *Social Forces* 79:191–228.

Bianchi, S.M., J.P. Robinson and M.A. Milkie. 2006. *Changing Rhythms of American Life*. New York: Russell Sage.

Bird, C.E. and A.M. Fremont. 1991. 'Gender, Time Use and Health'. *Journal of Health and Social Behavior* 32:114–29.

Bittman, M. and J. Wajcman. 2000. 'The Rush Hour: The Character of Leisure Time and Gender Equity'. *Social Forces* 79:165–89.

Blair-Loy, M. 2003. *Competing Devotions*. Cambridge: Harvard University Press.

Brines, J. 1994. 'Economic Dependency, Gender and the Division of Labor at Home'. *American Journal of Sociology* 100:652–88.

Bryant, W.K. 1990. *The Economic Organization of the Household*. New York: Cambridge University Press.

Caldwell, L.L. 2005. 'Leisure and Health: Why Is Leisure Therapeutic?' *British Journal of Guidance and Counseling* 33:7–26.

Caltabiano, M.L. 1994. 'Measuring the Similarity among Leisure Activities Based on a Perceived Stress-Reduction Benefit'. *Leisure Studies* 13:17–31.

Coleman, J.S. 1990. *Foundations of Social Theory*. Cambridge: Harvard University Press.

Coltrane, S. 2000. 'Research on Household Labor: Modeling and Measuring the Social Embeddedness of Routine Family Work.' *Journal of Marriage and the Family* 62:1208–33.

Connell, R.W. 2002. *Gender*. Cambridge: Polity Press.

Deutsch, F.M. 1999. *Having It All: How Equally Shared Parenting Works*. Cambridge, MA: Harvard University Press.

Duxbury, L. and C. Higgins. 2001. *Work-Life Balance in the New Millennium: Where Are We? Where Do We Need to Go?* Ottawa: Canadian Policy Research Networks.

Esteve, R., J. San Martin and A.E. Lopez. 1999. 'Grasping the Meaning of Leisure: Developing a Self-Report Measurement Tool'. *Leisure Studies* 18:79–91.

Ferree, M.M. 1991. 'The Gender Division of Labor in Two-Earner Marriages: Dimensions of Variability and Change'. *Journal of Family Issues* 12:158–80.

Frederick, Judith A. 1995. *As Time Goes By . . . : Time Use of Canadians: General Social Survey*. Ottawa: Statistics Canada.

Fritz, C. and S. Sonnentag. 2006. 'Recovery, Well-Being, and Performance-Related Outcomes: The Role of Workload and Vacation Experiences'. *Journal of Applied Psychology* 91:936–45.

Gauthier, A. 2002. 'Historical Trends in the Time Use Patterns of Canadian Youth'. Paper presented at the meetings of the Canadian Population Society, Toronto, Canada.

Hagan, J. and F.M. Kay. 1995. *Gender in Practice: A Study of Lawyers' Lives*. Oxford: Oxford University Press.

Hays, S. 1996. *The Cultural Contradictions of Motherhood*. New Haven, CT: Yale University Press.

Henderson, K.A. and D. Bialeschki. 1991. 'A Sense of Entitlement to Leisure as Constraint and Empowerment for Women'. *Leisure Sciences* 13:51–65.

Hilbrecht, M., J. Zuzanek and R.C. Mannell. 2008. 'Time Use, Time Pressure and Gendered Behavior in Early and Late Adolescence'. *Sex Roles* 58:342–57.

Hill, C.R. and F.P. Stafford. 1980. 'Parental Care of Children: Time Diary Estimates of Quantity, Predictability and Variety'. *Journal of Human Resources* 15:202–39.

Hochschild, A.R. 1989. *The Second Shift*. New York: Avon Books.

———. 1997. *The Time Bind: When Work Becomes Home and Home Becomes Work*. New York: Holt.

Iwasaki, Y. 2003. 'Examining Rival Models of Leisure Coping Mechanisms'. *Leisure Sciences* 25:183–206.

Iwasaki, Y. 2006. 'Counteracting Stress through Leisure Coping: A Prospective Health Study'. *Psychology, Health and Medicine* 11:209–20.

Iwasaki, Y., J. Mactavish and K. MacKay. 2005. 'Building on the Strengths and Resilience: Leisure as a Stress Survival Strategy'. *British Journal of Guidance and Counseling* 33:81–100.

Iwasaki, Y. and R.C. Mannell. 2000. 'The Effects of Leisure Beliefs and Coping Strategies on Stress-Health Relationships: A Field Study'. *Leisure: The Journal of the Canadian Association for Leisure Studies* 24:3–57.

Kay, F.M. and J. Hagan. 1999. 'Cultivating Clients in the Competition for Partnership: Gender & the Organizational Restructuring of Law Firms in the 1990s'. *Law and Society Review* 33:517–55.

Kordana, K.A. 1995. 'Law Firms & Associate Careers: Tournament Theory versus the Production-Imperative Model'. *Yale Law Journal* 104:1907–33.

Lee, Y. and B.P. McCormick. 2006. 'Examining the Role of Self-Monitoring and Social Leisure in the Life Quality of Individuals with Spinal Cord Injury'. *Journal of Leisure Research* 38:1–19.

Lee, Y.G. and V. Bhargava. 2004. 'Leisure Time: Do Married and Single Individuals Spend It Differently?' *Family and Consumer Science Research Journal* 32:254–74.

Leete, L. and J.B. Schor. 1994. 'Assessing the Time-Squeeze Hypothesis: Hours Worked in the United States, 1969–89'. *Industrial Relations* 33:25–43.

Lloyd, K.M. and C.J. Auld. 2002. 'The Role of Leisure in Determining Quality of Life: Issues of Content and Measurement'. *Social Indicators Research* 57:43–71.

MacEachen, E., J. Polzer and J. Clarke. 2008. '"You are Free to Set Your Own Hours": Governing Worker Productivity and Health through Flexibility and Resilience'. *Social Science and Medicine* 66:1019–33.

Mannell, R.C. and D.A. Kleiber. 1997. *A Social Psychology of Leisure*. State College, PA: Venture Publishing.

Marshall, K. 2006. 'Converging Gender Roles.' Perspectives on Labour and Income, July 7, Statistics Canada Catalogue No. 75-001-XIE.

Mattingly, M.J. and S.M. Bianchi. 2003. 'Gender Differences in the Quantity and Quality of Free Time: The U.S. Experience'. *Social Forces* 81:999–1030.

Mattingly, M.J. and L.C. Sayer. 2006. 'Under Pressure: Gender Difference in the Relationship between Free Time and Feeling Rushed'. *Journal of Marriage and the Family* 68:205–21.

Nomaguchi, K.M. and S.M. Bianchi. 2004. 'Exercise Time: Gender Differences in the Effects of Marriage, Parenthood, and Employment'. *Journal of Marriage and Family* 66:413–30.

Nomaguchi, K.M., M.A. Milkie and S.M. Bianchi. 2005. 'Time Strains and Psychological Well-Being: Do Dual-Earner Mothers and Fathers Differ?' *Journal of Family Issues* 26:756–92.

Robinson, J.P. and G. Godbey. 1997. *Time for Life: The Surprising Ways Americans Use Their Time*. University Park: Pennsylvania State University Press.

Sanchez, L. 1994. 'Gender, Labor Allocations, and the Psychology of Entitlement within the Home'. *Social Forces* 73:533–53.

Sayer, L.C. 2005. 'Gender, Time and Inequality: Trends in Women's and Men's Paid Work, Unpaid Work and Free Time'. *Social Forces* 84:285–303.

Schor, J.B. 1991. *The Overworked American: The Unexpected Decline of Leisure*. New York: Basic Books.

Simon, R.W. 1995. 'Gender, Multiple Roles, Role Meaning, and Mental Health'. *Journal of Health and Social Behavior* 36:182–94.

Sonnentag, S. 2003. 'Recovery, Work Engagement, and Proactive Behavior: A New Look at the Interface between Nonwork and Work'. *Journal of Applied Psychology* 88:518–28.

Spain, D. and S.M. Bianchi. 1996. *Balancing Act: Motherhood, Marriage and Employment among American Women*. New York: Russell Sage Foundation.

Suitor, J.J., D. Mecom and I.S. Feld. 2001. 'Gender, Household Labor, and Scholarly Productivity among University Professors'. *Gender Issues* 19:50–67.

Thompson, L. 1991. 'Family Work: Women's Sense of Fairness'. *Journal of Family Issues* 12:181–96.

Trenberth, L. and P. Dewe. 2002. 'The Importance of Leisure as a Means of Coping with Work-Related Stress: An Exploratory Study'. *Counseling Psychology Quarterly* 15:59–72.

Wallace, J.E. 2002. *Juggling it All: Exploring Lawyers' Work, Home and Family Demands and Coping Strategies, Report of Stage One Findings. Research Report 00-02 prepared for the LSAC Research Report Series: a Publication of the Law School Admission Council*.

———. 2005. 'Job Stress, Depression and Work-Family Conflict Amongst Lawyers: A Test of the Strain and Buffer Hypotheses'. *Industrial Relations.* 60:510–37.

Zijlstra, F.R.H. and S. Sonnentag. 2006. 'After Work Is Done: Psychological Perspectives on Recovery from Work'. *European Journal of Work and Organizational Psychology* 15:129–38.

Zukewich, Nancy. 2003. *Work, Parenthood and the Experience of Time Scarcity*. Cat. No. 89-584-MIE-No. 1. Ottawa: Statistics Canada.

Questions for Critical Thought

CHAPTER 26

1. How was the intensity of violence measured in Roth's study? What two variables were strongly related to a high intensity of violence? Why?
2. How are workers rewarded for taking violence graciously?
3. What two voices are highlighted in Roth's study? What are the similarities and differences between the narratives told?
4. According to Roth, what actions can and should be taken in order to diminish this type of workplace violence?
5. The job of taking care of the elderly and developmentally disabled is probably not more violent than it was previously. The problem seems to have intensified because these individuals are increasingly receiving professional institutional care rather than personal, family care. What are some limitations of framing this problem as a workplace issue? What about the people who perform this difficult care work in the home rather than at work? What can be done for them?

CHAPTER 27

1. Why and how has the 'new public management' approach forged public–private partnerships in processing Medicaid applications?
2. Explain how the chronic care application process is heavily textually mediated. What challenges does this pose both to applicants and to the care facilities that are the eventual beneficiaries of each applicants' Medicaid funds?
3. How does the 'let's be friends' framework differ from the former approach? How does it change the assumptions that caseworkers make about applicants? What concrete changes in the application process have resulted?
4. How are local application reformers working within two accountability circuits? Describe the two circuits and how they shape reformers' work, including their goals and the people they are accountable to.
5. The authors caution us to not read too much into the surface benefits of this newly formed public–private partnership, as the applicants' interests are not fully recognized. Rather, applicants 'benefit when their interests coincide with those of the organizations involved'. Discuss how this arrangement could be potentially beneficial and/or harmful to these future recipients.

CHAPTER 28

1. Compare the meanings of the word *profession* in common parlance and sociological usage.
2. Compare the trait and power definitions of professions. What are the strengths and weaknesses of each? Explain why they are not mutually exclusive.

3. What definition does Adams settle on? Be sure to explain how she draws on both Freidson and Weber.

4. Why did Adams measure professions through regulatory legislation? How does this relate to her definition of professions?

5. Compare Adams' findings about professional and occupational regulation. How do the rights and responsibilities of these two types of regulation differ? How do professionals achieve special status through the law?

6. What evidence is there that professions are declining in power? What does Adams have to say about this development?

CHAPTER 29

1. What is role strain? How do the different household roles of men and women (e.g. mother/father or responsibilities for different tasks) enable men and women to deal with role strain in different ways? How does this relate to leisure?

2. What do Wallace and Young find about the relationship between paid work and leisure activities for men and women? How do they explain this relationship?

3. How do Wallace and Young's findings support their hypotheses? How are their findings surprising?

4. What future research questions are opened up by Wallace and Young's surprising findings?

5. Discuss the limitations to Wallace and Young's data. Explain why their findings can or cannot be generalized to the experience of all men and women.

Part VIII

Aging and the Life Course

The average age of Canadians increases with each decade. However, aging is not merely a biological phenomenon—it also has cultural meanings and social-psychological outcomes that affect people as they age. Aging affects, and is in turn affected by, interactions between individuals and their family, friends, communities, and the whole of society. As with other topics, there are various sociological approaches to understanding aging. Functionalists sometimes contend that the devaluation of people as they age is harmful to society because older individuals have a wealth of knowledge and experience they can pass on. Conflict theorists view aging as problematic because the power and influence necessary to effect change decreases as people age. Symbolic interactionists focus on how an individual's roles change in response to aging. And applying feminist theory to the analysis of ageism can provide insight into the social forces that affect older women and their experiences in a gendered world.

Given the rapid aging of our society, Canadian sociologists are paying increased attention to the social process of aging and to related issues such as retirement and the older individual's sense of identity. Since a large portion of the senior population is composed of older immigrants, there has also been interest in how these older citizens experience aging in a foreign society. However, this section is not only about elderly people or even aging: it is about the life course, and how people's social roles, opportunities, and connections change as they pass through life.

The life course approach recognizes that people's lives are situated in particular times and places, so that the process of aging itself varies over time. It is a social and cultural, as well as biological, process. Moreover, people's life courses are affected by their past experiences and past decisions. They may be free to choose the next steps in their lives, but all choices are socially constrained by available opportunities. Thus, important life events such as marriage, parenthood, divorce, retirement, and widowhood are situated in time and place, and people's experiences of these events will also reflect their current age, resources, and available opportunities. It is a different experience to enter parenthood at 15 or 30, and to enter widowhood at 45 or 90, and different to enter these roles in a modern industrial society or a less-developed country.

The paper by Frank Trovato and Nirannanilathu Lalu shows that, in recent decades, the life expectancy gap between men and women has started to close, owing to increased cigarette smoking among women and reduced male mortality from accidents and violence. Laura Funk and Karen Kobayashi argue that researchers need a new way to study the decision to provide filial care work for aging parents. Rather than asking if the decision is a matter of free choice or obligation, they insist that the very meanings of 'choice' and 'obligation' are often blurred in novel ways across social and ideological contexts, and that this is what needs to be studied. Finally, Zenaida Ravanera and Roderic Beaujot show that levels of childlessness and views about it vary strongly by sex and level of education, and that these views change over the life cycle.

Childlessness and Socio-Economic Characteristics: What Does the Canadian 2006 General Social Survey Tell Us?

Zenaida Ravanera and Roderic Beaujot

Increase in Levels of Childlessness

About 22 per cent of Canadian women born at the beginning of the twentieth century were childless (see Figure 30.1), many of whom were in their child-bearing years around the time of the Great Depression. **Childlessness** decreased to lower than 15 per cent among women who gave birth in the baby boom years (1946–1966), started to increase for women born in 1952–56, and continued to increase in subsequent cohorts, with the childlessness of women born in the early 1960s approaching 20 per cent. While the women born in the 1970s and later have not as yet reached the end of their child-bearing years by 2006, if the trend continues, the percentage of childlessness in these younger cohorts may equal or surpass the level in the Great Depression. The trends of childlessness in other Western countries are similar to those in Canada. The countries where, for women born at the end of the 1960s, the proportion who are childless is 20 per cent or higher are Austria, Finland, England, West Germany, and possibly soon Ireland and the Netherlands (Sardon, 2006: 243–244). In contrast, childlessness in Portugal is under 10 per cent, and the United States, as well as Scandinavian countries except Finland, have levels closer to 15 per cent.

Childlessness is often generalized from data pertaining to women. But men and women need not have the same level of childlessness, and indeed, the data show that the proportion of childless men is higher than that of women (Figure 30.1). This difference could be partly explained by the older age when men become parents, and by the failure of some men to report in the survey their having fathered a child, especially if the child no longer lives with the father (Ravanera and Beaujot, 2010).

To overcome some of these shortcomings, this study uses the 2006 General Social Survey on Family Transitions to compare the influence of education and personal income on childlessness and on the intention to remain childfree for men and women, by age. We find that the relationship between gender and the effects of education changes across the life course. At age 30–39, the effect of education is similar for women and men; however, at age 40–49, education has the opposite effect. On the other hand, the effects of income are consistently opposite for men and women across the life course.

Childlessness and Constrained Decision Making

As with other related behaviour such as entering relationships and work patterns, childlessness can be seen as the result of decision-making processes that take place within constraints of the life course,

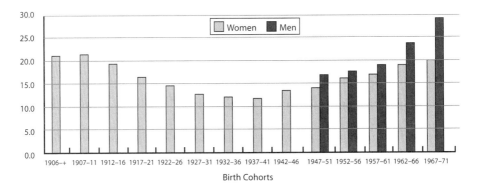

Figure 30.1 Proportion (%) Childless by Five-Year Birth Cohort
Canadian Women and Men

Source: 1991 Census PUMF for 1906 & earlier to 1946 birth cohorts; and 2006 GSS on Family transitions for 1947 to 1971 birth cohorts.

structures, and norms (Miller and Godwin, 1977; Beaujot, Ravanera, and Burch, 2007).

Young people give high priority to three life goals: having satisfying work, living in an enduring union, and having children (Lapierre-Adamcyk, 1990). These goals are largely placed in this order as priorities and within the life course sequence of events. Further, most young couples do not make a direct decision to be childless (Veevers, 1980: 20–29). Rather, childlessness results from a 'waiting game', or a series of postponements of child-bearing. The transition from wanting to not wanting children occurs in stages: the first is postponing child-bearing for a definite time; followed by postponement for an indefinite time; then, a period of deliberation of the pros and cons of parenthood; and finally, acceptance of permanent childlessness.

Schooling and work impose **structural constraints** on family life. These domains have drastically changed over the past decades, especially for Canadian women, whose school attendance and work participation have greatly increased (Clark, 2000; Beaujot, Ravanera, and Burch, 2007; Morissette, 2002; Beaujot, 2000). The changes for young men over the period 1981–2001 have been less positive: both the proportion of men working full time and the earning levels of those employed declined (Morissette, 2002: 33). Wages of newly hired employees have fallen substantially, and the

proportion of new employees, both males and females, hired for temporary jobs increased from 1989 to 2004 (Morissette and Johnson, 2005). The disadvantaged situation of recent entrants to the labour force affects entry into marriage and parenthood, which is especially dependent on men's earnings and career mobility (Oppenheimer and Lewin, 1999).

Orientation toward work and family also has an influence on child-bearing decisions. Hakim (2003) categorizes women into *family-centred*, *work-centred*, and *adaptive*, with the family-centred more likely to have children and the work-centred more likely to have fewer or no children.

Data and Methods

Our sample is taken from the 2006 **General Social Survey** on Family Transitions (GSS), which has as its target population all persons aged 15 years and older in Canada excluding residents of the Yukon, Northwest Territories, and Nunavut, and full-time residents of institutions (Statistics Canada, 2008). Our study uses data from 4,755 women and 3,411 men aged 30–49. Analysis is done separately for men and women and results are presented for 10-year birth cohorts, with information on 5-year birth cohorts included where deemed appropriate. Sampling weights were used in all the analyses.

Life Course Constraints: The Waiting Game

The intention to be childfree is low among young Canadians (Stobert and Kemeny, 2003). The 2006 GSS shows that at age 30–34, only 7 per cent of women and 10 per cent of men intend to be childfree, although 30 per cent of women and 48 per cent of men are actually childless (Figure 30.2).

Many people become parents in their thirties, and by ages 35–39, the proportion who are childless decreases to 19 per cent for women and 30 per cent for men. However, the proportion intending to remain childfree increases to 11 per cent for women and to 14 per cent for men. Few manage to become parents in their forties, so that at age 40–44, 19 per cent remain childless, and the proportion intending to remain childfree becomes 17 per cent for women and 18 per cent for men. At age 45–49, acceptance of permanent childlessness becomes evident: 17 per cent of women and 19 per cent of men are childless and 16 per cent intend to be childfree. If a real cohort had been followed from age 30 to age 49, the percentages would not be exactly the same as those presented in Figure 30.2; however, the trends in childlessness and intention to be childfree would be generally similar. These age-related trends in childlessness and intention to remain childfree reinforce findings from qualitative research that a high percentage of childlessness results from a 'waiting game' (Veevers, 1980).

Family life course stages influence childlessness—the married and formerly married have the lowest level of childlessness (Table 30.1), implying that marriage remains a pre-condition for having children. This is also evident from the expectedly higher proportion of childless women among the single and among those in common-law unions. Childlessness of women in common-law unions is more than twice that of married women, and men in common-law unions also have a higher level of childlessness than married men. Common-law unions may be seen as less permanent than marriage, and cohabiting couples may not hold the traditional family values that are associated with having children.

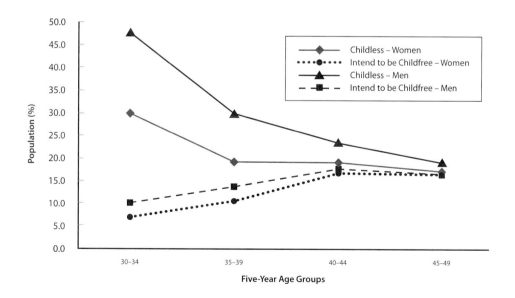

Figure 30.2 Proportion (%) Childless and Intending to be Childfree

Source: 2006 General Social Survey

Table 30.1 Proportion (%) of Childless Women and Men by Intention to Have Children*; Aged 30–49, by 10-Year Age Groups and Marital Status, 2006

Explanatory Variables	AGE GROUP 30–39				AGE GROUP 40–49			
	N	Total Childless	Intend to have		N	Total Childless	Intend to have	
			No Child	Children			No Child	Children
			WOMEN					
Total %	1,927	24.2	8.8	15.4	2,520	18.0	16.6	1.4
Married	1,178	12.5	3.8	8.7	1,620	12.4	11.4	1.0
Common-law	306	31.4	15.4	16.0	314	25.5	24.8	0.6
Wid/Div/Separated	142	14.7	7.7	7.0	354	10.2	9.6	0.6
Single	299	66.9	21.7	45.2	227	60.2	53.1	7.1
			MEN					
Total %	1,499	38.6	11.9	26.7	1,912	21.2	17.0	4.2
Married	867	23.0	5.7	17.3	1,253	9.6	8.1	1.5
Common-law	267	35.6	15.4	20.2	287	32.4	29.6	2.8
Wid/Div/Separated	60	35.0	8.3	26.7	169	15.4	11.8	3.6
Single	304	86.5	27.0	59.5	204	81.8	58.3	23.5

Note: *Excludes men and women with 'missing data' on intention to have children.

Source: 2006 General Social Survey on Family Transitions

Structural Constraints: Effects of Education and Personal Income

Education and personal income can influence childlessness in a number of ways: *postponement* of child-bearing occurs due to the large time investments associated with acquiring education and establishing careers; *affordability* refers to the ability to provide the financial resources required to raise children; and *values* associated with various levels of education and income could make child rearing and childfree life styles more or less preferable.

Our data reflect these trends. At age 30–39, the level of childlessness increases with education for both genders—11 per cent of lower-educated women are childless, compared with 32 per cent of women with university education (Table 30.2). Similarly, the proportion of university-educated men who are childless is highest at 47 per cent, whereas the proportion childless for men with the lowest level of education is 34 per cent. Those who did not pursue higher education became parents

while the highly educated men and women were still acquiring education. This postponement is also evident from the proportions intending to have children, which are highest for the university-educated women (22 per cent vs. 2 per cent for those with lowest education) and men (35 per cent vs. 22 per cent), an indication that men and women who did not have children in their twenties are intending to 'catch up' in their thirties.

However, the effect of education at age 40 to 49 differs by gender. Those who have postponed becoming parents would have had the time to do so in their thirties, and those who are still childless in their forties have remained so for other reasons. Women with the highest education have the highest proportion of those childless (25 per cent) and also the highest proportion of those intending to be childfree (23 per cent). In contrast, men with the highest education have the lowest proportion of those childless (20 per cent) and the lowest proportion of those intending to be childfree (15 per cent). However, the differences by levels of education are greater for women than for men.

The gender difference also holds true in the effect of personal income. For the two age groups, affluent women are more likely to be childless and intend to be childfree than are less-affluent women, whereas affluent men are more likely to have children and less likely to have the intention of remaining child-free than are less affluent men (Table 30.2).

The contrasting gender effects of education at older ages and of personal income at both ages cannot be fully explained by the process of postponement: these trends point to the effects of affordability and values. The division of tasks within couples may also be relevant. When men are seen as the main breadwinner, men with higher income can well afford to become a parent, especially with a partner who is expected to care for the child. Women with higher income bear a higher opportunity cost for becoming a parent; and affluent women may prefer and be able to afford to pursue childfree lifestyles.

Structural Constraints: Effects of Work Orientation or Work Status

That affordability is a consideration for having children is also evident in the influence of work status on the levels of childlessness and intention to be childfree. Men who are employed full time have the lowest level of childlessness, at 37 per cent for men aged 30–39 and 19 per cent for those aged 40–49 (Table 30.2). The proportion intending to remain childfree is also lowest for full-time employed men.

The work orientation of women has an influence opposite to that of men. Work-centred women have the highest proportion of those who are childless (Table 30.2). While they also have the highest proportion of those intending to have children among those aged 30–39 (24 per cent), the proportion intending to remain childfree (at 13 per cent) is double that of women who have a balanced work-family orientation (at 6 per cent). At age 40–49, the proportions of childless and intending to remain childfree are also highest among work-centred women, although the differences between the work-centred and balanced types are

smaller. That the highest levels of childlessness and intention to be childfree are among work-oriented women could again be an indication of the high opportunity cost of having a child, and could also mean that work-oriented women have a preference for a lifestyle unencumbered by children.

Summary and Conclusion

Most young people have a set of goals that includes having children—only about 7 to 10 per cent at age 30–34 explicitly state the intention to be child-free. However, this goal of having children is most commonly prioritized after the other lifetime goals of having satisfying work and an enduring relationship. As more young people, especially women, pursue higher education and delay their entrance into the labour force, marriage and child-bearing are also postponed. With this delay, an adjustment in the intention of having children is made, and thus, when those who are childless reach their mid-thirties, the proportion intending to remain childfree increases. For women and men who would have liked to have had children, the need to first establish themselves in the economic realm through education and work can be seen as constraints in the achievement of their fertility goals.

In the past two to three decades, the economic situation of young men has been at a disadvantage in comparison to women and to older men, which no doubt has led to the postponement of entry into stable relationships and parenthood. For some of these men, this has led to eventual childlessness. For women, high levels of childlessness are most apparent for those who have university education and high-paying jobs. This may be explained by the fact that, in the traditional family model wherein women do more of the unpaid work, the opportunity costs of becoming a parent are higher for women with high education and income (Ravanera, Beaujot, and Liu, 2009).

The intention to have no children sharply increases between the ages 35 to 40, indicating that social policies that would decrease the pressure to postpone child-bearing into the later thirties may also decrease childlessness. It is noteworthy that among women aged 30–39 with no

Table 30.2 Proportion (%) of Childless Women and Men by Intention to Have Children*; Aged 30–49, by 10-Year Age Groups and 'Structural' Variables, 2006

Explanatory Variables *Indicators of Structures at Individual Level*	AGE GROUP 30–39				AGE GROUP 40–49			
	Total Childless	Child	Intend to have		Total Childless	Child	Intend to have	
			No Child	Children			No Child	Children
WOMEN								
Respondent's Education								
Some HS or Lower	108	11.1	9.3	1.9	231	10.8	10.8	0.0
HS & Some College	442	19.9	9.0	10.8	735	16.2	14.7	1.5
College or Trade	676	22.2	7.2	14.9	886	15.9	14.5	1.4
University & Higher	675	31.8	10.2	21.6	626	25.4	23.3	2.1
Personal Income								
Less than $20,000	533	15.0	6.2	8.8	584	13.9	12.0	1.9
$20,000 to $49,999	742	26.0	10.0	16.0	912	16.1	14.3	1.9
$50,000 and over	348	38.5	10.3	28.2	505	26.5	25.9	0.6
Missing	303	19.5	6.6	10.9	520	17.5	16.5	1.0
Work-Family Orientation								
Family-centred	376	2.6	1.3	1.3	356	10.2	9.6	0.6
Balanced	561	17.5	59	11.6	737	15.4	14.2	1.2
Work-centred	910	37.0	12 7	24.3	1,240	21.0	19.3	1.7
Missing	60	26.3	18 8	7.5	187	23.5	21.4	2.1
MEN								
Respondent's Education								
Some HS or Lower	138	34.0	12.3	21.7	235	24.3	21.3	3.0
HS & Some College	423	38.8	13.5	25.3	561	20.8	16.2	4.6
College or Trade	448	32.3	10.9	21.4	563	21.6	18.0	3.6
University & Higher	469	46.5	11.5	35.0	498	19.7	15.3	4.4
Personal Income								
Less than $20,000	115	57.4	19.1	38.3	129	41.9	34.9	7.0
$20,000 to $49,999	521	44.2	131	31.1	515	27.6	21.4	6.2
$50,000 and over	671	32.0	8 9	23.1	993	16.6	14.1	2.5
Missing	193	35.2	14.5	20.7	274	16.4	10.9	5.5
Work Status in Past 12 Months								
Full-time	1,322	37.0	11.0	26.0	1,667	16.9	15.0	3.9
Part-time	59	62.7	20.3	42.4	72	33.3	25.0	8.3
Not Employed	99	48.5	19.2	29.3	138	39.9	31.9	8.0

Note: *Excludes women and men with 'missing data' on intention to have children.

Source: 2006 General Social Survey on Family Transitions

children, those with the highest education are the most likely to intend to have children. Social policies (such as child care and parental leave) could facilitate the achievement of this intention.

References

Beaujot, Roderic. 2000. *Earning and Caring in Canadian Families.* Peterborough: Broadview.

Beaujot, Roderic, Zenaida R. Ravanera, and Thomas K. Burch. 2007. Toward an HRSDC Family Research Framework. Paper presented at the Social Development Canada Expert roundtable on Challenges for Canadian Families, 1-2 December 2005. Population Studies Centre Discussion Paper No. 07-02: http://sociology.uwo.ca/popstudies/dp/dp07-02.pdf.

Clark, Warren. 2000. '100 Years of Education'. *Canadian Social Trends* 59, pp. 3–7.

Hakim, Catherine. 2003. 'A New Approach to Explaining Fertility Patterns: Preference Theory'. *Population and Development Review* 29(3), pp. 349–374.

Lapierre-Adamcyk, Evelyne. 1990. Faire face au changement démographique: la nécessaire participation des femmes. In R. Beaujot, Editor, *Faire Face au Changement Démographique.* Ottawa : Royal Society of Canada.

Miller, Warren B. and R. Kenneth Godwin. 1977. *Psyche and Demos: Individual Psychology and the Issues of Population.* New York: Oxford University Press.

Morissette, René. 2002. 'Cumulative Earnings among Young Workers'. *Perspectives on Labour and Income* 14(4), pp. 33–40.

Morissette, René and Anick Johnson. 2005. Are Good Jobs Disappearing in Canada? Statistics Canada Analytical Studies Branch research paper series, Catalogue no. 11F0019MIE — No. 239.

Ravanera, Zenaida R. and Rod Beaujot. 2010. Childlessness of Men in Canada's Second Demographic Transition. Paper to be presented at the 2010 Annual Meeting of the Canadian Population Society, June 1–3, Montreal.

Sardon, J.P. 2006. 'Evolution démographique récente des pays développés'. *Population* 61(3), pp. 225–300.

Statistics Canada. 2008. General Social Survey Cycle 20: Family Transitions (2006) Public Use Microdata File Documentation and User's Guide. Catalogue No. 12M0020G.

Stobert, Susan and Anna Kemeny. 2003. 'Childfree by Choice'. *Canadian Social Trends.* Summer 2003, pp. 7–10.

Veevers, Jean. 1980. *Childless by Choice.* Toronto: Butterworths.

CHAPTER 31

'Choice' in Filial Care Work: Moving beyond a Dichotomy

Laura M. Funk and Karen M. Kobayashi

For the first time in our nation's history, it is estimated that Canadian adults will spend more time caring for their aging parents than raising their children (McDaniel 2005). According to recent findings from the General Social Survey on social support, just over 10 per cent of the population aged 45 to 64 years are providing filial care to older parents (Stobert and Cranswick 2004). In this paper, the term **filial care work** is used to describe assistance and support provided by adult children for their adoptive, birth, or step-parents (i.e., it encompasses informal or family caregiving rather than formal or paid work).

Research shows that the majority of care for older adults has always come from family sources, and with the shift away from institutionalization in the 1980s, the probability of providing such care continues to increase (Marks 1996). Yet depending on the context in which care work for parents is performed, a caregiver's well-being, particularly his or her mental health, can be seriously compromised (Anderson et al. 1995; Cochrane et al. 1997; Lee 1999). As such, there has been keen interest in the factors that motivate and sustain adult children's caregiving behaviours and frame their subjective experiences.

In this paper, we argue that in order to understand filial caregiving, there is a need to move beyond a focus on a dichotomy between choice and obligation, as they are not **mutually exclusive** concepts. In doing so, we first illustrate how theoretical and empirical **discourse** maintains the idea of a dichotomy; then, we propose that the distinction between 'voluntary' and 'involuntary' motivations does not adequately capture the complexities of filial care work. Choice, we maintain, should be understood as both relational and contextual. Finally, we explore how the choice–obligation dichotomy operates ideologically, and discuss implications for the moral-political understandings of filial care work.

Deconstructing the Dichotomy

The dichotomy between choice and obligation does not adequately reflect the complexities of the family caregiving experience. Choice and obligation are not mutually exclusive; affection/love does not necessarily equate with choice (as with individualization) or with obligation (as with some feminist perspectives). McGrew (1998), for example, reveals how caregiving daughters respond to parental dependency with an 'impulse to care' (p. 49) that often precludes a conscious decision and is motivated by need, compulsion, socialization, and moral ideas; from this perspective, having to and wanting to are inextricably intertwined, and a sense of responsibility involves a complex combination of motivations to care for elderly parents, including external and internal, as well as obligatory and discretionary forces (Donorfio 1996).

In research by Funk (2008), 28 adult children were asked to talk about their sense of responsibility for their aging parents. Many participants made comments supportive of both choice and obligation within their interview. Asked to explain a sense of choice and/or obligation, at times, participants even used the same rationale: most notably, the idea that providing support for parents is entirely 'self-motivated' was used to support the idea of choice; at other times, participants spoke about how, because of the strength of their own personal values and beliefs, there was no other choice but to provide care. Further, some participants justified the presence of choice within obligation, or obligation within choice; others spoke about the 'everyday' choices made around the otherwise obligatory enactment of responsibility, and some spoke about choices made about how to cope and maintain a sense of control. There was also talk about how choices are made to 'take on' responsibilities, but that this creates a commitment with accompanying obligations. The fact that the same participants spoke of both obligatory and voluntary aspects within the same interview indicates that the concepts are not mutually exclusive in practice.

Rather, choice and obligation can be understood as both contextual and relational—that is, as manifesting in the interaction between or the intersection of macro (social, political, and cultural) and micro (family and relationship dynamics) contexts. A critical feminist perspective (as indicated above) highlights the importance of structural, ideological, and political contexts. In the following section, we illustrate how an in-depth understanding of the context of family relationships can enhance our understanding about choice and obligation in filial care work. In particular, data on filial relationships illustrate that the dichotomy between choice and obligation does not adequately reflect the complexities of decisions in the family caregiving experience.

A central focus of **life course** theorists is the principle of interdependent or 'linked' lives (Bengtson and Harootyan 1994; Elder 1994), whereby events in one family member's life have effects on other family members'. This is one way the *interrelationships* between family members have been explicated, in terms of their impact on filial care work. Parental need for support (e.g. due to the onset of chronic disease or disability) influences the choices of adult children around the timing of entrance into the caregiving role. More broadly, factors affecting the life transitions and circumstances of older Canadians, by impacting parents' need for support, affect children's sense of responsibility to provide care, as well as parents' expectations of appropriate levels and types of support.

Research on ethnocultural families in North America illustrates well the relational, interdependent nature of support in aging families. While values of filial responsibility are particularly salient, for example, in Korean American (Pyke 2000), Chinese Canadian (Ho et al. 2003), and Japanese Canadian (Kobayashi 2000) families, North American research on Chinese and South Asian immigrant families also indicates an equally strong sense of obligation on the part of parents to support young adult children (Gee and Mitchell 2003; Kamo 2000; Pacey 2002). These data suggest the need for further empirical research that helps us more fully understand the relational and interdependent nature of choice and obligation in ethnocultural family contexts.

Smart and Shipman (2004) summarize research indicating that individuals do not see family caregiving and kinship as contingent on one another (although much of this research focuses on marital partnerships rather than filial roles), but that kinship ties and family culture provide the contexts in which decisions are made. In other words, choices are 'taken in the setting of attentiveness to others' (Smart and Shipman 2004:493). Indeed, one criticism of the concept of caregiving is that it ignores reciprocal exchanges and interdependencies that are part of the context of meaning of normal family relationships and interaction (Henderson and Forbat 2002). From this perspective, filial responsibility is a commitment stemming from interactions and largely implicit negotiations over time in families (Finch and Mason 1991, 1993; Piercy 1998). McDaniel (2001) suggests that, in fact, a life course perspective considers 'the accumulation of choices made at earlier stages, as well as non-choices' (p. 198).

Ultimately, family relationships and dynamics are themselves rooted in structural (e.g. political, cultural, economic, ideological) contexts. However, our argument here is that the exploration of choice and obligation in filial care work would benefit from further examination of the family context in research—we need greater understanding of how choice and obligation are intertwined and embedded in family dynamics and family cultures over time; how the actions of one family member affect others (the life course concept of 'linked lives'); and how relational considerations, reciprocal exchanges, and symbolic interactions are fundamental to understanding the ways in which choice and obligation are experienced. Data on filial relationships, in this way, can help illustrate the ways in which a dichotomy between choice and obligation does not adequately reflect the complexities of family caregiving experiences.

The Choice–Obligation Dichotomy as Ideological

When choice and obligation are constructed as polar opposites, this dichotomy can be ideological when applied at the moral-political level. While the 2002 Romanow Report called for the expansion of formal care services, and while there is rapid aging of the population, cutbacks to home care programs in Canada over the past few years represent an example of the offloading of responsibility from the state onto the family. In this context, the dichotomy between choice and obligation can be, and indeed has been, used to justify this shift—family members are constructed as providing care out of a 'loving choice' as opposed to 'obligation'. This obscures the multitude of ways in which obligation and choice are intertwined at the individual level, and in the context of family relationships. Further, it obscures the underlying subtext of the discourse that, at the moral-political level, what can be constructed as behaviour motivated by individual choice is actually constructed as involving individual (as opposed to collective) obligation. However, a simple focus on the ways in which adult children *are* obligated to provide care for parents also does not fit well with many individuals' personal understandings of the complexities of their own filial relationships.

There has been some theoretical work that does highlight the important interconnections between choice and responsibility. In relation to care work specifically, McDaniel (2004) describes how, in the contemporary neo-liberal context, care 'becomes recoded as having little market value, to be provided out of love, voluntarily or for minimal compensation' (p. 38). In this context, care for aging parents, perceived as a choice by governments and individuals, is devalued in the sense of being an appropriate area for government intervention in the form of services. Yet while constructed as choice, McDaniel argues that the accompanying 'bullying normativities' put women in particular 'on the front lines of accountability' in this regard (p. 38). Parent care is simultaneously constructed as individual choice and as a generational (i.e., family-based) obligation or responsibility. In contrast, McDaniel (2001) promotes an understanding of individual life courses, constraints, and choices in the context of broader entitlements and opportunities that shift by gender and generational relations over time. That is, choices and constraints are viewed with a collective lens.

More broadly, the responsibilization perspective (e.g. Rose 1996) can also be used to examine the interconnections between choice and obligation. Familialism and individualism are competing ideals, yet paradoxically, both are used as justification for shifting additional responsibility for care from governments and formal settings to families. The result is a society in which we, as independent selves, should voluntarily choose and want to provide care, yet are simultaneously pressured into responsibility for family members as well as for self, and into independent yet 'responsible' choices (Rose 1996).

Conclusion

The discussion and debate about choice highlights the importance of understanding how normative and structural contexts affect how we view family commitments, how we view 'choice', and how we experience caregiving for aging parents.

In support of the work of individualization theorists, such a perspective does highlight changes that may have increased to some degree the amount of choice or flexibility in North American society, for at least some adult children (e.g. those with private resources). And, at the very least, it points to the potential for increased choice. However, given the weight of empirical research findings indicating constraints on choice, to maintain that family care work is 'voluntary' is perhaps overstated. However, such findings are often interpreted with reference to the obligatory nature of parent care, in contrast to choice and voluntary motivations.

Choice 'is not an individualized activity, but instead, one that takes place in a wider social arena' (Arksey and Glendinning 2007:172), as well as a more micro-level family context. Yet while there are myriad ways in which choice in filial care work is contextual, this does not necessarily mean it is subjectively experienced as obligation. Rather than perpetuating a dichotomy between 'choice' and 'obligation', there is a need to move beyond this in research on filial care work, and to acknowledge that the two concepts are not mutually exclusive as motivations for parent care.

Overall, a distinction between voluntary and involuntary motivations and the debate over whether there is greater or lesser choice in family care work today does not adequately reflect the complex realities of family caregiving experiences. Caregiving discussions need to move beyond the debate over choice. In particular, while it is important to consider the numerous ways individuals are constrained or supported in enacting care work, we should also consider how these broader dialogues are interpreted by adult children, and how they shape subjective experiences of care work and the well-being of those providing it. Gender and social class differences in this process are certainly implicated and need to be explored further. In addition, such an agenda behooves us to develop a deeper understanding of family care work than is currently characterized within quantitative research—that is, an agenda that moves us beyond a simplistic internal/external dichotomy of choice.

References

Anderson, C.S., J. Linto and E.G. Stewart-Wynne. 1995. 'A Population-Based Assessment of the Impact and Burden of Caregiving for Long-Term Stroke Survivors'. *Stroke* 26: 843–49.

Arksey, H. and C. Glendinning. 2007. 'Choice in the Context of Informal Care-Giving'. *Health and Social Care in the Community* 15:165–75.

Bengtson, V.L. and R.A. Harootyan. 1994. *Intergenerational Linkages: Hidden Connections in American Society*. New York: Springer.

Cain. R., M. Maclean and S. Sellick. 2004. 'Giving Support and Getting Help: Informal Caregivers' Experiences with Palliative Care Services'. *Palliative and Supportive Care* 2:265–72.

Cochrane, J.J., P.N. Goering and J.M. Rogers. 1997. 'The Mental Health of Informal Caregivers in Ontario: An Epidemiological Survey'. *American Journal of Public Health* 87:2002–2007.

Donomo, L.M. 1996. 'Filial Responsibility: Widowed Mothers and their Caregiving Daughters, a Qualitative Grounded Theory Approach'. Dissertation, University of Connecticut, Storrs.

Elder, G.H. Jr. 1994. 'Time, Human Aging, and Social Change: Perspectives on the Life Course'. *Social Psychology Quarterly* 22:233–45.

Finch, J. and J. Mason. 1991. 'Obligations of Kinship in Contemporary Britain: Is there Normative Agreement?' *British Journal of Sociology* 42:345–67.

————. 1993. *Negotiating Family Responsibilities*. London, UK: Tavistock/Routledge.

Funk, L.M. 2008. 'Responsibility for Aging Parents: Independence and Obligation within Filial Relationships'. Dissertation. University of Victoria, Victoria, BC, Canada.

Gee, E.M. and B.A. Mitchell. 2003. 'One Roof: Exploring Multi-Generational Households in Canada'. Pp. 291–311 in *Voices: Essays on Canadian Families*, edited by M. Lynn. Scarborough, ON: Nelson Thomson Learning.

Henderson, J. and L. Forbat. 2002. 'Relationship-Based Social Policy: Personal and Policy Constructions of "Care"'. *Critical Social Policy* 22:669–87.

Ho, B., J. Friedland, S. Rappolt and S. Noh, 2003. 'Caregiving for Relatives with Alzheimer's Disease: Feelings of Chinese-Canadian Women'. *Journal of Aging Studies* 17:301–21.

Kamo, Y. 2000. 'Racial and Ethnic Differences in Extended Family Households'. *Sociological Perspectives* 43:211–29.

Kobayuhi, K. 2000. 'The Nature of Support from Adult *Sansei* (Third Generation) Children to Older *Nisei* (Second Generation) Parents in Japanese Canadian Families'. *Journal of Cross-Cultural Gerontology* 15:185–205.

Lee, C. 1999. 'Health, Stress and Coping among Women Caregivers: A Review'. *Journal of Health Psychology* 4:27–40.

Marks, N.F. 1996. 'Caregiving across the Lifespan: National Prevalence and Predictors'. *Family Relations* 45:27–36.

McDaniel, S. 2001. 'Born at the Right Time? Gendered Generations and Webs of Entitlement and Responsibility'. *Canadian Journal of Sociology* 26:193–214.

McDaniel, S. 2004. 'Generationing Gender: Justice and the Division of Welfare'. *Journal of Aging Studies* 18:27–44.

McDaniel, S. 2005. 'The Family Lives of the Middle-Aged and Elderly in Canada'. Pp. 195–211 in *Families: Changing Trends in Canada*, edited by M. Baker. Toronto, ON: McGraw-Hill Ryerson.

McGrew, K. 1998. 'Daughters' Caregiving Decisions: From an Impulse to a Balancing Point of Care'. *Journal of Women and Aging* 10:49–65.

Pacey, M. 2002. *Living Alone and Living with Children: The Living Arrangements of Canadian and Chinese-Canadian Seniors*. Hamilton, ON: McMaster University.

Piercy, K. 1998. 'Theorizing about Family Caregiving: The Role of Responsibility'. *Journal of Marriage and the Family* 60:109–18.

Pyke, K. 2000. '"Normal American Family" as an Interpretive Structure of Family Life among Grown Children of Korean and Vietnamese Immigrants'. *Journal of Marriage and the Family* 62:240–55.

Romanow, R.J. 2002. *Building on Values: The Future of Health Care in Canada: Final Report of the Commission on the Future of Health Care in* Canada. Ottawa, ON: Government of Canada.

Rose, N. 1996. 'Governing "Advanced" Liberal Democracies'. Pp. 37–64 in *Foucault and Political Reason: Liberalism, Neo-Liberalism and Rationalities of Government*, edited by A. Barry, T. Osborne and N. Rose. Chicago, IL: University of Chicago Press.

Smart, C. and B. Shipman. 2004. 'Visions in Monochrome: Families, Marriage and the Individualization Thesis'. *British Journal of Sociology* 55:491–509.

Stein, C.H., V.A. Wemmerus, M. Ward, M.E., Gaines, A.L. Freeberg and T.C. Jewell. 1998. '"Because they're my Parents": An Intergenerational Study of Felt Obligations and Parental Caregiving'. *Journal of Marriage and the Family* 60:611–22.

Stobert, S. and K. Cranswick. 2004. 'Looking After Seniors: Who Does What for Whom?' *Canadian Social Trends: Statistics Canada: Ottawa, Ontario* 74:2–6.

From Divergence to Convergence: The Sex Differential in Life Expectancy in Canada, 1971–2000

Frank Trovato and Nirannanilathu Lalu

Currently, **life expectancy** at birth in the industrialized countries ranges in the upper seventies for men and above 80 years for women (van Hoorn and Broekman, 1999; Population Reference Bureau, 2005). During the last quarter of the twentieth century, an unexpected reversal in the long-established pattern of this differential was noted: the female advantage in the average length of life declined steadily, in some cases since the early 1970s and in others since the early 1980s (Trovato and Lalu, 1996a).

Early in the twentieth century, the male–female **mortality** differential was only between 2 and 3 years. After the 1920s, however, it rose gradually to about 4.5 years in the 1950s, and to about 7 years in 1971. By the early 1980s, it had reached a peak point, and has declined thereafter to its current level of about 5.3 years. The Canadian experience parallels that of most other industrialized countries. In Sweden, for example, the difference in life expectancy between the sexes surpassed the 3-year mark by the mid-1950s; it rose to approximately 5.5 years in the early 1970s, then declined to just under 5 years by 1999 (Trovato and Heyen, 2003). For the United States, the historical pattern of change in this differential is remarkably similar to that of Canada (Smith, 1993: 83). In this country, the peak point occurred between the late 1970s and the early 1980s, at 7.70 years. It then dropped to approximately 5.4 years by 2000.

The investigation in this paper expands on recently published works in this area of mortality analysis (e.g. Trovato and Lalu, 1996a; 1996b; 1998; Pampel, 2002; 2003a; 2003b; Waldron, 1993; Nathanson, 1995). Rather than examining an aggregate of countries, as is customarily done in this literature, here we look at the specific case of Canada over roughly a 30-year interval, from 1971 to 2000. Observed narrowing and widening of the difference in life expectancy between men and women must necessarily obtain from temporal shifts in sex differences in mortality from major causes of death. We examine, through statistical decomposition, the contribution of 10 causes of death to the change in the sex differential in life expectancy in Canada during this period. Conceptually, this analysis is situated in the context of the sociological literature concerning gender and the sex differential in mortality in industrialized countries. Specifically, we focus on the question of how change in the status of women pertains to changes in the sex differential in mortality and life expectancy, paying particular attention to the role of smoking.

A significant portion of the narrowing of sex difference in life expectancy in recent years is expected to be strongly linked to reductions in sex differences in death rates from chronic/degenerative diseases, particularly circulatory diseases and cancers, which account for a disproportionate number of deaths. In Canada, nearly two-thirds of the 218,000 deaths in 2000 were due to these two categories of disease (World Health Organization, 2005).

Both cardiovascular and cancer mortality are strongly associated with long-term tobacco use

(Doll and Peto, 1981; Peto, Lopez, Boreham, Thun and Heath, 2000; Ravenholt, 1990; Bartecchi, MacKenzie and Schrier, 1994; Waldron, 1976; 1986; 1995; 2000; Wister, 2005). In the United States, smoking caused approximately 435,000 deaths during 2000 (Mokdad, Marks, Stroup and Gerberding, 2004). Given the effect of smoking on health, we surmise that change in sex differences in smoking is related to change in the sex differential in life expectancy.

As in most industrialized countries, accidents in Canada claim a large number of lives annually (World Health Organization, 2005). Many such cases tend to be heavily concentrated in the young adult years, especially in men (Waldron, 1976; 1983; 1993; Perls and Frets, 1998; Owen, 2002). Alcohol is often implicated in many motor vehicle accidents. Although suicide and homicide rates have been declining recently, they remain an ongoing public health concern. In 2000, there were over 3,600 suicides and nearly 500 homicides in Canada (World Health Organization, 2005). We expect that change in sex differences in mortality from such causes would account for some of the observed narrowing of the sex differential in life expectancy in Canada in recent years.

Societies in the Western world, including Japan, have passed through three stages of **epidemiological transition**: 'the age of pestilence and famine', 'the age of receding pandemics', and 'the age of man-made and degenerative diseases' (Omran, 1971). As part of this process, populations experience widening sex differences in mortality, resulting from faster life expectancy gains among women, brought on by large-scale improvements in maternal mortality. As socio-economic modernization intensifies, men experience life changes that on the whole serve to slow their mortality improvements as compared to women. Part of this involves men's greater risk of death from accidents on the road and in the workplace, coupled with the adoption of unhealthy behaviours, most notably smoking and alcohol (Preston, 1976).

Recently, scholars have proposed additional stages of epidemiological transition. In 1986, Olshansky and Ault introduced 'the age of delayed degenerative diseases' as a fourth stage, in which a large proportion of deaths annually result from chronic and degenerative ailments relatively late in life. In this stage, survival improvements in men and women tend to occur at more or less the same pace of intensity. Reflecting on these features, plus the fact that many deaths in high-income countries are due to modifiable risks associated with lifestyle and personal habits, Rogers and Hackenberg (1987) suggested we are now in a 'hybristic' stage, characterized by a predominance of chronic/degenerative diseases related to aging coupled with a growing number of morbidities linked to unhealthy behaviours and lifestyles. Mokdad and colleagues (2004) show that in the United States, for example, the leading causes of death in 2000 were tobacco use (435,000 deaths), poor diet and physical inactivity (400,000), alcohol consumption (85,000), motor vehicle crashes (43,000), use of firearms (29,000), sexual behaviours (20,000), and illicit drug use (17,000). Taken together, these trends suggest that a large proportion of all deaths in Canada are due to preventable and modifiable lifestyle-related causes, of which lung cancer, heart disease, accidents, and violence are important examples.

Smoking and the Sex Differential in Life Expectancy

Besides these epidemiological features of the industrialized countries, such societies are also in the midst of a 'second **demographic transition**' (van de Kaa, 1987; 1999; 2004; Lesthaeghe and Surkyn, 1988), characterized by a pluralization of living arrangements among young adults, a pervasive tendency to postpone marriage, a large percentage of couples living in cohabiting unions, declining marriage rates, increased divorce probabilities, very high levels of contraceptive use, sub-replacement fertility rates, increased proportions of couples remaining childless, and an increasing tendency among couples for child-bearing outside of traditional marriage. As part of this configuration of social change, gender roles in these societies have become increasingly egalitarian (Davis, 1984; McDonald, 2000).

Perhaps the observed convergence in life expectancy between men and women in recent years relates in part to the changing status of women in these societies. In addressing this question, we restrict ourselves to two strands of theorizing, based largely on the recent works of Pampel (2002; 2003a; 2003b) and Nathanson (1995), though clearly the studies of other researchers are also relevant (e.g. Waldron, 1976; 1986; 1991a; 1991b; 1993; Veevers and Gee, 1986; Verbrugge, 1976). Pampel's research emphasizes smoking diffusion as the mechanism for the reduction in death-rate differentials between men and women; Nathanson's explanation stresses change in the position of women as a central factor.

An important indicator of the changing status of women is their degree of involvement in the paid labour force. In Canada, the participation rate for women aged 25 to 44 now stands at 80 per cent; in the 1950s it was only about 20 per cent (Roy, 2006). For the most part, this change has been beneficial for women, resulting in greater economic independence and increased well-being for their families (Sorensen and Verbrugge, 1987; Repetti, Matthews and Waldron, 1989). However, as part of this transformation, aspects of women's lifestyles may change; women may adopt some of the less positive features of the male gender role, thereby acquiring some of the mortality risks traditionally associated with men (Lopez, Caselli and Valkonen, 1995). To the extent that this is happening, women would at some point be expected to show some degree of erosion in their overall survival probabilities in relation to men (Nathanson, 1995).

One detrimental behaviour that has been increasingly adopted by women is cigarette smoking (Waldron, 1991a; 1991b; 1995; Lopez, Caselli and Valkonen, 1995; Pampel, 2002; 2001a; 2003a; 2003b; Rogers, Hummer, Krueger and Pampel, 2005; Patel, Back and Kris, 2005). The wide-scale adoption of cigarettes by women may reflect in part a rejection of traditional norms for appropriate female behaviour (Waldron, 1991b).

In Nathanson's (1995) conceptual model, change in the position of women in society (in terms of the division of labour, family status and political power) is viewed as a potential determinant of increased smoking prevalence. Nathanson (1995) hypothesized that countries with relatively high levels of gender equality would have a larger proportion of women smoking, which would in turn result in slower gains in female life expectancy at age 40. Nathanson's cross-national analysis revealed that in countries where the level of female smoking in 1970 was relatively high, women's life expectancy gains between 1970 and 1988 were slower than in those countries where smoking prevalence was low. For example, Japan, with very low female smoking rates, showed the largest increases in female life expectancy during this period. Denmark had the highest smoking prevalence for women, and it recorded the slowest gain in female life expectancy.

At the population level, the negative health effects of tobacco consumption are typically felt decades after the onset of widespread smoking adoption (Hegmann, Fraser, Kenny et al., 1993; Lopez, 1995; Nathanson, 1995; Pampel, 2002). In a study of 22 high-income countries between 1975 and 1995, Pampel (2002) found support for the proposition that rising levels of female smoking over the course of the latter part of the twentieth century, and the consequent lagged increases in female lung cancer and other smoking-related diseases in the 1970s and thereafter, fully accounts for the recently observed narrowing of the sex difference in mortality. In other words, it was concluded that all of the observed narrowing in the sex gap in mortality between 1975 and 1995 that was noted across industrialized countries has resulted from convergence in smoking prevalence between men and women: 'The results . . . do not suggest that cigarette smoking fully accounts for the sex differential in mortality between males and females; rather, smoking fully explains the recent narrowing of the sex differential' (96). Thus, according to Pampel (2002), the female relative advantage in life expectancy has fallen because of women's adoption of smoking over the second half of the twentieth century and its consequent lagged negative effects on their survival probabilities. This suggests that smoking-related mortality should account for much of the decline in Canada over recent decades in the sex differential in life expectancy.

Mortality and population data were obtained from the World Health Organization electronic database (World Health Organization, 2005). Cause-specific death rates by age (0, 1–4, 5–9, . . . 85+), sex, and period were computed, and used to generate appropriate abridged multiple-decrement life tables (see Table 32.1). International Classification of Diseases codes were grouped into 10 cause-of-death categories: (1) heart disease; (2) other diseases of the circulatory system; (3) lung cancer; (4) breast cancer; (5) prostate cancer; (6) all other cancers; (7) cirrhosis of the liver; (8) accidents and violence (excluding suicide); (9) suicide; and (10) all other causes of death (residual).

Observed differentials in life expectancy at birth between females and males were decomposed into the independent contributions of these 10 cause-of-death components using a method adapted from one originally proposed by Das Gupta (1993), intended for the decomposition of rates. The decomposition was executed in two steps. First, we decomposed the sex gap in life expectancy within a discrete period (i.e., 1971, 1981, 1991, and 2000, separately) to examine the contribution of each cause to the difference in life expectancy. Since male death rates from virtually all causes of death are greater than those of females, the contribution of most causes would be

Table 32.1 Decomposition of the Female–Male Differential in Life Expectancy at Birth (e0) by Period and Its Change Due to 10 Cause-of-Death Components; Canada, 1971 to 2000

	PERIOD				CHANGE		
	(1) **1971**	**(2)** **1981**	**(3)** **1991**	**(4)** **2000**	**(5)** **1971–1981**	**(6)** **1981–1991**	**(7)** **1991–2000**
Female life expectancy	76.649	79.244	80.999	82.216	2.595	1.755	1.217
Male life expectancy	69.479	71.915	74.438	76.869	2.436	2.523	2.431
Difference: Female/Male	**7.170**	**7.329**	**6.561**	**5.347**	**0.159**	**−0.768**	**−1.214**
DECOMPOSITION							
Heart disease	2.956	2.800	2.067	1.468	−0.156	−0.733	−0.599
Other circulatory	0.394	0.403	0.352	0.302	0.009	−0.051	−0.050
Lung cancer	0.681	0.885	0.838	0.527	0.204	−0.047	−0.311
Breast cancer	−0.493	−0.535	−0.596	−0.511	−0.042	−0.061	0.085
Prostate cancer	0.228	0.286	0.394	0.364	0.058	0.108	−0.030
Other cancers	0.344	0.591	0.742	0.838	0.247	0.151	0.096
Cirrhosis of liver	0.145	0.188	0.140	0.120	0.043	−0.048	−0.020
Accidents/violence (−suicide)	1.415	1.131	0.770	0.615	−0.284	−0.361	−0.155
Suicide	0.272	0.394	0.432	0.364	0.122	0.038	−0.068
Other causes	1.228	1.186	1.422	1.260	−0.042	0.236	−0.162
Total	**7.170**	**7.329**	**6.561**	**5.347**	**0.159**	**−0.768**	**−1.214**

Note: The decompositions under columns (1) to (4) express the number of years of life expectancy or fraction thereof attributable to sex differences in a given cause of death.

Source: Authors' computations based on data from the World Health Organization (2005).

positive (i.e., to increase the female advantage in life expectancy). However, in some cases the contribution can be negative. One obvious example of this is breast cancer. Being predominantly a female problem, this type of mortality can only reduce the female advantage in life expectancy. On the other hand, prostate cancer, being strictly a disease that afflicts males, would always have a positive impact on the life expectancy differential (i.e., to increase the female survival advantage). A second part of the decomposition looked at the change over time in the contribution of given cause-of-death components to the change in the female–male difference in life expectancy. By this approach we were able to ascertain whether a specific category of mortality served to either widen or narrow the sex gap in life expectancy across any two discrete time periods.

Findings

In Canada, as in other industrialized countries, the sex differential in life expectancy at birth widened during most of the twentieth century. However, a narrowing of this differential has occurred recently. In this study we examined this situation for Canada. Decomposition analysis showed that a large portion of the decline in the sex gap in life expectancy between 1981 and 2000 was accounted for by reduced sex differences in mortality rate with respect to heart disease, lung cancer, accidents, and violence (excluding suicide). The significant effects of heart disease and lung cancer uncovered here are consistent with the recent literature in this area, which shows that these causes of death are highly connected to tobacco use (Nathanson, 1995; Waldron, 1993; Pampel, 2002; 2003a; 2003b). Thus, increased smoking among women in conjunction with reduced smoking among men during the second half of the twentieth century explains a large part of the decline in the sex differential in expectancy since the early 1980s. But smoking cannot explain the entire decline in this measure because, as

indicated by the decomposition analysis, a substantial portion of the narrowing in the sex difference in life expectancy is attributable to men's larger improvements in mortality risk from accidents and violence.

We can think of at least two possibly contradictory reasons for this. First, men may be changing their conception of masculinity and may be gradually abandoning some of the more 'lethal' traditional aspects of the male gender role. Perhaps they are becoming less aggressive and less inclined to take unnecessary risks; perhaps men are more aware of safety concerns. Should these tendencies be real, they would help explain the decline in male death rates from accidents and violence noted in this study and, to a lesser extent, from reductions in suicide and homicide since the early 1980s.

On the other hand, male gains in life expectancy in recent decades may have resulted not from fundamental change in male gender role orientations and attitudes, but principally from the implementation of public health measures, which by their very nature influence men (and women) to change their behaviour. For example, one can think of mandatory safety belt legislation for drivers and mandatory use of helmets for bikers as public health measures that would have the effect of reducing the incidence of fatal accidents. Similarly, legislation prohibiting smoking in public places plus educational campaigns about its dangers to health may have lowered the desire for smoking in men. This type of explanation places the emphasis on forces external to men as the root agent of change.

We cannot at this time resolve these two contradictory possibilities without more in-depth sociological research. From our statistical analysis we can only establish that there has been a larger than expected reduction in mortality risk among men as compared to women from accidents and violence, lung cancer, and heart disease, and that the changes in these three causes of death explain most of the decline in the sex gap in life expectancy in Canada between 1981 and 2000.

References

Bartecchi, C.F., T.D. MacKenzie and R.W. Schrier. 1994. 'The human costs of tobacco use. Part I'. *New England Journal of Medicine,* Vol. 330, No. 13, pp. 907–12.

Coale, A.J. 2003. 'Increases in expectation of life and population growth'. *Population and Development Review,* Vol. 29, No. 1, pp. 113–20.

Das Gupta, P. 1993. *Standardization and Decomposition of Rates: A User's Manual.* U.S. Bureau of the Census, Current Population Reports, Series P23–186. Washington, D.C.: U.S. Government Printing Office.

Davis, K. 1984. 'Wives and work: Consequences of the sex role revolution'. *Population and Development Review,* Vol. 10, No. 3, pp. 397–417.

Doll, R. and R. Peto. 1981. 'The causes of cancer: Quantitative estimates of avoidable risks of cancer in the United States today'. *Journal of the National Cancer Institute,* Vol. 66, No. 6, pp. 1191–308.

El-Badry, M.A. 1969. 'Higher female than male mortality in some countries of South Asia: A digest'. *Journal of the American Statistical Association,* Vol. 64, No. 328, pp. 1234–44.

Enterline, P.E. 1961. 'Causes of death responsible for recent increases in sex mortality differentials in the United States'. *Milbank Memorial Fund Quarterly,* Vol. 39, pp. 312–28.

Hegmann, T.T., A.M. Fraser, R.P. Kenny et al. 1993. 'The effect of age at smoking initiation on lung cancer risk'. *Epidemiology,* Vol. 4, pp. 444–48.

Kramer, S. 2000. 'The fragile male'. *British Medical Journal,* Vol. 321, 23–30 Dec., pp. 1609–12.

Lesthaeghe, R. and J. Surkyn. 1988. 'Cultural dynamics and economic theories of fertility change'. *Population and Development Review,* Vol. 14, No. 1, pp. 1–45.

Lopez, A.D. 1983. 'The sex differential in mortality in developed countries'. In *Sex Differentials in Mortality: Trends, Determinants and Consequences.* A.D. Lopez and L.T. Ruzicka (eds.). Canberra, Australia: Australian National University Printing Press, pp. 43–120.

———. 1995. 'The lung cancer epidemic in developed countries'. In *Adult Mortality in Developed Countries: From Description to Explanation.* A.D. Lopez, G. Caselli and T. Valkonen (eds.). Oxford: Oxford University Press, pp. 111–34.

Lopez, A.D., G. Caselli and T. Valkonen. 1995. 'Moving from description to explanation of adult mortality: Issues and approaches'. In *Adult Mortality in Developed Countries: From Description to Explanation.* A.D. Lopez, G. Caselli and T. Valkonen (eds.). Oxford: Oxford University Press, pp. 3–18.

Luy, M. 2003. 'Causes of male excess mortality: Insights from cloistered populations'. *Population and Development Review,* Vol. 29, No. 4, pp. 647–76.

Madigan, F.C. 1957. 'Are sex mortality differentials biologically caused?' *Milbank Memorial Fund Quarterly,* Vol. 35, No. 2, pp. 202–23.

Maxim, P and C. Keane. 1992. 'Gender, age, and the risk of violent death in Canada, 1950–1986'. *The Canadian Review of Sociology and Anthropology,* Vol. 29, No. 3, pp. 329–45.

McDonald, P. 2000. 'Gender equity in theories of fertility transition'. *Population and Development Review,* Vol. 26, No. 3, pp. 427–40.

Meslé, F. 2004. 'Life expectancy: A female advantage under threat?' *Population & Societies,* June. Monthly bulletin of the Institut national d'études démographiques (INED).

Mokdad, A.H., J.S. Marks, D.F. Stroup and J.L. Gerberding. 2004. 'Actual causes of death in the United States, 2000'. *Journal of the American Medical Association,* Vol. 291, No. 10, pp. 1238–45.

Nathanson, GA. 1984. 'Sex difference in mortality'. *Annual Review of Sociology,* Vol. 10, pp. 191–213.

Nathanson, C.A. 1995. 'The position of women and mortality in developed countries'. In *Adult Mortality in Developed Countries: From Description to Explanation.* A.D. Lopez, G. Caselli and T. Valkonen (eds.). Oxford: Oxford University Press, pp. 135–57.

Noymer, A. and M. Garenne. 2000. 'The 1918 influenza epidemic's effects on sex differentials in mortality in the United States'. *Population and Development Review,* Vol. 26, No. 3, pp. 565–81.

Olshansky, S.J. and B.A. Ault. 1986. 'The fourth stage of epidemiologic transition: The age of delayed degenerative diseases'. *The Milbank Quarterly,* Vol. 46, No. 3, pp. 355–91.

Omran, A.R. 1971. 'The epidemiologic transition: A theory of the epidemiology of population change'. *Milbank Memorial Fund Quarterly,* Vol. 49, No. 4, pp. 509–38.

Owen, I.P.F. 2002. 'Sex differences in mortality rate'. *Science,* Vol. 297, 20 Sep., pp. 2008–09.

Pampel, F. 2002. 'Cigarette use and the narrowing sex differential in mortality'. *Population and Development Review,* Vol. 28, No. 1, pp. 77–104.

———. 2003a. 'Declining sex differences in mortality from lung cancer in high-income nations'. *Demography,* Vol. 40, No. I, pp. 45–65.

———. 2003b. 'Age and education patterns of smoking among women in high-income nations'. *Social Science and Medicine,* Vol. 57, No. 8, pp. 1505–14.

Patel, J., P.B. Bach and M.G. Kris. 2005. 'Lung cancer in U.S. women: A contemporary epidemic'. *Journal of the American Medical Association,* Vol. 291, No. 14, pp. 1763–68.

Perls, T.T. and R.C. Fretts. 1998. 'Why women live longer than men'. *Scientific American Presents,* Vol. 9, pp. 100–04.

Peto, R., A.D. Lopez, J. Boreham, M. Thun and C. Heath Jr. 2000. *Mortality from Smoking in Developed Countries, 1950–2000: Indirect Estimates from National Vital Statistics.* Oxford: Oxford University Press.

Population Reference Bureau. 2005. *World Population Data Sheet.* Washington, D.C.: Population Reference Bureau.

Preston, S.H. 1976. *Mortality Patterns in National Populations.* New York: Academic Press.

Ravenholt, R.T. 1990. 'Tobacco's global death march'. *Population and Development Review,* Vol. 16, No. 2, pp. 213–40.

Repetti, R.L., K.A. Matthews and I. Waldron. 1989. 'Employment and women's health: Effects of paid employment on women's mental and physical health'. *American Psychologist,* Vol. 44, No. 11, pp. 1394–401.

Retherford, R.D. 1975. *The Changing Sex Differential in Mortality.* Westport and London: Greenwood Press.

Riley, J.C. 2001. *Rising Life Expectancy: A Global History.* Cambridge: Cambridge University Press.

Rogers. K.G. and K Hackenberg. 1987. 'Extending epidemiologic transition theory: A new stage'. *Social Biology,* Vol. 34, Nos. 3–4, pp. 234–43.

Rogers, R.G., R.A. Hummer, P.M. Krueger and F.C. Pampel. 2005. 'Mortality attributable to cigarette smoking in the United States'. *Population and Development Review,* Vol. 31. No. 2, pp.259–92.

Rogers, R.G., R.A. Hummer and C.B. Nam. 2000. *Living and Dying in the USA: Behavioural, Health, and Social Differentials of Adult Mortality.* San Diego: Academic Press.

Roy, F. 2006. 'From she to she: Changing patterns of women in the Canadian labour force'. *Canadian Economic Observer,* Vol. 19, No. 6, pp. 1–10.

Salomon, J.A. and C.J.L. Murray. 2002. 'The epidemiologic transition revisited: Compositional models for causes of death by age and sex'. *Population and Development Review,* Vol. 28, No 2, pp. 205–28.

Smith. D.W.E. 1993. *Human Longevity.* New York: Oxford University Press.

Sorensen. G. and L.M. Verbrugge. 1987. 'Women, work, and health'. *Annual Review of Public Health,* Vol. 8, pp. 235–51.

Stolnitz. G. 1956. 'A century of international mortality trends, Part II'. *Population Studies,* Vol. 10. No. 1, pp. 17–42.

Trovato, F. and N.B. Heyen. 2003. 'A divergent pattern of the sex difference in life expectancy: Sweden and Japan, early 1970s–late 1990s'. *Social Biology,* Vol. 50, Nos. 3–4, pp. 238–58.

Trovato, F. and N.M. Lalu. 1996a. 'Narrowing sex differences in life expectancy in the industrialized world: Early 1970s to early 1990s'. *Social Biology,* Vol. 43, Nos. 1–2, pp. 20–37.

———. 1996b. 'Causes of death responsible for the changing sex differential in life expectancy between 1970 and 1990 in thirty industrialized countries'. *Canadian Studies in Population,* Vol. 23, No. 2, pp. 99–126.

———. 1998. 'Contribution of cause-specific mortality to changing sex differences in life expectancy: Seven nations case study'. *Social Biology,* Vol. 45, Nos. 1–2, pp. 1–20.

Tuljapurkar, S., N. Li and C. Boe. 2000. 'A universal pattern of mortality decline in the G7 countries'. *Nature,* Vol. 405, No. 6788, pp. 789–92.

Vallin, J. 1983. 'Sex patterns of mortality: A comparative study of model life tables and actual situations with special reference to the case of Algeria and France'. In *Sex Differentials in Mortality: Trends, Determinants and Consequences.* A.D. Lopez and L.T. Ruzicka (eds.). Canberra, Australia: Australian National University, Department of Demography, pp.443–76.

———. 1993. 'Social change and mortality decline: Women's advantage achieved or regained?' In *Women's Position and Demographic Change.* N. Federici, K. Oppenheim Mason and S. Sagner (eds.). Oxford: Clarendon Press, pp. 190–212.

———. 2002. 'Mortalité, sexe et genre'. In *Demographie: Analyses et synthèse. III. Les determinants de la mortalité.* G. Caselli, G. Wunsch and J. Vallin (eds.). Paris: INED, pp. 319–50.

Vallin, J. and F Mesle. 2005. 'Convergence and divergence: An analytical framework of national and sub-national trends in life expectancy'. *Genus,* Vol. LXI, No. 1, pp. 83–124.

Van de Kaa, D. 2004. 'Is the second demographic transition a useful research concept?: Questions and answers'. *Vienna Yearbook of Population Research 2004.* Vienna Institute of Demography. Vienna: Austrian Academy of Sciences.

———. 1987. *Europe's Second Demographic Transition.* Population Bulletin 42. Washington: Population Reference Bureau.

———. 1999. 'Europe and its population: The long view'. In *European Populations: Unity in Diversity.* D. van de Kaa, H. Leridon, G. Gesano and M. OkoIski (eds.). Dordrecht, The Netherlands: Kluwer Publishers, pp. 1–76.

van Hoorn, W. and R. Broekman. 1999. 'Uniformity and diversity scenarios for mortality'. In *Europe: One Continent, Different Worlds, Population Scenarios for the 21st Century.* J. de Beer and L. van Wissen (eds.). Dordrecht, The Netherlands: Kluwer Publishers. pp. 71–90.

Veevers, J.E. and E.M. Gee. 1986. 'Playing it safe: Accident mortality and gender roles'. *Sociological Focus,* Vol. 19, No. 4, pp. 349–60.

Verbrugge, L.M. 1976. 'Sex differentials in morbidity and mortality in the United States'. *Social Biology,* Vol. 23, No. 4, pp. 275–96.

Waldron, I. 1976. 'Why do women live longer than men?' *Social Science and Medicine,* Vol. 10, Nos. 7–8, pp. 349–62.

Waldron, I. 1986. 'The contribution of smoking to sex differences in mortality'. *Public Health Reports,* Vol. 101, No. 2, pp. 163–73.

———. 1991a. 'Effects of labor force participation on sex differences in mortality and morbidity'. In *Women, Work, and Health.* M. Frankenhaeuser, U. Lundberg and M. Chasney (eds.). New York: Plenum, pp.17–38.

———. 1991b. 'Patterns and causes of gender differences in smoking'. *Social Science and Medicine,* Vol. 32, No. 9, pp. 989–1005.

———. 1993. 'Recent trends in sex mortality ratios for adults in developed countries'. *Social Science and Medicine.* Vol. 36, No. 4, pp. 451–2.

———. 1995. 'Contributions of biological and behavioural factors to changing sex differences in ischaemic heart disease mortality'. In *Adult Mortality in Developed Countries: From Description to Explanation.* A.D. Lopez, G. Caselli and T. Valkonen (ads.). Oxford: Oxford University Press, pp. 161–78.

———. 2000. 'Trends in gender differences in mortality: Relationships to changing gender differences in behaviour and other causal factors'. In *Gender Inequalities in Health.*

E. Annandale and K. Hung (ads.). Buckingham: Open University Press, pp. 150–81.

White, K.M. 2002. 'Longevity advances in high-income countries, 1955–96'. *Population and Development Review,* Vol. 28, No. 1, pp. 59–76.

White, K.M. and S.H. Preston. 1996. 'How many Americans are alive because of twentieth century improvements in mortality?' *Population and Development Review,* Vol. 22, No. 3, pp.415–29.

Wilmoth, J.R. 1998. 'The future of human longevity: A demographer's perspective'. *Science,* No. 280, pp. 395–97.

Wister, A.Y. 2005. *Baby Boomer Health Dynamics: How Are We Aging?* Toronto: University of Toronto Press.

World Health Organization. 2005. *Electronic Mortality Data Base.* WHO: Geneva. http://www3.who.int/whosis/menu.cfm?path=whosis,mort&language=english.

Questions for Critical Thought

CHAPTER 30

1. Very few people consciously decide to be childless. Describe the 'waiting game' and how the intention to be childless evolves over the life course.
2. How do marriage, education, and income/work status affect childlessness?
3. How does the relationship between income and education differ by gender?
4. Compare this paper with Albanese's paper in Part V. How do they inform each other? Compare their policy recommendations.
5. The data used in this paper does not actually follow the same adults over their life course. Instead, it is cross-sectional, meaning that it measures the attitudes and circumstances of people of different ages. In effect, it measures different generations but assumes that they are all walking along the same life course path. What are some problems with assuming this? How else could you interpret the authors' findings, particularly the shift that occurs in people in their forties? How do Ravanera and Beaujot defend their assumption?
6. Consider Funk and Kobayashi's discussion about choice and obligation. How do their insights relate to Ravanera and Beaujot's discussion of constrained choice? If all of the respondents are on the same life course, can we trust that people in their forties really want to be childfree? Discuss.

CHAPTER 31

1. Describe the arguments and evidence used to depict filial care as a matter of discretion and choice. Be sure to discuss the individualization thesis.
2. Describe the arguments and evidence used to depict filial care as a matter of non-discretion and structured obligation. Be sure to discuss structures and normative ideologies, on both the macro and micro levels.
3. What are some methodological problems with measuring whether people are really obligated or free to choose? How are people's subjective experiences of free choice methodologically difficult to determine but also important to getting past the choice/obligation dichotomy?
4. Compare how the individualization thesis and critical feminist perspectives construct a dichotomy between choice and obligation by discussing how each theory would answer each of these questions: How are seemingly free choices built on compulsions? Where do those compulsions come from? What alternatives exist to express those compulsions in different ways?
5. What are some policy implications of maintaining and moving past the choice/obligation dichotomy?

6. This article articulates a core theoretical dilemma in sociology: the agency/structure debate. Caring for our parents is not the only issue in which it is hard to discern agentic, self-motivated, freely made choice from structurally enforced obligation. Consider another issue in which it is hard to know how limited or free a person is to choose. How does Funk and Kobayashi's work help you see how choice and obligation are mutually involved?

CHAPTER 32

1. According to Trovato and Lalu, which social and health factors are most responsible for men's life expectancy? How have these factors contributed to changes in men's mortality rate over the years?
2. According to Trovato and Lalu, which social and health factors are most responsible for women's life expectancy? How have these factors contributed to changes in women's mortality rate over the years?
3. According to Trovato and Lalu, what factors are responsible for the narrowing of the mortality gap between men and women? Is the gap narrowing largely because men are living longer? Or because women are dying earlier? Or both? Explain.
4. What trends do Trovato and Lalu examine regarding the smoking prevalence in men and women?
5. Discuss the epidemiological transitions Trovato and Lalu include in their paper. How do these affect the sex differential?

Part IX

Health

In Canadian society, good health is one of people's most important, continuing concerns, and as a society, we spend more on health than on any other public service. As sociologists, we understand that good health is important to people, and we understand too that social processes—including professional health care—influence people's access to good health. However, the chapters in this section focus on other sociological concerns and insights related to health.

As Reza Nakhaie and Robert Arnold show in their paper, social capital—in the form of close and loving social relations—makes an important contribution to people's continuing good health. We already know from previous research that poverty and inequality have a negative impact on people's health. Nakhaie and Arnold argue that everyone—even poor people—can benefit from social capital and the meaningful interactions, trust, and affection they provide. This position is supported by Anthony Lombardo's paper in this collection (Chapter 10). There, the author notes that men who have sex with men are presented as more likely to have risky and therefore dangerous sex if they lack the intimacy and trust that make for good health.

We like to think that health professionals do their job in rational and systematic ways, using scientific evidence to provide better health. However, scientific professional knowledge is not always purely rational; it can have ideological undertones, as we see in the paper by Carol Berenson about a recent increase in professionals supporting the idea of suppressing menstruation. Given a history of gendered misjudgments by doctors dating back at least to Freud, women have every right to wonder about the ideological motivations that promote certain medical points of view about women's bodily functioning. They are right to be especially suspicious about those pertaining to the sexual and reproductive organs, and Berenson questions whose interests are served when doctors weigh in on such issues.

As we have seen, sociologists view the human body as a biological entity whose well-being is altered by social determinants such as social capital ('love') and social inequality. They also view the human body as a political and ideological entity that is contested by various professional experts, as with menstrual suppression. Finally, sociologists view the body as a cultural entity with socially shared meanings, and it is this fact that Rebecca Scott and Jeff Stepnisky address in their papers.

Scott is interested in examining the social and cultural meanings attached to the post-childbirth, no longer functioning placenta—in some eyes, a bit of biological waste, but in others, an object imbued with awesome value. Stepnisky explores biocitizenship and the attribution of social meanings to medical events such as illness—especially mental illness. He notes that, as biocitizens, we invest our bodies and their functioning with personal meaning for our identity. An individual might ask, then, 'How can I "recover" from an illness that has become part of my personal identity—one of my prime identifying features as a biocitizen?'

CHAPTER 33

Biocitizenship and Mental Health in a Canadian Context

Jeff Stepnisky

This paper uses the concept of **biological citizenship**, or 'biocitizenship', to examine the report of the Standing Senate Committee on Social Affairs, Science and Technology (2006), *Out of the Shadows at Last: Transforming Mental Health, Mental Illness and Addiction Services in Canada*. Chaired by Senator Michael Kirby, the report (known informally as the 'Kirby report') was compiled after extensive cross-Canada consultations with a variety of stakeholders. In addition to describing the current functioning of the mental health system in Canada, and its impact on users, *Out of the Shadows* was part of a larger project to develop a Mental Health Commission of Canada, which was in fact established in 2007. The report and the commission aim to provide a national vision for mental health care. In the process, the report introduces a new understanding of what it means to be a Canadian citizen; hence its wide sociological relevance.

Recent scholarship has introduced the concept of biological citizenship to describe emerging forms of relationship between citizen and state that depend upon biomedical knowledge about the body and its capacities (Heath et al, 2007; Petryna, 2002; Rose & Novas, 2005). This concept is an addition to other widely discussed forms of citizenship. Civic, political and social citizenship, for example, indicate a contract in which rights are protected and guaranteed by the state (e.g. free speech, the right to vote, and the

right to welfare and unemployment benefits) in exchange for citizen obligations (e.g. payment of taxes, mandatory education, and military service) (Turner, 1993). Within the more recent concept of cultural citizenship, the relationship between state and citizen includes questions of identity. Here, it is not enough for a state merely to ensure civic, political, and social rights; it must also ensure that cultural or ethnic identities are recognized and protected. The idea is significant because it suggests that *full citizenship* is not merely contractual but also emotional, and that the accounting of any form of citizenship cannot be reduced to a list of rights and duties.

Biological citizenship emerges out of the recognition that people are increasingly crafting identities around problems of biological—and for the purposes of this analysis, mental—health. One's biological well-being does not merely stand in support of other capacities and identities, but becomes an identity in itself that gives rise to 'biosocialities' and lifestyles crafted around problems of illness and health (Rabinow, 1992). This said, biocitizenship is not simply a description of the increasing importance of biological self-understanding to identity. It emerges when these identities intersect with the politics of citizenship. Individuals and groups, having forged a biological identity, make claims on the state in the name of health and well-being.

Rose and Novas (2005) detail the elements of biological citizenship. For the purposes of this brief analysis, I focus on three. Biological citizenship is *individualist*, *activist*, and based in *science education*. The focus on individualism distinguishes contemporary biocitizenship from previous forms in which population health was regulated from above—through, for example, eugenics programs. The current form of biocitizenship emerges as the social welfare state disappears and government transfers responsibility for well-being to individual citizens. The Kirby report is committed to this individualism. In the context of mental health, it defines individualism as the capacity for autonomous self-care and as such aims to develop 'services and supports that encourage the involvement of individuals with mental illness and addiction and are based on the principles of recovery, self-help and independent living and functioning' (p. 73).

As a component of this individual autonomy, the report places the concept of choice front and centre. Choice, as conceived here, is both a political and a psychological ideal. It is political because the report suggests that all modern, democratic political systems are obliged to provide citizens with a wide range of options, even in terms of mental health care. At present, the report says, Canadian mental health care fails because it limits choice. Insofar as psychiatric care is determined, as it were, from above, by psychiatrists and administrators, the mentally ill are left out of the democratic, choice-making loop. This exclusion is especially pressing in a culture in which illness increasingly becomes a central component of identity.

The current system also fails because, in limiting choice, it exacerbates mental illness; this is where the Kirby report makes choice a psychological ideal. The report theorizes that

> [v]iewed from the perspective of fostering recovery, choice is both a means to an end—a more responsive service—and also an end in itself. This is because being able to make choices is a manifestation of the rights and responsibilities of adulthood and of full citizenship. *The availability and exercise of choice is itself a potential contributor to the recovery process.* (italics added, p. 46)

Choice is linked to mental health. Having choice is not just a political obligation; it also serves the therapeutic goal of promoting well-being. The design of mental health institutions that provide choice allows people to exercise their political rights as citizens, but it also promotes the kind of well-being that produces citizens. This theme is picked up again in Chapter 10 of the Kirby report, which champions self-help as a central component of the emerging ethic of Canadian mental health. Self-help refers to developing a mental health program of one's own choosing, and the act of designing one's own style of care in turn contributes to the enhancement of well-being.

Individualization is engendered and supported by science education and activism. Science education creates a citizenry that adopts the accounts, classifications, and categories embedded in biomedical knowledge. Biological citizens understand themselves as biological beings entrusted with the responsibility of biological self-care. At the same time, this understanding creates the condition in which biological citizens become activists, in two senses. First, they are active in managing and taking responsibility for their own mental health. Second, in the more obviously political sense, the biological citizen, as part of a larger collective of those similarly afflicted, lobbies government for research and action against mental illness (see Heath et al. [2007] for further examples). The Kirby report participates in this activist spirit. It is not in itself an activist entity, but it serves as a middle ground between government decision-making bodies and the citizenry. Its consultations capture the concerns and sentiments expressed by the mentally ill and their caregivers and recommend both research and investment on their behalf.

The report also supports science education by placing a premium on knowledge. One of its central recommendations is to create a national mental health 'information exchange'. The purpose of this exchange would be to overcome the fragmentary state of knowledge about mental health and health care in Canada, thereby generating knowledge about 'best practices'. It would provide a forum in which the latest research findings would be made widely accessible. This, it seems, would primarily serve professionals within the mental health field, though it is driven by the goal of producing a mental health system that is more responsive to the needs of individual consumers.

More relevant to the needs of the citizenry, the Kirby report recommends the creation of a national anti-stigma campaign (see White [2009] for an extensive discussion). The recommendation is offered in the spirit of creating a Canadian populace educated about mental health. The Kirby report imagines such a campaign having a profound influence on Canadian citizens, and it begins with several rousing claims for inclusion:

> From coast to coast we have met politicians, government officials, mental health service providers and professionals, and many, many ordinary Canadians who are willing to help make change a reality, to help bring people living with mental illness into the mainstream of Canadian society. (Committee, p. xvii)

> To the people of Canada, I say welcome us into society as full partners. (Witness to the Committee, p. xix)

The anti-stigma campaign will aim to create this inclusive atmosphere by disseminating scientific facts about mental illness (i.e., it's not a person's 'fault', it's biological). This educative process is intended to develop a Canadian population who not only are sensitive to the serious nature of mental illness, but also recognize the unique contributions made by the mentally ill to Canadian society. As one witness to the committee put it, Canadians should recognize the ways in which the mentally ill contribute to the 'cultural mosaic of a community' (p. 449). As an extension of the value placed on *cultural* multiculturalism, this recommendation introduces a *biological* multiculturalism, in which one's biological type constitutes a unique identity that offers unique cultural contributions.

Further still, the report calls for a transformation of every Canadian's self-understanding. Kirby states that stigmatization will be reduced by showing Canadians that they are all susceptible to mental illness: 'Accepting the possibility that any one of us can experience mental illness, that . . . we "are all at risk at different times in our lives" helps to remove the stigma engendered through seeing it as "them" and "us"' (p. 63).

The Kirby report emphasizes that people do not become mentally ill through a fault of their own; it is not something that they could have chosen against. Rather, mental illness can affect any person at any time in their life. All Canadians are potentially mentally ill. In other words, the citizenry is not divided between those who are ill and those who are well, but rather is imagined as a collective of the already ill and the potentially ill. Thus, the claims that ill persons make on government are of concern to all Canadians. Indeed, from this perspective, we are all already biological citizens.

In this essay, I have used the concept of biological citizenship to establish the basis for an analysis of an emerging program for the treatment and management of mental health in Canada. This is not simply a matter for those who are already ill, but involves the reconceptualization of Canadian citizenship itself. To be a good citizen is to protect oneself and others against mental illness and to cultivate mental well-being. It must be understood that, at present, the Kirby report represents a vision of mental health care rather than an institutionalized set of practices. Further analysis should focus on the ways in which these ideals become components of everyday psychiatric care. Moreover, the present analysis is limited because, in adopting the concept of biocitizenship, it has more or less equated psychological problems with physical problems. Thus, the concept of biocitizenship requires further nuance. To this end, what is hinted at in the Kirby report is that contemporary Canadian citizenship requires the exercise of particular psychological capacities: the ability to make choices, to think rationally, to exhibit moderate (rather than excessive) displays of emotion. For various socio-historical reasons, these capacities can no longer be taken for granted as part of the human makeup. Instead, these capacities must be cultivated through the kinds of self-care advocated in the report. Further analysis requires, then, a description of the ideals under which the biological

citizen operates. Equally, it requires information about the particular techniques that individuals use to generate the capacities necessary for the exercise of biological citizenship in the first place.

References

Heath, D., Rapp, R. & Taussig, K. 2007. Genetic citizenship. In D. Nugent & J. Vincent (eds.) *A Companion to the Anthropology of Politics*, Oxford: Blackwell, pp. 152–167.

Petryna, A. 2002. *Biological Citizenship: Science and the Politics of Health after Chernobyl.* Princeton, NJ: Princeton University Press.

Rabinow, P. 1992. Artificiality and enlightenment: From sociobiology to biosociality. In J.C. Kwinter (ed.) *Incorporations.* New York: Zone, pp. 234–253.

Rose, N. & Novas, C. 2005. Biological citizenship. In A. Ong & S. Collier (eds.) *Global Assemblages: Technology, Politics, and Ethics as Anthropological Problems*, Oxford: Blackwell, pp. 439–463.

Standing Senate Committee on Social Affairs, Science and Technology. 2006. *Out of the Shadows at Last: Transforming Mental Health, Mental Illness and Addiction Services in Canada.* Ottawa, ON: The Senate, available at http://www.parl.gc.ca/39/1/parlbus/commbus/senate/com-e/soci-e/rep-e/rep02may06-e.htm.

Turner, B. 1993. *Citizenship and Social Theory.* London: Sage.

White, K. 2009. Out of the shadows and into the spotlight: The politics of (in)visibility and the implementation of the Mental Health Commission of Canada. In K. White (ed.) *Configuring Madness: Representation, Context & Meaning.* Oxfordshire, UK: Interdisciplinary Press, pp. 225–249.

CHAPTER 34

Love and Changes in Health

Reza Nakhaie and Robert Arnold

Over half a century ago, sociologist Pitirim Sorokin (1954) insisted that 'love is a life-giving force, necessary for physical, mental and moral health' (1954:xi). He saw love as possessing 'curative power' to decrease or eliminate illness and unnecessary death (1954:45, 61). For him, love was 'one of the best therapies for curing many mental disorders; for the elimination of sorrow, loneliness, and unhappiness, for the mitigation of hatred and other antisocial tendencies; and above all for the ennoblement of human personality, for the release in man of his creative forces . . .' (1948:225).

Sorokin's belief that love was a major factor in health has been supported by a significant amount of later work. Neurological studies have shown that a loving relationship affects the brain, influencing emotion, motivation, memory, and attention. It can help inhibit destructive feelings and behaviours, and it can reduce stress, thus improving health status (see Esch & Stefano, 2005a; 2005b).

The perception of being loved may induce feelings of closeness, connectedness, protection, spirituality, trust, and well-being. Such feelings can make the immune system function better and help battle diseases (see Esch & Stefano, 2005a). A loving relationship may well provide the most intense form of social support, and thus may well produce psychological and physical benefits not available through other forms of life experience.

In a related matter, the feeling of loving and being loved by a divine power is shown to be strongly related to self-rated health among 205 family practice outpatients (Levin, 2001). This would not be surprising to Sorokin, for whom romantic love is a partial reflection of divine love.

The link between love and health has been examined in studies of 'broken heart syndrome', which arises after the unexpected death of a loved one. This can lead to stress cardiomyopathy, in which stress hormones flood the body, stunning the heart and requiring hospitalization and prolonged rest (see Hill, Eric & Olson, 2008). Durkheim observed earlier that the disappearance of a family member 'increases the chance that others may commit suicide' (1951:198). He stressed that individuals 'cling to life more resolutely when they belong to a group they love . . .' (Durkheim, 1951:209).

In our own research, we have examined the effect of love on changes in health among 9,442 people who responded to Canada's National Population Health Survey in 1996 and 2000. This study focuses on individuals who were age 25 and over in 1996. We assessed health changes by comparing scores on an index regularly used by Statistics Canada, called the HUI3, based on eight aspects of health: vision, dexterity, hearing, emotion, speech, cognition, ambulation, and pain. In each area, five or six levels are distinguished, and for each level a score is assigned: 1.00 for perfect health, and reduced scores for lower levels (for detailed descriptions see Feeny, 2005). The eight ratings are combined and the overall score is calibrated so that 1.00 represents perfect health, 0 represents death, and negative scores represent states of health rated by respondents to earlier studies as worse than death.

Over the four-year period examined here, the standard deviation of the change scores is .184. As an illustration of a change of about one **standard deviation**, consider someone who had not required a hearing aid, had full use of both hands, and was rated as happy and interested in life. If, four years later, he required a hearing aid to handle conversations among three or more people, had limited use of his hands (although he could

function independently without tools), and he was only somewhat happy, the change in the HUI3 would be –.181.

For predicting changes in health, our measure of love is whether people say that there is someone they love and who loves them in return. Love, as discussed here, is not specifically romantic love. Being married, which sometimes means being 'in love' is an important predictor of it, but so also are family contacts, being female, being elderly, and being born in Canada. Moreover, the concept may involve a felt sense of 'divine love', since, as will be shown, it is influenced by religious service attendance. We think this measure capture Sorokin's notion of altruistic and **psychosocial** love.

Many predictors of change in health were considered, but only those reported in Table 34.1 had effects that could not easily come up by chance. Figure 34.1 shows their relationships schematically.

Figure 34.1 shows that perceived love helps improve health, as indicated by the positive sign, and food insecurity results in a decline in health, as shown by the negative sign. Age and daily smoking also negatively influence health status. Presence of a loving relationship is itself influenced by being married and in contact with family members as well as attending religious services. Being older, female, and born in Canada also all increase the odds on saying that a loving relationship is part of one's life. Unsurprisingly, those with higher incomes report less insecurity about food. Daily smoking increases food insecurity. In contrast, older respondents, cushioned by government pensions, with greater savings than those younger than themselves, with lower debt-to-asset ratios and often with declining expenses for other things, are less likely to report food insecurity.

The importance of love for health may be seen by comparison to other predictors as shown in Table 34.1. A two-step movement on the food insecurity scale, from sometimes being short of money for food but not without food, to frequently being without food, has about the same effect on health as perceived love. The influence of daily smoking is only about a third as great as that of perceived love. No one would think of analyzing health status without considering smoking,

Table 34.1 Determinants of Perceived Love, Food Insecurity, and Changes in Health Status

	PERCEIVED LOVE				FOOD INSECURITY			CHANGE IN HEALTH STATUS		
	Odds Ratios	B	SE	sig	OLS bs	SE	sig	OLS bs	SE	sig
Family contacts	17.247	2.858	0.199	***						
Religious service attendance	1.245	0.220	0.075	***						
Married	1.927	0.656	0.176	***						
Perceived love								0.033	0.016	*
Ln(income) in $10,000					−0.346	0.066	***			
Food insecurity								−0.018	0.006	***
Age	0.962	−0.039	0.012	***	−0.004	0.001	***	−0.011	0.001	***
Female	1.534	0.428	0.181	***						
Born in Canada	1.742	0.555	0.231	**						
Daily smoker			w		0.083	0.014	***	−0.011	0.005	*
Intercept	−0.701	0.496	0.400		0.966	0.066	***	0.068	0.016	***
R-squared					0.099			0.074		
McFadden's pseudo R-squared	0.093									

* p <.05; ** p <.01; *** p<.001
B = beta
SE = standard error
Sig = significance level
OLS bs = ordinary least squares (blossom statistics)
Ln = natural log(arithm)

yet here a loving relationship has greater influence. Daily smokers' habit is costly: those who smoke a pack of 20 cigarettes a day can easily spend $300 Canadian each month (at about $10 a pack). Smoking is a difficult habit to break, so those who smoke regularly may find that it puts considerable pressure on their finances; that being so, they might be expected to have higher food insecurity than others.

Discussion and Conclusion

Results from this study support previous international studies that have indicated that social capital causally affects changes in health status. Moreover, under our model, a loving relationship is shown to be directly related to changes in health status. Marital status, family contact, and religious service attendance are also related to changes in health status through perceived love. Apart from the well-established predictors of age and smoking, health status is a function of subjective perception of love and economic insecurity. Therefore, in answer to Tina Turner's famous song lyric, 'What's love got to do with it?', we can say that it can help to maintain or enhance health. However, its effect is due not only to romantic love but to something like what Sorokin called altruistic love.

The evidence points to the importance of strong ties that are developed by loving relationships that also ensure trust and allow for easy communication of problems and solutions. Such relationships are developed most easily among groups whose membership is homogeneous and who associate with each other over a period of time. These bonding relationships allow for moral support and meeting of needs that will help to ensure well-being.

In a few other studies, people have been asked specifically about being loved. Medalie and

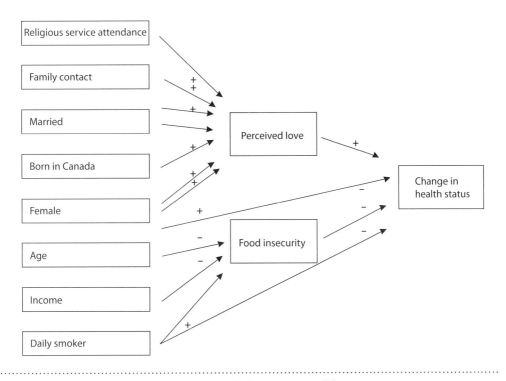

Figure 34.1 Schematic View of Predictors of Change in Health Status

Goldbourt (1976) followed 10,000 American men for five years, and reported that new cases of angina were less common among those who answered the question, 'Does your wife show you her love?' in the affirmative. In a later study (Medalie, Stange, Zysanski & Goldbourt, 1992) the same question helped to predict new cases of duodenal ulcers. In one study, Harvard students were followed up 35 years later, and those with warm relationships with mothers and fathers were substantially less likely to have been diagnosed with serious illnesses (Russek & Schwartz, 1997). In another study, Johns Hopkins medical students completed a 'closeness to parents' scale, which helped to predict who got cancer decades later (Graves, Thomas & Mead, 1991).

The link between feeling loved and changes in health may also reflect the respondent's loving of others. Many loving relationships are reciprocal; thus the variable we have used may be picking up benefits of loving as well as those of being loved. The literature on **altruism** has concentrated on the effects of volunteering, but has shown positive associations, as long as the demands of others have not become overwhelming (e.g. Schwartz, Meisehelder, Yunsheng & Reed, 2003; Brown, 2003; Post, 2005).

As shown in Table 34.1, the most impressive predictor of feeling loved is family contacts. Being married is also a significant predictor, further underscoring the importance of the family. As well, females are more likely than males to report feeling loved and cared for. This feeling may reflect a greater female tendency to form emotionally close, mutually self-disclosing and supportive relationships (Fehr, 2004). However, there has been debate about whether males form their intimate relationships in a different way (see Wright, 1998).

Another predictor of perceived love is religious service attendance. In this case, perceived love may point to a felt sense of divine love, to love from other members of the religious community, or both. Churches, mosques, synagogues, and temples may foster a sense of support that leads individual members to feel loved. Involvement in these services may lead to positive emotions such as love and contentment (see Ellison & Levin, 1998). People often organize part of their social lives around their religious groups, and all of the major religions teach that caring, loving, or compassionate relationships should flow from one's faith.

The link between food insecurity and changes in health may reflect both the effects of inadequate nutrition and the effects of the stress that an uncertain, and sometimes inadequate food supply can create. Reduced social assistance payments and reduced eligibility for unemployment insurance may very well exacerbate the problem (Hurtig, 2008; Osberg, 2006). We remark in passing that, in the absence of publicly funded medical care, the importance of social status variables to an understanding of changes in health might be considerably greater.

Policies aimed at family support and family unification appear important for the health of Canadians. This does not mean that we should download further health care work onto family members. If they are not committed to helping or the individual receiving help does not perceive that the help is motivated by love, the effect of the family may diminish significantly. Nor does it mean that if we can only help people to have better relationships, we can cease to be concerned about basic economic needs: food insecurity, in particular, has shown itself to be an important predictor of changes in health. However, we believe that our findings do suggest that we may expand our understanding of changes in health by reviving the tradition of assessing the social effects of love.

References

Brown, S. L. (2003). An altruistic reanalysis of the social support hypothesis: The health benefits of giving. *New Direction for Philanthropic Fundraising* 42:49–57.

Durkheim, E. (1951). *Suicide*. New York: Free Press.

Esch, T. & S. Tefano, G. B. (2005a). Love promotes health. *Neuroendocrinology*, 26(3):264–266.

———. (2005b). The neurobiology of love. *Neuroendocrinology Letters*, 26(3):175–192.

Ellison, C. G., & Levin, J. S. (1998) The religion–health connection: Evidence, theory, and future directions. *Health Education and Behavior*, 25:700–720.

Feeny, D. (2005). The health utilities index: A tool for assessing health benefits. *PRO Newsletter*, 34:2–6.

Fehr, B. (2004). Intimacy expectations in same-sex friendships: A prototype interaction-pattern model. *Journal of Personality and Social Psychology*, 86:265–284.

Graves, P. L., Thomas, C. B. & Mead, L. A. (1991). Familial and psychological predictors of cancer. *Cancer Detection and Prevention*, 15:59–64.

Hurtig, M. (2008). *The Truth about Canada*. Toronto: McClelland and Stewart.

Leonard, R. & Onyx, J. (2003). Networking through loose and strong ties: an Australian qualitative study. *Voluntas: International Journal of Voluntary and Nonprofit Organizations*, 14:189–203.

Levin, J. (2001). God, love and health. *Review of Religious Research*, 42:277–93.

Medalie, J. H. & Goldbourt, U. (1976). Angina pectoris among 10,000 men. II: Psychosocial and other risk factors as evidenced by a multivariate analysis of a five-year incidence study. *American Journal of Medicine*, 60:910–921.

Medalie, J. H., Stange, K. C. Zysanski, S. J. & Goldbourt, U. (1992). The importance of biopsychosocial factors in the development of duodenal ulcer in a cohort of middle-aged men. *American Journal of Epidemiology*, 136:1280–1287.

Osberg, Lars. (2006). Pulling apart—the growing gulfs in Canadian Society. *Policy Options*, April–May, 51–54.

Post, S. G. (2005). Altruism, happiness, and health: It's good to be good. *International Journal of Behavioral Medicine*, 12:66–77.

Russek, L. G. & Schwartz, G. E. (1997). Feelings of parental caring predict health status in midlife: A 35-year follow-up of the Harvard mastery of stress study. *Journal of Behavioral Medicine*, 20:1–13.

Schwarz, C., Meiseheleder, J.B., Yunsheng M. & Reed, G. (2003). Altruistic social interest behaviors are associated with better mental health. *Psychosomatic Medicine*, 65:778–785.

Sorokin, P. A. (1948). *The Reconstruction of Humanity*. Boston. Beacon.

———. (1954, 2002). *The Ways and Power of Love: Types, Factors, and Techniques of Moral Transformation*. London: Templeton Foundation Press.

Statistics Canada (1996). *The National Population Health Survey Overview 1996–1997*. Ottawa.

Wright, P. H. (1998). Towards an expanded orientation toward the study of sex differences in friendship. In Canady, D. J. & Dindia, K. (eds.), *Sex differences and similarities in communication*, pp. 41–64.

CHAPTER 35

Menstruation by Choice: The Framing of a Controversial Issue

Carol Berenson

As social constructions, frames are not merely ideological; rather they 'do' things. According to Epstein (2007), frames 'provide a diagnosis of a social situation, they propose solutions, and they can serve as a call to arms' (58). At the same time that frames enable their users to garner support and demobilize opponents, they also act as constraints by shaping the very limits of what is conceived as feasible action. In order to take hold and be sustainable, frames must be personally compelling, empirically defensible, and culturally coherent (58).

With this in mind, I examine a document entitled 'The Canadian Consensus Guideline on Continuous and Extended Hormonal Contraception' (SOGC 2007), published in the *Journal of Obstetrics and Gynaecology Canada*. Authored by a group of leading obstetricians and gynaecologists from the Society of Obstetricians and Gynaecologists of Canada (SOGC), the guidelines represent the most recent evidence on the use of hormonal birth control to suppress menstruation. This practice is not without controversy within the medical community, as various players, pro- and anti-suppression (Derry 2007; Edelman 2002; Nelson 2005; Stubbs, Mansfield & Kernoff 2006; Sucato & Gerschultz 2005) are currently formulating and defending their positions (Hitchcock 2008). My analytic interest is to do with how the issues of concern that count as relevant in the menstrual suppression discussion are framed by this particular group of experts. Epstein's criteria for sustainability are salient here, given that menstruation by choice is currently hovering at the brink of the cultural landscape. Whether or not it eventually takes hold as a viable cultural practice for women might well depend on how frames such as these stand up to Epstein's criteria.

Frame #1:
Manipulating Technology or 'How to Cheat on the Pill'

As the title of the document in question indicates, for these experts, menstrual suppression is first and foremost about manipulating technology. Specifically, the SOGC statement sets physician guidelines for the use of 'combined hormonal contraceptives' (CHCs) as menstrual suppressants. Although CHCs can be delivered via various methods, such as pills ('combined oral contraceptives' or COCs), patches, and vaginal rings, these devices all fit into the same category because they share a 'combined' hormonal configuration. More important for the discussion at hand, the CHCs also all have a seven-day 'hormone-free interval' (HFI) built into their regimes. During this time, a pseudo period (or withdrawal bleeding) will occur, and it is this bleeding that physicians are being advised about suppressing in the guidelines document. Continuous and/or extended regimes (C/E) are proposed in order to either completely or intermittently stop the menses.

The biomedical framing of menstrual suppression as first and foremost a technological issue might be culturally compelling for a few reasons. First, biomedical technology in general is well entrenched in contemporary Western societies where progress itself is inextricably intertwined with advancements in this arena (Rabinow 1992). Second, the specific technology being discussed in the case of menstrual suppression is taken for granted in many women's lives these days. North American women have had access to CHCs for a considerable length of time (50 years in the case of COCs) and feel quite comfortable with them as a result. Culturally, the matter-of-fact acceptance of hormonal contraception (particularly pills) as the most effective, simplest, and safest form of birth control seems quite widespread.

So, the technology of note here is well entrenched in the culture already—it is now simply a matter of shifting its use from one purpose (preventing pregnancy) to another (manipulating menstruation) (Loshny 2004).

Frame #2: Not Menstruating as the New 'Normal'

This frame involves constructing menstruation itself as abnormal for contemporary women. The frame builds on a history of pathologizing (Ehrenreich & English 1973, 20; de Beauvoir 1952; Tavris 1992) and medicalizing (Berenson, Miller & Findlay 2009; Figert 1996; Morgan 1998; Riessman 2003) women's reproduction, moving that discussion into a new frontier by arguing that menstruation is not only problematic or pathological, but actually abnormal, hence nonessential in today's women's lives. This then is a decidedly contemporary conversation in that it implicitly challenges traditional thinking that would see menstruation as not only natural and normal, but essential to being a woman.

The main line of discussion towards normalizing not menstruating involves an increasingly popular historical narrative that compares pre-industrial, hunter-gatherer women with their twenty-first-century counterparts (see also Coutinho & Segal

1999). Whereby the former would likely have had about 150 ovulatory cycles (due to early and frequent pregnancies), today's women experience some 450 periods because of 'earlier menarche, delayed first birth, low parity, and late menopause' (S5). The hunter-gatherer women are held as normative in this discussion, the implication being that women were never meant to menstruate with the frequency that today's women experience over the course of their lifetimes.

On one hand, here menstruation is understood as entirely about fertility, as those not wanting a pregnancy have no good reason to menstruate (S19). At the same time, the document also presents menstruation as a risk to fertility by citing a study that links it to pelvic inflammatory disease (PID), a sexually transmitted infection, as it creates a 'favourable environment to the ascending infection' (S20). Although these constructions of the link between menstruation and fertility are contradictory, taken together they stand to produce a compelling case for why today's young women might see suppressing menstruation as both viable and safe.

Frame #3: Women Want This

This frame locates women's wishes, rights, and entitlements at the heart of the menstrual suppression matter. The argument here states that there is a 'renewed interest of late' (S6) on the part of women (particularly adolescents) in 'having control over their menstrual cycles' (S6).

Numerous critiques of power in the clinical setting have called for more equitable and respectful relations between doctors and their female patients (Ratcliff 2002, 32–38). One outcome of these critiques has been a demand for informed consent as a basic guiding principle shaping relations between patients and various biomedical factions (Rothman 1991; Seaman 1980). In framing menstrual suppression as something that women want, then, doctors are presumably no longer paternalistically telling them what to do or failing to see them as capable of informed decision making.

Framing menstrual suppression as something that women want also moves the issue from the realm of the medical to that of personal preference or lifestyle choice. The document is introduced as a set of guidelines for providers on the use of C/E CHCs to 'prevent pregnancy, and to delay menses that affect health-related quality of life' (S1), and further repeated references to women's lifestyle choices are made throughout. The specifics of what constitute health-related quality of life issues are not articulated in this document, leaving wide open the list of potential reasons for suppressing menstruation.

The discussion concludes by advising that 'health care providers should be aware of the option of using C/E CHC and consider offering it to women for contraception, medical reasons, and personal preferences' (S6). While this advice may ensure that women are aware of their options, it also constructs options that are beyond the realm of individual women to imagine or want in the first place. This non-medical/non-contraceptive use of birth control pills, which draws in potentially all women for potentially all reasons, also stands to generate huge profits for the pharmaceutical industry.

Frame #4: 'We Have No Reason to Believe' That This Is Risky

The primary concern raised by the framing of menstrual suppression as likely not risky is the long-term safety of C/E CHCs. The authors of the guidelines identify the lay public, so-called special interest groups, the media, and government regulatory agencies as various factions that have raised this concern (S19). The scientific question of the safety of taking hormones without breaks (HFIs) over an extended period of time is rife with lack of evidence, a fact that the authors repeatedly reference. The question of empirical credibility is therefore front and centre here, making the framing of the long-term use of C/E CHCs and risks particularly challenging.

Although acknowledged, 'non-knowledge' (see Petryna 2002 for a discussion of this phenomenon) is diminished in a couple of ways in this frame. First, it is argued that 'new products could never enter the marketplace if complete assurance of long-term safety were a pre-marketing requirement' (S19). Hence, it is unreasonable to expect this level of knowledge if we want the kind of progress that would allow women this opportunity to improve their health-related quality of life. Second, the authors posit that it makes sense to extrapolate what we do know about the long-term effects of regular birth control pills to this new regime, given that the technologies here are so similar.

In terms of specific risks, the main health concerns connected to the long-term use of COCs are cardiovascular diseases and cancers, both of which are discussed in the guidelines in terms of the available evidence on COCs. In both of these cases, the likelihood of C/E CHCs increasing risks is dismissed as minuscule. The knowledge gap between the old and new pills makes the discussion hypothetical, and the 'no reason to believe' frame is the most that can be said on these health risks.

As the writers of the report are well aware, the critics converge around the question of risks connected with C/E CHCs. Therefore, this frame will presumably need ongoing attention and updates as the prevalence of physicians' prescribing practices increases. In the meantime, the 'no reason to believe' frame certainly enables doctors to go ahead with these prescribing practices.

Frame #5: The Benefits Outweigh the Costs

Adriana Petryna (2002) argues that the language of costs and benefits is characteristic of Western science, which is firmly ensconced in 'capitalist social contexts and values' (51). In keeping with Petryna's claim, the SOGC document not only considers health and lifestyle issues; it also makes explicit the economic costs and benefits of menstrual suppression. Numerous citations that variously consider the economics of the issues connected to menstrual suppression are discussed in the report in framing its 'cost-effectiveness' (S25). Regardless of how they are defined, in all cases the benefits are seen to outweigh the costs.

One of the things making this a particularly compelling frame is that both society-at-large and individual women are seen as gaining from women's suppressing their menstrual cycles. Specifically, the stated benefits of menstrual suppression to society include reduced stresses on the health system (which is more frequently used by heavy bleeders than those with light periods) and less absenteeism from work and/or school. For individual non-menstruating women, there are significant cost-saving benefits in the form of less need to purchase 'menstrual-hygiene' products (S25) or the analgesics and/or iron supplements that some women may need to take in conjunction with their periods. Finally, individual women also stand to benefit through their high levels of productivity and 'the qualitative benefits in lifestyle' (S25) from not menstruating, the specifics of which go unnamed in this document (as mentioned previously).

This framing of the issue relies on the earlier frames in order to work, both enabling and constraining what gets included in the discussion in order to ensure that the benefits outweigh the costs. It also extends these frames by moving the discussion explicitly into the economic realm. In the current environment of neo-liberal thinking and economic belt-tightening, this framing of the issue of menstrual suppression stands to resonate considerably. The cost/benefit analysis is also compelling because individuals and the larger society are taken into account here. It will be interesting to see if and how this frame is sustained and/or shifted as the current economic challenges play out.

Conclusion

The five frames articulated in this discussion provide a basis from which to further explore and analyse the terrain of positions—pro and anti, biomedical and otherwise—on the issue of menstruation by choice. Outlining the polarized positions provides a way of establishing the basic parameters of this debate as it is newly unfolding, and perhaps more broadly, of shedding light on the rise or demise of a cultural practice as it begins to appear on the social horizon.

References

Berenson, C., Miller, L.J. & Findlay, D.A. 2009. Through Medical Eyes: The Medicalization of Women's Bodies and Women's Lives. In (eds.) Bolaria & Dickinson, *Health, Illness, and Health Care in Canada* (Fourth Edition). Toronto: Nelson Education Ltd.: 239–58.

Coutinho, E.M., and Segal, S.J. 1999. *Is Menstruation Obsolete?* New York: Oxford University Press.

de Beauvoir, S. 1952. *The Second Sex.* New York: Vintage Books.

Derry, P.S. 2007. Is Menstruation Obsolete? *British Medical Journal,* 5 May.

Edelman, A. 2002 Menstrual Nirvana: Amenorrhea through the Use of Continuous Oral Contraceptives. *Current Women's Health Report,* 2(6): 434–38.

Epstein, Steven. 2007. *Inclusion: The Politics of Difference in Medical Research.* University of Chicago Press.

Ehrenreich, Barbara and English, Deirdre. (1973). *Complaints and Disorders. The Sexual Politics of Sickness.* New York: The Feminist Press at CUNY.

Figert, Ann. 1996. *Women and the Ownership of PMS: The Structuring of a Psychiatric Disorder.* Hawthorne, N.Y.: Aldine De Gruyter.

Hitchcock, Christine L. 2008. Elements of the Menstrual Suppression Debate. *Health Care for Women International,* 29(7): 702–19.

Loshny, Helen. 2004. From Birth Control to Menstrual Control: The Launch of the Extended Oral Contraceptive, Seasonale. *Canadian Woman Studies,* 24(1): 63–67.

Morgan, K.P. 1998. Contested Bodies, Contested Knowledges: Women, Health, and the Politics of Medicalization. In (Ed.) Sherwin, *The Politics of Women's Health.* Philadelphia: Temple University Press: 83–121.

Nelson, A. 2005. Extended-Cycle Oral Contraception: A New Option for Routine Use. *Treatments in Endocrinology,* 4(3): 139–45.

Petryna, Adriana. 2002. *Life Exposed: Biological Citizens after Chernobyl.* Princeton University Press.

Rabinow, Paul. 1992. Artificiality and Enlightenment: From Socio-Biology to Biosociality. In (eds.) Crary & Kwinter, *Zone 6: Incorporations.* MIR Press: 234–52.

Ratcliff, Kathryn Strother. 2002. *Women and Health: Power, Technology, Inequality, and Conflict in a Gendered World.* Boston: Allyn and Bacon.

Riessman, C.K. 2003. Women and Medicalization: A New Perspective. In (Ed.) Weitz, *The Politics of Women's Bodies.* New York: Oxford University Press: 46–63.

Rothman, David J. 1991. *Strangers at the Bedside: A History of How Law and Bioethics Transformed Medical Decision Making.* New York: Basic Books.

Seaman, Barbara. 1980. *The Doctors' Case Against the Pill.* Garden City, N.Y.: Doubleday & Company, Inc.

SOGC (Society of Obstetricians and Gynaecologists of Canada). 2007. Canadian Consensus Guideline on Continuous and Extended Hormonal Contraception. *Journal of Obstetrics and Gynaecology Canada,* 29(7): 1–32.

Stubbs, M.L., Mansfield, P. & Kernoff. 2006. Our Menses, Ourselves: Research and Commentary from The Society for Menstrual Cycle Research. *Sex Roles,* 54: 311–13.

Sucato, G.S. & Gerschultz, K.L. 2005. Extended Cycle Hormonal Contraception in Adolescents. *Current Opinion in Obstetrics and Gynaecology,* October, 17(5): 461–65.

Tavris, Carol. 1992. *The Mismeasure of Woman.* New York: Simon and Schuster.

CHAPTER 36

· ·

Placentations

Rebecca Scott

In sociology, **placentas** are rather unconventional objects of study. There has been some interest in the rituals and mythology that sometimes *surrounds* the placenta, but placentas *in and of themselves* make very few appearances indeed, even in sociological studies of pregnancy. Why is this the case? Perhaps since mother and fetus stage such an ineffable drama, this third, rather repugnant entity seems incidental and insignificant. However, if humanity is the object of sociological thought, and placentas play such integral and necessary role in the reproduction of humanity, then a sustained sociological engagement with them could prove very fruitful indeed.

I use the notion of **placentation** to do this. In biology, placentation refers to the process of the formation of the placenta: the dividing and multiplying of cells to form structures that enable the maternal–fetal exchange of nutrients and wastes. Yet placentation is not only biological; rather, it is the result of productive work done in the different socio-cultural, technical, theoretical, and even political realms implicated in and by the placenta. In this way, placentation is also multiple: there are many placentations, many different processes of placental formation. These placentations are ontologically distinct—what it means *to be* a placenta is different for each—but mutually informed. Placentation, in other words, is a dynamic ontology of placental becoming that traverses many realms. Placentations are examples of what Charis Thompson (2005) has called 'ontological choreography'—that is, 'What might appear to be an undifferentiated hybrid mess is actually a deftly well-balanced coming together of things that are generally considered parts of different ontological orders (part of nature, part of the self, part of society)' toward the production of some entity (p. 8). In this chapter, I argue that the manner in which the placenta traverses these realms begs a reformulation of a number of key topics and debates in sociology.

What might be called the 'natural' or 'material' production of the placenta is a form of placentation. The human placenta is made from what are called trophoblast cells, which are the first cells to differentiate (i.e., become uniquely suited to a particular physiological function) from a fertilized egg. Trophoblasts are commonly said to 'invade' or migrate into the tissues of the lining of the maternal uterus and 'remodel' the existing arteries, allowing for later increased pressure and volume of maternal blood flow to the placenta. Trophoblasts form two disks of tiny tree-like structures, called villi, that contain placental capillaries and blood vessels. The disks fuse around the edges, creating what is called an 'intervillous' space. This space is 'perfused' with maternal blood that circulates around the villi, the blood vessels of which eventually meet at the umbilical cord. By this means, the fetus derives nutrients, oxygen, and other blood-soluble substances from, and rids wastes into, maternal blood. In other words, mother, baby, and placenta all participate in these processes of production and exchange (Fox and Sebire, 2007).

Yet placentas are also produced in 'cultural' or 'social' ways. The placenta is sometimes believed to have magical powers as a spirit double that can heal or harm (Ober, 1979; Jones and Kay, 2003; Gideon, 1962; Helsel and Mochel, 2002; Croft Long, 1963). Often, this necessitates rituals, particularly relating to its disposal (Gideon, 1962; Helsel and Mochel, 2002; Davidson, 1985; Jones and Kay, 2003). The placenta may be buried, sometimes in a specific place such as under a cemetery gate or under a tree, with specific objects, or after preparing it with herbs (Davidson, 1985, p. 77). The placenta is also sometimes placed in a stream, disposed of at sea, burned, hung from a tree, eaten, or used in medicinal preparations (Davidson, 1985; Jones and Kay, 2003; Abel et al., 2001). Sociologically, the significance attributed to these practices varies. Some suggest that they index gender relations, arguing that whether a culture is 'high' or 'low' ritual with regard to the placenta corresponds to the social status of women (Jones and Kay, 2003). Others recall Mary Douglas's (1966) work on the 'purification' of objects that provoke fear and disgust because they exist in luminal, 'in between' spaces—in the case of the placenta, between two individuals (Davidson, 1985). In contrast to these serious matters, the placenta may in some environments be ascribed no mystical significance at all. It is frequently deemed 'hospital waste', refuse that is 'abandoned'. Yet this also means it can then be freely collected by hospital staff for later scientific research or banking purposes (Annas, 1999), activities that are possible because placentas have

'vitality': they retain living qualities that can be made to be productive in laboratory settings through, for example, cell culturing (see Graham et al., 1993). In this way, the placenta can also become 'biovaluable' for research scientists and exchangeable in markets (Waldby, 2002).

Understandings of placentas' material qualities—as liminal, as waste, as vital—inform practices surrounding them, yet here is no knowledge about the material properties of the placenta that exists outside of social relations that produce this knowledge. This slippage permits the dramatically different kinds of significance ascribed to the placenta: from sacred to garbage. It means that realms that are commonly understood in both sociology and science to be separate—'nature' and 'culture'—spill into each other in ways that show that, in fact, they are not separate at all. Rather, placentas are what Donna Haraway (2008) calls naturecultures.

There are also theoretical placentations, most often motivated by feminist theory. A provocative question might be asked: is the placenta a feminist organ? Simone de Beauvoir (1953) provides one answer, arguing that the growing fetus is a kind of parasite that threatens to subsume a pregnant woman's body and therefore her subjectivity. In contrast, Luce Irigaray, Kelly Oliver (1998), JaneMaree Maher (2002), and Anne Elvey (2003) have argued that the placenta is an emblem of feminist understandings of embodied subjectivity. As an 'intercorporeal' (Weiss, 1997; Elvey, 2003; Maher, 2002) organ that 'does not belong to one body' (Maher, 2002, p. 97), the placenta points to the ways in which the body cannot be understood as a singular entity. Rather, all bodies are simultaneously fused and separate (Bollinger, 2007) and continuous with all things, including nature. This resonates with feminist politics that emphasize the interconnectedness of oppressions and feminist ethics that emphasize mutual care and responsibility. In this way, in addition to the nature/culture debate, placentations are implicated in and challenge understandings of the body, feminism, and subjectivity.

Scientific methods and knowledge also participate in placentations. For example, placentation has been shown by scientists to be an extremely complex immunological event. The immune system is thought to establish boundaries of 'self' and to identify, attack, and clear anything within the body that is 'non-self'. However, this understanding does not fit well with what is known about the placenta. The placenta is made from fetal cells that bear a combination of both maternal and paternal DNA. These cells therefore contain some paternal antigens—molecules that trigger the immune system—that are 'foreign' to the mother. In this way, the placenta has been described as a *semiallogeneic graft* (Fox and Sebire, 2007. p. 385), *allogeneic* meaning of foreign origin (Choudhury and Knapp, 2001, p. 114), and *semi* referring to the partial maternal origin of fetal genes. Considering the presence of these foreign antigens, why are the fetus and placenta not rejected by the mother's immune system? Scientists surmise there must be restraints on the immune system in successful pregnancies, but these mechanisms are largely as yet unknown. Some scientists have proposed a *fetal parasite model* (Roberts et al., 1996) to explain this complex immunological event, suggesting that the fetus and placenta function like successful parasites that operate 'under the radar' of the maternal immune system.

This may also mean that 'unsuccessful' pregnancies fail to avoid activation of the maternal immune system. Pre-eclampsia, a disease of pregnancy and major cause of maternal mortality worldwide (Sibai et al., 2005), provides an illustration. As noted, uterine blood vessels are remodelled during placentation by trophoblast cells. Inadequate or abnormal transformation of the arteries has been shown to be present in women with pre-eclampsia (Sibai et al., 2005), possibly due to maternal immunosuppression of the trophoblast cells. When this happens, the placenta goes not get enough oxygen and the cells begin to die. This results in the shedding of the dead cells into the maternal system, leading to a systemic maternal immune response, seizures and coma, and finally, death. There is no cure for this dangerous syndrome except, as is frequently noted, delivery of the placenta.

Placental immunology and pre-eclampsia therefore demonstrate the ways in which a third

key topic in sociology is complicated by the placenta: the distinction between 'self' and 'other'. Placental immunology defies both conventional understandings of self and other as discrete, *and* feminist understandings of self and other as interconnected. The placenta is and is not separate and connected, familiar and foreign.

The placenta too is a shape-shifter through space and time. It even defies its own genetic lineage. For example, mosaicism, the presence of cells that are genetically distinct from the individual in which they reside, is present in pregnancy at a number of different sites (Hird, 2004). Pieces of freely circulating genetic material, called free fetal DNA, which come from the shedding of dead placental debris, are also known to circulate in maternal blood and can remain in the blood for as long as 27 years after the birth of the baby (Bianchi, 1996; Aractingi et al., 2000). Likewise, although placental cells are of fetal origin and genetic 'defects' present in the fetus are normally also present in the placenta and vice versa, in some cases, genetic abnormalities are confined only to the placenta, creating a condition called confined placental mosaicism (Kalousek and Vekemans, 1993). Interestingly, the placenta has shown to be a resilient organ in expressing mutations that would, if expressed in the fetus, likely lead to loss of the pregnancy: it has been estimated that only 16 to 21 per cent of pregnancies with confined placental mosaicism show pre- or perinatal complications (Kalousek and Vekemans, 1996). The placenta, therefore, also challenges the supposed direct translation and primacy of the genetic code, the code of life, the code that makes you essentially and undeniably you. Instead, placental, maternal, and fetal genes are a sometimes rather random mash-up.

The placenta is also a species shape-shifter. Human placentas, in fact, are not even entirely human. This is because knowledge about the human placenta is bound up in animal placentas. 'Animal models' for human systems are used extensively in research in reproductive sciences (Carter, 2007) because they enable experiments that could never be ethically performed on humans. If we understand that scientific knowledge is a form of placentation, and that placentations help to make new human beings, then we will also understand that animals help to make human beings. In this way, the human/non-human divide, so central to sociology, is not respected by placentas.

Finally, placentas may also be 'produced' in the strongest sense of the word. A number of researchers have found ways to culture placental cells, creating trophoblast cell lines that can reproduce indefinitely (for example, see Graham et al., 1993). These placentations make placentas whose natural habitat is not the womb but the laboratory. Researchers have also used placental tissues to make therapeutic tissue products that can be used in reconstructive or cosmetic surgery (Flynn, 2006; Flynn and Woodhouse, 2008). The placenta, then, goes on to become entirely something else and its process of becoming continues anew, raising new ontological choreographies and a whole host of new questions.

In these ways, placentations are achievements of the active co-production of matter, practices, and relations that shift through time and place. In other words, placentas are 'working objects' (Daston and Galison, 1992, 2007), a notion that captures the sense in which entities have agency (they help to make babies; they do work

in laboratories in scientific experiments), are a produced effect or outcome (as in, 'working the land'), and are contingent upon 'upkeep' work through time ('working' being a present continuous verb). Importantly, what I have shown is that this co-production is not neutral, but, because it takes place on heterogeneous terrains, open to contestation and change. In other words, placentations are driven by what Annemarie Mol calls 'ontological politics': the notion that reality is not given, but emerges from relations between matter and practice in ways that are political because they could be otherwise. To use the language of Karen Barad (2008a, 2008b, 2007) and Donna Haraway (2008, 1994), placentations can be 'reentangled' in new and transformative ways. As I have shown, placentations have implications for the ontological politics surrounding the nature/culture divide; conceptions of feminism; understandings of the body, of subjectivity, self, and other; genetics; and the human/non-human divide. So while few sociologists would pay any attention to the placenta's role in the momentous event of birth, it is absolutely central to our being, and it defies us to pin down exactly what that being entails.

References

Annas, George. 1999. 'Waste and Longing: The Legal Status of Placental Blood Banking'. *Legal Issues in Medicine* 340(19): 1521–1524.

Barad, Karen. 2008a. 'Living in a Posthumanist World: Lessons from Schrödinger's Cat'. Pp. 165–176 in *Bits of Life: Feminism at the Intersections of Media, Bioscience, and Technology*, edited by A. Smelik and N. Lykke. Seattle: University of Washington Press.

Bianchi, D. W. 2004. 'Circulating Fetal DNA: Its Origin and Diagnostic Potential—A Review'. *Placenta* 25(Supplement A: Trophoblast Research):S93–S101.

Bollinger, Laurel. 2007. 'Placental Economy: Octavia Butler, Luce Irigaray, and Speculative Subjectivity'. *Literature Interpretation Theory* 18:325–352.

Carter, A.M. 2007. 'Animal Models of Human Placentation—A Review'. *Placenta* 28A(21):S41–S47.

Choudhury, Shormila R. and Leslie A. Knapp. 2001. 'Human Reproductive Failure II: Immunogenetic and Interacting Factors'. *Human Reproduction Update* 7(2):135–160.

Croft Long, E. 1963. 'The Placenta in Lore and Legend'. *Bulletin of the Medical Library Association* 51(2):233–241.

Daston, Lorraine, and Peter Galison. 1992. 'The Image of Objectivity'. *Representations* (40): 81–128.

———. 2007. *Objectivity*. New York: Zone Books.

Davidson, J.R. 1985. 'The Shadow of Life: Psychosocial Explanations for Placenta Rituals'. *Culture, Medicine and Psychiatry* 9:75–92.

de Beauvoir, Simone. 1953. *The Second Sex*. 1st American ed. New York: Knopf.

Douglas, Mary. 1966. *Purity and Danger: An Analysis of Concepts of Pollution and Taboo*. New York: Praeger.

Elvey, Anne. 2003. 'The Material Given: Bodies, Pregnant Bodies and Earth'. *Australian Feminist Studies* 18(41):199–209.

Flynn, Lauren and Kimberly A. Woodhouse. 2008. 'Adipose Tissue Engineering in Engineered Matrices'. *Organogenesis* 4(4):228–235.

Flynn, Lauren. 2006. 'Decellularized Placental Matrices for Adipose Tissue Engineering'. *Journal of Biomedical Materials Research* 79(2):359–369.

Fox, H. and N.J. Sebire. 2007. *Pathology of the Placenta*. Philadelphia: Saunders Elsevier.

Gideon, Helen. 1962. 'A Baby Is Born in the Punjab'. *American Anthropologist* 64(6):1220–1234.

Graham, Charles H., Teresa S. Hawley, Robert G. Hawley, John R. MacDougall, Robert S. Kerbel, Nelson Khoo and Peeyush K. Lala. 1993. 'Establishment and Characterization of First Trimester Human Trophoblast Cells with Extended Lifespan'. *Experimental Cell Research* 206:204–211.

Haraway, Donna J. 2008. *When Species Meet*. Minneapolis: University of Minnesota Press.

———. 2008b. 'Posthumanist Performativity: Toward an Understanding of How Matter Comes to Matter'. Pp. 120–156 in *Material Feminisms*, edited by S. Alaimo and S.J. Hekman. Bloomington, IN: Indiana University Press.

———. 2007. *Meeting the Universe Halfway: Quantum Physics and the Entanglement of Matter and Meaning*. Durham: Duke University Press.

———. 1994. 'A Game of Cat's Cradle: Science Studies, Feminist Theory, Cultural Studies'. *Configurations* 2(1):59–71.

Helsel, Deborah G. and Marilyn Mochel. 2002. 'Afterbirths in the Afterlife: Cultural Meaning of Placental Disposal in a Hmong American Community'. *Journal of Transcultural Nursing* 13(4):282–286.

Hird, Myra J. 2004. 'Chimerism, Mosaicism and the Cultural Construction of Kinship'. *Sexualities* 7(2):217–232.

Irigaray, Luce. 1993. *Je, tu, nous: Toward a Culture of Difference*. New York: Routledge.

Jones, Elaine and Margarita A. Kay. 2003. 'The Cultural Anthropology of the Placenta'. Pp. 101–116 in *The Manner Born: Birth Rites in Cross-Cultural Perspective*, edited by L. Dundes. Walnut Creek, CA: AltaMira Press.

Kalousek, Dagmar, K. and Michel Vekemans. 1996. 'Confined Placental Mosaicism'. *Journal of Medical Genetics* 33: 529–533.

Maher, JaneMaree. 2002. 'Visibly Pregnant: Toward a Placental Body'. *Feminist Review* 72:95–107.

Mol, Annemarie. 1999. 'Ontological Politics: A Word and Some Questions'. Pp. 74–89 in *Actor Network Theory and After*, edited by J. Law and J. Hassard. Malden, MA: Blackwell Publishers.

Ober, William. 1979. 'Notes on Placentophagy'. *Bulletin of the New York Academy of Medicine* 55(6):591–599.

Oliver, Kelly. 1998. *Subjectivity without Subjects: From Abject Fathers to Desiring Mothers*. Lanham, MD: Rowman & Littlefield.

Roberts, R.M., S. Xie and N. Mathialagan. 1996. 'Maternal Recognition of Pregnancy'. *Biological Reproduction* 54(2):294–302.

Sibai, Baha, Gus Dekker and Michael Kupferminc. 2005. 'Pre-eclampsia'. *Lancet* 365:785–799.

Thompson, Charis. 2005. *Making Parents: The Ontological Choreography of Reproductive Technologies*. Cambridge: MIT Press.

Waldby, Catherine. 2002. 'Stem Cells, Tissue Cultures and the Production of Biovalue'. *Health*: 6(3):305–323.

Weiss, Gail. 1999. *Body Images: Embodiment as Intercorporeality*. New York: Routledge.

Questions for Critical Thought

CHAPTER 33

1. Define what Stepnisky and the authors whom he draws on mean by 'biological citizenship'.
2. According to Stepnisky, how does the Kirby report redefine what it means to be a Canadian citizen? What elements and psychological characteristics does it assume that a Canadian citizen ideally needs? How are we all biocitizens, even if illness is not part of our identity?
3. Explain the important status that choice has in the Kirby report. Why does the report argue that choice is so important for patients, the health care system, and a democratic society in general?
4. Why does the Kirby report emphasize the importance of knowledge to the new Canadian biological citizen? How will more knowledge help both health care professionals and mental illness patients?
5. What is biological multiculturalism? How is it conceptually similar to and different from cultural multiculturalism?
6. According to Stepnisky, what are the possible consequences of Canadians understanding themselves as potentially mentally ill rather than simply not mentally ill? Be sure to include what you have learned about the social construction of stigma and the normalcy/ deviance divide.

CHAPTER 34

1. What specific positive and negative medical outcomes are related to feeling love/loved or to losing love?
2. What characteristics (age, gender, etc.) are associated with perceived love? Explain.
3. What characteristics (age, gender, etc.) are associated with food insecurity? Explain.
4. Can perceived love counteract the negative health effects of food insecurity? Explain, using statistical evidence.
5. Nakhaie and Arnold transform various variables into indicators of two explanatory/inter-mediary concepts: perceived love and food insecurity. However, not all of the variables were entirely explained by either of these. Age and smoking had independent effects on change in health status. Explain how age and smoking are related to the explanatory variables and change in health status. Include the kind of relationship (positive or negative) and why it exists.

CHAPTER 35

1. Berenson's piece is not the only one in this volume to analyze the competing framing of issues (e.g. Adorjan; Chen; Hallgrimsdottir, Phillips and Benoit). According to Berenson, why do frames matter? How are the cultural texts Berenson studies similar and different

from those studied in other papers in this volume? (Consider content, function/purpose, readership, distribution, etc.) How might the texts Berenson studies be more or less powerful (i.e., able to have wide-reaching effects) than other kinds of texts?

2. Why is the framing of menstrual suppression as a technology issue, as a cost/benefit calculation, or within any of the other frames, culturally compelling, according to Berenson? What existing cultural forms does she argue are being drawn on?

3. Consider the contradictory elements that frame 2 (not menstruating as the new 'normal') and frame 3 (women want this choice) draw upon. How does the document Berenson studies manage to both preserve and criticize the traditional relationship between doctors and women?

4. The third frame highlights how much women want to suppress their menstrual cycles. Who else stands to benefit from women chemically suppressing their menstrual cycles? Using Epstein's criteria as Berenson has, explore why these other interests might not have made it into the dominant frame.

5. Berenson pointed out the lack of firm evidence that menstruating too much is dangerous (frame 2), or that suppressing menstruation is safe (frame 4). How does the framing of the issue invite readers to ignore the lack of firm evidence and accept the pro-suppression argument as valid?

6. Consider how frames help each other: how does the 'no reason to believe that this is risky' frame support the 'benefits outweigh the costs' frame. What if the lack of firm evidence was taken seriously? How might this change the cost/benefit analysis?

CHAPTER 36

1. What is a placentation in the strict biological sense? According to Scott, how are there multiple placentations? Use some of her examples to demonstrate how they each concern distinct processes.

2. Compare the material production of the placenta to its social/cultural production. How do these different placentations concern distinct processes and yet also overlap with one another? Be sure to discuss the concept of 'natureculture'.

3. How does placental immunology and pre-eclampsia challenge our theoretical understanding of the division between self and other?

4. How does the DNA involved in placentations challenge our understanding of selfhood?

5. Why and how are placentations political (open to contestation and change)?

6. Scott is drawing on a distinct notion of agency. She asserts that biological entities are active and productive, and that animals help 'make' human beings through their contributions to scientific placentations. Using some of Scott's examples, compare her notion of agency to traditional sociological conceptions of agency. What are some strengths and weaknesses of conceptualizing agency in this way?

Part X

Inequality and Stratification

One of the longest-standing objects of sociological analysis is the unequal distribution of strategic resources. Conditions of inequality are rarely random; they are often ordered around sets of traits that are used to distinguish individuals from one another and rank them. Communities stratify traits by rewarding some but disregarding, or even punishing, others with social stigma or material deprivation. Technically, any human trait that is variable could be subject to stratification, though not all are. For example, there is no special stigma attached to people who like mustard rather than ketchup, or vice versa. Some traits that are stratified are entirely socially acquired, while others have biological aspects. But the fact that certain traits are biological does not mean that they are naturally ranked; all traits must be imbued with cultural meaning to be ranked. And the fact that socially acquired traits aren't biological does not make them easier to change. Even though they are not biological, we are often 'born with them' in the sense that we inherit them from the communities in which we are born and socialized. It is very difficult to 'upgrade' to more socially valued, materially rewarded traits.

Humans are stratified by traits in various ways. One of the most obvious of these is the distribution of material resources. Throughout this collection, many authors refer to the ideology of neo-liberalism, crediting it with increasing material inequality within societies. In this section, Justin Paulson and Carlo Fanelli describe the neo-liberal policies increasingly in place within Canadian cities and how they impoverish some while enriching others. Pat Armstrong's piece takes on the persistent problem that women's work is, on average, paid less than men's work.

Stratification is also evident in how risk is distributed. In their paper, Arlene Tigar McLaren and Sylvia Parusel consider the risks that traffic poses to families as they bring children to and from school. By comparing two neighbourhoods that are differentiated by social class, they demonstrate that getting to school is a riskier endeavour for the children in one neighbourhood than for those in the other, and conclude that traffic risks are disproportionately experienced by lower-income and female parents.

Another way of measuring inequality is by considering the stratification of social power—the ability of those who are empowered to control and shape the lives of those who lack power. Jacqueline Kennelly describes how a variety of traits and activities became objects of extreme policing and scrutiny during the Vancouver 2010 Olympic Games. Affluent tourists were protected from the unsightly poverty of the Downtown Eastside, but at the expense of the city's low-income residents. While one group of people were served by a police force that reordered the city simply for their viewing pleasure, other groups were displaced by the same force from the only areas that provided the services they needed. These latter groups were targeted and even criminalized for doing unsightly (not necessarily criminal) things, or merely looking like they were the type of people who might engage in such behaviour.

Examining inequalities requires us to ask a radical question: Who benefits from the current social order? Answering this question does not imply that those who benefit are bad people or that they have intentionally planned or perfectly manipulated the social order to benefit from it. That being said, people who benefit from stratification often do take part in defending and maintaining their advantages in various ways. To understand what or who is to 'blame' for inequalities, we must also ask historical questions about how these conditions emerged, and how they continue to be systemically reproduced.

CHAPTER 37

Pay Equity: Yesterday's Issue?

Pat Armstrong

Understanding **pay equity** requires understanding the complex evolution of women and work. It really requires looking back to at least the nineteenth century in Canada and the establishment of the Royal Commission on the Relations between Capital and Labour. The commission heard testimony both about women's abysmally low wages and about how men were paid significantly more than women, even when performing the same job. The development of pay equity is dependent on evidence, argument, and collective as well as individual action. It is also dependent on renewing strategies as conditions and ideas change, as work is restructured, and as employers' strategies result in inequities.

Equal pay for work of equal value, or 'pay equity' as we call it in Canada, is based on comparisons of work predominately done by women with work predominately done by men. It does not challenge the wages paid for men's jobs but does say that women's jobs should be paid on the same basis as men's jobs. It assumes that legislation applied to all employers can create a level playing field. This failure to challenge the assumed market determination of men's jobs has been one reason some feminists have rejected pay equity strategies.

Pay equity supports the continuing segregation of the labour force that leaves women doing women's work at women's wages. This is the case even if the nature of the work and the forms of pay alter and even if some women and some jobs

at least are treated more equitably. Evidence on an overall **gender wage gap**, as well as on differences in the way individual women and men are paid, has been produced for a long time, and it has been used by women for a long time to improve their pay. But evidence alone does not do the trick. It is a necessary but not sufficient factor.

It was evidence of women's low wages and poor conditions, *combined* with their growing activism and their work during World War I, that led to the introduction of minimum wages and conditions for women across much of Canada. These state interventions, based on notions of need, improved women's wages because women are the majority of those earning the lowest wages. For this reason, minimum wage legislation remains critical for women today. This strategy also demonstrated that women's concentration in particular sectors could be redressed, at least to some extent, by ensuring that the lowest paid would not be totally impoverished. But it still left most women with wages lower than those of most men.

Minimum wage, though, was not intended to create equity. Evidence demonstrating an overall wage gap between women, once more combined with efforts by women's groups and unions at the local and international level, led to the first legislation promoting equity in pay.

Equal pay for equal work and then for basically similar work was another step forward. It was easier for activists to demand equity in the context of a post-war world concerned more with justice than it had been before or probably has since. But the legislation of equal pay for equal work is often easy to avoid and undermine due to the difficulty of defining 'equal work'. Light and heavy cleaning is the classic example, with the women cleaning toilets defined as doing light cleaning and paid less than the men cleaning the halls, work defined as heavy. And equal pay cases often require the demonstration of the employer's intent, something that is hard to prove, and that in any case is often not the clear cause of the division and inequality between men's and women's jobs. Moreover, equal pay is a strategy primarily focused on individuals and usually requires that individuals take the risk of complaining. And even in the rare instances of success, the gains are too often restricted to a single individual. The battle is still necessary for those individuals, however.

The evidence of the limits of this strategy, made clear in the 1970 Report of the Royal Commission on the Status of Women, led to recommendations that the Canadian government legislate equal pay for work of equal value. The experience of individual women then became the basis for establishing the way entire female-dominated occupational categories are underpaid relative to male jobs.

The challenge was to have gendered wage difference legally recognized as systemic discrimination—discrimination that required redress through equal pay for work of equal value and that did not require demonstrating employer's intent. The journey to this legal recognition has been a long one, characterized by compromise and steps backward and by both explicit and hidden justifications for the job segregation that is combined with the undervaluing of women's work.

Let's start with women's bodies. It was possible to establish that biological difference could not be used as the major explanation for the division of labour by sex, and it is hard for anyone today to justify pay inequity on the basis of male or female bodies, although we are seeing some reemergence of these kinds of biological claims often appearing in hidden forms. For example, the fact that women have babies and are frequently tasked with rearing

them as well as doing domestic work is too often used as an explanation for inequality by people discussing this issue. This argument ignores the structural and attitudinal factors that help maintain the division in domestic work. Treating the gendered division of domestic life as if it is natural, or entirely separate from the gendered division of the workplace, makes it possible for employers to claim they have no responsibility for workplace divisions, as if they are simply an unavoidable result of the sexism 'out there'. Notions about women's bodies also contribute to the undervaluing of women's skills, with assumptions often made that women who provide care, cook, clean, or do laundry (either paid or unpaid) are simply doing what comes naturally, and that these are not skills that need to be specially compensated like men's skills in the workplace outside the home.

Then there is also the persistent argument that women do not need the money they are earning from paid work. Of course, men are not paid on the basis of need, but the assumption has historically been pervasive. While the perspective that women work for 'pin money' is not often heard in current times, the argument justifying unequal pay as a choice often masks this assumption. The argument goes, that women choose to take low-paying jobs and part-time, precarious employment due to a lack of need for money, in the process crowding into job ghettos of their own making. For decades, feminist scholars have worked to show not only that women's so-called choices are highly circumscribed by structural and cultural constraints as well as by discrimination but also that there is little justification for making women's 'choices' have such low-paying consequences. Why should a women have to choose to be a fire-fighter—assuming she is allowed to make that choice—rather than a nurse in order to be paid decent wages, or choose to care for plants rather than children in order to make more than a minimum wage? But this argument too still has legs and is reappearing in various forms.

Level of education has become increasingly ineffective as a justification for unequal pay, given that women's graduation rates are equal to or higher than those of men. Nonetheless, the evidence still shows that, even with the same amount of formal education, women are paid less than men. Even more than this, men can have *less* education than women and *still* make more than them. Nurses, for example, have to have post-secondary education but fire-fighters do not, yet fire-fighters are paid more than nurses.

Level of experience is still used to support the fairness of pay inequities, although there is little difference in the numbers of women and men who have at least 10 years of experience in the same job and there is little strong evidence to show that there is any constant relationship between experience beyond 10 years and wages. For example, in our recent study of workers in long-term care, the majority of women had worked in long-term care for more than 20 years, yet their wages were much lower than those of men with less experience who are materials handlers.

The arguments presented here are ultimately irrelevant because they relate to the characteristics of individuals, their capacities, and their choices. In contrast, pay equity is about jobs. It is about comparing the skill, effort, responsibility, and working conditions in female-dominated jobs with those in male-dominated jobs, a comparison that has nothing to do with individuals but rather is focused entirely on the work. Nor does the debate about how much of the gendered pay gap can be explained by experience, education, or choice have much to do with pay equity. The overall wage gap is what is used to establish the existence of systemic discrimination. Pay equity legislation addresses a pay equity gap, the one between jobs, not between people in specific workplaces where job requirements can be assessed.

The various forms of legislation on pay equity mark major steps forward, reflecting years of hard preparatory work by pay equity coalitions and researchers, years of legal decisions such as in the case of *Action travail de femme vs. CN*, leading to an accumulation of rights. Based on arguments for social justice, each form of legislation nevertheless represents compromises. Although many women, and some men, benefit, not only in terms of pay but also in terms of respect, many are still left out and the need for new strategies remains.

As the federal Task Force on Pay Equity has made clear over the years, the recognition of systemic discrimination, of the need for compulsory action and real penalties and the establishment of independent, powerful tribunals, and commissions, as well as gender-sensitive job evaluation, are critical components. So is the inclusion of the public and private sectors, part-time employees, and single occupants of traditional female jobs. Unions need to be integrated into the negotiations, but the process cannot be left to unions alone. Equally important, the task force also emphasized that equity must be maintained, not assumed to be negotiated once and for all.

Maintenance, though, is no simple task, in part because jobs change, history is forgotten, and employers develop strategies to avoid the consequences of legislation. And all previous legislation, as the task force recognized, has had limitations, especially when it comes to the most marginalized.

According to most recent census data, women are the majority in all but three of the 20 lowest-paid occupations, and in two of the remaining three their numbers are the same as they are in the overall labour force. The reverse is the case with the 20 highest-paid jobs. This ratio is part of the same old pattern, with some changes in quantity and form. Many more women have moved into self-employment, where they are most likely to be 'own account'—doing jobs they formerly did as employees—and thus remain outside pay equity legislation. Or they have temporary jobs, with the same consequences. The privatization of many government services has also meant that women have moved outside the protection of legislation and that few of them have union protection. We also don't know how many are in the informal economy or in jobs in small workplaces that are outside the law, or how many are covered but have no real access to compensation because of the poor application of the law.

What is needed is not only to ensure the enforcement and maintenance of the laws as they exist but also, as the task force made clear, to expand them to include other forms of work not covered by current legislation, other approaches to pay equity and other forms of discrimination. The time has come to do this.

Deregulation and cut-throat competition briefly lost their shine in the economic crisis of 2009, during which there was some revival of the old Keynesian notion that argues for the need to spend during economic downturns. But the winds have shifted and now the attack is once again on the public sector and some forms of regulation that are claimed to inhibit economic recovery. Even as our political community has picked up some of Keynes' ideas, we seem to have forgotten his other argument that especially in tough times it is smart to keep money in the hands of the consumer who will spend, and we know that it is women who spend, not because they enjoy shopping for its own sake but for the survival of themselves and their families. It is time to once again level the playing field of work by ensuring that all employers pay equally for jobs of equal value. We need to do this women's work, but not for women's wages.

CHAPTER 38

Red Zones, Empty Alleys, and Giant TVs: Low-Income Youths' Spatial Accounts of Olympic Host Cities

Jacqueline Kennelly

Henri Lefebvre suggests that space cannot be understood as a fixed and unchanging entity within the social world of relations. Rather, it is infinitely mutable, multiple, and overlapping. This is not to suggest that space is infinitely malleable in the sense that any one person might have the same degree of control as any other over its quality and characteristics. Lefebvre (1991) links the production of space to property relationships and the forces of production. Bourdieu (1984) understands social spaces to be distinguished by the relative accumulation of economic, cultural, and social capital of those inhabiting the spaces. In the case of young people, there is the more or less consistent reality that their experiences of space are 'subject to surveillance and control by adults' (Valentine, Skelton, and Chambers, 1998, p. 9).

The Olympics, as a global spectacle of mass proportions, exerts its own particular pressures on urban spatial sites within host cities. These effects can be understood, in part, through the lens of globalization and in particular the resultant neo-liberal impacts on city spaces (see, for e.g. Harvey, 2006). However, there is another aspect of Olympic effects that I wish to highlight here: the specific manifestation unique to *spectacle* itself. Following on the ideas of Guy Debord (n.d.), I suggest that the hosting of the Olympics by global cities such as Vancouver results in particular reorganizations of space, some temporary, some more permanent, that have specific and concrete implications for low-income young people living within host cities. As Debord notes, the effects of such a spectacle generate an illusion of togetherness, exemplified through the repeated mantras of nationalistic pride and patriotism expounded throughout the event itself. But the reality, at least for certain segments of the population, is an intensification of *separation*, experienced in part through the changing spatial realities of the Olympic host city.

Through participant accounts and images, this paper will explore the specific manner in which low-income young people experienced these effects in Vancouver, both during the 2010 Winter Olympics and in the period directly preceding. Tracing encounters with police, crowds, surveillance, and their own restricted mobility within the Olympic city, the young people's stories document the unequal spatial distributions that become intensified during spectacular neo-liberal mega-events such as the Olympic Games.

Methodology: Spatial Ethnography of Everyday Perceptions

The research has thus far been carried out over two time periods. The first took place approximately a year before the Vancouver 2010 games began (February to April 2009). The second took place during the games themselves (February 2010). During these two fieldwork periods, I or a research assistant conducted **focus groups**, interviews, and a longer-term arts-based project. In total, 33 youth (ages 15 to 24) participated in the first phase of the research, and 27 youth participated in the second phase, bringing the total to 60 participants over the two phases.

In addition to the fieldwork with youth participants, I conducted interviews with 'key informants' during both field periods. These were adults who were in some manner associated with the topic of this research, and included City of Vancouver and Vancouver School Board staff, youth workers, youth advocates, members of Olympic watchdog organizations, and city planners. I also kept field notes of my observations of the city of Vancouver both before and during the games themselves.

Spatial Reorganization in the Global Olympic City

Although the Vancouver police chief maintained that his police force would not implement restrictive legislation that was introduced just prior to

the games (Vancouver police won't . . ., 2009), the experiences of many of the youth who participated in this project suggest that the police presence was certainly a noticeable one, both in the period leading up to the games and during the games themselves. Alison, age 24, recounted her experiences walking through the core of the Downtown Eastside immediately after the opening ceremonies:

Alison: It was just bizarre, like it was really ominous. We were walking down Hastings [the main street in the Downtown Eastside] . . . and there's all these tour buses [that are marked with] Vancouver 2010, we're walking down and there's the Money Mart, and then there's the shelter, that you actually can't really see because they've built this fake little wall thing so that the people going to the shelter there aren't really seen. But then you look to the right side of the street and you see this big condo building, and a big shiny new London Drugs, and it's just really bizarre. And then you continue to walk down past Abbott, and outside there's a bar that there's usually a lot of action going on there, like there's guys standing outside who are drinking at the bar. And then at the corner, there's usually people who are selling and using drugs. And there's *nobody*. . . . I have never seen those doorways, like in the five years that I have lived in downtown, I have never seen the doorways [empty like that] . . . Like nobody.

Jacqueline: And did you see police around?

A: Yeah. There was a paddy wagon parked right across the alley, there was an undercover police cruiser right at the corner, and then there was another police cruiser right behind the paddy wagon. So like the police dominance there was very well seen.

Alison's account simultaneously documents the effects of urban development that have been widely recognized as a consequence of hosting **mega-events** (Burbank, Andranovich & Heying, 2002; Broudehoux, 2007; Chalkley & Essex, 1999) *and* the symbolic and material consequences of policing practices during the events. She describes the markers of both the aspiring global Olympic city and the real city of entrenched poverty and historically situated disadvantage, literally located on opposite sides of the same street.

Alison's description highlights not only how the city has been irrevocably changed by the relentless gentrification that accompanies such global events (in the form of condominium and retail development), but that even those sites that have traditionally been the safe spaces for those otherwise shut out of gentrification's benefits have been transformed, literally emptied of their previous inhabitants. She links such effects to the presence of police paddy wagons and cruisers; later in the interview, she recounts stories of people being arrested and held for the duration of the games for minor offences that would normally be disregarded in the context of that particular neighbourhood. While the presence of police in this neighbourhood is not unusual, the accompanying shift in the spatial realities for its low-income residents is one powerful effect that can only be associated with the hosting of the Olympic Games.

Low-income young people faced similar spatial pressures in the year directly preceding the games. During the fieldwork period conducted throughout the year before the Olympics began, Richard recounted a spatial practice utilized by police, called 'red zoning'. A **red zone** is an area that the police have designated as 'out of bounds' to particular youth who have been banished by police for partaking in illegitimate (though not always criminal) behaviour. Such practices can have the result of 'pushing' low-income young people away from the areas where they can access services such as housing or drug treatment, and into the Downtown Eastside, where, as Richard points out, 'you can get caught up in anything'. The youth strongly believed that such practices were linked to Olympic pressures to 'clean up the streets', pushing them out of sight to locations where their presence would not disturb affluent tourists.

Interestingly, space is not only *emptied* of low-income youth and other marginalized residents as a result of policing in the context of the games, but also, paradoxically, filled. Sandy, age 23,

described how she and her friends had been continually moved on from the steps of the Vancouver Art Gallery prior to the start of the games. Once the games began, however, her experiences in this space changed:

> Sandy: Oh, that [being moved on by the police] doesn't usually happen anymore, with that big TV screen there [near the steps of the Vancouver Art Gallery].
>   Jacqueline: Oh yeah. OK. Why?
>   S: Because the TV screen's there. . . . It's a big fucking TV screen, have you seen it?
>   J: Yeah yeah, but why does that matter?
>   S: Because now we're not loitering. [laughs] Now we're not loitering *because* we're watching TV. Isn't that awesome?

The Vancouver Art Gallery might be considered one of Vancouver's '**zones of prestige**' (Newman, 2007, following Maguire, 2005), a 'culturally impressive institution or space' (Newman, 2007, p. 261) that a city uses to boost its reputation both nationally and globally. Located in the heart of the downtown Vancouver shopping district, and surrounded by Robson Square, headquarters for Olympic celebrations within the city, it is a key symbolic locale for Vancouver's global city aspirations. It is thus not insignificant that Sandy, a visibly homeless active drug user, was no longer being asked to vacate the steps. This may have been due to the public scrutiny in place during the games and enforced through global media coverage, which both key informants and youth participants in this research noted may have stopped police from being overzealous in their treatment of homeless people. However, Sandy believes that the presence of a giant TV screen held greater explanatory force. As she noted, 'Now we're not loitering *because* we're watching TV'; in other words, the Olympic spectacle had transformed this central urban space from a site of intense surveillance and policing, and into a space of consumption. This meant that street-involved young people could enjoy the steps of the art gallery with relatively little interference, something they were not free to do during the period leading up to the Olympics.

Photo 38.1 Art-based activity in the fieldwork period that took place the year before the games captures the 'emptying' spatial effects of mega-events such as the Olympics.

The presence of thousands of spectators, from Canada and around the world, also changed the space of the city for the young people in this study. When asked during a focus group what it was like for them in the city while the games were on, the first response of the participants was a sense of overwhelming unease with the sheer numbers of people on the city streets:

- 'It's like a can of tuna fish.'
- 'I bump into a couple of people.'
- 'I don't know, just it's too busy. Insanely busy, I don't like it.'
- 'I can't walk from A to B.'
- 'I even start sweating lots, there's just too many people, squished up too much.'

For youth who did venture out into the city to take part in the celebrations, there remained a risk of being harassed if they were perceived to be 'out of place' (Wright, 1997). One young woman and her boyfriend, who were both Aboriginal, were told by the police that they didn't look as if they belonged in the affluent west-side neighbourhood where they had finally secured permanent housing, with the assistance of various youth service agencies.

Conclusions

The preceding accounts document a variety of spatial implications for low-income young people of their cities hosting the Olympic Games. Spatial effects can be seen through the 'emptying' of some spaces, and, paradoxically, the 'filling' of others. As global cities attempt to capitalize on such 'prestige projects' (Newman, 2007), the police often act as agents of the spatial reorganization that permits the city to 'look its best' when the 'world is watching' (see McCann, 2009). Both gentrification effects and the sheer numbers of people that descend upon a city during an Olympic Games are also implicated in reorganizing urban space. Each result in specific effects for the city's marginalized inhabitants, including low-income, homeless, and street-involved young people. These are not the stories of youthful heroism and athletic endeavour that the International Olympic Committee uses to market its brand; nonetheless, these youth are the recipients of Olympic legacies within the city they call home.

References

Bourdieu, P. (1984). *Distinction: a social critique of the judgement of taste* (R. Nice, Trans.). Cambridge, Massachusetts: Harvard University Press.

Broudehoux, A. (2007). Spectacular Beijing: the conspicuous construction of an Olympic metropolis. *Journal of Urban Affairs, 29*(4), 383–399.

Burbank, M. J., Andranovich, G., & Heying, C. H. (2002). Mega-events, urban development, and public policy. *The Review of Policy Research, 19*(3), 180–202.

Chalkley, B., & Essex, S. (1999). Urban development through hosting international events: a history of the Olympic Games. *Planning Perspectives, 14*(4), 369–394.

Debord, G. (no date). *Society of the spectacle*. London: Rebel Press.

Harvey, D. (2006). Neo-liberalism as creative destruction. *Geografiska Annaler 88 B*(2), 145–158.

Lefebvre, H. (1991). *The production of space* (D. Nicholson-Smith, Trans.). Malden, MA: Blackwell Publishing.

McCann, E. J. (2009). City marketing. In R. Kitchin & N. Thrift (Eds.), International Encyclopedia of Human Geography, Vol. 2, 119–124. Toronto: Elsevier.

Newman, P. (2007). 'Back the bid': the 2012 Summer Olympics and the governance of London. *Journal of Urban Affairs, 29*(3), 255–267.

Valentine, G., Skelton, T., & Chambers, D. (1998). Cool places: An introduction to youth and youth cultures. In T. Skelton & G. Valentine (Eds.), *Cool places: Geographies of youth cultures* (pp. 3–32). New York: Routledge.

Vancouver police won't force homeless into shelters. (2009, December 7). CBC news. Retrieved February 4, 2010 from http://www.cbc.ca/canada/british-columbia/story/2009/11/25/bc-homeless-legislation-protest.html.

Wright, T. (1997). *Out of place: homeless mobilizations, subcities, and contested landscapes*. Albany, NY: State University of New York Press.

Parents and Traffic Safety: Unequal Risks and Responsibilities to and from School

Arlene Tigar McLaren and Sylvia Parusel

Introduction

As an icon of modern society, the automobile represents for many people personal freedom, convenience and pleasure, the good life, and national progress. This rosy picture ignores the fact that the 'lived experience of dwelling with cars' is complex, ambiguous and contradictory (Sheller 2004: 222). The contradictions are perhaps no more apparent than in the case of parents who depend on cars to carry out domestic responsibilities yet must go to great lengths to protect their children inside and outside cars from auto-saturated streets. Though the car has become increasingly embedded in family life, scholars have paid remarkably little attention to **parental traffic safeguarding**—the ways in which parents protect their children's diverse mobilities from the dangers of motorized traffic in variable social and automobilized environments—and the complex ways this phenomenon relates to the production and reproduction of the automobility system.

Despite the fact that collisions are a leading cause of death and injury among children in many places around the world, scholars, experts, and media say relatively little about traffic danger. In Canada in 2007 alone, 99 children aged 0–14 were killed in motor vehicle collisions and 626 were seriously injured (Transport Canada 2010), totalling altogether over 700 children. These statistics do not take into account minor injuries, countless near misses, and the never-ending discipline required by parents as both drivers and non-drivers to avert collisions in protecting their children.

To begin to untangle the complex interactions between automobility and urban parental traffic safeguarding, it is necessary to locate them in their social and geographical contexts. Based on a comparison of two elementary schools located on the east and west sides of Vancouver, British Columbia, this paper explores parents' concerns about traffic danger in their children's school journey. We examine how auto-dominated urban environments intertwine with social inequalities (in particular, gender and social **class**) to produce unequal risks and responsibilities in parental traffic safeguarding practices. Our analysis illustrates the ways in which the automobility system—which includes trucks as well as cars and other forms of private motor vehicles—shapes parenting and how traffic safeguarding, as part of the work of parenting, constitutes automobility and its illusion of safety. In what follows, we first introduce automobility and the feminist theories that inform this paper; second, we outline the methods of our case study; third, we examine two sites of the school journey (neighbourhood streetscapes and school entrances); and fourth, we provide some conclusions.

Automobility and Parental Traffic Safeguarding

According to Urry (2004: 27), automobility can be conceptualized as 'a self-organizing autopoietic, non-linear system that spreads world-wide, and includes cars, car-drivers, roads, petroleum supplies and many novel objects, technologies and signs'. As a powerful and hegemonic system that has transformed daily life, automobility is the result of historical struggles and continues to be contested locally and globally (Paterson 2007; Conley and McLaren 2009). Norton (2008) shows, for example, how motordom in the 1920s in the United States fought to gain control of public streets, which had once belonged to pedestrians. By inventing jaywalking and reinventing child safety education, traffic safety campaigns successfully redistributed responsibility for traffic threats away from motor vehicles and toward pedestrians (including children) and their 'reckless' behaviour. As a result, traffic safety became a foundation of the automotive city.

But even as children's pedestrian and bicycle injury and death rates have declined over time while car ownership has risen, streets have not necessarily become safer for children. A decrease in children's death and injury rates masks 'the larger problem of the removal of these users from the transportation system' (McMillan 2005: 442) when parents restrict their children's mobility for fear of exposing them to traffic dangers (Hillman et al. 1990).

In borrowing from Beckmann (2004), we argue that traffic safety practices are not primarily about safety, but are actually about the *illusion* of safety, which serves to accelerate traffic and foster automobility. Beckmann (2004: 95) argues that the vast auto networks of accident-workers 'cleanse the road, repair the car, heal the victims and lock up irresponsible drivers—suggesting that afterwards driving has become safe.'

Automobility works because the social organization of road accidents denies the risks of driving and aims to reconstruct the 'illusion of safety'. Similarly, we suggest that the vast range of traffic safety measures that remove children from the street create an illusion of safety that denies the actual risks of traffic. Such measures serve the automobility system and traffic flow by displacing the responsibility for collisions away from motor vehicles and onto children and their parents, and by concealing the cost of children's immobilization and parents' safeguarding on everyday lives.

While research shows that legal and cultural discourses typically hold parents accountable for any traffic mishaps that befall children (Jain 2004; Bonham 2006), few scholarly studies (for an exception, see Thomsen 2005) have examined the actual practices and concerns of everyday parental traffic safeguarding of young children. The sociological literature has rarely acknowledged the complexities, and the inequalities (such as gender and social class), of parental safeguarding, which include the costs of time (planning, organizing, chauffeuring, escorting, confining), money, and worry.

Feminist theorists have long recognized gender as an underlying principle of domestic organization that assigns mothers, more than fathers, an unequal and invisible burden of responsibilities (Fox 2009), but theorists have not adequately explored the ways in which parental traffic safeguarding is part of domestic work. Our research illustrates how parental traffic safety practices are gendered, with mothers predominantly responsible for organizing children's school journey. In keeping with feminist theorizing that highlights how gender intersects with other social inequalities (Fraser 1997), our study also explores how parental traffic safeguarding is linked to specific neighbourhoods marked by social class differences. Our analysis adds to the growing body of evidence mapping the different ways that urban design and transportation systems of local neighbourhoods intertwine with social class in determining fatality and injury rates (Short and Pinet-Peralta 2010). But instead of focusing on collision rates in differing local contexts, we examine parental safeguarding that seeks to prevent collisions in the first place.

Method

Our study is based on **fieldwork** (including interviews, site observations, document analysis) of two elementary schools in Vancouver, British Columbia, which we selected to consider social class differences between the east and west sides of Vancouver (see Parusel and McLaren [2010] for further discussion). The east side of Vancouver is composed of relatively low-income residents and recent immigrants from diverse countries. The west side consists of relatively high-income residents, reflecting British heritage but also with recent influxes of wealthy immigrants from such countries as China and Korea.

Between June 2007 and September 2008, we conducted in-depth interviews with 10 parents at the east side (ES) school and 12 parents (including a focus group of six mothers) at the west side (WS) school. All interviews were audio-taped and took place in homes or cars, or at the schools. We also asked the parents to fill out a brief demographic sheet to provide a profile of the interviewed parents at each school. We recruited parents through the schools, using several different procedures such as attending Parent Advisory Council (PAC) meetings, sending notices home with children, and speaking with parents and caregivers at the school entrances.

Corresponding to research that shows a general pattern of mothers being more involved in their children's schooling than fathers (O'Brien 2008), nearly all the parents we interviewed at the WS school were mothers (11 out of 12). In contrast, at the ES school almost as many fathers (four) as mothers (six) were involved in our research. These gendered patterns of the interview participants mirror the differentiated practices of traffic safeguarding at the two schools that we analyze below.

Streetscapes and Parental Traffic Safeguarding

By taking into account the dynamics of gender and social class in different auto-centred environments at the two schools, we explore how automobility shapes parents' traffic safeguarding practices in distinct ways and how these practices contribute to automobility's illusion of safety. We illustrate our arguments by focusing on two sites—neighbourhood streetscapes and school entrances—in children's journeys between home and school.

Parents at both schools were concerned about the dangers of the highly trafficked streets in their school neighbourhoods. Their worries differed, however, as a result of the distinct forms of the

automobility system in their local streetscapes, which were linked to social class. In the relatively working-class neighbourhood of the ES school, parents were especially anxious about the dangers of nearby truck routes, whereas in the relatively middle-class neighbourhood of the WS school, parents focused most of their concerns on parental chauffeuring at the school entrance.

One ES school mother explained that the school's location near truck routes creates a particularly dangerous 'energy level' of traffic:

> We're just bounded by two very busy roadways that have big trucks. It's not just cars, it's these big trucks just going quickly. And sometimes just not stopping, you know. . . . just, the energy level—suddenly you're just having to really be aware of crossing the street. (Christina)

She added that, in dissecting the community, the road system undermines cohesiveness: 'You have these really busy streets, which seems almost unnatural for the area and . . . it kind of dissects the community . . . you're part of a highway, but you're supposed to be a community.' Truck routes—characterized by heavy vehicles, high speeds, and traffic volumes that correlate positively with traffic danger (Hillman et al. 1990)—heighten parental worries about safeguarding such that parents talked, for example, about not being able to trust traffic lights and about never allowing their children to walk by themselves to school. The truck routes that carve their way through this neighbourhood correspond to the general pattern in Vancouver, in which truck routes are more prevalent on the east side than west side, creating unequal risks and responsibilities—linked to social class—for parents in safeguarding their children.

As a result of a highly developed chauffeuring culture, the greatest worry for parents at the WS school was the risk posed by parental traffic at the school entrance. During daily drop off and pick up times, we observed fleets of cars converging onto the streets adjacent to the school. Drivers regularly got in one another's way, took up pedestrian space, and endangered themselves and others. One mother said: 'It's a free-for-all.

Whoever gets there first, people double-park, and it's not really very safe' (Lisa).

At the WS school, in most instances, it was mothers, not fathers, who were primarily involved in chauffeuring and traffic safeguarding their children (including mothers who actively volunteered in the school traffic safety committee). The mothers' unequal safeguarding responsibilities vis-à-vis fathers' were partly a reflection of social class privilege intertwined with gender. A key difference between the traffic safeguarding practices at the two schools is that ES school mothers were less available as chauffeurs, escorts, or school volunteers due to, for example, employment schedules and shift work. Their families were less modelled on the two-parent Anglo, male breadwinner family structure than at the WS school, where English-speaking mothers were available to participate in school affairs, and where various forms of economic, social, and cultural capital were available for investment in traffic safeguarding.

Ironically, at the WS school, it was usually mothers as chauffeurs, constituting automobility, who created the greatest concerns about traffic dangers. At both schools, it was primarily mothers vigilantly practising traffic safeguarding who helped to create the illusion of safety. Without such practices, the roads would have been far more dangerous for children than they already were. And again, it was typically mothers walking their children to school, or allowing them to walk or bicycle independently, or organizing Walk to School Weeks, who challenged and resisted auto hegemony.

Conclusion

Our study illustrates the ways in which the automobility system engenders parental traffic safeguarding practices in specific contexts, while showing conversely how these practices, both informally and formally, contribute to sustaining the automobility system and its illusion of traffic safety. As a lynchpin of the automobility system that enables traffic to flow on public streets, parental traffic safeguarding is also ridden with contradictions and conflicts that, depending on geographical and social contexts, entail particular forms of unequal risks and responsibilities as well as resistances to motor vehicle dominance.

If we are to move 'beyond the car', as some argue we should (e.g. Dennis and Urry 2009), mobility alternatives need to take into account parents' and children's traffic safety experiences. Once auto hegemony loosens its grip on transportation and urban design, parenting—especially mothering—may also be transformed by the reduced need for intense, worrisome, and socially unequal traffic safeguarding.

References

Beckmann, J. (2004) Mobility and safety, *Theory, Culture & Society* 21(4/5), pp. 81–100.

Bonham, J. (2006) Transport: Disciplining the body that travels, in S. Böhm, C. Jones, C. Land and M. Paterson (Eds.) *Against Automobility*, pp. 57–74 (Oxford: Blackwell/Sociological Review).

City of Vancouver (2009) Truck route map (updated Jan 2009). http://vancouver.ca/engsvcs/transport/traffic/pdf/english_map.pdf. Accessed 12 March 2010.

Conley, J. and McLaren, A.T. (Eds.) (2009) *Car Troubles: Critical Studies of Automobility and Auto-Mobility* (Farnham: Ashgate).

Dennis, K. and Urry, J. (2009) Post-car mobilities, in J. Conley and A.T. McLaren (Eds.) *Car Troubles: Critical Studies of Automobility and Auto-Mobility*, pp. 235–252 (Farnham: Ashgate).

Fox, B. (2009) *Family Patterns, Gender Relations*, 3rd edition (Don Mills: Oxford University Press).

Fraser, N. (1997) *Justice Interruptus: Critical Reflections on the 'Postsocialist' Condition* (New York: Routledge).

Hillman, M., Adams, J. and Whitelegg, J. (1990) *One False Move . . . A Study of Children's Independent Mobility* (London: Policy Studies Institute).

Jain, S.S.L. (2004) Dangerous instrumentality: The bystander as subject in automobility, *Cultural Anthropology* 19(1), pp. 61–94.

McMillan, T.E. (2005) Urban form and a child's trip to school: The current literature and a framework for future research, *Journal of Planning Literature* 19(4), pp. 440–456.

Norton, P.D. (2008) *Fighting Traffic: The Dawn of the Motor Age in the American City* (Cambridge Mass.: The MIT Press).

O'Brien, M. (2008) Gendered capital: Emotional capital and mothers' care work in education, *British Journal of Sociology of Education* 29(2), pp. 137–148.

Parusel, S. and McLaren, A.T. (2010) Cars before kids:

Automobility and the illusion of school traffic safety, *Canadian Review of Sociology* 47(2), pp. 129–147.

Paterson. M. (2007) *Automobile Politics: Ecology and Cultural Political Economy* (Cambridge, UK: Cambridge University Press).

Sheller, M. (2004) Automotive emotions: Feeling the car, *Theory, Culture and Society* 21(4/5), pp. 221–242.

Short, J.R. and Pinet-Peralta, L.M. (2010) No accident: Traffic and pedestrians in the modern city, *Mobilities* 5(1), pp. 41–59.

Thomsen, T.U. (2005) Parents' construction of traffic safety: Children's independent mobility at risk?, in T.U. Thomsen, L.D. Nielsen and H. Gudmundsson (Eds.), *Social Perspectives on Mobility*, pp. 11–28 (Aldershot: Ashgate).

Transport Canada (2010) *Canadian Motor Vehicle Traffic Collision Statistics: 2007* http://www.tc.gc.ca/eng/roadsafety/tp-tp3322-2007-1039.htm. Accessed 5 July 2010.

Urry, J. (2004) The 'system' of automobility, *Theory, Culture & Society* 21(4/5), pp. 25–39.

CHAPTER 40

Municipal Malaise: Neo-liberal Urbanism in Canada

Carlo Fanelli and Justin Paulson

We use the term **neo-liberal urbanism** to refer to a range of uneven processes unfolding in the urban environments in which we live and work. These include the privatization, restructuring, and elimination of public goods and municipal services; the shifting of the cost of maintenance of public resources onto the working class; the increasing precariousness of work in sectors previously thought to be more secure; the devolution of responsibilities onto local governments without matching fiscal support; the reining in of the influence of public sector unions and community groups; the scaling back of social entitlement programs; and the expansion of so-called 'public–private partnerships' that shift a significant part of the responsibility for urban governance from communities to corporations.

Although there has been much talk in academic circles about the recession and ongoing economic crisis marking the end of neo-liberalism, we find through our studies of Toronto, Vancouver, and Ottawa (the first-, third-, and fourth-largest census metropolitan areas in Canada) that these processes not only continue apace but remain orthodox responses to budgetary shortfalls. The experiences of both public sector workers and users of public services in these cities vividly demonstrate the malaise confronting Canadian cities today.

Neo-liberal Ascent in Historical Perspective

Every recession in Canada since the mid-1970s has been used as a pretext to restructure the relations between capital, labour, and state, and to radically reorient social policies to the benefit of the ruling class. Throughout the 1980s and 1990s, federal and provincial governments responded to economic crisis by curbing real wages, razing social programs, and selling off assets, while adhering tightly to a kind of market fundamentalism. At the same time, the weakening of socialist elements within the labour movement, political parties, and academe cleared the way for neo-liberalism's ascendancy in political, corporate, and academic discourse.

The 'common sense' promoted by neo-liberalism maintains a cult-like privileging of individual economic liberties and personal responsibility; the idealization of the private sector as a measuring stick for public sector remuneration; the 'need' to shift from the universal, public provision of social services to market provision with attached user fees; the competitive lowering of taxation between jurisdictions; and tax-shifting from businesses to consumers and from property owners to the users of city services. The material fallout accompanying such ideological purity is clear: although productivity output per employee between 1980 and 2005 in Canada rose by more than 37 per cent, real median wages have been stagnant since 1982. In short, with employee productivity rising and outpacing growth in wages, workers are receiving even fewer of the profits they produced. By the mid-1990s, income inequality in Canada reached levels not seen since the 1930s (Baragar 2009).

For several decades, this process has been trickling down to our cities. While the federal and provincial governments have a variety of relatively flexible revenue sources (such as income, sales, corporate, resource, and import taxes—tools that remain at their disposal whether or not they choose to use them), only eight cents on every dollar collected go back to Canada's municipalities. For our cities, property taxes remain the major source of funding, and from this, they must provide for their public utilities, public works, parks and recreational facilities, waste management, transit services, public housing, and other social and community services. However, since the 1980s, successive governments at both the federal and provincial levels have looked to 'correct' their budget deficits by 'downloading' services to cities, transferring greater amounts of fiscal responsibility onto municipalities without providing for additional capacities to share or generate revenue.

Toronto, Vancouver, and Ottawa

In response to the current economic slump, Toronto, Vancouver, and Ottawa—the first-, third-, and fourth-largest census metropolitan areas in Canada—are all struggling to simultaneously cut costs, meet the increasing demands on city services, and keep taxes low. When the math

doesn't add up, neo-liberal orthodoxy directs that public sector workers and the provision of public goods are to be sacrificed. Thus we see in each city a variety of moves to cut access to social services and reduce commercial property taxes in favour of increased subsidies and financial support for businesses, while seeking concessions from the city's unionized and non-unionized workforces. Each of these cities has also been seeking greater contracting out of public services, so-called public–private partnerships ('P3s'), and in some cases the privatization of municipal assets.

Powerful business and conservative lobby groups such as the Vancouver Board of Trade, Vancouver Fair Tax Coalition, the Toronto Board of Trade, and the Empire Club of Canada, continue to press for decreased taxes on businesses with a corresponding shift of the burden onto consumers and residents, and we have not (yet) seen any social movements with enough influence to counter the trend. In shifting the financial burden from businesses and landlords to consumers and residents, the cities will continue to lose revenue and erode their own fiscal capacities; yet social insecurity stemming from the economic crisis, continued population growth, and decaying urban infrastructure have only amplified the importance of the disappearing funds and services.

Public sector unions generally, and the smaller, municipally based private sector unions in particular, have been on the defensive since the beginning of the crisis, and will likely remain targets to be squeezed for some time. The pressure on public workers has been fuelling increasingly bitter labour conflicts, including, in Toronto, the 2008 Toronto Transit Commission strike, the 2009 civic workers' strike, and the Zellers Warehouse strike; in Vancouver, the Metro civic workers' strike and lockout and the HandyDart strike; and, in Ottawa, the OC Transpo bus drivers' strike and the museum workers' strike.

Pressures on city governments to change working conditions, renege on pension promises, and decrease wages, especially in the context of battered unions in the automotive and manufacturing sectors, have been intensifying as the budget gaps in annual infrastructure and operating expenses versus revenue reinforce fiscal austerity. Indeed, if the 1990s recession witnessed a growing courageousness on the part of capital and the state to purge the federal and provincial public sectors of their unions, the first decade of the twenty-first century is witnessing an intensification of such attacks, first in the private sector and, now, in a stepped-up assault on what's left of municipal strongholds in the public sphere.

The HandyDart case is particularly interesting in the way it highlights the perils for workers when public services are contracted out. In nearly 30 years the union, whose members provide nearly 5,000 daily trips for seniors and the disabled, had never gone on strike. But when the government-funded service was contracted out to a subsidiary of a U.S. corporation, workers were asked to abandon their pensions, cap health benefits, accept limitations on transfer and promotion, and accept the dismissal of employees on long-term disability and maternity leave. (After a gruelling 10-week strike, the matter was sent to binding arbitration, to the satisfaction of neither party.)

The recent wave of strikes has also been notable for the lack of public support for public sector workers under attack. In all three cities we are studying, the implicit (and, at times, explicit) goal of city officials has been to simply offload costs onto labour, breaking the unions if necessary; part of the strategy has been to fight an ideological battle in the press against the unions and their workers (and, by extension, public goods and services in general). In many cases, the strikes are causing visible divisions within the working class: in Ottawa, for instance, there was little solidarity with the drivers' union amongst the bus riders (mostly working-class themselves), to whom there seems not to have been sufficient outreach before or during the strike.

This has repercussions that go beyond the bus drivers themselves, for it was the logic of neo-liberalism that won the day: unionized public sector workers were raked over the coals by the mayor and in the pages of the local newspapers, treated as if they were spoiled children who enjoyed holding a helpless city hostage until their demands were met. This was far from the truth, but the strike thus highlighted a particularly vexing problem for public sector unionism: although people want public services, they are not ipso facto willing to support those who provide them. Without cross-sectoral political or social movement unionism making a dent in popular consciousness, individual public sector strikes can easily be spun by the employer in such a way as to reinforce neo-liberal common sense rather than challenge it. In such a climate, any public sector strike that is not a clear win becomes part of a long-term defeat.

Countering the Trend

So how do we get from the cities we live in to the cities we want? In the absence of a credible alternative in public discourse, and a social movement pushing for it, processes of neo-liberal urbanism will continue apace. Every year there is public debate about which programs should be cut, which should be spared, and from where the additional revenue should come. Yet in most of our cities the argument for maintaining services and public goods comes from single-interest groups appearing before council to defend their turf, or to insist on a specific provision for them in the municipal budget. These are often important demands. Yet their piecemeal approach means that any successes in one area, as important as they may be, are simply offset in another—effectively pitting parks against ambulances, student transit passes against the actual number of bus trips, community centres against low personal tax rates. Thinking inside the box, the fight is then about which services get cut or privatized, and *whose* taxes and end-user fees get raised, and at what proportion.

Public sector workers are on the front lines of this battle. Currently in a defensive position as they come under attack at all levels (federal, provincial, and municipal), they of course must defend their members against rollbacks of hard-won benefits. Yet the vitriol directed at them is intense—as if they live lavish lives at the expense of non-unionized workers. The OC Transpo strike in Ottawa, the municipal workers' strike in Toronto, and the HandyDart strike in Vancouver suggest that there is much to do to overcome popular hostility toward striking workers.

Changing this attitude is not primarily the task of the unions themselves, but of a broader public that wants livable cities with a fair and just provision of services and common goods, well-managed in a way that fosters sustainable development and is accountable to the community. One way to do this is to make a strong public sector once again part of common sense, but this requires struggle: the recent economic crisis provided an opportunity to dislodge neo-liberal common sense, but it didn't change it automatically.

We believe that fixing our cities requires a new kind of broad social movement unionism in order to bring together workers, social justice activists, and community groups. In short, we ought to stop treating cities as the backbone of capital and treat them as the places where most Canadians live, work, and play. Our collective struggles have tended to take the form of demands *of* the city, while they ought to be based in class and **urban consciousness**, and to demand instead the opportunity to restructure the city to serve our needs rather than those of capital.

References

Albo, G. and B. Evans. (2009). 'And End to Neo-liberalism? Ontario Responds to the Crisis'. *Relay* 27, pp. 4–6.

Baragar, F. (2009). 'Canada & the Crisis?' In Guard, J. & W. Antony (eds.), *Bankruptcies & Bailouts*, pp.77–106. Halifax: Fernwood Publishing.

Bashevkin, S. (2006). *A Tale of Two Cities: Women and Municipal Restructuring in London and Toronto*. Vancouver: UBC Press.

Bermingham, J. (2009). 'Municipalities' Spending Outpacing Real Growth'. *The Province*. http://www2.canada.com/theprovince/news/story.html?id=b5f554d7-a75c-47ce-b5e9-ed95dedb026a. Accessed 10 November 2009.

Boudreau, J.A., R. Keil, and D. Young (2009). *Changing Toronto: Governing Urban Neo-liberalism*. Toronto: UTP Press.

Brown, L. (2010). 'Public Sector Workers Paying for Corporate Tax Cuts'. http://www.nupge.ca/content/public-sector-workers-paying-for-corporate-tax-cuts. Accessed 5 April 2010.

Caulfield, J. (2010). 'Toronto: The Form of the City'. In Hillier, H (ed.). *Urban Canada*, pp. 324–350. Oxford: Oxford University Press.

Chase, S. 'Budget Officer Warns of Tougher Times Ahead'. *Globe and Mail*. http://www.theglobeandmail.com/news/politics/budget-officer-warns-of-harder-times-ahead/article1348952/. Accessed 1 December 2009.

Cockburn, N. (2010). 'Council Passes Budget, 3.77% Tax Hike'. *Ottawa Citizen*. http://www.ottawacitizen.com/news/news/2497191/story.html. Accessed 29 January 2010.

Deslongchamps, A. (2010). 'Page Says Canada Has "No Targets" to Erase Deficit'. Bloomberg.com. http://www.bloomberg.com/apps/news?pid=newsarchive&sid=aqiPcqcsI9dU. Accessed 4 February 2010.

Enchin, H. (2010). 'HandyDart Arbitration'. *Vancouver Sun*. http://communities.canada.com/vancouversun/blogs/everybodysbusiness/archive/2010/02/01/handydart-arbitration.aspx. Accessed 4 February 2010.

Fanelli, C. (2009). 'The City of Toronto Fiscal Crisis: Neoliberal Urbanism and the Reconsolidation of Class Power'. *Interdisciplinary Themes* 1:1, pp. 11–19.

Federation of Canadian Municipalities (2008). Annual Report 2007–2008. http://www.fcm.ca/CMFiles/FCM_Annual%20Report%2007-08%20En1OHO-172009-73.pdf. Accessed 25 March 2010.

Hackworth, J. (2006). *The Neo-liberal City*. New York: Cornell.

Harvey, D. (2009). *Social Justice and the City*. Athens: University of Georgia.

Insin, E. (1998). 'Governing Toronto without Government: Liberalism and Neo-liberalism'. *Studies in Political Economy* 56, pp. 169–192.

Moloney, P. (2009). 'Borrowing Can't Fix Repair Backlog'. *Toronto Star*. http://www.thestar.com/news/gta/article/736354. Accessed 9 December 2009.

Sanger, T. and C. Crawley (2009). 'The Problem with Public–Private Partnerships'. *CCPA Monitor*. http://www.policyalternatives.ca/publications/monitor/problem-public-private-partnerships. Accessed 2 February 2010.

Questions for Critical Thought

CHAPTER 37

1. According to Armstrong, what is the pay equity movement? What comparisons, challenges, and assumptions does it make? Use examples from the article.
2. What arguments have classically been made to defend the fairness of pay inequity? How does Armstrong debunk them and refocus the pay equity debate?
3. Why is pay equity legislation so hard to enforce? What are some shortcomings of its scope?
4. Even if successful legislation and implementation were achieved, could we simply 'set it and forget it'? What are the challenges of maintaining pay equity?
5. Discuss the various reports that Armstrong cites for addressing pay equity. Describe the progress each report achieved, and the issues it failed to address.

CHAPTER 38

1. While the Olympic Games unites some people across some kinds of differences, in its reorganizing of urban space it also pushes other kinds of people apart. Which groups are united and which are separated?
2. How did the police enforce spatial reorganization around the 2010 Vancouver games? What were 'red zones' and what effect did they have on low-income youth?
3. Describe how spaces in Vancouver were simultaneously emptied and filled.
4. Consider Vancouver's attempt to '"look its best" while the "world is watching"' as a form of identity management. How do the 'wrong' kinds of people threaten to stigmatize Vancouver's identity as a global city? Based on Kennelly's description, what kinds of people, buildings, services, and practices were acceptable to support this image?
5. Kennelly points out that the Olympic Games is a youth-centred event, but that not all youth receive the same experience from it. Compare the different experiences and legacies that different kinds of youth take from the games.

CHAPTER 39

1. Discuss the contradictions between what the automobile symbolizes to many people and the actual experience of living with cars.
2. What is the automobility system? What forms of transportation are given privileged use of roads in our contemporary automobility system? Who is responsible for traffic safety?
3. How is the traffic safeguarding of children gendered? How does gender interact with social class in this context?
4. How are the streetscapes of the two schools different? How does social class contribute to these different streetscapes?
5. What unique traffic safeguarding work does each neighbourhood require of parents trying to transport their children to and from school every day?

6.   McLaren and Parusel point out that the leading cause of children's deaths in many countries is automobile collisions, yet media hardly ever discuss traffic danger. Consider how this relates to the phenomenon of moral panic (discussed in Part IV) and the social construction of social problems.

CHAPTER 40

1.   What is neo-liberal urbanism? Describe the contradictory pressures being experienced by municipal governments in Canada, as discussed by Fanelli and Paulson, and how the 'common sense' of neo-liberal ideology informs their typical responses to these pressures.
2.   How do neo-liberal policies benefit some at the expense of others?
3.   In debates about public sector budget cuts, the pragmatic defence is often that there isn't enough tax money to hold up past promises. How have changes to the distribution of wages and the tax burden since the 1980s dried up tax revenue in Canada despite a more productive economy? Where is the money going?
4.   How does the public (media, politicians, citizens) usually respond to public sector strikes? How are strikers perceived? Why is it problematic for citizens (who want public services) to not support those who provide them?
5.   Describe the case of HandyDart. Why did the company's workers strike? How did the employer use 'contracting out'?
6.   According to Fanelli and Paulson, how does the piecemeal approach to carving up the municipal budget pit community groups and needs against one another? How do the authors suggest we solve this?

Part XI

Sex and Gender

Sex and gender are two of the most ubiquitous categories used to order human life. These categories rest on the assumption that bodies have significant sex-based differences that necessarily produce different kinds of people. Specifically, our popular ontological assumptions maintain that there are exactly two kinds of people on the sex and gender continuum: men and women. You have likely learned that sex refers to real, biological divisions, while gender refers to social constructions and expectations. However, even the idea of two biological sexes is in part a social construction. Biological sex is comprised of a combination of biological markers—chromosomes, genitals, hormones, etc.—that don't always fit neatly within two mutually exclusive categories. Despite this complex reality, inter-sexed people face a world made for two mutually exclusive sexes, in which all individuals must check one of two boxes to indicate their sex on a number of bureaucratic forms, and use one of two sex-specific public washrooms.

The concept of gender casts a much wider net than that of biological sex linking biological bodies to certain cultural practices, abilities, and even moral conditions. Gender is also bound up with sexual orientation, the socially prevalent assumption being that it is natural for each gender to be sexually attracted only to its 'opposite'. This belief persists despite evidence that same-sex attraction and encounters are common in all sexual animals.

The two-sex and -gender division is rooted in socially embedded ideas and theories about different bodies, and a significant amount of sociological work is dedicated to pointing out how such ideas do not correspond to scientific evidence. A popular area of gender studies is devoted to revealing stated and unstated assumptions about sexed bodies. Much of this work involves difficult interpretive work—unpacking how common cultural forms tell stories about gender.

To this end, Riley Olstead and Kathy Bischoping examine common plot devices in mystery novels for what these devices tell readers about men and women. They find striking patterns—female characters being used in certain ways and male characters in others. These explorations uncover a gender-based ranking in which women are suspect and problematic, and men are calm, rational, and a source of solutions.

Similarly, Sara O'Shaughnessy uncovers a common gender narrative in a magazine depiction of life in Fort McMurray. She shows that men are portrayed as honest and hard working, while many of the women are dangerous sexual distractions plotting ways to 'catch' men. But she also uncovers a hierarchy within femininities ('good' and 'bad' women), according to which qualities in females are ranked. She finds a common story that much previous work has described: female bodies are most valued when devoted to selflessly supporting husbands and communities, while independent and unapologetically sexual female bodies are morally suspect and sanctioned with stigma. This last part is important. It is not enough to point out differences in representations: another crucial function of gender studies is linking representations with consequences.

In her paper, Kristen Hardy tracks how the condition of fatness historically inherited its stigma by being associated with inferior bodies. She also acknowledges that gender constructions rarely stand alone. Through a historical analysis, she draws connections between gender, race, and class to show how fat non-white, lower-class female bodies were a problem for the bourgeois political project of civilization and self-control.

But deconstructing sex and gender has consequences too. Lisa Taylor points out that feminism and gender studies have not simply deconstructed sex and gender, but have built a new normative framework that is often used to judge other cultures—other femininities—as barbaric and inferior. By considering the use of Western feminist ideas to justify the war in Iraq, she warns feminist academics that their constructions can also have damaging consequences.

Finally, Wesley Crichlow reminds us that gender studies isn't just about women. He explores how heterosexual and masculine ideals in Caribbean cultures contribute to risky sex and the spread of HIV/AIDS between male same-sex partners. Like Hardy and Taylor, Crichlow demonstrates the links between race, class, and sex/gender hierarchies.

Gold Diggers and Moms: Representations of Women's Identities in Fort McMurray in *Chatelaine*

Sara O'Shaughnessy

Introduction

As the most recent boom in Fort McMurray's oil industry surged to its apex in the mid-2000s, a number of articles in the media shifted the global gaze away from the unprecedented feats of oil extraction to the curious state of gender relations in a community facing a sudden influx of men—many of whom are mobile workers with families in their home towns. Numerous reports of unusually high divorce rates, infidelity, and gold-digging women emerged in media and local accounts (e.g. Edemariam 2007; Nikiforuk 2008; Fortney 2006). The most controversial of these is a 2006 article by Philip Preville in *Chatelaine*—a popular Canadian monthly women's magazine—entitled 'Down and Dirty in Fort McMurray' (Preville 2006). The notoriety of this article is evident in the reaction pieces and references to it in other media (e.g. Edemariam 2007; Fillion 2006; *Fort McMurray Today* 2006).

Preville purports to explore love and relationships in the context of a boomtown where many individuals lead dual lives, commuting long distances between their homes and their jobs. Yet, from the opening photograph depicting the body (face obscured by her hair) of a young woman 'grinding' between another female body and a male body, it is evident that the article will be focusing the author's perceptions of sexual relations in Fort McMurray. The main thrust of the article is, ostensibly, to explain the 'bizarre internal logic at work' that results from a 'gender ratio [that] is so lopsided that it throws things off-kilter, resulting in a strangely twisted and pernicious singles scene' (Preville 2006, p. 122) where women are competing for the attention of men despite being the minority gender.

In the following section, I use feminist **post-structuralist** discourse analysis, which Gavey describes as 'the careful reading of texts . . . with a view to discerning discursive patterns of meaning, contradictions, and inconsistencies' (1998, p. 467), to explore the gendered images embedded in the *Chatelaine* article. Following this analysis, I present the perspectives of the interview participants in relation to their hyper-represented discursive environments.

Frontier Masculinity and 'Male Spaces'

> Like an old Klondike boom town, this place attracts a lot of down-and-outers and unskilled workers. But extracting oil from the sands is far more complicated than panning for gold. (Preville 2006, p. 119)

The *Chatelaine* article in question draws heavily on the discourse of frontier masculinity—including adopting the vernacular commonly associated with popular representations of frontier times—to make sense of numerous phenomena in Fort McMurray. Most notable is Preville's depiction of the community and nearby oil industry as a 'male space' where the construction of opportunities and challenges are distinctly gendered. Indeed, the author paints a bleak picture of Fort McMurray's physical landscape:

> The place sure looks as if it was built by and for young males. It's a bachelor pad of a city, functional and grey and fusty, like a bare-walled room with an unmade bed. (Preville 2006, p. 119)

An aerial photograph of the town's core reasserts this imagery of Fort McMurray as a barren, isolated landscape, too hostile an environment for community and other social relationships to take root. The article highlights some of the more visible landmarks in the town: the Oil Can Tavern, the Boomtown Casino, and Cowboys Bar.

A core feature in the traditional conception of frontier masculinity is an emphasis on the frenetic, larger-than-life opportunities from resource development luring hordes of down-and-outers hoping to strike it rich—much of which is replicated in current boomtowns such as Fort McMurray. Given the complexity and scale of the oil sands, however, Fort McMurray is also attracting 'thousands of skilled tradesmen, engineers, managers and other highly paid professionals, most of them men, many of them young' (p. 119). The opportunities afforded by resource extraction are available almost exclusively to white, heterosexual men, but are always tempered by the dangers and seductions of the wild frontier. In fact, the focus of this article centres on the perception that '"[e]very guy in town has a good job"' (p. 124, quoting a local female resident) and that women's only access to the cash that flows from the oil sands is through (hetero-)sexualized relations with men, not through their performance of equally difficult and valued labour.

Abutting the narrative of the land of opportunity is the narrative of despoliation. This particular narrative is also imbricated with gendered notions of who and what is responsible for the breakdown of community values. As Preville notes,

> It's the same problem with any boom town: just about everyone—from the hookers on down—isn't from here and doesn't want to be from here. Their hearts are somewhere else. Like the oil companies and the escorts, they're just here to exploit a wellspring to their advantage, screw around a bit and leave. (p. 130)

Within the discourse of frontier masculinity, and replicated in Preville's article, responsibility for despoliation is deflected from men who work in the resource industry and capitalize on the abundant opportunities of the boom. The casinos, bars, and other sites of debauchery are strategically presented as a necessary vice for hardworking men who have limited time and opportunities to escape the brutal physical labour demands of their jobs. Though Preville acknowledges men's participation in gambling, cocaine, adultery, and other vices, the responsibility for this behaviour is not internalized as a reflection of the character of these men. It is presented as an inevitable result of the myriad external temptations that exist in the 'wilderness' of the northern frontier.

Good and Bad Women in the Frontier

> It's a gold strike for any single woman. There's bachelors in them thar' hills. (Preville 2006, p. 119)

Among the temptations facing men in frontier communities are women 'planting ideas in the heads of the guys who'll head home alone at closing time' (p. 126). In Preville's article, women are constructed as having very little access to the employment and income-earning opportunities afforded by the resource boom. None of the women presented are employed in the oil sector. Rather, they are overwhelmingly rendered part of the dangerous frontier wilderness. For example,

'Fort McMurray is a challenging place to be single if you're a man,' says Eunice Peterson . . . . That's putting it lightly. I spent a Friday night at Cowboys, the downtown club of choice for twenty- and thirty-somethings. It's a cavernous place with concrete floors and waitresses with straw cowboy hats and lots of cleavage. (p. 122)

In this statement, the author removes any sense of the 'waitresses' as subjective agents, and naturalizes them as fixtures of the bar, alongside the 'concrete floors'. This backgrounding of women as objects is a common theme within frontier masculinity. In popular accounts of the frontier era, as Wright (2001) and Stoeltje (1975) point out, women are not the heroes. Frontier mythologies, with few exceptions, place white males front and centre. These men are rugged, disaffected, and individualistic (Stoeltje 1975). Yet, they are also deeply moral and honest (Wright 2001). Women are, in effect, the antithesis to the traits valued in frontier masculinity—they are constructed as dependent and incapable of physical labour. At best, women serve as background characters, restricted to two opposite roles: the helpmate (or 'good woman') and the whore (or 'bad woman') (Stoeltje 1975). Their identities are inherently defined by their sexualized relationships with men.

The morality of male frontier heroes emerges through men's interactions with good women, who act as a civilizing force on the frontier. Good women act as subservient helpmates to the men, dutifully taking on the burden of maintaining their households and contributing to community well-being on behalf of their husbands, which permits the frontiersmen to retain a facade of autonomy. Moreover, the work performed by these good women provides a counterbalance to the plundering of the community's resources. Preville presents, these women as those who stand by their men dutifully and repress any complaints about their lack of opportunities or the boredom of living in such isolated sites.

Conversely, a bad woman on the frontier is described by Wright as 'socially tainted because of her independence; she is too cavalier about sex, she acts like a market competitor, she associates with questionable men, she seeks wealth and property' (2001, p. 153). Such women, frequently portrayed as whores in frontier representations, exist at the margins of society and do not perform the dutiful role of existing to support the male heroes. Bad women are defined by their independence and sexuality, whereas good women are devoid of sexuality and defined by their steadfastness. In effect, personal ambition, which, in the frontier context, necessarily conflates economic ventures with sexuality, is the defining feature of bad women. Because women are perceived as invariably dependent on men, personal economic ambitions are necessarily constructed as parasitic.

Preville draws heavily on the tropes of good and bad women to explicate the gendered subversion of the 'gold strike' in Fort McMurray. Women's personal ambition, oppositionally contrasted with selflessness and community-mindedness, inverts the inherent public–private gender divide by paralleling men's socially acceptable economic ambitions. Any women displaying personal ambition over commitment to family and community are conflated with **gold diggers**: 'There are guys in them thar' hills of this booming frontier town, but you'll need to step over the gold diggers, divorcées and escorts to get 'em' (p. 119).

Readers are cued to identify good women from bad women through the explicit reference to the bad women's sexualized physical appearances. The article begins with the physical description of 'Tori':

in her late 20s, pretty, with long blond hair and a full-figured medium-height frame. She's wearing a twin-set and a tight knee-length black skirt with matching stilettos . . . . Tori's business: she's an escort. (p. 119)

Similarly, Tori's boss, 'Paige', is described as having '"bleached blond hair and fake boobs", as she puts it, which gives her the aura of a porn star' (p. 126). Images scattered throughout the text show women engaging what the author deems sexually aggressive behaviour—dancing at nightclubs and arguing with a police officer.

Conversely, good women play down any notion of economic ambition or sexuality. Their descriptions and identities are hinged on their family and community commitments. For instance, a young mother is shown in a photograph playing with her son. Below this image is a photograph of a crowd of women and men dancing at a nightclub. The caption reads 'Single mom Erica Power, 23, above, with her son, Riley, 3, says women have become more aggressive as the town has grown more prosperous. Right, getting frisky at Cowboys' (p. 124). Fort McMurray's mayor, featured prominently in the article, is portrayed as the ultimate good woman. The readers are reminded that she has a 'local boy' partner and young child (p. 131). She is shown in a photograph, presumably in her office, focused on a document on the desk in front of her. The caption reads 'Melissa Blake, Fort McMurray's mayor, has fought tirelessly to provide improved roads, more housing, and better services for families and children' (p. 130).

Conclusion

Although women have largely been left out of the media narratives surrounding Fort McMurray's recent oil boom, it is the sins of commission, rather than the sins of omission (Geertsema 2009, p. 154), that have the greatest impacts on resident women's lives. Media representations of women's identities in Fort McMurray, as in the case of Preville's article, do not simply erase women's experiences; they replace them with marginalized subject positions that reinforce the primacy of the masculine protagonist. Using a feminist post-structuralist discourse analysis of print media reports on Fort McMurray, I argue that frontier masculinity is the primary organizing frame through which gender relations and identities in the community are constructed and represented to the outside world. The gold digger, the devoted mother, and the lady truck driver satisfy the global imagination of Fort McMurray as a modern day gold rush—a place of extremes that is more legendary than real.

References

Edemariam, Aida (2007) 'Mud, sweat and tears (the fall of Fort McMurray)', *The Guardian UK*, 30 Oct., p. 4.

Fillion, Kate (4 December 2006) 'Melissa Blake talks to Kate Fillion', *Maclean's*, vol. 119, pp. 16–19.

Fort McMurray Today (September 15, 2006) 'Chatelaine story under fire', [Online] Available at: http://today.ab.ca/ArticleDisplay.aspx?archive=true&e=1827850.

Fortney, Valerie (2006) 'Abundance of men skews Fort McMurray dating game', *Calgary Herald*, 10 Nov., p.1.

Gavey, Nicola (1989) 'Feminist poststructuralism and discourse analysis: contributions to feminist psychology', *Psychology of Women Quarterly*, vol. 13, pp. 459–475.

Geertsema, Margaretha (2009) 'Women and news: making connections between the global and the local', *Feminist Media Studies*, vol. 9, pp. 149–172.

Nikiforuk, Andrew (2008) *Tar Sands*. Greystone Books, Vancouver.

Preville, Philip (2006) 'Down & dirty in Fort McMurray', *Chatelaine*, vol. 79, pp. 118–131.

Stoeltje, Beverly J. (1975) '"A helpmate for man indeed": the image of the frontier woman', *The Journal of American Folklore*, vol. 88, pp. 25–41.

Wright, Will (2001) *The Wild West: The Mythical Cowboy and Social Theory*. Sage, Thousand Oaks.

CHAPTER 42

Hyperheterosexualization, Masculinity, and HIV/AIDS Challenges in the Caribbean

Wesley Crichlow

My objective in this study was to understand how cultural ideas of manhood and masculinity affected **HIV/AIDS** education in the Caribbean—especially, Trinidad and Tobago. Further, given the colonial and religious nature of Trinidad and Tobago, I wanted to untangle the multi-layered, complex historical social and political cannons through which identification/gay profiling, prejudice, **homophobia**, and power are produced, performed, and understood. As we will see, this paper is concerned with the power relations between black gay men in a hypermasculine, hypersexualized culture. Therefore, it is useful to know how this view of power and masculinity is learned and practised, and I will discuss these issues below.

The methodology I employed included both qualitative and multi-sited approaches that applied different methodological tools, discourse analysis, participant observation, and interviews in nature. In-depth interviews were conducted with 47 key informant male natives living in Trinidad and Tobago. **Field observation** action research, informal group interviews, media clippings, and archival searches were also employed. Interviews took place in public parks at night, in the private backyards/homes of key informants who provided a space for men to meet socially. Interviews also occurred at my home, at social events, in clubs, but never on the telephone. The spaces and places mentioned are important because I had to conduct these interviews on the informants' terms and in spaces of their comfort and could not organize a location, place, or time because these were set by the research subjects.

A total of 47 men were interviewed in Trinidad and Tobago. They ranged from ages 18 to 60, coming from varying ethnic, cultural, religious, class, and educational backgrounds. The project involved the continued exchange of data with some research subjects who agreed to assist with interpretation and wanted to be sure I did not misrepresent them. Some of the men identified as men who like to have sex with men, some as bullers, some as gay, and some said there was no need to use a label. Three of the men were homeless or living in public housing shelters. Ten of the subjects identified themselves as living with HIV/AIDS, but did not say where they were living or whom they were living with. Eight couples were interviewed, of whom two were identified as living together in intimate relationships under the same roof, while the other six couples were still living with their parents and families. Four men lived alone and were skilled professionals, while three others were sharing accommodations with friends. Ten were students attending college or university.

As Donna Hope (2001) reminds us in her work on homophobia in Jamaica, the intense paranoia that informs male homosexuality is a reflection of the hyperheterosexualization of Caribbean masculinity most apparent among working classes. Many Caribbean men understand their masculine gender identity in relation to how they see and understand women and their roles. Masculine gender identity, always in dialogue with female gender identity and with notions of heterosexual masculinity, is inevitably complex and multi-layered. Heterosexual conquests and a hatred of homosexuality (internalized homophobia and self-hate) are performed by men who do not want to be outed, in order to access their entire cache of masculinity and secure their manhood (Hope: 2001: 5).

The Implications for HIV/AIDS

The men I spoke to had their own understanding of the connection between their sexuality and HIV/AIDS. For example, one respondent said to me,

> I am 19 years old and I never thought of HIV/AIDS. It was just some letters that I saw as a white man thing. Before I found out I had HIV/AIDS, I always felt that I was immune to it because they say it is a gay, white man's disease. I do not fit that category, at least that is how I was thinking at the time. How in the hell did I get this thing? I didn't sleep with anybody other than black men. I was not prostituting. I wasn't shooting drugs. I was saying, what happened?

Another respondent, speaking of his intimate partner, said, 'I do not want him to leave me because I love him, so if he know I have HIV he will leave me, I want love not rejection, so I lie to him or anybody who love me and can take care of me.' Lying to find love despite their HIV status is understood not as unethical or immoral, but rather as a condition for survival and acceptance in a hetero-patriarchical and homophobic society. In such a society, gay and young heterosexual men are prisoners of a particular system of ideological thought and oppression that teaches all them not to tell the truth about themselves. As young men or boys, they measure themselves and self-worth in relation to others whom they estimate to be similar to them. This can only mean men and other boys, whom they look up to. Most of the respondents in the study are looking for love, affection, family approval, security, and public affirmation of their lives. They want to be loved and cared for, and they know the social, economic, violent, and

alienating consequences of telling their partners the truth about their HIV/AIDS status.

The AIDS epidemic claimed an estimated 24,000 lives in the Caribbean in 2005, making the disease the leading cause of death among adults aged 15 to 44 years. A total of 300,000 people are currently living with HIV in the region, including 30,000 people who became infected in 2005. Men play a key role in HIV transmission in the Caribbean, being the group most affected. Sexual contacts between men appear to be a major contributor, but it is precisely because homosexuality is illegal that it has become a major means of transmitting HIV/AIDS. Since homosexuality is a criminal offence, highly stigmatized, and perceived as delinquent behaviour, individuals are driven underground to engage in sex with other men, and social acceptance is gained by adopting a visibly heterosexual lifestyle. In some of the relationships between younger and older men, the older men are the more straight- or heterosexual-acting of the pair. Most older men did not identify themselves as gay because they feminized the younger men in their relationship; they were thus able to act out a **heterosexualization** and hetero-socialization of masculinity.

Barry Chevannes (2001) informs us that through the heterosexual socialization of Caribbean men, a hypermasculinity is constructed, maintained, and celebrated. He notes that not just having one's first sexual experience, but having a child and/or setting up an independent household, are marks of reaching adulthood, more so than other social factors and events such as jobs and education.

Power plays an important role in the social construction of masculinity. Wealthy hegemonic masculinity versus marginalized or working masculinity is only one of the many areas where power is exercised in male same-sex relations. The dominant Caribbean consumerist cultural ideal of what it means to be a man becomes the terrain on which all marginalized or subordinated masculinities are constructed and performed. This perspective allows us to understand how wealthy black men can subjugate black working class men in same-sex relationships without negotiation. Subjugation in this instance is not open to discussion—it just happens. Wealthy hegemonic masculinity relies on negative referents for its construction, power, and security, and contributes to relations of domination and subordination between rich and poor men.

Hegemonic discourses of masculinity clearly shape the way wealthy black men think about themselves as men and as providers; this self-perception is shaped by their class, age, income, education, argot, and sexuality. The older men on whose terms these sexual relationships are formed feel that they have to provide all the material possessions for the younger boys/men, which by extension confirms their sense of hypermasculinity and their ability to control the relationship without negotiation. Most young Caribbean men do not feel that they are really men unless they are sexually active and exhibit heterohypermasculine behaviour. Chevannes (2001) further writes that among Afro-Caribbean males, first sexual encounters take place on average between the ages of 14 and 16, with females following on average two years later. Unsafe sex is common, not exceptional, in this community.

The main reason young men say they engage in unsafe sexual practices is because they fear losing the older, more financially secure man who is providing for them. Their goal is to be given food, shelter, and clothing and to be cared for by an older man who has a house, a job, and a car. The male who provides is also the active, top, or insertive partner, while the younger and in some cases the lighter skin one is the passive, bottom, or receptive partner. When the older men were asked why they assumed the dominant role with younger boys or why they assumed the top role, they replied that they were seen as the masculine one and that they liked acting out the heterosexual roles within their relationship to reassure their masculinity. Indicative here is the articulation of penetration as power and maintenance of masculinity. All Caribbean men, gay and straight, view sexual relations as opportunities to demonstrate hypermasculinity, since effeminacy is shunned and ridiculed. This means taking risks, to show masculine courage.

Beyond that, concerns with secrecy lead to unsafe practices. Due to their family situations, many men are forced to meet for sex outside or in public spaces. These public spaces include cars, parks, under bridges, washrooms, abandoned buildings, bus station toilets, or near the river and beach areas. Some will also take the risk of having sex at the dance clubs they frequent, as the security guards close their eyes to it. One young man reported that he had sex with men for money and was subjected to all forms of abuse; he was once gang raped by three men who told him they would pay him if he allowed them to do it. He said that after he was raped, they laughed at him and walked away without paying him. He noted that when he engaged in sex with most men it was unsafe, because he made more money that way. The same young man also told me that he was taken into prostitution by some male street sex workers. He could not tell his parents (with whom he was still living) that he was doing such work. At the same time, he said he was threatened by the men that if he stopped prostituting for them, they would kill him or have the police arrest him.

The lives of the men I interviewed become endangered in the various settings they choose to operate in to conduct their sexual activities, and by unsafe sexual practices. The risks of acquiring HIV/AIDS are driven upward by a lack of legal and sexual protection, rampant homophobia, and an openness to having multiple partners (to maximize earnings). The result is a serious health care problem for the men and for the society as a whole.

Conclusion

Homophobia in the Caribbean occurs within a particular system of ideological thought and practice. No wonder the Caribbean has the highest HIV/AIDS rates outside of sub-Saharan Africa. Further, in recent decades, tourism has become the most important Caribbean industry. Studies suggest that tourist areas are epicentres of demographic and social changes linked to HIV risk, such as transactional sex, elevated alcohol and substance use, and migration within the island.

Despite this volatile situation, formative HIV prevention studies are very slow in examining tourist areas as ecologies that heighten HIV vulnerability. HIV/AIDS research needs to place emphasis on the context of sexual vulnerability in tourist areas and develop multi-level interventions that are sensitive to this context. We need to understand the social setting to understand why these men are particularly vulnerable to HIV/AIDS.

Finally, homosexuality must be legalized and the multi-layered hypermasculine gender roles and sexual taboos, embedded in a traditional colonial system, must be challenged, changed, and unlearned in order to develop successful human rights and HIV/AIDS education that gets the message across: hypermasculinity does not discourage homosexuality—it drives it underground, thus raising the risks of STD infection, especially from HIV/AIDS. Caribbean masculinity also thrives on risk taking; men's masculinity is tied to how dominant or hypermasculine they are and how much risk they are willing to engage in. The challenge, therefore, is to develop HIV/AIDS strategies sensitive to the many forms that dominant masculinity takes, while also embracing softer masculinities. The fight against HIV/AIDS will also have to involve a fight against homophobia.

References

Chevannes, Barry. *Learning to Be a Man: Culture, Socialization, and Gender Identity in Five Caribbean Communities*. Barbados: University of the West Indies Press, 2001.

Crichlow, Wesley. *Buller Men and Batty Bwoys: Hidden Men in Toronto and Halifax Communities*. Toronto: University of Toronto, 2004.

Government Printer of Trinidad & Tobago. Immigration Act, Chapter 18/1, 1980.

Hope, Donna. 'Of Chi-Chi-Chi Men: The Threat of Male Homosexuality to Afro-Jamaican Masculine Identity'. Paper presented at the Annual Caribbean Studies Association Conference, St. Marten, 2001.

Ministry of National Security. *First Annual Report of the Police Complaints Authority, Trinidad and Tobago, 1996/97*.

The Gay Chat Room Group For LGBTQ persons of Trinidad. 33 Murry Street Wood Brook Port of Spain. Republic of Trinidad & Tobago. 2007.

CHAPTER 43

Contested Imaginaries: Reading Muslim Women and Muslim Women Reading Back: Transnational Feminist Reading Practices, Pedagogy, and Ethical Concerns

Lisa Taylor

Within the context of the current global and geopolitical landscape and the '**war on terror**', there are competing imaginaries—Western imperialist, **Orientalist**, imperialist feminist as well as transnational feminist, anti-colonial, and Islamic—that form a contested terrain of knowledge production upon which the lives, histories, and subjectivities of Muslim women are discursively constituted, debated, claimed, and consumed through a variety of literary, academic, and visual forms of representation. This chapter is part of a larger project of both critically examining the ways these forms of representation are taken up in various educational sites and exploring pedagogies focused on the politics and ethics of reading (Zine, Taylor & Davis, 2007; Zine & Taylor, forthcoming).

Writing Muslim Women: Imperialist Feminists and Native Informants

Since 9/11 and the ongoing 'war on terror', narratives by and about Muslim women have been increasingly commodified, circulated, and uncritically consumed, particularly in the West. As part of this process, an explosion of books promising to take the Western reader 'behind' or 'beyond' the veil of Muslim society and to 'demystify' the lives of Muslim women have become fodder for a fetishistic voyeurism rooted in the Orientalist and Western feminist preoccupation with 'unveiling' Muslim women's bodies and lives. Of particular interest and concern to us is the predominant paradigm framing the production, circulation, and reception of these narratives: this paradigm positions Muslim women as the objects of concern, expertise, civilization (Razack, 2008), and liberation by secular Western feminists. A great deal of earlier feminist writing about Muslim women occurs within the genre of 'imperialist feminism'. Sudbury (2007) problematizes this scholarship as feminist analyses that erase the historical and structural conditions underpinning the North–South balance of power and social configurations:

> To bemoan the oppression of Third World women without acknowledging the role of racism, colonialism and economic exploitation is to engage in what black British feminist filmmaker Pratibha Parmar calls 'imperial feminism', a standpoint which claims solidarity with Third World women and women of color, but in actuality contributes to the stereotyping of Third World cultures as 'barbaric' and 'uncivilized'.

Transnational femini (1991), Amos and Parma and Razack (2008) have inism for its represent ized Muslim women tru of the North–South balance corresponding construction of Muslim World' women as an abject, essentialize egory of other. Such representation plays into the Manichean racial and religious divide underscoring the 'clash of civilizations' thesis (Huntington, 1996) and holds Muslim women's lives and experiences in a seemingly irreconcilable tension with dominant Western sensibilities and democratic values. In response, transnational feminist discourses have centred their politics of representation on exposing the North–South imbalance of power that has allowed feminist scholars of the North greater access to claim discursive authority over women in the South as the objects of academic enquiry, or, through more paternal and politicized tropes, to 'rescue the other'.

According to Lazreg, imperialist feminist writers showcase women to 'vent their anger at their societies' and in so doing enact a form of 'epistemic violence'. This refers to a broader notion of violence that is not simply physical but that takes place through the construction of knowledge and fixing of identity categories. She argues that while these women 'appear on the feminist stage as representatives of the millions of women in their own societies, to what extent they do violence to the women they claim authority to write and speak about is a question that is seldom raised' (1988: 89). The Western/Orientalist construction of Muslim women, therefore, with the help of dubious, yet first-hand, corroboration from such 'native informants', helps maintain a certain academic currency for these archetypes as central narratives, despite the fact that they present distorted and static images that serve to essentialize Muslim women as abjectly different. As a result, Muslim women have been viewed and consumed with a mixture of imperial fascination and ethnocentric pity, thus locating them at the nexus of contradictory desires on the part of Western feminists who, on the one hand, want to liberate

...ese women and yet, at the same time, express aversion and pass judgment on many aspects of their lives and identities.

In her essay 'Eating the Other', bell hooks (1992) takes up these contradictory impulses, arguing that 'The desire to make contact with those bodies deemed Other with no apparent will to dominate, assuages the guilt of the past, even takes of the form of a defiant gesture where one denies accountability and historical connection' (p. 25). In the context of the Western feminist imaginary and the representation of Muslim women, discursive moves such as those hooks describes serve to shore up the positional superiority of white Western feminists vis-à-vis 'other' women. This creates a space of innocence where the complicity of imperial feminists in creating this subaltern archetype can be forgotten or denied.

Playing the role of the 'native informant', some Muslim feminist scholars have also framed their analysis of Islam and gender in imperialist feminist terms, thus replicating, rather than undermining, the colonial discourse on Muslim women (Zine and Bullock, 2002). In particular, sensationalist biographic 'tell all' books like Canadian journalist Irshad Manji's *The Trouble with Islam* (2003) or Dutch politician Ayaan Hirsi Ali's *Infidel* (2007) represent insider 'truths' about Islam and Muslims through what Marnia Lazreg (1988) has termed a 'search for the disreputable' (p. 89).

From Post-colonial Critique to Anti-colonial Praxis: Pedagogical Interventions

The hegemony of these neo-Orientalist imaginaries within the contemporary political and discursive landscape therefore must be continually challenged in order to make space for new articulations of Muslim women's lives and lived experiences. While this discursive space will always bear the imprint of imperial legacies and contemporary forms of Islamophobia, new pedagogies of dissent are needed to counter the continuing miseducation within the political and public sphere. We see this as a form of anti-colonial **pedagogy**

that moves beyond the space of post-colonial critique toward anti-colonial praxis. In other words, this involves moving from theory to action, from deconstruction to asserting new political projects and more textured subjects.

The task for anti-racist feminist cultural and knowledge workers is to intervene in these public pedagogies by building communities capable of critically and reflexively reading and imagining within and against our complex social locations. This project returns us to the pedagogical challenge implied in Spivak's famous query: 'Can the subaltern speak?'. We need to address the related question, 'Can the subaltern be heard?'. That is, what pedagogical conditions and reading strategies, what forms of critical reflexivity, visual, literary, aesthetic, and epistemic literacy might ground a practice of listening and imagining for First World 'embedded' readers (Hunt & Rygiel, 2006)? Spivak's question draws our attention to the question of epistemic and material violence within the cultural politics of representation and imagination; in other words, how are the repertoires through which readers in the West are hegemonically taught to imagine, interpret, write, read, and claim knowledge of Muslim women complicit with larger imperial projects of political, economic, and military domination? Signalling the double meaning of representation (*darstellen*—portraying—and *vertreten*—acting as proxy), she proposes an ethical practice in which readers resist the tendency to constitute broad, monolithic identities in the name of whom we *read as, read about,* and *speak/act on behalf of* (Spivak, 1988, pp. 276–279; 1990, pp. 108–110). These modalities of reading are learned and contested within the public pedagogies, particularly within the current context of war and empire, and have immediate consequences in terms of the forms of violence and resistance they incite and license. Our pedagogy begins with the recognition that even resistant texts cannot secure deconstructive readings, but they are always already 'worlded' (Said, 1993) within particular material and discursive 'relations of exchange' (Amireh & Majaj, 2000, p.12) as well as within reading formations that produce particular reading dispositions and desires. Writing back to empire is not necessarily politically effective: just as our students have learned to read texts by and about Muslim in particular ways, so we as educators need to develop a pedagogy of anti-imperial, anti-Orientalist, transnational feminist reading.

What we are proposing, then, is an anti-colonial pedagogy grounded in a close attention to the political, aesthetic, and psychic dynamics of reception and response (Taylor, 2007), one that takes up Spivak's challenge for educators and students to critically historicize the geopolitical locations from which they read, speak, and make knowledge claims. The critical multimodal literacies we see emerging in the work of contemporary feminist post-colonial educators and artists imply a combination of strategies. On the one hand, this approach involves interdisciplinary strategies learned from post-colonial criticism, including Said's (1978, 1993) contrapuntal analysis that geopolitically and discursively situates texts, juxtaposing narrative from different sides of the 'activated imperial divide' in ways that contextualize and deconstruct their apparent neutrality. On the other hand, there is a need for feminist anti-colonial pedagogies that both examine the production of differently embodied reading subjectivities (i.e., how different reading identities and interpretive claims are normalized) and build critically reflexive politically engaged communities of practice.

References

Ali, A. H. (2007). *Infidel: My Life*. London: The Free Press.

Amireh, A. and Majaj, L. S. (eds.). (2000). *Going Global: The Transnational Reception of Third World Women Writers*. New York and London: Garland Publishing.

Amos, V. and Parmar, P. (1984). 'Challenging Imperial Feminism'. *Feminist Review, No. 17, July*. Pp. 3–19.

Brooks, G. (1995). *Nine Parts of Desire*. New York: Anchor Books.

Dabashi, H. (2006). 'Native Informers and the Making of the American Empire'. *Al-Ahram Weekly Online*, No. 797, 1–7 June. Retrieved November 1, 2006, from http://weekly.ahram.org.eg/2006/797/special.htm.

Eisenstein, Z. (2006). 'Is "W" for Women?' In K. Hunt & K. Rygiel (eds.), *(En)gendering the War on Terror: War Stories and Camouflaged Politics*. Surrey, UK: Ashgate Publishing (pp. 191–200).

Esguerra, A. Y. (2006). 'The Day After: A Cento Based on Hate Crimes Filed Shortly after 9/11'. In S. Husain (ed.), *Voices of Resistance: Women on War, Faith and Sexuality*. Emeryville, CA: Seal Press.

Goodwin, J. 1995. *Price of Honor: Muslim Women Lift the Veil of Silence on the Islamic World*. New York: Penguin Books.

hooks, b. (1992). *Black Looks: Race and Representation*. Toronto: Between the Lines.

Hunt, K. & Rygiel. K. (2006) 'Engendered War Stories and Camouflaged Politics'. In K. Hunt & K. Rygiel (eds.), *(En)Gendering the War on Terror, War Stories and Camouflage Politics*. Surrey, UK: Ashgate Publishing (pp. 1–24).

Husain, S. (2006). *Voices of Resistance: Muslim Women on War, Faith, and Sexuality*. Emeryville, CA: Seal Press.

Keshavarz, F. (2007). *Jasmine and Stars: Reading More Than Lolita in Tehran*. Chapel Hill: University of North Carolina Press.

Lazreg, M. (1988). '"Feminism and Difference" The Perils of Writing as a Muslim Woman on Women in Algeria'. *Feminist Studies*, Vol. 14, No. 1. Pp. 81–107.

Manji, I. (2003). *The Trouble with Islam Today: A Wake-Up Call for Honesty and Change*. Toronto: Random House of Canada.

Mohanty, C. (1991). 'Under Western Eyes: Feminist Scholarship and Colonial Discourses'. In C.T. Mohanty , A. Russo, & L.Torres (eds.), *Third World Women and the Politics of Feminism*. Bloomington: Indiana University Press (pp. 51–80).

Nafisi, A. (2003). *Reading Lolita in Tehran: A Memoir in Books*. New York: Random House.

Razack, S. (2008). *Casting Out: The Eviction of Muslims from Western Law and Politics*. Toronto: University of Toronto Press.

Said, E. (1979). *Orientalism*. New York: Vintage Books.

———. (1993). *Culture and Imperialism*. New York: Knopf.

Spivak, G. C. (1988). 'Can the Subaltern Speak?' In C. Nelson & L. Grossberg (eds.), *Marxism and the Interpretation of Culture*. Urbana: University of Illinois Press (pp. 271–313).

Sudbury, Julia. 2007. 'Building Women's Movement Beyond "Imperial Feminism"', *San Francisco Chronicle* . 27 March, 2000. Retrieved April 4, 2011, from: http://www.commondreams.org/views/032800-103.htm.

Taylor, L. K. (2007). 'Reading Desire: From Empathy to Estrangement, from Enlightenment to Implication.' *Intercultural Education*, Vol. 18, No. 4. Pp. 297–316.

Zanganeh, L. A. (Ed.). (2006). *My Sister Guard Your Veil; My Brother Guard Your Eyes: Uncensored Iranian Voices*. Boston: Beacon.

Zine, Jasmin. (2002). 'Muslim Women and the Politics of Representation'. *American Journal of Islamic Social Sciences*, Vol. 19, No. 4. Pp. 1–23

Zine, J. & Bullock, K. (eds.) (2002). 'Editorial: Re-Framing Women and Islam'. *American Journal of Islamic Social Sciences*. Special Issue: Women and Islam. Vol. 19, No. 4. Pp. i–iii.

Spinsters and Suspects: Gender and Moral Citizenship in Poison Pen Mystery Novels

Kathy Bischoping and Riley Olstead

Long organized around an interest in making sense of the issues of modern life, the mystery genre should hold particular affinity for sociologists (Klein, 'The Woman Detective' 8). While the genre's particular problematic revolves around puzzles of crime (Marling 4), sociologists can regard crime as a plot device that invites reflections on the puzzles of the moral order—on the tensions in, and antagonisms to, modern communities, including questions of whether and how social cohesion may be restored. Mysteries offer a promising site of inquiry into ways in which we work through 'not only the problem of the crime but also the problems of the social system' (Klein, 'The Woman Detective' 27).

Here, we hone in on works in which anonymous communication—whether it be in the form of poison pen letters in a village 'cozy' mystery or the e-mail correspondence of an urban stalker—is a central plot device, a lens allowing us to focus on characters' questions about who constitutes their community and how moral bonds can be sustained.

We root our analysis in an approach to media that is feminist (Modleski) at the same time as it draws on Durkheim's conceptualization of social cohesion in modern life and his perspective on the basis of morality. We employ Durkheim to underscore our view of the social contract as 'not physical but moral; that is, social' ('Suicide' 252). As Durkheim describes it, social cohesion is occasioned 'not by a material environment brutally imposed', but through collective association and conscience that exceeds the sum of individual interests ('Suicide' 252). Our analysis seeks evidence of how moral bonds in modern communities are sustained through shared civic identification as members of an 'imagined community' (Cormack 42; Anderson; Radway).

Our findings indicate specific ways in which discourses about gender in mysteries organize the ways in which the social can be meaningfully talked and reasoned about (Hall 44). This isn't altogether surprising. Earlier feminist work has shown gender relations of power to be linked to depictions of gender in the mass media (Modleski), and has demonstrated how media play a fundamental role in shaping the meanings of **masculinity** and **femininity** (Van Zoonen 42). Earlier research has shown how gender stereotyping and gendered subjectivities are prevalent throughout the mystery genre (Klein, 'The Woman Detective', 'Diversity and Detective Fiction'; Reddy 176), with one example being the tendency to position men as authority figures, relegating women to the domestic sphere (Kinsman 13).

Our distinctive contribution is to show how moral stories about anonymous antagonisms to the social contract are fundamentally stories about gender. Women may not turn out to be the criminals in all of these stories, but in a deeper sense, their gender is always suspect in these works, which ineluctably bind meaningful articulations of gender to normative definitions of moral citizenship. That's not to say that audiences uniformly and uncritically accept the positions that media transmit (Miller and Philo 24). Indeed, as mystery readers know, puzzles are often solved by heightened reflexivity and willingness to question assumptions. Nevertheless, our point is that the genre reproduces discourses that reasonably influence readers' active interpretation of the depictions set before them. As readers bring the storylines to life through the act of reading, they participate in what Radway, considering the romance genre, conceives of as a practice of citizenship, engaging with a particular form of cultural competence that serves as a bond between groups of readers who will never meet in person (18).

Importantly, the specifics of discourses on morality and gender are multiple in these works, reflecting, as Durkheim points out, that morality is socially specific (Durkheim, 'Moral Education' 3). We identified three distinct, ideal-typic social settings in which three distinct ideal-typic women dwell. The *Spinster Suspect* character is frequently found in village settings of the early modern period (though she may be created in the twenty-first century), while the *Urban Victim* and *Self-Made Subject* ideal types more commonly emerge in stories about the city during the modern and the late modern period (Giddens; Beck). Despite the apparent transition from early- to late-modernity, in our reading we found that the three ideal-types don't follow an evolutionary logic. They can coexist within a novel.

Methods

For our analysis, we took notes on 37 mystery novels and 1 short story whose plots revolved around anonymity, as well as 1 non-anonymous early stalker novel. We also took notes on anonymous communication in some 10 other works by major literary figures such as Honoré de Balzac and O. Henry. In sum, these works can't be said to represent the population of published anonymous communication mystery novels. Instead, they are a convenience sample of works, some included in online lists of stalker fiction that we culled for works in which anonymous communications were central, and others having a sufficiently large potential readerships for their publishers to upload them, permitting us to locate them in a search for 'anonymous letter'. (We should note

that many of the works are by authors who have received significant mystery writers' awards or topped best-seller lists.)

The analysis that follows features one of our ideal-types, the *Spinster Suspect*. For readability, we use acronyms for the mystery titles, listing them after the references at the end of this chapter.

The Spinster Suspect

The *Spinster Suspect* is most often found in 'cozies', a mystery sub-genre featuring the social norms, roles, and practices of a conservative, close-knit community—for instance, an archaeological dig (MM), a Lake District village (CG), or a suburb of London that is repeatedly characterized as 'Victorian' (MS). Often early in these works, the cohesion of these insular communities is threatened when poison pen letters are sent, accusing community members of wrongdoing. Although the recipients may burn the letters (GN), the 'filth' (MWU 23) has contaminatory power, poisoning the community and setting in motion a course of events that may culminate in murder.

Traditional forms of knowledge, routine practices, and long-established stratifications define and organize the communities depicted. These social settings generally reflect qualities associated with the early modern period, with traditional rural ways of life juxtaposed with an emerging modern urbanity. The anonymous missive signals instability in this social order, alerting the community to the presence of an unfaithful subject, inimical to the group's solidarity. Thus one novel's letter-recipient suddenly 'felt she understood now why Judas' betrayal was especially dreadful. He had been the friend who sat at table' (TWML 3). (This stands in sharp contrast to the construction in the second ideal-type, the *Urban Victim*, in which urban characters expect anonymous relations to be the norm.)

What is intriguing is how this moral problem is staged and treated in terms of gender. In *Spinster Suspect* works, anonymity is constructed as a form of passive hostility, particular to women. Characters almost exclusively position spinsters as the natural authors of these troublesome letters: 'Usually female of a certain age, frustrated in some way. Typically a spinster' (MS 165). Spinsters are written of as 'dessicated women' (MF 75), including the 'craggy virgin' (DHH 6) and the 'evil-minded old blossom' (MWU 187).

Although spinsters are considered to cause trouble, to the point of being responsible for the very condition of society, paradoxically, women aren't taken especially seriously. In this aspect, they parallel the rural village setting of many a cozy. Consider, for instance, Agatha Christie's 1942 work, *The Moving Finger,* in which air force veteran Jerry is sent by his London doctor to convalesce in little Lymstock, or, in other words, 'to be a vegetable' (MF 131) While there, Jerry reacts to a series of poison pen letters, first conflating the 'backward' village with immature women:

> These things probably happen fairly often in out-of-the-way villages. Some hysterical woman with a taste for dramatizing herself was probably at the bottom of it. (MF 11)

The associations Jerry draws between women and rural space, combined with the characterizations of his love interest, Megan, as variously 'a stricken gazelle', 'a meditative bird', a 'catfish', and the like (MF 49, 82, 176), all reflect the culturally salient equation of femininity with wilderness, the countryside, and further 'natural environments' (Wilson 7–8). Though today's social theorists consider this gender-space formulation inaccurate (Champion 2), cozy mysteries draw upon it as a frame by which to spatially essentialize and oppose rural and urban characters' actions and behaviour.

The equation of masculinity with the urban (Saegert) and with science, rationality, separation from nature, and the capacity to dominate it (Little and Leyshon 263) is underscored through characters such as Jerry and a 'tall, soldierly' inspector with 'quiet reflective eyes and a straightforward, unassuming manner' (MF 61) or a cosmopolitan diplomat, equally adept in Latin and martial arts (GN). (In the remarkable climax of *The Moving Finger,* in which an elderly spinster fond of knitting fleecy wool reveals the murderous letter-writer to be a male lawyer, Agatha Christie demonstrates how reliably readers take these gendered assumptions for granted).

Women, by contrast, are 'childish and silly' (MF 11). One way in which this is expressed in the novels is through the regular construction of women as primed to spread gossip, often in chains, such as, 'She told Nessie Currie, who told everyone in Patel's grocery' (DPP 6) or,

> Later that evening Mrs Gurney told Jessie Peck, who was a cousin of hers, and Jessie Peck told her sister-in-law who worked Tuesdays and Thursdays for Miss Eccles. . . . Just how many people the sister-in-law told cannot be estimated. Her name was Hilda Price, and she was a strong persevering talker. (PP 33)

It interested us that *Spinster Suspect* representations of women and gossip deployed seemingly contradictory propositions. On the one hand, as feminist scholars have noted, gossip is routinely associated with women and stigmatized as a sign of childish heedlessness (Adkins; Tebbutt) and justifiable powerlessness. On the other hand, it is treated as a weapon with which the social order is assailed. Thus, a gossiping woman is not unlike a child playing with a gun, especially in a village setting, where close ties fray under mutual suspicions, shame, and fear. It would interest Durkheim that egoistic suicidality, or murder disguised as such, appeared in eight of the works we read.

The routine connection of women to gossip naturalizes them as the agents of small communities' social upheaval. After the apparent suicide of a letter recipient, *The Moving Finger*'s Jerry thinks, 'Just for a moment, I hated Lymstock and its narrow boundaries, and its gossiping, whispering women' (MF 52). In contrast, men are generally depicted as law-abiding, intelligent, and respectful of communal bonds. It is not unusual that male mystery characters serve as superintendents, detectives, or as the official or unofficial safekeepers of community (Kinsman 19). Tellingly, resolution of the problem in these stories is often accomplished through the displacement of the feminine at the same time as the moral grounds of the traditional village are supplanted by a more modern, scientific, deductive, and masculinist order. Thus, a male detective urges his female mystery-writing friend to, 'put your prejudices aside and think it out. What's happened to you that you can't put two and two together?' (GN 394). In story after story, cohesion in the village is recovered on the basis of legal-rational bonds (Weber 224).

Conclusion

We have found that mystery novels employ a variety of interpretive structures, routinely positioning women—in the ideal-type explored above, rural spinsters—as inimical to the moral order. Indeed, we are struck by the regularity of such depictions and the way in which characters in mysteries use 'women as social problem' as a category through which the general social group solidifies its social identity (Berger 41–42). As the *Spinster Suspect* storyline shows, women need not actually perpetrate crime in order to be the prime suspects. Further, locating women as gossiping troublemakers normalizes a version of morality as masculine. Whether readers of these novels accept or reject the positions presented to them, it is the basic familiarity of these gendered meanings that is the thread connecting the mystery readership as a moral community.

References

Adkins, K. 'The real dirt: Gossip and feminist epistemology'. *Social Epistemology* 16.3 (2002): 215–232.

Anderson, B. *Imagined Communities*. New York: Verso, 2006.

Beck, U. *The Risk Society*. London: Sage, 1992.

Berger, A. *Durkheim Is Dead!: Sherlock Holmes Is Introduced to Sociological Theory*. Lanham, MD.: Rowman and Littlefield Publishers, Inc., 2003.

Champion, T. and G. Hugo. *New Forms of Urbanization: Beyond the Urban–Rural Dichotomy*. Aldershot, UK: Ashgate Publishing Ltd., 2003.

Cormack, P. *Sociology and Mass Culture: Durkheim, Mills and Baudrillard*. Toronto: University of London Press, 2004.

Durkheim, É. *Suicide: A Study in Sociology*. J.A. Spaulding and G. Simpson (trans.). New York: Free Press, 1897.

———. *Moral Education: A Study in the Theory and Application of the Sociology of Education*. E. K. Wilson and H. Schnurer (trans.). New York: Free Press, 1925.

Giddens, A. *The Consequence of Modernity*. Oxford: Polity Press, 1990.

Hall, S. *Representation: Cultural Representations and Signifying Practices*. London: Sage Publications, 1997.

Kinsman, M. '"Different and yet the same": Women's worlds/women's lives and the classroom', pp. 5–21 in K. G. Klein (ed.), *Diversity and Detective Fiction*. Bowling Green, KY: Bowling Green State University Popular Press, 1999.

Klein, K. G. *The Woman Detective: Gender and Genre*. Urbana: University of Illinois Press, 1995.

———. (ed.). *Diversity and Detective Fiction*. Bowling Green, KY: Bowling Green State University: Popular Press, 1999.

Little, J. and M. Leyshon. 'Embodied rural geographies: Developing research agendas'. *Progress in Human Geography* 27.3 (2003): 257–272.

Marling, W. 'Dashiell Hammett'. Retrieved 30 April, 2010, from http://www.detnovel.com.

Miller, D. and G. Philo, 'The effective media', pp. 21–32 in Philo, G. (ed.) *Message Received: Glasgow Media Group Research 1993–1998*. New York: Addison Wesley Longman, 1998.

Mitchell, W., P. Crawshaw, R. Bunton, and E. Green. 'Situating young people's experiences of risk and identity'. *Health, Risk and Society* 3.2 (2001): 217–233.

Modleski, T. *Feminism without Women: Culture and Criticism in a Postfeminist Age*. New York: Routledge, 1991.

Radway, J. *Reading the Romance: Women, Patriarchy, and Popular Literature*. Chapel Hill, NC: University of North Carolina Press, 1984.

Reddy, M. 'The feminist counter-tradition in crime: Cross, Grafton, Paretsky, and Wilson'. pp. 174–197 in R. G. Walker and J. M. Frazer (eds.), *The Cunning Craft: Original Essays on Detective Fiction and Contemporary Literature Theory*. Macomb, IL: Western Illinois University Press, 1990.

Saegert, S. 'Masculine cities and feminine suburbs: Polarized ideas, contradictory realities'. Signs 5.3 (1980), 'Women and the American City' Supplement: S96–S111.

Tebbutt, M. *Women's Talk: A Social History of 'Gossip' in Working-Class Neighbourhoods, 1880–1960*. Aldershot, UK: Scholar Press, 1995.

Van Zoonen, L. *Feminist Media Studies*. London: Sage, 1994.

Weber, M. 'Types of authority and characteristics of bureaucracy', pp. 224–229 in H. Gerth and C. W. Mills (eds.), *Max Weber: Essays in Sociology*. New York: Oxford University Press, 1973.

Wilson, E. *The Sphinx and the City*. London: Virago, 1991.

Primary Materials Cited

CG   Edwards, Martin. 2006 [2005]. *The Cipher Garden.* London: Allison & Busby.

DHH   Brand, Christianna. 1996 [1941]. *Death in High Heels.* New York: Carroll & Graf.

DPP   Beaton, M. C. 2004. *Death of a Poison Pen.* New York: Warner Books.

GN   Sayers, Dorothy. 1986 [1936]. *Gaudy Night.* New York: Harper Collins.

MF   Christie, Agatha. 2000 [1942]. *The Moving Finger.* London: Penguin.

MM   Christie, Agatha. 1984 [1935]. *Murder in Mesopotamia.* New York: Berkley.

MS   Heley, Veronica. 2002. *Murder by Suicide.* New York: HarperCollins.

MWU   Allingham, Margery. 2007 [1948]. *More Work for the Undertaker.* London: Vintage.

PP   Wentworth, Patricia. 1985 [1957]. *Poison in the Pen.* London: Hodder.

TWML Granger, Ann. 2004. *That Way Murder Lies.* New York: St. Martin's Press.

CHAPTER 45

Fleshy Histories: Fatness, Sex/Gender, and the Medicalized Body in the Nineteenth Century

Kristen A. Hardy

Introduction

Modern biomedicine has contributed significantly to the pathologization of bodies deemed 'fat', characterizing them as appropriate sites for therapeutic intervention. A substantial collection of research has emerged in recent decades, often subsumed under the rubric of 'fat studies', which seeks to critique scientific and medical paradigms of fatness from positions both biological and sociological.

Scholars such as Paul Campos, J. Eric Oliver, and Michael Gard and Jan Wright are among those who have produced widely read and well-received exposés of the often-flawed science and partisan motivations behind medical constructions of fatness as inherently unhealthy. Still other researchers, including Sander Gilman and Hillel Schwartz, have considered some of the historical precursors to the contemporary rhetoric of the '**obesity** epidemic',

laying bare the role of societal prejudices in the representation of fat bodies as problematic.

The specialized terminology of contemporary medicine—'overweight', 'obesity', 'morbid obesity'—created to cast particular bodies as fundamentally 'abnormal' by virtue of their weight, size, and/or shape, speaks to the cultural importance attached to measuring and quantifying the degree of otherness of certain bodies. Further, fat bodies have long been constituted and 'disciplined' through biological and medical thought and practice in ways that frequently reflect the presence of broader sex-stratified bodily and behavioural ideals, which are themselves rooted in specific histories and ways of seeing.

Focusing on the nineteenth century, I wish to consider how particular historical shifts in epistemology, medicine, and socio-political thought have participated in a casting of certain sized and weighted bodies as deviant, not simply in relation to an abstract model of 'health', but in specific, gendered ways.

Grounds of Possibility: Epistemologies, Politics, and Medicalized Bodies

The very notion of a 'normate body'—in other words, the assumption that the diversity of bodies encountered in the life-world ought to conform to an identifiable standard configuration—is predicated upon a particular regime of truth. Such truth-regimes embody the historically and culturally specific grounds of possibility for the articulation of sensible statements about phenomena—in other words, they make it possible for (only) certain types of claims to be asserted, understood, and accepted as valid in any given socio-cultural context (Foucault, *Archaeology of Knowledge* 211).

In *The Birth of the Clinic*, Michel Foucault locates one such epistemic transition in the late eighteenth century, when modern clinical medicine came into existence. The new 'anatomo-clinical' perspective, which continued to blossom during the nineteenth century and beyond, emphasized the physician's penetrating perception into the truth of health and illness through a sensate encounter with disease. Specifically, Foucault identifies the clinical crux as *le regard*, the 'pure gaze' of the doctor, supposedly rendering visible the true character of bodies and their conditions. He notes, in this respect, the increasing importance conferred upon the physician's discernment of *signs* (rather than patient-reported *symptoms*) as characteristics of this regime of the gaze (*Birth of the Clinic* 107–123). Yet, in anatomo-clinical medicine, Foucault explains, the sign 'assumes shape and value only within the questions posed by medical investigation' (162). Thus, in a very tangible sense, medical professionals participated in the creation of specific pathologies in and of the body, and, in so doing, solidified the consignment of authority about bodies largely to the external 'expert' observer.

Paralleling these historical changes in the nature of medical perception was the unfolding of a socio-political trajectory that functioned to manage subjects via the regulation of life itself. The development of an 'anatomo-politics' of the individual body emphasized the exercise of disciplinary power to optimize the usefulness and docility of embodied subjects. The eighteenth century witnessed the rise of the 'bourgeois body', whereby this emerging class, lacking the aristocracy's claims to a blood-based superiority, became focused instead upon the creation of a body which, in Foucault's words, 'looked to its progeny and the health of its organism' for power and perpetuity (*History of Sexuality* 128). The bourgeoisie's emphasis was not, Foucault maintains, on the actual maximization of labour *capability*, but rather upon the political and economic *symbolism* of those bodies that culturally signified physical health, strength, and longevity (125).

As well, the latter part of the eighteenth century saw the emergence of what Foucault termed 'biopolitical' strategies, which, in supplementing disciplinary practices, were directed toward the management of the health of populations on the aggregate level via technologies of 'regularization' (Foucault, *Society Must Be Defended*). In so doing, society moved increasingly toward what disability-studies researcher Lennard Davis has termed a 'utopia of the norm' (12). Governance of the population through cultivating the health and vitality of the collective has, further, often been articulated through twinning discourses of nationalism with those of science, crafting the body-politic through the biomedical politicization of bodies.

Differentiating Bodies: Sex, Race, and Anatomical Hegemony

The bodies that served as the objects of medical investigation, disciplinary control, and biopolitical governance during this era were invariably inscribed with another socially consequential distinction—that of *sex*. Examining an extensive collection of historical texts and illustrations, historian Thomas Laqueur posits a transition from a 'one-sex' world view in which males and females were conceived of as differing manifestations of a single bodily prototype, to an increasing dominance of a 'two-sex' model, in the late eighteenth and nineteenth centuries, in which male and female subjects became increasingly conceptualized as wholly different from one another, a distinction that was attributed to supposedly immutable biology. In this respect, Laqueur observes that the notion of two incommensurable sexes 'were, and are, as much the products of culture as was, and is, the one-sex model' (153).

The specific ways in which putative sexual differences have been utilized in support of a modern androcentric social order have been explored at some length by science historian Londa Schiebinger in her influential monograph, *Nature's Body*. In particular, Schiebinger's work makes evident the intimate linkages between scientized sexism and a similarly discursively justified racism. During the nineteenth century, European women and non-Europeans of both sexes—particularly those of African descent—were objects of especially close attention from practitioners in the biological sciences. While there was a strong political investment in establishing the biologically rooted 'natures' of white women and non-white men, an intense interest in the *comparative* anatomy of African women (particularly the Khoikhoi or 'Hottentots') and their white European counterparts also flourished; genital features, pelvis configurations, and distributions of body fat in breasts and buttocks preoccupied Western medico-scientific men. As Sander Gilman has stressed, black women and their ostensibly 'overdeveloped' bodies came to represent sexual surfeit, further emphasizing the 'natural' modest and non-passionate character of the white bourgeois lady (Gilman, *Difference and Pathology*). White women of the lower classes in Europe fared midway between these points, with 'African-like' physical characteristics alleged to prevail in the 'degenerate' working-class prostitute. Both the accumulation of flesh and, particularly, its apportionment in a manner that emphasized secondary sexual characteristics, marked certain classed and raced bodies as improper and inferior.

Mainstream medical literature of the period often plainly linked physical features, particularly those of women, with mental 'aberrations' or supposed deficiencies of the will; nymphomania and lesbianism were prominent among such 'problems'. In other cases, men were the object of concern; Jewish men, for example, were popular nineteenth-century targets of gendered and racialized psycho-biology, with a supposed predisposition to certain physical qualities—fatness among these—taken as evidence of the essentially effeminate character of Jewish males (Gilman, 'Fat as Disability').

Sized and Sexed Bodies: Pathologizing Corporeal Difference

The foundational role of new orientations and multiple contributors toward the establishment of particular 'disordered' bodies is reflected in the nineteenth-century emergence of a pervasive discursive linkage between fatness and pathology. Of course, Western medical interest in fat bodies had earlier precursors (Bray). However, the epistemological changes of the eighteenth and nineteenth centuries, coupled with shifting societal concerns, were necessary for the specific subsequent manifestations of this biomedical interest. The movement from essentialized, abstract diseases to embodied conditions whose management was intimately linked to the symbolic health of the bourgeoisie and the collective well-being of the nation, presented medicine with the possibility of seeing body fat as a *necessarily* problematic presence within living, sexed bodies. Under this new regime of medical perception, rather than awaiting a subjective presentation of 'dis-ease' by a patient, particular tissue configurations could be discerned by the medical gaze as abnormalities.

From a broader socio-cultural perspective, the modern-day meme that, in earlier times, 'fatness signified wealth', obscures the more complex class politics at play. While few eighteenth- and nineteenth-century bourgeois subjects would have courted confusion with underfed and overworked farm-turned-factory labourers, neither did they seek conflation with the 'idle rich' of the hoary aristocracies. The cultivation of association with *industry*—in the multiple meanings of that term—gave a distinctive moral cast to the bourgeoisie's wealth and power, with an implicit self-justification of earned, not inherited, abundance. The very antithesis of the energetic masculine industrialist, the image of the frivolous, lackadaisical, and over-fed effeminate aristocrat, coupled with the growing stress on controlling the habits and practices of the body, carved out a space for the emergence of the body-as-project. In the case of male citizens of the European colonial powers, this emphasis became increasingly interlinked with the theme of 'imperial masculinity', with its stress upon a cultivated physique as an essential aid to moral and mental discipline. Together, these developments laid fertile ground for negative readings of fat bodies as insufficiently controlled, unsuitably self-indulgent, and often inappropriately gendered.

Nineteenth-century biopolitical strategies also opened the possibility of attempting to regularize bodies on a collective scale along any of a variety of axes, including gender and weight conformity. As Gilman observes, campaigns for weight modification through diet and/or other means became a way 'to intervene so as to improve the private life of the individual and thus the health of the nation' (*Fat: A Cultural History* 4). Both the fat woman and the fat man possessed bodies that could be read as evidence of their failure as biocitizens, but in sex-specific ways to which each was thought bound by anatomical destiny. While 'obese' females were thought to procreatively endanger the health of the nation and the race, 'excessively' fleshy males also fell outside of the bounds of normative, economically and socially generative masculinity, and were feared to induce a collective vulnerability in the populace. Thus, not only was fatness believed to impair both sexes, anti-fat reasoning and rhetoric simultaneously acted to reaffirm disparate gender roles on the basis of biology, vesting men's biopolitical value in their production, and women's in their reproduction.

The Ambiguity of Fat and the Medical Gaze

In spite of these negative characterizations, within the nineteenth-century medical-aesthetic evaluation of the body, fatness could occupy an ambivalent status. While, as noted above, racialized and classed women, such as the African Khoikhoi and European prostitutes, were thought to be marked by an 'unnatural' fatness, the healthy and beautiful white bourgeois lady could also be recognized by her moderate, attractive plumpness, which signalled her capacity to aid in the healthy reproduction of the nation and the race (Gilman, *Picturing Health* 92). Given that female fatness could thus be read as a sign of vitality *or* degeneracy, it was imbued with an element of deception and, by extension, threat. The ambiguous voluptuosity of women, from this perspective, necessitated the expert eye of the medical practitioner to discern life-giving health or species-defiling disease within fleshy female bodies.

Thus, while fat men in the nineteenth century were indeed subject to a process of pathologization undergirded by social, cultural, and political norms, fat female bodies were even more consistently and profoundly rendered as objects and pressed to bear a surplus of meaning, reducing women's already-limited agency within a medicalized regime of truth and power/knowledge. As fatness was pathologized along lines of sex and gender, the latter were simultaneously co-constituted by discourses and practices relating to fatness. Thus, fat tissue and its distribution within individual bodies and among human populations increasingly emerged in the nineteenth century as a crucial component of the enactment of sexed bodies and gendered subjectivities.

References

Bray, George A. 'Obesity: Historical Development of Scientific and Cultural Ideas,' *International Journal of Obesity* 14 (1990): 909–926.

Campos, Paul. *The Obesity Myth: Why America's Obsession with Weight Is Hazardous to Your Health.* New York: Gotham Books, 2004.

Davis, Lennard J., editor. *The Disability Studies Reader*. London: Routledge, 1997.

Foucault, Michel. *The Archaeology of Knowledge*. Translated by A. M. Sheridan Smith. London: Routledge, 1989 [London: Tavistock, 1972].

————. *The Birth of the Clinic: An Archaeology of Medical Perception*. New York: Pantheon, 1973.

————. *The History of Sexuality: An Introduction* (Vol. 1). Translated by Robert Hurley. New York: Vintage Books, 1990 [New York: Pantheon Books, 1978].

————. *'Society Must Be Defended': Lectures at the Collège de France, 1975–1976*. Translated by David Macey. New York: Picador, 2003.

Gard, Michael, and Jan Wright. *The Obesity Epidemic: Science, Morality and Ideology*. London: Routledge, 2005.

Gilman, Sander L. *Difference and Pathology: Stereotypes of Sexuality, Race, and Madness*. Ithaca, NY: Cornell University Press, 1985.

————. *Fat: A Cultural History of Obesity*. Cambridge: Polity Press, 2008.

————. 'Fat as Disability: The Case of the Jews,' *Literature and Medicine* 23 (2004): 46–60.

Laqueur, Thomas. *Making Sex: Body and Gender from the Greeks to Freud*. Cambridge, MA: Harvard University Press, 1992.

Oliver, J. Eric. *Fat Politics: The Real Story behind America's Obesity Epidemic*. New York: Oxford University Press, 2006.

Schiebinger, Londa. *Nature's Body: Gender in the Making of Modern Science*. Boston: Beacon Press, 1993.

Schwartz, Hillel. *Never Satisfied: A Cultural History of Diets, Fantasies and Fat*. New York: Macmillan, 1986.

Questions for Critical Thought

CHAPTER 41

1. Why does Preville consider the gender relations of Fort McMurray to be 'bizarre'? How are they different from more mainstream, stereotypical relations?
2. What is 'frontier masculinity', and how does Preville use it to portray Fort McMurray?
3. 'Women are, in effect, the antithesis to the traits valued in frontier masculinity.' Explain O'Shaugnessy's meaning here.
4. According to O'Shaughnessy, women can play only one of two background roles in narratives of frontier masculinity: 'good' and 'bad' women. Explain the difference between these two roles, using examples from the text.
5. Compare and contrast the content of Preville's article (as analyzed by O'Shaughnessy) to Barron and Lacombe's discussion of the moral panic over 'nasty girls' in section four. Do you think Preville's article is contributing to a moral panic? Explain.

CHAPTER 42

1. Discuss how masculinity is socially constructed in the Caribbean culture. Is it similar to or different from the social construction of masculinity in North American culture?
2. What is hyperheterosexualization? How does this threaten gay men's masculine identities?
3. How do Caribbean men reaffirm their own masculinity in their same-sex relationships? What risks does this relationship dynamic pose to their partners? And conversely, how does this make it necessary for their partners to lie about their HIV/AIDS status?
4. Crichlow argues that there are multiple masculinities, and that, within cultural structures, they are not all equal. Describe the different masculine identities Crichlow exposes in his paper, and how they are located hierarchically in relation to each other.
5. Discuss the different Caribbean masculinities with attention to how they contribute to men's exposure to sexual risks and their power to minimize them.
6. How does the criminalization of homosexuality contribute to the spread of HIV/AIDS in the Caribbean, and homosexual men's (regardless of their masculine identity) dramatically higher likelihood of getting HIV/AIDS?

CHAPTER 43

1. What is 'imperialist feminism'? What are the implications for Muslim women when Western women pursue imperial feminist political projects?
2. Discuss the contradictory impulses at the root of imperialist feminism.
3. Muslim women are not simply the passive victims of imperialist feminism. Some of them take part in it by being 'native informants'. What are native informants and how, according to Taylor, do they commit epistemic violence on other Muslim women? How does the native informant help legitimize imperialist feminism?

4.   Taylor points out that it is hard to change the way people think of Muslim women through writing alternative narratives about them. As she points out, the critical question is, 'Can the subaltern be heard?'. She focuses on the problem that people may read and interpret texts in a way that the authors do not intend and can't control. Discuss the particular 'reading modality' that she takes issue with, and how she proposes educators and students grapple with it.

CHAPTER 44

1.   According to Bischoping and Olstead, why should the content of mystery novels interest sociologists? What does crime achieve as a plot device?
2.   Why did the authors choose plots involving anonymous communication? What did they find to suggest that these are fundamentally stories about gender? Be sure to discuss Durkheim's concepts of social cohesion/morality and to use examples from the text.
3.   What do Bischoping and Olstead mean when they refer to the act of reading as a 'practice of citizenship'?
4.   Compare and contrast the portrayal of men and women in the mystery sub-genre 'cozies', which the authors focus on in their paper. What, or who, is the problem in these stories? How is the problem resolved?
5.   Bischoping and Olstead note that reading reflexively is an important part of engaging with mystery novels. If mystery readers do indeed read these novels differently than other texts (take for example any of the cultural texts analyzed in this volume), is the effect of the content on the reader the same? Explain.

CHAPTER 45

1.   What is the 'normate body', and what relationship does it have to the 'bourgeois body' of the eighteenth century? Be sure to consider the division between the bourgeois/capitalist and aristocratic/royal bodies.
2.   What kind of 'truth regime' is the normate body located within? Who has the power to define the normate body under this regime, what kind of tools do they use, etc.? How did this truth regime work with governments to produce a rise in biopolitical strategies in pursuit of the 'utopia of the norm'?
3.   A common theme throughout this collection is that our understandings of the world matter because they shape our actions toward the world and other people. Compare the one-sex and two-sex medical world views, as explored by Hardy. Consider the consequences of each, drawing on examples in the paper.
4.   How did sex, race, and class of fat bodies converge in the eighteenth century to attract a biomedical scrutiny of fatness?
5.   Even though fatness became a problem for both genders, under the two-sex model it posed different dangers to each. Explain these respective dangers. What do these dangers reveal about the different kinds of work that is valued from male and female bodies?

6.   Modern medicine (and our trust in it) is premised on rational, disinterested investigation, which generates unbiased truth. However, Hardy and other fat studies scholars suggest that medical investigators were subject to societal prejudices in medicalizing fat bodies. Recall the concept of reflexivity, explored throughout this volume. How could reflexivity help medical researchers and practitioners in producing knowledge?

Part XII

Immigration, Race, and Ethnicity

Like sex and gender, race and ethnicity are among the major bases of division in human societies. People generally consider race to be the more 'real', biophysical category, like sex, while ethnicity is the work of culture and social construction, like gender. However, race does not comprise the purely objective biophysical or genetic characteristics that make us truly biologically different, since genetic differences *within* 'races' are much larger than the differences *between* them. This means that any given Asian is likely to be more genetically similar to some Africans or Caucasians than to fellow Asians. The genetic differences between races just seem large because they are often the most visible to us: skin colour, facial shape, body shape, etc.

Unlike sex and gender, race and ethnicity have an intimate connection to geography. In an obvious way, we know that people of different races and ethnicities are geographically ordered; Africans come from African countries, Indians from India, Peruvians from Peru, Québécois from Quebec, etc. Most contemporary states govern not just over a geographic territory but also a *nation*, a group of people who imagine themselves as an internally similar community (due to shared blood lineage, various cultural traits, or a mix of both) united against an outside world of others. Nation-states are some of our most powerful contemporary organizations and they are built to serve and protect ethnically and racially homogeneous communities.

For multi-ethnic countries (such as India, especially when it included what is now Pakistan) or multi-racial countries (such as Canada and the United States), the battle for who counts as a member of the nation, who gets included in governance or resource distribution, can be fierce. The lives of ethnic and racial minorities are often made difficult as they are treated by the majority population as 'them' in opposition to 'us'. These groups face a wide range of challenges living in a community that is not made to include them. These challenges include, but are not limited to, barriers to essential resources such as good jobs, housing, health care, and education, as a result of discrimination, segregation, and exclusion. The consequent divisions among groups and individuals are difficult to repair, as Jeffrey Denis notes in his paper on the legacy of residential schools in Canada. By comparing white and Aboriginal reactions to the Canadian prime minister's apology for the abusive treatment of Aboriginals in residential schools, Denis shows that the dominant group can not simply dispense of a serious, deeply historical problem by offering an apology and some money. Aboriginal responses show that much more is needed from the government to heal the traumatic legacy of the schools. But white responses reveal that it is difficult for those from the dominant cultural group to know how to right a wrong committed by past generations, or to imagine how they are responsible for the structural social advantages their group enjoys.

Given the strong connections between group membership and territory, many of these same barriers exist for people who decide to migrate to a new country. As Alan Simmons points out, some nations are more welcoming to new members than are others, though none are perfectly open. In his paper, Simmons evaluates how Canada fares as a welcoming nation to the many immigrants on which it depends for economic development.

The chapters in this section stress that immigrants and racial or ethnic minorities cannot be viewed as mere specimens of victimhood and objects of pity. They remind us that the individuals in these groups are agents, actively responding to and challenging the barriers they face. To this end, Cora Voyageur argues that the academic community needs to adjust the deficit lens with which it tends to study the First Nations community in Canada, in order to see the range of possibilities that has opened up for First Nations people in recent years and how groups and individuals are responding. Vic Satzewich and William Shaffir provide this kind of investigation into recent Canadian immigrants. Focusing on the power of religious and ethnic organizations in the local community, they highlight the resourcefulness of immigrants and their determination to succeed in their new country. One way that immigrants help each other is by banding together and offering mutual help when their host country does not provide the support they need. But this is not to say that all immigrants to Canada form distinct enclave communities. Monica Boyd and Emily Laxer discuss how immigrants and their children integrate into the Canadian political system as voters and candidates. They find that by the third generation, if not before, the descendants of immigrants are indistinguishable from other native borns in terms of their political engagement.

Bridging Understandings: Anishinaabe and White Perspectives on the Residential School Apology and Prospects for Reconciliation

Jeffrey S. Denis

Introduction

> Today, we recognize that this policy of assimilation was wrong, has caused great harm, and has no place in our country.

So said Prime Minister Stephen Harper on 11 June 2008, as he apologized to the Aboriginal peoples of Canada for the **residential school** system that the federal government funded and Christian churches operated for more than a century, as a tool of Aboriginal **assimilation**.[1] To begin to understand what this event meant to Aboriginals and non-Aboriginals, I interviewed 70 First Nations and Métis residents, including 14 residential school survivors, and 70 white (Euro-Canadian) residents of Northwestern Ontario (Treaty #3 territory) about their views on the apology, the associated monetary settlement, and ways to facilitate healing and reconciliation.[2] Despite some overlap in perspectives and within-group variations, Aboriginals and whites tend to frame these issues in incompatible ways. Although most residents view the apology as necessary, whites tend to see it as a final act of 'closure', whereas Aboriginals tend to see it as one step in an ongoing 'healing journey'. While most agree that monetary compensation cannot erase survivors' pain, many whites think it is excessive but many Aboriginals feel it is insufficient. When asked about follow-up actions, a majority of whites say we should 'stop dwelling on the past' and 'just move on', whereas most Aboriginals offer practical suggestions for healing, such as restructuring the Truth and Reconciliation Commission and enhancing cultural and language programs. Ultimately, the dominant white frame reflects a Canadian style of 'laissez-faire' (Bobo et al. 1997) or 'color-blind' (Bonilla-Silva 2010) racism—an ideology that justifies racial inequality, avoids responsibility, and defends dominant group interests without sounding 'racist'.

Findings

1. Framing the Apology

On the day of the apology, across Canada, large groups gathered in community centres, hockey arenas, and band offices. In Fort Frances—a pulp and paper mill town of 8,103 (Statistics Canada 2007)—I attended the 'Hope, Honour, Healing' event at the Rendezvous banquet hall, steps from the former St. Margaret's Residential School (1902–1974), with over 100 Anishinaabe and their supporters to collectively prepare, watch, and reflect as the prime minister and all the opposition leaders said they were 'sorry' and the leaders of five Aboriginal organizations responded on national television. As the sweet scent of burning sage wafted across the hall, some cried, others cheered, and still others fled, too emotional to bear the words they had so longed to hear.

Down the street, at the local public health unit, my partner asked some white co-workers in the break room if they had seen the apology. 'What apology?' one replied. 'For the residential schools', she said. 'Oh, that? We didn't go . . . What were residential schools again?' And they returned to their discussion of cookbooks.

This anecdote illustrates an important point:

Table 46.1 Residential School Attendance and Responses to the Residential School Apology and Settlement among Aboriginal and White Interviewees (N=140)

RESIDENTIAL SCHOOL ATTENDANCE	ABORIGINAL INTERVIEWEES (%)	WHITE INTERVIEWEES (%)
Attended residential school	20	0
At least one immediate family member (parent, sibling, spouse) attended residential school	76	2
At least one extended family member attended residential school	90	8
Responses to the Apology		
Watched in a large group setting	28	8
Surprised	30	6
Emotional	30	6
Predominantly positive	18	40
Predominantly negative	10	24
Indifferent	0	8
Mixed	72	28
Responses to the Settlement		
Compensation fair or adequate	8	40
Compensation not enough	40	12
Compensation too much	0	38
Indifferent about compensation	0	6
Money won't take away the pain	66	54
Negative stories or views about uses of money	14	20
Applied for compensation – self	20	0
Applied for compensation – close family member	58	6
Eligible for compensation but did not apply – self or close family member	20	0
What, if anything, should be done to follow up on the apology?		
Just move on	10	56
Governments, churches, and/or local residents should take specific follow-up actions	82	36
Don't know or vague response	8	8
Mentions TRC	12	8
Skeptical of TRC	12	2

while most Aboriginal people viewed the apology as an historic event, were highly engaged with it, and made sure to watch or listen, a substantial number of whites were indifferent and only paid attention after the fact, if at all.

When later asked how they felt about the apology, some Aboriginals were positive, others negative, and the majority ambivalent (see Table 46.1). A few said that it was exactly what they wanted to hear and would help them heal. Others are so wounded by residential schools or their **intergenerational** effects that no matter what anyone says or does, it may never be enough; they reject the apology as 'a bunch of BS'. Yet, most Aboriginal people had mixed and nuanced responses. They said things like:

The apology was 'a long time coming'.[3]

It's an important 'step' in our 'healing journey'.

We'd like to believe it was 'heartfelt', but will have to wait and see if the government makes good on it and assess its sincerity by the 'actions' that follow.

Some whites shared these views. But, although many whites had, on the surface, positive interpretations of the apology in that they said it was 'good' and 'necessary', their responses were often short and defensive and their wording negative:

'I don't have a problem with that.'

'When you do something wrong, you should apologize, right?'

What does this abruptness and defensiveness mean? When probed further, some whites responded to the effect of 'Look, we've apologized. It's over and done. What more do they want? Move on!' In other words, the apology was 'good' because, in their minds, it put the issue to rest and they no longer had to deal with it. A minority also gave purely negative responses:

Why should the prime minister apologize for 'something he didn't do'?

'I never had nothin' to do with them going to that school!'

Thus, although opinions vary within the Aboriginal and white populations, the modal (most frequent) responses differ in content, tone, and style.

2. Framing the Settlement

Much the same can be said about reactions to the monetary settlement.[4] Just as most whites and Aboriginals agree that an apology was necessary, there is a high consensus that money alone cannot purge the pain. However, the *meaning* of the compensation differs between groups.

Some Aboriginals view it as a positive gesture, more important for its symbolism than its market value. Others complain it is 'not enough' and still others call it 'hush money', arguing that 'the government is just trying to buy us off.'

Some whites agree that the settlement is 'too little, too late'. Their modal response is that compensation is appropriate, but, as with the apology, their wording and tone tend to be defensive and negative:

'I don't have an issue with that.'

'I think there's nothing wrong with that, but I . . . I . . . I . . .'

Unlike Aboriginals, a substantial minority of whites also complain that the money is either 'too much' or should not be given at all because (1) Why should they, as 'taxpayers', pay for their ancestors' mistakes?; (2) Residential school teachers presumably had 'good intentions'; (3) Aboriginals' stories of abuse are allegedly exaggerated; (4) Residential school attendees are 'all dead now anyway'.[5]

Some whites and a few Aboriginals also oppose compensating *individuals* who might 'drink or gamble [the money] away'. These views reflect well-known stereotypes. Yet, when survivors are asked what they have done (or will do) with the money, the most common responses are sharing it with family and buying a new motor vehicle.

In any case, the residential school issue is *not* about money from the perspective of most Aboriginals. It is about seeking recognition for wrongdoing, acknowledgment of guilt, and acceptance of responsibility; healing emotional and spiritual wounds; and working toward reconciliation. A few thousand dollars is nice to have, but it is not what they are seeking.

3. Next Steps

As part of the settlement agreement, the federal government created a Truth and Reconciliation Commission (TRC) with a five-year mandate to 'witness, support, promote and facilitate truth and reconciliation events' and 'create as complete an historical record as possible of the [residential school] system' for 'public . . . use and study' (Truth and Reconciliation Commission of Canada n.d.: p. 1). After a bumpy start, including the resignation of its first chair, the commission began hearings in Winnipeg in June 2010.

Yet, when interviewees are asked what else, if anything, should be done to follow up on the apology, only a handful seem aware of the TRC and most are skeptical of its current structure and mandate. For instance, some worry that the commission hearings will be just another form of 'entertainment reconciliation' whereby Aboriginals tell their sad stories and others pity them, but nothing really changes. Genuine truth and reconciliation, they say, would also involve confession by residential school teachers, priests and nuns, bush pilots who flew children from remote reserves to the schools, and policy-makers who designed the schools or neglected to close them despite the reported abuse and abysmal living conditions. Non-Aboriginal Canadians, they argue, must acknowledge their complicity in the system and their resulting privileges and must find ways to apply the apology on a local level. Unless the commission facilitates this process, questions about its legitimacy will remain.

More generally, the biggest gap in understandings emerges around this question of 'next steps'. A majority of whites say we should 'stop dwelling on the past' and 'just move on'. One retired white teacher argues, 'It's part of our history. They've done their apology. Why beat a dead horse?' Her adult daughter agrees: 'Let it go and move on.' In contrast, most Aboriginals cite specific actions that governments, churches, and others could do to live

out the apology. Many Aboriginals and a few whites say the apology will be seen as sincere in the long run only if the government honours its treaty commitments, signs the United Nations Declaration on the Rights of Indigenous Peoples, fills the chasm in education and child welfare funding, and provides replacement infrastructure for the 118 First Nations still lacking clean drinking water. Many also recommend increased funding for Aboriginal healing services and cultural and language programs to revitalize the vital components of Aboriginal life that residential schools sought to destroy.

On a local level, there are concerns that the Fort Frances public schools did not pause to watch the apology live on TV and that Town Council and the local Catholic Church have not offered their own apologies. Indeed, when I requested an interview from a white woman who, according to two independent sources, taught at the local residential school, she denied it and told me to 'find somebody else'. Although the Fort Frances Museum did host an exhibit on the residential school system in summer 2008, and the Right Relations Circle (a small local anti-racist group) has educated itself about residential schools and initiated activities to promote better relations between whites and Aboriginals, there is still much work to do before the gap in understanding can be bridged.

Conclusions

Aboriginals and whites tend to view residential school issues through incompatible frames. The traditional Anishinaabe frame is holistic, fluid, and processual. From this perspective, the apology is an early step in the 'healing journey', which will take 'seven generations' to complete. Healing is an individual and collective process and does not end with the prime minister's words, for history is alive and shapes the future. Above all, an apology *becomes* real by the actions that follow.

In contrast, the dominant white frame is individualistic, dualistic, and ahistorical. It suggests that the 'past is past'; that it has no bearing on the present and after an apology has been made, nothing more can be done; and that we start anew from a blank slate. These views reflect a broader trend of 'laissez-faire' or 'colour-blind' racism, which I have found throughout my research (Denis 2010). Many whites claim to be egalitarian, saying we all should be treated the same, but, in a historical context, this translates into a rejection of treaty rights, a denial of First Nations sovereignty, a blaming of Aboriginals themselves (rather than historical or structural factors) for their poverty, and resentment toward those who exercise their rights or seek a more equal share of power and resources. When it comes to residential schools, many whites say they support reconciliation in principle—and often point to Aboriginal friends or family members as evidence—but, in practice, they prefer to 'just move on' and avoid concrete initiatives to rectify historical injustices. While purporting to take the moral high ground, this racial ideology is a barrier to truth and reconciliation and ultimately serves the interests of white power and privilege.

The fundamental divide, then, is not so much based on 'blood' or 'skin' as on racial ideologies and clashing frames that sustain or challenge the hierarchical racial system. For the residential school apology to be accepted and for reconciliation to occur, a paradigm shift will be needed by many white Canadians who have long repressed their history and its relevance for the contemporary social structure and disparate life chances of Aboriginals and non-Aboriginals. As the historically more powerful group, which has benefited in some ways from colonization, whites have a responsibility to support Aboriginals in their healing journeys and, in so doing, to begin to heal ourselves.

Notes

1. 'Aboriginal' refers to the original inhabitants of present-day Canada and their descendants (First Nations, Métis, and Inuit peoples). More specific terms (Anishinaabe, Ojibwa) are used where appropriate.
2. The interviews were conducted between March 2008 and July 2009. They are based on a theoretical sample with multiple independent snowballs and saturation logic (Biernacki & Waldorf 1981; Small 2009; Wilson & Chaddha 2009). Thus, the percentages in Table 46.1 should be taken as rough rather than precise estimates.
3. Unless otherwise indicated, words in quotation marks are *actual* interview quotations.
4. The 2005 settlement agreement included a one-time Common Experience Payment of $10,000 for anyone who could prove they attended residential school, $3,000 for each additional year after that payment, and an Independent Assessment Process for survivors alleging serious physical or sexual abuse (CBC 2008).
5. In fact, 85,000 (more than half of the total) are still alive.

References

Benford, Robert D., and David A. Snow. 2000. 'Framing Processes and Social Movements: An Overview and Assessment'. *Annual Review of Sociology 26*: 611–39.

Biernacki, Patrick, and Dan Waldorf. 1981. 'Snowball Sampling: Problems and Techniques in Chain Referral'. *Sociological Methods and Research 10*(2): 141–63.

Bobo, Lawrence, James Kluegel, and Ryan A. Smith. 1997. 'Laissez-Faire Racism: The Crystallization of a Kinder, Gentler Anti-Black Ideology'. Chapter 2 in *Racial Attitudes in the 1990s: Continuity and Change*, edited by Jack Martin and Steven A. Tuch. Westport, CT: Greenwood.

Bonilla-Silva, Eduardo. 2010. *Racism without Racists: Color-Blind Racism and Racial Inequality in Contemporary America*, 3rd edition. New York: Rowman & Littlefield.

Canadian Broadcasting Corporation (CBC). 2008. 'Indian Residential Schools: Agreement in Principle: FAQs'. From the *Truth and Reconciliation: Stolen Children* series. June 6.

Denis, Jeffrey S. 2010. 'Contact and Prejudice: Coexisting in a Northern Ontario Milltown'. Paper presented at the 105th annual American Sociological Association conference, Atlanta, August 17.

Feagin, Joe R. 2010. *The White Racial Frame: Centuries of Racial Framing and Counter-Framing*. New York: Routledge.

Goffman, Erving. 1974. *Frame Analysis: An Essay on the Organization of Experience*. New York: Harper Colophon.

Grand Council of Treaty Number 3 (GCT3). 2010. 'New Support Program Targets Residential School Survivors'. Press Release, March 10.

Kelly, Diane M. 2008. 'Residential School Apology: Statement to the Gatherings of Treaty #3 Citizens'. Grand Council of Treaty #3, June 11.

Palys, Ted. 1997. *Research Decisions: Quantitative and Qualitative Perspectives*, 2nd edition. Toronto: Harcourt Canada.

Small, Mario. 2009. '"How Many Cases Do I Need?" On Science

and the Logic of Case Selection in Field-Based Research'. *Ethnography* 10(1): 5–38.

Statistics Canada. 2007. *2006 Community Profiles*. Statistics Canada Catalogue No. 92-591-XWE. Ottawa: Government of Canada.

Truth and Reconciliation Commission of Canada (n.d.) *Schedule N of the Indian Residential Schools Settlement*

Agreement: Mandate for the Truth and Reconciliation Commission [PDF] Retrieved on Apr 14th, 2011 from: http://www.trc.ca/websites/trcinstitution/File/pdfs/SCHEDULE_N_EN.pdf

Wilson, William Julius, and Anmol Chaddha. 2009. 'The Role of Theory in Ethnographic Research'. *Ethnography* 10(4): 549–64.

CHAPTER 47

....

The Informal Settlement Sector: Broadening the Lens to Understand Newcomer Integration in Hamilton

William Shaffir and Vic Satzewich

Previous research on newcomer **settlement** has already identified some of the main challenges that newcomers face when it comes to integration into Canadian society (Wayland 2006). This research points to the significance of language barriers, but also to barriers related to educational credential recognition, Canadian work experience, and translating the skills and experience associated with jobs and careers prior to coming to Canada into comparable jobs and careers here in Canada. Our research is not intended to reproduce these findings. Instead, we are interested in understanding how newcomers go about trying to solve the challenges they face when it comes to settlement and integration through their participation in religious organizations and ethnically specific associations.

We conducted 30 interviews in November and December 2009 with persons connected with the immigration field in Hamilton. The sample included immigrants that arrived in Hamilton under a variety of immigration programs, professionals familiar with the immigration scene, and leaders of churches and ethnic community associations.

In this paper, we are drawn by two main questions:

- What role do religious institutions and ethno-cultural associations play in helping newcomers adjust and integrate into Hamilton society?
- What is the relationship between the formal settlement sector and religious institutions and ethno-cultural associations in the city?

We conceive of settlement as a process through which newcomers interact with a variety of individuals and both formal and informal organizations in order to live and work in a new land. We define the formal settlement sector as those organizations that receive government or foundation funding to provide services to newcomers. The Settlement and Integration Services Organization (SISO) is one of the cornerstones of the formal settlement sector in the city, but the sector also includes organizations such as St. Joseph Immigrant Women's Centre, Circle of Friends for Newcomers, l'Association canadienne-française de l'Ontario, Centre de santé communautaire, and

Mohawk College. The informal settlement sector consists of those organizations and institutions that are not funded by government or foundation resources but that nevertheless play a role in the settlement and integration of newcomers.

While settlement services are provided to newcomers by various institutions and agencies in Hamilton, newcomers are not simply passive recipients of these services. Nor are they passive victims of the various barriers that have been identified in the literature. Newcomers have 'agency': they have the ability to act and react, and to change their circumstances and surroundings. As a result, it is important to understand settlement and integration from the perspective of newcomers, and the ways they go about solving the various challenges posed by the barriers they face in the course of living in a new city and country. Our focus is on the ways that two sets of institutions within the informal settlement sector, faith organizations—churches, temples, gurdwaras, and mosques—and ethno-cultural associations help newcomers solve various settlement issues.

Support Provided by the Informal Settlement Sector

Hamilton's SISO is a community-based organization that helps to mediate newcomers' experiences and facilitates their integration and serves as the formal face of settlement services in Hamilton. Mandated to 'provide programs and services to culturally and racially divergent immigrant and refugee communities' in Hamilton, and to enable 'all people to fully participate in the social, economic, and cultural life of the society' (SISO, n.d.), the organization claims to have achieved credibility and widespread respect for its professionalism and strong commitment to community. Representatives of this organization are typically the first people with whom immigrant newcomers interact upon arrival.

While services to newcomers offered through SISO dominate Hamilton's immigration scene, it is easy to overlook the support the newly arrived gain by connecting with a religious institutions or ethno-cultural association. It is essential to recognize the informal services of religious institutions and ethno-cultural associations established by immigrants themselves, and the stabilizing role they play in providing much-needed emotional support and opportunities in helping newcomers find direction.

Faith-Based Institutions and Social Integration

Generally speaking, immigrants arriving in Hamilton enjoy government-sponsored programs that would make earlier waves of immigrants envious. These services mainly address newcomers' instrumental needs, however, and newcomers identify faith institutions as consistently helping them to fulfill their expressive needs. Providing spiritual sustenance and emotional comfort, these institutions morph into informal organizations offering guidance and networking opportunities to meet newcomers' concerns. As explained by an Imam at a local mosque: 'Those who are coming, they trust the mosque more than other organization, because of that spiritual link. The mosque helps many of them find work.' He continues:

> What happens is those that have companies or some small business, they come here to pray. When they come, they come to greet Imam, they give me their card. They prefer to have someone recommended by me. They have stores, gas stations. 'Imam, I need a serious person, someone who is honest.' And I know people who come to pray, they are educated. I can recommend them for a job.

The particular blend of spiritual, emotional, and instrumental support within the informal environment of places of worship is precisely what makes these institutions particularly significant vehicles to enhance settlement. As explained by one member of a non-denominational church in the city:

> Some people are lucky to have family here, but there are others who come here strictly on their own. . . . And there is trepidation when you come from a foreign

country. You don't know how to talk, how to express yourself and yet when you meet your own people, and you talk, you feel more comfortable. . . . [The church], it's accepting. . . . They come here because it is not formalized. It is not rushed. There are no exams. It's like a free open school. It's open 24/7. They can come here any time. (Church official)

The relevance of faith institutions for newcomers was underscored by both religious officials and immigrants. They are valued for the spiritual guidance they offer, while providing an anchor enabling newcomers to better position themselves to meet their new challenges. Contrasting the support offered for immigrant newcomers by SISO and the mosque, one Imam in Hamilton remarks:

The mosque is spiritual—this is the main difference. . . . Mosque is special for newcomers because all Muslims are attached to a mosque. . . . When there are spiritual things, the families, the children, and education, all this is what the mosque provides—religious side. The second, and this is the most important, those that are coming new, they trust the mosque more than any organization because of that spiritual link. So this is the difference.

The powerful influence of the faith institutions shines through in their latent consequences. They serve as meeting places providing opportunities for people to associate with others who share such similarities as ideas, ways of life, and ethnic and racial backgrounds. An official from a Sikh temple makes this point when he notes, 'We meet people's emotional needs. It's more emotional. . . . What is important for newcomers is the emotional connection.' He adds:

. . . some of them have never been out of [their home] country, so it's their first trip ever overseas. They have difficulties. But when they come in here they face the difficulties with others. This is home. You're with people you understand. So this is their second home.

A recently arrived immigrant who came as a skilled worker observed:

I go to an Adventist church. . . . It's one of the things I really appreciate because when you are new in a country, in a place, you feel really uprooted, you feel like disoriented, and have many fears. When I went to that church, those people are really friendly. They help us. For example, they offer to pay because they have a private school, they said that you can send you children to the private school and the church will pay.

The challenges of immigration can be accentuated when newcomers are also visible minorities. While many newcomers with whom we spoke attended churches that had a diverse membership, it is also clear that there is a place for faith institutions that define themselves as catering to a specific group:

They come here to this church because they are more comfortable fitting in with somebody of your own race, not culture, race. But you also know that there is a connection between Afro-Caribbeans because we all probably originated from Africa. You know, so there is a connection, and the comfort level. We may not be able to speak French, but there is still a connection. . . . This is predominantly a black church. These are black people from Africa, and we provide an association of comfort. (Church official)

Ethno-Cultural Associations

Some critics argue that Canadian immigration and multiculturalism policies weaken the country's social fabric. Specifically, multiculturalism presumably encourages immigrants to cling to their past instead of gradually eliminating their old self-conceptions and fashioning a distinctive Canadian identity (Bissoondath 1994). The discussion has centred on whether multiculturalism interferes with the process via which immigrants view themselves as contributors to Canadian society.

Contrary to what some critics of multicultural policy suggest, the ethno-cultural organizations we encountered are promoting integration rather than acting as barriers to integration. The following example serves as a case in point:

> Most of the events also we're doing, we're trying to focus on how to integrate these families, especially their kids, within the society with the idea of giving, because this idea is missing from back home. Volunteering is non-existent in the same concept we know here. People are just busy . . . with wars, with their problems, with how to get their food. . . . If you talk to some from the Middle East countries, 'Can you volunteer some hours to society?' they would laugh. It's a joke. 'Like I'm not getting any payment for that?' 'No.' So that another challenge we're trying to change, or at least growing them this concept. . . . (Ethno-cultural association leader)

Ethno-cultural community organizations and associations are also important in that they assist new arrivals with securing employment, whether permanent or temporary. As in faith-based institutions, newcomers actively develop informal networking groups that often help them find work.

As one official who works in the settlement sector observes, this informal approach resonates particularly with newcomers for whom the bureaucratic structure is both foreign and off-putting. As the official explains, it is to these informal networks that newcomers gravitate and where information gained is regarded to be reliable:

> There are formal and informal networks. Newcomers come in and function on informal networks, organizations function more on formal networks.
> Think about cab drivers. Who are the cab drivers in Hamilton? The whole cab driver system is set up by a lot of new immigrants. Why? Because they come in and can't find a job. Credentials aren't recognized. So they have links to who runs the cabs. Cabs need to be serviced. . . . So what do the guys do?

> They help each other out. They don't need to go to the bigger places to get their cabs serviced. On a Sunday afternoon, they go to somebody's back yard . . . . And they help each other out because they recognize we're all together in this boat. . . .
> Think of your relationships in your family. And you've been entrenched in this community for a long time. You go visit a family member and you have a whole extended family. This is your support network. But because you're entrenched in the community, those support networks work upwardly, vertically, and those support networks work horizontally. When new immigrants come in, they may still be able to establish the horizontal networks but some of the vertical pieces aren't available because they don't know people at the top. . . .I see them [immigrants] establish horizontal networks and groups. It happens with the church, it happens with the mosque, it happens with the various associations.

Despite the fact that these informally established networks may not provide the most accurate and credible advice, they nevertheless remain a primary source of information:

> Now sometimes when you go to informal networks, is the information you get there valid? Not necessarily. Is the information you get there good? Not necessarily. Is it the information you believe? Absolutely. Because if you think about how people are, we work in groups. So you go to a group, you feel comfortable. And if you have large organizations and somebody walks through the door and they don't see anybody in there that makes them feel comfortable, why would they want to go back? (Settlement sector worker)

Conclusion

We conclude that, far from being passive recipients of services that government-supported and private organizations make available, immigrant newcomers display resourcefulness, ambition, and creativity as they interact with outside officials and co-ethnics to pave a path, however wide or narrow, to face the challenges before them. These traits are especially evident in their organization of services provided by their places of worship and ethno-cultural community associations. Though these services are not mandated as part of the formal immigrant settlement sector, they nonetheless provide networks facilitating newcomer integration.

There has been a move in recent years away from talking in reified terms about 'social structures'—divorce rates, division of labour, racism—as if there were mysterious forces somehow acting on human beings. More and more, social scientists appreciate that it is human beings who act and who, through the ways in which they define situations and construct lines of action for themselves, create and constantly recreate social structures. Toward this end, we would be amiss in characterizing immigrants as cultural dupes, forever buffeted by outside forces over which they exercise little, if any, control. Instead, the clear conclusion derived from our analysis is that immigrant newcomers are imaginatively resourceful and to be admired for the entrepreneurial skills they display. In this regard, they become micro-managers of their destiny, seeking to ensure that they acquaint themselves with, and benefit maximally from, programs in place to cushion their transition.

References

Bissoondath, Neil. 1994. *Selling Illusions: The Cult of Multiculturalism.* Toronto: Stoddart.

Wayland, Sarah. 2006. *Unsettled: Legal and Policy Barriers for Newcomers to Canada.* Community Foundations of Canada and the Law Commission of Canada.

Available at http://www.cfc-fcc.ca/socialjustice/pdf/LegalPolicyBarriersReview.pdf.

Settlement and Integration Services Organization (SISO). n.d., Information Brochure. Hamilton: Settlement and Integration Services Organization.

CHAPTER 48

The New Relationship between the Social Sciences and the Indigenous Peoples of Canada

Cora J. Voyageur

Introduction

Social science has a long history of researching **First Nations** subjects. The bulk of the early research comprised ethnographic case studies in anthropology, such as Franz Boas' research on the Kwakiutl of British Columbia. As sociology developed into its own discipline, it offered an important perspective from which to explore the relationships within the First Nations community and the relationship between First Nations people and mainstream society. This paper highlights some of the changes that can help set the stage for a new relationship between First Nations people and the social science community.

Social Change

First Nations people are more visible in Canadian society than ever before. This is due, in part, to the tremendous population growth of the First Nations in Canada. The community has rebounded from near elimination; according to the 1911 Census of Canada, its population shrank to a mere 105,611 (Saku, 1999) from an estimated 2 million prior to European contact (Thornton, 1987). The First Nations population has tripled in the past 30 years and now stands at approximately 700,000 (Statistics Canada, 2008). Many individuals and families have left rural or remote reserves and have integrated into urban areas, thus increasing their presence in mainstream Canada.

The past few decades have witnessed a dramatic increase in First Nations students' participation in post-secondary education. The 2006 census identified 42,900 First Nations individuals holding at least one university degree (Statistics Canada, 2007). This is an increase of 14,055 or 49 per cent over a five-year period. The distribution of First Nations students across post-secondary disciplines is also improving, with less clustering in social work and education and more representation across a wide variety of fields such as engineering, law, business, and medicine. These trends bode well for those graduates who want to return to work in First Nations communities after completing their training.

Economic Change

First Nations communities and individual business owners are increasing their involvement in the mainstream economy. In fact, there are more than 30,000 Aboriginal-owned businesses across the country.

Aboriginal financial institutes have been created in each province and these First Nations-controlled institutions offer employment, training, and capital to First Nations. The creation of First Nations banking institutions is another positive development that supports the First Nations economy. The oil-rich Samson Cree Nation at Hobbema, Alberta, created the Peace Hills Trust Company in 1980, while the Saskatchewan Indian Equity Foundation and the Toronto Dominion Bank partnered to form the First Nations Bank of Canada in 1996.

There is money to be made and partnerships to be struck in the First Nations community. Mainstream banks have discovered that First Nations businesses are lucrative. First Nations ventures that might not have been funded in the past because they were viewed as too risky, simply because they were First Nations enterprises, are now viewed as viable and attractive by investors and corporations.

The First Nations community is enthusiastic about business, as shown by band-owned businesses, joint ventures with non–First Nations organizations, and individual entrepreneurs. However, enthusiasm is not enough to move the First Nations community ahead politically, economically, or socially. Policy changes are needed to enable opportunities to be acted upon, and those changes come as a result of political change.

Political Change

The politics and policies that rule the First Nations' world are not easy to live by. The political, economic, and social rules that control their lives come from outside the community and from people who know little about First Nations culture. Yet, in spite of these repressive rules, First Nations people have still been able to raise their profile in mainstream society. For example, they have earned seats in mainstream politics. These politicians are able to inject indigenous interests and perspectives into caucus debates, and to bring their peoples' insights into the policies and functioning of the larger polity. Meanwhile, First Nations governments and political organizations such as the Assembly of First Nations and tribal councils negotiate, advocate, and lobby for policy changes affecting their constituents.

Self-government is never far from the minds of First Nations people. Self-government agreements enhance First Nations' ability to influence the politics and legislation of the larger society to better take into account First Nations' interests. One legislative accomplishment—the Sechelt Indian Band Self-Government Act—attracted considerable interest from First Nations leaders and was an early model of self-government. The preservation and recognition of Aboriginal and treaty rights is of prime importance to the First Nations community. Although the federal government entered into treaties with the First Nations people, many provincial governments hold the view that they have no legal obligation to honour them.

Legal Change

The Supreme Court of Canada (SCC) has handed down some landmark court decisions that have advanced First Nations rights. For example, in 1977, the Supreme Court ruled in the landmark *Drybones* case that individual Indians have the same human rights as other Canadians. More specifically, the court found that Section 94[b] of the Indian Act was a violation of the Canadian Bill of Rights since it denied Indians 'equality before the law'.

The court's decision in the *Calder* (also known as the *Nisga'a*) case in 1973 was instrumental in making the federal government recognize Aboriginal rights. The SCC ruled that there was a legal notion of Aboriginal rights, but only three justices said there were existing rights while the other three said that such rights had been extinguished. The SSC's unanimous decision in another British Columbia case, *Delgamuukw* (also called *Gitxsan-Wet'suwet'en*) in 1997, proclaimed that in the absence of treaties, Aboriginal title to land was not extinguished and that the First Nations are entitled to use such ancestral lands. More recently, the issue of consultation has taken centre stage in the relationship between First Nations and industry. Government policies now require that all provincial, regional, and district staff who are planning industrial management activities examine whether those actions infringe upon Aboriginal or treaty rights.

Given these important social, economic, political, and legal changes, it is important that academics engage in the process by in changing the portrayal of First Nations people in their academic work. I believe that social scientists must adjust the lens through which they view and represent First Nations people in their curriculum, research, publications, and dissemination of data.

Curriculum

First, we must integrate information on First Nations peoples and their issues into the postsecondary curriculum. This inclusion will make students aware of the issues that concern the Aboriginal community. To do this properly, we must ensure that our teaching material is based on fact and not on opinion or conjecture. In addition, our course readings must be updated regularly since there is a tremendous amount of research being conducted in the First Nations community and each new publication can change the dialogue.

Professors must speak to the diversity in the First Nations community rather than speaking of it as a homogenous group. Canada's 625 First Nations are geographically and culturally different and govern more than 2,200 parcels of land across Canada. First Nations in Canada have 11 language families and speak 53 languages (Elliot, 1992).

It is also crucial that professors take a balanced approach in teaching about First Nations people. This means that the curriculum must not focus entirely on the negative aspects of the community. Stories of resiliency, community initiatives, and other successes can be included in classroom teachings. Also, field trips or guest lectures by First Nations members or elders can allow students to experience or connect to tradition and cultural activities.

Research

Second, academics who wish to conduct research in the First Nations community must invest time, money, and energy to build a relationship with the community. This will entail numerous visits to get to know the community's people, values, culture, and concerns. The community's perspectives must also be reflected in the resulting reports and publications. The research itself should be community driven rather than researcher or agenda driven, and research projects should preferably deal with a practical question rather than a theoretical one. Research needs to be relevant to the community, so the research community must enter into win-win relationships with the First Nations community.

Many First Nations communities have implemented their own research protocols, which dictate that the chief and council must approve all research projects conducted with a community's members. Other communities have adopted the National Aboriginal Health Organization's principles for research, which include ownership, control, accessibility, and possession of data (OCAP). This means that First Nations communities are research partners and not merely subjects. Research must be conducted *with* the community and not just *on* it.

Publishing and Dissemination of Data

Third, the academic community learns of new research findings through conferences and scholarly publications. In these venues, researchers are addressing an audience of peers who are familiar with the discipline's theory, terminology, and jargon. As a result, they are able to present their information in a narrow and specialized format. However, this type of data presentation would not be appropriate or understandable to the First Nations community.

One of the OCAP principles is accessibility. This means that research findings from studies conducted in the First Nations community must be distributed in formats that are easily obtained by community members. For example, they can be shared through community presentations, on posters and CDs, or in DVDs, pamphlets, or booklets. The information must also be disseminated in terms that are understandable to people who have been studied.

Fortunately, there is remarkable growth in the number of publications by indigenous scholars in the areas of sociology, politics, law, history, economics, family, and gender. These books, journals, and articles provide a unique insight into local, regional, national, and international phenomena from an indigenous perspective. Indigenous scholars must continue to research and publish their findings to help set the tone of the academic discourse. Finally, social scientists need to ensure that the indigenous voice comes through in their own published materials. First Nations subjects should always be able to recognize themselves in research publications about them.

Conclusion

Many changes have occurred in the First Nations community over the last few decades, and these changes have altered its relationship with mainstream society and the academy. First Nations marginalization has diminished substantially and opportunities have opened for communities and individuals to an extent unimaginable even 20 years ago.

First Nations people are gaining educational credentials, starting businesses, being elected into mainstream politics, and interacting with mainstream society in ways never seen before. They are raising their profiles and working to shatter the stereotypes held by some mainstream citizens. Their burgeoning population means that they will be more visible in Canadian society, while increased political, economic, and legal power has given them more authority over themselves and their communities.

Today, First Nations people can dictate the parameters of the research conducted in their communities—even whether their communities participate at all. In the past, the First Nations did not have this luxury since decisions were generally made by the government on their behalf or by the researcher. The new relationship that the First Nations seek with the academy means that they will be telling their own story in terms that meet their own levels of accuracy and satisfaction. Social scientists must move away from the archaic model of the First Nations community as being one-dimensional and as a ready pool of research subjects. Researchers have a responsibility to the community they study and the way they portray it in their findings.

References

Aboriginal Business Canada. *Aboriginal Entrepreneurs in Canada: Progress and Prospects.* Ottawa: Aboriginal Business Canada, 2000. Catalogue No. 1206-260X

Attorney-General of Canada v. Lavell; Isaac v. Bedard (1973), 38 D.L.R. (3d) 481.

Calder v. Attorney-General of British Columbia, 34 D.L.R. (3d) 145, (1973).

Delgamuukw v. British Columbia, 3 S.C.R., 1010, (1997).

Drybones v. R. [1970] S.C.R. 282.

Elliot, D.W. 1992. *Law and Aboriginal People of Canada.* North York: Captus Press.

First Nations Bank of Canada. Accessed September 4, 2008. http://www.firstnationsbank.com.

Indian and Northern Affairs Canada (INAC), *Basic Departmental Data, 2005.* Ottawa: Departmental Statistics Section, Information Quality and Research Directorate, Information Management Branch, INAC, 2007. Catalogue No. R12-7/2003E

Royal Commission on Aboriginal Peoples. 1996a. *Report of the Royal Commission on Aboriginal Peoples, Vol. 2: Restructuring the Relationship.* Ottawa: Minister of Supply and Services Canada

Saku, James. 1999. 'Aboriginal Census Data in Canada: a Research Note'. *The Canadian Journal of Native Studies*, 19(2) pp. 365–379.

Statistics Canada. 2007. *Canada (Code01)* (table). *Aboriginal Population Profile.* 2006 Census. Statistics Canada Catalogue no. 92-594-XWE. Ottawa. Released January 15, 2008. http://www12.statcan.ca/census-recensement/2006/dp-pd/prof/92-594/index.cfm?Lang=E. Accessed 19 April 2011.

———. 2008. Aboriginal Peoples in Canada in 2006: Inuit, Métis and First Nations, 2006 Census: First Nations People. Accessed September 19, 2008. http://www.statcan.ca/Daily/English/0 506283d050628d.htm.

Thornton, Russell. 1987. *American Indian Holocaust and Survival: A Population History Since 1492.* Norman: University of Oklahoma Press.

Voyageur, Cora J., and Brian Calliou. 2007. 'Aboriginal Economic Development and the Struggle for Self Government'. In *Power and Resistance: Critical Thinking about Canadian Social Issues*, 4th edition, Wayne Antony and Leslie Samuelson (eds.). Halifax: Fernwood Publishing, 135–160

Weir, Warren. 2007. *First Nation Small Business and Entrepreneurship in Canada.* Vancouver: National Centre for First Nations Governance.

CHAPTER 49

Changing Canadian Immigration and Foreign Worker Programs: Implications for Social Cohesion

Alan Simmons

Canada actively seeks highly skilled immigrants from around the world, admits the family members of these immigrants, and provides asylum for refugees. Up to one quarter of a million new immigrants are admitted annually. Canada also admits large numbers of temporary foreign workers and accepts many foreign students. This all suggests a very positive attitude to admitting foreigners. However, on more careful inspection, it is clear that Canada promotes a mix of 'welcome/stay out' policies (Abu Laban 1998). All those admitted are carefully selected. Some, such as less skilled foreign workers, are admitted only temporarily to work under conditions that most Canadians would not accept.

This paper examines new developments in Canada's welcome to foreigners, the nation-building ideology that shapes these developments, and how the developments impact social cohesion.

New Developments

It is useful to distinguish the following three periods of policy development.

1. The 1960s and Following Decades

The main plank of Canadian international migration policy is an immigration program that has been in place since the 1960s. It recruits, selects, and admits for settlement principal applicants and their immediate family members. This policy emerged following the end (in 1962) of racist national preferences for immigrants. It operates through a **points system** for selecting immigrants without reference to their country of origin or ethnicity. Initially, the points system was designed to select immigrants with job skills relevant for Canada's industrialization programs in the 1960s (Hawkins 1988).

Other important features of Canadian policy have also been in effect for years. Dependent parents and other family members may be sponsored for immigration in the Family Class. **Refugees** are admitted from abroad under particular conditions and are also admitted from within Canada if their claims are approved. Two foreign worker programs have been in place for some time: the Seasonal Agricultural Workers Program (established in 1966) currently brings in temporary farm workers from the Caribbean, Mexico, and Central America; the Live-in Caregiver Program (established in 1992 as a revision to the 1973 Non-Immigrant Employment Authorization Program) brings in nannies, mostly now recruited in the Philippines. In addition, Canada has a long history of granting visas to foreign students.

The vast majority of immigrants from the mid-1970s on have come from non-European origins: Africa, Asia, the Caribbean, and Latin America. As a support to **social cohesion** and the peaceful incorporation of new immigrants, the official policy discourse—backed by the 1988 Multiculturalism Act, anti-racist law, and affirmative action provision for visible minorities—emphasizes, as a way of 'selling diversity', that Canada is a multicultural country in which all national, ethnic, and religious backgrounds are welcome (Abu-Laban and Gabriel 2002).

2. The 1990s

The 1990s brought a set of changes in emphasis in international migration policies (Simmons 1999). The most important was a shift in selection criteria to privilege the immigration of very highly educated workers (those with college and university degrees). Refugees and Family Class immigration inflows were correspondingly reduced, on the grounds that individuals in these streams are not selected for their skill levels.

3. 2005 and Following

Since 2005, the following very important policy developments have emerged.

- Employers who wish to hire more temporary foreign workers are being given state approval to do so, leading to a continuing rise over time in the number of foreign workers admitted (Table 49.1).
- Related to the above, there is a widening spread in the skill levels of foreign workers. Most foreign workers enter, as before, through the Live-in Caregiver and Seasonal Agricultural Workers programs. However, increasing numbers enter outside these established programs as truck drivers and insulators. Some are teachers, specialists in business services, mechanical engineers, and computer systems analysts; namely individuals who have skills similar to those selected as immigrants (Table 49.1).
- The process of selecting foreign workers is changing. Companies can recruit them directly outside the country, provided that they first demonstrate that job openings they have advertized in Canada remain unfilled.
- The Canadian Experience Class of immigration was added in 2007 to permit skilled foreign workers who have successfully completed a period of work in Canada to then apply for permanent residence

Table 49.1 Numbers and Characteristics of Canadian Foreign Residents and Immigrants, 2005 and 2008

Number of Temporary Foreign Residents	2005	2008
Foreign workers	142,130	363,494
Foreign students	100,769	242,861
Total	242,899	606,355
Occupations of Foreign Workers in Alberta		
Live-in caregivers	916	
Agricultural workers	563	
Professional business services to management	469	
Post-secondary teaching & research assistants	263	
Labourers in food, processing	236	
University professors	168	
Truck drivers	137	
Insulators	127	
Mechanical engineers	125	
Computer systems analysts	119	
Total - Top 10 occupations	3,123	
Total - Other and unspecified occupations	6,815	
Total	9,938	
TOTAL IMMIGRANTS	**212,873**	**247,243**
Immigrants by Class (selected classes only)		
Declining inflows:		
Skilled workers - principal applicants	52,269	40,729
Refugees landed in Canada	19,935	7,202
Stable inflows:		
Family class	63,361	65,187
Government-assisted refugees	7,424	7,425
Rising inflows:		
Provincial nominees - principal applicants	2,643	11,799
Live-in caregivers - principal applicants	3,063	6,272

At the time of writing, data on detailed occupational breakdown were not available for 2008.

as immigrants. Foreign students with Canadian post-secondary college or university diplomas are also allowed to remain in Canada, obtain work experience, and later apply for immigrant status.

- The Provincial Nominees Class, added in 2008, permits provinces to play a role in fast-tracking the admission of immigrants with job skills that the employers in their jurisdictions require. The numbers admitted in this new class are still small but rising very rapidly (Table 49.1).
- The number of immigrant applicants directly selected on the basis of their very high levels of skills has been falling in recent years (Table 49.1).

The Role of Nation-Building Ideology

In the late 1980s and early 1990s, Canada adopted a neo-liberal nation-building ideology that included powerful assumptions about the role that international migration could play in expanding Canadian exports and economic growth (Simmons 2010, Chapter 4). This ideology assumes that nations are like business firms: they will succeed by achieving greater sales (i.e., expanding exports), relying more on markets and private enterprise to allocate resources for economic growth, and cutting government costs. The adoption of this ideology led to diverse labour policies, including attracting highly qualified immigrant workers; expanding post-secondary training to increase worker productivity; adopting new labour-saving technologies; meeting the immediate demands for labour through temporary foreign worker programs; exporting jobs by adopting trade policies that will encourage some industries to relocate production and jobs to low-wage countries and encourage consumers to import low-priced goods from abroad; and avoiding potentially costly efforts to increase child-bearing in Canada (Simmons 2010, Chapter 10). Concurrent with the shift to the neo-liberal nation-building model, Canada entered its first 'free trade' agreement, the Canada United States Free Trade Agreement, in 1988; signed the North American Free Trade Agreement in 1994, and adopted new immigration rules in the early 1990s intended to recruit more highly skilled immigrants and to reduce sponsored family and refugee inflows (Simmons 1999).

The currently dominant nation-building ideology also presupposes that multicultural social cohesion will arise in large part automatically. It assumes that the world will furnish Canada with 'designer immigrants' who will arrive as if made-to-measure for Canada's needs (Simmons 1999). The immigrants will have high levels of education to quickly integrate and contribute to Canada's knowledge-based economy. They will have the ability to pay significant fees to cover state costs for processing their applications. And, they will have the capacity to cover their own settlement costs. For all these reasons, it is assumed that native-born citizens will appreciate immigrant contributions, welcome them with open arms, and facilitate their harmonious incorporation.

The post-2005 policy changes are new strategies adopted within the neo-liberal nation-building framework. Consider these examples.

- Foreign workers programs are expanding because the state is increasingly responsive to the short-term labour needs of private companies. The response mechanism involves fast government approval of applications from private companies that need particular kinds of workers who are not available locally. It promotes 'just-in-time' cost-efficiency principles to solving labour shortages. Foreign workers are hired when needed, and then sent home to avoid costs to state welfare or unemployment programs when not (Sharma 2006).
- Decision making regarding the admission of new immigrants is being partly decentralized from the federal state to other stakeholders. Provinces make decisions on whom to admit in the Provincial Nominees Class. Firms make decisions about which skilled foreign workers they want brought in. Universities and colleges make decisions about which foreign students they want to admit. Later, the skilled foreign workers and foreign students can become eligible for immigration status within the Canadian Experience Class.
- When immigrants enter through the Canadian Experience Class, the costs of their selection and training are downloaded from the federal state to private firms and individuals. Private firms select foreign workers and provide them with on-the-job experience. Colleges and universities select the foreign students and educate them, with a relatively high portion of the costs being covered by the foreign students themselves, who pay higher fees than Canadians.

Challenges to Social Cohesion

Canada's recent immigration and foreign workers policies generate large negative implications for social cohesion. Consider these points.

- Contrary to hopes and earlier patterns, recently arrived immigrants are not doing well in the Canadian job market (Picot, Hou, and Coulombe 2007). This is despite the fact that they are more highly trained. The downward trend in the jobs and incomes of newly arrived immigrants has been underway since the 1990s and continues. This frustrates the immigrants, contributes to a loss of potential for Canada, and poses challenges to social cohesion.
- Social cohesion in Canadian society is being challenged by the marginalization of recently arrived immigrants (Reitz and Banerjee 2007). These individuals' low wages force them to reside in low-cost residential areas, mostly located in the outer suburbs of the cities where they settle (Hulchanski 2007). They live close to other immigrants and have less daily contact with and supports from native-born Canadians, factors that may reduce their networks for finding good jobs (Qadeer and Sumar 2006).
- The state is seeking to improve immigrant job outcomes through strategies that may lead to widening inequalities between immigrants and foreign workers. The number of immigrants entering in the Skilled Worker Class declined by more than 20 per cent over the period 2005–2009 while, over the same period, the number of foreign workers (potentially immigrants in the Canadian Experience Class) and the number of immigrants in the Provincial Nominees Class have been rising (Table 49.1). These may be the early signs of a strategy that will develop significantly in the future, in which selection of immigrants is being decentralized significantly to private firms. These firms select foreign workers, of whom the more skilled can become eligible

to be landed immigrants after they have proved their ability to work in Canada, while others, the less skilled, will be restricted to (repeat) contracts as 'foreign workers' who are to be sent home when not required. The selection of immigrants is also being decentralized to provinces that use their own selection criteria related to local labour markets. These new strategies may perhaps better respond to both short- and long-term labour market demands, but they do not respond to other disparities and related social cohesion problems. If anything, the inequalities are likely to increase between highly skilled immigrants admitted directly from abroad (often after a long wait), highly skilled foreign workers and Canadian-trained foreign students who are working in Canada in the hope of being admitted later as immigrants, and less skilled foreign workers who are in Canada on temporary (or repeat temporary) work permits.

- Foreign worker programs may look like a promising avenue from a neo-liberal perspective, but the experience in Canada and elsewhere suggests that they create enormous social cohesion problems. Foreign workers are often not protected by the same labour rights codes and constitutional guarantees provided to Canadian workers. If foreign workers protest their working conditions or report that they need medical attention for injury or sickness, they may be sent home (Basok 2002). Trial programs bringing in foreign workers for diverse low-skilled jobs result in an unfair and exploitative situation, as these workers can have their contracts renewed and contribute over many years to Canada without ever obtaining the right to remain and enjoy the benefits of permanent residence and citizenship (Nakache and Kinoshita 2010). These outcomes are directly exclusionary. Indirectly, they can reinforce gender and racial stereotypes and negatively affect the fight against prejudice in Canada (Preibisch and Binford 2007).

Canadian labour organizers and labour rights groups in Canada have joined with migrant workers to promote better working conditions (Preibisch 2007), but this has not yet solved the basic injustice for workers who renew their contracts many times over and contribute to Canada but are excluded from remaining as citizens.

Solutions to the preceding social cohesion problems will require rather substantial changes to Canada's overall approach to welcoming foreigners and to the nation-building ideology that shapes the current approach.

References

Abu-Laban, Yasmeen and Christina Gabriel. 2002. *Selling Diversity: Immigration, Multiculturalism, Employment Equity, and Globalization*. Peterborough, ON: Broadview Press.'

Abu-Laban, Yasmeen. 1998. 'Welcome/STAY OUT: The Contradictions of Canadian Integration and Immigration Policies at the Millennium'. *Canadian Ethnic Studies* 30:3:190–211.

Basok, Tanya. 2002. *Tortillas and Tomatoes: Transmigrant Mexican Harvesters in Canada*. Montreal and Kingston: McGill-Queen's University Press.

Hawkins, Freda. 1988. *Canada and Immigration: Public Policy and Public Concern*, Second Edition. Montreal & Kingston: McGill-Queen's University Press.

Hulchanski, J. D. 2007. *The Three Cities within Toronto: Income Polarization among Toronto's Neighbourhoods, 1970–2000*. Toronto: University of Toronto, Centre for Urban and Community Studies.

Nakache, Delphine, and Paula J. Kinoshita. 2010. The Canadian Temporary Foreign Worker Program: Do Short-Term Economic Needs Prevail over Human Rights Concerns? Montreal Institute for Research on Public Policy. *Ideas Analysis Debate*, Number 5. http://www.irpp.org/pubs/IRPPstudy/IRPP_Study_no5.pdf.

Picot, Garnett, Feng Hou, and Simon Coulombe. 2007. *Chronic Low Income and Low-Income Dynamics among Recent Immigrants*. Ottawa: Statistics Canada, Analytical Studies Branch Research Paper Series.

Preibisch, Kerry. 2007. 'Globalizing Work, Globalizing Citizenship: Community-Migrant Worker Alliances in Southern Ontario'. Pp. 98–114 in *Organizing the Transnational: Labour, Politics, and Social Change,* edited by Luin Goldring and Sailaja Krishnamurti. Vancouver: UBC Press.

Preibisch, Kerry and Leigh Binford. 2007. 'Interrogating Racialized Global Labour Supply: An Exploration of the Racial/National Replacement of Foreign Agricultural Workers in Canada'. *Canadian Review of Sociology and Anthropology* 44:1:5–36.

Qadeer, Mohammad and Sandeep Kumar. 2006. 'Ethnic Enclaves and Social Cohesion'. *Canadian Journal of Urban Research* 15:1–17.

Reitz, Jeffrey and Rupa Banerjee. 2008. 'Racial Inequality, Social Cohesion and Policy Issues'. Pp. 489–546 in *Belonging? Diversity, Recognition and Shared Citizenship in Canada*, edited by Keith Banding, Thomas Courchene, and F. Leslie Seidle. Montreal: Institute for Research on Public Policy.

Sharma, Nandita R. 2006. *Home Economics: Nationalism and the Making of 'Migrant Workers' in Canada*. Toronto: University of Toronto Press.

Simmons, Alan. 1999. 'Economic Integration and Designer Immigrants: Canadian Policy in the 1990s'. Pp. 53–69 in *Free Markets, Open Societies, Closed Borders? Trends in International Migration and Immigration Policy in the Americas,* edited by Max J. Castro. Coral Gables, FL: North-South Center Press; University of Miami.

———. 2010. *Immigration and Canada: Global and Transnational Perspectives*. Toronto: Canadian Scholars' Press.

CHAPTER 50

Voting across Immigrant Generations

Monica Boyd and Emily Laxer

Introduction

Interest in the voting patterns of successive **immigrant** generations rests on two rationales. First, voting is an important indicator of political participation and second, political participation is widely considered a crucial mechanism in securing immigrants' economic, social, and political foothold in the host society (Ramakrishnan 2005). In recent years, a similar rationale has directed attention to the political participation of immigrants' children. The focus also reflects the recent rapid growth in the numbers of immigrant offspring as a result of sustained post–World War II migration. Most immigrants to Canada are adults; they bring young children with them and they bear Canadian-born children. Census data for 2006 tell us that these offspring (those arriving before age 15 and those who are born in Canada) represent nearly one-third (32 per cent) of the population aged 15 and older. The size of this sector of the population is almost twice that of the foreign born who come as late adolescents or as adults (17.5 per cent of those aged 15 and older).

The growing research on immigrant offspring brings an additional lens to discussions of political participation. It is commonly acknowledged that the integration of immigrants takes time; indeed, integration—defined as the notion that diverse members of a society have equal access to resources by virtue of being incorporated into core institutions—may take more than one generation to be achieved. The question of whether and to what extent immigrant offspring participate in political institutions thus becomes framed within the larger context of immigrant integration. In particular, do immigrant offspring participate more, or less, compared with immigrants who arrived in adulthood or compared to those whose ancestors have been in Canada for several generations? Using information from the 2002 Ethnic Diversity Survey (EDS), we answer this question by looking at generational differences in voting.

Generation Status, Political Participation, and Voting Patterns

In discussing variability across generations in the propensity to vote, a specific vocabulary is employed. In the vast North American literature on immigrant offspring, immigrants and their offspring are classified according to the distance of each generation from the original migration experience. The *first generation* to arrive in a country is identified by that label. Their children, born in the same destination country, are called the *second generation*; their children in turn are referred to as the *third generation* and so on. In actuality, refinements can be made within these broad categorizations; we discuss these sub-categories later.

How do these generational distinctions relate to voting? According to the orthodox accounts of acculturation and integration (Alba and Nee 1997; Gans 1992), participation progressively increases as successive generations of immigrant origin groups become more acculturated to dominant host society values and become increasingly indistinguishable, in their socio-economic status and behaviours, from the average person in the host society. With respect to political participation, immigrants are thought to be the *least* likely to vote, either because the emphasis on economic integration leaves them little time for political activities (Mollenkopf et al. 2006) or because impediments exist, including low proficiency in the official language(s) (Baer 2008), lack of familiarity with the political norms and processes of the host society (Jedwab 2006; White et al. 2006), and restricted access to occupational networks promoting civic engagement due to poor labour market outcomes. Scholars adhering to this view expect second and third generations to exhibit higher rates of political engagement than the foreign born.

This scenario is called the 'straight line' model since it depicts the level of political participation as incrementally increasing with each successive generation. The second generation has higher rates of voting than the first; the third generation has higher voting rates than the second, and so on. However, the voluminous literature on immigration offspring points to at least two additional possibilities (for others, see Ramakrishnan 2005). Fuelled by higher levels of education, rapid acculturation, and a drive to have a higher stake in election outcomes, the second generation may actually have the highest voting rates of all generation groups. Here, the model is one of an inverted V, in which the second generation, and perhaps the 1.5 generation, are more likely to vote than are immigrants arriving as adults or the third and later generations. Alternatively and in contrast to this 'second generation advantage' model, under conditions of structural impediments and strong hierarchical stratification systems, the second generation may be denied opportunities to participate in the larger society. Consequently, they may be far less likely to vote. In this scenario, called the 'second generation decline' or the 'segmented assimilation' model (Zhou 1997), the generation-specific voting rates are represented by a V, where voting rates for the second generation are the lowest for all generational groups.

To date, studies of voting behaviour across immigrant generations in Canada do not support the straight line model. But which of the other models hold is less certain. In their analysis of the 1984 Canadian National Election Survey, Chui et al. (1991) find that the second generation offspring are more likely than both their parents and members of more established generational cohorts to vote, contact politicians, and volunteer in election campaigns. This support for the second generation advantage model contradicts the expectation derived from the straight line model that deeply rooted Canadians are the most participatory. A more recent analysis of the 2004 Canada Election Study finds no difference in federal voting rates between the second generation and the third-plus generation after controlling for age, religion, and ethnic origin groups (Soroka, Johnston and Banting 2007). A third study offers support for the second generation decline model by finding that visible minority second generation offspring have lower voting percentages, reporting that they voted less in the 2000 federal election compared to immigrants arriving before 1991 and compared to the third-plus white generation (Reitz and Banerjee 2007). However, the findings of the third study should be tempered by the fact that the visible minority second generation is very young when compared to the age composition of immigrant visible minority groups or the third-plus white population (see Jedwab 2008; Palmer 2006). Young persons generally have lower voting rates. In the 2000 federal election, the voter turnout for those aged 18–24 was approximately 25 per cent, compared with nearly two-thirds of the general population (Elections Canada no date).

Our Study and Findings

These studies indicate that although the straight line model appears not to hold in Canada, the jury is still is out with respect to which of the remaining two models best describe voting patterns across immigrant generations. To shed additional light on this debate, we conducted a multivariate analysis of the 2002 Ethnic Diversity Survey (EDS) for persons aged 25 and older. The EDS asks respondents if they voted in the last federal, provincial, and municipal elections; it also collects a large amount of information on the social and economic characteristics of these respondents. This information is used to assess if differences in the likelihood of voting across generational groups simply reflects differences between generations with respect to factors known to influence voting propensities. For example, highly educated persons are more likely to vote than less educated persons. If generations that are the most removed from the migration experience are better educated than recently arrived immigrants, education compositional differences across generations might underlie the observed generational differences in voting.

Unlike previous Canadian studies that focused on a limited number of generations, the EDS allows us to study variations across eight generational groups: the first generation (immigrants arriving as older adolescents or as adults), distinguished by three periods of arrival; the 1.5 generation (foreign born arriving before the age of 15); the second generation (those born in Canada to two foreign-born parents); the 2.5 generation (those born in Canada with one foreign-born parent); the third generation (those born in Canada to two native-born parents); and the fourth-plus generation (those born in Canada to two native-born parents and four native-born grandparents. Compared with previous studies, we also have a greater number of demographic, social, and economic variables known to differ between generations and also to influence voting propensities.

We adjust for the influence of these factors using logistic regression analysis (DeMaris 1992) in which the outcomes are 'voted in the past election' versus 'did not vote'. (Individuals who are not citizens of Canada are excluded from the analysis.) Although we use the survey weights to obtain a representative population, we apply normalized weights where the mean is 1. We then use inferential statistics, applying a bootstrapping methodology to adjust for the sampling design, to determine if the differences between the logits are statistically significant for our sample, using the voting patterns of the fourth-plus generation as our reference group. The (ns) notation indicates that logit differences from the fourth-plus generation are not statistically significant.

We report these results in Table 50.1, showing logits and the hypothetical percentages that would be observed if all the generations were alike with respect to age, provincial and large Census MetropolitanArea residence, marital status, composition of the nine visible minority groups and the non-visible minority group, home language, dual versus single Canadian citizenship, education, and income. When logits are not statistically significant, we do not present the percentages since the analysis tells us there is no real meaningful difference from the fourth-plus generation.

After the existing demographic, social, and economic differences between generations are taken into account, few differences exist across generations, relative to the voting rates of the fourth-plus generation. Overall, the voting patterns weakly support a second generation advantage model. In terms of voting in the last federal election, both the second and the 2.5 generations have higher calculated percentages of voting, relative to the fourth generation, and this also occurs for the second generation at the municipal election level. Throughout, the most recently arrived immigrants continue to have substantially lower percentages of voting in the past federal, provincial, and municipal elections.

Discussion

We use the term 'weak support' to describe the second generation advantage model for two reasons: first, the pattern whereby the percentages voting are higher for the second generation is observed at the federal and municipal level, but not in provincial elections. Second, the likelihood of voting among many other generation groups is similar to that observed for the fourth-plus generation. This means that there is not an incremental increase in voting from those most recently arriving to the second generation, followed by incremental declines for successive generations. Instead, the pattern is one in which the likelihood of voting is very similar among most generational groups, with the exception of the second generation and immigrants who recently arrived.

Although space constraints limit a full discussion, somewhat greater variation is found when looking at the actual voting rates without taking compositional differences into account. But

Table 50.1 Loqistic Regression Logits[a,b] and Calculated Hypothetical Percentages of Voting in the Last Election by Generation, Persons Age 25 Years and Older, Canada, 2002

	LOGITS[a] (1)	PERCENTAGES (2)
Federal Election		
4th-plus generation	(RG)	84
3.0 generation	0.172 (ns)	(ns)
2.5 generation	0.194*	86
2.0 generation	0.329***	88
1.5 generation	0.128 (ns)	(ns)
1.0 generation – arrived before 1981	0.275 (ns)	(ns)
1.0 generation – arrived 1981–1990	-0.091 (ns)	(ns)
1.0 generation – arrived 1991+	-1.020***	65
Provincial Election		
4th-plus generation	(RG)	85
3.0 generation	0.118 (ns)	(ns)
2.5 generation	0.108 (ns)	(ns)
2.0 generation	0.198 (ns)	(ns)
1.5 generetion	-0.097 (ns)	(ns)
1.0 generation – arrived before 1981	0.008 (ns)	(ns)
1.0 generation – arrived 1981–1990	-0.088 (ns)	(ns)
1.0 generation – arrived 1991+	-0.986***	67
Municipal Election		
4th-plus generation	(RG)	72
3.0 generation	0.060 (ns)	(ns)
2.5 generation	0.070 (ns)	(ns)
2.0 generation	0.165*	75
1.5 generation	-0.137 (ns)	(ns)
1.0 generation – arrived before 1981	0.104 (ns)	(ns)
1.0 generation – arrived 1981–1990	-0.144 (ns)	(ns)
1.0 generation – arrived 1991+	-0.733***	55

*p<.05   **p<.01   ***p<.001

(RG) Reference group. All logits are expressed in relation to the 4th-plus generation.

(a) Net of sex, age, age squared, province & city of residence, marital status, visible minority status, home language, citizenship (dual versus sole Canadian citizenship), highest level of education, and income.

(b) Logistic regressions run separately for voting yes/no in most recent federal, provincial, or municipal elections.

Source: Master File of the Ethnic Diversty Survey, housed in the University of Toronto Research Data Centre

here the variation is mostly between the foreign born who have arrived in different decades. Our research finds that much of the variation across generations can simply be attributed to group compositional differences in characteristics that are associated with voting or not.

Overall, there is no evidence for the second generation decline model, in which immigrant offspring are less likely to be politically engaged, at least in terms of voting. However, different origin groups may have different norms, expectations, and practices regarding political participation generally and voting in particular (Jedwab 2006; White et al. 2006). If these norms are transmitted to offspring, then there may be voting patterns across generations that are specific for country of origin groups. Clearly more research remains to be undertaken if we are to understand the full complexity of voting patterns across immigrant origin generations in Canada.

References

Alba, Richard, and Victor Nee. 1997. 'Rethinking Assimilation Theory for a New Era of Immigration.' *International Migration Review* 31: 826–874.

Baer, Douglas. 2008. *Community Context and Civic Participation in Immigrant Communities: A Multi-Level Study of 137 Canadian Communities.* Working Paper Series, Metropolis British Columbia, Centre of Excellence for Research on Immigration and Diversity. No. 80-03.

Chui, Tina W. L., James E. Curtis, and Ronald D. Lambert. 1991 'Immigrant Background and Political Participation: Examining Generational Patterns'. *The Canadian Journal of Sociology*, 16(4): 375–396.

DeMaros, Alfred. 1992. *Logit Modeling: Practical Applications.* Quantitative Applications in the Social Sciences No. 86. Newbury Park: Sage Publications.

Elections Canada. no date. Voter Turnout at Federal Elections and Referendums, 1867–2008. Accessed June 30, 2010, from: http://www.elections.ca/content.asp?section=pas& document=turnout&lang=e&textonly=false.

Gans, Herbert J. 1992. 'Second Generation Decline: Scenarios for the Economic and Ethnic Futures of the Post-1965 American Immigrants'. *Ethnic and Racial Studies* 15 (April): 173–192.

Jedwab, Jack. 2006. The 'Roots' of Immigrant and Ethnic Voter Participation in Canada. *Electoral Insight,* December 2006. Accessed April 14, 2011, at: http://www.elections.ca/res/eim/article_search/article.asp?id=143&lang=e&frmPageSize=5.

Jedwab, Jack. 2008. 'The Changing Vertical Mosaic: Intergenerational Comparisons in Income on the Basis of Visible Minority Status in Canada, 2006'. Association for Canadian Studies, 6 October, 1–9.

Mollenkopf, John, Jennifer Holdaway, Philip Kasinitz, and Mary Waters. 2006. 'Politics among Young Adults in New York: The Immigrant Second Generation', Pp. 175–193 in Taeku Lee, S. Karthick Ramakrishnan, and Ricardo Ramirez (eds.), *Transforming Politics, Transforming America.* University of Virginia Press.

Palmer, Douglas L. 2006. *Where Reitz Is Wrong: Visible Minority Responses to the Ethnic Diversity Survey.* Report prepared for Canadian Heritage, Citizenship and Heritage Sector, Strategic Policy and Management.

Ramakrishnan, S. Karthick. 2005. *Democracy in Immigrant America: Changing Demographics and Political Participation.* Stanford, California: Stanford University Press.

Reitz, Jeffrey and Rupta Banerjee. 2007. 'Racial Inequality, Social Cohesion and Policy Issues in Canada'. Pp. 489–545 in Keith Banting, Thomas J. Courchene, and F. Leslie Seidle (eds.), *Belonging? Diversity, Recognition and Shared Citizenship in Canada*, Montreal: Institute for Research on Public Policy.

Soroka, Stuart N., Richard Johnston, and Keith Banting. 2007. 'Ties That Bind? Social Cohesion and Diversity in Canada'. Pp. 561–600 in Keith Banting, Thomas J. Courchene, and F. Leslie Seidle (eds.) *Belonging? Diversity, Recognition and Shared Citizenship in Canada.* Montreal: Institute for Research on Public Policy.

White, Stephen, Neil Nevitte, André Blais, Joanna Everitt, Patrick Fournier, and Elisabeth Gidengil. 2006. Making Up for Lost Time: Immigrant Voter Turnout in Canada. *Electoral Insight*, December 2006. Accessed April 14, 2011, at: http://www.elections.ca/res/eim/article_search/article.asp?id=144&lang=e&frmPageSize=5.

Zhou, Min. 1997. 'Segmented Assimilation: Issues, Controversies and Recent Research for the New Second Generation'. *International Migration Review* 31: 975–1008.

Questions for Critical Thought

CHAPTER 46

1. In what ways were Aboriginal and white interpretations of the apology similar? In what ways were they different? Use examples from Denis' paper.
2. In what ways were Aboriginal and white interpretations of the settlement similar? In what ways were they different? Use examples from Denis' paper.
3. In what ways were Aboriginal and white interpretations of next steps similar? In what ways were they different? Use examples from Denis' paper.
4. What are some problems with the current truth and reconciliation process, according to Denis' respondents? How do they argue it could be better?
5. Denis argues that Aboriginal and white approaches to the residential school issue are 'incompatible'. What makes them incompatible rather than just different? What policies do they each suggest? Can those policies be pursued simultaneously? Are the approaches as incompatible as he makes them seem?
6. What was your position on residential schools and/or the apology before reading this article? Has reading about other points of view changed your mind, and if so, how? Why or why not?
7. What is 'neo-liberal'/'colour-blind'/'democratic' racism? How is it different from more blatant kinds of racism with which you may be more familiar? Use examples from the article.

CHAPTER 47

1. How is Shaffir and Satzewich's research on immigrant integration different from past research (which mostly focused on barriers)?
2. What is the difference between the formal and informal settlement sectors? What kinds of organizations and people are there in each?
3. What are some of the main ways that religious and cultural centres help newcomers integrate into Hamilton? Be sure to discuss both instrumental and expressive needs.
4. Why do immigrants prefer getting help through informal networks? What are some advantages and disadvantages of seeking advice and help from informal networks rather than organizations?
5. Shaffir and Satzewich discuss the multiculturalism debate and assert that their data demonstrates that, far from keeping immigrants in their own ethnic enclaves, religious and ethno-cultural groups help immigrants integrate into Canadian society. Yet they don't overtly argue that these organizations help immigrants meet natives of different races or cultures. Do you think that their data provides strong evidence for one side of the multiculturalism debate, or perhaps more mixed evidence for both sides? Be sure to use evidence from the paper to support your answer.

CHAPTER 48

1. Choose a few of the social, economic, political, or legal changes pointed out by Voyageur that you think have been most important and consequential for Canadian Aboriginals. Describe them and why you think they have been so consequential.
2. Voyageur asserts that academics have a role to play in portraying Aboriginals in a way that better represents their contemporary reality. Why?
3. What suggestions does Voyageur make to improve the representations of contemporary Aboriginals in the academic curriculum? How are these suggestions helpful, how are they not so helpful, and what other suggestions can you think of?
4. Voyageur stresses that data must be disseminated to the Aboriginal communities from which they are derived *in a format that is accessible to them*. Should this apply only to Aboriginal communities, or would it also be valuable to all sociological research subjects? Discuss. Be sure to clarify how research findings can be valuable to the research subjects.
5. According to Voyageur, how have the social, economic, political, or legal changes that Aboriginal communities have undergone changed the power they have vis-à-vis the researcher? What impact does this have on the kind of relationships researchers can and cannot have with the Aboriginal communities they study?

CHAPTER 49

1. According to Simmons, how are Canada's immigration policies 'welcome/stay out' policies?
2. Compare the points system to temporary worker programs. What kinds of workers does each target? What kinds of jobs do the workers fill? What kinds of rights do they enjoy? Are these two kinds of immigrants equal?
3. According to Simmons, the dominant nation-building ideology relies on using the individual firm as a metaphor for the country. Discuss the effectiveness of this metaphor. How are firms and countries different from and similar to one another? What are their goals/purposes? How are they governed? All in all, do you think that this metaphor is useful or misleading? Explain.
4. According to Simmons, why are recent immigrants (despite having skills and credentials that make them highly employable) not succeeding in the labour market?
5. What are some advantages of foreign worker programs for the firms that hire them? What are the disadvantages of such programs for Canada's social cohesion?

CHAPTER 50

1. Why is it important for immigrants to vote?
2. Why is it that first generation immigrants are less likely to vote than native-born Canadians? What structural or social constraints deter them from participating?

3. Explore the competing models of immigrant voting by generation—the straight line, inverted V, and V models. Which model(s) does Boyd and Laxer's evidence not support?

4. Why do Boyd and Laxer say that there is only weak support for one of the models?

5. The data that Boyd and Laxer analyze measure many different age groups at once and assume that all age groups are following the same life course path (e.g. today's immigrants will produce children who behave like today's second generation immigrants). What problems do Boyd and Laxer note with this assumption? What further research do they suggest to deal with this problem?

Part XIII

Globalization

In its most common definition, the term *globalization* refers to the process by which diverse populations around the world come increasingly into contact with one another through the movement of people, ideas, and goods. You can think of the process as a kind of synchronization: our local lives are more and more connected to, and thus subject to changes in, distant communities.

Globalization isn't a new phenomenon. Trade routes linking distant countries and even continents have existed for hundreds, possibly thousands, of years. Colonization, one of the biggest global projects in recent history, was responsible for establishing many of these links. From the fifteenth to the nineteenth century, the armies of Western European countries conquered and reordered colonies all over the world in their own image: invaded lands included all of North and South America, Africa, Australia, and parts of Asia. An influx of European ideas changed the colonized people's cultures, and the extraction of their resources changed their economies. Currently, globalization researchers and analysts are embroiled in debates about just how much more substantial our current level of globalization is compared to past globalized periods, and which characteristics are distinctive to our contemporary form of globalization.

Suzan Ilcan and Rob Aitken open this section by explicating an early period of contemporary globalization. They argue that many important communication and co-operation strategies developed in the post–World War II period, which demanded substantial global organization to manage the massive population of displaced people. Out of this period came a number of institutions whose purpose was to create global order.

When talking about globalization and world order, it is important to specify what kinds of international connections and order are being formed. Nathan Young considers the situation of smaller Canadian communities that have lost their economic security as a result of globalization. This paper points out some of the problems arising from how easily communication and economic connections can shift within the current global order. As more and more communities are able to connect with each other from greater distances, locally connected centres lose their importance. New, more lucrative opportunities arise elsewhere and capital flies from the community, leaving rural, isolated towns with the challenge of reimagining their functionality in order to survive.

Further challenges come with how easily it is to make connections across the globe. Not only can valued aspects of our lives and community easily move abroad and leave us behind, but we can also be more exposed to dangerous elements from the global arena, such as infectious diseases or terrorists. Given the deep integration of global travel networks into our way of life, the need to shut these down for security reasons creates an impossible dilemma. While Harris Ali points out that health concerns are often silenced in the name of sustaining global movement, Claudio Colaguori and Carlos Torres explore how the 'war on terror' has been used to reorder a number of public and private aspects of life, sometimes drastically limiting individuals' freedom and rights.

CHAPTER 51

United Nations and Early Post-war Development: Assembling World Order

Suzan Ilcan and Rob Aitken

Introduction

The notion of world order remains important to the fields of **international relations** (including development) and globalization studies. As Mitchell Dean notes, world order is a political mythology that enables certain forms of global political action. This chapter contributes to recent attempts, like Dean's, to situate this political mythology in a more complicated critical context. We advance the argument that a liberal governing rationality of rule shaped nascent development practices—that is, specific social and political efforts that consist of governmental actors establishing new ideas and visions for directing and vitalizing vulnerable populations, created various institutional sites, and managed vulnerable and 'other' populations central to emerging conceptions of post-war world order. From our perspective, world order is not a singular kind of project rooted in the power of the U.S. state, but is an assemblage cobbled together out of diverse forms of expertise and initiatives pursued in and across a variety of different institutional sites.

Based on archival and historical research, the chapter examines the **United Nations** (UN) institutions and their post-war development efforts that influenced the notion of **world order** and constituted certain populations for this world order. It analyzes the ways in which certain populations were conceived and administered through liberal and authoritarian governing techniques organized around two UN initiatives key to both post-war planning and early discourses of development: the work related to (1) the role of **mass communication** in the post-war moment associated with both the United Nations Information Organization (UNIO) and the United Nations Educational Scientific and Cultural Organization (UNESCO), and (2) the United Nations Relief and Rehabilitation Administration (UNRRA). More specifically, we argue that a broader conception of world order was assembled in relation to very particular, and quite distinct, rationalities of how populations should be addressed, 'improved', and made vital. The mass communication initiatives first initiated at UNIO and later codified at UNESCO, for example, sought out 'other' populations in terms of a notion of social security and social governance. UNRRA, in contrast, invoked a conception of biopolitical management in its attempt to link human life and world order and to manage certain populations through this linkage. Although both initiatives foregrounded a relationship between population and world order, they assembled this relationship in heterogeneous ways.

I. Social Governance and World Order: Early Mass Communication Initiatives

One of the places where concepts of world order were worked out relates to the role of social citizenship/social security in post-war planning. As Janine Brodie (2008) has noted, the 1930s and 1940s witnessed a novel reformulation of the relationship between state, citizen, and security. This entailed a reworked conception of citizenship in which risk was placed not directly on individuals but was diffused across the social body in techniques of social insurance and social security (see Rose 1999). What we want to argue in this section of the chapter is that a particular rationality of social governance was key to another set of UN initiatives that sought to address post-colonial populations as part of a process of post-war planning: early UN mass communications initiatives organized around UNIO and UNESCO. UNIO was formed in 1941 mainly as a centralized clearinghouse for Allied war information and propaganda pursuits but ultimately became involved in post-war information planning practices. Such practices eventually entailed developing plans regarding the broader role of information in any reconstructed post-war world order. With its emphasis on information broadly constituted—including radio, film, print publications, and mass communications in all its forms—UNIO became interested in a series of broad issues that would be taken up more fully by UNESCO. After the preparatory commission on UNESCO had finished its work, UNIO was disbanded and many of its personnel and interests were directly incorporated into UNESCO.

UN mass communication initiatives centred around UNIO and UNESCO, which helped form a very ambitious plan for the role that communication might play in a reconstructed post-war order. Partly, this ambition was reflective of a broader optimism for the international possibilities of the 'new' communication technologies. As communications advocates argued, the internationalist interest in communication in the interwar period was animated by both deep concern about the global political and economic crises as well as the opportunity to contribute to a reconstructed international economic order. As expressed by one activist, the movement was inextricably bound into stories of (and hopes for) 'the widening horizons of commerce, the complexities of manufacture, and the range of communications: indeed in

all the steam and smoke, dazzle and speed, of the world at hand, and all the strange and sweep of affairs more distant' (qtd. in Sexton 2008, p. 78).

This enthusiasm was particularly targeted to post-colonial populations. Julian Huxley, the first Director of UNESCO, was keen to deploy new technologies 'in all backward sectors . . . to let in light on the world's dark areas' (Huxley 1946, p. 17). Huxley's optimism was tempered, however, by an Orientalist concern that these communication techniques would not be able to overcome difference. For Huxley, 'primitive' cultures were so marked by strangeness, so *different* from the universal culture he sought to promote, that he feared an intractable cultural divide (p. 17; see also Cooper 1946, p. 316).

Despite these concerns, UNIO and UNESCO became preoccupied with the possibilities of communication as a set of technologies with which a new world order could be constituted. For example, UNIO engaged in the massive distribution of educational materials to various educational and labour fields (UNIO 1945). Furthermore, these institutions began to articulate a role for communication in targeting post-colonial populations in relation to forms of social governance. This view assumed mass communications as a kind of rationality through which the requirements of citizenship could be made visible to everyday populations. 'I suggest', Grierson noted, that the key to communication lies 'in the realm of the imaginative training for modern citizenship and not anywhere else' (Grierson 1966a, p. 327; see also Grierson 1966b, 1970).

In film, in particular, Grierson identified what he conceived as an instrument capable of locating citizens within the fabric of the social body. In his ambitious vision, film could mobilize the citizen and 'the far reaches of his social self, however local it may immediately appear. He understands how common to all the world are his problems' (1946, p. 164). Grierson framed film as the practice capable of constituting the visual order necessary to provoke the 'deep alterations' in the categories of citizenship and engagement that the new social world required (1946, p. 163).

Mass communication practices were capable of targeting and addressing post-colonial populations and, by extension, were implicated in both emerging discussions of world order and nascent formulations of development. This is true, albeit in a quite distinct manner, of another key site related to post-war planning: the practices of biopolitical management organized through UNRRA.

II. Expertise and Biopolitical Management: UNRRA Initiatives

UNRRA was the first interwar international organization to deal with international welfare. It was established in 1943 to finance relief and rehabilitation supplies and services in those liberated countries that requested help (Armstrong-Reid and Murray 2008, p. 4) and to care for and resettle specific populations during the interwar and immediate post-war reconstruction and development period (see Ilcan and Lacey 2011). During its five-year existence, from 1943 to 1948, UNRRA relocated and managed millions of persons within the occupied territories in Europe, Southeast Asia, and the Pacific. It set up holding camps to care for the health and well-being of displaced persons, enabled the expert training of local personnel in wartorn countries, and upheld liberal approaches to post-war relief, reconstruction, and development.

UNRRA engaged in a form of politics, biopolitical management, which entails the administration of the processes of the life of populations, including processes that sustain or impede the optimization of the health and welfare of populations (see Dean 2010; Lui 2004, pp. 116–135). This form of politics began shortly after the establishment of UNRRA. At this time, UNRRA set up its Central Tracing Bureau to locate missing, displaced persons with the aim of caring for and repatriating them. UNRRA's notion of care was formulated around international attempts to deal with the population of refugees and displaced persons, which approached 21 million by mid-1943. The organization's key focus centred on the category of 'displaced persons' as a result of the war, which permitted UNRRA to act on certain kinds of populations. A document titled 'Eligibility for UNRRA Care' (UNRRA 1947) stressed that UNRRA would provide care to the population of displaced persons based on certain ideas of displacement in relation to nationality. Stateless persons, nationals of non-enemy countries, and former residents of Estonia, Latvia, and Lithuania (except those of German extraction) were, for example, eligible for UNRRA care if they were 'displaced from their former country or place of origin or former residence by action of the enemy'.

As an integral element of post-war world order and planning, UNRRA facilitated the control of the population of displaced persons by resettling them in camps or assembly centres. In Europe, for example, UNRRA teams entered Italy in mid-1944 and Germany and Austria in the spring of 1945 to gather displaced persons and relocate them to assembly centres. Displaced persons were thought of in terms of population and nationality; these terms, we argue, were fused in UNRRA's biopolitical management of assembly centres and in the broader discourses of post-war reconstruction and development. At each assembly centre, UNRRA administrators focused on the species body by highlighting biological processes (births, mortality, levels of health)— what Foucault (1978, p. 139) calls the 'biopolitics of the population'. In calculating the life of a population, UNRRA officials collected information on the nutritional, medical, and welfare services available to the population of displaced persons, and charted the total number of births, still births, and pregnant women.

The biopolitical management of displaced persons, as a population, necessitated authoritative experts to collect, tabulate, and calculate data that would distinguish particular features of this population. In each assembly, records were kept on unaccompanied children by age and nationality, and on the largest national group. It was through the calculation of such biopolitical information that the domain of assembly centres could be inscribed, visualized, compared with other centres, and its populations assembled. As Rose (2009) stresses, the strategies of calculating the life of a population aimed to identify and control that population.

During the interwar and early post-war period, UNRRA's relief and rehabilitation efforts were increasingly implicated in divisive practices that encouraged and even forced displaced persons to accept repatriation, such as those in the British zone of Germany. A 1946 UNRRA policy document emphasized: 'every effort will be made to preserve . . . the cultural, welfare and educational organizations existing for Displaced Persons. Such organizations will be forbidden to indulge in political activity or to act in such a way as to discourage repatriation' (UNRRA 1946, p. 2). In situations where repatriation was deemed unlikely, UNRRA officials considered it imperative for displaced persons to work full-time on the understanding that it would increase their chance 'to be accepted as an immigrant in another country' over those who were 'idle for a long period' (UNRRA 1947). Displaced persons were often compelled to work full-time as a condition of their receipt of food ration cards (United Nations 1946, p. 2). Until its decline, and as part of building post-war world order, UNRRA initiated health, shelter, food, and resettlement plans through biopolitical management efforts that aimed to direct and shape the population of displaced persons.

Conclusion

As we have demonstrated, emerging notions of world order were tied to a series of preoccupations post-war planners had regarding vulnerable populations and how they could be managed as part of that order. The practices and knowledge related to the management of these populations—knowledge that would form the basis of development—were an integral part of the early conceptions of post-war world order. In this context, the mass communication initiatives first beginning at UNIO and later codified at UNESCO sought out 'other' populations in terms of a notion of social security and social governance. By contrast, UNRRA's international welfare experts and biopolitical management efforts attempted to shape the settlement and well-being of the population of displaced persons for the building of post-war world order. In short, post-war world order was not merely a matter of representation; it was also a matter of intervention. Taking seriously the importance of this diverse assemblage, we argue, permits an understanding of how certain experts, populations, information, and forms of communication entered into the fields, activities, and early development projects of world order.

References

S. Armstrong-Reid and D. Murray (2008) *Armies of Peace: Canada and the UNRRA Years.* Toronto: University of Toronto Press.

J. Brodie (2008) 'From Social Security to Public Safety: Security Discourses and Canadian Citizenship', *University of Toronto Quarterly* 78 (2): 687–708

J.M. Cooper (1946) 'Problems of International Understanding', *Proceedings of the American Philosophical Society* 90(4), Symposia on Present Day Social and Economic Aspects of National Health, and The United Nations Educational, Scientific and Cultural Organization, and American Participation in Its Activities, pp. 314–317

M. Dean (2010) *Governmentality: Power and Rule in Modern Society,* 2nd edition. Los Angeles: Sage.

M. Foucault (1978) *The History of Sexuality: An Introduction.* New York: Pantheon.

J. Grierson (1938) 'The Course of Realism', in *Footnotes to the Film,* Ed. Charles Davy. London: Lovat Dickson Ltd, pp. 137–161.

———. (1946) 'Postwar Patterns', *Hollywood Quarterly* 1(2): 159–165.

———. (1966a) 'The Challenge of Peace', in *Grierson on Documentary,* Ed. Forsyth Hardy. London: Faber and Faber, pp. 317–328.

———. (1966b) 'The Documentary Idea: 1942', in *Grierson on Documentary,* Ed. Forsyth Hardy. London: Faber and Faber, pp. 248–258.

J. Huxley (1946) *Unesco: Its Purpose and Philosophy.* London: Preparatory Commission of Unesco.

S. Ilcan and A. Lacey (2011) *Governing the Poor: Exercises of Poverty Reduction, Practices of Global Aid.* Montreal and London: McGill-Queen's University Press.

R. Lui (2004) 'The international government of refugees', in *Global Governmentality: Governing International Spaces,* Eds. W. Larner and W. Walters. London: Routledge, pp. 116–135.

N. Rose (1999) *Powers of Freedom: Reframing Political Thought.* Cambridge: Cambridge University Press.

————. (2009) *The Politics of Life Itself*. Princeton and Oxford: Princeton University Press

J. Sexton (2008) *Alternative Film Culture in Inter-War Britain*. Exeter: University of Exeter Press.

UNIO (1945) Minutes: Documentary Committee Meeting. 4 December.

United Nations (1946) Policy Instruction No. 2 on the Treatment of Displaced Persons. Issued by Headquarters, Control Commission for Germany (British Element).

UNRRA (1946) Eligibility for UNRRA Care: Analysis Field Order No. 16. 14 May.

————. (1947) Guidance to Camp Commanders and UNRRA Team Directors on Announcement of New Policy towards DPS. Washington: UNRRA.

CHAPTER 52

Policing Terrorism in the Post-9/11 Era: Critical Challenges and Concerns

Claudio Colaguori and Carlos Torres

The Advent of the Post-9/11 Era

Since the terrorist attacks of September 11, 2001, many countries have substantially revised their national policy with regard to policing terrorist activities. The practices involved in combating what is commonly known as the 'war on terrorism' have been controversial and divisive. The state's role in protecting against terrorist attacks has conflicted with its duty to preserve human rights and endorse international law, which has created a paradoxical situation that remains problematic and continues to be a central political issue long after the events of 9/11. The security response to the events of 9/11 has been of such magnitude that it has caused a shift in state priorities and has been cast as a turning point in modern history. The twenty-first century was thus birthed an era of *hypersecurity* (Colaguori, 2005) and radical new interpretations of the rules of warfare, public security, citizenship rights, and state power. The official state response to the events of 9/11 has intensified political debate around numerous issues, from public safety and security to human rights and global poverty. Does the nation-state have justification in reorganizing itself as a surveillance society to face the threat posed by **terrorism** even if this comes at the expense of basic individual liberties and the erosion of democracy? Does the state not have a responsibility to protect its own citizens from terrorist violence? These are the questions that continue to be faced as the war on terror continues to define **geopolitics** at the beginning of the twenty-first century.

The post-9/11 world is an era with its own distinct geopolitics, characterized by intensifications of various forms of conflict. These conflicts include increasing competition over global resource extraction; a growing gap between richer and poorer; various forms of resistance to what is seen as Western imperialist hegemony; and the now infamous 'war on terror', which has further intensified pre-existing tensions in the Middle East and elsewhere. Some argue that these local conflicts have been exacerbated by the U.S.-sponsored international war on terror, while others maintain that the coordinated anti-terrorist efforts of nation-states across the globe have successfully implemented systems for the detection and thwarting of potential terrorist attacks. From new anti-terrorist laws and public policies that work through police intelligence and military efforts all the way to the securitization of public spaces ranging from airports to downtown streets—the focus on policing terrorism has drastically shifted the priority of the state from liberty to security.

It is important to recognize that the post-9/11 era is distinguished by its marked contrast from the era that immediately preceded it. In the 1990s, the dominant political discourse celebrated the ideal of civil society, which was seen to emerge from the globalization of freedom and democracy and the fall of communism. This fin-de-siècle optimism was captured in Francis Fukuyama's (1992) 'end of history' thesis, which understood the fall of Soviet communism (in 1991) as signifying the triumph of free-market capitalism (rather than simply the successful progression of a social movement against communist state oppression). The free-market doctrines that were implemented to further capitalist globalization formed the economic underpinnings of the project of neo-liberalism. There was, however, something missing from the new geopolitical scenario from a capitalist state hegemony point of view. The twentieth century was marred by military conflict that culminated in the Cold War political division of the world into a capitalist bloc set against a Soviet bloc. After the fall of the Soviet bloc, communist nations no longer represented an identifiable threat. When neo-liberal free-market projects failed to deliver a greater economic 'trickle down' to the masses of the global under-wealthed, the events of 9/11 created a pretext for a new type of political consolidation of power. This was achieved through a recasting of the geopolitical spectrum once again into an us-versus-them adversarial contest, also known as the friend/enemy distinction (Schmitt, 1996 [1927]). The reinvention of political hostilities was based not on capitalism versus communism but on a 'clash of civilizations' (Huntington, 1996) between Western capitalist democracy and Islamic fundamentalism—a contest that created new global divisions and the justification for radical forms of state authoritarianism, from the violation of the civil rights of citizens in their home nation to the reinvention of international law and the construction of the adversary as an 'unlawful combatant', a non-citizen, or what Giorgio Agamben (1998) has termed *homo sacer* ('accursed man').

This paper will discuss the challenges and controversies involved in policing terrorism and introduce the reader to the debate between security and liberty—the protection of society from terrorist violence versus the protection of human rights and individual freedoms. The role of the state in balancing this precarious situation has become one of the principal concerns in the analysis of state power in the precarious geopolitics of the post-9/11 era.

The Challenges of Policing Terrorism

The majority of critical analyses of the post-9/11 political state focus on how the practices of state power have extended the repressive dimension of political control at the expense of individual liberty. Functionalist analyses have focused more on the practical problem of how to deal with and respond to the threat posed by terrorist activities, which remains a significant public concern, even if the actual number of deaths caused by terrorist activities is substantially lower than the number of deaths by other means.

However, 'terrorism', referring to the violent actions of fringe groups who work outside of conventional political processes and generate public fear as part of a revolutionary strategy, has now become redefined by many nation states as a type of military strategy, as a mode of warfare. This remains a central problem since the conflict that exists between al Qaeda (and its affiliates) and the United States does not conform to the conventional definition of war. There is no central battlefield and no recognizable army on the 'terrorist' side, and the established rules of warfare, including protocols covered under the Geneva Convention, have been declared invalid and not legally binding.

The threat the West faces in the war on terror conflict is actually a concerted effort of groups from various nations that may be aligned ideologically, even if they do not form a coherent army. This mass participation poses significant problems in the policing of terrorism insofar as it presents an enemy that defies the traditional norms of military engagement. The post-9/11 war on terror has been referred to as **asymmetrical warfare** because of its diffusion across time and space, and because the 'enemy' does not conform to the definition of a state-sponsored army. The main action in the war is the U.S.-led military intervention in Afghanistan and Iraq, a force countered by a network of grassroots armed resistance movements in these nations that has proven to be effective at resisting traditional military domination. Because the war on terror is based on an ideological conflict between Western and Islamic nations, it has also attracted followers who do not reside in the lands where warfare is being played out, and who have carried out terrorist acts of resistance and destabilization on various continents in the non-Islamic world. This sequence of global attack and resistance of course was sparked by the now infamous attacks on the World Trade Center and the Pentagon on September 11, 2001, and intensified by the 2004 train bombings in Madrid and the 2005 public transit attacks in London, as well as by a number of terrorist attacks in Southeast Asia.

It is important to focus on the *asymmetrical* aspect of the war on terror as one of its central difficulties, as the spatial element of the conflict poses problems for policing terrorism from a military and public security standpoint. An asymmetrical military situation is characterized by a loosely defined terrain of battle, an imbalance of firepower between combatants, and a variation in combat strategies, methods, and rules of engagement. Terrorist attacks against conventional military incursions into Afghanistan, for example, may be countered abroad by 'forms of violent action directed against highly visible public targets' (Gurr, 1988: 31) in countries that do not include the homeland of the terrorists themselves. The theatre of war is thus vast, wide-ranging, and impossible to police. Second, the imbalance of firepower between combatants means there will often be dramatic disproportionality in the actions of the better- and worse-equipped sides, leading to gross differences in victimization. Finally, a variation in combat strategies, methods, and rules of engagement means a continued lack of clarity in the traditional proprieties of warfare that go back

at least as far as the Geneva Conventions. This covers matters such as the treatment of war prisoners and the exposure of civilians to harm.

Asymmetrical war also means that the terrorist enemy is not highly visible. In contrast to conventional soldiers who wear the familiar garb of an army, terrorist antagonists are concealed, normalized, and/or inconspicuously merged with the general population. A key strategy of policing the war on terror has to do with the proactive detection and prevention of future terrorist attacks. This is achieved through the intensive monitoring and surveillance of communications, the securing/guarding of public spaces, the monitoring of people who enter potentially sensitive areas, and the gathering of information from suspects and/or about planned suspected activities.

The element of concealment and surprise—another feature of assymetricality—is what makes the war on terror so difficult to manage militarily. It is also what makes it notoriously problematic on the Western home front since identification and detainment of the enemy requires the casting of a wide net on presumed suspects, and as is the case with all forms of war, suspicion is rampant. We encounter the problem of the securitization of the public, including the surveillance of public space; conflicts with innocents through security screening techniques based on ethnic profiling; the costly and dehumanizing arbitrary detention of domestic and foreign travellers; the lengthy and notorious detention and torture of captured suspects who are deemed 'unlawful combatants' and are thus deprived of virtually any legal protections; authoritarian forms of restrictions on normal personal freedoms such as membership on U.S. 'no-fly lists'; lengthy detentions and unlawful deportations of suspects; the increased surveillance of information channels, including the persecution of investigative journalists who are critical of the abuses of security protocols by state agents; the redefinition of civil rights protest groups as potential terrorist groups; and a litany of other human rights violations on a global scale. Numerous nations continue to use their versions of anti-terror legislation to police and punish the dissident activities of citizens who have nothing to do with terrorism or any identifiable terrorist group. The extent to which the new policing powers that governments claim in the war on terror are being exploited to further hegemonic political aims remains an ongoing concern insofar as it has fuelled corruption, fostered abuse of the rule of law, and worked against the promotion of democracy.

Conclusion

The 'war on terror' has been notoriously controversial since it began. Policing terrorism continues to present numerous challenges both at home and in the war zones of Afghanistan and Iraq. Such policing has been criticized for being costly both in an economic sense and in terms of the inherent restrictions it places on human liberty. It is difficult to determine whether or not the anti-terror efforts have been worth the costs paid by Western societies. At one level, there have been very few terrorist attacks that have been successfully carried out since the anti-terror efforts began, and none on North American soil. Whether or not this is actually due to successful policing and military efforts is difficult to ascertain. At another level, the wars against terrorism being waged in Afghanistan in particular, and to a lesser extent in Iraq, have been criticized as actions that have increased military recruitment in Muslim countries and increased anti-Western sentiment and thus have actually multiplied terrorist threats as well as killed, injured, and displaced thousands of innocents. After almost a decade of the same counter-terrorist strategies and hyper-security policies from Western nations, and the fears and failures inherent in them, it remains to be seen whether a new paradigm of world security and civility will emerge in the near future.

References

Agamben, Giorgio. 1998. *Homo Sacer: Sovereign Power and Bare Life*. Stanford: Stanford University Press.

Colaguori, Claudio. 2005. 'The Prison Industrial Complex and Social Division in Market Societies: The Hyper-Security State, Crime and Expendable Populations', pp. 353–370 in L.A. Visano, ed., *Law and Criminal Justice: A Critical Inquiry*. Toronto: Athenian Policy Forum Press.

Fukuyama, Francis. 1992. *The End of History and the Last Man*. London: Penguin Books.

Gurr, Ted Robert. 1988. 'Some Characteristics of Political Terrorism in the 1960s', pp. 31–57 in Michael Stohl, ed., *The Politics of Terrorism*, 3rd ed. New York: Marcel Dekker.

Huntington, Samuel. 1996. *The Clash of Civilizations and the Remaking of World Order*. New York: Simon and Schuster.

Schmitt, Carl. 1996 [1927]. *The Concept of the Political*. Chicago: University of Chicago Press.

Weber, Max. 1978 [1947]. *Economy and Society: An Outline of Interpretive Sociology*, Volume 1. Berkeley: University of California Press.

CHAPTER 53

Infectious Disease, Environmental Change, and Social Control

Harris Ali

Introduction

Throughout history, significant changes in the character and types of relationships that human beings have had with nature—particularly animals and the wilderness—have led to changes in the development and spread of infectious diseases. McMichael (2001) outlines how, for instance, a change 10,000 years ago in settlement patterns from nomadic hunting and gathering to settled agrarian-village living enabled countless strains of bacteria and viruses to jump from domesticated herd animals and rodents to relatively stationary human beings. Indeed, many existing infectious diseases that affect human beings today, including smallpox, measles, tuberculosis, leprosy, influenza, the common cold, malaria, dengue fever, and the bubonic plague, can be traced to this historic period of transition. Subsequently, other changes such as an increase in trade, travel, and military movements via the great powers of the Roman Empire and China, beginning around 2000 years ago, and the expansion of colonialism during the seventeenth to nineteenth centuries, led to further changes in the patterns of infectious disease spread. McMichael (2001) speculates that we may be entering a fourth transitional period in the ever-changing environment–human relationship—a new epoch informed by globalization.

Some significant evidence supports this claim. Consider the fact that over the last quarter-century, the world has witnessed an unprecedented number of 'new and (re) emerging' diseases. Examples of these abound: HIV/AIDS, **severe acute respiratory syndrome** (SARS), *E. coli* 0157:H7, *Clostridium difficile*, West Nile virus, Lyme disease, antibiotic-resistant tuberculosis, the Ebola virus, and avian influenza (Levy and Fishchetti, 2003; Nikiforuk, 2006). In what follows, I briefly explore various aspects of the hypothesized relationship between globalization and infectious disease emergence by broadening the focus of discussion to consider the implications of globalization, and the associated developments of urbanization, neo-liberalization, and post-9/11 securitization, for understanding new and emerging diseases.

Globalization

Held et al. (2002), conceptualize globalization as the general transformations involved in the organization of human affairs that occur because of, and through, the linking together and expansion of human activity across regions and continents. In these terms, the international spread of infectious diseases such as SARS or influenza A/H1N1 is clearly a globalized phenomenon in several respects. First, it can be noted the networks of social contacts involved in the spatial diffusion of these diseases were quite extensive, involving long and extended chains of transmission connecting southern China to Toronto, or Mexico City to northern Canada (with reference to the SARS and influenza A/H1N1, respectively). At the same time, the intensity and velocity of the globalized flows of infectious disease were critically involved in the spread of these diseases, with the increased volume of passenger flow, coupled with the increased speed of jet travel, effectively heightening the risk of global infection. Furthermore, with globalization, the number of opportunities for the global spread of disease multiply. In the past, if the crossover to human beings of the SARS coronavirus from the civet cat, or influenza A/H1N1 virus from the pig, occured in some remote location, this would result only in a localized and contained outbreak in an isolated village—an event that would ultimately burn itself out and prevent the diseases from spreading beyond the confines of that locale. Today, however, because of globalized connectivity, such protective insularity and isolation no longer exist to the extent they once did, and an outbreak of a disease in a remote area is more likely to spread to more populated areas and therefore have a much greater potential for global impacts (Ali and Keil, 2008).

Urbanization, the Built Environment, and Infectious Disease

The United Nations (2007) has noted that, as of the year 2008, more than half of the world's population will live in cities. This development has important implications for the spread of infectious diseases. With their large number of people and crowded conditions, cities are well suited to the survival needs of pathogens. Furthermore, the physical environment of cities, including their infrastructure and transportation patterns, serve to open up new avenues for spatial diffusion and proliferation. In a sense, due to the very nature of their built infrastructure, cities are consciously constructed as both internally and externally connected entities, and it is this connectedness that makes human beings vulnerable to infectious disease spread. This built environment influence was seen in at least a couple of ways with respect to the 2003 multi-nation SARS epidemic. First, a community outbreak among 300 residents of the Amoy Gardens apartment complex in Hong Kong was found to have occurred because of transmission of the virus through a vertical sewage pipe that connected the washrooms, positioned one atop the

other (Ng, 2008). Second, the international spread of SARS was clearly dependent on air travel, thereby implicating the built infrastructure of airports as connecting hubs (Ali and Keil, 2010). Notably, the spread of SARS illustrated how the location of major hubs in certain types of cities—that is, what are referred to as 'global cities'—was instrumental in spreading the disease through the global network of connections between Hong Kong, Toronto, and Singapore (Ali and Keil, 2006).

Neo-liberalization and Infectious Disease Flow

Toward the goal of completely eliminating state intervention in the provision of goods and services (i.e., the economy), neo-liberal policies and activities often promote the privatization of state functions, including the outsourcing and downloading of state functions to private agencies and the elimination of environmental, industrial, trade, and health regulations viewed as costly barriers to privatized profit maximization. Although these are all matters of a political nature that seem distant from the types of issues related to disease flows, neo-liberalization has in fact had a significant impact on infectious disease flows by influencing the health and economic policies and regulations that ultimately channel these flows through the environment. An example will help illustrate this point.

In the summer of 2000, the town of Walkerton, Ontario, experienced an outbreak of E. coli 0157:H7 that was causally related to the Ontario government's neo-liberal policy, known at the time as the 'Common Sense Revolution' (Ali, 2004). The outbreak event, resulting from the contamination of drinking water by the bacteria, notably occurred at a time when drinking water management in the province was being deregulated and privatized. As a consequence of such systemic changes, the provincial government agencies and laboratories that were responsible for the testing of samples from municipal drinking water supplies were being downsized and subject to heavy staff cuts. These government services had in fact just been privatized at the time of the outbreak, and rural municipalities such as Walkerton—with a sparse population and therefore a weak tax revenue base—simply could not afford the costs of regular privatized water testing (a monitoring function previously performed by the provincial government). In part as a consequence of these developments, the contamination of the drinking water was not detected in a timely fashion, and even when detected, efforts to curb the flow of the pathogen were hindered by a lack of resources resulting from budget and staff cuts.

Securitization and Infectious Disease Flow

Social control has always been an important aspect of the state's approach to dealing with infectious disease, and this is clearly seen in the case of the 2003 SARS epidemic with regard to the adoption of contact tracing–based social distancing methods (i.e., quarantine and isolation) by state-run public health agencies. Social control however, has also led to tension with other governance functions with which the state is involved—primarily, the maintenance of continued economic growth. That such tension still persists today is evidenced by the fact that travel advisories were issued by the World Health Organization—warning travellers not to travel to SARS-affected areas such as Toronto. Such advisories were politically contentious and were met with disapproval by Canadian officials who feared severe economic consequences to the hospitality, tourism, and other sectors of its domestic economy. Security from public health threats has increasingly been recognized as a precondition for the stabilization of economic activity, and in this light security measures may be somewhat grudgingly tolerated by state actors. This toleration of security measures may have intensified to an all-encompassing embrace after the events of September 11, 2001, as a newly renewed emphasis on issues of surveillance, vigilance, and security now play a prominent role in an environment of crisis politics sometimes referred to as the 'new normal' (Hooker and Ali, 2009). Within this

world view, public health and terrorism issues become conflated under the mantle of 'national security'. The explicit reframing of public health as a security issue may be seen, for example, in a report developed for the U.S. Central Intelligence Agency that framed the possibility of new infectious diseases as a threat to the nation (CIA, 2003) or in the fact that public health emergencies figure prominently in Canada's first national security policy (Van Wagner, 2008). Furthermore, it has been noted that in the post-9/11 era, a focus on bioterror and infectious diseases as security threats has led to a renewed interest in traditional social control measures associated with national security, such as border control and intelligence capabilities (King, 2002). Examples of the adoption of such measures can be seen in the national and international response to the spread of SARS.

A notable example of this emphasis on enhanced surveillance is evident in the recommendation of the World Health Organization that airports in SARS-affected areas adopt certain monitoring practices, including temperature screening of departing and transiting passengers, the provision of information leaflets to travellers, exit questioning, and the completion of a mandatory health declaration form by passengers (Ali and Keil, 2010).

Conclusion

Over the last quarter century, as globalization has intensified, significant changes have occurred that have had important implications for the genesis and spread of infectious diseases as well as the response to these developments. The increased speed of travel, a greater degree of human migration, intensified urbanization, and increasing human encroachment on untouched natural habitats have all enhanced the potential for pathogens to spread internationally in very short periods of time. Furthermore, interactions of these developments with other contemporary dimensions of societal change, such as neo-liberalization and securitization, have contributed to a situation of enhanced vulnerability to disease spread as new opportunities and pathways are opened up in response to these interactions.

References

Ali, S. Harris (2004) 'A Socio-Ecological Autopsy of the *E. coli* 0157:H7 Outbreak in Walkerton, Ontario, Canada'. *Social Science and Medicine* 58(12):2601–12.

Ali, S. Harris and Roger Keil (2010) 'Securing Network Flows: Infectious Disease and Airports'. In S. Graham and S. Marvin (eds.) *Disrupted Cities: When Infrastructure Fails.* New York: Routledge. Pages 97–110.

———. (2008) *Networked Disease: Emerging Infections in the Global City.* Oxford: Wiley-Blackwell.

Ali, S. Harris and Roger Keil (2006) 'Global Cities and the Spread of Infectious Disease: The Case of Severe Acute Respiratory Syndrome (SARS) in Toronto, Canada'. *Urban Studies* 43(3):491–509.

CIA (Central Intelligence Agency) (2003), *SARS: Lessons from the First Epidemic of the 21st Century: A Collaborative Analysis with Outside Experts (Unclassified).* 29 September, Office of Transnational Issues.

Held, D., A. McGrew, D. Goldblatt and J. Perraton (2002) 'Rethinking Globalization'. In D. Held and A. McGrew (eds.) *The Global Transformation Reader: An Introduction to the Globalization Debate*, 2nd edition. Oxford: Blackwell.

Hooker, Claire and S. Harris Ali (2009) 'SARS and Security: Health in the New Normal'. *Studies in Political Economy* 84(Autumn):101–26.

King, Nicholas B. (2002) 'Security, Disease, Commerce: Ideologies of Postcolonial Global Health'. *Social Studies of Science* 32(5/6):763–80.

Levy, Elinor and Mark Fischetti (2003) *The New Killer Diseases: How the Alarming Evolution of Germs Threatens Us.* New York: Three Rivers Press.

McMichael, A.J. (2001) 'Human Culture, Ecological Change and Infectious Disease: Are We Experiencing History's Fourth Great Transition'. *Ecosystem Health* 7(2):107–15.

Nikiforuk, Andrew (2006) *Pandemonium: Bird Flu, Mad Cow Disease and Other Biological Plagues of the 21st Century.* Toronto: Viking Press.

Ng, M.K. (2008) 'Globalization and SARS and Health Governance in Hong Kong under "One Country, Two Systems"'. In S. Harris Ali and Roger Keil (eds.) *Networked Disease: Emerging Infections in the Global City.* Oxford: Wiley-Blackwell. Pages 70–85.

United Nations Population Fund (2007) 'UNFPA State of World Population 2007: Unleashing the Potential of Urban Growth', www.unfpa.org/swp/2007/english/introduction.html, Accessed 1 April 2008.

Van Wagner, Estair (2008) 'The Practice of Biosecurity in Canada: Public Health Legal Preparedness and Toronto's SARS Crisis' *Environment and Planning A* 40(7): 1647–1663.

CHAPTER 54

Does a Place Like This Still Matter? Remaking Economic Identity in Post-Resource Communities

Nathan Young

Introduction

The images of rural Canada that most of us grew up with have largely faded into history. For example, the past 35 years have witnessed a steep decline in small-scale family farming, as the economics of agriculture in a globalized world have privileged large, industrialized farms with lower costs per unit of production. The same trend can be observed in resource industries such as fisheries, in which the increasing costs of licences and equipment are driving out smaller operators and processors. In short, rural Canada is in the midst of profound changes, one result of which is that many traditional industries no longer employ the numbers they once did.

The causes of these changes have been well-documented elsewhere (e.g. Boyens 2003; Young 2008; Parkins and Reed, forthcoming). The great unanswered question, however, is: What comes next for rural Canada? British sociologist Terry Marsden has argued that the pressures of economic **globalization** are pushing rural regions across the developed world away from **production activities** (agriculture, natural resources, manufacturing), and toward **consumption activities** (tourism, recreation, arts and culture) whose geographical distribution is uneven but that are potentially quite lucrative. But while Marsden's (1999) 'consumption countryside' is readily observable in the tamer rural spaces of Europe, given Canada's vast distances and landscapes, most rural communities in this country are unable to follow places such as St. Jacob's, Ontario, and Nelson, British Columbia, down this path. For most rural towns and villages in Canada, the future remains uncertain.

This short chapter looks at what happens to people's identities under these conditions of uncertainty, based on field research carried out in 2004–2007 in two isolated communities in British Columbia—Port Hardy and Bella Coola (see Figure 54.1). Both communities are classic resource towns that have been particularly dependent on forestry and fisheries. I argue that the decline of older economic identities tied to resource industries has been traumatic but at the same time has opened up space for new and competing visions of the future and community revitalization.

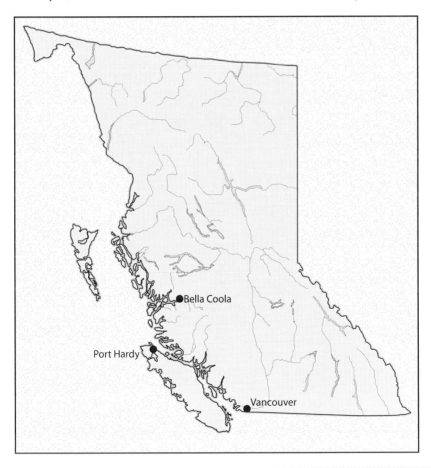

Figure 54.1

Port Hardy and Bella Coola as Places that Mattered

The economic system that dominated in much of rural British Columbia into the 1990s was deeply exploitative, both environmentally and economically (Marchak 1983). Variously labelled Fordist, corporatist, or command-and-control, this system was based on a *centre–periphery* model, in which local production was tightly controlled by government and corporate officials headquartered in cities (Markey et al. 2005). Recently, this economic system has weakened and been partially replaced by one that is more flexible but less reliant on local labour, preferring to use temporary or non-resident 'fly-in/fly-out' workforces (Young 2008; Markey 2010).

One consequence of these changes is that a wedge has been driven between space and place in many rural regions. When asked about community identity, the most common response from interview participants was some variant on 'this is a fishing and logging town'. In many cases, however, this rote answer later gave way to one that touched upon the deeper relationship between the community (place) and the region (space):

> The reason that we're here is because of all this. *[Gestures towards landscape].* I don't think that people [in the cities] understand that at all. . . . We're not just points on the map. . . . People [in the cities] ask: 'Why would you want to live there, in the middle of nowhere?' But we're here not because it's far [but] because it's close to what we do, you dumb-dumbs!
> (Male business operator, Bella Coola)

The importance of the link between the community and the region is also demonstrated in comments about what has changed over the past decade and more. In the following interview excerpts, economic identity is framed around the perceived role of the community as the master of the region. This is significant because, under the Fordist economic system, both communities were centres for public and private regional administration within the overall centre–periphery arrangement.

> It seems strange to say right now, but this place used to be exciting. . . . This is all gone now. Bella Coola *was* the centre of the central coast [region], [but] not anymore. . . . We're a bit on our own now, and some people feel really lost.
> (Female community leader and business owner, Bella Coola)

> I don't know how successful Port Hardy can be even in keeping what's still here. . . . We're just less important than before.
> (Male business leader, Port Hardy)

The sentiment that 'this used to be an important place' is now common across many parts of rural Canada (e.g. Sinclair 1999). As economic changes undermine the traditional role of rural communities as producers of wealth, many rural people resist these changes by engaging in 'place-making' activities—reimagining the value of the community in a way that reasserts that 'this place matters' (Gille and O'Riain 2002). This type of imaginative place-making can be a tool for economic development, because it can spur new ideas and rally a community around a collective vision of the future. On the other hand, place-making can cause division, confusion, and conflict as rural people grapple with alternative futures.

Place-Making: Visions of Rootedness and Flow

I argue that the shock of economic change is engendering two general forms of place-making imagination in Bella Coola and Port Hardy. The first, and more conservative (in the traditional sense of the term), envisions the establishment of 'contained spaces'—spaces of intense locality that are separate or somehow removed from the (global) market economy. This imagination is more prominent among community leadership in Bella Coola. The second form of place-making is better recognizable in Port Hardy, and envisions intensified community participation in global economies. Both visions are ways of asserting the value of the community despite recent experiences of spatial and economic devaluation.

Finding Virtue in (Enclosed) Places: Visions of Rootedness

David Harvey (1996) has argued that one of the most significant reactions to globalization—to the speeding up and spreading out of economic and cultural activities—has been for people to embrace ideas about boundaries, stability, and control. The interview research found ample evidence of this in both communities. Foremost, the imagination of contained spaces involves an affirmation of locality. Even if the economic value of the community has been diminished (in the eyes of outsiders), locality is seen as a source of untapped worth and wealth. In the words of one Port Hardy business owner,

> I think it's time we started looking inwards for answers [to economic problems] rather than outwards. Outwards hasn't done us much good, right? . . . Even if everything closed down tomorrow we could be self-sufficient. You can't say that about the cities, right? We could live here on what's here. And probably prosper better than we have yet, too.
>
> (Male business owner, Port Hardy)

A concrete example of place-making in this way involves the recent founding of an agricultural society in Bella Coola, which was established in 2003 on a narrative of **self-sufficiency**. In the words of a leader of this group,

> The goal is to have this place become in some way self-sufficient. We can farm anything and everything [in this climate and soil] except tropical fruit.
>
> (Female community leader, Bella Coola)

Self-sufficiency in this case has obvious connections to **subsistence** activities (although it is important to note that settler communities on the Pacific coast have less of a tradition of subsistence

work than those on the Atlantic). However, subsistence does not appear to be the main goal of the society. Another active member described the intent as follows:

> I don't think the goal is to close down the grocery store [for lack of business]. It's about breathing life back into the history of this place. . . . Restoring a bit of pride in this place. . . . Showing ourselves that we can do things together without relying on outside help.
>
> (Male community leader, Bella Coola)

Open Spaces: Visions of Movement and Flow

In contrast to the visions of contained spaces, both Port Hardy and Bella Coola are also home to strong visions of open movement and flow. These imaginations are experiences in place-making as well, in that they advance an identity for the community within a larger spatial framework (in this case, *as part of* rather than separate from larger economies). In similar fashion to the imagination and establishment of contained spaces, the construction of 'open' spaces encapsulates a desire to reassert that 'this place matters' in the wider economy.

The imagination of movement and flow is often expressed in abstract visions of connection and connectivity. For instance, in several of the interviews conducted with community leadership in Bella Coola, the decline in the community is framed as a problem of connectivity with extra-local actors and markets.

> For me, the priorities for this place ought to be: one, to get a fixed link to Vancouver Island [from Vancouver]. That'll put more traffic on the ferry [to Bella Coola]. Two, to build an alternative [road] route out of here. Three, to get a satisfactory level of electronic communication in here. . . . These moves would go a long way to helping us out economically. . . . We just need to get more connected.
>
> (Male community leader, Bella Coola)

Such visions of connectivity are also strongly held in Port Hardy. For example, at the time of interviewing in Port Hardy, in 2005–2006, several community leaders spoke of recent local efforts to develop a foreign investment strategy to take advantage of perceived global interests in the community:

> It's a big wide world right now. But we're not used to thinking that way, eh? I know it sounds funny to talk about it this way [right now], but there's never been more opportunity. If we can get our act together, the [foreign investment strategy] will open doors for us we never knew existed before.
>
> (Male community leader, Port Hardy)

One of the great injustices of traditional resource production was that local wealth was exported into international markets without local participation or involvement. The retrenchment of these institutions, therefore, is seen by some as both a crisis and a long overdue liberation. According to this view, it has already been proven that communities such as Port Hardy and Bella Coola have resources that the world wants, and now there is a unique opportunity to make these connections directly. The value of place can be unleashed if it has more rather than less contact with the global.

Conclusion

Rural people are not just the victims of change, but also its authors, which means that what comes next in rural Canada will have much to do with the vision and creativity of the regions' residents. Fieldwork in Port Hardy and Bella Coola, British Columbia, identified two predominant 'identity responses' to the sudden demotion of these communities from status as regional centres in a vibrant if problematic resource economy. The first response involves a valourization of locality and place. This narrative, which is more evident in Bella Coola, puts a strong emphasis on self-sufficiency. Against the idea that the community has been abandoned, adherents to this view recast the community as a privileged place that can take care of itself. The second response, more prominent in Port Hardy, envisions a future of direct connectivity with the global economy. This narrative sees the retrenchment of corporate and government institutions as an opportunity (albeit one tainted by hardship) for the community to negotiate its own external relationships and become more integrated with global and regional economies. In a sense, these visions compete with one another. In another sense, however, they are in fact rather similar, as both are exercises in 'place-making' or reasserting the value of the community in the face of changes that have left these places without obvious economic roles.

References

Boyens, I. 2003. *Another Season's Promise*. Toronto: Penguin Books.

Gille, Z. and S. O'Riain. 2002. Global Ethnography. *Annual Review of Sociology* 28: 271–295.

Harvey, D. 1996. *Justice, Nature and the Geography of Difference*. Cambridge, MA: Blackwell.

Marchak, P. 1983. *Green Gold: The Forestry Industry in British Columbia*. Vancouver: UBC Press.

Markey, S. 2010. Fly-In, Fly-Out Resource Development: A New Regionalist Perspective on The Next Rural Economy. In G. Halseth, S. Markey, and D. Bruce (eds.) *The Next Rural Economies: Constructing Place in Global Economies*. CABI: Cambridge, MA, 239–250.

Markey, S., Pierce, J., Vodden, K., and Roseland, M. 2005. *Second Growth: Community Economic Development in Rural British Columbia*. Vancouver: UBC Press.

Marsden, T. 1999. Rural Futures: The Consumption Countryside and Its Regulation. *Sociologia Ruralis* 39(4): 501–520.

Parkins, J. and Reed, M. Forthcoming. *The Social Transformation of Rural Canada*. Vancouver: UBC Press.

Sinclair, P. 1999. A Future without Fish? In D. Newell and R. Ommer (eds.) *Fishing People, Fishing Places*. Toronto: U of T Press, 321–339.

Young, N. 2008. Radical Neoliberalism in British Columbia. *Canadian Journal of Sociology* 33(1): 1–36.

Questions for Critical Thought

CHAPTER 51

1. What do Ilcan and Aitken mean by 'world order'?
2. How were early mass communication strategies (like that of UNIO and UNESCO) used to reconfigure the relationships between citizen, state, and security? What were the strategies' goals? Consider various examples, such as education or film.
3. What were the biopolitical strategies of UNRRA? Compare and contrast the biopolitical strategies discussed by Ilcan and Aitken to those discussed in another paper in this volume that has used the term *biopolitical* (e.g. Stepnisky or Hardy).
4. The emerging relationship between vulnerable/wartorn countries and powerful/war-winning countries is central to Ilcan and Aitken's argument. Describe this relationship and how it affects development. How is this relationship still present between developed/rich countries and underdeveloped/poor countries? Has it changed?
5. Ilcan and Aitken point out that the UN employed communication and biopolitical strategies to care for various populations. Imagine for a moment what these populations (post-war/displaced people) needed. How did the UN's strategies help meet some of those needs? How did they not help meet others?

CHAPTER 52

1. According to Colaguori and Torres, how is the post-9/11 world different from the pre-9/11 world?
2. How was the geopolitical spectrum changed by 9/11? Who are the new global enemies? How have they been used to justify authoritarian state policies?
3. Discuss the security and liberty dilemma in Western nations.
4. People can hold different opinions regarding the security/liberty dilemma depending on what issue is being discussed. Compare the dilemma as it pertains to global health (see Ali's paper in this section) and terrorism. Do you support different sides of the dilemma for each issue? Discuss.
5. How does terrorism defy traditional conceptions of war? What are the limitations of established war conventions and laws (such as the Geneva Convention) when it comes to terrorism?
6. How is the war on terror asymmetrical? How does this asymmetry invite states to violate human rights?
7. Colaguori and Torres briefly suggest that the practical challenges of the war on terror may be exploited and abused in a way that damages democracy and rule of law. How do you think politicians could carry out such abuse? Do you know of any contemporary examples where you think this has happened? If so, discuss.

CHAPTER 53

1. How has the changing relationship between humans and nature affected infectious diseases throughout history? Use examples from Ali's paper.
2. Ali argues that the main impact globalization has had on infectious disease is through increased connectivity. Explain how connectivity (on both a global level and an urban level) affects disease flows, using an example from the paper (e.g. SARS or H1N1).
3. How do deregulation and neo-liberal policies increase connectivity and thus disease flow? Why is social control important in reducing the impact of infectious disease?
4. Ali also points out the importance of political policies in affecting the flow of infectious diseases. In many ways, the 'common sense revolution' and the 'new normal' are opposite ways of dealing with disease. Compare and contrast the policies emerging from these two perspectives. What do they each achieve? What are the costs of each?
5. Consider the dilemma experienced by Toronto's health officials during the SARS outbreak: on the one hand, spreading SARS endangers people's lives; but on the other, a quarantine can jeopardize the jobs of people in some domestic industries. Discuss this dilemma and any ideas you may have about how to resolve it.

CHAPTER 54

1. How has globalization made the future increasingly uncertain for rural Canadian communities? What are some opportunities that have arisen from the retrenchment of certain economic organizations?
2. Explain why some argue that rural communities need to move from production to consumption economies. Is this a reliable way forward for all rural communities? Why or why not?
3. What are 'place-making' activities? How are they sources of both development and division for communities?
4. Compare the two alternative place-making projects that Young explores in Bella Coola and Port Hardy. How do they each propose that the community relate to the global economy?
5. Young focuses on identities, but action is also very important to place-making projects. How do the two place-making identity projects discussed in the article lead to different actions on behalf of the communities?

Part XIV

States and Government

For humans, living together in large communities is not easy. There are some problems that just can't be resolved by individuals alone—they require collective coordination and action. Communities have always had political processes for getting us to co-operate, and for making decisions regarding collective resources, deciding on and enforcing right and wrong, and working out disagreements. We are embedded within a number of these systems within all of the groups we live in: our friendships, families, workplaces, and countries all have to develop ways to deal with collective challenges. Consider the difference between families or friendships that you have experienced: they foster more or less co-operation and sharing between members, and some ignore disagreements until they blow up into conflict that breaks the group apart, while others develop ways to deal with these conflicts before they do serious damage. Modern nation-states face challenges similar to those we experience in our face-to-face relationships. Bureaucratic governments and elected officials are tasked with managing order among huge groups of people, and as in friendships, families, and workplaces, there are many ways in which a country can structure its political processes.

But these giant social units face unique problems. On a basic level, it is hard to coordinate millions of people who live at large distances from each other, and who will likely never even meet, let alone be able to discuss every nationally relevant issue in depth together. As Kevin Walby and Michael Haan point out, the attempt to obtain even basic information about citizens poses intractable problems. Accurate information is absolutely key to the development of effective government policy, and yet we can never acquire all of the needed information in such large communities. This paper shows that as states fumble through making their data on populations manageable (in this case, by counting castes in India), they actively take part in enforcing and changing the ways citizens understand themselves and each other.

Nation-states also face the problem of responding to citizens' will. In democracies, we assume that governments are to be responsive to the desires of their citizens, acting on behalf of them rather than ruling over them as royalty or dictators. But in reality, the responsiveness of policy to public opinion is erratic. Dissecting the relationship between government policies, public opinion, and economic trends, Robert Andersen and Josh Curtis's findings suggest that public opinion is somewhat responsive to material conditions, but that Canadian government policies often did the opposite of what citizens wanted during the years of their study.

The challenge to express the will of the citizens is made even more difficult when our collective life has different effects on different segments of the population; we can become very divided as governments make decisions that can benefit some individuals and groups at the expense of others. And what could be harder than dealing with a divided nation? Imagine trying to coordinate *multiple* divided nations, whose interests can be drastically different. As we saw in the section on globalization, many supra-national organizations have formed in the last few decades. Ivanka Knezevic considers the challenges and contradictions inherent in transitioning previously sovereign European countries into a coordinated European Union.

But bureaucratic states and supra-states do not have a monopoly on governing social change and collective order. Dominique Clément asks us to pay attention to the role that contemporary social movements play in governing and changing our collective lives.

CHAPTER 55

Counting, Caste, and Confusion during Census Enumeration in Colonial India

Kevin Walby and Michael Haan

Introduction

Censuses are massive attempts to count and categorize widely scattered groups of people, and late-nineteenth century enumerations in India were no exception. None of the data categories from this era in India was as confusing as **caste**; when British colonial censuses were first taken in India in 1871, caste data could not possibly have been compiled into a national list, because many castes only appeared in one or two parts of India. By 1921, however, this had all changed; there were national lists to streamline the upcoming headcount and to massage the collected data. But how did this radical transformation occur? To answer this question, we draw upon archival research conducted at the British National Library in London. We examine the correspondence of census officials as well as numerous reports concerning caste data in the Indian censuses. What we find is that caste data were read with an eye to creating a national social hierarchy, but that this often contradicted the local and regional character of caste.

We became interested in this topic, in part, because of the writings of Ian Hacking (1990) on what he calls 'making people up'. Hacking discusses how knowledge practices such as census taking create categories that have no innate footing but become powerful ways to characterize, classify, and count groups of people. When applied to populations through various social practices, classificatory frameworks loop back to guide and govern the lives of the people they purport to describe.

Caste interpretations in the Indian censuses are a key example of this process. Below, we argue, following Curtis (1994: 418), that censuses are 'made, not taken, fabricated through processes that select, and do not simply reflect dimensions of social organization', and that this had a profound impact on how caste was subsequently conceptualized. Although there are no doubt religious and economic antecedents to caste categories, how caste is understood today was and is mediated by the process of census enumeration. Caste was not created by the census, but attempts at redefining caste were made during the process. These reclassifications altered the way India was envisioned by the colonial government. More broadly, by documenting the case of British colonial censuses in India, we suggest that historical sociology provides a context for understanding how pervasive categories and classifications that seem 'natural' today were shaped in the past.

Caste and the Indian Colonial Censuses

For a good part of India's colonial history, British rule was exercised through the East India Company, a quasi-governmental commercial company operating in India. As early as 1687, the company was counting people in the regions under its control. In 1806, for example, the court of directors of the East India Company wrote to their servants in Bengal that they wanted a statistical survey of the country carried out. The East India Company lost its trade monopoly in 1813. Following the company's demise, a national census was one of the first proposed activities of the Indian colonial government. Due to the uprisings of 1857, however, the national census initiative planned for 1861 was suspended in 1859, and plans for a general census were postponed.

Discussions about a national census soon resumed. India's first census was prefaced by provincial pilot tests, but there was no consistency across the provinces concerning the category of caste. Categories were borrowed from regional census efforts, or from other knowledge sources. For instance, the *Report of Census of the Island of Bombay 1864* noted, 'The castes and races have been grouped in the way followed in the Mortuary Registration' (p. ix). Administrators recognized the lack of consistency, yet the records indicate no efforts to come up with an alternative, leaving local enumerators to improvise, which resulted in irreconcilable caste schedules.[1] Nor were local peoples receptive to the early provincial census efforts. For example, during the 1866 Census of Calcutta, 'The general impression that prevailed amongst the lower classes of Natives [was] that the object of the census was the imposition of some new tax' (*Report on the Census of Calcutta* 1866: 1). This quotation not only demonstrates the existence of local opposition to the census, but reflects the paternalistic outlook of colonial administrators.

Eventually, the Government of India allowed a general enumeration to be taken in 1871. The London Statistical Society was called upon to help design the first Indian national census, forming a subcommittee to design a template. The society had been helping the British government since 1841 with its censuses across England. Near London, at Haileybury College, administrators were introduced to statistical knowledge for the purpose of assisting with colonial governance in India.

There was debate about what the census schedule should look like. The least objectionable schedule recommended by the London

Statistical Society was designed by W.C. Plowden, who served as the 1871 census commissioner for the northwestern provinces. Several of the 1871 census questions were open-ended, in that many questions had no fixed response categories. Enumerators were instructed to write down the responses of the enumerated, regardless of any apparent absurdities. If the person did not know his or her age (and most respondents did not), the enumerator was told to estimate. The 1871 census was nowhere near nationally synchronous. Many provinces adapted the census procedures to suit local conditions, whereas other provinces asked only a portion of Plowden's recommended items. Later commentators said that the only consistency in the 1871–1872 Indian census was the 'uniform absence of uniformity' (Ibbetson 1883: 10).

Caste data were disastrous. One problem was that local provincial officials patterned their *own* categorization on pre-existing understandings of caste, which were not nationally consistent. The consensus among census officials was that the main problem with caste calculations was 'due partly to the intrinsic difficulties on the subject, and partly to the absence of a uniform plan of classification' (Waterfield 1875: 27). The shortcomings of India's first 'national' census led to a flurry of recommendations from British colonial administrators and statistical experts. As Plowden (1873: lxxviii) put it, 'The whole question of caste is so confused, and the difficulty of securing correct returns on this subject is so great, that I hope on another occasion no attempt will be made to attempt to obtain information as to the castes and tribes of the population.'

Administrators wanted to prevent a repeat of the 1871 debacle. Seeking national-level statistics were of little use as long as many categories remained local. The administrative solution was to abstract caste from its locality and project it to aggregate India. By unyoking caste from its geographical location and centralizing its classifications, the Indian census officials detached caste from its indigenous meaning and used it to reinforce their own ideas about India. Many caste names disappeared in the abstraction process. Of the nearly 2,000 castes listed in 1881, for instance, the general report for that same year identified only 207 castes (Maheshwari 1996: 106).

Another issue that troubled administrators was that some enumerators were introducing caste names to people when those caste names had no prior usage in those communities, a practice that occurred throughout the censuses of 1881 and 1891. The 1881 *Report on the Census of the Panjab* discusses the perils of determining the 'degree of discretion to be allowed to the enumerators and supervising staff in rejecting answers given by the people and recording what they believe to be the truth' (Vol. 1: 485). In Panjab, an indigenous tribe known as the Syals was labelled as Rajputs, even though 'not one man in a hundred of the Syals is aware that he is a Rajput' (p. 189). Due to this caste confusion, Plowden sent a letter to the undersecretary of state for India in 1888, calling for caste to be removed from the next census. Another census official, J.A. Baines, argued in 1899 correspondence, 'I am inclined to advise the omission of caste from the Imperial schedule, and to make use of the returns of 1891 as a standard until 1911.' The tension between the pragmatics of administration on the ground and the broad imperial objectives of accumulating knowledge for the governance of populations led Plowden and Baines to suggest removing caste from the census. As a category, it just didn't map onto Indian reality.

Making People Up through Anthropometry

Enter H.H. Risley. Risley, then president of the Asiatic Society of Bengal and director of ethnography for India, had an understanding of caste that used anthropometric measures. Risley believed that he could learn something about groups of people by measuring their skulls and noses with calipers and other instruments. Riding on the success of his ethnography *Tribes and Castes of Bengal* (1891), Risley altered how caste was imagined and measured in the censuses by promoting his ideas about caste. Critical of the 1891 national census, Risley argued (as he had published in 1890: 747) that the 'non-scientific' theories of caste were

insufficient, and that an understanding of caste with anthropometric measures was required. As an example of Risley's discourse concerning caste, he argued 'the Aryan type, as we find it in India at the present day, is marked by a relatively long (dolichocephalic) head, a straight, finely cut (leptorhine) nose, a long symmetrically narrow face, a well-developed forehead, regular features and a high facial angle.' Risley (1908: 110) saw what he called the 'remarkable vitality of caste' in the bodies of Indians themselves, but this was quite a different vision of caste than existed previously in India.

Risley introduced a deeper connection between race and caste in the census. For Risley, this was a matter of racial science, but of politics as well. Administrative scientists and anthropologists in colonial India rarely addressed the political implications of their research concerning caste, although Risley made his political intentions public. He argued (1890: 757) that having statistical knowledge of India was a question of governance and who to include in the polity. The danger of extending representative political institutions to Indians was that 'the adoption of a wider franchise may give undue leverage to the caste organization.' Risley was concerned that indiscriminate democracy would give Indians power over the British in India, and thus, statistical information was needed to help discriminate between citizens who should and should not be represented by the government. According to Dirks (1992: 71), 'Risley's liberalism is complicit in the general project of British colonialism.'

Risley was critiqued by local caste associations and Indian scholars. C. Varma (1893: 1) writes that Risley 'committed very many blunders to which he was probably led by wrong information supplied to him by his correspondents and informants.' Ghurye (1932) also critiqued Risley's methods, questioning the validity of anthropometric measures. Yet Risley held sway due to his service record as well as his academic work, an influence he used to submerge the arguments of Plowden and Baines for abandoning caste.

Despite Risley's championing of putatively scientific categories and measurements of caste, a total agreement on how to categorize caste never emerged. Concerning the census in 1921,

Commissioner Marten could only conclude that 'the enormous complexity of the caste system makes it impossible to combine large groups of the population on the basis of caste. No satisfactory method of classifying castes for the purposes of demographic statistics has been discovered' (Marten 1924: 224).

Conclusion

Inventing a classificatory grid for making sense of the people of India produced new ways of visualizing the colonial territory. Plowden, Baines, and others were skeptical about the merits of naturalizing caste through statistical science. They were against enumeration of caste on pragmatic grounds concerning cost and time. Those who argued in favour of augmenting the enumeration of caste, such as Risley, turned to **anthropometry** to create a different vision of caste, aggregated from local variations.

As Hacking (1983: 280) puts it, 'Enumeration demands *kinds* of things or people to count. Counting is hungry for categories. Many of the categories we now use to describe people are byproducts of the needs of enumeration.' India was an experimental ground for administrative science, so much so that Hacking (1990: 17) argues, 'India evolved one of the great statistical bureaucracies.' Yet, for all the energy put into counting and categorizing caste in colonial India, the colonial state produced an administrative space that was neither statistically sound nor foolproof. Confusion was the rule, not the exception.

Note

1. The term 'schedules' refers to the collection of questions asked, the information probed for, and the formatting of answers in the census interview.

References

Baines, J. 1899. 'Correspondence Concerning Arrangement for the Census of 1901, to the Under Secretary of State for India'. July 1899. From the British Library, Asia, Pacific & Africa Collections, London.

Curtis, B. 1994. 'On the Local Construction of Statistical Knowledge: Making Up the 1861 Census of the Canadas'. *Journal of Historical Sociology* 7(4): 416–424.

Dirks, N. 1992. 'Castes of Mind'. *Representations* 37(1): 56–78.

Ghurye, G. 1932. *Caste and Race in India*. London: Routledge.

Hacking, I. 1990. *The Taming of Chance*. Cambridge: Cambridge University Press.

———. 1983. 'Biopower and the Avalanche of Printed Numbers'. *Humanities in Society* 5(4): 279–295.

Ibbetson, D. 1883. *Report on the Census of the Panjab, Taken on the 17th of February 1881*. Volume 1. Text and appendices C and D (tables and instructions). Lahore: Superintendent of the Central Jail Press.

Marten, J. 1924. *1921 Census of India—Report*. Calcutta: Superintendent Government Printing.

Maheshwari, S. 1996. *The Census Administration under the Raj and After*. New Delhi: Concept Publishing.

Plowden, W. 1873. *Census of the Northwest Provinces, 1872, General Report*. Allahabad: North-Western Provinces Government Press.

Report of Census of the Island of Bombay 1864. 1864. Bombay: Education Society's Press.

Report on the Census of Calcutta in 1866. 1866. Calcutta: Thacker, Spink and Co. Press.

Risley, H. 1890. 'The Race Basis of Indian Political Movements'. *Contemporary Review* 57: 752–767.

———. 1891. *The Tribes and Castes of Bengal*. Calcutta: Bengal Secretariat Press.

———. 1908. *The People of India*. Calcutta: Thacker, Spink & Co.

Varma, C. 1893. *Criticisms of Mr. Risley's Articles on Brahmans, Kayasthas & Vaidyas as Published in his Tribes and Castes of Bengal*. Calcutta: Samya Press.

Waterfield, H. 1875. *Memorandum of the India Office on the Census of British India 1871–72*. London: Her Majesty's Stationery Office.

CHAPTER 56

Canada's Rights Revolution: Social Movements and Social Change, 1937–1982[1]

Dominique Clément

In February 1987, a group calling themselves the Raging Grannies joined an anti-uranium rally in Victoria after the BC government decided to lift its **moratorium** on uranium mining. Dressed in purple, yellow, and blue flowered hats and long white gloves, and carrying leather purses, the Grannies sang their trademark songs 'Uranium Tango' and 'Jealousy' to the amusement or—for the musically inclined—the horror of the protestors. After having whipped the crowd into energetic applause, the Grannies announced that they had their own briefs to present to the legislature, and with stupendous aplomb they produced a laundry basket and a clothesline, which they stretched from one end of the stone steps to the other. Clothes pegs were unpacked, along with a selection of undies, including long johns, boxers, and bikinis, which they clipped on the line. The crowd roared and the media dutifully covered the event.

The Raging Grannies are a typical example of a social movement organization (SMO). While SMOs certainly do not *constitute* a **movement** in and of themselves, they form an important dynamic within the overall movement. Movements are defined by the beliefs they propagate and their ability to mobilize collective action around those beliefs, but all movements are composed of the people who struggle to articulate and apply, sometimes imperfectly, those beliefs. SMOs mobilize the resources of a movement, and are carriers of movement ideas, and are thus useful windows for studying social movements. Also, unlike an **interest group**, which assumes a clear distinction

between civil society and the state and focuses its efforts on promoting the interests of its members, the Grannies, who seek to promote the principles of the peace movement, challenge public–private divisions. For them, promoting social change has become a way of life. Participation in the Grannies is a way for its members to find a role for themselves in a society where the elderly, particularly women, are expected to sit quietly on the sidelines. Yes, they seek to change the minds of policy-makers. But most of their efforts are directed inward. Understanding the complexities of social activism is, I believe, an important contribution that historians and sociologists can make to understanding the dynamics of local, national, and international social movements.

My book *Canada's Rights Revolution* (Clément 2008) engaged not only with the study of social movements, but with human rights as well. Consider, for a moment, the tragic circumstances surrounding the life of Lal Jamilla Mandokhel. In March 1999, Lal Jamilla, a 16-year-old girl in Pakistan, was repeatedly raped. Her uncle filed a complaint with the police. Police officers detained her attacker, but handed Lal Jamilla over to her tribe. The council of elders decided that Lal Jamilla had brought shame on the tribe, and that the only way to overcome the shame was to put her to death. She was shot dead on the orders of the council (Freeman 2002: 1).

Is this a violation of human rights? The answer would seem obvious, but in fact there are rigorous debates about whether human rights is a Western idea, and whether or not human rights principles apply in situations such as that of Lal Jamilla. The study of human rights is the study of a particular social context. That is not to say I am a cultural relativist—far from it. Too often has this line of argument been used to justify horrors such as those visited upon young Lal Jamilla. But to ignore the social context in which human rights evolve is to shield ourselves from the necessary application of human rights in our everyday lives.

In writing the book, I had two objectives. The first was to explore some of the most controversial human rights violations in Canadian history. I examined controversies such as denominational education, domestic terrorism, criminalization of narcotics, civilian review of the police, national security policies, and **welfare** policy reform. Each of these controversies highlights how people struggled to apply vague human rights principles to concrete issues their communities faced.

Throughout its history, the human rights movement in Canada was ideologically divided, fighting similar issues from different perspectives. For example, in the case of single mothers in Ontario before 1987, a particularly notorious regulation called the 'man in the house rule' stated that if there was evidence that a woman receiving welfare had a male living with her, she would lose her welfare support (the same rule did not apply to men). It was a regulation deeply rooted in the **breadwinner** ideology, and presumed that a sexual relationship implied a financial one. It resulted in welfare officials scrutinizing women's sexual activity; in order to receive welfare, women had to appear as chaste as possible. The records produced by welfare officials whose job it was to investigate welfare fraud make for fascinating reading. In attempting to determine if a man was living in the house, they reported everything from open beer cans to raised toilet seats.

Civil liberties organizations such as the Canadian Civil Liberties Association (CCLA) and the British Columbia Civil Liberties Association (BCCLA) fought to have this odious regulation reworked in 1987 to include spouses of men and women, so that it no longer targeted only sexual relationships and women. But neither association dealt with the amount of welfare people received—only with the administration of welfare. In contrast, *human rights* groups such as the Ligue des droits de l'homme or the Newfoundland Human Rights Association fought vigorously to raise the amount of welfare. In the mid-1970s, the Toronto Social Planning Council estimated that welfare recipients received barely 60 per cent of the funds necessary to maintain a basic standard of living (see Clément 2008: 163). Whereas human rights groups argued that individuals had a right to economic security, and could not exercise their political and civil rights without proper resources, their civil libertarian counterparts considered these questions as matters of public policy, not rights.

My second objective was to study professional social movement organizations. These organizations are important vehicles for promoting social change. But how did they conceive of social change? In an era made famous by activism and social ferment, what challenges faced social movement organizations?

I argued that the idea of human rights is highly statist, and that the evolution of human rights has been intimately linked with the rise of the modern state. But grassroots activism, not the state, was at the heart of the most profound human rights advances in Canadian history. Still, most activists embraced a minimalist approach to human rights. Human rights activists have long recognized that economic or gender inequalities lead to rights violations. But human rights advocates too often assume that correlative duties that emerge from moral human rights claims rely on the *state*. This, I believe, is problematic. Human rights advocacy is inherently directed toward state power; rights discourse is thus a potentially poor vehicle for limiting economic or private power. So, for instance, the human rights groups I examined in my book did not campaign around ensuring that corporations did not deprive others; nor did they seek to challenge private forms of oppression, such as male power within the family. By locating duties only within the state, the potential for challenges to economic and private power are severely limited.

Ultimately the book was about asking a more fundamental question: To what degree can rights discourse promote social change? Human rights encourage the perception of social change as legal change. I argued that individuals and groups can make rights-claims and that such claims have a powerful moral force, but they have not been recognized as *rights* until enforced by the state.

This is, in my mind, the basis for a sociology of human rights. Far too few social historians or sociologists study human rights in Canada, and this is an area that is ripe for future studies. . . . Legal scholars and political scientists have dominated the study of human rights and, as a result, such studies tend to focus on the courts and governments—almost as if the state alone were responsible for human rights innovations.

I had to submit numerous freedom of information (FOI) requests, which was by far the most torturous aspect of my research. Innocuous material such as information about funding for SMOs is restricted by law, even 40 years after the fact. The problem in essence is that access laws do not specify which materials should be restricted, and have created a blanket prohibition that is excessively broad. Frankly, I've come to the conclusion that we should consider discouraging graduate students from pursuing research projects that require FOI application. The worst situation, in my experience, is in British Columbia. Three years ago, the BC Archives began enforcing an obscure part of the provincial FOI laws that requires users to permit civil servants to 'audit' (inspect) their home and offices, including their computers, to confirm their security measures. This is a remarkably invasive requirement to obtain access to documents that were at one time in the public domain and are hardly national security threats. It is a shocking invasion of privacy, and I can't help but think that this can only act to the detriment of producing research on BC history. And the policy doesn't even achieve the standards of basic due process, since only people in Vancouver or Victoria are subject to arbitrary inspections because the province will not pay the archivists to go anywhere else.

One of the reasons I wrote *Canada's Rights Revolution* as a series of case studies was to link the English and French experiences in Canada. Far too many contemporary studies of Canada, historical

or sociological, which purport to be 'national', are in fact studies of English Canada supported by weak explanations for why the author has not incorporated the francophone experience.

This year's short-list for the Canadian Historical Association's book prize does not include a single book written in French; every book is regional or based on English Canada. In the past 10 years, almost all the books short-listed for the prize were explicitly about either English Canada *or* Quebec. The very few books that did claim to be 'national' either did not draw on both English and French language sources or, in the case of English-language books, offered weak explanations for not including Quebec. The Canadian Sociological Association's John Porter Prize reflects exactly the same trend: since 1983, only one French-language book has won the prize, and except for Allan Greer's book on the Lower Canada rebellion of 1837, as far as I can tell, mine is the only one to link the English and French experiences and draw on sources in both languages. Certainly within the literature I know very well—the sociological literature on social movements and human rights in Canada—I can think of very few studies that are not limited to either English or French Canada or that effectively draw on literature in both languages.

Can we truly claim to be offering national studies when we ignore the entire literature written in French? Surely we are neglecting an incredible amount of literature on Canada.

To return to my earlier point, is the francophone experience really so different that it requires separate consideration? I worry about such broad generalizations, especially in any study dealing with the post–World War II period. My book shows how the Ligue des droits de l'homme, a unilingual francophone rights association in Montreal, engaged with the same debates as its counterparts across Canada and abroad, and regularly interacted with people outside Quebec. It's an old expression, but the term 'two solitudes' seems apt for describing a great deal of academic writing today, at least in studies on human rights and social movements.

My point is not to disparage regional studies or studies that rely on English-language sources. Far from it. But if we are going to engage in studies of social movements or human rights in Canada, or any similar national study, especially in the post-1960s period, we need to engage with the literature and sources in both languages. This is not only because it is critical to engage with the broader academic community studying Canada, but also because experiences across the country are increasingly comparable and can inform each other. With various broad historical changes (the advent of new technologies and demographic mobility since the 1960s, to name only two examples) developments in Montreal and Trois Rivières are no longer so different or isolated from those in Smithers BC or St. John's.

Note

1. Excerpts from the John Porter Tradition of Excellence Book Awards lecture at the 2010 Canadian Sociological Association conference. The book discussed in this paper is the winner of the 2009 John Porter Award: Dominique Clément, *Canada's Rights Revolution: Social Movements and Social Change, 1937–1982* (Vancouver: UBC Press, 2008).

Reference

Michael Freeman, *Human Rights: An Interdisciplinary Approach* (Cambridge: Polity Press, 2002), 1.

CHAPTER 57

The Economy and Public Opinion on Welfare Spending in Canada

Robert Andersen and Josh Curtis

Introduction

This paper examines the relationship between economic and political conditions and **public opinion** on welfare spending in Canada from 1980 and 2005. Many commentators argue that elected officials attempt to maximize their chance of re-election by implementing policies that reflect public opinion (Stimson 1995; Erikson, MacKuen and Stimson 2002; Wlezien 2004; Weakliem, Andersen and Heath 2005; Brooks and Manza 2007). Others suggest that the direction of causation is predominately the other way around; that is, economic and political contextual factors influence public opinion (Andersen and Fetner 2008; Kenworthy and McCall 2008). Regardless of the causal interpretation one prefers, a general shift to the right in electoral politics and growing income **inequality** within most modern democracies over the past few decades (Fisher and Hout 2006; Goesling 2001; Firebaugh 2000), including Canada (Banting 2006; Myles 2010; Osberg 2007) underscore the importance of assessing the interplay of public opinion, political and economic conditions, and policy.

Economic Conditions, Political Climate, and Public Opinion

Public opinion on what is an acceptable level of inequality varies across time, social groups, and cultures (Noll and Roberts 2003; Osberg and Smeeding 2006). Some research indicates that national differences in public opinion are negatively related to level of economic development, **welfare state** involvement (Kelley and Evans 1993), and presence of a Soviet-communist past (Kelley and Zagorski 2005; Fisher and Heath 2006). Other research suggests that attitudes toward redistribution are influenced by the type of political regime— e.g. social democratic, conservative, liberal— that people experience (Svallfors 1997; Papadakis 1993; Jaeger 2006). In this regard, Svallfors (1997) argues that social democratic countries are characterized by strong public support for welfare-state intervention and income equality. Countries with more liberal economies, on the other hand, tend to show very little public support for government redistribution and income distribution.

Public opinion research also demonstrates fluctuations in support for public spending within countries. Using Finnish survey data collected from 1975 to 1993, Shivo and Uusitalo (1995) demonstrate that public opinion tends to be more favourable toward redistribution in times of economic recession. Svallfors (1991, 1995) has similar findings for Sweden. Similarly, Soroka and Wlezien (2004) suggest that Canadian public opinion responds to the structuring role of institutions. More specifically, they state, 'As in the US and the UK, the Canadian public appears to respond thermostatically to changes in public spending, and Canadian policymakers appear to respond to public preferences. The underlying details are not the same, however, and the pattern of results across the three countries is suggestive about the structuring role of institutions' (Soroka and Wlezien 2004:533).

Research Questions

Our goal is to assess the relationship between public opinion on welfare spending on the one hand and economic and political conditions on the other, in Canada during the period from 1980 to 2001. This period is of particular interest because it was characterized by a rightward shift in Canadian politics and a corresponding rise in inequality. Specifically, we ask:

1. Was there a relationship between public opinion and political context? In particular, did public opinion move in tandem with the political regime (i.e., Liberal versus Conservative federal government) and the level of public expenditures?
2. Did public opinion follow trends in the economy?

We expect that public opinion will be most in favour of spending when the economy is performing well. We are particularly interested in the roles of the **unemployment** rate and median income, two commonly used indicators of the performance of the economy. We expect that public opinion was most favourable toward spending when the unemployment rate was low and median income was high. We also expect public opinion was most favourable toward spending when income inequality was high. We propose two possible reasons for this relationship: (a) people with higher incomes feel morally obligated to help eradicate inequality as it rises, or to keep it under control for instrumental reasons such as keeping some if the ills of inequality (e.g. crime, a lack of social cohesion) under control; (b) those with lower incomes favour social spending for instrumental reasons, in particular because they stand to benefit from it.

Methods

Our public opinion data were collected by the commercial polling firm Environics between 1980 and 2001. Data from 18 polls are used in the analysis. The questionnaire item upon which our measure of public opinion is based was identical in all years under study. The question was worded as follows: 'Keeping in mind that increasing services could increase taxes, do you think the federal government is spending too much, just the right amount, or should be spending more'.

Our contextual data were obtained from Human Resources and Skills Development Canada (2010), and included the effects of average median family income, level of income inequality (measured by the ratio of average incomes for the 10th and 90th percentiles), the unemployment rate, and the amount of public expenditures on social programs relative to GDP.

Findings

We start by exploring simple trend data in Figure 57.1. Panel (a) reveals a rising trend in social spending in Canada from the early 1980s until 1994 and then a sharp decline afterwards until spending reaches approximately the same level as in the 1980s. Other research indicates that this decline was largely due to the paring back of benefits for the unemployed and single parents (Battle et al. 2005; Banting 2006; Osberg 2007). Although these benefits fall primarily under provincial responsibility, the replacement of the Canada Assistance Program with the Canada Health and Social Transfer suggest that the federal government also played a role in the decline (see Frenette et al. 2009). This preliminary evidence suggests, then, that 1994 was a critical turning point in the extent of public spending in Canada.

Panel (b) of Figure 57.1 suggests that the trend in public opinion on social spending followed quite closely with the trend in public expenditures. The early 1990s were characterized by a precipitous decline in support for welfare spending until 1994, when it rises sharply until reaching—and even slightly surpassing—the level of support in the late 1980s and early 1990s. Most importantly, as in the case of social expenditures, the critical turning point in public opinion appears to occur around 1994. After this time, public opinion on social spending begins to climb back to levels similar to the levels of support in the late 1980s.

In other words, there is some evidence that the preference for spending among the Canadian population increased during times of declining spending, especially since the 1990s. At the very least, these data fail to support the common argument that the decline in public expenditures

reflected Canadians' preferences. Still, this finding is not inconsistent with Wlezien's (1995) idea of a responsive public. That is, 'when policy increases (decreases), the preference for more policy decreases (increases)' (Soroka and Wlezien 2004).

Figure 57.1 also demonstrates interesting trends in some important economic indicators during the same 1980–2004 period. Particularly interesting are the increases in both median income and income inequality in the mid-1990s—panels (c) and (e). With respect to median income, it is also striking how the rising trend occurs after a gradual decline starting in 1980. The trend in the unemployment rate shown in panel (d) appears to be almost a mirror image of the trend in public opinion. On the other hand, the level of income inequality was relatively stable until around 1995. Finally, the marked change in the patterns observed above corresponds quite closely to the period of Liberal governments from 1993 onwards. In short, the tentative evidence presented thus far suggests that public opinion was strongly influenced by the state of the economy.

Multinomial Log-Linear Models Predicting Public Opinion

We now turn to more rigorous tests of the relationships between the national context variables and public opinion. Specifically, we fit multinomial log-linear models to carry out our tests. These are statistical models that allow us to assess simultaneously the impact of all of the context variables on the number of respondents that fall into each of the categories of the public opinion spending question. Likelihood ratio tests for the terms in the models and measures of goodness of fit are shown in Table 57.1. These tests determine whether including a particular variable in the statistical model improves the fit of the model to the actual data.

Now a completely new story emerges. Although the descriptive analyses indicated that public opinion tracks well with social spending, the multinomial logit models suggest otherwise. When controlling for economic conditions, including public expenditures does not significantly improve the fit of the model predicting public opinion.

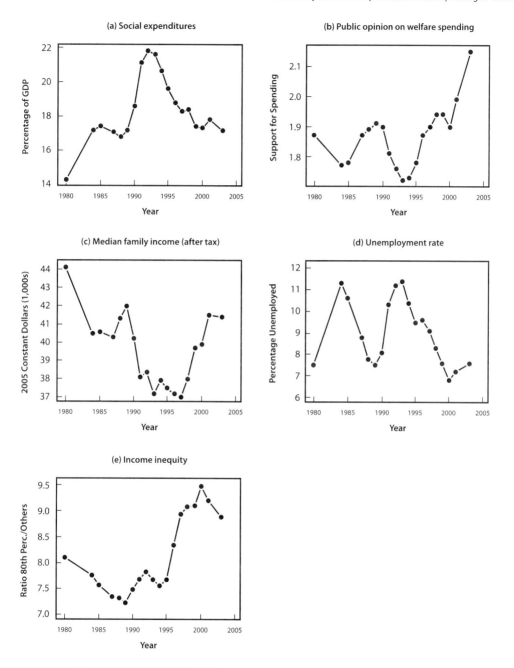

Figure 57.1 Trends in Welfare Spending, Public Opinion on Spending, and Various Economic Indicators

Nevertheless, the role of governing party remains important. Even more noteworthy, however, is the persistent influence of economic conditions. Particularly important is the unemployment rate, though median income and income inequality are also important predictors of public opinion.

Table 57.1 Likelihood Ratio Tests for Terms in the Multinomial Log-Linear Model Fitted to the Public Opinion Data

CONTEXT VARIABLE	CHI-SQUARE
Public expenditures	4.0
Liberal government	13.9***
Median income	6.8*
Income inequality	30.1***
Unemployment rate	118.6***
Pseudo-*R2*	0.85
Number of respondents	34,020
Number of polls	18

*p<.05; **p<.01; ***p<.001
Note: All tests for model terms have two degrees of freedom

To understand the contextual influences on public opinion, Figure 57.2 presents predicted percentages derived from the statistical model for each of the categories of the dependent variable through the range of the context variables (see Fox and Andersen 2006 for more details). Simply put, the public is much more favourable toward welfare spending when median family income and income inequality are high. Most obvious is the increase in the number of 'not enough' responses as both income and income inequality rise. More importantly, the strong relationship between public opinion and the unemployment rate is very clear. The limited role of public expenditures on public opinion is also very clear in the fact that the lines representing each of the response categories are almost completely horizontal. Finally, although it is a statistically significant relationship, public opinion appears to have changed very little with changes in government.

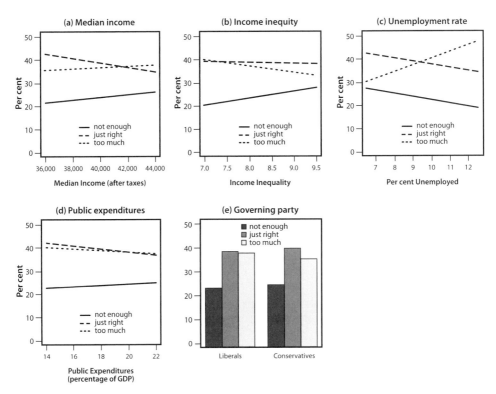

Figure 57.2 Predicted Public Opinion Regarding Public Spending on Welfare by Median Income, Income Inequality, Unemployment Rate, Public Expenditure, and Governing Party. Fitted Values Derived from the Multinomial Log-Linear Model Predicting Public Opinion.

Conclusions

The fact that public opinion follows the unemployment rate and median income suggests that it reflects changes in the business cycle. In short, when the economy is performing poorly, people tend to be less likely to support increases in spending on welfare. Contrary to the views of policy-makers, we propose quite a different story for the mechanisms underlying the positive relationship between income inequality and public opinion on spending. Our data suggest that people want to remedy inequality. We speculate on two possible reasons for the increasing desire to eradicate inequality as it rises. Both of these arguments are based on the premise that people become more aware of inequality and its effects as it becomes larger. First, people of higher incomes may feel increasingly obligated on moral grounds to help those in poor economic conditions as the level of inequality becomes more apparent. Second, as inequality increases, those at the bottom of the income distribution may become more aware of their own position and thus become increasingly more likely to support social spending on the grounds that it might some day help them or people like them.

References

Andersen, Robert and Tina Fetner. 2008. 'Economic Inequality and Intolerance: Attitudes toward Homosexuality in 35 Democracies'. *American Journal of Political Science* 52(4): 942–58.

Andersen, Robert and John Fox. 2001. 'Pre-election Polls and the Dynamics of the 1997 Canadian Federal Election'. *Electoral Studies* 20: 87–108.

Banting, Keith G. 2006. 'Dis-embedding Liberalism? The New Social Policy Paradigm in Canada'. In David A. Green and Jonathan R. Kesselman, eds. *Dimensions of Inequality in Canada*. Vancouver: UBC Press, pp. 417–52.

Battle, Ken, Michael Mendelson, and Sherri Torjman. 2005. 'The Modernization Mantra: Toward a New Architecture for Canada's Adult Benefits'. *Canadian Public Policy/Analyse de Politiques* 31: 431–37.

Brooks, Clem and Jeff Manza. 2007. *Why Welfare States Persist: The Importance of Public Opinion in Democracies*. Chicago: University of Chicago Press.

Erikson, R.S., M.B. MacKuen and J.A. Stimson. 2002. *The Macro Polity*. New York: Cambridge University Press.

Firebaugh, Glenn. 2000. 'The Trend in Between-Nation Income Inequality'. *Annual Review of Sociology* 26: 323–39.

Fisher, Stephan and Anthony Heath. 2006. 'Decreasing Desires for Income Inequality?' In P. Esther, M. Braun, and P. Mohler (eds.), *Globalization, Value Change, and Generations: A Cross-National and Intergenerational Perspective*. Leiden, Netherlands: Brill Academic Publishing, pp. 207–32.

Fisher, Claude S. and Michael Hout. 2006. *Century of Difference. How America Changed in the Last One Hundred Years*. New York: Russell Sage Foundation.

Fox, John and Robert Andersen. 2006. 'Effect Displays for Multinomial and Proportional-Odds Logit Models', *Sociological Methodology* 36: 225–56.

Frenette, Marc, David A. Green, and Kevin Milligan. 2009. 'Taxes, Transfers, and Canadian Income Inequality'. *Canadian Public Policy/Analyse de Politiques* 35: 389–411.

Goesling, Brian. 2001. 'Changing Income Inequalities within and between Nations: New Evidence'. *American Sociological Review* 66(5): 745–61.

Human Resources and Skills Development Canada. 2010. http://www.hrsdc.gc.ca/ Retrieved 14 May 2010.

Jaeger, M.M. 2006. 'What Makes People Support Public Responsibility for Welfare Provision: Self-Interest or Political Ideology?' *Acta Sociologica* 49(3): 321–38.

Kalterthaler, Karl and Stephen Ceccoli. 2008. 'Explaining Patterns of Support for the Provision of Citizen Welfare'. *Journal of European Public Policy* 15(7): 1041–68.

Kelley, Jonathan and M.D.R. Evans. 1993. 'The Legitimation of Inequality: Occupational Earnings in Nine Nations'. *American Journal of Sociology* 99(1): 75–125.

Kelley, Jonathan and Krzysztof Zagorski. 2005. 'Economic Change and the Legitimation of Inequality: The Transition From Socialism to the Free Market in Poland and Hungary, 1987–1994'. *Research in Social Stratification and Mobility* 22: 321–66.

Kenworthy, Lane and Leslie McCall. 2008. 'Inequality, Public Opinion and Redistribution'. *Socio-Economic Review* 6: 35–68.

Korpi, Walter and Joakim Palme. 1998. 'The Paradox of Redistribution and Strategies of Equality: Welfare State Institutions, Inequality, and Poverty in the Western Countries'. *American Sociological Review* 63(5): 661–87.

———. 2003. New Politics and Class Politics in the Context of Austerity and Globalization: Welfare State Regress in 18 Countries, 1975–95. *American Political Science Review* 97: 425–46.

Myles, John. 2010. 'The Inequality Surge: Changes in the Family Life Course Are the Main Cause'. *Inroads: The Canadian Journal of Opinion* 26 (Winter/Spring): 66–73.

Noll, Heinz-Herbert and Lance W. Roberts. 2003. 'The Legitimacy of Inequality on Both Sides of The Atlantic. A Comparative Analysis of Attitudes in Canada and Germany'. *The Tocqueville Review* 24(2): 154–89.

Osberg, Lars and Timothy Smeeding. 2006. '"Fair" Inequality? Attitudes toward Pay Differentials: The United States in Comparative Perspective'. *American Sociological Review* 71 (3): 450–73.

Osberg, Lars. 2007. 'A Quarter Century of Economic Inequality in Canada 1981–2006'. Halifax, NS: Dalhousie University, unpublished manuscript.

Papadakis, Elim. 1993. 'Class Interests, Class Politics and Welfare State Regime'. *The British Journal of Sociology* 44(2): 249–70.

Sihvo, T. and H. Uusitalo. 1995. 'Economic Crises and Support for the Welfare State in Finland: 1975–1993'. *Acta Sociologica* 38: 251–62.

Soroka, Stuart N. and Christopher Wlezien. 2004. 'Opinion Representation and Policy Feedback: Canada in Comparative Perspective'. *Canadian Journal of Political Science* 37: 531–59.

Stimson, James A. 1995. 'Opinion and Representation'. *American Political Science Review* 89(1): 179–83.

Svallfors, Stefan. 1991. 'The Politics of Welfare Policy in Sweden: Structural Determinants and Attitudinal Cleavages'. *The British Journal of Sociology* 42(4): 609–34.

———. 1995. 'The End of Class Politics? Structural Cleavages and Attitudes to Swedish Welfare Policies'. *Acta Sociologica* 38(1): 53–74.

———. 1997. 'Worlds of Welfare and Attitudes to Redistribution: A Comparison of Eight Western Nations'. *European Sociological Review* 13(3): 283–304.

Van Oorschot, W. (2002). 'Individual Motives for Contributing to Welfare Benefits in the Netherlands'. *Policy and Politics* 30: 31–46.

Weakliem, David, Robert Andersen and Anthony Heath. 2005. 'By Popular Demand: The Effect of Public Opinion on Income Inequality'. *Comparative Sociology* 4: 261–84.

Wlezien, Christopher. 1995. 'The Public as Thermostat: Dynamics of Preferences for Spending'. *American Journal of Political Science* 39: 981–1000.

———. 2004. 'Patterns of Representation: Dynamics of Public Preferences and Policy' *Journal of Politics* 66: 1–24.

CHAPTER 58

Social Europe and Eastern Europe: Post-Socialist Scholars Grapple with New Models of Social Policy

Ivanka Knezevic

Capitalist Economy, Market, and Social Policy

The project of 'Social Europe', a common standard for social and citizenship rights in all member countries of the **European Union (EU)**, is a policy not seriously supported by the EU governing bodies. It is, nevertheless, presented as a significant improvement for the new member and applicant countries. Its acceptance is a condition of joining the EU. However, since its goal is to complement, rather than correct, the effects of an unregulated market, its provisions are not only below the existing levels of social policy in most of the old EU member countries, but also below the levels of social policy that Eastern Europe enjoyed during its relatively recent socialist past.

Capitalist economy cannot be maintained without social policy (Drahokoupil 2007, 404)—a point that many neo-liberal commentators neglect. Functioning of the economy depends on broader social institutions (such as the availability of **labour** and a country's legal system), so it can never be maintained by isolated, pure market relationships of supply, demand, and exchange.

Especially important for the maintenance of a capitalist economy is availability of labour. Polanyi calls labour a 'fictitious commodity' (quoted in

Drahokoupil 2007, 40): although it is bought and sold in markets, it cannot be reproduced in them. Workers must have stable non-economic conditions to reproduce their physical and mental labour power, and to produce and bring up a new generation of workers. If the provision of these conditions is left solely to the market, labour may even be destroyed through over-exploitation. For this reason, social institutions surrounding a capitalist economy always include policies for the decommodification of labour: making sure that the employees' ability to shelter, feed, and rest themselves and their children does not depend solely on what they earn in the labour market. Public services, such as health care and education, and income supplements, such as unemployment insurance, welfare, and pensions, both serve this purpose.

In the past several decades, the increasing influence of corporate interests, cash-strapped governments, and neo-liberal ideology have decreased the scope of these non-market means of survival. This has been described as 'recommodification' of labour. The change has been particularly noticeable in European states, which traditionally tried to weather economic crises by implementing public works and maintaining income supplements, but have since the 1980s increasingly opted for their reduction (i.e., recommodification of labour) as a way out of economic difficulties (Bailey 2009, 49).

One of the most important decisions about any **social policy** is whether it should apply to all citizens or only to those who are for some specific reason unable to earn necessary goods and services by commodifying (selling) their labour. This is the difference between 'universalistic' and 'targeted' social policies. Universalistic benefits are meant to improve social citizenship for all. Targeted measures are meant to ensure that previously excluded groups (e.g. women, ethnic minorities, disabled, aged) 'catch up' to the already existing level of social citizenship.

The EU favours targeted social policies by making them—and not the universalistic policies— subject to its 'hard' (i.e., mandatory) policy-making process. This implies that the general level of social citizenship in the EU is already satisfactory and that only identifiable excluded populations need help to 'catch up' with it.

In recent decades, the difference between market-complementary and market-corrective social policies has become increasingly important. As the power of large corporations grew (because of monopolization and global mobility of capital), the neo-liberal ideology representing their interests became increasingly influential. This ideology incorporates a firm belief that an absence of market regulation can solve all economic and social problems. This has led to a preference for market-complementary policies—those that equip workers to compete in the market more efficiently: education, training, and active labour market policies (incentives to accept any work rather than remain unemployed).

At the same time, labour laws in Europe have been changing. At the beginning of the 1980s, all EU countries had legislation that strongly favoured standard, full-time, permanent employment. They have since allowed non-standard, part-time, temporary work. The post-socialist states, trying to fit in with the EU, have done the same. This means that the employment gained through active labour market policies is likely to be non-standard: part-time, poorly paid, and insecure. The EU, however, does not see this as a problem, but instead hails the increased prevalence of non-standard work as 'flexibilization of the labour market' (Baloković 2008, 226).

The European Union: An Empire, Its Social Project, and Its Institutions

The best way to understand how joining the EU changes policy-making in the new member states is to think of the EU as an empire, as Hayden (2008) does. Hayden defines empires as 'sets of mechanisms to bring separate nations, and usually separate polities, into one cooperative framework for generating, collecting and centralizing wealth'. The goal of imperial rule is 'not so much divide and conquer as balance and thereby exploit' (p. 85). This is exactly the kind of relationship that exists between the 'old member' states, on one hand, and the 'new member' and post-socialist 'candidate' states, on the other. Candidate states are required to follow EU policies, even before they join the organization.

The EU declares that its membership is contingent on policy changes that supposedly bring political cultures of candidates closer to the EU values of democracy, freedom, human rights, social justice, the rule of law, and the protection of minorities. This smug ideology, which declares the EU to be 'a union founded on values' (Hayden 2008, 88) is in marked contrast to European history. The complex history of Europe, its unpleasant episodes, and its past full of divisions and conflict, are swept under the carpet by the obsessive repetition of progressivist, Eurocentric phrases (Velikonja 2007, 145). This obfuscation reflected in the expression *acquis communautaire* (community acquisitions), denoting the accumulated legislation of the EU, which all members accept when they join. This hides the fact that these documents are by no means of the same legal status, and that they are enforced (or not) by a spectrum of mandatory, voluntary, and unspecified procedures.

What, then, are those common values of social policy that the EU asks its new members to embrace?

Many observers connect the Social Europe project to the European social model (ESM). Esping-Andersen (1990) first defined the ESM as a fairly comprehensive, universalistic system of decommodifying policies, somewhere between the more extensive Scandinavian and the more restricted Anglo-American model. As an ideal type, in Max Weber's sense of the word, ESM is a useful tool to analyze social-policy systems of various countries.

However, two problems arise when it is used as a normative concept: an ideal to aspire to and be measured against. First, the term is used in public debates about the EU social policies, but it does not appear in any EU legal document. This creates an ungrounded expectation that ESM will be applied in the EU policies. Second, the use of this now outdated concept masks the fact that the real EU social policies have long since shifted toward the more restricted Anglo-American model.

What procedural means are available to implement the EU social project? The EU uses 'hard' (binding) and 'soft' (non-binding) policy tools.

The main 'hard' policy tools are the 'social funds', from which resources are transferred to member states for specific social-policy purposes. All the social funds in the last 10 years have been used to fight the social exclusion of identifiable social groups (e.g. women, ethnic minorities such as Roma, the disabled, and the elderly).

While targeted policies are a part of 'hard' EU decision making, universalistic policies (such as education, health care, pensions, welfare, employment conditions, and benefits) are relegated to the 'soft' policy-making process called the 'open coordination method' (Lendvai 2005, 7). This is a sort of international 'hall of shame', where member states discuss benchmarks and 'best practices', and where laggards are brought into line by peer pressure, without any legal sanctions. This non-binding mechanism allows the EU not to enforce even its supposedly most important piece of social legislation—the Charter of Fundamental Rights of the European Union (European Union 2000, 21), which proclaims a variety of human, civil, and cultural rights.

While national state policies have been recommodifying labour since the 1980s, the EU social-policy decision making is dominated by actors who represent corporate and neo-liberal interests: they have no interest in pursuing the decommodifying policies that the Charter allows.

There are also institutional reasons why a decommodifying social project cannot succeed at the level of the EU. The size of the EU budget (compared to national state budgets) is small. This effectively prevents implementation of large-scale, universalistic, decommodifying measures. Since the EU parliamentarians and officials are not elected by popular vote, they are not motivated to promote universalistic issues (Bailey 2009, 149–153).

Post-Socialist Discussions of Social Policy

Authors from the EU member states (including the post-socialist ones) use two well-known frameworks to evaluate social policies: the neo-liberal and the traditional social democratic one. While the former dominates political debates, the latter is used in most research on the topic. This model's critical approach to the dominant market-complementary social project may be explained by two social conditions of academic work: a greater knowledge of alternate social projects than the general public is likely to have, and a greater freedom from direct political pressure. Academics do not negotiate with the EU for support and resources, as politicians must, and can thus afford to be more critical of its demands (Matonytė 2006).

Discussions of social policy in 'candidate' and 'possible candidate' countries are either completely neo-liberal, or carefully non-judgmental toward the EU principles and policies. The traditional socio-democratic perspective is absent.

Šošić's (2005) proposal for reforms of labour policies in Croatia shows complete trust in the power of the market to solve problems of poverty and long-term unemployment. They are to be solved by twin strategies of flexibilization of the labour market (so that the long-term unemployed find non-standard work and take themselves off social services registers) and a shorter period of entitlement to unemployment benefits. In this kind of argument, the usual criteria of quality of work are turned on their heads. Job stability becomes a problem (called 'insufficient dynamism of the labour market') and shuttling between standard and non-standard employment is not seen as a hardship (Šošić 2005, 78).

Other commentators from the EU candidate countries follow a carefully neutral and non-judgmental approach. One could almost call it 'factual', but that would hide the fact that social policies are results of political negotiations and decisions, and are grounded in ideological assumptions that are not factual, objective, or unproblematic. As Kolin's (2008) review of the commodifying EU social policies shows, this approach often leads to theoretical difficulties. The author does not mention that the concept of social exclusion—central to the 'hard' EU social policies—is polar (i.e., it divides society into sharply defined interest groups, squabbling for bigger slices of the social pie) and open to culturalist interpretation (which focuses attention on social acceptance, lifestyle, and identity, and away from difficulties on the labour market). There is no critique of the EU's preference for privatization of social services (politely called 'cooperation with the civil society') and its basis in the fiction that capitalism can ever provide full employment (Kolin 2008, 200–201).

Concluding Remarks

The social policies that the EU implements are targeted at 'excluded' populations, and are explicitly non-universal. They are essentially post-materialist: based on the assumption that all members of society have sufficient material resources for comfortable living, so that their political interests are now focused on non-material issues of discrimination, identity, and social exclusion.

We contend, however, that universal social policies should not yet be abandoned. Global recommodification of labour, justified by the continuing influence of neo-liberalism, makes universal social policies necessary. Full social citizenship for all is a goal that should not be abandoned and that cannot be achieved by targeted social policies. These policies are actually inefficient. Because they have to identify and reach their targets precisely, they need complex and expensive administration. Because they address excluded populations, they need extensive resources to include them in a variety of social activities needed to produce the desired outcomes (Lendvai 2005, 5). This suggests a need for reorientation to universalist social justice, now so conspicuously absent from political debates both at the level of the EU and in its individual member states. Both the universalistic and the targeted policies are necessary for development of meaningful social citizenship.

In practice, the insufficiency of the EU social policies means that the present generation of citizens of the new member states should pay for an allegedly prosperous, market-dominated future for subsequent generations. This is ironic, given that the Stalinist willingness to sacrifice the present generation for the sake of the future was such a mainstay of the Western critique of Stalinism throughout the Cold War.

References

Bailey, David J. 2009. *The Political Economy of European Social Democracy: A Critical Realist Approach*. London and New York: Routledge.

Baloković, Snježana. 2008. 'Programi pomoći Republici Hrvatskoj u sustavu socijalne sigurnosti: CARDS—regionalni program pomoći', *Revija za socijalnu politiku* (15: 2), 225–242.

Drahokoupil, Jan. 2007. 'Analysing the Capitalist State in Post-Socialism: Towards the Porterian Workfare Postnational Regime', *International Journal of Urban and Regional Research* (31: 2), 401–424.

Esping-Andersen, Gøsta. 1990. *The Three Worlds of Welfare Capitalism*. Cambridge: Polity Press.

European Union, European Parliament. 2000. *Charter of Fundamental Rights of the European Union*, Nice. Online. http://www.europarl.europa.eu/charter/pdf/text_en.pdf

Hayden, Robert M. 2008. 'Highways, Roadblocks and Empires', *Sociologija* (L: 4), 337–358.

Kolin, Marija. 2008. 'Obrasci života u siromaštvu i nove paradigme Evropske unije', *Sociologija* (L: 2), 191–206.

Lendvai, Noèmi. 2005. 'Socijalna politika u Srednjoj i Isto noj Europi i ulazak u Evropsku Uniju: Vrijeme za razmišljanje', *Financijska teorija i praksa* (29: 1), 1–12.

Matonyté, Irmina. 2006. 'Why the Notion of Social Justice is Quasi-Absent from the Public Discourse in Post-Communist Lithuania', *Journal of Baltic Studies* (37: 4), 388–411.

Šošić, Vedran. 2005. 'Siromaštvo i politike na tržištu rada u Hrvatskoj', *Financijska teorija i praksa* (29: 1), 75–94.

Velikonja, Mitja. 2007. *Evroza: kritika novog evrocentrizma*. Beograd: Krug.

Questions for Critical Thought

CHAPTER 55

1. What does Hacking mean when he says: 'Counting is hungry for categories'? How does this relate to 'making people up'?
2. What were some problems that the colonial government encountered when they tried to count and classify national castes in India? What were some of the ways they tried to deal with those problems?
3. 'By unyoking caste from its geographical location and centralizing its classifications, the Indian census officials detached caste from its indigenous meaning and used it to reinforce their own ideas about India.' Explain this process with examples from the text, paying particular attentions to which indigenous meanings of caste were erased and which ideas about India were reinforced.
4. What is anthropometry and how did H.H. Risley believe it could help measure caste more accurately? How did it introduce a deeper connection between caste and race?
5. How did the census change the meanings of caste in Indian society?

CHAPTER 56

1. What are social movement organizations, and how are they related to social movements? How are they different from interest groups?
2. How does the example of the 'man in the house' rule demonstrate that the human rights movement in Canada was ideologically divided?
3. How is the idea of human rights 'statist'? How does this limit the forms of justice that the idea can be used to pursue?
4. Discuss the methodological challenges that Clément experienced in her historical research.
5. Why does Clément argue that we need to engage in studies of social movements and human rights in both of Canada's national languages (English and French)?

CHAPTER 57

1. Explain some of the competing theories about the relationship between public opinion and policies that the authors describe.
2. According to the trend data, how did Canadian public spending change over the years of Andersen and Curtis's study (1980–2001)? How did Canadian public opinion on spending change over the years studied? What does this suggest about the relationship between opinion and policy? What theory does it contradict?
3. According to the trend data, how did median income and income inequality change over the period studied? What does this suggest about the relationship between economic context and public opinion?

4. How are the findings from the two different models (i.e., simple trend data and multinomial log-linear model data) different? What different stories do they tell about the relationships between public opinion and public expenditures/governing party/economic context?

5. 'Both of these arguments are based on the premise that people become more aware of inequality and its effects as it becomes larger.' Evaluate this assumption. How is it possible for people to 'see' inequality? How is it difficult to see increases in inequality?

CHAPTER 58

1. Explain what Knezevic means when she states, 'Capitalist economy cannot be maintained without social policy.'

2. Compare and contrast universalistic and targeted social policies.

3. How do the ideas of Social Europe or the European social model compare with actual social policies in the European Union? What is the danger in trusting that these concepts represent the EU's actual governance practices?

4. Describe the open coordination method of the EU and its 'soft' policy procedures. According to Knezevic, is this method successful?

5. What are the neo-liberal strategies for solving poverty?

Part XV

Environment

Earth's environment is currently subject to abuse by a host of human activities, and responsibility for remedying this abuse generally parks at the doors of the state and the civil society. Too often, we continue to let private industry—the main perpetrator of environmental damage—off the hook. Why is this the case?

In this section, Katja Neves' paper reminds us that the line distinguishing society from nature has been an important concept for humanity throughout its history. It was the assumption of this difference that made possible the efforts by humanity, especially during the last five centuries, to dominate nature via science and technology. Pre-industrial people are much less likely than 'modern' industrial people to see and accept such a differentiation, as they believe it is necessary for humans to live in harmony with nature. As Neves points out, Herman Melville in his classic novel *Moby Dick* was one of the first and most important Western novelists to remind us about the interdependence and interaction between the human and natural worlds.

Along similar lines, Mark Vardy asks a central question in connection with the difficulty humans face in dealing with impending ecological disaster: namely, how should we respond—ethically, socially, and politically—to environmental issues that are just as real as those we deal with in our everyday lives, but that are harder to see because they operate on a time scale much longer than any human life? We have as much trouble getting outside our own time frame as we do getting outside our own cultural assumptions and defining social institutions, such as the market economy. Moreover, we make our decisions—or fail to make them—in a context of interdependency that is not only global but also interspecies.

When we forget this interdependency, humans are likely to take dangerous chances with life and nature, as Wilhelm Peekhaus illustrates in his discussion of the risks associated with agricultural biotechnology. Humanity, he argues, simply does not know the full measure of risk associated with genetic engineering, a relatively new field of science that is more powerful than it is precise. For this reason, there is a great need for the regulation of this industry; it is crucial that we assess and prevent dangerous risks rather than suffer the consequences for a lack of vigilance and assign blame later.

Raising important questions about accountability for environmental problems such as climate change, Sherrie Steiner's paper focuses on the international 2009 United Nations Climate Change

Conference in Copenhagen. Steiner notes that the process of assessing accountability and consequent responsibility for restitution is made all the more difficult by the power contest between nation-states and multinational industries, and between more and less developed countries regarding the allocation of restrictions.

Finally, Mark C.J. Stoddart and Laura MacDonald note that environmental activism can play an important role in calling environmental offenders to account, and that the Internet may provide opportunities to mobilize support well beyond what the traditional media make possible. That said, it is too soon to tell whether, and under what circumstance, the Internet will fulfill this important mandate, because we cannot tell who will access which websites. So far, the mass media and their owners still exercise disproportionate control over the information people receive, and the views they hold, about the environment.

CHAPTER 59

'How Can You Decide about Us without Us?': A Canadian Catastrophe in Copenhagen

Sherrie M. Steiner

The unfolding oil spill tragedy in the Gulf of Mexico draws attention to how environmental issues undermine quality of life even in affluent countries and create problems of governance associated with external **accountability**. President Obama has been under immense political pressure to hold BP, Halliburton, and Transocean Ltd. accountable for the spill, and to ensure the future safety of offshore oil drilling (Walsh, 2010). The environmental challenges associated with **climate change** are far more severe even than this spill, threatening the very infrastructure that supports life on Earth (Wilson, 2006).

Rather than remain a detached observer, Paul Wapner calls on environmental scholars to struggle to find a language to communicate what we see—to 'leave our comfort zone and disorient ourselves from a world largely tone-deaf to the magnitude and depth of our environmental challenges' (Wapner, 2008:13). Radical environmental changes must be met with equally radical political responses if governance is to be effective. '[O]ur notions of realism must shift', says Wapner (p. 11). The responsible environmental scholar must search for a language that renders radical insights as what 'they really are, namely, the most realistic orientations these days' (p. 10). Toward that end, I use words such as *catastrophe* as a rhetorical tool to make visible impediments and opportunities for global governance in the context of climate change.

Globalization is a situation of 'governance without government' (Mayntz, 2002). Power has been shifting away from the nation-state's ability to hold multinational corporations accountable to serve the interests of citizens within their respective borders. As such, we have left the 'statist' period of thinking, in which countries are the strongest arbiters of power.

Globalization is proceeding in accordance with some measure of accountability. Bäckstrand (2008) describes *climate* governance as taking the form of 'multistakeholder' hybrid partnerships, 'market' private partnerships, and 'elite' governmental partnerships. Although this global regime absorbs norms of the dominant states to bring a measure of transparency, participation, and reasoned review to ensure greater accountability and responsiveness to globalization, Kingsbury and Stewart (2008:2) make the case for viewing much global governance as *administrative* in character.

While this curb on public power promotes more orderly patterns of globalization, the highly fragmented, horizontally organized regimes function with considerable autonomy, outstripping any global governmental ability to control and legitimate regulatory decisions (Kingsbury and Stewart, 2008:5; Wallach, 2002). Administrating globalization so that it unfolds with a measure of decency and order leaves accountability gaps that have drawn sharp criticism from concerned non-governmental organizations, politicians, and citizens and media who question the nature and direction of globalization itself. Democratic norms continue to expand, but the pace is slow, the process is mostly internal, and the accountability gaps in governance remain large (Bäckstrand, 2008; Newell, 2008).

Legitimacy

In the absence of a world government, climate governance has to rely almost entirely upon non-hierarchical modes of steering globalization (Risse, 2004) that are characterized by multiple sites of governance with power diffused among multiple actors (Bäckstrand, 2008:82). As long as actors perceive the overall quality of this **social order**'s institutions and norms to be legitimate, actors will voluntarily comply with the political order even at great cost (Weber, 1921/1980; Hurd, 1999). Legitimacy depends upon both a procedural logic (predictable rules determined by legitimate actors) and a consequential logic (rules lead to collective problem-solving) (Bäckstrand, 2008:79). Democratic social orders are perceived as legitimate because the rulers are accountable to citizens who participate in rule-making through representation—mechanisms that are absent from transnational governance (Risse, 2004:7). Hence, the situation of governance without government faces legitimacy problems. Scholars have suggested a variety of democratic innovations to address this 'democratic deficit' and enhance the legitimacy of global governance. Some focus more on 'input legitimacy'—concerned with the participatory quality of the decision-making process leading to laws and rules. Others focus more on 'output legitimacy'—concerned with the problem-solving quality of laws and rules. Both are critical for maintaining a legitimate political order (Scharpf, 1999; Risse, 2004:8).

Strengthening accountability of climate partnerships enhances the legitimacy of the climate regime (Bäckstrand, 2008; Newell, 2008). But there are a variety of ways in which individuals who exercise power can be constrained by external means or internal norms—that is, held accountable. Despite its desirability, strengthening accountability can be a complex, messy process with well-intentioned actors working at cross-purposes. Koppell (2005) identifies five dimensions of accountability (transparency, liability, controllability, responsibility, and responsiveness) to explain how conflicting expectations borne of different conceptions of accountability can undermine a global organization's effectiveness.

There are competing models of accountability, with intergovernmental networks favouring delegation models and NGOs favouring participation models (Grant and Keohane, 2005). Steffek and Ferretti (2009) identify potential trade-offs between these two approaches, with international non-governmental organizations (INGOs) torn between their deliberative and watchdog functions. INGOs often tackle the most difficult accountability challenges, representing the 'voices of the weak and powerless'. Willetts (1996:54) refers to them as the 'conscience of the world', noting that they exercise a form of accountability that is *claimed from below* rather than *conferred from above* (quoted in Newell, 2008:124). INGOs face their own problems of internal accountability (Risse, 2004:12), but nevertheless, their effectiveness often rests upon their claim to moral authority and their use of shaming tactics to affect the reputation of organizations through media exposure (Keohane, 2004:25).

INGOs are more single-minded and agile than states, giving them an advantage in media struggles. They actively lobby governments and, because they command the allegiances of up to billions of people, they are able to influence public opinion. Reputational accountability is relatively unreliable but nevertheless significant, affecting inclusion/exclusion in relevant networks requiring cooperation and negotiation (Bäckstrand, 2008:81; Keohane, 2004:26). To capture the hearts and minds of the people, INGOs target the global cultural realm and appeal to moral norms, symbols, and scientific argument to pursue environmentally sound practices. Their activities represent a significant form of world politics even though it is not a matter of state activity. Groups such as Greenpeace capture media attention with spectacular visuals, inviting the public to bear witness. Their activities augment statist politics with civic life politics, playing on the fact that governments and corporations are vulnerable to public opinion. Their lobbying has been crucial to the advancement of environmental law and practice.

INGOs use knowledge as a form of power to shape the nature and terms of the debate through evolving norms and ideas that may strengthen or undermine the legitimacy of the global system (Risse, 2002). Disclosure of information has become such a heavily relied upon tool used to strengthen accountability that transparency has become a moral and political imperative in environmental governance (Gupta, 2008). Global environmental politics has taken a 'procedural turn' where 'getting the process right' is so over-emphasized that 'governance-by-disclosure' may become counterproductive, diverting time and resources from substantive outcomes and ultimately undermining the emancipatory potential of information (Gupta, 2008).

Copenhagen

'Governance-by-disclosure' certainly characterizes events at the 2009 United Nations Climate Change Conference in Copenhagen (known informally as the Copenhagen Summit)—although reporters referred to it as 'negotiation-by-leak' (Vidal and Watts, 2009). The leaks began on the second day of the conference and gradually increased until, by the end, there was a flood—making this the leakiest international conference in history (Vidal and Watts, 2009). As transparency demands increased, deliberative decision making increasingly moved behind closed doors, creating further objections. For example, during the famous all-night drama that saved the deal from complete collapse, Latin American nations and the small island nations objected to the way the accord had been reached: '"We're offended by the methodology. This has been done in the dark" fumed the Bolivian delegate' (Vidal and Watts, 2009:2). Friends of the Earth called it a 'secret backroom declaration that failed to take into account the needs of more than a hundred countries' (Vidal and Watts, 2009:4). As Richard Black (2010:1) notes, Gro Harlem Brudtland compared the atmosphere at the Copenhagen summit 'to student politics in the 1960s—"chaotic, wearing, tiring, disappointing"—and said it was one in which countries had little room for real negotiating'.

Efforts to strengthen accountability were evident, but as the summit progressed, 7,000 representatives from civil society were reduced to 1,000 and then to 90 by the last day. INGO representation was cut back according to membership size, a reduction that hit Asian and African INGO's the hardest (Vidal and Watts, 2009:3). Posters protesting the clamp down bore messages such as 'How can you decide about us without us?', 'Civil society silenced', and 'Civil society has been removed from the negotiations'.

Canada's performance in Copenhagen was particularly disturbing. Climate Action Network, an organization made up of 450 NGOs, identified Canada as the most obstructive participant in the talks, awarding Canada the Colossal Fossil award for doing the least to mitigate climate change and doing the most to obstruct an ambitious agreement (Hance, 2009a). There were 192 countries at the summit, and Canada walked away with over a third of the 'fossil awards' given to countries that most impede progress. On 11 December, Toronto Mayor David Miller accepted the Casket of Shame award on behalf of Canada with the statement, 'I'm embarrassed to be Canadian' (Hance, 2009b).

When Canadian cabinet documents were leaked on 15 December, INGOs said what no state-actor could: that these documents imply Canada was negotiating in bad faith and that other countries would likely find this disturbing and upsetting. 'Canada's performance here in Copenhagen builds on two years of delay, obstruction and total inaction. This government thinks there's a choice between environment and economy, and for them, tar sands beats climate every time' said Ben Wikler of the INGO Avaaz (Hance, 2009a:1). Canada's environmental minister offered zero progress on financing, offered no targets, and made no references to science in his presentations. This despite international criticism and a Proceeding of the National Academy of Sciences identifying Alberta's tar sands as one of the world's largest industrial sources of greenhouse gases—emitting an estimated 40 million tons every year (Hance, 2009c).

Canada is the only country to join, and then drop out of, the Kyoto Treaty, and Canada's emissions have risen by 26 per cent since 1990 (10 per cent more than the United States, which never signed on to Kyoto). Canada's international reputation took a beating over its stance on climate in Copenhagen. Eric Walton, Green Party Critic for International Affairs, is concerned this will 'negatively impact on our diplomatic ability to advance Canada's interests and could even lead to future tariff penalties on our exports' (quoted in Faulkner, 2009).

Is George Monbiot (2009) of the *Guardian* right when he says the tar barons are holding Canada to ransom? Is Canada turning itself into a corrupt petro-state? What happened to the image of Canada as peacekeeper, as friendly, decent, civilized, fair, and well governed? In a global world of deepening interdependence—where governance must progress without government, the cultivation of trust is essential for progress on international negotiations. Trust may not be a good survival tactic, but it is essential for the socializing effects of processes of accountability within systems of corporate governance (Roberts, 2001). The international community needs trustworthy Canadians capable of strengthening global climate governance in a world without government.

Conclusion

Many had high hopes for the Copenhagen Summit. It was the last governmental-level meeting of the parties to the United Nations Framework Convention on Climate Change before the Kyoto Protocol needs to be renewed in 2012. It was hoped that delegates meeting in Copenhagen (7–13 December, 2009) would develop a framework for climate change mitigation. By most counts, the summit was perceived as a failure.

When it comes to climate change, there are few mechanisms that ensure that those potentially affected by the international norms have a say in making the rules (Risse, 2004:9). If including stakeholders in deliberations increases input legitimacy, who decides who the stakeholders are (Risse, 2004:10)? Keohane reminds us that common values are lacking in what is a highly interdependent and violence-prone system. 'A universal global society remains a dream, and one that may be receding from view rather than becoming closer' (Keohane, 2004: 6). Global society will therefore be *partial* rather than universal; so how do we determine which entities have the right to hold agents accountable if the agents do not recognize a corresponding obligation (Keohane, 2004:12)?

Should those who are defining (and often making) the choices be fully accountable for their actions (Held, 2002:26)? A key question for global governance is 'What do adapted democratic principles imply about desirable patterns of accountability in world politics?'

References

Bäckstrand, Karin. 2006. 'Democratising Global Governance? Stakeholder Democracy after the World Summit on Sustainable Development'. *European Journal of International Relations* 12 (4): 467–498.

———. 2008. 'Accountability of Networked Climate Governance: The Rise of Transnational Climate Partnerships'. *Global Environmental Politics* 8 (3): 74–102.

Black, Richard. 2010. '"Arrogance" Undid Climate Talks'. *BBC News*. 29 May.

Cox, Bruce. 2010. 'Strength Out of Failure'. *Greenpeace Magazine* 11 (6): Spring/Summer.

Faulkner, Anne. 2009. 'Canada's Reputation in Peril'. *Green Party of Canada. Media Release*. December 7.

Grant, Ruth W. and Robert O. Keohane. 2005. 'Accountability and Abuses of Power in World Politics'. *American Political Science Review* 99 (1): 29–43.

Gupta, Aarti. 2008. 'Transparency Under Scrutiny: Information Disclosure in Global Environmental Governance'. *Global Environmental Politics* 8 (2): 1–7.

Hance, Jeremy. 2009a. 'Canada at Copenhagen: "Delay, Obstruction, and Total Inaction"'. *Mongabay.com,* December 21.

———. 2009b. 'Canada's Reign of Shame in Copenhagen'. *Mongabay.com*, December 11.

———. 2009c. 'Oil Sands Pollution in Canada Worse Than Industry and Government Claim'. *Mongabay.com*, December 7.

Held, David. 2002. 'Law of States, Law of Peoples: Three Models of Sovereignty'. *Legal Theory* 8: 1–44.

Hurd, Ian. 1999. Legitimacy and Authority in International Politics. *International Organization* 53 (2): 379–408.

Keohane, Robert O. 2004. 'Global Governance and Democratic Accountability', pp. 261–287 in *Government and Opposition* by David Held and Mathias Koenig-Archibugi (eds.) London: London School of Economics.

Kingsbury, Benedict and Richard B. Stewart. 2008. 'Legitimacy and Accountability in Global Regulatory Governance: The Emerging Global Administrative Law and the Design and Operation of Administrative Tribunals of International Organizations', pp. 1–20 in Flogaitis Spyridan (ed.), *International Administrative Tribunals in a Changing World*. London: Esperia.

Koppell, Jonathan G.S. 2005. 'Pathologies of Accountability: ICANN and the Challenge of "Multiple Accountabilities Disorder"'. *Public Administration Review* Vol. 65 (1): 94–108.

Mayntz, Renate. 2002. 'Common Goods and Governance', pp. 15–27 in Adrienne Heritier (ed.), *Common Goods. Reinventing European and International Governance*. Lanham, MD: Rowman and Littlefield.

Monbiot, George. 2009. 'Canada's Image Lies in Tatters: It Is Now to Climate What Japan Is to Whaling'. *The Guardian*, 30 November.

Newell, Peter. 2008. 'Civil Society, Corporate Accountability and the Politics of Climate Change'. *Global Environmental Politics* 8 (3): 122–153.

Risse, Thomas. 2002. Transnational Actors and World Politics', pp. 255–274 in Walter Carlsnaes, Thomas Risse, and Beth A. Simmons (eds.), *Handbook of International Relations*. London: Sage.

———. 2004. *Transnational Governance and Legitimacy*. Center for Transatlantic Foreign and Security Policy. Retrieved 27 May, 2010.

Roberts, John. 2001. 'Trust and Control in Anglo-American Systems of Corporate Governance: The Individualizing and Socializing Effects of Processes of Accountability'. *Human Relations* 54 (12): 1547–1572.

Scharpf, Fritz W. 1999. *Regieren in Europa*. Frankfurt: Campus Fachbuch.

Steffek, Jens and Maria Paola Ferretti. 2009. 'Accountability or "Good Decisions"? The Competing Goals of Civil Society Participation in International Governance'. *Global Society* 23 (1): 37–57.

Vidal, John and Jonathan Watts. 2009. 'Copenhagen: The Last-Ditch Drama That Saved the Deal From Collapse'. *Guardian.Co.Uk*, 20 December.

Wallach, Lori M. 2002. 'Accountable Governance in the Era of Globalization: The WTO, NAFTA, and International Harmonization of Standards'. *University of Kanas law Review* (50): 823.

Walsh, Eric. 2010. 'Obama: Gulf Drilling Only If Ensure No More Spills'. *Reuters*. Retrieved 28 May, 2010.

Wapner, Paul. 2008. 'The Importance of Critical Environmental Studies in the New Environmentalism'. *Global Environmental Politics* 8 (1): 6–13.

———. 1996. *Environmental Activism and World Civic Politics*. Albany, NY: State University of New York Press.

Weber, Max. 1921/1980. *Wirtschaft und Gesellschaft*. Tübingen: J.C.B. Mohr.

Wilson, Edward O. 2006. *The Creation: An Appeal to Save Life on Earth*. New York: W.W. Norton and Company.

CHAPTER 60

The Production of Modernity in Classic American Whale Hunting

Katja Neves

Sociology first emerged as a social science aiming to describe and explain the historical phenomenon of **modernity** (Sayer 1991). Modernity refers to a series of social, institutional, and economic transformations that began to unfold during the period of Enlightenment in Europe, and that became increasingly global throughout the twentieth century (Giddens 1991; 1998). According to the founders of sociology, these historical transformations entailed the institutionalization of the **nation-state** and democracy, the industrialization of production and establishment of capitalism, and the rationalization and disenchantment of human existence. Thus, Émile Durkheim sought to explain what held together modern societies when religion, feudal hierarchy, and community solidarity ceased to be the main sources of social organization and cohesion. Karl Marx endeavoured to understand the social effects of substituting direct exchanges of goods and services with exchanges mediated by money, especially the unequal and exploitative relations this created between capitalist owners of means of production and salaried workers (i.e., the proletariat). Max Weber, in turn, proposed that Protestant beliefs and norms concerning human conduct and salvation helped foster the rise of capitalism. Weber also studied the newly instituted bureaucracies of nation-states, arguing that their deeply rationalizing logic was tantamount to imprisoning humans and human imagination in iron cages.

More recently, Bruno Latour (e.g. 1993, 2004) demonstrated that science has contributed greatly to the production and reproduction of modernity. Modernity, Latour argues, is founded on a set of premises and practices that create the illusion that society and nature are completely independent entities, and that a very clearly demarcated boundary divides them. Science plays a particularly important role in this context by furnishing society–nature dichotomies with purportedly objective studies and discourses that reinforce the notion that the world is indeed constituted by such discrete entities. This is a uniquely modern phenomenon since previous historical periods tended to grant a much higher degree of integration to all sorts of beings (human, nonhuman, spiritual, and material). According to Latour (2004), the modern divide has been used to legitimize human domination and exploitation of **ecosystems** and peoples around the world. Moreover, these dichotomies have become so deeply embedded in the modern world that they are effectively very similar to national constitutions: 'Just as the constitution of jurists defines the rights and duties of citizens and the State, the working of justice and the transfer of power, so this Constitution . . . defines humans and nonhumans, their properties and their relations, their abilities and their groupings' (Latour 1993: 15).

In parallel and in tension with the society–nature divide, the modern constitution also institutes and regulates a second dichotomy. This one draws a line between the world of discrete entities mentioned above and a world of '**hybrid networks**' punctuated by blurred boundaries between humans and non-humans, societies and natures, biological organisms and machines (see Figure 60.1).

Hybrid networks are inhabited by all the creatures and artifacts that emerge from encounters and associations of the human and the non-human, the biological and the technological, the social and the ecological. They involve the work of translation, whereby humans, plants, non-human animals, machines, ecosystems, and so on become so inextricably connected that they can only be conceptualized as collectives. Although the world has always been inhabited by such creatures, modernity has tended to deny their existence, keeping them hidden behind imagined and objectified human–nature separateness.

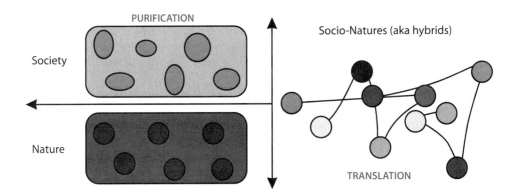

Figure 60.1 The Interplay between Society and Nature

In short, the ontological and political foundations of modernity stem from the establishment, orchestration, and performance of these two sets of dichotomies. Nevertheless, the orchestration of these dichotomies is extremely unstable and contingent, as the world of hybrids constantly threatens to reveal the spuriousness of the modern constitution. Without such orchestration, Latour argues, we would 'stop being wholly modern' and our future would begin to change (Latour 1993: 11). Dismantling these dichotomies would challenge the status quo of the elites and economic interests that most stand to gain from the modern constitution and the concomitant exploitation of both humans and non-humans on a planetary scale. Even in the context of contemporary nature conservation, variations of the modern constitution continue to re-create environmental problems around the globe (e.g. Neves 2004; 2006; Neves 2010; see also Igoe, Neves, Brockington 2010).

Whereas Latour has provided extensive evidence that science plays a crucial role in creating and perpetuating the illusion that there is a clear divide between nature and society, as well as between discrete entities and hybrids, I suggest that the production of commodities within capitalism plays a no lesser role by bringing the modern constitution into material, embodied, and symbolic-ideological existence. This argument takes Latour further, and is also seen in more recent contributions by Noel Castree (2000; 2002), who pioneered the synthesis between Latourian and Marxian scholarship. While Castree argues that the material, symbolic, and ideological production of nature in capitalism renders invisible the extent to which humans and non-humans co-construct one another, thus further legitimizing human domination of endless 'natures', I extend his argument to show that these processes ultimately amount to the production and reproduction of the epochal configuration we tentatively call modern.

The case of classic American industrial whale hunting provides comprehensible evidence in support of these novel claims and their empirical substantiation (see Neves 2010; see Neves forthcoming for in-depth analysis). Not only do these materials show the role that early capitalist industrial processes played in furthering the illusion that a clear divide separates the world of humans (society) from the world of non-humans (nature), they also unveil a parallel world of hybrid networks in which human–whale dichotomies were much harder to sustain. Revealing tensions between the two offers important insight for political ecologists and promotes greater levels of social reflexivity in regard to our relations with non-humans (see Beck 1992).

Borrowing Latour's terminology, one can argue that classic industrial capitalist commodities were traditionally produced as 'risk-free objects' or as 'matters of fact'. In a Latourian framework, risk-free objects (or matters of fact) are those that appear as independent, discrete entities because their connection to the humans and natures that produced them have been erased. They are risk-free matters of fact because nothing in them indicates that they are actually the product of complex associations between humans, technologies, and natures—in other words, that they are hybrids. Moreover, they are perceived as risk free because their social, political, and environmental impacts (either effective or potential) are also concealed. To be sure, in the context of capitalism, commodities appear in markets as if by magic, expunged of the complex human–non-human matrices out of which they come to be. Karl Marx called this process the **fetishization of commodities**.

Latour argues that in parallel to risk-free objects, modernity constantly produces 'risky objects' or 'matters of concern'—more often than not, concurrently. The history of the nuclear industry is an example: nuclear power sites were presented as risk-free matters of fact until the Chernobyl accident of 1986 showed their full complexity as risky objects. These objects call into question the kinds of dichotomies mentioned above, on which the modern constitution relies. Managing the tension that exists between both types of objects has been a central concern within modern systems of governance. This includes the systems of governance on which the expansion of capitalism has rested historically, such as the current case of neoliberalism. Hence, my work expands Castree's argument that the capitalist 'production of nature' entails the co-construction of a joint human and non-human world, to argue that what are in fact being produced through the implementation of the modern constitution at different historical junctures are distinct epochs of human–non-human collectives (e.g. premodern, modern, postmodern).

Whale-derived commodities, such as oil, provide an excellent means to illustrate the ways in which early industrial capitalism contributed to the material implementation and legitimation of the modern constitution. Whale oil was such an important source for illumination and machine lubrication during the early years of the Industrial Revolution that whaling became a major global economic enterprise during the eighteenth and nineteenth centuries.

As Melville has aptly described in his famous book *Moby Dick* (1851 [1981]), the activity of whale hunting was extremely brutal both for the humans who killed the whales and for the whales—though no doubt in highly unbalanced terms. Men were often at sea for periods of up to four years, living in highly precarious conditions of lack of proper nutrition, isolation, and constant danger of deadly accidents. The hunt itself was extremely painful for the whales, who often suffered in agony for hours on end (see Neves 2005 for a detailed description). Processing the whales once they were hunted was no easier task. It was in fact so laborious and messy that the whalers' clothes had to be thrown away as they were drenched in foul smells, blood, and whale oil. The whale oil that was sold in markets contained the suffering and pain of whales as well as the hard labour and sacrifice of humans. It was the product of a complex matrix of human–non-human associations.

And yet, whale oil reached the consumer completely stripped of any trace of these entanglements, abstracted from the encounters out of which it came into existence. Most people used their lamps in the evening without having the slightest idea of the biological origin of the oil, of how it was produced, or even how it had travelled around the world to reach the consumer. Whale oil was thus perceived abstractly in fetishized form as a material resource, extracted from an equally abstract and homogenized nature, and brought directly into the social world of human consumption. In the meantime, entire species of whales were hunted to the brink of extinction.

My use of Latour's opus allows us take the sociological understanding of fetishized commodities one step further to discuss their role in the production of modernity. By appearing in markets completely detached from the human, material, and ecological context of their production, industrial commodities are the material manifestation and implementation of the modern constitution. Insofar as these commodities appear to constitute discrete entities, they arrive in markets as risk-free objects, with their true social and ecological costs rendered invisible. Consequently, imagined dichotomies between society and nature are reproduced, as is a global mode of production and governance that relies on destructive relations with ecosystems and exploitative relations amongst humans. These, as Latour (2004) has argued, are the core features of the modern constitution and, one might add, a major contributing factor to our current socio-environmental predicament.

However, whale hunting also produced another type of commodity that is best described as a risky object or matter of concern: the maritime whaling novel of which Melville's *Moby Dick* (1851 [1981]) is the best-known example—though merely one among many of its kind. Such writing captures the full context in which whale products such as oil, baleen, and ivory were produced. They reveal in intimate detail the inextricable connections that existed between whales, humans, society, and nature, thus carrying the potential of bringing into question the kinds of modernist dichotomies that ruthlessly legitimize the exploitation of humans and non-humans within capitalist frameworks. I propose that the genius of books like Melville's lies in their revolutionary potential to carry out Latour's call to show the simultaneity of the production of worlds of discrete entities and worlds of hybrids within modernity (Latour 2004). In agreement with Latour's call for such a political ecology, I contend that it is our role as sociologists to unveil and explain these processes and, in so doing, help nurture higher degrees of reflexivity concerning the politics and implications of distinct epochs of human–non-human collectives.

References

Beck, Ulrich 1992. *Risk Society: Towards a New Modernity.* London, Thousand Oaks: Sage.

Castree, Noel 2000. Marxism and the Production of Nature. *Capital & Class* 72: 5–33.

———. 2002. False Antitheses? Marxism, Nature and Actor Networks. *Antipode.* 34(1): 111–146.

Giddens, Anthony 1991. *Modernity and Self-Identity: Self and Society in the Late Modern Age,* Palo Alto, CA: Stanford University Press.

———. 1998. *Conversations with Anthony Giddens: Making Sense of Modernity.* Stanford, CA: Stanford University Press.

Haraway, Donna 1991. A Cyborg Manifesto: Science, Technology, and Socialist-Feminism in the Late Twentieth Century. In Donna J. Haraway, Ed., *Simians, Cyborgs and Women: The Reinvention of Nature,* pp. 149–181. New York: Routledge.

———. 2008. *When Species Meet.* Minneapolis, MN: University of Minnesota Press.

Igoe, J., Neves, K., Brockington, D. 2010. Engaging the Hegemonic Convergence of Capitalist Expansion and Biodiversity Conservation: A Theoretical Framework for Social Scientific Investigation. *Capitalism and Conservation,* special issue of *Antipode* 42(3): 486–512.

Latour, Bruno 1993. *We Have Never Been Modern.* Cambridge, MA: Harvard University Press.

———. 2004. *Politics of Nature: How to Bring the Sciences into Democracy.* Cambridge, MA: Harvard University Press

Melville, Herman 1851 [1981]. *Moby Dick: The Whale.* Bantam Classics; Reissue edition.

Neves, K. Forthcoming. *'A Whale of a Thing': The Production, Reproduction, and Liquidation of Modernity from Whale Hunting to Whale Watching.*

Neves, K. 2010. Cashing in on Cetourism: A Critical Engagement with Dominant E-NGO Discourses on Whaling, Cetacean Conservation, and Whale Watching. *Capitalism and Conservation,* special issue of *Antipode* 42(3): 719–741.

Neves-Graca, K. 2006. Politics of Environmentalism and Ecological Knowledge at the Intersection of Local and Global Processes. *Journal of Ecological Anthropology* 10: 19–32.

———. 2005. Chasing Whales with Bateson and Daniel. *Ecological Humanities Corner of the Australian Humanities Review Journal* (35) June 2005.

———. 2004. Revisiting the Tragedy of the Commons: Whale Watching in the Azores and its Ecological Dilemmas. *Human Organisation* 63(3): 289–300.

Sayer, Derek 1991. *Capitalism and Modernity: An Excursus on Marx and Weber.* New York: Routledge

CHAPTER 61

'Keep It Wild, Keep It Local': Comparing News Media and the Internet as Sites for Environmental Movement Activism for Jumbo Pass, British Columbia

Mark C.J. Stoddart and Laura MacDonald

Social movements rely on the mass media to gain visibility for their issues, to reach potential supporters, and to engage opponents and governments in public debate (Doyle, Elliott, and Tindall 1997; Gamson 2007; Hannigan 2006; Hutchins and Lester 2006; Rossiter 2004; Stoddart 2005). Traditionally, the relationship between social movements and journalists has been characterized as one of 'asymmetrical dependency' (Carroll and Ratner 1999; Gamson and Wolfsfeld 1993). This is because social movement organizations that seek media attention must make their issues newsworthy enough to gain coverage.

The emergence of the Internet as an 'alternative public sphere' may be changing the nature of the relationship between social movement actors and news workers (della Porta and Mosca 2005; Hackett and Carroll 2006; Lester and Hutchins 2009; Owens and Palmer 2003). The Internet may give environmental organizations greater independence and power to raise substantive issues, promote citizen engagement, and speak directly to supporters rather than traditional mass media. In this paper, we examine the case of **eco-political** conflict over Jumbo Pass—the site of a proposed ski resort in British Columbia—to analyze how the Internet may function as a more open public sphere than traditional mass media for environmentalist communication.

Methodology

Our study incorporates a textual analysis of news articles published in major national and provincial newspapers in combination with an analysis of websites produced by local and provincial environmental organizations involved in the Jumbo Pass conflict (Macdonald 2003; Mason 2002; Prior 1997; Silverman 2001). We used the Factiva database to sample articles from the *Globe and Mail*, the *National Post*, and the *Vancouver Sun* and performed an Internet ethnography on the selected websites. All of the newspaper texts as well as the data from the websites were imported into NVivo 8 software for qualitative analysis, where they were coded and analyzed. Coding focused on several elements of the data, including the following: which organizational actors appeared as news sources, how the Jumbo Pass landscape was defined by different news sources, which claims and counter-claims were made about ecological degradation in the area, which forms of land use were seen as appropriate for the two areas, and which mechanisms of political decision making about the area were discussed.

Results

Tourism, Development, and Ecological Risk in the Purcells

Mass media

In the mass media news narrative, several different discourses define the meaning of the Jumbo landscape and describe which modes of interaction with this mountain environment should be viewed as appropriate or inappropriate. The most prevalent theme, which is primarily articulated by environmentalists, is of Jumbo Pass as a wilderness landscape in need of protection from skiing development. The local grizzly bear population is a particularly important focal point for environmentalist **claims-making**. This is consistent with prior research on the symbolic work that animals are called upon to do within environmental politics (for example, see Philo and Wilbert 2000; Wolch and Emel 1998). Moreover, environmentalist news sources gain entrée as 'authoritative knowers' (Ericson, Baranek, and Chan 1989) and political representatives for non-human animals. This dominant environmentalist discourse defines resort-based skiing as an ecologically illegitimate mode of interaction with the mountain landscape.

A recurring pro-resort discourse, which is articulated by Jumbo Glacier Resort project proponents, as well as by some journalists, focuses on how the resort will bring tourism and economic development to a region with a declining forestry economy. Here, skiing is defined as a mode of 'attractive development' (Luke 2002), which values non-human nature for the experience it provides, rather than as a resource pool for forestry or mining. In this discourse, skiing is an economically beneficial, rather than pro-environmental, mode of interaction with mountainous nature.

Websites

Websites also focus primarily on protecting grizzly bears from the negative environmental impacts that would result from resort development (Jumbo Creek Conservation Society 2010; Wildsight 2010). In contrast to the newspaper data, however, climate change is an additional environmental issue associated with development and is depicted as an issue of urgency. Glaciers in the region of the proposed resort are predicted to be entirely melted within four decades, a prediction that challenges the claims that are made by resort proponents that Jumbo is the perfect site for year-round glacier skiing. Websites provide scientific evidence that support their claims about grizzly bears and climate change, and scientists are frequently cited as authoritative voices (Nelson EcoSociety 2010; Valhalla Wilderness Society 2010; Wildsight 2010).

Websites also often provide an alternative to the proposed Jumbo Resort. Although viewers are not directly encouraged to visit the local ski hills, these venues are described as being under capacity, which suggest that Jumbo Resort is an excessive development project for this wilderness area. This discourse focuses on Jumbo Resort as a specific example of ecologically illegitimate ski development, rather than framing skiing in general as a problem, and creates space for greater alignment between environmental organizations and environmentally aware skiers.

Repertoires of Protest

Mass media

Less than a third of the newspaper articles mention the specific strategies and protest tactics environmentalists used to bring attention to the Jumbo Pass conflict. The tactics that do receive coverage include blockades, petitions, and NHL defenceman Scott Neidermeyer's endorsement of the campaign. In contrast to prior research on movements and media, there is little difference in the number of articles that focus on different tactics, which suggests that the choice of tactics used by environmentalists is not a significant factor in determining whether Jumbo Pass becomes news (Boykoff 2006; McCarthy et al. 1996; Smith et al. 2001).

The blockades were initiated by an attempt to begin 'temporary' construction in the Jumbo Pass area and involved protesters physically obstructing the access road. While the blockades were useful for gaining media access, the main environmental discourse in these articles focused on the notion that the project is 'controversial', while

giving little attention to substantive claims about grizzly bear impacts, wilderness values, or calls for local decision making. The news stories that focus on blockades appear to be consistent with prior research suggesting that reliance on particularly dramatic protest tactics may risk minimizing attention to the substantive claims of social movement groups (Doyle 2003; Gitlin 1980).

Websites

Letter writing is the most popular form of protest that is incorporated into the websites. Postal and/or e-mail addresses, sample letters, instructions on how to write the letter, and direction on what points to include are often provided (Jumbo Creek Conservation Society 2010; Valhalla Wilderness Society 2010; Wildsight 2010). In addition, several celebrities are incorporated into the websites as supporters or volunteer spokespeople, including Neidermeyer, whose picture serves as the link to the 'take action' page on the Jumbo Creek Conservation Society (JCCS) webpage. This encourages letter writing and indicates that these groups are making use of celebrities in a direct way to get people involved in activism, rather than only as a hook to gain news coverage and raise awareness of the issue, as is often the case when environmental issues are incorporated into the 'politicized celebrity system' (Boykoff and Goodman 2009; also see Brockington 2008).

Local Democracy and Environmental Governance

Mass media

A significant body of research examines the degree to which non-state actors are gaining increasing access to—and power within—processes of environmental governance (Bardati 2009; Bulkeley and Betsill 2005; Mascarenhas and Scarce 2004; Parkins and Davidson 2008). Other work has similarly queried the connections between environmentalism and a 'reconceptualization of citizenship as participatory, expansive, solidaristic, and ecological' (Adkin 2009, 4; also see Salazar 2009; Spaargaren and Mol 2008). In line with this recent academic research, questions of local decision making within environmental governance are central to the news narrative of Jumbo Pass.

However, the meaning of local decision-making varies across news articles and is contested by different groups. An article from 2004, for example, describes how the provincial government is shifting decision-making power over the proposed resort to the Regional District of East Kootenay (RDEK), which is a regional governing body. The government frames this move as a sign of respect and empowerment for local communities. Environmentalists' initial response to this move is that the province is 'trying to "pass the buck" for an unpopular decision' onto a local system that is not well equipped to understand the complexities of the issue (Hartwig qtd Hume 2004a, A11).

Environmental discourse quickly shifts, however, and links local decision making to widespread opposition to the project in nearby communities. Local decision making is preferred to provincial decision making because it gives members of East Kootenay communities greater control over development in the region. In opposition to the environmentalist discourse of local decision making as democratic, several op-ed pieces reframe local control over the project as undemocratic, claiming that local governments are easily manipulated by environmentalists.

Websites

The need to keep the decision for or against the resort local is repeatedly stressed on the websites. Website viewers are encouraged to demand that the decision be kept local through tactics such as letter writing. In taking the situation into their own hands in order to further expose government officials with respect to their stance on the issue, JCCS and Wildsight provide a list of the RDEK board members and whether they voted to keep the decision local or pass the decision to the provincial level. This is a good example of information provision on the Internet that would not likely occur via traditional media such as newspapers (della Porta and Mosca 2005).

Conclusion

In the news narrative constructed around the Jumbo Pass conflict, environmentalists are able to gain entrée to news narratives—often without aid of dramatic protest actions. The relationship between environmentalists and news media, as illustrated in this particular case, appears to be one in which environmentalists are treated as 'authorized knowers' and are given the power to speak on behalf of non-human nature (Ericson, Baranek, and Chan 1989; also see Cottle 1993). Rather than reflecting a relationship of asymmetrical dependency, this analysis is more consistent with Cottle's (2008) recent suggestion that the relationship between movements and media are changing due to several factors, including generational shifts among news-workers.

Despite this, websites provide space for a greater range of claims and more nuanced claims than are admitted into the newspaper narrative. This is evident from the detailed information that is provided in the websites with respect to scientific knowledge and local democracy. The Internet allows movements to disseminate the kind of information they feel is most valuable to gain support for their claims: for example, plebiscite and third-party polls that were conducted that clearly identify opposition to resort from local citizens, not just from dedicated environmentalists (Valhalla Wilderness Society 2010; Wildsight 2010). This level of provision of information and the incorporation of e-mail writing are unique to the Internet as a new medium for activism (Arquilla and Ronfeldt 2001; Rohlinger and Brown 2009). They extend the communicative capacity of environmental organizations beyond the limitations imposed by the genre conventions of the mass media by directly mobilizing supporters to acts of 'low-cost activism', such as letter writing or contributing donations (Tindall 2002).

While activist-produced websites are obviously useful tools for environmental groups, as illustrated in the case of Jumbo Pass, their utility should not be overstated. Without further research on the different audience size and makeup of mass media and activist-produced media, we cannot make confident assertions about the efficacy of environmentalist-produced webpages as a communication medium. However, it is probable that newspapers reach both a larger audience and a more general audience than that reached by environmentalist websites. By contrast, activist-produced websites may be limited to speaking to smaller, more attentive audiences (Rauch 2007). If this is the case, social movement communication strategies should focus on how these different media may be used to complement each other. For example, mass media coverage may provide the necessary motivation for sympathetic audience members to seek out the more detailed content of activist-produced websites (Owens and Palmer 2003).

References

Adkin, Laurie E. 2009. Ecology, Citizenship, Democracy. In *Environmental Conflict and Democracy in Canada*, edited by L.E. Adkin. Vancouver: UBC Press.

Arquilla, John & David Ronfeldt, eds. 2001. *Networks and Netwars: The Future of Terror, Crime and Militancy*. Santa Monica: RAND.

Bardati, Darren R. 2009. Participation, Information, and Forest Conflict in the Slocan Valley of British Columbia. In *Environmental Conflict and Democracy in Canada*, edited by L.E. Adkin. Vancouver: UBC Press.

Boykoff, Jules. 2006. Framing Dissent: Mass-Media Coverage of the Global Justice Movement. *New Political Science* 28 (2):201–228.

Boykoff, Maxwell T., and Michael K. Goodman. 2009. Conspicuous Redemption? Reflections on the Promises and Perils of the 'Celebritization' of Climate Change. *Geoforum* 40:395–406.

Brockington, Dan. 2008. Powerful Environmentalisms: Conservation, Celebrity and Capitalism. *Media, Culture & Society* 30 (4):551–568.

Bulkeley, Harriet, and Michele Betsill. 2005. Rethinking Sustainable Cities: Multilevel Governance and the 'Urban' Politics of Climate Change. *Environmental Politics* 14 (1):42–63.

Carroll, W.K., and R.S. Ratner. 1999. Media Strategies and Political Projects: A Comparative Study of Social Movements. *Canadian Journal of Sociology* 24 (1):1–34.

Cottle, S. 1993. Mediating the Environment: Modalities of TV News. In *The Mass Media and Environmental Issues*, edited by A. Hansen. New York: Leicester University Press.

———. 2008. Reporting Demonstrations: The Changing Media Politics of Dissent. *Media, Culture & Society* 30 (6):853–872.

Della Porta, Donatella, and Lorenzo Mosca. 2005. Global-Net for Global Movements? A Network of Networks for a Movement of Movements. *Journal of Public Policy* 25 (1):165–190.

Doyle, Aaron. 2003. *Arresting Images: Crime and Policing in Front of the Television Camera*. Toronto: University of Toronto Press.

Doyle, Aaron, Brian Elliott, and David Tindall. 1997. Framing the Forests: Corporations, the B.C. Forest Alliance, and the Media. In *Organizing Dissent: Contemporary Social Movements in Theory and Practice*, edited by W.K. Carroll. Toronto: Garamond Press.

Ericson, R.V., P.M. Baranek, and J.B.L. Chan. 1989. *Negotiating Control: A Study of News Sources*. Toronto: University of Toronto Press.

Gamson, W.A. 2007. Bystanders, Public Opinion, and the Media. In *The Blackwell Companion to Social Movements*, edited by D.A. Snow, S.A. Soule and H. Kriesi. Oxford: Blackwell.

Gamson, W.A., and G. Wolfsfeld. 1993. Movements and Media as Interacting Systems. *Annals of the American Academy of Political and Social Science* 528:114–125.

Gitlin, Todd. 1980. *The Whole World Is Watching: Mass Media in the Making & Unmaking of the New Left*. Berkeley: University of California Press.

Hackett, Robert A., and William K. Carroll. 2006. *Remaking Media: The Struggle to Democratize Public Communication*. New York: Routledge.

Hannigan, John A. 2006. *Environmental Sociology: A Social Constructionist Perspective*. 2nd ed. London Routledge.

Hume, Mark. 2004. B.C. Backs Resort in Pristine Area. *The Globe and Mail*, 15 October, A11.

Hutchins, Brett, and Libby Lester. 2006. Environmental Protest and Tap-Dancing with the Media in the Information Age. *Media, Culture & Society* 28 (3):433–451.

Jumbo Creek Conservation Society (JCCS). (2010). http://www.keepitwild.ca.

Lester, Libby, and Brett Hutchins. 2009. Power Games: Environmental Protest, News Media and the Internet. *Media, Culture & Society* 31 (4):579–595.

Luke, Timothy W. 2002. On the Political Economy of Clayoquot Sound: The Uneasy Transition from Extractive to Attractive Models of Development. In *A Political Space: Reading the Global through Clayoquot Sound*, edited by W. Magnusson and K. Shaw. Montreal & Kingston: McGill-Queen's University Press.

Macdonald, Myra. 2003. *Exploring Media Discourse*. London: Arnold.

Mascarenhas, Michael, and Rik Scarce. 2004. 'The Intention was Good': Legitimacy, Consensus-Based Decision Making, and the Case of Forest Planning in British Columbia, Canada. *Society and Natural Resources* 17:17–38.

Mason, Jennifer. 2002. *Qualitative Researching*. 2nd ed. London: Sage Publications.

McCarthy, John D., Clark McPhail, and Jackie Smith. 1996. Images of Protest: Dimensions of Selection Bias in Media Coverage of Washington Demonstrations, 1982 and 1991. *American Sociological Review* 61 (3):478–499.

Nelson EcoSociety. (2010). http://ilovenelson.com/eco-society-update-4.

Owens, Lynn, and L. Kendall Palmer. 2003. Making the News: Anarchist Counter-Public Relations on the World Wide Web. *Critical Studies in Media Communication* 20 (4):335–361.

Parkins, John, and Debra Davidson. 2008. Constructing the Public Sphere in Compromised Settings: Environmental Governance in the Alberta Forest Sector. *Canadian Review of Sociology* 45 (2):177–196.

Philo, Chris, and Chris Wilbert, eds. 2000. *Animal Spaces, Beastly Places: New Geographies of Human-Animal Relations*. London & New York: Routledge.

Prior, Lindsay. 1997. Following in Foucault's Footsteps: Text and Context in Qualitative Research. In *Qualitative Research: Theory, Method and Practice*, edited by D. Silverman. London: Sage.

Rauch, Jennifer. 2007. Activists as Interpretive Communities: Rituals of Consumption and Interaction in an Alternative Media Audience. *Media, Culture & Society* 29 (6):994–1013.

Rohlinger and Brown. 2009. Democracy, Action, and the Internet after 9/11. *American Behavioral Scientist* 53 (1):133–150

Rossiter, David. 2004. The Nature of Protest: Constructing the Spaces of British Columbia's Rainforests. *Cultural Geographies* 11:139–164.

Salazar, Debra. 2009. Saving Nature and Seeking Justice: Environmental Activists in the Pacific Northwest. *Organization & Environment* 22 (2):230–254.

Silverman, David. 2001. *Interpreting Qualitative Data: Methods for Analysing Talk, Text and Interaction*. 2nd ed. London: Sage.

Smith, Jackie, John D. McCarthy, Clark McPhail, and Boguslaw Augustyn. 2001. From Protest to Agenda Building: Description Bias in Media Coverage of Protest Events in Washington, D.C. *Social Forces* 79 (4):1397–1423.

Spaargaren, Gert, and Arthur P.J. Mol. 2008. Greening Global Consumption: Redefining Politics and Authority. *Global Environmental Change* 18:350–359.

Stoddart, Mark C.J. 2005. Wilderness or Working Forest? British Columbia Forest Policy Debate in the *Vancouver Sun*, 1991–2003. *Research in Social Movements, Conflict and Change* 26:187–206.

Tindall, David B. 2002. Social Networks, Identification and Participation in an Environmental Movement: Low-Medium Cost Activism within the British Columbia Wilderness Preservation Movement. *Canadian Review of Sociology & Anthropology* 39 (4):413–452.

Valhalla Wilderness Society. (2010). http://www.vws.org.

Wildsight. (2010). http://www.wildsight.ca.

Wolch, Jennifer, and Jody Emel, eds. 1998. *Animal Geographies: Place, Politics, and Identity in the Nature–Culture Borderlands*. London & New York: Verso.

Regulating Agricultural Biotechnology in Canada: Paradoxes and Conflicts of a Closed System

Wilhelm Peekhaus

Introduction

The resounding message articulated in virtually every policy document drafted over the last two decades by various federal governments in respect of **biotechnology** is that this science and its attendant technological applications will drive economic growth, improve our health, increase agricultural production levels, and aid in environmental remediation. Yet the championing role successive Canadian governments have adopted with regard to biotechnology has resulted in a systemic contradiction with the government's crucial regulatory role.

Taking this internal paradox as its starting point, this chapter seeks to demonstrate a number of implications for the regulation of genetically engineered feed and foods in this country that flow from the federal government's dual role of regulator and promoter of this technoscience. In the following sections, emphasis is placed on locating the major gaps in our regulatory approval processes that have emerged as a result of the tensions inherent in these contradictory roles. In particular, attention will focus on the imprecision of **genetic engineering** technologies and the flawed concept of **substantial equivalence** that underpins Canada's regulatory regime with regard to genetically engineered food and feed products. Having established these fundamental weaknesses, the final section of the chapter will consider briefly how the regulatory system disallows consideration of the broader social justice, politico-economic, and **ethical** concerns that attach to biotechnology.

Regulatory Responsibility and Contradictory Roles

At the federal level in Canada, Health Canada and the Canadian Food Inspection Agency (CFIA) are the two main entities responsible for regulating biotechnology. Health Canada is mandated with assessing the safety of genetically engineered foods meant for human consumption. The CFIA approves field trials and commercial growing (i.e., unconfined release) and is responsible for variety registration of most new seeds in this country. The CFIA, rather than Environment Canada, is responsible for assessing the environmental safety of genetically engineered organisms under jurisdiction of the Seeds Act (R.S.C. 1985, c. S-8.). The Chrétien government left the regulation of biotechnology firmly in the hands of Agriculture and Agri-Food Canada and Health Canada, completely ignoring the recommendation issued by the House of Commons Standing Committee on Environment and Sustainable Development to move regulatory oversight for biotechnology to Environment Canada. This department would have been given increased power through a proposed new section to the Canadian Environmental Protection Act, which would have regulated genetically engineered organisms as potentially 'toxic substances' that would have required a departmental environmental assessment. Given the possibility of more stringent regulation, as well as the usurpation of a major Agriculture Canada policy mandate, it is perhaps not surprising that this option never made it beyond policy debates (Abergel & Barrett, 2002; Kuyek, 2002).

As mentioned above, Canadian biotechnology policy suffers from an internal tension between, on the one hand, the federal government's role in assessing and regulating all products developed and marketed for human and animal consumption as well as environmental release and, on the other hand, its task of promoting economic growth. Part of the problem stems from the fact that contemporary regulatory agencies are compelled to establish a solid working relationship with the industries they regulate in order to ensure an effective and enforceable system of regulation.

However, such a 'co-management' arrangement leads to problems of capture of state regulators by industry (Clark, 2002; Leiss, 2000, 2001; Salter, 1993). Specific to agricultural biotechnology, this tension is particularly evident within the CFIA, where its regulation and promotion warrants continue to be sources of significant criticism and concern about how well the agency discharges its regulatory duties. Indeed, this is one of the major critiques levelled in a report issued by The Royal Society of Canada, which was commissioned by the federal government in 2000 to examine and analyze Canada's regulatory system with regard to genetically engineered food products. Aside from such inherent conflicts of interest among biotechnology regulators in this country, or perhaps as a direct result, the Canadian regulatory regime in respect of agricultural biotechnology is also susceptible to scientific critique.

The Imprecision of Genetic Engineering Techniques

In Canada, we regulate the product and not the process; that is, regulatory oversight is triggered by the end product rather than the processes by which it is created. As a result, our regulatory system fails completely to adequately consider the secondary effects that accrue from manipulation of an organism at its genetic level, despite the fact that genetic engineering affects an organism's metabolic pathways in ways that are often quite difficult to detect and determine (Ferrara & Dorsey, 2001). Precise placement of engineered genetic constructs is critical to proper gene expression. However, far from being a precise technique, the insertion of genes into new cellular environments carries with it the potential for unexpected and contingent consequences. The use of 'gene guns' and various vectors (the four major types are plasmids, bacteriophages and other viruses, cosmids, and artificial chromosomes) to transfer foreign genetic material into another cell is imprecise and random with respect to placement of the transgene packet in the target plant chromosome.

This randomness can result in physical disruption in the genome (insertional mutation at the site of transgene insertion or at random locations throughout the genome) or in the regulation of the gene, which compromises the safety of the genetically engineered plant. Because transgenes are inserted into or proximate to functional gene sequences, insertion site mutations have the potential to cause inadvertent loss, acquisition, or misexpression of critical traits. Interaction effects might also occur between the inserted genes and the thousands of other genes in the organism being genetically altered. Endogenous genes might be inactivated or, conversely, silent genes activated. Other unintended effects could include modified metabolism, novel fusion proteins, the production of new substances, the induction of unanticipated changes in the manner in which the plant functions or interacts with other organisms or the environment, or alterations to the toxicity or nutritional value of the genetically engineered plant (Ho, 1999; Ho, Ryan, & Cummins, 1999; Jiao, Si, Li, Zhang, & Xu, 2010; Lotter, 2009; The Royal Society of Canada, 2001; Wilson, Latham, & Steinbrecher, 2006; Zolla, Rinalducci, Antonioli, & Righetti, 2008).

The overall message emanating from the unfortunately scant scientific literature evaluating the implications of genetic engineering processes is articulated nicely by Latham and his colleagues

(2006, p. 5): 'Even with the limited information currently available it is clear that plant transformation is rarely, if ever, precise and that this lack of precision may cause many of the frequent unexpected phenotypes that characterise plant transformation and that pose a significant biosafety risk.' Yet one is left wondering just to what extent these findings are reflected in regulatory decisions given that our regulatory regime is triggered by the presence of a novel trait in a plant and *not* by the process or method employed to introduce that trait.

Substantial Equivalence

Part of the rationale offered for the decision to regulate the genetically engineered product rather than the process by which transgenes are incorporated into host plants is found in the controversial concept of 'substantial equivalence', which, as a safety assessment criterion, is defined as 'the equivalence of a novel trait within a particular plant species, in terms of its specific use and safety to the environment and human health, to those in that same species, that are in use and generally considered as safe in Canada, based on valid scientific rationale' (Canadian Food Inspection Agency, 2006, para. 1).

In essence, a particular genetically engineered crop is considered substantially equivalent if there exists a conventionally or organically grown counterpart. But to compare transgenic products, such as Bt (*Bacillus thuringiensis*) products that produce toxins, to other products, even an insecticide, is to draw a false analogy. Certainly both can wreak havoc on the environment, but the latter does not pose the same threat of long-term genetic consequences as the former (Critical Art Ensemble, 2002). The Royal Society report is similarly critical of the CFIA for incorrectly applying the concepts of 'familiarity' and 'substantial equivalence' such that regulatory approvals are '*based upon unsubstantiated assumptions* about the equivalence of the organisms by analogy with conventional breeding' (Royal Society of Canada, 2001, p. 182; emphasis added).

As the drafters of this report contend, equivalence claims cannot be made a priori but instead

require an integrated approach of rigorous scientific evaluation that seeks to uncover how phenotypes are affected by genomes and their variants at multiple levels (DNA structure, gene expression, protein profiling, and metabolic profiling) (Royal Society of Canada, 2001; Wills, 2001). Other researchers express their opposition to substantial equivalence in even more critical terms, arguing that it 'is a pseudo-scientific concept because it is a commercial and political judgment masquerading as if it were scientific. It is, moreover, inherently anti-scientific because it was created primarily to provide an excuse for not requiring biochemical or toxicological tests. It therefore serves to discourage and inhibit potentially informative scientific research' (Millstone, Brunner, & Mayer, 1999, p. 526).

Concerns in Respect of Agricultural Biotechnology beyond Science

But beyond apprehensions about the scientific vigour of our regulatory regime, people's concerns about the impacts and risks of biotechnology also encompass wider normative questions of social justice and economics, conceptions of nature, and cultural values. Part of the problem is the way that biotech proponents, who yield from industry, government, and science, frame biotechnology issues. 'Biotechnology offers putative solutions which predefine the problems to be solved. Its reified problem-definition in turn influences forms of public participation and safety regulation' (Levidow, 1999, p. 64). This type of framing completely excludes alternative definitions of the problem. Instead, **risk assessment** is completely embedded in a foundation that contemplates the potential dangers of agricultural biotechnology from the perspective of industrialized monoculture, rather than from a perspective that admits consideration of the broader environmental, not to mention social and politico-economic, impacts that follow in the wake of this type of intensive agriculture.

The result of this approach is that potential detrimental effects of new genetically engineered plants are considered tolerable if they can be dealt with by subsequent technological advances. Of course, the problem is deeper and older than the advent of biotechnology. From the earliest phases of industrialization, the social, political, and environmental effects of technological development were interpreted as secondary effects that would be resolved through additional technological innovation (Moser, 1995). But biotechnology and genetic engineering bring with them their own set of spiralling demands for ever-greater technological applications, leading many to suggest that the 'chemical treadmill' of industrial agriculture will be replaced by Levidow's 'genetic treadmill', in which corporations respond to the negative repercussions of biotechnology through new generations of the technology that created the problems in the first place. The upside for biotechnology firms in such a circular system is that dependence on technological solutions ensures a continued generation of new markets (Levidow, 1999; Levidow & Tait, 1995; Schmitz, 2001).

Moreover, proponents of biotechnology, particularly those from industry, frequently employ discursive strategies designed to characterize all opposition to biotechnology as uninformed, irresponsible, and even hysterical. According to former Monsanto CEO Robert Shapiro, 'those of us in industry can take comfort. . . . After all, we're the technical experts. We know we're right. The 'antis' obviously don't understand the science, and are just as obviously pushing a hidden agenda—probably to destroy capitalism' (as quoted in Smith, 2003, p. 252). The Canadian federal government has voiced similar sentiments: 'A complicating factor [to gaining public acceptance of biotechnology] is that people often do not know about or do not understand the benefits to them of various biotechnology applications' (Industry Canada, 1998, p. 3).

Completely disregarding the possibility that citizens might have legitimate concerns about biotechnology, the federal government would prefer to retain a paternalistic perception of Canadians, who, in its view, are merely ignorant of the presumed advantages this apparently beneficent technology will provide to the country. Indeed, no Canadian policy document raises concerns about biotechnology and its applications, at least not in any substantial depth. The consistent government line is that biotechnology is largely safe and the Canadian regulatory system will protect Canadians. What such statements and positions miss is that those individuals who are critical of agricultural biotechnology are interested in emphasizing and interrogating issues that professional science has excluded rather than merely debating scientific knowledge per se (Cozzens & Woodhouse, 1995).

Conclusion

While there is certainly a vocal opposition in Canada that is battling to inject important considerations into the debates around biotechnology, the government nonetheless occupies a potent gatekeeper function that heavily influences what knowledge is considered legitimate or not. And despite common laments about citizen apathy toward government, health and safety regulators continue to engender a substantial amount of trust among the broader population, which in turn translates into significant power to shape broader public discourses in respect of biotechnology. As we saw above, genetic engineering technologies are having difficulty meeting the scientific expectations promoted by their industry developers and government cheerleaders. Since the benefits ascribed to agricultural biotechnology are susceptible to challenge precisely on scientific grounds, the one and only domain that industry and government concede as legitimate for assessing biotechnologies, it seems obvious why these actors steadfastly refuse to admit broader social and economic issues into the debate.

Against such a backdrop, we, as social subjects, must demand that the regulatory process incorporate complementary and more reflexive analyses that consider and make allowance for the impact social effects exercise on the trajectory of biotechnological development, and, conversely, the effects that biotechnology has on shaping society. By conceptualizing technological development in this recursive manner, opportunities arise to alter or even resist a particular path that might otherwise appear beyond control—that is, we open pathways for resistance.

References

Abergel, E., & Barrett, K. (2002). Putting the cart before the horse: A review of biotechnology policy in Canada. *Journal of Canadian Studies*, 37(3), 135–161.

Boucher, L.J., Cashaback, D., Plumptre, T., & Simpson, A. (2002). *Linking in, linking out, linking up: Exploring the governance challenges of biotechnology*. Ottawa: Institute on Governance.

Burkett, P. (1996). On some common misconceptions about nature and Marx's critique of political economy. *Capitalism Nature Socialism*, 7(3), 53–80.

Burkett, P. (1999). *Marx and nature: A red and green perspective*. New York: St. Martin's Press.

Canadian Biotechnology Advisory Committee (2002). *Improving the regulation of genetically modified foods and other novel foods in Canada: Report to the Government of Canada Biotechnology Ministerial Coordinating Committee*. Ottawa: Government of Canada.

Canadian Food Inspection Agency (2006). Biology document BIO2006-07: The biology of *Triticum turgidum* ssp. durum (durum wheat). Retrieved 5 July, 2007, from http://www.inspection.gc.ca/english/plaveg/bio/dir/dir0607e.shtml.

Clark, E. A. (2002). *Government and GM. . . . for whom . . . by whom?* Paper presented at the Association Canadienne Francaise pour l'Avancement des Sciences, Laval, QC.

Committee on Environmental Impacts Associated with Commercialization of Transgenic Plants, & National Research Council (2002). *Environmental effects of transgenic plants: The scope and adequacy of regulation*. Washington, D.C.: National Academy Press.

Cozzens, S. E., & Woodhouse, E. J. (1995). Science, government, and the politics of knowledge. In S. Jasanoff, G.E. Markle, J.C. Petersen & T. Pinch (Eds.), *Handbook of science and technology studies* (pp. 533–553). Thousand Oaks, CA: Sage Publications.

Critical Art Ensemble (2002). *The molecular invasion*. Brooklyn: Autonomedia.

Diamond, N. (1981). The politics of scientific conceptualization. In L. Levidow & B. Young (Eds.), *Science, technology and the labour process: Marxist studies* (Vol. I, pp. 32–45). Atlantic Highlands, NJ: Humanities Press.

Doern, G.B., & Reed, T. (2000). Canada's changing science-based policy and regulatory regime: Issues and framework. In G.B. Doern & T. Reed (Eds.), *Risky business: Canada's changing science-based policy and regulatory regime* (pp. 3–28). Toronto: University of Toronto Press.

Engels, F. (1940). *Dialectics of nature* (C. Dutt, Trans.). New York: International Publishers.

Ferrara, J., & Dorsey, M. K. (2001). Genetically engineered foods: A minefield of safety hazards. In B. Tokar (Ed.), *Redesigning life?: The worldwide challenge to genetic engineering* (pp. 51–66). Montreal: McGill-Queens's University Press.

Foster, J.B. (2000). *Marx's ecology: Materialism and nature*. New York: Monthly Review Press.

Government of Canada (2004). *Biotechnology transforming society: Creating an innovative economy and a higher quality of life: Report on biotechnology (1998–2003)*. Ottawa: Government of Canada.

———. (2007). *Mobilizing science and technology to Canada's advantage*. Ottawa: Government of Canada.

Hindmarsh, R. (2001). Constructing bio-utopia: Laying foundations amidst dissent. In R. Hindmarsh & G. Lawrence (Eds.), *Altered genes II: The future?* (2nd ed., pp. 36–52). Melbourne: Scribe Publications.

Ho, M.-W. (1999). *Genetic engineering: Dream or nightmare? Turning the tide on the brave new world of bad science and big business* (2nd ed.). Dublin: Gateway.

Ho, M.-W., Ryan, A., & Cummins, J. (1999). Cauliflower mosaic viral promoter—A recipe for disaster? *Microbial Ecology in Health and Disease, 11*, 194–197.

Industry Canada (1998). *The 1998 Canadian Biotechnology Strategy: An ongoing renewal process*. Ottawa: Government of Canada.

Jiao, Z., Si, X.-X., Li, G.-K., Zhang, Z.-M., & Xu, X.-P. (2010). Unintended compositional changes in transgenic rice seeds (*Oryza sativa L.*) studied by spectral and chromatographic analysis coupled with chemometrics methods. *Journal of Agricultural and Food Chemistry*, 58, 1746–1754.

Kleinman, D.L., & Kloppenburg, J., Jr. (1991). Aiming for the discursive high ground: Monsanto and the biotechnology controversy. *Sociological Forum*, 6, 427–447.

Kloppenburg, J. R., Jr. (2004). *First the seed: The political economy of plant biotechnology* (2nd ed.). Madison: The University of Wisconsin Press.

Kuyek, D. (2002). *The real board of directors: The construction of biotechnology policy in Canada, 1980–2002*. Sorrento, BC: The Ram's Horn.

Latham, J.R., Wilson, A.K., & Steinbrecher, R.A. (2006). The mutational consequences of plant transformation. *Journal of Biomedicine and Biotechnology*, 2006, 1–7. Retrieved 26 April, 2011 from http://downloads.hindawi.com/journals/jbb/2006/025376.pdf.

Leiss, W. (2000). Between expertise and bureaucracy: Risk management trapped at the science–policy interface. In G.B. Doern & T. Reed (Eds.), *Risky business: Canada's changing science-based policy and regulatory regime* (pp. 49–74). Toronto: University of Toronto Press.

———. (2001). *In the chamber of risks: Understanding risk controversies*. Montreal: McGill-Queen's University Press.

Levidow, L. (1999). Democratizing technology—or technologizing democracy? Regulating agricultural biotechnology in Europe. In R. von Schomberg (Ed.), *Democratising technology: Theory and practice of deliberative technology policy* (pp. 51–69). Hengelo, Netherlands: International Centre for Human and Public Affairs.

Levidow, L., & Tait, J. (1995). The greening of biotechnology: GMOs as environment-friendly products. In V. Shiva & I. Moser (Eds.), *Biopolitics: A feminist and ecological reader on biotechnology* (pp. 121–138). London: Zed Books.

Levins, R., & Lewontin, R. C. (1985). *The dialectical biologist*. Cambridge, MA: Harvard University Press.

———. (1994). Holism and reductionism in ecology. *Capitalism Nature Socialism*, 5(4), 33–40.

———. (1997). The biological and the social. *Capitalism Nature Socialism*, 8(3), 89–92.

Lotter, D. (2009). The genetic engineering of food and the failure of science—Part 1: The development of a flawed enterprise. *International Journal of the Sociology of Agriculture and Food, 16* (1), 31–49.

Marcuse, H. (1968). *Negations: Essays in critical theory* (J.J. Shapiro, Trans.). London: Penguin Books.

McMurtry, J. (2002). *Value wars: The global market versus the life economy*. London: Pluto Press.

Millstone, E., Brunner, E., & Mayer, S. (1999). Beyond 'substantial equivalence'. *Nature, 401*, 525–526.

Moser, I. (1995). Introduction: Mobilizing critical communities and discourses on modern biotechnology. In V. Shiva & I. Moser (Eds.), *Biopolitics: A feminist and ecological reader on biotechnology* (pp. 1–24). London: Zed Books.

Munn-Venn, T., & Mitchell, P. (2005). *Biotechnology in Canada: A technology platform for growth*. Ottawa: The Conference Board of Canada.

Munro, M. (2005, December 29). Modified wheat takes root with little opposition: Keeps growing when sprayed with herbicides. *National Post*, p. A8.

Riley, S. (1999, October 27). Seeds of discontent blowing past cabinet. *The Ottawa Citizen*, p. A14.

Royal Society of Canada (2001). *Elements of precaution: Recommendations for the regulation of food biotechnology in Canada*. Ottawa: Royal Society of Canada.

Salter, L. (1993). Capture or co-management: Democracy and accountability in regulatory agencies. In G. Albo, D. Lagille & L. Panich (Eds.), *A different kind of state? Popular power and democratic administration* (pp. 87–100). Toronto: Oxford University Press.

Schmitz, S.A. (2001). Cloning profits: The revolution in agricultural biotechnology. In B. Tokar (Ed.), *Redesigning life?: The worldwide challenge to genetic engineering* (pp. 44–50). Montreal: McGill-Queen's University Press.

Smith, J.M. (2003). *Seeds of deception: Exposing industry and government lies about the safety of the genetically engineered foods you're eating*. Fairfield, IA: Yes! Books.

Statistics Canada (2000). *Federal government personnel engaged in scientific and technological (S&T) activities, 1990–1991 to 1999–2000*. Ottawa: Government of Canada.

Wills, P.R. (2001). Disrupting evolution: Biotechnology's real result. In R. Hindmarsh & G. Lawrence (Eds.), *Altered genes II: The future?* (2nd ed., pp. 53–68). Melbourne: Scribe Publications.

Wilson, A. K., Latham, J. R., & Steinbrecher, R. A. (2006). Transformation-induced mutations in transgenic plants: Analysis and biosafety implications. *Biotechnology and Genetic Engineering Reviews*, 23, 209–234.

Wynne, B. (1995). Public understanding of science. In S. Jasanoff, G.E. Markle, J.C. Petersen & T. Pinch (Eds.), *Handbook of science and technology studies* (pp. 361–388). Thousand Oaks, CA: Sage Publications.

Zolla, L., Rinalducci, S., Antonioli, P., & Righetti, P. G. (2008). Proteomics as a complementary tool for identifying unintended side effects occurring in transgenic maize seeds as a result of genetic modifications. *Journal of Proteome Research*, 7, 1850–1861.

CHAPTER 63

··

The Science and Politics of Polar Ice

Mark Vardy

Introduction

This paper examines the configurations of science and politics related to two events: increased melting of Arctic sea ice, and increased melting of Greenland and West Antarctic ice sheets. At issue are the different temporal scales in which not only science and politics but also sea ice and ice sheets operate. As will be discussed in further detail below, sea ice and ice sheets are different entities with different material characteristics, and although they are both changing with the changing climate, they figure into science and politics in much different ways. While the configuration of science and politics in the case of the sea ice maintains the hegemonic ordering of politics as the space properly defined by territorially based nation-states and the state system (Walker 2010), the case of the ice sheets indicates a possible way of opening up space in which a different form of politics can be articulated.

Insights from Science and Technology Studies

The field of science and technology studies does not regard science as having essential characteristics that demarcate it from other ways of knowing. Rather, science is treated as a social practice that generates knowledge through practical activity. This does not mean there are no insights gleaned from science, but rather that such knowledge is 'situated' within specific and historically located ways of knowing (Haraway 1987). In other words, the world becomes known through our engagement with it, but this knowledge is always contingent upon the social practices it arises within. Science can also be considered as one way of engaging with the materiality of the earth system. In this view, objects and things are granted a form of agency, not as conscious beings that act with intentionality, but as 'actants' that will behave in manner according to their own proprieties despite any claims made on their behalf (Latour 2000; Callon 1999). This is similar to the point made by environmental sociologist Raymond Murphy (2009: 37–38): the world exceeds our knowledge of it, and regardless of the accumulation of scientific knowledge about the earth system, the natural world still possesses a radically unknown and unknowable potential to disrupt social understandings and habitual ways of going on with everyday life.

This paper treats ice sheets and sea ice as material actants in the networks of relations that comprise the political, which, just like science, is not essentialized but constituted through ongoing practices. The relationship between science and politics employed here draws upon Barry

(2001), who uses Agamben (1993) to argue that politics can be thought of as the historically variable ensemble of institutions and practices—such as political parties, electoral systems, and nation-states—that are currently given, often in hegemonic fashion, as comprising modern liberal democracies, while 'the political' is the contestation of what constitutes politics. Given the vast range of practices that could potentially be considered as legitimate politics, limitations are applied to what counts as politics. This setting out and maintenance of boundaries between what is and what is not considered to be legitimate politics is precisely the realm of the political. As the history of science shows, science can be used to legitimate repressive or anti-democratic politics. However, as mentioned above, science can also introduce new understandings of phenomena, offering up a new sense of the material world. The question of whether science actually contributes to the opening up or the closing down of spaces of meaningful discussion and debate about what politics should be is 'partly empirical' because science is practiced in many different forms for many different purposes (Barry 2001).

Sea Ice and Ice Sheets

A clear distinction must be drawn between ice sheets and sea ice. Whereas ice sheets are land-based remnants of the last ice age covering Greenland and the Antarctic continent, sea ice freezes every winter on the ocean. A significant amount of the total sea ice is formed in winter and melts in summer, with a smaller proportion remaining year-round. Satellite images and accounts from the Inuit show that the extent of the Arctic sea ice summer melt has increased over the past several decades (Markus et al. 2009; Maslanik et al. 2007; Ford et al. 2008). The season in which the Canadian Arctic is navigable is getting longer, making destinations such as mines and off-shore fossil fuel drilling sites more accessible. One of the ways in which nation-states are responding to reduced sea ice is to lay claim to the ocean floor under the Arctic, where a significant amount of the world's known remaining known fossil fuels are said to exist (Johnston 2010).

Under the United Nations Convention of the Law of the Sea (UNCLOS), nation-states have access rights to an 'exclusive economic zone' that extends 200 nautical miles off their respective coastlines, and in which they have sole authority to extract fossil fuels from the sea floor. Article 76 of UNCLOS allows a nation-state to extend its exclusive economic zone if it demonstrates that the continental shelf on which it sits extends past the 200 nautical mile limit. The five countries that have coastlines on the Arctic (Russia, the United States, Denmark, Norway, and Canada) are currently preparing to make precisely this claim. If successful, the fossil fuels currently in international Arctic waters would almost all fall under the sovereignty of one or another nation-state. Rather than openly compete with one another over claims for the sea floor, the five Arctic coastline countries agreed in 2008 to co-operatively pursue claims through UNCLOS, which specifies the scientific basis on which claims can be submitted (Huebert 2009: 95–98; Macnab 2009). Canada set aside $40 million to be spent from 2008 to 2013 (the deadline for Canada's submission to UNCLOS) to scientifically map the sea floor to demonstrate the extent of its continental shelf (Able, Courchen, Seidle, & St-Hilaire 2009: 588), and is co-operating with the two nations it shares Arctic borders with, the United States and Denmark, to map the sea floor in the Beaufort Sea and off Greenland (Huebert 2009: 100). The co-operation among the five countries that have coastline on the Arctic could be interpreted as a way for the nations to secure their individual claims in a broader context that includes non-Arctic nations that have expressed interest in maintaining the international status of the Arctic (Young 2009).

As can be seen in this brief outline, as one response to melting sea ice, Canada is re-inscribing a modernist politics of asserting sovereign authority over territory through the practice of science. In what way does the science of the ice sheets, to which this paper now turns, open up the possibility of articulating a different politics?

The science of ice sheets is complex and uncertain but of importance because of the potential contribution the melting ice makes to rates of sea level rise. The Greenland and West Antarctica ice sheets contain 75 per cent of the world's fresh water, enough to increase sea levels by many tens of metres (Bindschadler 2008: 76). Indeed, it is thought that sea levels rose by some 60 metres with the melting of the ice sheets after the last ice age (Oldfield 2005: 118). The questions some scientists are now asking is: are the ice sheets are melting, and if so, how fast?

Ice sheet dynamics are complex and a relatively recent subject of study that spans many disciplines. One way of approaching this complexity is to begin with an article published in the journal *Science* in 2002 that describes a new finding: surface meltwater channelling down through Greenland ice sheets to the bedrock underneath (Zwally et al 2002). Increased quantities of meltwater acting as lubricant between the ice sheet and bedrock raised the possibility that, together with other factors such the dislodging of buttressing ice shelves due to a slight increase in ocean temperature, ice sheets could disintegrate in a rapid non-linear fashion, sliding into the ocean in massive discharges of ice rather than simply melting (Hansen et al 2007a; 2007b; Pittock 2008). More recent investigations argue the contribution of melt-water to increasing ice sheet disintegration was overestimated (Sundal et al. 2011). This is not to say that the issue has been resolved or that surface meltwater is the only dynamic that needs to be addressed; indeed, the different material configurations of ice sheets in Greenland and the Antarctic raise a number of complex considerations (e.g. the West Antarctic ice sheet is anchored below sea level). Despite the uncertainties associated with the particular dynamics, the overall trend appears consistent. For example, based on the varying amount of gravitational pull exerted by the ice sheets on two satellites flown in parallel from 2002 to 2009, scientists calculated the Greenland ice sheet went from melting at 137 gigatonnes per year in 2002–2003 to 286 gigatonnes per year in 2007–2009 (Velicogna 2009). Other studies using other measurement techniques corroborate the finding that ice sheets are losing mass at an accelerated rate (Rignot 2008; Bindshadler 2008). The trend in scientific peer-reviewed journals that consider the ice sheets is toward quadratic, not linear, projections of future sea level rise (Overpeck & Weiss 2009).

Importantly, some scientists argue that estimates of rates of future sea level rise contained in the first four reports (up to 2007) issued by the Intergovernmental Panel on Climate Change (IPCC) were based on general circulation models (GCMs) that could not account for ice sheet dynamics or non-linear disintegration (Bindschadler 2008: 75; Hansen et al 2007a; Smith et al 2009). This particular argument can be contextualized by sociological investigations that found that GCMs were authoritative in the IPCC partly for extra-scientific reasons, such as serving as a central node in the networks of diverse and diffuse scientific communities that comprise climate science (Shackley et al. 1998, 1999). Indeed, the role that these accounts of how knowledge is produced through social practices is critical to understanding the limits of how the dynamics of the earth system is currently understood. A June 2010 workshop convened by the IPCC produced a report titled *Sea Level Rise and Ice Sheet Instabilities* that recognizes the historical inadequacy of the ability of GCMs to accurately model ice sheet dynamics. The report concludes that while more work is needed to understand the vast complexities that attend understanding ice sheet dynamics, the contribution the ice sheets might make to sea level rise is an issue of some concern.

Conclusion

Ice sheets, as actants with the potential to suddenly begin acting on a temporal scale directly relevant to that of humans, open up the political to contestation: are our current politics capable of responding to non-linear earth system events without imposing the modernist authority of territorially based nation-states? The response seen thus far to reductions in sea ice does not bode well. As briefly outlined above, one way that nation-states are responding to the reduction of Arctic sea ice is by deploying science to map the sea floor to extend claims of sovereignty over larger territorial extents. In this response, the political space for meaningful discussions and debates about how to respond to changing earth system conditions is not opened up. This entrenchment of authoritative relations would be a troubling response to increased sea level rise. While the complexities of both human politics and the earth system, not to mention the relationships between them, make any attempts to forecast certainties nearly impossible, and while it would be naive to suggest events would or should follow a deterministic route, what seems clear is that many millions of the world's most vulnerable people would be greatly impacted by sea-level rise, perhaps leading to mass migrations (Perch-Nielsen et al. 2008). Should the response mirror the self-interested entrenchment of national borders seen in response to melting sea ice, hard lines would be drawn that could be used as a basis for enacting violence. Moreover, non-linear ice sheet disintegration is but one example of the potential for the earth system to act in unexpected or unanticipated ways. The volatility of the changing earth system suggested by non-linear ice sheet disintegration speaks of the need, articulated by theorists such as Walker (2010) and Agnew (2009), to enact a critical politics that engages with the limits of modernist tropes about the sovereignty of territorially based nation-states over the earth, as well as to engage critically with specific findings in the earth sciences (Clark 2011).

References

Abele, Frances et al. 2009. 'The New Northern Policy Universe'. Pp. 561–594. In *Northern Exposure: Peoples, Powers and Prospects in Canada's North*. Edited by Frances Abele, Thomas J. Courchène, F. Leslie Seidle, and France St-Hilaire. Montreal: Institute for Research on Public Policy.

Agamben, Giorgio. 1993. *The Coming Community*. Translated by Michael Hardt. Minneapolis: University of Minnesota Press.

Agnew, John. 2009. *Globalization and Sovereignty*. Lanham, MD: Rowman & Littlefield.

Barry, Andrew. 2001. *Political Machines: Governing a Technological Society*. London: Athlone Press.

Bindschadler, Robert. 2008. 'Why Predicting West Antarctic Ice Sheet Behavior Is So Hard: What We Know, What We Don't Know and How We Will Find Out'. Pp. 75–80. In

Sudden and Disruptive Climate Change: Exploring the Real Risks and How We Can Avoid Them. Edited by Michael C. MacCracken, Frances Moore, and John C. Topping, Jr. Sterling, VA: Earthscan.

Callon, Michelle. 1999. 'Some Elements of a Sociology of Translation: Domestication of the Scallops and the Fishermen of St. Brieue Bay'. Pp. 67–83. In *The Science Studies Reader.* Edited by M. Biagioli. New York: Routledge.

Clark, Nigel. 2011. *Inhuman Nature: Sociable Life on a Dynamic Planet.* Thousand Oaks, CA: Sage.

Ford, James D., Tristan Pearce, Justin Gilligan, Barry Smit, and Jill Oakes. (2008). 'Climate Change and Hazards Associated with Ice Use in Northern Canada'. *Arctic, Antarctic, and Alpine Research* 40(4):647–659.

Hansen, J., et al. 2007a. 'Climate Change and Trace Gases'. *Philosophical Transactions of the Royal Society A: Mathematical, Physical and Engineering Sciences* 365(1856):1925–1954.

Hansen, J., et al. 2007b. 'Dangerous Human-Made Interference with Climate: A GISS Model Study'. *Atmospheric Chemistry and Physics* (7):2287–2312.

Haraway, Donna. 1988. 'Situated Knowledges: The Science Question in Feminism and the Privilege of Partial Perspectives'. *Feminist Studies* 14(3): 575–599.

Huebert, Rob. 2009. 'Canada and the Changing International Arctic: At the Crossroads of Cooperation and Conflict'. Pp 77–106. In *Northern Exposure: Peoples, Powers and Prospects in Canada's North.* Edited by Frances Abele et al. Montreal: Institute for Research on Public Policy.

IPCC, 2010. *Workshop Report of the Intergovernmental Panel on Climate Change. Workshop on Sea Level Rise and Ice Sheet Instabilities* Edited by T.F. Stocker et al.. IPCC Working Group I Technical Support Unit, University of Bern, Bern, Switzerland.

Johnston, Peter F. 2010. 'Arctic Energy Resources and Global Energy Security'. *Journal of Military and Strategic Studies* 12(2). http://www.jmss.org/jmss/index.php/jmss/issue/view/46/showToc.

Latour, Bruno. 2000. 'When Things Strike Back: A Possible Contribution of "Science Studies" to the Social Sciences'. *British Journal of Sociology* 51(1): 107–123.

Macnab, Ron. 2009. '"Use It or Lose It" In Arctic Canada: Action Agenda or Election Hype?'. *Vermont Law Review.* 34(1): 3–14,

Markus, T., Stroeve, J.C., & Miller, J. 2009. 'Recent Changes in Arctic Sea Ice Melt Onset, Freezeup, and Melt Season Length. *Journal of Geophysical Research—Oceans* 114. Accessed online at http://www.agu.org, no pagination.

Maslanik, J.A. et al., W. 2007. 'A Younger, Thinner Arctic Ice Cover: Increased Potential for Rapid, Extensive Sea-ice Loss.' *Geophysical Research Letters* 34(24). Accessed online at http://www.agu.org, no pagination.

Murphy, Raymond. 2009. *Leadership in Disaster: Learning for a Future with Global Climate Change.* Montreal, Kingston: McGill-Queen's University Press.

Oldfield, Frank. 2005. *Environmental Change: Key Issues and Alternative Approaches.* Cambridge University Press.

Overpeck, J. & Weiss, J. L. 2009. 'Projections of Future Sea Level Becoming More Dire'. *Proceedings of the National Academy of Sciences* 106(51):21461–21462.

Perch-Nielsen, S., Battig, M., & Imboden, D. 2008. 'Exploring the Link between Climate Change and Migration.' *Climatic Change* 91(3-4): 375–393.

Pittock, Barrie A. 2008. 'Ten Reasons Why Climate Change May Be More Severe Than Expected'. Pp. 11–28. In *Sudden and Disruptive Climate Change: Exploring the Real Risks and How We Can Avoid Them.* Edited by Michael C. MacCracken, Frances Moore, and John C. Topping, Jr. Sterling, VA: Earthscan.

Rignot, Eric. 2008. 'Changes in the Greenland Ice Sheet and Implications for Global Sea Level Rise'. Pp. 63–74. In *Sudden and Disruptive Climate Change: Exploring the Real Risks and How We Can Avoid Them.* Edited by Michael C. MacCracken, Frances Moore, and John C. Topping, Jr. Sterling, VA: Earthscan.

Shackley, S., J. Risbey, P. Stone, and B. Wynne. 1999. 'Adjusting to Policy Expectations in Climate Change Modeling—An Interdisciplinary Study of Flux Adjustments in Coupled Atmosphere-Ocean General Circulation Models'. *Climatic Change* 43(2):413–454.

Shackley, S., P. Young, S. Parkinson, and B. Wynne. 1998. 'Uncertainty, Complexity and Concepts of Good Science in Climate Change Modelling: Are GCMs the Best Tools?' *Climatic Change* 38(2):159–205.

Smith, J. B. et al. 2009. 'From the Cover: Assessing Dangerous Climate Change through an Update of the Intergovernmental Panel on Climate Change (IPCC) "Reasons for Concern"'. *Proceedings of the National Academy of Sciences* 106(11): 4133–4137

Sundal, A.V., et al., P. 2011. 'Melt-induced Speed-up of Greenland Ice Sheet Offset by Efficient Subglacial Drainage'. *Nature* 469(7331): 521–524.

Velicogna, I. 2009. 'Increasing Rates of Ice Mass Loss from the Greenland and Antarctic Ice Sheets Revealed by GRACE' *Geophysical Research Letters* 36(19): L19503.

Walker, R.B.J. 2010. *After the Globe, before the World.* New York: Routledge.

Young, Oran R. 2009. 'The Arctic in Play: Governance in a Time of Rapid Change'. *The International Journal of Marine and Coastal Law* 24: 423–442

Zwally, H. J., et al. 2002. 'Surface Melt–Induced Acceleration of Greenland Ice-Sheet Flow'. *Science* 297(5579):218–222.

Questions for Critical Thought

CHAPTER 59

1. What does Steiner mean when she says that the world currently has global *governance* without global *government*?
2. What is accountability? Explain how and to whom the current global governance process is or is not accountable.
3. What roles do INGOs play in global governance?
4. Throughout this paper, Steiner deals with the problem of legitimacy. Central to this is the push and pull between the *process* of decision making and its *outcomes*. Ensuring that one of these is fair does not ensure that the other is. Discuss the process versus outcomes debate using examples from Steiner's paper.
5. According to Steiner, how did Prime Minister Stephen Harper represent Canada at the Copenhagen climate talks? What role did Canada play in these talks? How does this role affect Canada's image and thus diplomatic position in the global governance context?

CHAPTER 60

1. According to Neves, how did science contribute to modernity? What dichotomies did it create and maintain?
2. According to Neves, what are hybrid networks and how do they threaten the modern constitution? How do risky objects/matters of concern reveal them?
3. How does modern capitalism create risk-free objects/matters of fact? How does commodity fetishism take part in this process?
4. According to Neves, what are the dangers in ignoring the relationships (human and non-human) that produce our commodities?
5. Consider the things you habitually buy/use. Are you familiar with how any of them are made or where they come from? Describe a risky and a risk-free object in your life. Which kind of object do you more commonly use?

CHAPTER 61

1. Why is the traditional relationship between social movements and journalists one of asymmetrical dependency? How do Stoddart and MacDonald hypothesize that the Internet may change this?
2. Compare and contrast the representation of the Jumbo Pass territory and its ideal uses in the mass media and on websites: What claims were made? What evidence was offered to substantiate those claims?
3. Compare and contrast the representation of activist tactics in mass media and on websites.
4. Compare and contrast the representation of the issue of local governance in mass media and on websites.

5. Do Stoddart and MacDonald's findings offer support for the hypothesis that the Internet provides an alternative public sphere? What are some strengths and limitations of using websites as a public sphere? How do the authors suggest that social movements can use websites and mass media *together*?

CHAPTER 62

1. According to Peekhaus, why does the government play contradictory roles with regard to biotechnology?
2. Peekhaus argues that part of the regulation problem stems from the relationship between regulatory agencies and the industries that they regulate. Describe the co-management relationship. How is a co-operative relationship between regulatory agencies and industries helpful for regulation? How is it not helpful? What would be some strengths and weaknesses with developing a less co-operative relationship between the two parties?
3. What is the difference between regulating the product and the process? According to Peekhaus, why does the process of genetic engineering deserve more critical attention?
4. Analyze the assumption of substantial equivalence. What are some of its logical flaws? Why is it a dangerous assumption? Why are people so eager to use this assumption even if it is logically unsound and dangerous?
5. According to Peekhaus, why does genetic engineering not solve the real problems being caused by certain industrial agricultural practices? How are industrial agriculture practices trapped on a 'treadmill'? Who benefits from this treadmill?

CHAPTER 63

1. Discuss how and why science and politics move on different temporal scales. How do these scales compare with that of the earth?
2. What challenges does our political system face when trying to deal with issues that unfold on a different temporal scale than that of everyday life? What about when those issues suddenly convert to an urgent, fast-paced temporal scale?
3. According to Vardy, why are ice sheets and sea ice actants with agency?
4. What opportunities does the melting of sea ice open up? Why are nations scrambling to claim the Arctic floor?
5. Vardy points out that science has been used to justify and legitimate claims to land ownership. What are the strengths of this approach (as opposed to, say, warring over it)? On the other hand, what are the weaknesses? Is ownership a scientific issue or a political one? Can science provide just procedures for converting communal property to private property?
6. Vardy argues that we are dealing with ice melting in a 'modern' way. What does he mean by this? How does Neves' description of modernity (in this section) compare with Vardy's?

Part XVI

Media

On its own, 'media' may seem to be an elusively general term. What, or who, is it that people are talking about when they say something like, 'How could you not have heard?! It's all over the media!', or 'The media is perverting today's young people!'. What is 'the' media? Is there only one? And if not, how can many small, disconnected media sometimes produce such similar messages that we talk about them as if they are one united causal agent?

To unpack this nebulous concept, perhaps it is helpful to remind ourselves that the root form of the word media is *medium*—referring to an instrument, or means, to accomplishing some end. Media outlets, then, such as newspapers and magazines, are different channels through which we communicate messages to each other. Conversations or written letters exchanged between friends are also media, though these aren't usually the forms of communication that people consider 'the' media.

Ever since the invention of the printing press, the role of impersonal media such as newspapers has grown in developed societies around the world. The printing press enabled people to make multiple copies of written messages instead of copying them one at a time, by hand. Not only was it time consuming to create individual handwritten copies, but there were likely to be large differences between the copies. Thanks to the printing press, one message could be copied exactly and distributed among a huge number of people. Over time, this spread of homogeneous messages enabled a degree of synchronization among vastly different and separated groups. This is what is meant by 'mass' media—messages created by a few producers and distributed widely to a large number (mass) of readers, listeners, or viewers. The media can act as gatekeepers, as they choose which messages get shared with large audiences. In reality there isn't one homogeneous audience, but instead various, segmented audiences. By creating separate messages for different audiences (for example, compare the content of men's magazines with women's magazines), mass media can over-exaggerate the differences between groups and contribute to deepening those differences instead of reducing them.

Subsequent to the printing press, many other forms of media were invented through technological developments—forms such as film, radio, and television. 'The' media usually refers to these plethora of communication channels through which we share messages. Since the end of the last century, Internet technology has been rapidly reshaping many of the ways we communicate. The main difference between the Internet and earlier forms of media is its decentralization: anyone can create a message, or respond to anyone else's message, and groups and individuals can create websites to disseminate their own messages. This dramatically revises the relationship between producers and consumers, shifting it to a much more personal level in which the individual has control. This trend has intensified with the rise of social media, which individuals use to produce content about themselves, for each other. We use sites such as Facebook or Twitter to see what our friends are communicating, through status updates, blog posts, pictures, videos, comments, etc., and to communicate back to them (our own, personalized audience) through the same channels.

The four articles in this section discuss a number of these aspects of the mass and social media. Linda Quirke describes how parenting magazines managed to recreate the role of parenthood as a goal-oriented process. She argues that through focusing on the responsibility of parents to deliberately foster children's cognitive development, this medium promoted a shift in values from family fun to family learning.

Rima Wilkes and her collaborators describe how newspapers present protest events by Canadian indigenous peoples. They explore how the craft of packaging stories for audiences results in some kinds of stories, or aspects of stories, receiving attention while others are ignored.

The importance of this uneven coverage is brought home by Hallgrimsdottir and her collaborators, which compare the stories told about sex workers in journalistic sources (both on- and offline) to the stories sex workers tell about themselves. Content analyses such as these highlight how professional media producers can easily misrepresent reality in ways that promote damaging stigmas about marginalized groups or individuals.

But would more democratically produced media reduce this filtering and asymmetrical agenda-setting? Michèle Ollivier and her collaborators address this question by examining the online research network PAR-L, whose goal is to preserve contact among feminist researchers in Canada. The answer, we discover is 'yes and no'. On the one hand, this medium allows for direct discussion between users and for less censorship—which means that very different views can be exchanged on a topic. On the other hand, content is only as diverse as the users of the media, so some views are liable to be vastly overrepresented compared to others, and some users feel pressure to conform to more dominant views. Furthermore, power structures offline carry into online discussions, so discussants can use their personal authority to shut down discussion or dissenting views.

Fallen Women and Rescued Girls: Social Stigma and Media Narratives of the Sex Industry in Victoria, BC, from 1980 to 2005

Helga Kristin Hallgrimsdottir, Rachel Phillips, and Cecilia Benoit

The significance of the media as an arbiter of social experience is well recognized. The media—newspapers, television, radio and, more recently, the Internet—educate, inform, and entertain, all the while reflecting and refracting images and understandings of our social worlds with varying accuracy and truth. This paper compares media portrayals of people who work in the sex industry with these workers' self-reports of their personal backgrounds and experiences of what they do for a living. Our aim is first, to gauge the empirical distance between media depictions and workers' lived reality, and second, to understand how the media contributes to constructing, reproducing, and deepening the social stigmas associated with working in the sex industry. We argue that pulling apart the historical and spatial variability of these stigmas and explicating their links to socio-structural contexts is a crucial step toward understanding their social construction. Exposing the socio-structural and human architecture of sex industry stigmas opens them to reinterpretation: insofar as new understandings position sex industry workers as individuals deserving of similar rights and protections as other 'legitimate' workers, they have the capacity to facilitate a better and safer experience for this clandestine population.

We rely on two data sources for this paper. First, we analyze print media discussion of the sex industry in one metropolitan area of Canada—the Census Metropolitan Area of Victoria, BC—between 1980 and 2004 in a single regional daily newspaper, the Victoria *Times Colonist*. We then compare these media narratives with the self-reported experiences of sex industry workers in the same city and over a comparable time period.

We argue here that social stigmas are a central example of a normative knowledge that emerges out of and is reinforced by media practices that are aimed at making the news 'resonant'. Stigma has historically been defined as a social attribute that is deeply discrediting and reduces the bearer from a whole and usual person to a tainted and discounted one (Goffman, 1963). We elaborate on this conception in two ways. First, following Link and Phelan (2001: 366–67), we expand this definition to understand stigma as 'when elements of labelling, separation, stereotyping, status loss and discrimination co-occur'. This elaboration of the stigma concept links the meaning-making activity of media authors with the material consequences associated with labelling and social exclusion. Furthermore, felt stigma, the internalization of perceived stigmatized/discrimination, which incorporates both fear of experiencing discrimination and the interpretation of the self within dominant cultural scripts, can be damaging even in the absence of observable instances of discrimination (Cree, Kay, Tisdall, and Wallace, 2004; Crocker and Quinn, 2000; Gray, 2002; Scambler,

Peswani, Renton, and Scambler, 1990). Second, by analyzing how 'whore' stigmas are articulated in dominant media knowledge, and how they are historically variable in scope and content, this paper adds to a growing literature on the structural mediation of stigma (Bobo, 1999; Kusow, 2004; Riessman, 2000).

The subject index of the Victoria *Times Colonist* (*TC*) for the time period in question identified a total of 425 articles concerning the sex industry. Using an open-coding technique, we developed seven narrative categories: vectors of contagion, population at risk or endangered, sexual slavery, moral culpability, predatory pimps, criminal culpability, community failure, and other. Below, we track how these narrative strands were variously woven together to produce three kinds of storylines. Consistent throughout the entire study time period, however, is that, first, sex industry workers are portrayed as vectors of contagion, whether as moral pollutants or as sources of disease. Second, sex industry work is portrayed as both an acute and a serious social problem; alternative constructions are almost completely absent in media discourse for the entire period. Third, media narratives focus almost exclusively on outdoor sex work. Fourth, the dominant media motif is strongly gendered: virtually all the media coverage over the entire period focuses on women of different age groups (adults, teenagers,

and children) with men appearing only as clients, pimps, or law enforcers.

However, there are three notable shifts in these themes over the study period. Discourses assigning criminal culpability to sex industry workers disappear after the late 1980s, and discourses suggesting that moral culpability lies with individuals also decline rapidly. Replacing them are discussions that move responsibility away from individual workers and toward others, including clients, pimps, and the 'global sex trade'. An additional change is a decline in discussions suggesting that community support systems—religious organizations, schools, and families—are responsible for the sex industry problem. Table 64.1 tracks the shifts in media narratives over our 24-year period.

Media authors, in general, relied on one of three broad (and sometimes overlapping) narrative conventions when writing news stories about the sex industry in Victoria: contagion, culpability, and risk. Let us look at each of these narrative conventions in succession.

'Street prostitution with all its attendant blights, including violence, drug addiction, disease, and degraded neighbourhoods, has long been one of the most unsavoury problems affecting Canadian cities' (editorial, *TC*, 13 January, 1996). This suggestion that sex work is a 'reservoir' of urban malaise is apparent through the entire time period; however, it is primarily between 1980 and 1990

Table 64.1 Discussions of the Sex Industry in the Victoria *Times Colonist*, 1980–2004

THEME	1980–1990 (N = 115)	1990–2000 (N = 182)	2001–2004 (N = 128)
Vectors of Contagion	43 (37%)	51 (28%)	25 (20%)
Risk	0	33 (18%)	45 (35%)
Sexual Slavery	0	27 (15%)	31 (24%)
Moral Culpability	17 (15%)	18 (10%)	0
Community Failure	19 (17%)	11 (6%)	0
Predatory Pimps	0	42 (23%)	6 (5%)
Criminal Culpability	30 (26%)	0	0
Other	6 (5%)	0	21 (16%)

that the discussion centres most frequently on physical contagion and the need for spatial containment solutions: streets needed to be 'cleared of prostitution' (editorial, *TC*, 19 February, 1982) because 'neighbourhoods are blighted by prostitution' (editorial, *TC*, 12 May, 1984). More explicitly: 'Whores . . . not only . . . offend . . . the law, they are an embarrassment when the family goes downtown for dinner. They speak of the community's failure. They are also seen as a threat by some wives and mothers and they are bad for business' (editorial, *TC*, 22 October, 1981). Underscoring the need for the physical eradication of the sex industry are also media discussions that portray it as a vector of criminality: 'prostitution and violence related to prostitution are on the rise' (*TC*, 22 October, 1981). This finding is further emphasized by loading the discussions with metaphors of warfare and violence: 'Government street hookers say there will be a territorial war' (*TC*, 17 August, 1985), and 'teen sex rings' make for an 'eerie feeling of impending violence on city streets' (*TC*, 10 October, 1984).

A narrative convention around culpability is the most characteristic feature of discourses of sex industry work in the 1980s. There are two kinds of stories told here. First, sex industry workers are thought of as criminals.

However, those who work in the sex industry are far from common criminals. Rather, they are uniquely morally culpable in that they are believed to take pride in circumventing the law and avoiding arrest. This results in a situation where, because of their immunity to legal and moral norms, people who work in the sex industry are 'above the law': 'Police are hamstrung by the liberalization of prostitution laws' (*TC*, 21 November, 1981); similarly, the police chief of Victoria is quoted as saying, 'We don't have any prosecutorial tool we can use against them. I suppose we could lay charges, but what's the use?' Meanwhile, the Canadian Association of Police Chiefs states: 'Laws against soliciting by prostitutes are unenforceable . . . the situation is virtually out of control.' Furthermore, 'without better laws, they will continue to 'spread their joy, herpes, and other venereal diseases' (*TC*, 22 December, 1982).

Risk: Entrapment and Slavery as Routes to the Sex Industry

The prominence of stories around culpability diminishes in the 1990s, concomitant with the rise of theories of victimhood, as well as a shift in the focus of criminal prosecution: as workers are recast as victims, 'Johns' and 'pimps' become more central to discussions of criminal culpability. Instead of being culpable, sex workers appear to be legally and morally incapacitated, incapable of making safe and reasonable choices for themselves. This is conveyed in particular through stories that emphasize risk—of violence, of entrapment, and seduction.

Importantly, while contagion narratives suggest that workers pose a risk to innocent others, victimhood narratives tend to locate and bound risk within the confines of the sex industry: 'Predatory pimps target Victoria in teen recruiting' (*TC*, 14 February, 1997) and 'Prostitution circuit keeps girls in slavery' (*TC*, 24 August, 1997). Victimhood/risk stories are often racialized and highlight the vulnerability and youth of the women involved; references to global trafficking of women and children from less-advantaged countries 'prostituted girls are essentially slaves . . . in India and Thailand' (*TC*, 30 August, 1996) abound and a significant majority of all *TC* media stories appearing after the mid-1990s concern child and juvenile prostitution.

The narrative conventions outlined above amount to dominant scripts that organize and structure most discussions of the sex industry. As scripts, they offer the reader well-known protagonists (a wily prostitute who escapes the law; a damaged, drug-addicted, and desperate teenager), trajectories (an early loss of innocence entails permanent moral damage), and solutions (physical containment, confinement, moral rescue campaigns).

We now turn to presenting primary data based on in-person interviews with adults who work in the sex industry in the metropolitan area under study. Our aim here is to reveal how omissions and punctuations in media narratives perpetuate social stigmas, particularly through their reliance on scripts that represent sex industry workers as 'lost' or 'fallen' others and create and reinforce theories of contagion, victimization, and criminality. At the same time, these stigmas reassure a middle-class readership that the 'sex work problem' has little direct relevance to their own lives.

To begin, although a majority (80 per cent) of our total sample of 201 respondents identified as female (*n* = 160), reflecting other estimates of the gendered nature of the sex industry in Canada (Brock, 1998), a sizable minority (18 per cent) of males were also interviewed (*n* = 36). The remaining 2 per cent (*n* = 5) identified as male-to-female transgendered. Thus, one of the first notable media omissions is the experience of males, a gap that is, to a lesser degree, mirrored in the academic literature (Weitzer, 2000).

Also missing from the media stories is information on the everyday circumstances of our respondents, including their housing situation. While 63 per cent of all householders in the study area own their own dwellings, this was the case for only 3.5 per cent of our respondents. Furthermore, while three-quarters of them said they had a stable living situation, nearly 25 per cent stated that they lived in unstable or very unstable circumstances. It was also apparent from the open-ended comments that many of them were recipients of income assistance, including disability income assistance, which is further evidence of the on-average lower socio-economic status of this population. Finally, 28 per cent of the females and 14 per cent of the males were currently caring for dependent children, another fact that is not commonly noted in the media depictions.

In sum, while an unstable family background was certainly common among our respondents, and may represent partial convergence with some of the depictions of sex industry workers found in media coverage, a more accurate interpretation of the empirical data is that persons involved in the sex industry represent populations that face barriers to mainstream employment, are more likely to belong to discriminated identities, and come from current and historical backgrounds of economic and social hardship. Such an interpretation positions sex industry workers as structurally disadvantaged, not morally corrupt or helpless victims (Link and Phelan, 1995).

One of the greatest divergences between media and empirical depictions of the sex industry is in the descriptions of work activities and workers' feelings about what they do for a living. Whereas media depictions emphasize violence, forced or abusive circumstances, and the community nuisance caused by the street-level sex industry, workers paint a much more heterogeneous picture and were apt to talk about the many mundane and routine aspects of the work they do. They also hold varied views about their work, ranging from complacency and indifference to strong positions in favour of and against it.

Whereas media narratives generally offer only one kind of explanation for entry into the sex industry—entrapment—respondents described a variety of circumstances that precipitated their entry. Just over one-third said that they became involved in the industry because they were enticed by a presenting opportunity, such as having peers who were involved, seeing an employment ad, or having someone approach them with an offer of money for sex. For over one-quarter of respondents, however, economic duress—described as being 'unable to find a job', 'on welfare with small children', living 'on the streets with no income,' or having 'bills to pay'—was the main motivating factor, and in many cases economic need overlapped with opportunity. In addition to opportunity-based and economic reasons, a minority of respondents cited the risk factors alluded to in the media stories, such as dependency on illicit drugs and alcohol, as a motivating factor. A few respondents also described what might be characterized as forced or abuse-related involvement.

Media depictions do not emphasize the 'work' aspects of the sex industry. In contrast, the most important aspect of the sex industry for respondents was that it was a source of income. A majority of respondents were relatively long-term participants in the sex industry, with an average of eight years' involvement at the time of the interview. Respondents also reported a clear sense of what each service was worth, and that one of the main reasons that they sold sex was not to pay for drugs, but for normal, 'mundane' living costs—rent, food, and clothing.

Discussion and Conclusion

Our findings show that media narratives of the sex industry tell us little about the complexities of what sex workers do for a living. Instead, our primary data show that media narratives follow relatively rigid and standardized cultural scripts in which individuals in the sex industry are presented as morally lost and legally corrupt, and as vectors of social and physical malaise. These cultural scripts organize media narratives by directing what gets counted as newsworthy and what gets omitted from news accounts. Scambler and Scambler (1997: 112) refer to this as the 'paradox of attention': media attention is paid to the titillating and illicit aspects of trading sex for money, while its less glamorous, ordinary reality is ignored.

Our findings also suggest that the contents of these cultural scripts convey much about, first, how social stigmas become reproduced in media narratives, as well as how women's (not men's) sexuality is a specially privileged disciplinary discourse (Sanders, 2004). While the cultural scripts and narrative conventions shifted over the 24-year period under examination, creating new kinds of characters and constructing slightly different power relations between them, across the two decades there is a consistent focus on moral loss and contagion, reminding us that, for many readers, female workers' personhood is so intimately linked with their sexual selves that violation of sexual norms entails utter and complete loss of individuality. In addition, the dominating focus on street work, i.e., a public display of women's sexuality, suggests that sex work stigmas are a key disciplinary site of women's sexuality in general.

Media narratives offer a voyeuristic and consumerist interpretation of the sex industry, through which a mainstream audience is titillated with stories of culpable and wicked females (in the earlier time period) or the entrapment and seduction of innocent girls (in the later period). In so doing, these narratives reproduce social stigmas that suggest that sex industry workers are morally, mentally, and psychologically damaged, and, by focussing on individual pathologies and risk behaviours, obscure the various distal forces that shape both entry into the sex industry and the ordinary and mundane experiences within it (Weitzer, 2000). These narratives thus place the worker at the margins of society, as the stigmatized other, and direct the moral obligations of the audience in particular ways: abandoning fallen women and rescuing lost girls.

References

Barak, G. 1994. *Media, Process, and the Social Construction of Crime*. New York and London: Garland Publishing.

Benford, R.D. and D.A. Snow. 2000a. 'Framing processes and social movements: An overview and assessment'. *Annual Review of Sociology*, Vol. 26, pp. 611–39.

Benford, R.D. and D.A. Snow. 2000b. 'Clarifying the relationship between framing and ideology'. *Mobilization*, Vol. 5, No. 1, pp. 55–60.

Benoit, C. and A. Millar. 2001. Dispelling Myths and Understanding Realities: Working Conditions, Health Status, and Exiting Experiences of Sex Workers. Victoria, B.C.: Prostitutes Empowerment, Education and Resource Society (PEERS).

Berbrier, M. 1998. '"Half the battle": Cultural resonance, framing processes, and ethnic affectations in contemporary white separatist rhetoric'. *Social Problems*, Vol. 45, No. 4, pp. 431–50.

Bobo, L.D. 1999. 'Prejudice as group position: Microfoundations of a sociological approach to racism and race relations'. *Journal of Social Issues*, Vol. 55, No. 3, pp. 445–72.

Brock, D. 1998. *Making Work, Making Trouble*. Toronto: University of Toronto Press.

Crée, V.E., H. Kay, K. Tisdall, and J. Wallace. 2004. 'Stigma and parental HIV'. Qualitative Social Work, Vol. 3, No. 1, pp. 7–25.

Crocker, J. and D.M. Quinn. 2000. 'Social stigma and the self: Meanings, situations, and selfesteem'. In *The Social Psychology of Stigma*, T.F.K. Heatherton, R.E. Hebl, M.R. Hulland, and J. Jay (eds.). New York: Guilford Press, pp. 153–83.

Gitlin, T. 2003. *The Whole World Is Watching: Mass Media in the Making and Unmaking of the New Left*. Berkeley: University of California Press.

Goffman, E. 1963. *Stigma: Notes on the Management of Spoiled Identity*. Englewood Cliffs, N.J.: Prentice-Hall.

Gray, D.E. 2002. '"Everybody just freezes. Everybody is just embarrassed": Felt and enacted stigma among parents of children with high-functioning autism'. *Sociology of Health and Illness*, Vol. 24, No. 6, pp. 734-39.

Hall, S.M. 1978. *Policing the Crisis: Mugging, the State, and Law and Order*. London: Macmillan.

Jenness, V. 1990. 'From sex as sin to sex as work: Coyote and the reorganization of prostitution as a social problem'. *Social Problems*, Vol. 37, No. 3, pp. 403–20.

Kitzinger, J. 2000. 'Media templates: Patterns of association and the (re)construction of meaning over time'. *Media, Culture, and Society*, Vol. 22, No. 1, pp. 61–84.

Kubal, T.J. 1998. 'The presentation of political self: Cultural resonance and the construction of collective action frames'. *Sociological Quarterly*, Vol. 39, No. 4, pp. 539–54.

Kusow, A.M. 2004. 'Contesting stigma: On Goffman's assumptions of normative order'. *Symbolic Interaction*, Vol. 27, No. 2, pp. 179–97.

Link, B.C. and J. Phelan. 1995. 'Social conditions as fundamental causes of disease'. *Journal of Health and Social Behaviour*, Extra Issue, pp. 80–94.

Link, B.C. and J. Phelan. 2001. 'Conceptualizing stigma'. *Annual Review of Sociology*, Vol. 27, pp. 363–85.

Lowman, J. 1987. 'Taking young prostitutes seriously'. *The Canadian Review of Sociology and Anthropology*, Vol. 24, No. 1, pp. 99–116.

Lundman, R., O. Douglass and J. Hanson. 2004. 'News about murder in an African American newspaper: Effects of relative frequency and race and gender typifications'. *The Sociological Quarterly*, Vol. 45, No. 2, pp. 249–72.

MacKinnon, C. 1987. *Feminism Unmodified: Discourses on Law and Life*. Cambridge, Mass.: Harvard University Press.

Mirola, WA. 2003. 'Asking for bread, receiving a stone: The rise and fall of religious ideologies in Chicago's eight-hour movement'. *Social Problems*, Vol. 50, No. 2, pp. 273–93.

Pateman, C. 1988. *The Sexual Contract*. Cambridge: Polity Press.

Riessman, C. 2000. 'Stigma and everyday resistance practices: Childless women in South India'. *Gender and Society*, Vol. 14, No. 1, pp. 111–35.

Sacks, V. 1996. 'Women and AIDS: An analysis of media misrepresentations'. *Social Science and Medicine*, Vol. 42, No. 1, pp. 59–73.

Sanders, T. 2004. 'A continuum of risk? The management of health, physical and emotional risks by female sex workers'. *Sociology of Health & Illness*, Vol. 26, No. 5, pp. 557–74.

Scambler, G. and A. Hopkins. 1986. 'Being epileptic: Coming to terms with stigma'. *Sociology of Health and Illness*. Vol. 8, No. 1, pp. 26–43.

Scambler, G., R. Peswani, A. Renton and A. Scambler. 1990. 'Women prostitutes in the AIDS era'. *Sociology of Health and Illness*, Vol. 12, No. 3, pp. 260–73.

Scambler, G. and A. Scambler (eds.). 1997. *Rethinking Prostitution: Purchasing Sex in the 1990s*. London: Routledge.

Seale, C. 2003. 'Health and media: An overview'. *Sociology of Health and Illness*, Vol. 25, No. 6, pp. 513–31.

Shaver, F.M. 2005. 'Sex work research: Methodological and ethical challenges'. *Journal of Interpersonal Violence*, Vol. 20, No. 3, pp. 296–319.

Snow, D.A. and R. Benford. 1988. 'Ideology, frame resonance, and participant mobilization'. *International Social Movement Research*, Vol. 1, pp. 197–217.

Snow, D.A., B.E. Rochford, S.K. Worden and R. Benford. 1986. 'Frame alignment processes, micromobilization, and movement participation'. *American Sociological Review*, Vol. 51, No. 4, pp. 464–81.

Statistics Canada. 2001, 'Community profiles: Victoria, B.C.', Retrieved May 5, 2006. http://www12.statcan.ca.myaccess. library.utoronto.ca/english/profil01/CP01/Details/Page. cfm?Lang= E&Geo1 = CMA& Code 1 = 935_&Geo2 = PR&Code2 = 59&Data = Count&SearchText = victoria&SearchType = Begins&SearchPR=01&B1= All&Custom=).

Stenvoll, D. 2001. 'From Russia with love? Newspaper coverage of cross-border prostitution in Northern Norway, 1990-2001'. *European Journal of Women's Studies*, Vol. 9, No. 2, pp. 143–62.

Watkins, S.C. and R. Emerson. 2000. 'Feminist media criticism and feminist media practices'. *Annals of the American Academy of Political and Social Science*, Vol. 571, No. 1, pp. 151–66.

Weitzer, R.J. 2000. 'Deficiencies in the sociology of sex work'. *Sociology of Crime, Law and Deviance*, Vol. 2, pp. 259–79.

CHAPTER 65

Feminist Activists Online: A Study of the PAR-L Research Network

Michèle Ollivier, Wendy Robbins, Diane Beauregard, Jennifer Brayton, and Geneviève Sauvé

This paper presents an analysis and discussion, based largely on the results of an online survey, of one of Canada's first, longest-lived, and most successful feminist discussion lists. PAR-L, a bilingual electronic network of individuals and organizations interested in feminist action and research on policy issues in Canada, was founded as an e-mail list in March 1995 by the former Canadian Advisory Council on the Status of Women (CACSW), where the two principal authors of this paper were employed. Our main goal was to provide a space where community- and university-based researchers and activists across Canada could come together to exchange information, discuss ideas, and create closer links with one another.

PAR-L's importance to the women's movement in Canada is indicated by quantitative measures—subscribers to the e-mail list number over 1,500, the list archives contain 15,000 messages posted over the decade 1995–2005, and PAR-L Partners include 21 Canadian feminist research organizations—and by qualitative ones—PAR-L is identified as a 'life-line', a 'key resource', and even 'a national treasure' by survey respondents.

The 2002 survey had two main objectives: (1) to assess the effectiveness of PAR-L as a tool for feminist activism; and (2) to get feedback from subscribers. Our report is based on data collected from questionnaires posted to the list in the spring and fall of 2002.

How well has PAR-L achieved its goals of providing a space where feminist researchers and activists can come together to exchange information, create networks, and discuss women-centred policy issues? Is the list an effective tool for increasing women's equality and creating social change? In survey research conducted in 1996 (Ollivier and Robbins, 1999), where we examined who subscribes to the list and whose voices are heard, we showed that we were partly successful in achieving our goals.

In the spring of 2002, we posted a second questionnaire to the list. Perhaps because the questionnaire was posted late in the spring, we received only 57 answers, compared to the 91 that we had received in 1996. We posted the questionnaire again in the fall and we received additional responses from 30 subscribers, for a total of 87.

Analysis of the socio-demographic characteristics of respondents to the survey suggests that the PAR-L membership is far from being representative of the Canadian population. Almost all of those who answered are female (one is male and one did not answer the question about gender), and all but two are residents of Canada. All but five (94 per cent) have attained a university or community college degree, compared to 53 per cent of women aged 25 and over in Canada (Statistics Canada, 2000). Only 22 per cent declare personal annual incomes below the average mean personal income of $25,000 for Canadian women aged 25 to 54, and 46 per cent earn over $45,000 a year (Statistics Canada, 2000). All but one own a personal computer (compared to 49 per cent of Canadian women, see Denis and Ollivier, 2003).

However, other results suggest that among feminist researchers and activists, PAR-L contributes to bridging the gap between women from different age groups, geographical locations, and professional situations. Only 18 per cent of respondents are under 30 years old, compared to the 32 per cent of Canadian women who are between the ages of 15 and 25. With regard to language, 75 per cent speak only English at home, 11 per cent speak both English and French, 8 per cent speak only French, and the rest (6 per cent) speak a combination of French, English, and other. One identifies as an Aboriginal, four as visible minorities, and seven as persons with disabilities. Although young women and French-speaking participants are under-represented, their contribution to discussions over the year has been significant. With regard to professional situation, only 49 per cent are affiliated with (employed by or attending) a university, college, or other academic institution. Among those who are in the paid labour force, 20 per cent work for a college, university, or other academic institution, 27 per cent work for a women's organization or a community group, 28 per cent are freelance, and 10 per cent work for the government. The ability of PAR-L to bring together women working in universities, community groups and other settings remains in our view one of its main strengths and accounts for its originality.

PAR-L is perceived as a valuable source of information on political and scholarly events, employment opportunities, political campaigns, action alerts, legislative policy issues, and resources for research and action-including reports of research in progress, bibliographical references, and electronic links. It is sometimes described as an alternative to mainstream media by those seeking information on issues of interest to feminists in Canada. Participants discussed the usefulness of PAR-L in allowing them to know which women's issues are currently being argued and discussed, and what political actions are taking place. They praised the list's selective focus on women's issues and its up-to-the-minute topicality for feminist policy, action, and research: 'It allows me to have my finger on the pulse of the issues and activities within the women's movement.'

Many academic feminists use PAR-L as a pedagogical resource or use the messages posted on the list to inform and enrich their own research. Feminist professors talked specifically about the importance of using PAR-L information in their classes, as the content is both current and feminist. They also discussed the value of job postings, calls for conference papers, and summaries of recent scholarship for themselves and their students who, they reported, 'love these contacts'. In addition, several graduate students discussed the usefulness of PAR-L information for their own academic work and for staying well informed on issues relevant to feminist activism. For example, one subscriber reported: 'I have recently learned to use the PAR-L e-mail Archive, and it has helped me to write a section for an academic paper.'

Community activists, policy analysts, and freelancers also discussed the usefulness of PAR-L information in their professional lives. They described how many postings are helpful to their work, especially discussions of current events and messages pertaining to new initiatives, policy statements, upcoming conferences or events, and new resources for research and action. They also discussed the value of being able to receive and disseminate job postings and various other professional advertisements. Finally, some participants view PAR-L as a model and a 'key resource' that helps and influences them in their online work. The survey results also show that PAR-L information and exchanges are sometimes used as a source of inspiration for new projects and initiatives.

Finally, a number of participants expressed an appreciation for how the information posted on PAR-L sometimes pushes them toward concrete actions, such as signing petitions, writing letters, or taking a political stand on particular issues.

PAR-L provides a discussion forum where participants have an opportunity to articulate their positions on key feminist issues. The expression of competing views among feminist researchers and activists coming from very different horizons provides an alternative to the monolithic and often distorted image of feminism conveyed by mainstream media. This appears to be a particularly useful feature of the list, since many women, taken by the immediate necessities of research and action, rarely have the opportunity to participate in meaningful debates on feminist issues. PAR-L is often praised as a 'good list' because it is moderated (messages are screened by the moderators for relevancy) and allows for respectful exchanges between members with differing feminist opinions and perspectives: 'Generally, I think you do a great job of striking a balance between allowing debates to continue and encouraging them to be civil and respectful.'

Among those who did not explicitly answer that they had modified their position on an issue as a result of PAR-L, a number of respondents expressed an appreciation for how the variety of perspectives in the list discussions helped them to formulate a position or an opinion on specific subjects. Being exposed to competing feminist views challenged them to question their own beliefs and values, making them more aware, in certain cases, of their oppressive attitudes:

> PAR-L allows participants to 'keep in touch' with the feminist movement in Canada, with feminist activism/grassroots, and with academic feminism. Consistent with our objectives, PAR-L is considered by respondents as an important networking tool that is conducive to creating connections and exchanges within the feminist community.

Networking goes beyond participants exchanging messages on the list. Among those who answered the survey, 57 per cent (49) say that they have corresponded privately with other PAR-L members whom they met through the list. When asked to elaborate on the nature of this correspondence, they gave the following answers by order of importance: requesting a permission; requesting information or clarification; requesting resources, advice, or assistance; offering support; offering thanks; networking; furthering or continuing the discussion; finding specific people; and renewing contact with long-lost friends. Communicating privately allows individuals and groups to form new connections and ties with other feminists, linked by a shared membership in PAR-L. Some respondents described how private correspondence led not only to connections and

exchanges, but also sometimes to various types of professional opportunities and invitations.

Communicating privately, however, does not always lead to satisfying and respectful exchanges. One subscriber, for example, reported having had a bad experience as a result of this type of exchange, even though both people presumably shared a commitment to feminist analysis and action.

PAR-L provides some respondents with a way to minimize their sense of isolation (as feminists) and to feel more connected to the 'feminist community' in Canada. It allows subscribers from across Canada to be aware of the differing issues and events of concern to women at the provincial, national, and international levels. PAR-L also provides a safe space where feminist voices can be heard and positions articulated.

Similarly, some respondents discussed the impact PAR-L discussions and exchanges has had on their personal lives. They have named how, in various ways, being subscribers has contributed to their sense of well-being and of connectedness to a larger community. It should be stressed that the psychological benefit to individual activists is one aspect of online activism that is rarely mentioned as a positive outcome in the literature on Internet use for social change. As we have discussed and documented above, the literature concentrates on group, rather than individual, empowerment, access, and validation. It tends to highlight 'social goods' in the public sphere of work and citizenship, rather than in the personal realm of beliefs, values, and psychological or moral support. Thus, benefits are typically registered in terms of the strengthening of social ties, rather than in the perhaps more subjective reports and measures of individual psychological well-being and mental health.

Finally, there is evidence that women and men connected to PAR-L act as 'bridges' (Wood, 1998) to some individuals and organizations who, for a variety of reasons, cannot access PAR-L, either because they are not connected, not well connected (e.g. slow connections or low e-mail storage space), or are unable to keep up with the mail volume on the list. Among those who answered the survey, 72 per cent (61) regularly forward PAR-L messages by e-mail, photocopy, or fax to other parties such as friends, colleagues, or other listservs.

Respondents were also asked to describe any aspect of the list that they find problematic. There are two thematic areas of concern. First, PAR-L subscribers complain about technical problems and the sheer volume of messages. Second, they experience dissatisfaction with communication policies and the conduct of participants on the list. Their answers point to some of the challenges of running a feminist e-mail list, where internal issues of power and exclusion are as much a source of concern as political intervention in public affairs.

A large number of answers concerned technical issues such as bulky headers, the digest format, and the transmission of French characters. The volume of mail sent by PAR-L was also considered a problem by many respondents. More interesting were comments on the nature and tone of our exchanges. Several comments pertained to uncertainty about, and inadequate enforcement of, the norms of conduct governing interaction on the list. This problem involves four distinct processes.

A first source of frustration is lack of adherence by subscribers to the list guidelines, especially those concerning the format of messages. This includes editing messages before replying to them, providing a clear title, mentioning the location where an action is taking place in the title of the message, and writing the sender's e-mail address at the bottom of the message. These guidelines are contained in the introductory PAR-L welcome message, as well as being posted in the Help Desk section of the PAR-L website. Subscribers were most annoyed by messages where the subject line does not clearly indicate the nature of the posting.

A second problem concerns inconsistent enforcement of list policies by the list moderators. In principle, the list has a relatively narrow focus, since it is devoted to discussion of policy, action, and research on issues of concern to women in Canada. Because women represent about 52 per cent of the Canadian population, however, any issue is bound to affect us one way or another. Moderators have rejected messages on issues such as water management in Toronto, animal rights, and grants for artists in Halifax, only

to receive angry replies that these were feminist issues since they have an impact on women's lives. When we posted messages of support for Robert Latimer and on conflict in the Middle East, we also received angry messages saying that these were off topic. Where do you draw the line? There is no clear answer to this question. Compounding the difficulty, PAR-L has two moderators who alternate moderating the list every other week and sometimes have slightly different interpretations of the list guidelines. This situation may contribute to the feeling of alienation expressed by some respondents, who feel that the norms and guidelines governing interaction are sometimes applied in an arbitrary way.

A third source of frustration concerns the tone of certain exchanges and the questionable conduct of a few participants on the list. While many respondents praised the list for providing a space where diverse opinions can be expressed in a manner that is respectful of differences, others were highly critical of the tone of some of the exchanges. Our list guidelines specify that personal attacks and flaming are not allowed on the list, but it is difficult to avoid the expression of strong feelings entirely. Making room for different styles of speech is an issue of internal inclusion, as norms of dispassionate and articulate speech are culturally specific and tend to vary along class lines (Young, 2000).

The comments also illustrate a fourth source of frustration. While PAR-L subscribers represent a relatively privileged segment of the Canadian population, they also differ on a wide range of characteristics, including geographical location, age, gender, race/ethnicity, linguistic proficiency, professional qualifications, disability, sexual orientation, etc. Offline social locations are associated with various levels and types of social power, which may influence whose voices are heard in the discussions. The cohabitation of diverse standpoints within a common space inevitably creates tensions and opportunities for internal forms of exclusion.

For example, several respondents described the list as **elitist**. This feeling was most often associated with two problems: first, with the fact that PAR-L exchanges are sometimes perceived as favouring an academic or intellectual type of feminism over a community-based feminism, and second, with situations in which older or 'mainstream' feminists react strongly to some postings and use their authority to suppress discussions.

In addition, while men are welcome on the list, they constitute a small minority of subscribers. Strong and prolonged intervention on their part was mentioned as a source of frustration by some women. However, one female subscriber described feeling frustrated by the absence of 'male feminists' in PAR-L discussions.

Overposting by some groups or individuals, and cross-posting of information between related discussion forums, were also mentioned as sources of frustration. Some PAR-L members are subscribed to similar feminist discussion groups, such as Womenspace, and are bothered by the repetition of information. Furthermore, while participants appreciate discussions that allow them to form their own opinion on current issues, they have different levels of tolerance for how long it should be allowed to go on. A few think that our interventions designed to keep discussions from becoming too heated are unfair and result in the silencing of dissenting voices.

These comments, coupled with the desire expressed by many respondents to filter messages by region, language, or types of issues to meet their special information needs, illustrate the tension between the goal of maintaining a broad membership among feminists across Canada on the one hand, and the tendency toward the increasing segmentation of special interests on the other. Reaching across to a **diversity** of feminists in Canada is both a source of enrichment and a source of frustration, as participants need to deal with irrelevant information, conflicting views, and different interpretations of the norms of conduct.

As our research results clearly suggest, even amongst feminists, whose work involves a critique of power and exclusion, equality and inclusion necessarily remain ideals to strive for rather than permanent achievements. Overall, comments on problematic aspects of the PAR-L list support the conclusions of other studies of the Internet. While some features of Internet technology may provide a means to empower those who have been marginalized, enhance **democracy**, and foster the emergence of more fluid communities, technology in and of itself does not eliminate power differentials and problems of external and internal exclusion. Evidence surfaced in the PAR-L survey in the form of statements of feelings of alienation expressed by some young feminists, comments on the list being somewhat elitist, and complaints about the use of authority to stifle discussion.

Achieving equality remains a clear, central objective of feminist praxis. However, eliminating difference per se is not and should not be an option. Equality is not a synonym for sameness, and homogeneity was never the goal. Individual autonomy and equality of access are in a fine balance with collective norms of behaviour and a sense of belonging. As indicated by PAR-L members' comments, the pluralism of voices is, at the same time, a source of frustration and a means of broadening our understanding. As argued by Young (2000), social difference may be viewed as a resource for democratic communication. The co-presence of differences within a shared space creates tensions, sometimes threatening the very existence of our community, but it also leads to the renewal of discourses and practices.

References

Abbott, J.P 2001. 'Democracy@internet.asia? The challenges to the emancipatory potential of the Net: Lessons from China and Malaysia'. *Third World Quarterly*, Vol. 22, No. 1, pp. 99–114.

Bury, R. 1999. 'X-clusively female: The Cyberspaces of the David Duchovny Estrogen Brigades'. *Resources for Feminist Research*, Vol. 27, Nos. 1–2, pp. 25–47.

Colline, PH. 1991. 'Learning from the outsider within: The sociological significance of black feminist thought'. In *Beyond Methodology: Feminist Scholarship as Lived Research*. M.M. Fonov and J.A. Cook (eds.). Bloomington and Indianapolis: Indiana University Press, pp. 35–59.

Denis, A. and M. Ollivier. 2003. 'How wired are Canadian women: The intersection of gender, class and language in information technologies'. In *Out of the Ivory Tower: Taking Feminist Research to the Community*. A. Martinez and M. Stuart (eds.). Toronto: Sumach Press, pp. 251–69.

Engel, M. and C. Fisher. 1998. 'Women & wires: Feminist connections and the politics of Cyberspace'. *WE International*, Nos. 42–43, pp. 32–34.

George, E. 2000. 'De l'utilisation d'Internet comme outil de mobilisation: Les cas d'ATTAC et de SalAMI'. *Sociologie et sociétés*, Vol. 32, No. 2, pp. 171–87.

George, E. 2002. 'La question des inégalités au coeur des usages de l'Internet'. COMMposite, Vol. 1. Available at: http://commposite.org/2002.1/articles/george6.html. Consulted on May 23, 2006.

Gersch, B. 1998. 'Gender at the crossroads: The Internet as cultural text'. *Journal of Communication Inquiry*, Vol. 22, No. 3, pp. 306–21.

Hargittai, E. 2000. 'Standing before the portals: Non-profit content in the age of commercial gatekeepers'. *Info*, Vol. 2, No. 6, pp. 543–50.

Harmon, A. 1998. 'Sad, lonely world discovered in Cyberspace'. *New York Times*. Aug. 30, Section 1, p. 1.

Herring, S. 1996. 'Gender differences in computer-mediated communication: Bringing familiar baggage to the new frontier'. In *CyberReader*. V. Vitanza (ed.). Boston: Allyn and Bacon, pp. 144–54.

Hsiung, E-C. and Y.-L. R. Wong. 1998. 'Jie Giu connecting the tracks: Chinese women's activism surrounding the 1995 World Conference on Women in Beijing'. *Gender & History*, Vol. 10, No. 3, pp. 470–97.

Klein, H.K. 1999. 'Tocqueville in Cyberspace: Using the Internet for citizen associations'. *The Information Society*,

Vol. 15, No. 4, pp. 213–20.

Knouse, S.B. and S.C. Webb. 2001. 'Virtual networking for women and minorities'. *Career Development International*, Vol. 6, No. 4, pp. 226–28.

Kutner, L.A. 2000. 'Environmental activism and the Internet'. *Electronic Green Journal*, Vol. 12. Available at: http://egj.lib.uidaho.edu/egjl2/kutnerl.html. Consulted on May 23, 2006.

Ollivier, M. 2004. 'Méthodologies féministes à l'ère de la mondialisation : ébauche d'un bilan critique'. *Cahiers de recherche du GREMF*, No. 88, pp. 45–70.

Ollivier, M. and W. Robbins. 1999. 'Electronic communications and feminist activism: The experience of PAR-L'. *Atlantis*, Vol. 24, No. 1, pp. 39–53.

Poxon, J.L. and K. O'Grady. 1999. 'Internet mailing lists and feminist research, pedagogy, and activism'. *Resources for Feminist Research*, Vol. 27, Nos. 1–2, pp. 121–25.

Scott-Dixon, K. 1999. 'Ezines and feminist activism: Building a community'. *Resources for Feminist Research*, Vol. 27, Nos. 1–2, pp. 127–32.

Smith, D. 1974. 'Women's perspective as a radical critique of sociology'. *Sociological Inquiry*, Vol. 44, No. 1, pp. 7–13.

Statistics Canada. 2000. *Women in Canada 2000: A Gender-Based Statistical Report*. Ottawa: Minister of Industry.

Wood, P. 1998. 'Changing the world electronically'. *WE International*, Nos. 42–43, pp. 35–39.

Young, I.M. 2000. *Inclusion and Democracy*. Oxford: Oxford University Press.

Zelwietro, J. 1998. 'The politicization of environmental organizations through the Internet'. *The Information Society*, Vol. 14, No. 1, pp. 45–56.

CHAPTER 66

'Keeping Young Minds Sharp': Children's Cognitive Stimulation and the Rise of Parenting Magazines, 1959–2003

Linda Quirke

This study is an exploration of the changing ethos of **parenting**, based on an examination of parenting magazines and articles. Drawing upon the work of authors who argue that childrearing is

becoming a more intensive endeavour, I examine changes in the publication rates and the specific content of parenting articles. I argue that the substantial growth of parenting magazines in a number of English-speaking industrialized countries is indicative of a larger concern about 'parenting' as a deliberate undertaking or strategy. Consistent with others who document a heightened concern with children's cognitive development, I find that, over time, Canadian parenting articles increasingly emphasize schooling and children's academic skills.

Magazines as data sources comprise a number of limitations. They are directed at middle-class audiences, who are most likely to turn to expert childrearing advice (Wrigley, 1989; Smith, Van Loon, DeFrates-Densch, and Schrader, 1998; Bigner and Yang, 1996). Magazine content is not directly correlated with actual childrearing practices. Yet, the content of these articles is a measure of what is of interest to the lay public; the sheer popularity of these publications suggests that they resonate with parents. Despite their limitations, material presented in childrearing manuals and parenting magazines are an 'approximation of the dominant cultural model of raising children' (Hays, 1996: 52). Together with other data sources, such as ethnographic work (see Lareau, 2000; 2003) and time series data (e.g. Sayer, Bianchi, and Robinson, 2004; Bianchi and Robinson, 1997), parenting magazine data represent another method for studying changing childrearing practices and philosophies over time.

The vast majority of articles studied were short, and conveyed one main theme, such as alerting parents to depression among children (coded as 'psychology/emotions'), or discussing when babies should babble (coded as 'development'). It was not uncommon for more than one theme or category to be mentioned within the text of one article. A secondary or tertiary 'theme' might be mentioned in passing, but was not fully discussed or developed. Often, whatever topic occurred first in the text of the article also received the greatest attention, emphasis, and depth. It was rarely the case that more than one focus vied for prominence within the space of one article. For example, an article titled 'Curb the Chemicals' focused mainly on the risk to children's health of ingesting harmful chemicals found in household solvents. While the article mentioned children's development being potentially harmed by exposure to such chemicals, this point was not emphasized, and was made only in passing. The article was coded into the category 'health and safety', rather than 'development', as the major focus was the overall risk of harmful chemicals to children's health. Articles were simple and formulaic in their attempt to present one main point of information; authors rarely shifted from a primary focus. The short, simple, often mechanical presentation of information within magazine articles minimized discretion in terms of coding.

The analysis of parenting magazines reveals three trends. First, the growth of parenting magazines has outstripped overall growth in periodicals and magazines. Second, parenting magazines are increasingly catering to niche markets. Certainly, generic magazines such as *Parents* or *Today's Parent* draw a large readership, and remain the mainstay of the industry. The circulation numbers of generic publications are impressive, while smaller niche magazines remain deliberately small. However, the sheer proliferation of niche-oriented publications is of note. Magazines are segmented according to geography, with publications that offer advice, information, and resources pertinent to particular areas and cities. Magazines are also segmented according to the traits of both parents and children alike. Parenting publications focus on addressing the needs of particular kinds of families and children. The permutations of the combinations of locales, parent, and child characteristics, respectively, are staggering. Finally, this analysis reveals a trend toward publications that emphasize parents' role in fostering their children's academic and cognitive development.

Inside Canadian Parenting Articles

Keen attention to children's cognitive and academic progress is not limited to magazines like *Parent & Child*, such as those discussed above. A preliminary analysis of Canadian parenting articles reveals a shift in emphasis since the mid-1970s from traditional topics of safety and 'fun' activities

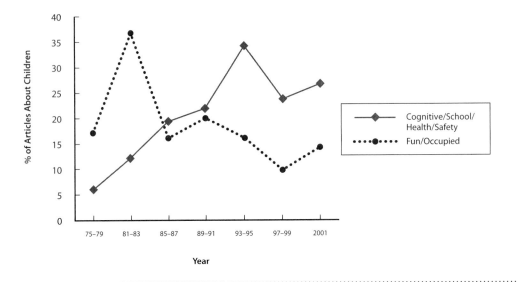

Figure 66.1 Parenting Article Focus

Source: *Canadian Magazine*, 1975–2001

to keep children occupied, to an emphasis on stimulating children cognitively. Figure 66.1 displays the most popular categories or topics over time: the proportion of articles focusing on schooling and cognitive development, health/safety, and fun/occupied. There was not an apparent change over time in the frequency of articles that focused on other topics, such as physical exercise, day care or hygiene/fashion.

In the mid-1970s and early 1980s, more than half of parenting articles focused on children's health and safety, or on fun activities to keep children amused or occupied. For instance, 'health/safety' articles might focus on car seats, nutritious snacks for children, or childhood obesity. 'Fun/occupied' articles discuss gifts children could make, and summer projects to fend off the 'I'm bored' syndrome. In the 1970s, focus on children's cognitive development or school experiences is minimal; just 5 per cent of all articles about children deal with either schooling or children's cognitive development. The focus is on keeping children amused, rather than learning.

In the 1980s, children's activities are often framed in terms of having fun, keeping children

occupied and out of their parents' (usually mothers') hair. Yet, increasingly focus is placed on children's brains. In one 1985 article, the preschooler's mind is described as 'a magical maze' (Rae, 1985: 71). In order to enrich their children, parents are encouraged to 'use every opportunity to talk with preschoolers' throughout their waking hours and during everyday pursuits such as toilet training, eating, and dressing (Rae, 1985: 74). As such, children's intellectual traits are increasingly highlighted.

Parents are also encouraged to take concrete steps to expose their children to new and stimulating activities that will enrich their learning potential. These efforts are not limited to children who appear to hold the most intellectual promise; all children will benefit from such enrichment. Moreover, parents are encouraged to expose their children to books, as 'it's never too soon to gently nurture a young child's love of books' (Morgan, 1985: 015).

Throughout the 1980s, articles emerge that encourage parents to set up their own home reference libraries, with academic resources such as dictionaries, a thesaurus, atlas, and medical dictionary. This effort is designed to set 'a positive example for your children, encouraging them to develop good study and research skills' (Matte, 1983: 01). Parents' role in their children's education is increasingly presented as one of intervention, rather than passivity. Experts claim that parents can prevent such ills as math anxiety early on, before children attend school. Articles instruct parents about how to talk to their child's teacher, as well as recognize signs that their child is losing interest in school. Parents are coached to actively guide 'even the average student' through the university admission process (Habs Johnston, 1989: 111).

Articles that simply focus on fun activities for children (e.g. birthday parties, leisure activities) persist throughout the 1990s, but in smaller numbers than in the 1970s and 1980s. In contrast, articles dealing with children's cognitive development and schooling flourish in the 1990s. A definitive shift occurs whereby emphasis on simply keeping children occupied and amused gives way to a primary focus on stimulating children cognitively.

As such, the actual activity of cooking is secondary to the cognitive skills that it fosters. Similarly, more recent articles are more overt in their emphasis on making good use of children's time away from school, with a focus on keeping young minds sharp over the summer holidays. In 'Brain Maintenance', authors point out that 'Elementary school students forget so much over the summer in math and reading that it can take as long as a month in the fall for them to catch up to where they were in June' (Noakes and Keating, 2001b: 125). Parents are urged to stimulate children's minds while they are out of school by prompting them to read each day, keep a journal, and by taking children to visit museums or historic sites.

Other magazine articles such as 'Can Music Help Kids with Math?', 'Literacy for Little Ones', and 'Learning Begins at Home' emphasize parents' role in stimulating their children cognitively at home. For instance, in 'Grill Guide', parents are filled in on the workings of children's cognitive development, and are given tips on how to respond to children's seemingly endless litany of questions (Noakes and Keating, 2001a). Parental advice focuses explicitly on children's cognitive development by dealing with such subjects as 'How Do Kids Learn?' Many of these articles aim to help parents bolster their children's academic performance. In addition to providing 'grade booster' tips on how to foster children's concentration on homework and academic development in the home, articles also provide tips for getting involved with their child's school directly. Articles such as 'Make This Your Child's BEST School Year Ever' and 'Choose Your Child's Teacher' encourage parents to intervene directly in their child's schooling. Other authors offer advice about speaking with teachers, encouraging parents to check their child's progress weekly with the classroom teacher.

Since 1975, the proportion of articles dealing with such traditional topics as health and keeping children occupied has diminished, giving way to a larger share of articles that focus on stimulating children cognitively. Since the 1970s, the proportion of articles focusing on schooling or cognitive development has increased dramatically. Currently, more than one quarter of parenting articles emphasize cognition or schooling. Articles with a traditional focus on children's physical well-being, or keeping children occupied, comprise a smaller proportion of parenting articles since the 1980s. Overall, interest in children's cognitive or academic needs has grown steadily, while emphasis on simply amusing children has waned since the 1980s.

Discussion

This analysis yields two main conclusions. First, the expansion of parenting magazines can be understood as an indicator or measure of public interest in childrearing. The considerable growth in the number of these magazines suggests a heightened concern or attention to 'parenting' as a concerted activity. Given the niche marketing within the parenting magazine sector, parents can tailor their magazine purchases to match their individual child's attributes. From this perspective, a baby is no longer simply an American Baby, and parents are no longer simply Parents, but parents of children with particular, individualized traits. As such, parents are thus encouraged to think of their children as unique and particularized, rather than generic or ordinary. While more research is necessary, this preliminary analysis suggests that a growing number of magazines focus specifically on fostering children's cognitive development and academic performance. The increasing incidence of parenting magazines in America, England, Australia, and Canada cannot tell us directly about how people in those countries are raising their children. However, the impressive expansion of the market for these publications signals a broad concern about, or interest in, parenting as a deliberate or concerted endeavour.

The second main finding from this research is that topics such as schooling and children's cognitive development are enjoying an increasing emphasis within Canadian parenting articles. To be sure, a content analysis of parenting articles does not indicate actual childrearing techniques in Canada. Yet, this material is instructive, comprising an approximation of current childrearing norms (Hays, 1996). This research suggests that the social context of childrearing in Canada is one of heightened concern for children's academic chances. Within parenting articles, parents are encouraged to foster their children's cognitive development through everyday interactions and exposure to enriching activities and environments. They are also advised to stimulate their children cognitively in the home, and become involved with their child's school progress. This emphasis on children's schooling and intellect is perhaps most explicit when parents are told that they should cognitively stimulate their preschool children in anticipation of later schooling. Meanwhile, less attention is given to simply keeping children amused or occupied.

Why have parents become more attuned to the performance and success of their offspring? I argue that there is a greater widespread preoccupation about the importance of educational credentials. As Wrigley (1989) suggests, parents' concern for children's cognitive development has grown as children's life chances are increasingly influenced by their performance in school. Formal education has taken on more importance than ever; while in the Canada of the 1940s and 1950s staying in school until grade nine was considered sufficient, this is now no longer the case (Sutherland, 1997). Post-secondary education is increasingly being seen as the base requirement for job success in future economic markets. Nationally, 88 per cent of Canadian parents expect their children to attend either college or university (Davies, 2005). Clearly, childrearing today exists in a climate of heightened interest and concern for children's educational chances.

Children's cognitive development takes on greater importance in the light of securing social advantage. Generations ago, parents could pass on property or their physical or financial capital to their children in order to secure their social advantage (Wrigley, 1989; Lareau, 2003). Today, however, parents cannot transmit their status directly to their children, as they cannot provide them with educational credentials. Admission to successive levels of schooling must be secured through academic grades and performance—which children alone can provide (Chin, 2000). Parents must labour tirelessly to provide children with every possible opportunity for advantage in their uncertain ascent through the series of educational contests within the school system (Chin, 2000; Lareau, 2000; 2003). As Wall (2006) argues, educational materials urge parents to see their children as opportunities for investment; parental behaviour in the early years of a child's life is now cast as a crucial element in securing children's eventual intellectual potential and material success.

Parenting magazines, and their shift in focus toward children's cognitive development, signal a larger public concern with children's cognitive and academic development. The shift from keeping children amused to actively fostering children's academic progress supports the findings of authors who argue that not only is parenting becoming more intensive over time, it is also increasingly becoming characterized by a heightened preoccupation with children's cognitive development (Lareau, 2000; 2003; Wrigley, 1989). The findings of this study suggest that there is a changing ethos of childrearing in Canada. Parents are actively encouraged to foster their children's cognitive development, with the aim of enhancing and maximizing their children's chances for academic success.

References

Arendell, T. 2001. 'The new care work of middle class mothers'. In *Minding the Time in Family Experience: Emerging Perspectives and Issues*. K. Daly (ed.). Contemporary Perspectives in Family Research, Vol. 3. New York: JAI Press, pp. 163–204.

Atkinson, M. and S. Blackwelder. 1993. 'Fathering in the 20th century'. *Journal of Marriage and Family*, Vol. 55, No. 4, pp. 975–86.

Babbie, E. 2001. *The Practice of Social Research*. 9th ed. Belmont, Calif.: Wadsworth/Thomson.

Beckett, B. 1979. 'Is heaven like a toy library?' *Canadian Living*, April, pp. 27–30.

Bianchi, S. and J. Robinson. 1997. 'What did you do today? Children's use of time, family composition, and the acquisition of social capital'. *Journal of Marriage and Family*, Vol. 59, No. 2, pp. 332–44.

Bigner, J. and R. Yang. 1996. 'Parent education in popular literature: 1972–1990'. *Family and Consumer Sciences Research Journal*, Vol. 25, No. 1, pp. 3–27.

Canizaree, S. 2002. 'My son doesn't know all his letters'. *Parent & Child*, Vol. 10, No. 2, pp. 30, 32.

Chin, T. 2000. 'Sixth grade madness': Parental emotion work in the private high school application process'. *Journal of Contemporary Ethnography*, Vol. 29, No. 2, pp. 124–63.

Chin, T. and M. Phillips. 2004. 'Social reproduction and childrearing practices: Social class, children's agency and the summer activity gap'. *Sociology of Education*, Vol. 77, No. 3, pp. 185–210.

Clarke-Stewart, K. 1978. 'Popular primers for parents'. *American Psychologist*, Vol. 33, No. 4, pp. 359–69.

Cook, D. 2004. *The Commodification of Childhood: The Children's Clothing Industry and the Rise of the Child Consumer*. Durham: Duke University Press.

Davies, S. 2005. 'A revolution of expectations? Three key trends in the SAEP data'. In *Preparing for Post-secondary Education: New Roles for Governments and Families*. R. Sweet and R Anisef (eds.). Montreal and Kingston: McGill-Queen's University Press, pp. 149–65.

Dickinson, H. 1993. 'Scientific parenthood: The mental hygiene movement and the reform of Canadian families, 1925–1950'. *Journal of Comparative Family Studies*, Vol. 24, No. 3, pp. 387–402.

Duxbury, L. and C. Higgins. 2001. *Work-life Balance in the New Millennium: Where Are We? Where Do We Need to Go?* Ottawa: CPRN Discussion Paper No. W/12.

Epstein, J. 1987. 'Parent involvement: What research says to administrators'. *Education and Urban Society*, Vol. 19, No. 2, pp. 119–36.

Fox, B. 2001. 'The formative years: How parenthood creates gender'. *The Canadian Review of Sociology and Anthropology*, Vol. 38, No. 4, pp. 373–90.

Habs Johneton, G. 1989. 'University bound? Tips to help even the average student get accepted at the right school'. *Canadian Living*, Nov., pp. 27–30.

Hardyment, C. 1983. *Dream Babies: Child Care from Locke to Spock*. London, U.K.: Jonathan Cape.

Hays, S. 1996. *The Cultural Contradictions of Motherhood*. New Haven, Conn.: Yale University Press.

Knaak, S. 2005. 'Breast-feeding, bottle-feeding and Dr. Spock: The shifting context of choice'. *The Canadian Review of Sociology and Anthropology*, Vol. 42, No. 2, pp. 197–216.

Lareau, A. 2000. *Home Advantage*. 2nd ed. Oxford: Rowman and Littlefield.

Lareau, A. 2002. 'Invisible equality: Social class and childrearing in Black families and White families'. *American Sociological Review*, Vol. 67, No. 5, Oct., pp. 747–76.

Lareau, A. 2003. *Unequal Childhoods: Class, Race and Family Life*. Berkeley, Calif.: University of California Press.

Marshall, H. 1991. 'The social construction of motherhood: An analysis of childcare and parenting manuals'. In *Motherhood: Meanings, Practices and Ideologies*. A. Phoenix, A. Woollett and E. Lloyd (eds.). London: Sage Publications, pp. 66–85.

Matte, A. 1983. '"When did we get the maple leaf flag?": For quick answers to everyday questions, set up your own home reference library'. *Canadian Living*, June, pp. 01–02.

Mayall, B. 2002. *Towards a Sociology of Childhood: Thinking from Children's Lives*. Buckingham, U.K.: Open University Press.

Morgan, J. 1985. 'Give a child a good book . . . and watch her soar!' *Canadian Living*, March, pp. 015–017, 019.

Noakes, S. and J. Keating. 2001a. 'Grill guide'. *Canadian Living*, Jan., p. 27.

Noakes, S. and J. Keating. 2001b. 'Brain maintenance'. *Canadian Living*, June, p. 125.

Rae, J. 1985. 'Share your child's secret world . . . Learn to communicate with your preschooler . . . and enrich both your lives'. *Canadian Living*, April, pp. 71–72, 74, 76–77, 79, 81.

Sayer, L., S. Bianchi and J. Robinson. 2004. 'Are parents investing less in children? Trends in mothers' and fathers' time with children'. *American Journal of Sociology*, Vol. 110, No. 1, pp. 1–43.

Schaub, M. 2004. 'Parenting cognitive development from 1950 to 2000: The institutional effects of mass education and the social construction of childhood and parenting'. Paper presented at the American Sociological Association Annual Meeting, San Francisco, Calif., pp. 1–40.

Smith, M.C., E Van Loon, N. DeFrates-Densch and T. Schrader. 1998. 'Content changes in parent education books for parents of adolescents'. *Family and Consumer Sciences Research Journal*, Vol. 27, No. 2, pp. 194–213.

Stern, B. 1993. 'Kids break for cooking'. *Canadian Living*, March, pp. 39, 41.

Stevens, M. 2001. *Kingdom of Children: Culture and Controversy in the Homeschooling Movement*. Princeton, N.J.: Princeton University Press.

Sutherland, N. 1997. *Growing Up: Childhood in English Canada from the Great War to the Age of Television*. Toronto: University of Toronto Press.

Thorpe, K. and K. Daly. 1999. 'Children, parents and time: The dialectics of control'. In *Through the Eyes of the Child: Revisioning Children as Active Agents of Family Life*. C. Shehan (ed.). New York: JAI Press, pp. 199–224.

Ulrich's International Periodicals Directory. 1959–2003. New York: Bowker.

Urwin, C. and E. Sharland. 1992. 'From bodies to minds in childcare literature: Advice to parents in inter-war Britain'. In *In the Name of the Child: Health and Welfare, 1880–1940*. R. Cooter (ed.). New York: Routledge, pp. 174–99.

Urquhart, E 1985. 'Music hath charms . . . to start your child on a lifelong love affair'. *Canadian Living*, Feb., pp. 05–08.

Wall, G. 2004. 'Is your child's brain potential maximized? Mothering in an age of new research'. *Atlantis*, Vol. 28, No. 2, pp. 41–50.

Wall, G. 2006. 'Engineering children: Conceptions of children in early years discourse'. Paper presented at the Canadian Sociology Association Annual Meeting. York University, Toronto, pp. 1–16.

Wrigley, J. 1989. 'Do young children need intellectual stimulation? Experts' advice to parents, 1900–1985'. *History of Education Quarterly*, Vol. 29, No. 1, pp. 41–75.

Zelizer, V 1985. *Pricing the Priceless Child: The Changing Social Value of Children*. Princeton, N.J.: Princeton University Press.

Zuzanek, J. 2000. *The Effects of Time Use and Time Pressure on Child–Parent Relationships*. Health Canada Research Report. Waterloo, Ont.: Otium Publications.

CHAPTER 67

Packaging Protest: Media Coverage of Indigenous People's Collective Action

Rima Wilkes, Catherine Corrigall-Brown, and Daniel J. Myers

Despite comprising just slightly less than 4 per cent of the population, indigenous peoples have nevertheless engaged in widespread **mobilization** in Canada. And, as our review of these actions and the scholarly literature about them will show, much of this mobilization has generated significant media interest.

The media package news stories in a variety of ways. Packaging elements can include the volume of coverage (the number of stories), page placement, and headlines (both size and content), as well as the length of story and the inclusion of visuals. Events that are the subject of more news coverage are more likely to garner attention (e.g. see Alimi, Gamson, and Ryan 2006; Amenta et al. 2009; Lee and Craig 1992; McKay 1996). Ongoing coverage of an event or issue signals its importance (Carvalho 2008; Carvalho and Burgess 2005), and increases the likelihood that a broader range of readers will receive at least some information about the event, even if they are not daily consumers of newspapers or other news sources. The location and accompanying visual features of an article are also important (Ryan 1991). There is also general agreement that the single most effective way for a story to garner attention is through front-page placement (Davis and McLeod 2003; Tuchman 1978). While packaging is by no means the only important aspect of coverage, it is one about which little is known (except see Amenta et al. 2009) and is a neglected topic in the literature (Amenta et al. 2009).

In light of the importance and lack of attention to media packaging of protest, what accounts for different quality and quantity of media packaging an event or issue will receive? Two major theories have been advanced to explain how the media gathers and selects what news is 'fit to print'. First, the media follow a set of 'news routines', which lead them to select and feature certain types of stories and events. Second, the media seeks to present stories that are dramatic and sensational, providing high 'news values'. Each of these theories leads to different expectations about how indigenous people's collective action will be covered in the media.

There is strong evidence from a host of empirical studies (McCarthy, McPhail, and Smith 1996; Myers and Caniglia 2004; Smith et al. 2001; Wilkes and Ricard 2006) demonstrating the important relationship between event characteristics and the media's organizational practices. In particular, the 'news gathering' perspective with its emphasis on news routines and news values suggests not only that media attention will vary across events, but also that different events will receive different *types* of media attention including different media packaging.

News routines are the day-to-day organizational and structural aspects of news production. Because newspapers still have to be published irrespective of whether a given day has any newsworthy events, events occurring before slow news days (usually Mondays) are more likely to be included in the newspaper than those occurring on busier news days (Myers and Caniglia 2004; Oliver and Myers 1999). A number of scholars have also pointed out that reporters have regular newsbeats—either locations (such as city hall) where they routinely go (see, e.g. Oliver and Myers 1999; Ryan 1991) or issues for which they are regularly responsible. In the case of the latter, the assignment of a 'beat' reporter is a signal of an issues' perceived importance (Eliasoph 1988).

Staff time and resources are also saved (and page space used up) when editors use reports furnished by newswires (Ryan 1991). Newswire reports provide news from faraway locations as well as more generic human-interest stories. Yet, because the news is subject to its own distinct internal organizational dynamics, the competitive nature of journalism is such that newswire reports are not often featured as prominently as those written by in-house staff (Sumpter 2000). The use of newswires also reflects editors' judgment

about whether or not an event merits having a journalist investigate and write an original story. Finally, different newspapers have different style formats ranging from tabloid to broadsheet, longer or shorter average story length, and more or fewer visuals. Papers also have different audience mandates that require different types of news ranging from nationally relevant to smaller and more local interest stories.

Clearly the filtering these types of routine elements provide is likely to shape the type of packaging a story receives (it is also likely that some events will receive more coverage than others). In terms of the day of publication, indigenous people's collective action events that appear in the Monday edition of the paper should be given more prominent packaging than those that appear in stories on other days of the week. An article that is written by a beat reporter should also receive more prominent packaging than should one written by an in-house reporter (as opposed to a wire). Finally, we might also expect to find some differences across papers in terms of the kinds of events and the kind of attention each receives.

In addition, because newspapers are a consumer product, they also need to feature stories that are of interest to their readers to maintain their circulation numbers. A story is said to have 'news value' if it has some or all of the following characteristics: relevance, immediacy, novelty/innovation, and drama (Boyd 1994; Bridges 1989; Bridges and Bridges 1997; Shoemaker and Reese 1996). In terms of relevance, events that involve more people will appear to be more relevant and important to a broader spectrum of readers than events involving a small group (see, e.g. Mueller 1997; Neveu 2002). Immediacy refers to the 'newness' and timeliness of a story. Recent 'episodes' are more newsworthy than ongoing 'issues'. Novelty refers to anything that is seen to depart from the usual. In the case of protest, scholars have noted for some time now that marches and demonstrations are relatively routine and predictable ways to air grievances (McCarthy, McPhail, and Crist 1999; see also Tilly 1978). This normalization of protest may be a primary reason why the empirical evidence does not show a significant difference between **media coverage** of different event forms, such as marches, demonstration, vigils, and literature tables (e.g. Oliver and Maney 2000; Oliver and Myers 1999). Finally, events are perceived as dramatic if they involve violence, death, and/or destruction—'If it bleeds it leads' (Gitlin 1980). For example, Myers and Caniglia (2004) found that riots with higher levels of violence and greater numbers of arrests were more likely to be reported in the *New York Times*.

Many First Nations activists are well aware of the media's need for dramatic and newsworthy events and of the importance of the media more generally. Accordingly, they have tailored their protests in ways that facilitate bold headlines and front-page placement. Lubicon Chief Bernard Ominyak and his supporters were clearly aware of this need when, in order to draw media attention to their land dispute with the Alberta government, they parodied the 1988 Calgary Olympic torch run logo 'Share the Flame' by changing it to 'Shame the Flame'. The 1985 blockades of Lyell Island by Haida people resulted in media images of elders adorned in traditional Haida dress being arrested and hauled away from the site. The associated content appears to have been supportive, suggesting that the Haida had little choice but to engage in civil disobedience ('So what choice do the Haida have?' *Vancouver Sun* November 21, 1985:A5). Similarly, in 1987 widespread media interest was also generated when Peguis Chief Louis Stevenson extended a controversial invitation to South African Ambassador Glenn Babb to tour his reserve in northern Manitoba.

While the above events are dramatic and contentious and should have garnered prominent packaging, they are also notable for their absence of violence. In contrast, protracted standoffs such as those at Oka, Mercier, Ipperwash, and Gustafsen Lake could be labelled as contentious, though in global terms they are still marked by extremely low levels of violence. Furthermore, even though these events may have started out as direct action, even their participants ultimately ended up having some relationship with the media. For example, in the case of Oka, not only did the warriors have a spokesperson (Ellen

Gabriel) and in some cases refused to talk with reporters whom they found unsympathetic, but some media photographs also show warriors reading the newspaper or watching TV while defending the barricades. We therefore investigate the extent to which the factors associated with quality and quantity of coverage received by the standoffs is similar to, or different from, other events.

We collected data on events that took place from 1985 to 1995. This time period was selected because it was a major period for mobilization by indigenous peoples in Canada (Ramos 2006). We also discuss the coverage received by several more recent events in the discussion section of this paper. Data were collected from two major daily newspapers, the *Globe and Mail* and the *Vancouver Sun*. The *Globe and Mail*, based in Toronto, is one of two national newspapers and has the second highest circulation of any newspaper in the country. Canada's other national newspaper—the *National Post*—did not exist during the period considered for this study. We selected the *Globe* due to its national presence and the *Vancouver Sun* because it is located in British Columbia, the province in which the most protests by indigenous peoples have taken place. The *Vancouver Sun* is the largest circulating paper in Vancouver. While there are clearly many other papers that could have been selected, and some that likely provided more detailed coverage of particular events, we elected to go with these two papers on the grounds that they are papers that a wide number and range of Canadians read.

To find information about indigenous people's collective action events, we searched both the titles listed on the paper index and also used a keyword search of the electronic versions of Canadian Newsstand—an index of major daily newspapers. We searched the electronic index using general keywords, such as 'Native', 'Aboriginal', 'First Nation', 'Indian', and 'protest', 'demonstration', 'blockade'. We then refined the search to locate all possible articles about each individual event using event-specific keywords (e.g. 'Mohawk' and 'Oka'). Finally, to ensure that we had as comprehensive a database as possible, we also searched using multiple spellings of proper names, such as 'Gitksan' and 'Gitxsan'.

Because only a very limited number of events received coverage beyond that provided within the calendar year of the event's occurrence we restricted the number of articles collected about particular events to those published within the same calendar year that the event took place. In cases where the event lasted for more than one year, we included articles published until the final year of the protest. This limited our data set to articles with a primary focus on the given event (with a few exceptions which focused on several events at the same time). Past events mentioned in passing, years later, were therefore excluded from our sample. While this means that our data do not speak to shifts in coverage over time, from a practical point of view these shifts only apply to a small number of events. Our final data set consists of 1,801 articles about 230 events reported on in the *Globe and Mail* and the *Vancouver Sun*.

In addition to descriptive statistics, we use a range of multivariate methods to analyze the data. Because the number of articles is a count (and the mean of this variable exceeds the variance) we use negative binomial regression. The models for front page and picture variables involve dichotomous dependent variables, and we therefore use binary logistic regression. However, to account for the correlation between outcomes corresponding to the same event, we used logistic generalized estimating equations (GEE) with an exchangeable correlation structure.

Discussion

In summary, the results clearly indicate that while tactic escalation increases the amount of coverage, only disruptive tactics are more likely to appear on the front page. Whether an article will be accompanied by a picture is largely determined by news routines as opposed to tactics. The results also show that the coverage of standoffs is much less predictable than other types of events.

The events we consider in the paper end in 1995. How might these results look had we considered a more recent set of events? In the interim, other events (we have found at least 130 additional events from 1996 to 2008), such as the ongoing land conflict at Caledonia and the 2001 blockade at Sun Peaks, BC, have taken place. We have little reason to believe that tactic escalation is less important now than it was during the late 1980s and early 1990s. However, the results for the inclusion of visuals might be quite different had we considered more recent events. The advent of online news media has dramatically changed the nature of news production. The transfer of high-quality images is much simpler and less costly than it was in the past. News routines may therefore have less to do with whether an article is accompanied by a picture. Nevertheless, additional research is clearly needed to ascertain the extent to which these hypotheses hold true.

While a number of studies have considered single and high-profile events, no study has attempted to consider the range of events in their entirety. What factors distinguish the quality and quantity of coverage an event receives? Our results show that in the case of collective action by Indigenous peoples, the size and length of the event have very little association with coverage. These results stand in contrast to the results of studies of collective action by other groups (e.g. McCarthy et al. 1996; Mueller 1997; Smith et al. 2001), likely because in comparison, the protests under consideration in this study are very small.

Despite the small size of many of the events in this study, they received a large quantity of coverage. Therefore, it seems that the use of contentious tactics provides an excellent strategy for overcoming the disadvantage of small size. In addition, the fact that prolonged standoffs (recognizing that this may not have been activist's initial intent) with authorities generated prominent packaging is clearly in line with previous research linking violence to media coverage (McAdam and Su 2002). However, the findings also show that being contentious or unusual is not a guarantee of high-profile packaging. If this were the case, there would have been a strong relationship between land occupations and **media packaging**. The tactics that did generate prominent packaging—road and rail blockades—can be distinguished from land occupations in terms of their capacity to disrupt the lives of outsiders. As long as it is an extended event, tactics such as preventing people from getting to work or home or preventing supplies from reaching their destinations, work well in this regard.

The findings underscore the need to pay more attention to differences in media attention across events. While contention is clearly associated with differential packaging, the magnitude of difference in the effect sizes is worth commenting on.

Standoffs generated significantly more attention across multiple packaging elements than other forms of contention. Although there were several hundred events, they generated nearly 40 percent of the articles and half of all front-page coverage. This means that the difference in packaging across events, like academic citations patterns or salaries, is exponential rather than linear (see also Biggs 2005; Taleb 2007).

References

Alfred, T. 2001. 'Deconstructing the British Columbia Treaty Process'. *Balayi: Culture, Law and Colonialism* 3:37–66.

Alfred, T. and J. Corntassel. 2005. 'Being Indigenous: Resurgences Against Contemporary Colonialism'. *Government and Opposition* 40:597–614.

Alfred, T. and L. Lowe. 2005. 'Warrior Societies in Contemporary Indigenous Communities'. Report to the Ipperwash Inquiry, 65 pp.

Alimi, E., W.A. Gamson and C. Ryan. 2006. 'Knowing Your Adversary: Israeli Structure of Political Opportunity and the Inception of the Palestinian Intifada'. *Sociological Forum* 4:535–57.

Allison, P. 1999. *Logistic Regression Using the SAS System*. North Carolina: SAS Institute.

Amenta, E., N. Caren, S.J. Olasky and J.E. Stobaugh. 2009. 'All the Movements Fit to Print: Who, What, When, Where, and Why SMO Families Appeared in the *New York Times* in the Twentieth Century'. *American Sociological Review* 74:636–56.

Andrews, K.T. 2008. 'Making the News: Movement Organizations, Media Attention, and the Public Agenda'. Unpublished manuscript obtained from author.

Armstrong, R. and T. Rogers. 1996. *A First Nation Typology: Patterns of Socio-Economic Well-Being*. Ottawa: Department of Indian Affairs and Northern Development.

Barakso, M. and B.F. Schaffner. 2006. 'Winning Coverage: News Media Portrayals of the Women's Movement, 1969–2004'. *Press/Politics* 11:22–44.

Biggs, M. 2005. 'Strikes as Forest Fires: Chicago and Paris in the Late 19th Century'. *American Journal of Sociology* 96:144–85.

Blomley, N. 1996. '"Shut the Province Down": First Nations Blockades in British Columbia, 1984–1995'. *BC Studies* 111:5–35.

Boyd, A. 1994. *Broadcast Journalism, Techniques of Radio and TV News*. Oxford: Focal.

Boyle, M.P., M.R. McCluskey, D.M. McLeod and S.E. Stein. 2005. 'Newspapers and Protest: An Examination of Protest Coverage from 1960 to 1999'. *Journalism and Mass Communication Quarterly* 82:638–53.

Bridges, J.A. 1989. 'News Use on the Front Pages of the American Daily'. *Journalism Quarterly* 66:332–37.

Bridges, J.A. and L. Bridges. 1997. 'Changes in News Use on the Front Pages of the American Daily Newspaper, 1986–1993'. *Journalism and Mass Communication Quarterly* 74:826–39.

Burstein, P. and S. Sausner. 2005. 'The Incidence and Impact of Policy-Oriented Collective Action: Competing Views'. *Sociological Forum* 20:403–19.

Carvalho, A. 2008. 'Media(ted) Discourse and Society: Rethinking the Framework of Critical Discourse Analysis'. *Journalism Studies* 9:161–77.

Carvalho, A. and J. Burgess. 2005. 'Cultural Circuits of Climate Change in U.K. Broadsheet Newspapers, 1985–2003'. *Risk Analysis* 25:1457–69.

Davis, H. and L.S. McLeod. 2003. 'Why Humans Value Sensational News: An Evolutionary Perspective'. *Evolution and Human Behavior* 24:208–16.

Edwards, P. 2001. *One Dead Indian: The Premier, the Police and the Ipperwash Crisis*. Toronto: McClelland and Stewart.

Eliasoph, N. 1988. 'Routines and the Making of Oppositional News'. *Critical Studies in Mass Communication* 5:313–34.

Frideres, J.S. and R.R. Gadacz. 2008. *Aboriginal Peoples in Canada*. Toronto: Pearson Education Canada.

Gitlin, T. 1980. *The Whole World is Watching*. Berkeley, CA: University of California Press.

Grenier, M. 1994. 'Native Indians in the English-Canadian Press: The Case of the "Oka Crisis"'. *Media, Culture and Society* 16:313–36.

Kalant, A. 2007. *National Identity and the Conflict at Oka*. New York: Routledge.

Khawaja, M. 1994. 'Resource Mobilization, Hardship, and Popular Collective Action in the West Bank'. *Social Forces* 73:191–211.

Koopmans, R. and S. Olzak. 2004. 'Discursive Opportunities and the Evolution of Right-Wing Violence in Germany'. *American Journal of Sociology* 110:198–230.

Lambertus, S. 2004. *Wartime Images, Peacetime Wounds: The Media and the Gustafsen Lake Standoff*. Toronto: University of Toronto Press.

Lee, J. and R.L. Craig. 1992. 'News as an Ideological Framework: Comparing US Newspapers' Coverage of Labor Strikes in South Korea and Poland'. *Discourse and Society* 3:341–63.

Long, D. 1997. 'Culture, Ideology, and Militancy: The Movement of Native Indians in Canada, 1969–91'. Pp. 118–34 in *Organizing Dissent*, edited by W. Caroll. Toronto: Garamond Press.

Maxim, P., J. White and D. Beavon. 2003. 'Dispersion and Polarization of Incomes among Aboriginal and Non-Aboriginal Canadians'. Pp. 222–47 in *Aboriginal Conditions: Research as a Foundation for Public Policy*, edited by J. White, P. Maxim and D. Beavon. Vancouver: University of British Columbia Press.

McAdam, D. 1996. 'The Framing Function of Movement Tactics: Strategic Dramaturgy in the American Civil Rights Movement'. Pp. 338–56 in *Comparative Perspectives on Social Movements*, edited by D. McAdam, J.D. McCarthy and M. Zald. Cambridge, UK: Cambridge University Press.

McAdam, D. and Y. Su. 2002. 'The War at Home: Antiwar Protests and Congressional Voting, 1965–1973. *American Sociological Review* 67:696–721.

McCarthy, J.D., C. McPhail and J. Crist. 1999. 'The Emergence and Diffusion of Public Order Management Systems: Protest Cycles and Police Response'. Pp. 49–69 in *Globalization and Social Movements*, edited by H. Kriesi, D. Della Porta and D. Rucht. London: McMillan.

McCarthy, J.D., C. McPhail and J. Smith. 1996. 'Images of Protest: Dimensions of Selection Bias in Media Coverage of Washington Demonstrations, 1982 and 1991'. *American Sociological Review* 61:478–99.

McKay, J. 1996. 'Reflecting the Hazard or Restating Old Views: Newspapers and Bushfires in Australia. *International Journal of Mass Emergencies and Disasters* 14:305–19.

Miller, J. 2005. 'Ipperwash and the Media: A Critical Analysis of How the Story was Covered'. Report submitted to Aboriginal Legal Services of Toronto.

Mueller, C. 1997. 'International Press Coverage of East German Protest Events, 1989'. *American Sociological Review* 62:820–32.

Myers, D. and B. Caniglia. 2004. 'National Newspaper Coverage of Civil Disorders, 1968–1969'. *American Sociological Review* 69:519–43.

Neveu, E. 2002. 'The Local Press and Farmers' Protests in Brittany: Proximity and Distance in the Local Newspaper Coverage of a Social Movement'. *Journalism Studies* 3:53–67.

Niezen, R. 1998. *Defending the Land: Sovereignty and Forest Life in James Bay Cree Society*. Boston, MA: Allyn & Bacon.

Okamoto, D. 2003. 'Toward a Theory of Panethnicity: Explaining Asian American Collective Action'. *American Sociological Review* 68:811–42.

Oliver, P. and G. Maney. 2000. 'Political Processes and Local Newspaper Coverage of Protest Events: From Selection Bias to Triadic Interactions'. *American Journal of Sociology* 106:463–505.

Oliver, P. and D. Myers. 1999. 'How Events Enter the Public Sphere: Conflict, Location, and Sponsorship in Local Newspaper Coverage of Public Events'. *American Journal of Sociology* 105:38–87.

Ramos, H. 2006. 'What Causes Canadian Aboriginal Protest? Examining Resources, Opportunities and Identity, 1951–2000'. *Canadian Journal of Sociology* 31:211–34.

Ramos, H. 2008a. 'Aboriginal Protest'. Pp. 55–70 in *Social Movements*, edited by S. Staggenborg. Don Mills: Oxford University Press.

Ramos, H. 2008b. 'Opportunity for Whom? Political Opportunity and Critical Events in Canadian Aboriginal Mobilization, 1951–2000'. *Social Forces* 97:795–823.

Ryan, C. 1991. *Prime Time Activism: Media Strategies for Grassroots Organizing*. Boston, MA: South End Press.

Sanders, D.E. 1985. 'The Indian Lobby and the Canadian Constitution, 1978–82'. Pp. 151–89 in *Indigenous Peoples and the Nation-States: Fourth World Politics in Canada, Australia and Norway*, edited by N.Dyck. St. John's, NF: Institute of Social and Economic Research, Memorial University of Newfoundland.

Santoro, W.A. 2002. 'The Civil Rights Movement's Struggle for Fair Employment: A "Dramatic Events-Conventional Politics" Model'. *Social Forces* 81:177–206.

Shoemaker, P. and S. Reese. 1996. *Mediating the Message: Theories of Influence on Mass Media Content*. White Plains, NY: Longman.

Skea, W.H. 1993. 'The Canadian Newspaper Industry's Portrayal of the Oka Crisis'. *Native Studies Review* 9:15–31.

Smith, J., J. McCarthy, C. McPhail and B. Augustin. 2001. 'From Protest to Agenda-Building: Description Bias in Media Coverage of Protest Events in Washington, D.C.' *Social Forces* 79:1397–423.

Snow, D.A. and C. Corrigall-Brown. 2004. 'Why Frames Sometimes Fall on Deaf Ears: The Problems of Misalignment, Scope, Exhaustion, and Relevance'. Pp. 222–38 in *Rhyming Hope and History: Activists, Academics, and Social Movement Scholarship*, edited by D. Croteau, W. Hoynes and C. Ryan. Minneapolis, MN: University of Minnesota Press.

Snow, D.A., R. Vliegenthart and C. Corrigall-Brown. 2007. 'Framing the French Riots: A Comparative Study of Frame Variation'. *Social Forces* 86:385–415.

Staggenborg, S. 1993. 'Critical Events and the Mobilization of the Pro-Choice Movement'. *Research in Political Sociology* 6:319–45.

Steele, S. 1997. 'Gustafsen Lake Standoff: 15 Charged'. *MacLean's*, June 2.

Stuart, C. 1993. 'The Mohawk Crisis: A Crisis of Hegemony: An Analysis of Media Discourse'. M.A. thesis, University of Ottawa.

Sumpter, R.S. 2000. 'A Case Study: How to Get on or Stay off the Front Page'. *Newspaper Research Journal*, 9 pp.

Taleb, N.N. 2007. *The Black Swan: The Impact of the Highly Improbable*. New York: Random House.

Tilly, C. 1978. 'The Routinization of Protest in Nineteenth Century France'. CRSO Working Paper 181, 12 pp.

Traugott, M. 1993. 'Barricades as Repertoire: Continuities and Discontinuities in the History of French Contention'. *Social Science History* 17:309–23.

Tuchman, G. 1978. *Making the News*. New York: Free Press.

Vliegenthart, R., D. Omegema and B. Klandermans. 2005. 'Media Coverage and Organizational Support in the Dutch Environmental Movements'. *Mobilization* 10:365–81.

Wetzel, C. 2009. 'Theorizing Native American Land Seizure: An Analysis of Tactical Changes in the Late Twentieth Century'. *Social Movement Studies* 8:15–32.

Wilkes, R. 2004. 'First Nation Politics: Deprivation, Resources, and Participation in Collective Action'. *Sociological Inquiry* 74:570–89.

Wilkes, R. 2006. 'The Protest Actions of Indigenous Peoples: A Canadian–U.S. Comparison of Social Movement Emergence'. *American Behavioral Scientist* 50:510–25.

Wilkes, R. and D. Ricard. 2006. 'How Does Newspaper Coverage of Collective Action Vary?: Protest by Indigenous People in Canada'. *The Social Science Journal* 44:231–51.

Wolfsfeld, G. 1997. *Media and Political Conflict: News from the Middle East*. Cambridge, UK: Cambrdige University Press.

York, G. 1989. *The Dispossessed: Life and Death in Native Canada*. Toronto: McArthur.

York, G. and L. Pindera. 1991. *People of the Pines*. Toronto: Little Brown and Company.

Young, C. 2009. 'Model Uncertainty in Sociological Research: An Application to Religion and Economic Growth'. *American Sociological Review* 74:380–97.

Questions for Critical Thought

CHAPTER 64

1. According to Hallgrimsdottir, Phillips, and Benoit, what is the value of comparing depictions of sex workers in the media to the workers' own depictions of their lives? Consider how this relates to the 'insider/outsider' investigator problem brought up in McGuire's paper in Part I.
2. Describe the three narrative conventions that enframe depictions of sex workers in the media that Hallgrimsdottir, Phillips, and Benoit analyze. Use examples from the paper.
3. Based on the demographic information collected by Hallgrimsdottir, Phillips, and Benoit, how are the identities of sex workers different from media depictions? What kinds of sex workers do media typically focus on and ignore?
4. How do sex workers' own accounts of their lives differ from media depictions of their lives? What are some aspects that are under-represented and overrepresented in media depictions?
5. Discuss how sex workers' depictions of their lives are diverse and at times even contradictory. Consider the difficulties this poses for constructing a coherent narrative of sex work and, thus, policy.
6. If media depictions do not accurately represent sex work and workers, what do Hallgrimsdottir, Phillips, and Benoit suggest is a better narrative or interpretation of their experiences? Do you think their interpretation is a good representation of the data that they have presented? How else could you make sense of the data, to tell a more representative story?

CHAPTER 65

1. How do members report using the PAR-L network? How do different kinds of members use the network differently?
2. Discuss the difficulty of deciding what is on or off topic. How is this similar to or different from the process used by other media outlets?
3. How does authority and inequality operate on the PAR-L network? What groups are divided against others, or marginalized? How does this affect discussions?
4. In some ways the Internet democratizes discussions, by decentralizing the power to build and share messages with others. However, this decentralization presents new difficulties for discussions, even as it enables them. What are some drawbacks that members identify with the PAR-L medium that do not apply to other media outlets?
5. Consider other media outlets with which you are familiar. How have they integrated some of the capacities of the Internet (like those discussed in this paper) to enhance the engagement of their audiences with their content and each other?

CHAPTER 66

1. What are some strengths and weaknesses of Quirke's use of parenting magazines as a data source to answer her research question?
2. What three trends does Quirke identify in parenting literature over the period of time studied? Explain the change in content (from fun to cognitive development) that she finds.
3. How does Quirke explain the rising social interest in children's cognitive development?
4. According to Quirke, why are cognitive abilities of children more important in securing social advantage than they were previously? How did parents pass on their social advantage in the past?
5. Consider other sources of parenting advice. Where else do parents seek/get messages about how to parent? If Quirke had researched messages about parenting in these sources, do you think she would have found the same focus on cognitive development? What other messages about child rearing do you think she would have found in these other media?

CHAPTER 67

1. What are some important packaging elements that the media uses to package news stories, and how do they affect the spread and perceived importance of news stories?
2. Explain the news routines theory of how media gathers and selects news. How does this theory predict that indigenous people's collective actions would be packaged?
3. Explain the news values theory of how media gathers and selects news. How does this theory predict that indigenous people's collective actions would be packaged?
4. Discuss the relationships that the authors found between event characteristics and media attention in indigenous people's collective actions. Which characteristics increased media attention? Which ones decreased media attention? Which ones had no effect on media attention?
5. How do the various findings support either theory (news routines or news values) of how media gather and select news? Which theory do you think best explains how Canadian media gather and select news on indigenous people's actions?

Glossary

Aboriginal Canadians: Indigenous people recognized in the Canadian Constitution Act, 1982, section 25 and 35, as Indians (First Nations), Métis, and Inuit.

Accountability: Often used synonymously with such concepts as responsibility, liability, and other terms associated with the expectation of account-giving. As an aspect of governance, it has been central to discussions related to problems in the public sector, non-profit, and corporate worlds.

Accountability circuit: A system in which representatives are required to answer to the represented on the disposal of their powers and duties, act upon criticisms or requirements made of them, and accept (some) responsibility for failure, incompetence, or deceit.

AIDS (Acquired immune deficiency syndrome): A disease transmitted through the blood and other bodily fluids (often through sexual contact) that destroys the body's natural immunity to infection so that the person is susceptible to and may die from a disease such as pneumonia and aggressive behaviours.

Africentric: An emphasis among African-descended people worldwide on shared African origins, taking pride in these and having an interest in African history and culture.

Agency: Often juxtaposed with structure emphasizing human action. It is sometimes defined through the psychological and social psychological makeup of the actor, to imply the capacity for willed or voluntary action.

Altruism: Behaviour which takes account of the interests of others, usually treated as in opposition to egoism, selfishness, and individualism.

Anomie: Also referred to as 'normlessness'. A state of being when people have no clear guidance for their daily behaviour, and are unable to select right and wrong actions. In sociology the term is most frequently identified with the work of Émile Durkheim and Robert Merton.

Anthropometry: The taking of measurements of the human body or its parts. Comparisons can then be made between individuals of different sexes, ages, and races to determine the difference between normal and abnormal development.

Arranged marriage: Marriage planned and agreed upon by the families or guardians of the couple concerned.

Assimilation: Refers to the decline of an ethnic distinction and its corollary, cultural and social differences. *Decline* in this context means that a distinction attenuates in salience—that the occurrences for which it is relevant diminish in number and contract to fewer and fewer domains of social life.

Asymmetrical warfare: War between belligerents whose relative military power differs significantly, or whose strategy or tactics differ significantly. This is in contrast to *symmetric warfare*, in which two powers have similar military power and resources and rely on tactics that are similar overall, differing only in details and execution.

Biological citizenship: A concept that emerges out of the recognition that people are increasingly crafting identities around problems of biological (including mental) health.

Biotechnology: The use of biological processes for medical, industrial, or manufacturing purposes.

Breadwinner: The main wage earner in a household. Traditionally, this was considered to be the man, but increasingly women are becoming the primary earners and households are relying on dual or multiple earners (multiple breadwinners) to provide the standard of living they need (or want).

Canadian Charter of Rights and Freedoms: A piece of Canadian legislation that seeks to protect individual rights and freedoms. The Charter expresses fundamental laws that help build the kind of community Canadians would like to enjoy.

Capitalist economy: An economic system based on private legal ownership of the major means of production and primary use of hired workers to make and sell commodities in competitive markets to generate profits for owners.

Caste: Hereditary social status in society, which is often linked with ideas of spiritual purity and socio-economic stratification. In Hindu Indian society, movement and marriage between castes are not acceptable.

Census: A periodic enumeration of the population, primarily intended to collect information to identify eligible voters and taxpayers. It is sometimes used to identify people eligible for military service, and incidentally many other useful facts, e.g., about housing conditions.

Childlessness: The state of not having any children.

Chomsky, Noam: He developed the concept of a transformational grammar, embodying his theories about the relationship between language and mind, and an underlying universal structure of language. Unlike supporters of behaviourism, Chomsky argued that the human capacity for language is partially innate. His ideas greatly influenced psychologists concerned with language acquisition.

Claims-making: The process by which individuals or groups assert grievances about the troublesome character of people or their behaviour; claims-making thus involves the promotion of a particular moral vision of social life and, thus, is any action taken to propagate a view of who or what is deviant and what should be done about it.

Class: The relative location of a person or group within a larger society, based on wealth, power, prestige, or other valued resources.

Climate change: The term commonly used to refer to changes to the Earth's climate over many years, centuries, or longer.

Collective consciousness: The English translation of Émile Durkheim's term *conscience collective*, which he defined in *The Division of Labor in Society* (1893) as 'the set of beliefs and sentiments common to the average members of a single society'. Collective consciousness, Durkheim argued, is a far more significant determinant of individual behaviour where mechanical solidarity is the norm—reflecting in part the absence of a strong social basis for individualism.

Consumption activities: Activities such as tourism, recreation, arts, and culture that provide monetary value for the economy.

Crime: The violation of laws, or more precisely those social norms that have become subject to state control and legal sanctions reliant on punishment. Crime is thus distinct from deviance, which describes any violation of social norms, including those that are merely subject to societal or group disapproval.

Critical race theory: A movement that studies and attempts to transform the relationship between race and power by examining the role of race and racism within the foundations of modern culture.

Democracy: A form of government in which people choose their legislators and executive leaders. Rule of the people, as opposed to rule by one (autocracy) or a few (oligarchy).

Demographic transition: The pattern of transition, observed in many areas of the developed world, between two demographic regimes: the first, termed *traditional*, in which levels of fertility and mortality are high; and the second, or *modern*, regime, in which levels of fertility and mortality are low.

Deviance: Behaviour that is at odds with social norms.

Discourse: Written or spoken language, especially when it is studied in order to understand how people use language.

Diversity: The variety and tolerance of different social groups (or social types) in a particular locale.

Duality: The quality or character of being two-sided.

Durkheim, Émile: The most famous French sociologist (1858–1917), long acknowledged as the founding figure of functionalism.

Eco-politics: Political policy motivated by concerns for the environment.

Ecosystem: A biological environment consisting of all the organisms living in a particular area, as well as all the nonliving, physical components of the environment with which the organisms interact, such as air, soil, water, and sunlight.

Elitism: The restriction of an activity to a privileged group or the belief that participation in key social institutions ought in principle, always and everywhere, to be confined to the elite—a minority that possesses a disproportionate share of resources or power within a group or society.

Embodiment: The acquisition and use of knowledge that cannot be easily dissociated from the personal qualities of its bearer; the result of people disciplining themselves physically and emotionally to internalize a particular mindset

Empirical research: Research that occupies a close relationship to sensory experience, observation, or experiment.

Epidemiological transition: A phase of development witnessed by a sudden increase in population growth rates brought about by medical innovation in disease or sickness therapy and treatment, followed by a relevelling of population growth from subsequent declines in procreation rates.

Epistemology: The philosophical theory of knowledge—of how we know what we know.

Equality: The state of being equal, especially in status, rights, or opportunities.

Ethics: Moral principles that govern a person's behaviour or the conducting of an activity.

Ethnocentric: A perspective from which other races and cultures are evaluated in comparison to one's own.

Ethnography: A term usually applied to the acts both of observing directly the behaviour of a social group and producing a written description thereof; sometimes also referred to as fieldwork.

European Union (EU): An economic and political association of certain European countries as a unit with an agreement for internal free trade and common external tariffs.

Femininity: The characteristics belonging to, and considered appropriate to, the female sex.

Feminism: Theoretical paradigm that focuses on the social construction and consequences of gender inequality.

Fetishization of commodities: In the context of capitalism, the appearance of commodities in markets as if by magic, expunged of the complex human and non-human matrices out of which they come to be.

Field observation: A formal experiment conducted outside the laboratory, in a natural setting.

Fieldwork: Data collection for any study that involves talking to people or asking them questions about their activities and views, sometimes including attempts at systematic observation of their behaviour. Fieldwork ranges from large-scale survey interviewing by hundreds of professional interviewers to the lone researcher recording information collected through participant observation in a small-scale case study.

Filial care work: The assistance and support provided by adult children for their adoptive, birth, or step-parents (i.e., it encompasses informal or family care-giving rather than formal or paid work).

First Nations: A term of ethnicity referring to the Aboriginal peoples in Canada who are neither Inuit nor Métis.

Fish, Stanley: U.S. literary theorist and cultural critic. In critical theory, he is best known for the concept of the interpretive community, which displaces the problem of how meaning is produced onto society itself and makes meaning the practical production of readers rather than texts.

Front de libération du Québec (FLQ): A left-wing ethnic nationalist and ethnic socialist paramilitary group in Quebec, active between 1963 and 1970, which is widely regarded throughout Canada as a terrorist organization.

Focus groups: A qualitative method of data collection that involves interactive discussion among a small number of people.

Gender: A socially determined set of qualities and behaviours expected from males and females.

Gender gap: A late-twentieth-century concept used to describe the contemporary result of the historic legacy of the sexual division of labour. The industrialized society and economy in nineteenth-century North America designated gender-specific political and economic arenas and activities for women and men. The result of such gender-based segregation of work reinforced the notion of women working outside the home as remaining fundamentally unpaid family workers inside the home, thus obstructing women's achievement of individual economic freedom in the workplace.

Gender wage gap: A difference between a man and woman's fixed regular payment earned for work or services, typically paid on a daily or weekly basis.

General Social Survey: A sociological survey used to collect data on demographic characteristics and attitudes of residents of the United States and Canada. The survey is conducted face-to-face through in-person interviews of a randomly selected sample of adults aged 18 and older. The data collected about this survey includes both demographic information and respondents' opinions on matters ranging from government spending to the state of race relations to the existence and nature of a higher power.

Genetic engineering: The techniques involved in altering the characters of an organism by inserting genes from another organism into its DNA. This altered DNA (known as *recombinant DNA*) is usually produced by gene cloning.

Globalization: A complex series of economic, social, technological, cultural, and political changes associated with the increasing interdependence, integration, and interaction among people and companies in disparate locations.

Goffman, Erving: The most influential micro-sociologist during the 1960s and 1970s, Goffman pioneered the dramaturgical perspective for sociology.

Gold digger: A term originally applied to a gold miner. With the rise of pop culture, it has been applied to women who are perceived to associate with or marry a rich man in order to get valuables from him through gifts or a divorce settlement.

Habitus: A structure of the mind characterized by acquired sensibilities, dispositions, and tastes. Also a mechanism through which objective social structure becomes a part of individual subjectivity; often associated with particular class locations.

Hegemonic ideology (hegemony): The phenomenon of a social class, state, or nation exerting dominance or power over other levels of government through the control of ideological and material production.

Heterosexualization: The process in which individuals are socially conditioned to adopt heterosexual practices by ignoring and suppressing their sexual feelings toward the same sex and then using these suppressed emotions toward the opposite gender. *Hyperheterosexualization* is an excess of this.

Homophobia: The psychological fear of homosexuality.

Human capital: The economic value that is derived from the actual application of knowledge, collaboration, and process management.

HIV **(Human immunodeficiency virus):** The virus that causes AIDS.

Hybrid network: A network inhabited by all the creatures and artifacts that emerge from encounters and associations of the human and non-human, the biological and the technological, the social and the ecological.

Identity: The way in which an individual views himself or herself, or the ways in which others view the individual.

Ideology: The way in which a group views and makes sense out of the world, which serves to justify the existence of the group and its accompanying values and beliefs.

Immigrant: A person who migrates to and settles in a country other than that of their birthplace and upbringing.

Impression management: A dramaturgical concept, introduced by Erving Goffman in *The Presentation of Self in Everyday Life* (1959). It highlights the ways in which persons in the company of others strive to present an image of themselves in particular ways.

Inequality: A condition in which rewards or opportunities for different individuals within a group or groups in a society are unequal.

Intergenerational: Existing or occurring between or across different generations of people.

International relations: The discipline that studies interactions between and among states, and more broadly, the workings of the international system as a whole. It can be conceived of as a multidisciplinary field, gathering together the international aspects of politics, economics, history, law, and sociology.

Labour: The portion of the work force working for wages.

Leisure: Time spent not working for pay. The time used for idle, unpaid, and economically unproductive activities.

Liberalism: An ideology that attempts to ensure that individuals and groups can resist any authoritarian demands. In practice, this has most commonly meant a split between a public world and a private world where rights are defined, the most common of which are to private property, as well as the free exercise of religion, speech, and association.

Life course: A system of socially embedded transitions and processes of age-grading, such as when to leave home and marry. Varies across time and location in response to changing demographics, cultural, socio-economic, and political environments.

Life expectancy: The number of further years of life a person can expect at a given age. The measure is calculated from a life table, and since it is expressed as an average for persons of that age and sex in a country, it depends upon prevailing levels of mortality at different ages within the population or sub-population to which the individual belongs.

Likert scale: A widely used technique for scaling attitudes. Respondents are presented with a number of items, some positively phrased and some negatively phrased, which have been found to discriminate most clearly between extreme views on the subject of study.

Macrosociology: The study of whole societies, the totality of their social structures, and their social systems.

Marx, Karl: A German social theorist, founder of revolutionary communism and, in sociology, of historical materialism. His ideas played a significant role in the development of modern communism and socialism.

Marxism: The political and social theory based on the works of Karl Marx and Friedrich Engels. Marxism stresses the exploitative effects, such as inequality of wealth, produced by the capitalistic economic system.

Masculinity: The characteristics belonging to, and considered appropriate to, the male sex.

Mass communication: Large-scale organizations that use one or more technologies (print, radio, or television) to communicate with large numbers of people.

Media coverage: Reporting of public activities by the mass media (including press, television, and other forms of news journalism).

Media packaging: The style or format in which mass media present news items, for the purposes of influencing public perception of the issue.

Mega-events: High profile, one-time events of a limited duration hosted by a city that receives global media attention. Mega-events typically circulate among host cities rather than recurring in the same city multiple times. The Calgary Stampede, for example, is not a mega-event. The frequency of a mega-event is often determined by a fixed schedule, such as the four-year cycle of the Winter and Summer Olympic Games.

Merton, Robert K.: One of the most influential American sociologists and a leader in modern science studies. Merton's contributions to sociological thought are diverse, though broadly influenced by the functionalism of the 1940s and 1950s.

Microsociology: Sociology concerned with action, interaction, and the construction of meaning.

Mobilization: The process by which a group goes from being a passive collection of individuals to a collection of active participants in public life.

Modernity: Typically denotes a post-traditional, post-medieval historical period—in particular, one marked by progress away from agrarianism via the rise of industrialism, capitalism, secularization, the nation-state, and its constituent institutions and forms of surveillance.

Modernization theory: Theory emphasizing that positive change in social conditions is related to the modernization of attitudes and beliefs.

Moral panic: An overreaction of the community, mass media, and government to a disturbance which is, in reality, much more minor than how it is portrayed.

Moratorium: A temporary prohibition of an activity.

Mortality: The death rate. It is typically standardized by age and sex, to facilitate comparisons between areas and social groups. It provides a measure of health risks, improvements in the quality of health care, and the comparative overall health of different groups in the population.

Movement: Movements are typically defined by the beliefs they propagate and the ability to mobilize collective action around those beliefs.

Mutually exclusive: Refers to two events that cannot occur at the same time (i.e., they have no common outcomes). The best example is tossing a coin, which can result in either heads or tails, but not both. Both outcomes cannot happen simultaneously.

Narrative: Another word for 'story'. A narrative usually follows a sequence of events from initial calm through ensuing conflict to eventual climax, conclusion, and (once more) calm.

Nation-state: A sovereign state in which most of the citizens or subjects are united also by factors that define a nation, such as language or common descent.

Nationalism: Sentiment, aspiration, and consciousness are all terms applied to what constitutes nationalism, or the valuation of the nation-state above all else. However, it also entails certain assumptions about the will to self-determination, the existence and indeed desirability of diversity, the superiority of the sovereign state over other forms of rule, and the centrality of national loyalty to political power as a basic form of legitimation.

Neo-liberal urbanism: A range of uneven processes unfolding in the urban environments in which we live and work.

Neo-liberalism: An intellectual and political perspective that is suspicious of state intervention in economy and society and advocates maximum scope for the free play of market forces.

Obesity: The condition of being overweight, generally defined as weighing 20 per cent or more above the recommended norm for the person's sex, height, and build. People who are overweight are at increased risk of disease and have a shorter life expectancy than those of normal weight.

Open-door policy: A company policy in which every manager's door is open to every employee at any time. The purpose of this policy is to encourage open communication, feedback, and discussion about any matter of importance to an employee. Companies adopt open-door policies to develop employee trust and to make certain that important information and feedback reach managers, who can utilize the information to make changes in the workplace.

Open-ended interviews: Interview that allows the subject to direct the path of the discussion through questions without a set of specific answers.

Orientalism: A term for the West's interest in, and sometimes imitation of, Eastern (Oriental) languages, cultures, and arts during the eighteenth, nineteenth, and twentieth centuries.

Parental traffic safeguarding: The ways in which parents protect their children's diverse mobilities from the dangers of motorized traffic in variable social and automobilized environments.

Parenting: The raising of a child by its parents, focusing on types of parental practices that are more or less likely to produce socially valuable outcomes.

Parsons, Talcott: His sociological theory (most often labelled structural-functionalism) was commonly seen as a product of modern, affluent U.S. society, where structural social conflicts had been largely eliminated and where there appeared to be a general social cohesion and shared adherence to democratic values. His focus was on ideas, values, norms, and the integration of individual actions. For Parsons, the prime task was to develop a set of abstract, generalizing concepts describing the social system.

Participant observation: A research method that involves acquiring observational data by directly participating in the real-life settings of the group being studied. By interacting with group members and participating in aspects of their everyday lives, the researcher seeks to acquire an intimate understanding of how the subjects define their life-worlds. The researcher's goal is to offer a fine-grained description and analysis of the experiences, behaviours, and perspectives of those being observed.

Pathology: The scientific study of organic diseases, their causes, and symptoms.

Patrilocal multigenerational family: The family created when, after marriage, the wife lives in her husband's household, near or with the husband's kin and extended family.

Pay equity: The term used in North America to refer to equal pay between men and women.

Pedagogy: The science or art of teaching.

Placenta: An organ within the uterus by means of which the embryo is attached to the wall of the uterus. Its primary function is to provide the embryo with nourishment, eliminate its wastes, and exchange respiratory gases. It also functions as a gland, secreting progesterone and oestrogens which regulate the maintenance of pregnancy.

Placentation: The formation or arrangement of a placenta in a woman's or female animal's uterus.

Points system: A system used in the immigration process for distributing and allocating resources, or for ranking or evaluating candidates on the basis of points allocated or accumulated.

Population statistics: Related to demography; statistics are used to analyze population changes or trends.

Pornography: Visual or aural material presenting erotic behaviour that is intended to be sexually stimulating, and is lacking in artistic or other forms of merit. It is often considered to be demeaning to both sexuality and to the body.

Post-structuralism: A doctrine that rejects structuralism's claims to objectivity and emphasizes the plurality of meaning.

Presentation of self: An individual's efforts to present a self acceptable to others in the context of social interactions. The concept was elaborated by Erving Goffman in his classic *The Presentation of Self in Everyday Life* (1959). Goffman argued that individuals are usually successful in this process, which is why social interactions usually proceed in a routine and regular fashion.

Production activities: Activities such as agriculture, natural resources, and manufacturing, by which one produces products for profit.

Prostitution: The provision of sexual favours for financial reward. It has nearly always involved the prostitution of women to men, though male prostitution, especially to male clients, is not uncommon.

Psychosocial: Involving or relating to both the psychological and social aspects of a patient's life.

Public opinion: The approval or disapproval of publicly observable positions and behaviour, as expressed by a defined section of a society, and usually measured through opinion polls.

Qualitative: Describes analysis that relies on descriptive accounts of behaviour, beliefs, feelings, or values, with few or no numerical data available for statistical analysis.

Quantitative: Describes analysis involving the numerical representation and manipulation of observations for the purpose of describing and explaining the phenomena that those observations reflect.

Racism: A form of prejudice based on the belief that certain racial groups are inherently superior to others. Racist discourse generally attributes such characteristics to biology, although cultural and historical arguments may also come into play.

Radical feminism: A loosely formed but highly visible movement within feminism calling for a substantial change to the structure of contemporary society.

Red zone: An area that the police have designated as 'out of bounds' to particular youth who have been banished by police for partaking in illegitimate (though not always criminal) behaviour.

Reflexive sociology: A sociological theory that aims at a study of the sociologist himself or herself. It is based on the idea that knowledge is filtered through the researcher's own concepts of the world.

Reflexivity: Tendency of a thing, whether an individual or an institution, to be directed back to itself in a manner that influences how it exists.

Refugee: A person who has been forced to leave his or her native country in order to escape war, persecution, or natural disaster.

Relativism: A term loosely used to describe intellectual positions that reject absolute or universal standards or criteria.

Residential school: Native residential schooling, a project intended to assimilate Aboriginals into Euro-Canadian society and Christianity, became part of Canada's history starting in the 1840s. The use of Native languages—known colloquially as 'talking Indian' was vigorously discouraged. The schools were run by churches of various denominations, and preaching frequently disparaged Aboriginal spirituality, calling it devil worship. Students were subjected to the denigration of Aboriginal identity and the promotion of Euro-Canadian values and practices.

Risk assessment: The process of estimating short- and long-term harmful impacts on human health or the environment that arise from exposure to hazards associated with a particular product or activity.

Risk society: A society in which perception of risk is extremely important. This perception causes insecurity among citizens and propels them to seek strategies of reducing the perceived risk.

Roles: Characteristics and expected social behaviours associated with professions, gender, etc.

Role strain: Every role brings with it a number of different partners, each with their own set of expectations. When these expectations are in disagreement, sociologists talk of role strain.

Science: The intellectual and practical activity encompassing the systematic study of the structure and behaviour of the physical and natural world through observation and experiment.

Self-sufficiency: The state of needing no outside help to satisfy one's basic needs, especially with regard to the production of food.

Separatism: The advocacy of a state of cultural, ethnic, tribal, religious, racial, governmental, or gender separation from the larger group, often with demands for greater political autonomy and even for full political secession and the formation of a new state.

Settlement: The process through which immigrants enter, adjust to, and function within their new host environment.

Severe Acute Respiratory Syndrome (SARS): A viral respiratory illness causing a condition similar to pneumonia combined with influenza-like symptoms. It is most readily transmitted through respiratory droplets, but may also be spread more widely through the air. SARS was first recognized in southern China in 2002 and caused worldwide concern in 2003.

Social cohesion: A condition of connectedness, unity, co-operation, and trust among people in a society.

Social constructionism: A general term sometimes applied to theories that emphasize the socially created nature of social life.

Social control: Social mechanisms that regulate individual and group behaviour in terms of greater sanctions and rewards. Informal social control is exercised by a society without explicitly stating these rules.

Social order: The presence of generally harmonious relationships; used synonymously with social organization. This condition exists when rules are obeyed and social situations are controlled and predictable. Rules serve not only to indicate which behaviours are acceptable, but also to allow participants to anticipate the behaviour of others.

Social policy: Guidelines and interventions for the creation, changing, and maintenance of living conditions that are conducive to human welfare. Thus, social policy is that part of public policy that has to do with social issues.

Social practice theory: A framework for social science researchers who attempt to describe how individuals in different societies across the globe shape and are shaped by the cultural atmosphere in which they live.

Socialization: Socialization is the process by which we learn to become members of society, both by internalizing the norms and values of society, and also by learning to perform our social roles (as worker, friend, citizen, and so forth).

Standard deviation: A measure of the amount by which observed data or scores deviate from the mean. A small standard deviation indicates that observations cluster around the mean, while a large one indicates that the data are spread far from the mean.

Status: Refers to the standing or position that a person occupies in the social structure, such as teacher or doctor. It is often combined with the notion of the social role to produce the idea of a status role.

Status groups: Competitive groups of people who enjoy the same status and seek to preserve their monopolistic privileges by excluding their rivals from enjoyment of certain resources.

Structural constraint: The level of restriction placed on indivuduals' options by their social role or by their lack of access to social, cultural, economic, or political resources.

Subsistence: The minimum level of wages and/or consumption necessary to ensure survival and the basic necessities of life.

Substantial equivalence: The equivalence of a novel trait within a particular plant species, in terms of its specific use and safety to the environment and human health, to those in that same species that are in use and generally considered as safe in Canada, based on valid scientific rationale.

Symbolic interactionism: A sociological approach to the study of human group life that emphasizes the centrality of activity, language, and human interchange. This perspective builds on the pragmatist philosophy with an emphasis on community, self, and reflective activity, and it relies on ethnographic research.

Systems theory: Also known as systemic, this theory studies both unified whole and self-organizing systems. The relationships in a system, or community, are interdependent and interactional. A society is more than the sum of all its members.

Terrorism: Use of violence, sometimes indiscriminately, against persons and property for the nominal purpose of making a political statement.

Traditional marriage: Marriage is traditionally conceived to be a legally recognized relationship, between an adult male and female, that carries certain rights and obligations.

Two worlds thesis: The idea that immigrants are caught between two worlds: their homeland and their host country.

Unemployment: The state of not working. Generally, individuals in this state are willing to work at a prevailing wage rate yet they are unable to find a paying job.

United Nations (UN): An organization of independent states formed in 1945 to promote international peace and security.

Unpaid work: Labour—especially care work and domestic work done by women—that earns no cash payment or wage.

Urban consciousness: Individuals' state of being cognitively aware of and alert to their situation in relation to their city.

The Vertical Mosaic: John Porter's classic tome that, in 1965, marked the coming of age of Canadian social science. This breakthrough book impressed through its original scope, insight, and innovative data analysis. In contrast to the image of a U.S. 'melting pot', Porter's findings were of a 'hierarchical relationship between Canada's many cultural groups'. Porter challenged the wisdom of 'multicultural' policies.

War Measures Act: A Canadian statute that allowed the government to assume sweeping emergency powers in the event of 'war, invasion or insurrection, real or apprehended'. The October Crisis of 1970 raised fears in Canada of a militant terrorist faction rising up against the government. Prime Minister Pierre Trudeau invoked the act to allow police more power in locating, arresting, and detaining the FLQ members.

War on Terror: An operation initiated by the United States government under George W. Bush, using legal, military, personal, and political actions to limit the spread of terrorism after 9/11.

Weber, Max: Weber, together with Émile Durkheim, is often regarded as the founder of modern sociology as a distinct social science. His work is the more complex and ambitious, still providing a rich source for interpretation and inspiration.

Welfare: A system whereby the state undertakes to protect the health and well-being of its citizens—especially those in financial need—by means of grants, pensions, etc.

Welfare state: A form of capitalist society in which the state takes responsibility for a range of measures intended to ensure the well-being of its members, through providing education for children, access to health care, financial support for periods out of the labour market, and so on.

Workplace violence: A current health and safety problem in businesses where employees are the victims of verbal and/or physical harassment from customers and/or clients.

World order: A political mythology that enables certain forms of global political action.

Zone of prestige: A culturally impressive institution or space that a city uses to boost its reputation both nationally and globally.

Credits

Tracey L. Adams, 'Profession: A Useful Concept for Sociological Analysis?', *Canadian Review of Sociology*, 47, 1 (2010): 49–70. Excerpted and reprinted by permission of John Wiley & Sons Ltd.

Michael C. Adorjan, 'Emotions Contests and Reflexivity in the News: Examining Discourse on Youth Crime in Canada'. Excerpted and reprinted by permission of the author. This paper appears as a condensed version of a complete paper, forthcoming as 'Emotions Contests and News Reflexivity' *Journal of Contemporary Ethnography*, 40, 2 (2011).

Patrizia Albanese, 'The More Things Change . . . The More We Need Child Care: On the Fortieth Anniversary of the *Report on the Royal Commission on the Status of Women*'. Excerpted and reprinted by permission of the author.

Harris Ali, 'Infectious Disease, Environmental Change and Social Control'. Excerpted and reprinted by permission of the author.

Robert Andersen and Josh Curtis, 'The Economy and Public Opinion on Welfare Spending in Canada'. Excerpted and reprinted by permission of the authors.

Pat Armstrong, 'Pay Equity: Yesterday's Issue?'. Excerpted and reprinted by permission of the author.

Maureen Baker, 'The Rise of the "Research University": Gendered Outcomes'. Excerpted and reprinted by permission of the author.

Christie Barron and Dany Lacombe, 'Moral Panic and the Nasty Girl'. *Canadian Review of Sociology*, 42, 1 (2005): 51–69. Excerpted and reprinted by permission of John Wiley & Sons Ltd.

Brenda L. Beagan, '"Even If I Don't Know What I'm Doing I Can Make It Look Like I Know What I'm Doing": Becoming a Doctor in the 1990s'. Excerpted and reprinted by permission of the author.

Nancy Beauregard, Andrée Demers, and Louis Gliksman, 'The Ecology of College Drinking: Revisiting the Role of the Campus Environment on Students' Drinking Patterns'. Excerpted and reprinted by permission of the authors.

Carol Berenson, 'Menstruation by Choice: The Framing of a Controversial Issue'. Excerpted and reprinted with permission of the author.

Monica Boyd and Emily Laxer, 'Voting across Immigrant Generations'. Excerpted and reprinted by permission of the authors. Funding for this for this project comes from the SSHRC research grant 410-09-2659 on 'Social and Economic Integration of Immigrant Children and Young Adults' awarded to Monica Boyd. The analysis of the Ethnic Diversity Survey is made possible by the joint university-SSHRC-Statistics Canada funding of the Research Data Centers and the availability of the EDS at the University of Toronto Research Data Centre.

Shaun Chen, 'Segregation versus Self-Determination: A Black and White Debate on Canada's First Africentric School'. Excerpted and reprinted by permission of the author.

Sinziana Chira, 'From International Universities to Diverse Local Communities? International Students in Halifax and Beyond'. Excerpted and reprinted by permission of the author.

Dominique Clément, 'Canada's Rights Revolution: Social Movements and Social Change, 1937–1982' Excerpted and reprinted by permission of the author.

Claudio Colaguori and Carlos Torres, 'Policing Terrorism in the Post 9/11 Era: Critical Challenges and Concerns'. Excerpted and reprinted by permission of the authors.

Wesley Crichlow, 'Hyperheterosexualization, Masculinity, and HIV/AIDS Challenges'. Excerpted and reprinted by permission of the author.

Bruce Curtis, 'Reading Reflexively'. Excerpted and reprinted by permission of the author.

Jeffrey S. Denis, 'Bridging Understandings: Anishinaabe and White Perspectives on the Residential School Apology and Prospects for Reconciliation'. Excerpted and reprinted by permission of the author.

Marjorie DeVault, Murali Venkatesh, and Frank Ridzi, '"Let's Be Friends": Working within an Accountability Circuit'. Excerpted and reprinted with permission of the authors. A longer version of this paper is forthcoming in Griffith, A.I. and Smith, D.E. (Eds.), *Governance and the Front Line*, University of Toronto Press.

Andrea Doucet, 'Gender Equality and Gender Differences: Parenting, Habitus, and Embodiment (The 2008

Porter Lecture)', *Canadian Review of Sociology*, 46, 2 (2009): 103–121. Excerpted and reprinted by permission of John Wiley & Sons Ltd.

Slobodan Drakulic, 'Nationalism from Below'. Excerpted and reprinted by permission of the author.

Peter Eglin, 'Intellectual Citizenship and Incarnation: A Reply to Stanley Fish'. Excerpted and reprinted by permission of the author.

Carlo Fanelli and Justin Paulson, 'Municipal Malaise: Neo-liberal Urbanism in Canada'. Excerpted and reprinted by permission of the authors.

Laura M. Funk and Karen M. Kobayashi, '"Choice" in Filial Care Work: Moving beyond a Dichotomy', *Canadian Review of Sociology*, 46, 3 (2009): 235–252. Excerpted and reprinted by permission of John Wiley & Sons Ltd.

Steve Garlick, 'Maintaining Control? Masculinity and Internet Pornography'. Excerpted and reprinted by permission of the author.

Helga Kristin Hallgrimsdottir, Rachel Phillips, and Cecelia Benoit, 'Fallen Women and Rescued Girls: Social Stigma and Media Narratives of the Sex Industry in Victoria, B.C., from 1980 to 2005', *Canadian Review of Sociology*, 43, 3 (2006): 265–280. Excerpted and reprinted by permission of John Wiley & Sons Ltd.

Kristen A. Hardy, 'Fleshy Histories: Fatness, Sex/Gender, and the Medicalized Body in the Nineteenth Century'. Excerpted and reprinted by permission of the author.

Rick Helmes-Hayes, 'Anticipating Burawoy: John Porter's Public Sociology'. Excerpted and reprinted by permission of the author.

Suzan Ilcan and Rob Aitken, 'United Nations and Early Post-war Development: Assembling World Order'. The research on which this chapter is based was supported by grant funds from the Social Sciences and Humanities Research Council of Canada (SSHRC) and SSHRC's Canada Research Chairs Program. Suzan Ilcan and Rob Aitken conducted archival research at the United Nations Archives (New York) in June/July 2009 and in August 2008 respectively.

Nedim Karakayali, 'Duality and Diversity in the Lives of Immigrant Children: Rethinking the "Problem of the Second Generation" in Light of Immigrant Autobiographies'. Excerpted and reprinted by permission of the author.

Jacqueline Kennelly, 'Red Zones, Empty Alleys, and Giant TVs: Low-Income Youths' Spatial Accounts of Olympic Host Cities'. Excerpted and reprinted by permission of the author.

Ivanka Knezevic, 'Social Europe and Eastern Europe: Post-Socialist Scholars Grapple with New Models of Social Policy'. Excerpted and reprinted by permission of the author.

Sarah Knudson, 'What a Girl Wants, What a Girl Needs: Examining Cultural Change and Ideas about Gender Equality in Relationship Self-Help Books, 1960–2009'. Excerpted and reprinted by permission of the author.

Matthew Lange, 'Education, Ethnonationalism, and Non-violence in Quebec'. Excerpted and reprinted by permission of the author.

Anthony P. Lombardo, 'Online Interactions among Men Who Have Sex with Men: Situated Performances and Sexual Education'. Excerpted and reprinted by permission of the author.

Patricia D. McGuire, 'Indigenous Spaces in Sociology'. Excerpted and reprinted with permission of the author.

Reza Nakhaie and Robert Arnold, 'A Four-Year (1996–2000) Analysis of Social Capital and Health Status of Canadians: The Difference that Love Makes'. Excerpted and reprinted by permission of the authors.

Nancy S. Netting, 'Love and Arranged Marriage in India Today: Negotiating Adulthood'. Excerpted and reprinted by permission of the author.

Katja Neves, 'The Production of Modernity in Classic American Whale Hunting'. Excerpted and reprinted by permission of the author.

Sara O'Shaughnessy, 'Gold Diggers and Moms: Representation of Women's Identities in Fort McMurray in *Chatelaine*'. Excerpted and reprinted by permission of the author.

Michèle Ollivier, Wendy Robbins, Diane Beauregard, Jennifer Brayton, and Geneviève Sauvé, 'Feminist Activists Online: A Study of the PAR-L Research Network', *Canadian Review of Sociology*, 43, 4 (2006): 445–464. Reprinted by permission of John Wiley & Sons Ltd.

Riley Olstead and Kathy Bischoping, 'Spinsters and Suspects: Gender and Moral Citizenship in Poison Pen Mystery Novels'. Excerpted and reprinted by permission of the authors.

Patrick Parnaby and Myra Leyden, 'Dirty Harry and the Station Queens: A Mertonian Analysis of Police Deviance'. Excerpted and reprinted by permission of the authors.

Wilhelm Peekhaus, 'Regulating Agricultural Biotechnology in Canada: Paradoxes and Conflicts of a Closed System'. Excerpted and reprinted by permission of the author.

Linda Quirke, '"Keeping Young Minds Sharp": Children's Cognitive Stimulation and the Rise of Parenting Magazines, 1959–2003', *Canadian Review of Sociology*, 43, 4 (2006): 387–407. Reprinted by permission of John Wiley & Sons Ltd.

Zenaida Ravanera and Roderic Beaujot, 'Childlessness and Socio-Economic Characteristics: What Does the Canadian 2006 General Social Survey Tell Us?'. Excerpted and reprinted by permission of the authors.

Stephen Harold Riggins, 'The Bonds of Things'. Excerpted and reprinted by permission of the author.

Reuben N. Roth, '"Suck it Up Buttercup": A Culture of Acceptable Workplace Violence in Group Homes'. Excerpted and reprinted by permission of the author. With the research assistance of Diane Rioux, B.A. Hons., and Cayley Koomans, B.A. Hons., Laurentian University.

Rebecca Scott, 'Placentations'. Excerpted and reprinted by permission of the author.

Sherrie M. Steiner, '"How Can You Decide about Us without Us?": A Canadian Catastrophe in Copenhagen'. Excerpted and reprinted by permission of the author.

Jeff Stepnisky, 'Biocitizenship and Mental Health in a Canadian Context'. Excerpted and reprinted by permission of the author.

Vic Satzewich and William Shaffir, 'The Informal Settlement Sector: Broadening the Lens to Understand Newcomer Integration in Hamilton'. Excerpted and reprinted by permission of the authors.

Frances M. Shaver, 'Legislative Approaches to Prostitution: A Critical Introduction'. Excerpted and reprinted by permission of the author.

Alan Simmons, 'Changing Canadian Immigration and Foreign Worker Programs: Implications for Social Cohesion'. Excerpted and reprinted by permission of the author. An earlier version of this paper, titled 'Trends in Canadian Foreign Workers Programs: An Analysis of Neo-Liberal Nation Building', was presented at the workshop Migration, Work and Citizenship: Toward Decent Work and Secure Citizenship, York University, Oct. 1–3, 2009. The present paper was presented at the Canadian Sociological Association Meetings, Montreal, May 31 to June 4, 2010. The author is indebted to Tanya Basok, Jenna Hennebry, and Vic Satzewich for oral comments and insights arising from their research on foreign workers.

Mark C.J. Stoddart and Laura MacDonald, '"Keep it Wild, Keep it Local": Comparing News Media and the Internet as Sites for Environmental Movement Activism for Jumbo Pass, British Columbia'. Excerpted and reprinted by permission of the authors. The authors would like to thank Dr. Howard Ramos for his input throughout this project. Financial support for this research was provided by Killam Trusts.

Lisa Taylor, 'Contested Imaginaries: Reading Muslim Women and Muslim Women Reading Back: Transnational Feminist Reading Practices, Pedagogy, and Ethical Concerns'. Excepted and reprinted by permission of the author.

Annette Tézli, 'Keeping the Family Intact—The Lived Experience of Sheltered Homeless Families'. Excerpted and reprinted by permission of the author.

Arlene Tigar McLaren and Sylvia Parusel, 'Parents and Traffic Safety: Unequal Risks and Responsibilities to and from School'. Excerpted and reprinted by permission of the authors.

Frank Trovato and Nirannanilathu Lalu, 'From Divergence to Convergence: The Sex Differential in Life Expectancy in Canada, 1971–2000', *Canadian Review of Sociology*, 44, 1 (2007): 101–122. Excerpted and reprinted by permission of John Wiley & Sons Ltd.

Mark Vardy, 'The Science and Politics of Polar Ice'. Excerpted and reprinted by permission of the author.

Cora J. Voyageur, 'The New Relationship between Social Sciences and the Indigenous Peoples of Canada'. Excerpted and reprinted by permission of the author.

Kevin Walby and Michael Haan, 'Counting, Caste and Confusion during Census Enumeration in Colonial India'. Excerpted and reprinted by permission of the authors.

Jean E. Wallace and Marisa C. Young, 'Work Hard, Play Hard?: A Comparison of Male and Female Lawyers' Time in Paid and Unpaid Work and Participation in Leisure Activities', *Canadian Review of Sociology*, 47, 1

(2010): 27–47. Excerpted and reprinted by permission of John Wiley & Sons Ltd.

Jean-Philippe Warren, 'Francophone and Anglophone Sociologists in Canada Diverging, Converging, or Parallel Trends?'. Excerpted and reprinted by permission of the author.

Rima Wilkes, Catherine Corrigall-Brown, and Daniel J. Myers, 'Packaging Protest: Media Coverage of Indigenous People's Collective Action', *Canadian Review of Sociology*, 47, 4 (2010): 327–357. Reprinted by permission of John Wiley & Sons Ltd.

Nathan Young, 'Does a Place Like This Still Matter? Remaking Economic Identity in Post-Resource Communities'. Excerpted and reprinted by permission of the author.